sexualities

in HISTORY

A READER

EDITED BY

KIM M. PHILLIPS AND BARRY REAY

Routledge
Taylor & Francis Group
New York London

Routledge is an imprint of the
Taylor & Francis Group, an informa business

Published in 2002 by

Routledge
Taylor and Francis Group
270 Madison Avenue
New York, NY 10016

Routledge
Taylor and Francis Group
2 Park Square
Milton Park, Abingdon
Oxon OX14 4RN

Routledge is an imprint of the Taylor & Francis Group.

Library of Congress Cataloging-in-Publication Data
Sexualities in history : a reader / edited by Kim M. Phillips and Barry Reay.
    p.   cm.
  Includes bibliographical references and index.
  ISBN 0-415-92934-2 — ISBN 0-415-92935-0 (pbk.)
  1. Sex—History. 2. Sex customs—History
  3. Sex and history. I. Phillips, Kim M. II. Reay, Barry.
HQ12 .S46 2001
306.7'09—dc21   2001019346

CONTENTS

Introduction   I
KIM M. PHILLIPS AND BARRY REAY

PART 1   RETHINKING SEX

1   Sexuality and History Revisited   27
JEFFREY WEEKS

2   Forgetting Foucault   42
Acts, Identities, and the History of Sexuality
DAVID M. HALPERIN

PART 2   SEXING THE BODY

3   Bodies That Don't Matter   71
Heterosexuality before Heterosexuality in Gottfried's Tristan
JAMES A. SCHULTZ

4   "Ut cum muliere"   90
A Male Transvestite Prostitute in Fourteenth-Century London
RUTH MAZO KARRAS AND DAVID LORENZO BOYD

5   Gender and Generation   105
Representing Reproduction in Early Modern England
MARY FISSELL

PART 3   CONTROLLING SEX

6   Bodies and Minds   129
    Sexuality and Renunciation in Early Christianity
    PETER BROWN

7   Family Life and the Regulation of Deviance   141
    JOHN D'EMILIO AND ESTELLE B. FREEDMAN

8   Sexuality in California's Franciscan Missions   166
    Cultural Perceptions and Historical Realities
    ALBERT HURTADO

PART 4   REDEFINING SEX

9   Redefining Sex in Eighteenth-Century England   185
    TIM HITCHCOCK

10 Sex for Thought   203
    ROBERT DARNTON

11 Parasexuality and Glamour   222
    The Victorian Barmaid as Cultural Prototype
    PETER BAILEY

PART 5   CONSTRUCTING SEX

12 Anne Lister's Construction of Lesbian Identity   247
    ANNA CLARK

13 Richard von Krafft-Ebing's "Step-Children of Nature"   271
    Psychiatry and the Making of Homosexual Identity
    HARRY OOSTERHUIS

14 Trade, Wolves, and the Boundaries of Normal Manhood   293
    GEORGE CHAUNCEY

15 Toward a "Value-Free" Science of Sex   327
    The Kinsey Reports
    JANICE M. IRVINE

PART 6   PUNISHING SEX

16   Negotiating Sex and Gender in the Attorney General's   359
     Commission on Pornography
     CAROLE S. VANCE

17   AIDS and the Discursive Construction of Homosexuality   375
     STEVEN SEIDMAN

18   Regulated Passions   386
     The Invention of Inhibited Sexual Desire and Sexual Addiction
     JANICE M. IRVINE

19   Hottentot 2000   407
     Jennifer Lopez and Her Butt
     MAGDALENA BARRERA

PART 7   UNSETTLING SEX

20   Leatherdyke Boys and Their Daddies   421
     How to Have Sex without Women or Men
     C. JACOB HALE

21   The Game Girls of VNS Matrix   434
     Challenging Gendered Identities in Cyberspace
     KAY SCHAFFER

     Notes on the Contributors   453
     Permissions Acknowledgments   457
     Index   461

INTRODUCTION

KIM M. PHILLIPS AND BARRY REAY

The making historically visible of heterosexuality is difficult because, under its institutional pseudonyms such as Inheritance, Marriage, Dynasty, Family, Domesticity, and Population, heterosexuality has been permitted to masquerade so fully as History itself—when it has not presented itself as the totality of Romance.[1]

—Eve Kosofsky Sedgwick

Several years ago, there was some rather acidic debate in the pages of the *New York Review of Books*. The exchange arose from the review of a two-volume survey of sexual practices in the United States, the published findings of a massive research project based at the University of Chicago involving several hundred interviewers and nearly 3,500 "scientifically selected respondents." The disagreement focused on a basic issue: Could people be trusted to tell the truth about their sex lives? The reviewer, a biologist and philosopher of science, accused the social scientists involved in the project of being hopelessly naive about people's capacity to delude both themselves and those asking the questions about their sexual practices. What prompted the furor was the uncritical use of another survey which found that nearly half of men aged in their eighties said that they still had sex with a partner. The attack widened into an assault on a particular kind of sociology. "It is frightening to think that social science is in the hands of professionals who are so deaf to human nuance that they believe that people do not lie to themselves about the most freighted aspects of their own lives."[2]

However, it could be argued that this intervention missed far more interesting aspects of what has come to be known as the "Sex in America Survey." The National Health and Social Life Survey of 1992—note that sex is not mentioned in the official title—was presented as a scientifically accurate survey, without any preconceived ideas on the part of the principal researchers. It clearly saw itself as the most accurate survey in U.S. history—better than Kinsey, Masters and Johnson, and Hite. The researchers randomly selected households throughout the United States and interviewed them. The sample did not include teens or those over sixty. The reported findings of this survey were likely to gladden the hearts of conservative Americans. People are faithful in marriage: more than 80 percent of women reported that they had had no other sexual partner while married. (The fact that some 40 percent of marriages in the United States end within ten years tends to undermine these findings somewhat.) Only 3 percent of adults said they had had five or more sexual partners in the past year. Those swinging singles are a myth: "In real life, the unheralded, seldom discussed world of married sex is actually the one that satisfies people the most." Only 29 percent of women said they always have an orgasm with a primary partner, yet these women "still seem happy with their sex lives." (It is interesting that *44 percent* of men thought that their female partners always had orgasms.)

Although the researchers claimed that they had no agenda, their report for popular consumption was shot through with a bias in favour of heterosexual sex, with marriage constantly looming large in their framework and terms of reference: "in selecting sex partners, people are also selecting partners with whom they might have children and with whom they might raise children." "At one time or another, almost everyone has felt excluded from the world of loving couples. Almost everyone has watched young lovers walk hand in hand through a park on a balmy spring afternoon or noticed how many women, young and old, beautiful and not so beautiful, sport wedding rings, or how many men, attractive or not, prominently display pictures of their wife and family in their office." One of the more featured "findings" was what is repetitively termed "vaginal sex." Some 80 percent of women and 85 percent of men said that "vaginal sex" was very appealing. "To our surprise, we discovered that although the sexual menu is long and varied, only one practice—vaginal intercourse—stood out as nearly universal. It is of course the only sexual activity that can result in the birth of a baby and it is the only practice that is universally and morally sanctioned by all religions. . . . Vaginal sex also is what most people imagine when they think of sex. It is the sexual activity that defines the loss of virginity, the one that teenagers dream of when they think of 'going all the way.'" (The survey also found that over 25 percent of men and 20 percent of women said that they had experienced anal sex at some time in their lives, but did not make a feature of this discovery.)[3]

The not so hidden agenda of this survey was to stress procreative, heterosexual sex. As Mary Poovey has pointed out in an analysis of the context and nature of the whole project, this view of sex represents a form of crude social determinism: as the researchers put it, "society's goal is to get people safely married and procreating."[4] The findings of such sexual surveys help to constitute the very (hetero)sexualities they purport to represent.

One of the benefits of studying history is that it enables recognition of the strangeness of contemporary society. Or, rather, it allows one to see that not only is the past different from the present, but that aspects of present culture that seem eternal or fundamental will prove transient. In the contemporary West, sexual desires, behaviors, and identities are largely organized around the two polar opposites of heterosexual and homosexual. The polarity by no means imparts equality, of course, with heterosexuality made powerful through its identification as "normal" and "natural," while homosexuality has been demonized as heterosexuality's dark twin, "deviant" and "unnatural." Not all Western contemporaries seem at ease with such limited choices and neatly defined categories. Bisexuality refuses "binary categories" and "one-to-one correspondences between sex acts and identities" in favor of polymorphous desires.[5] Indeed the sociologist Anthony Giddens has argued that an important characteristic of modern sexuality is its malleability. Sexuality is no longer a "natural condition," but rather "free-floating." It "functions as a malleable feature of self": what he has termed, with all its modern connotations, "plastic sexuality."[6] And yet, when all the qualifications have been made, there is no doubting the resilient power of the more conventional sexual imaginary. In an extended critique of Giddens, Lynn Jamieson has demonstrated a widespread adherence to many of the fixed gender stereotypes of compulsory heterosexuality—what has been termed heteronormativity.[7]

The idea that there are only two (or three) sexual identities, and that everyone must decide which is most appropriate for them, is very recent as the dominant mode of structuring sexuality. Late too is the notion that sexual object choice is defined by biological sex: a heterosexual desires members of the "opposite sex," a homosexual desires members of the "same sex," and a bisexual may desire either. By viewing sexualities in historical perspective, the relative novelty of such ideas quickly becomes apparent. Thus, "heteronormativity" becomes the "heterosexual imaginary."[8]

At first one might be tempted to impose current categories onto past individuals: after all, it is easy enough to single out individuals who evidently desired members of their own sex, the other sex, or both.[9] But, as tracing the history of those dominant terms quickly reveals, the emphasis on the biological sex of the desirer and the desired above all other considerations has not been with us very long. The gender of the parties has often been of greater concern: the pattern of dominant, masculine men desiring passive, feminine men, for example, has an immensely long and varied lineage. The social status of the parties, whether determined by class, age, occupation, or sex, has also acted as an organizing factor for sexualities, particularly in premodern Western societies. "Sex," as in biological distinctions of male and female, turns out to have only a little to do with sexualities.

The purpose of this reader is to demonstrate that sexualities are culturally constructed, and thus subject to fundamental historical change. The articles selected illustrate varying formations of sexualities at different moments in Western history, from ancient Athens to the late twentieth century, and locate explanations for the nature of the formations within specific historical contexts. The value of a historical approach to sexualities is immense, for our understanding both of the past and of the present. It forces the rethinking of a wide range of topics already established as subjects for historical investigation, including marriage, family, concepts of sex and gender, roles of men and women, class relations, race relations, religious ideologies, and relationships between the state and individuals: there is nothing narrow or overly specialized about sexualities as a subject for historical investigation.

A simple message of this book is the variability of sexuality. There are numerous ways of demonstrating this. Anthropologists can show that sexual practices that, on the face of it, are very similar to those in one's own society, are in fact invested with hugely variant meanings by other cultures. Historians can use the past in a comparable way to show the inconstancies of sex over time, that the meanings, languages, and practices of sex change. While this book recognizes that there may be imposed or dominant sexualities in any given period (sex reflecting power structures), it would question that there is any natural sexuality. The value for the present and future is in the acceptance of diversity that a historical perspective fosters. As it is "no longer possible to see sex as caught in the toils of nature, outside the bounds of history," writes Jeffrey Weeks in chapter 1 of this volume, "we can see the present not as the culmination of an unproblematic past but as itself historical," and "it may lead us to be a little more accepting of the diversity of the present." Once sexualities are seen as constructs, "a series of representations" with their own histories, many of our received wisdoms and certainties vanish.

But what precisely *is* the subject of this history? What constitute the "sexualities" that have been gaining such attention in recent scholarship?[10] The problems of defining the terms of debate are frequently acknowledged. As Weeks notes, "One of the problems with the new sexual history is that it is in danger of becoming a history without a proper subject." A history of sexuality is at once a history of a "category of thought," and a history of "changing erotic practices, subjective meanings, social definitions, and patterns of regulation whose only unity lies in their common descriptor." The problem is heightened by the fact that different cultures have assigned sexual meanings to phenomena no longer viewed in an erotic light, while other phenomena that are freighted with sexual overtones in the present had different meanings in the past. Arnold Davidson has provided the telling comparison between a seventeenth-century medical treatise on the use of flogging to facilitate erection, and late-nineteenth-century descriptions of masochism. The former, it was believed, involved a physiological (humoral) response to the stimulation of the blood: the latter was an expression of deep-seated (so to speak) sexuality. The difference between the two was the difference between therapy and identity.[11]

Though the flexibility and mutability of the term *sexualities* must be acknowledged, it is dissatisfying either to attempt no definition at all or to advance one that covers a broad range without seeking some unifying theme. Leaving the term undefined allows for writing histories of "sexualities" that are not about sex. While sex acts, identities, wider practices, thoughts, and arousal are optional within a definition of sexualities, sexual desire is the one essential component. Even if actual manifestations of desire (e.g., arousal, sex acts) are not present, associations with sexual desire are necessary to make an identity, a practice, or a thought sexual. It is not the leather boots or mask of the fetishist that is itself sexual, but the reminder of sexual desire that it prompts that makes it seem so to the viewer. That viewer need not have experienced that desire him or herself, but only know that such associations exist for some individuals for the sexual nature of the object to be acknowledged. Thus to study properly the history of sexualities, it is necessary to determine from wider contexts which phenomena were associated with desire and which were not.

The history of sexualities is broad, then, in taking in identities, orientations, sex acts, work-practices, images, bodies, thoughts, institutions, and systems of power, but focused in the constant connection with erotic desire. It is a history with a proper subject, though manifested in multitudinous ways. It is, indeed, one of the widest reaching, and thus among the most important, subjects of human history.

Like sexualities themselves, the history of sexualities changes with its social and intellectual context. Its beginnings are coeval with the emergence of sex as an autonomous phenomenon, a matter worthy for thought and study in its own right, rather than as an aspect of other topics or fields of study. Early historians of sexualities produced works ringing with Freudian theories of essential "drives" and "taboos," explaining historical phenomena with reference to ideas derived from psychology and sexology. "Whenever society attempts to restrict expression of the sexual drive more severely than the human constitution will stand, . . . [e]ither men will defy the taboos, or they will turn to perverted forms of sex, or they will develop psychoneurotic symptoms": this framework led G. Rattray Taylor to diagnose the medieval period as suffering from "an outbreak of mass psychosis," and as resembling "a vast insane asylum."[12] The Freudian influence can be dimly detected in sexual histories long after its mid-twentieth-century heyday, just as other ghosts from the early days of psychoanalysis lingered in the intellectual and popular consciousness. James A. Brundage's monumental 1987 study of sexual control under the medieval church claimed that "sex represents a rich source of conflicts that can disrupt orderly social processes. Human sexuality is too powerful and explosive a force for any society to allow its members complete sexual freedom."[13] But by the late 1960s and early 1970s the louder cries were those for sexual liberation, expressed by historians and Western popular culture at large. Vern L. Bullough, whose early career as a sex researcher was evidently hampered by those who felt that sex was not a respectable subject for historical study and termed him a "queer, pimp, fairy, pornographer," or worse, called for scholars to "break the taboo" of sex.[14] During the 1970s the women's movement and gay liberation provided the spur to more detailed and specific studies, with particular emphasis on ways in which sex had been used as a tool of oppression against these groups.[15] Such studies began to open up the study of sex in history, but generally left unexamined the fundamental meanings and categories of sexuality.

The English translation of the first volume of Michel Foucault's *The History of Sexuality* has long been recognized as a pivotal moment in sexual historiography, not only reworking the narrative of this history but also challenging the basic concepts used by its practitioners.[16] He first took apart the long-cherished belief that Western society had, especially in the nineteenth century, become repressed about sexuality, and showed that this "repression" was not a silencing of discussion about sex but rather an explosion of discourse. This view led Foucault to a second, more fundamental insight: "sexuality" is not a phenomenon that exists transculturally, transhistorically, almost autonomously from human society, but is itself a product of discourse and therefore subject to constant transformation and re-creation. This theory came to be called the "social constructionist" view of sexuality. Foucault then embarked on the project of examining sexual cultures through Western history, starting with Greece and Rome, but left the project unfinished at his death in 1984.[17]

Jonathan Ned Katz and Jeffrey Weeks have both pointed out that the destabilization of sexual categories had already been initiated by the time Foucault's book appeared, but it was Foucault and others such as Robert Padgug and Weeks himself who offered worked-through accounts of the theory.[18] By the early 1980s an alternative to the constructionist approach was already apparent, notable especially in studies of the history of "homosexuality."[19] These studies preferred to view sexual categories and orientations as stable across time, and to identify "gayness" or "lesbianism" in past societies. Authors of such "essentialist" works, as they were termed by their constructionist rivals (though rarely by themselves), looked to the past for validation.[20] This is unsurprising, especially given that most social constructionist work focused on the construction of "homosexuality," leaving heterosexuality undissected and thus powerful within the modern discourse on sexuality. During the 1980s and 1990s sexuality entered the mainstream of historical study, with an explosion of scholarly works focused on specific historical contexts adding depth and sophistication to the field, though theoretical debates continued to circle around the constructionist/essentialist quarrel. As scholars such as the philosopher Edward Stein have demonstrated, the parties to the debate wasted a good deal of time misconstruing or arguing past aspects of each other's arguments.[21] Though the debate is not played out yet, important works are emerging that indicate that a new phase has been entered. David Halperin's chapter in this reader, "Forgetting Foucault" (chapter 2), is notable for its critique of reductive uses of Foucault's work and suggestions for ways forward in the post essentialist-versus-constructionist climate.

Of course the readers of this book—you, touching the page—are situated in the history of sexuality. This is true in two senses. First, sexuality in Western culture today has a centrality, an importance rarely true of other societies and at other times in our history: it is central to our identity, our self-definition, our being. This centrality was not likely the case in the past. Our tendency to define ourselves by our sexuality—hetero, homo, bi, straight, queer, trans—simply does not apply to most of the Western past. Other definitions of self were used. Second, as already intimated, the academic study of sex is a late phenomenon. As Weeks has argued elsewhere, the treatment of sex as a thing in its own right, what he has described as a "continent of knowledge," a discipline with its own experts, is a recent development in historical terms.[22] Its short history dates from the nineteenth century, with the sexologists, the early sexual scientists, those who had the expertise to write and talk with authority about sex. However, these men (and they were males) had relatively little historical sense of sexuality. The actual historiography of sex—that is, historians dealing with sex—is an even more recent phenomenon, a product of the last twenty years.

These dual histories are linked; sex as self and sex as enquiry have not maintained discreet autonomies. Hence the recent discussion—in "My Best Informant's Dress: The Erotic Equation in Fieldwork" and *Taboo: Sex, Identity, and Erotic Subjectivity in Anthropological Fieldwork*—about the implications of sexual involvement in research. Does such interaction with informants, in oral history for example, *enhance* or *compromise* research?[23] Jane Gallop, a well-known feminist professor of English and comparative literature, has said that she sexualizes her teaching, arguing that the most productive form of university instruction occurs in the presence of an erotic current, "a consensual amorous relation" between student and teacher. (Perhaps unsurprisingly, she is the author of a book called *Feminist Accused of Sexual Harassment*.[24]) In 1991 the acting chair of the comparative literature department of the University of Massachusetts finished an article with a quantitative estimate of his gay sexual encounters in the 1970s and 1980s—"a conservative estimate would be three hundred a year between 1977 and 1983."[25] Two decades ago, these issues would never have been raised. Such examples illustrate that the centrality of sexuality in Western culture today applies equally to academia. And one of the most interesting aspects of this discourse is not the occurrence of these various sexual experiences but their open discussion in academic forums.

When, as a prologue to her devastating critique of modern scientific and medical notions of male-female duality, Anne Fausto-Sterling sketched out a brief overview of the history of sex and gender, she came up with a cartoon tracing the history of the West from the active/passive sexuality of the Greco-Roman world, and the reproductive sexual focus of the medieval and early modern periods, through the eighteenth- and early-nineteenth-century creations of the mollies and sapphists, to the more modern scientific categorizations of sexual types.[26] How do we tell this story? Is there a narrative—are there even several narratives—of the history of sex?

"We are preoccupied *with whom* we have sex, the ancients with the question of excess or over-indulgence, activity and passivity," Jeffrey Weeks has written.[27]

In ancient Athens sex was always "an action performed by one person upon another," where the active and passive partners held unequal status, so that the active one was deemed superior to the passive (the one whose body is at the service of another's pleasure.) All sexual encounters that preserved proper social hierarchies were thus, at least in theory, licit. An adult male citizen of Athens could properly have sex with any inferior, including women, adolescent males, noncitizens, and slaves. Illicit sex consisted of acts that broke such hierarchies, such as sex between two adult male citizens (because one man would have to be passive), or between two women (because one woman would have to be active), or where a superior was penetrated by an inferior. Sex "was not simply a private quest for mutual pleasure" but "a manifestation of public status." Ancient sex was a political act.[28]

This model of ancient sexuality has served the liberating purpose of cutting understanding of past sexualities free from modern paradigms. It can, however, be overstated. David Cohen, through studying the practice as well as the theory of Athenian law and stressing "honor" and "shame" over the more neutral "active" and "passive," has pointed out the considerable anxiety felt about the subjection of adolescent boys to the shameful state of being penetrated.[29] Another danger is in stereotyping all "the ancients." Amy Richlin has castigated Foucault for neglecting women especially, but also for producing an antiquity "without Jews . . . Africans, Egyptians, Semites, northern Europeans . . . children, babies, poor people, slaves. All the 'Greeks' are Athenians and most of the 'Romans' are Greeks."[30] Bernadette Brooten has been critical of those who have viewed the past through the "phallocentric lens of male pederasty," thus offering a male model of sexuality that, she argues, is not adequate to account for varieties of female same-sex sex and love.[31]

Historians are now shifting their efforts toward seeing that a range of sexual dispositions did exist in past Western cultures, and toward understanding how those "identities" (we stumble for the appropriate word) operated and were understood within the cultures under question. In chapter 2 Halperin demonstrates that one can find notions of sexual "disposition" or "subjectivity," not just acts, in the premodern world. The Greek and Roman figure of the *kinaidos* or *cinaedus* was a male characterized not by exclusive homoerotic attachment to men (for he could engage in sexual intercourse with women), but by his shameful—because *feminine*—pleasure in being penetrated by men. The *kinaidos*, then, does not stand as evidence for an eternal male "homosexual" type, for his identity is "not defined principally by his sexual subjectivity," but rather by his gender transgression. "It represents an extinct category of social, sexual, and gender deviance." The *kinaidos* is just one of many sexual identities that do not have exact modern counterparts: *moikhoi, moikheutria, tribades, hetaeristriai, viragines*, and even pederasts.[32] It is in such historically specific examples of alternatives to modern sexual types that historians will be able to make the strongest claims to the historical construction of sexuality.

We must be prepared to recognize that the cultures we are dealing with may actually have seen bodies differently from the way in which most of us see them today. James Schultz tackles this problem in chapter 3 in a highly original fashion. What did it mean to be "heterosexual," in the imprecise sense of directing one's sexual desires toward certain men if one is a woman or certain women if one is a man, in a period before the invention of "heterosexuality" in the precise sense of taking "sexual object choice as the primary criterion of classification"? The modern heterosexual regime is dependent on nineteenth- and twentieth-century scientific models that privilege biological sex over cultural gender as a marker of differences between male and female.[33] As Schultz demonstrates, influenced by the work of Judith Butler, medieval regulatory schemas did *not* produce the same male and female bodies that modern ones do. In contemporary heterosexuality it is imperative that anatomical sex differences be noted and incorporated within desiring impulses. In *Tristan*, however, desirable male and female bodies are not explicitly distinguished by sex, for "a beautiful man and a beautiful woman *should* look the same." Desire, rather, is prompted by class on the one hand, and gender, marked by clothing, on the other. Where modern sexual desire focuses on the desiring subject—one desires members of the *opposite* sex, or the *same* sex as oneself—desire in *Tristan* is governed by the object. Thus women are desired in one way and men in another, and though women are usually desired by men and men by women it is possible for a male subject to convey the mode of desire for a male object. This study is especially valuable because it grapples with the problem of understanding constructions of sexuality in a culture that looks superficially, and deceptively, similar to our own. Schultz describes the phenomenon as heterosexuality before heterosexuality; the point is that our concept of heterosexual desire does not adequately describe what was occurring in this premodern context.

In a culture that did not know modern heterosexuality, activities that in today's world constitute clear breaches of the heterosexual marital paradigm, such as same-sex intercourse, transvestism, and prostitution, cannot be expected to have had the same meanings as they have developed. As Ruth Karras and David Lorenzo Boyd argue in chapter 4 in their exploration of the 1394 case of John/Eleanor Rykener, labels such as "bisexual," "transvestite," and "prostitute" cannot adequately convey the fourteenth-century London court's notion of Rykener's transgressions. His/her case offers a microcosmic view of medieval English sexualities and the gulfs that lie between the medieval and the modern.

A cheap trick in a first lecture in a course on the history of sexuality is to show the audience an overhead of an early modern drawing of the vagina, taken from Thomas Laqueur's influential book *Making Sex*. The uninitiated nearly always take it for a penis, for we simply do not view this image in the same way as did the sixteenth-century male medical experts. Laqueur has proposed a basic division between what he has described as a pre-Enlightenment "one-sex" perception of the body and the post-Enlightenment "two-sex model." Before the late eighteenth century, a woman was portrayed in the medical texts as a man with sex organs inverted: the vagina was an interior penis, the ovaries were testicles. Male and female were the same sex with different genders. The rigid modern two-sex correlation between gender and sex, male and female as different sexes with different genitals, as "organically one or the other of two incommensurable sexes," was not part of the premodern mindset.[34] The eighteenth century, according to the argument, effected the emergence of the modern framework of two sexes and two genders, where women and men have different bodies, and gender corresponds to this anatomical difference.

The changing construction of women's bodies was closely linked to the rise of the male pleasure principle. A "two-seed" model of reproduction accompanied the one-sex model. Women's orgasms had, since Greek antiquity, been deemed necessary for conception, as both women and men produced an essential seed.[35] There was a stress on female pleasure (as a means to reproduction). The radical transformation of the "neck of the womb" into the "vagina," which Mary Fissell (chapter 5) locates in the late seventeenth and early eighteenth centuries, reconceptualized the female genitals as primarily passive vessels designed for man's pleasure and active reproductive drive. Fissell demonstrates that popular childbearing guides and domestic conduct books from this period asserted male "control over female sexuality." Female sexual pleasure, despite the sixteenth-century "discovery" of the clitoris, went into a decline in importance from which it has perhaps yet to recover.[36]

As Jacques Donzelot once put it, the priest preceded the doctor as the manager of sexuality.[37] Sex has long existed in an environment of Christian-inspired church and state intervention, "regulating desire, reforming practice," as Merry Wiesner-Hanks has rather aptly termed it.[38] Peter Brown's chapter, "Bodies and Minds" (chapter 6), explores the influence of early Christian thought on sexuality within a late Roman culture that was receptive to the ideal of bodily control and renunciation but had not previously made such a deep connection between sexual impulses and the self. The innovation of the early Christians was in the compaction of the body and the mind, and the formation of the idea that if the body could be set free from sexual compulsions the mind, or the self, would be freed from earthly society and finally from the "chill contagion of the grave." One implication of the new austere regime was that an altered gender system—based more powerfully in bodily and reproductive differences between men and women—produced a dominant sexual culture of marital relationships and declared illicit all acts and desires that fell beyond the marital sexually dimorphic model.

The typically medieval sexual culture that awkwardly attempted to reconcile the celibate ideal with the marital ideal was simplified by Protestantism's rejection of perpetual celibacy, the Counter Reformation's tightening of grip over reproductive sexuality through extended use of the Inquisition, and state-directed attempts to control the realm through control of the family.[39] The early modern focus on marital sexuality was hardly new, but its place at the pinnacle of acceptable sexual life was. Conditions in the New England colonies took the Old World's esteem for marital sexualities and gave it added force. The difficulties of survival in a new society made families essential as economic units of production and consumption. The Puritan ideology strengthened the importance of the "reproductive matrix." As John D'Emilio and Estelle Freedman demonstrate in chapter 7, much of the "regulation of deviance" practiced in seventeenth-century New England was aimed at channelling all sexual activity within the functionally and ideologically desirable marital matrix. Even individuals who transgressed the sexual boundaries could be fully incorporated within respectable society, provided they redeemed themselves through marriage. By the late seventeenth century, with the early exigencies of survival receding, white colonists turned greater attention to condemnation of interracial sexual activity as a second stage of social formation, using such sexual prohibitions and denigration of black slaves' sexuality in particular as one mode of asserting white domination.

The patterns of regulation varied. Robert Muchembled has argued for nothing short of a French cultural revolution between 1550 and 1750. Sexual and bodily matters were treated with new decorum. Church and state inculcated a sense of sin. In England, the more strongly enforced moralities of the sixteenth and seventeenth centuries contrasted with the relative laxity of the eighteenth century, when there was far less control of popular mores.[40] In chapter 8 of this book Albert Hurtado deals with Spanish efforts to colonize sex in California, where Christianity and race made for a complex sexual encounter. For much of Western history sexual behavior has been governed by a range of punishments and controls, demonstrating a will to enforce an always gendered and frequently racial morality.

While the sexual histories that we provide are provisional—shifting as we write and you read—there are pivotal points in this narrative. One claimed moment is the eighteenth century, at the transition between the early modern and the modern. The reconfiguration of women's bodies and the shift from the two-seed to one-seed models of conception, discussed earlier, are aspects of the eighteenth-century redefinition of sex outlined by Tim Hitchcock in chapter 9. He also argues that a fundamental shift occurred at this time toward a phallocentric penetrative model of sexuality that he cleverly links to a range of demographic, social, and cultural changes. Even if many historians remain unconvinced of the scale, concentration, and consistency of this eighteenth-century revolution in constructions of sexuality, such bold interpretations have certainly forced a rethinking of our taken-for-granted categories and the manner in which many view the Western past.[41]

Like several terms encountered in the history of sexuality, *pornography* did not appear until the nineteenth century. Sexually explicit material certainly existed in the period before the late eighteenth and nineteenth centuries. We know that classicists have had great trouble translating some of the Latin in Catullus: "*Paedicabo ego vos et irrumabo*," meaning, according to a recent translation, "I will bugger you and I will fuck your mouths."[42] We know of the sixteenth-century poems and engravings (of sexual positions) of the Italian Pietro Aretino.[43] But the significant thing about this early "pornography" was that it was presented mainly in terms of reproduction (medical advice for the married has been described as "concealed pornography"[44]) or was used to attack the crown, the church, or aspects of society. In chapter 10, Robert Darnton describes one eighteenth-century French work in which a Jesuit priest flogs a young woman while giving her a radical philosophy lesson. "Strange as it may seem to a modern reader, the sex and the philosophy go hand in hand throughout the novel. The characters masturbate and copulate, then discuss ontology and morality." Much of this literature was so hostile to the church that it seemed to be more about religion than sex. In other words, before 1800, as the historian Lynn Hunt has expressed it, pornography was "most often a vehicle for using the shock of sex to criticize religious and political authorities." It rarely existed purely for sexual titillation. Pornography as an end in itself is another recent construct.[45]

One of the more interesting developments in the history of sex is a newer historiography that posits the multiplicities of Victorian sex. For Foucault, and for those who have been influenced by him, the Victorian period saw an outpouring of discussion and classification of sex—in the debates, surveys, and legislation dealing with population, public health, women's and children's work, prostitution, and venereal disease; in the copious medical advice literature and advertisements concerning sexual matters. Foucault was not arguing for freedom of sexuality in the Victorian period—indeed all sorts of controls and categorizations were being made—but there was certainly no silence about sex.[46] *Parasexuality* is Peter Bailey's useful term for a type of Victorian sexuality, quite open in its expression, flirtatious, but stopping short of more serious sexual involvement. Parasexuality is sex "deployed but contained"—"everything but." Bailey (chapter 11) has advanced the barmaid as the object of desire in parasexuality, but it could just as likely have been a music hall entertainer (male or female), an acrobat, actor or actress, or performers of anything from opera to minstrelsy. Parasexuality, then, could be applied beyond the bar, to dance halls, theaters, parks, races, and streets—anyplace where the sexes gathered and interacted without necessarily progressing to more serious (heterosexual) sex. It is particularly interesting as a phenomenon because it hovers somewhere in the middle of theories of repression and permissiveness. Parasexuality represents a certain amount of freedom of interaction, but with simultaneous control. It is a concept that also encourages historians of all periods to consider alternative definitions of sexuality.

Martha Vicinus has argued that when writing histories of lesbianism it is important not to essentialize: to search for the emergence of some rigidly defined ideal. Historians have looked for mannish lesbians (including examples of women who passed as men), romantic friendships between women, and self-identified lesbians. The figure of the butch, because she is readily identifiable, has received undue attention in lesbian history. But what about women who were married to men and had relationships with women? Historians should be open to a wider range of possibilities, for "sexual behaviour is polymorphous, changeable and impossible to define absolutely."[47]

For some time, historians have argued that the lesbian role did not exist until the late nineteenth century, when it was identified by the sexologists. Before that, the history of lesbianism focuses on what have been termed romantic friendships: close romantic relationships that probably did not involve actual physical sex and were certainly not stigmatized until lesbianism was discovered. But the problem with this sort of argument, Terry Castle has pointed out, is that we might have argued the same about the friendships of Anne Lister in the early nineteenth century if her diaries had not been discovered.[48] That is why the diaries of this early-nineteenth-century Yorkshire gentlewoman are so important. It is clear that she engaged in what we (though not she) would term lesbian behavior. Indeed as Anna Clark argues in chapter 12, Lister constructed a kind of lesbian identity based on her reading of such behavior in the classics, her interaction with other, similar women, and an awareness of her own same-sex desires. She was cautious about declaring herself. But she had no trouble interacting in what could be seen as something approaching a lesbian subculture. Even more interesting, her diary reveals a range of such sexuality. Lister was what would later be termed a stone dyke: she penetrated her lovers but would not let them penetrate her (womanize her, as she put it). She had a long-term lover who was married—that is, who was engaging in, for want of better terms, heterosexual and homosexual sex: her husband gave her venereal disease, which she passed on to Lister. Lister unofficially married a woman whom she lived with as a female companion, and she knew of others in similar situations. But Lister also had relationships with what we would term "heterosexual" women: young women who later married, and a widow with a child. Women flirted with her as they might with a man.

As we have already seen, the nineteenth century was also the era of sexology, which has to be seen as another important moment in the history of sex. The terms *heterosexual, homosexual, bisexual, sadist, masochist*—indeed *sexuality* itself—all date from that period.[49] It was an ambivalent legacy. As several historians have shown, sexology opened out the subject of sex, enabling sex to be taken seriously, and recognizing a wide range of desires and practices. Sexuality was established as being worthy of serious study and as being central to both the individual and society. By collating, listing, and publishing case histories of their patients, sexologists put into discourse a wide range of different sexualities. Yet this very categorization could be restrictive: stigmatizing, denying historical change and variability, establishing the tyranny of the norm—"seeking to produce" what Joseph Bristow has termed "some everlasting truth about the sexual capacity of human beings."[50] This move by medicine and science into the sexual arena meant in effect that something called sexuality was located and defined, boundaries were set up, and deviancy was mapped. The normal and the abnormal were medically and scientifically inscribed. Hence the title of Richard von Krafft-Ebing's 1894 book: *Psychopathia sexualis, with Especial Reference to the Antipathic Sexual Instinct: A Medico-Forensic Study*. The sexologists essentially created the pervert; there were no perverts before they were identified. And there was no normality before normality's other, perversion, was discovered. The sexologists helped to create the strict categories of the twentieth century: "normal" heterosexual married sex versus its perversions—fetishism, homosexuality, and other forms of "degenerate" behavior.

One of the dangers of this argument has always been that it precluded agency on the part of the so-called perverts. And yet the readers of Krafft-Ebing took heart from his case studies, sending letters to him recounting their own life situations. In chapter 13 Harry Oosterhuis shows that the work of Krafft-Ebing provided the opportunity for self-awareness and self-expression. Men used its findings to argue that their same-sex desires were inherited and therefore natural. Readers used its case studies to locate like-minded communities, and they provided them with the feeling that they were not isolated. There is little recorded evidence that women used the book in the same manner, although they may have privately done so, despite its male focus. Whatever the attentions of the compiler, the stories provided narratives similar to "coming out." As Oosterhuis explains, these autobiographies did not so much represent lives that had been lived but people trying to give meaning to their lives and construct a sexual identity in keeping with their desires. Jennifer Terry has recently argued similarly of twentieth-century medico-scientific sex surveys.[51] The history of sexuality contains a continuous dialectic between the urge to control and human agency.

It is ironic that the most comprehensive histories we have are of same-sex attractions, and predictable that they deal disproportionately with male homosexuality. Randolph Trumbach has claimed that in the eighteenth century, particularly in London, homosexuality emerged as an identity or culture, or subculture. According to this interpretation, the birth of modern homosexuality began in what were called the molly houses, clubs where men met and had sex together. The molly houses contained, or were visited by, what were called mollies, some of whom were male prostitutes, effeminate men who dressed and behaved like women. Thus there developed—both in terms of self-identification and stigmatization—what could be described as a male homosexual subculture. Trumbach's claim, then, is that the birth of the modern homosexual dates from the eighteenth century. He has written of two worldwide systems for organizing homosexual behavior, and sees 1700 as witnessing the replacement of the old system with the new.[52]

Historians are always tempted by such turning points, but we should remain somewhat skeptical about the extent of claimed change. The impossibility of simplistic stories of the transformation of sexuality is demonstrated by George Chauncey's study of early-twentieth-century New York, which traces the emergence of an identifiable gay male culture in that city between the 1890s and the 1930s, centred in the Bowery, the bars, speakeasies, clubs of Harlem and Greenwich Village, and Times Square. It is a history of the migrant, black, and working-class areas, but involves middle-class men as well. There were cruising areas (pick-up points) in the streets and parks, and men had sex in bathhouses and in the backrooms of saloons. (It is interesting that this world was also the world of developing twentieth-century hetererosexual freedom.) Gay men had codes of self-presentation so that they could recognize one another.[53]

One of the most interesting findings in Chauncey's book is that the division into the binary, heterosexual and homosexual, was very recent—as late as the 1950s for working-class culture, he suggests. Before that there were various forms of male sexuality. There were the fairies (sometimes called faggots or flaming faggots, or pansies), identifiable as queer mainly because of their effeminacy. The abnormality of the fairy lay in his womanlike appearance and behavior. Then there were the men who had sex with the fairies, called trade, but they were not considered to be abnormal or homosexual, provided they were masculine in appearance and were the penetrator in the relationship. They assumed the male role and used the fairy as they would a woman. Indeed their choice of sexual partner could equally be male or female. They were often sailors, soldiers, policemen, or the single men who lived in the numerous lodging houses—including the YMCAs, which were notorious pick-up points. Then there were the queers. They were interested in men but did not assume the effeminate behavior of the fairies. They were probably more numerous than the fairies, but less visible. Finally, there were the wolves. They were conventionally masculine, but showed a preference for men or boys—as Chauncey expresses it, they were not labelled homosexual but their preference was obvious.

As Chauncey's contribution in this volume (chapter 14) shows, the world of the fairy was far removed from any strict division between deviant homosexuality and compulsory heterosexuality. Some men were seen as womanlike and effeminate, but the men who sought them out for sex were not considered homosexual or unmanly. What was important in this culture was whether a person acted like a male or a female (that is, gender) rather than their sexual orientation (whether they were gay or straight). The penetrator, because penetration was associated with dominance, did not compromise his masculinity. A fairy was a fairy not because he engaged in what we would term homosexual activity but because he was the passive partner—womanlike. Men went with fairies much as they went with female prostitutes. In other words, although on the face of it this was activity we would identify as male homosexuality, in fact the attitudes, desires, and identities involved in this activity were not the same as many would now mean by the term.

It is often observed that in the nineteenth and twentieth centuries the personnel of science and medicine replaced the churches' ministers and priests as the custodians, confessors, and controllers of sex—though this is not to minimize the continuing power of religious morality upon sexual mores. One of the main ways in which sex became part of the medical and scientific domain, and in the process came to be seen as central to modern society and individual identity, was through the sex survey.[54] The sex survey helped to establish sex as that "continent of knowledge" referred to at the start of this introduction. It accomplished this by establishing (legitimating) the scientific and medical experts of sex, by revealing beliefs and practices, and by structuring attitudes. It is important to be aware of the discursive power of the sex survey: since several of the surveys were published as massive sellers, they were a powerful—though always ambivalent—means of shaping attitudes. In chapter 15 Janice Irvine discusses the Kinsey surveys, the most famous published sex research of the twentieth century. As Irvine discusses, the methodologies and findings of the Kinsey project were complex—the implications of the Kinsey reports and the team's own private sexualities are still debated—but the reports firmly established sex in the public domain. One of Kinsey's more controversial findings was the seven-point continuum of sexual activity that ranged from exclusive heterosexuality at one end to exclusive homosexuality at the other; that is, male and female same-sex behavior was a natural feature of human sexuality. Nearly 50 percent of the male sample had experienced some combination of hetero- and homosexual relations while adults. Not surprisingly, these claims provoked a backlash.[55]

In the twentieth century we also return to pornography and the sexual anxieties that it has produced. Pornography, in the sense of sex for sex's sake, emerged most clearly for the first time in the nineteenth century in what Steven Marcus has described as pornotopia, literature in which "almost every human consideration apart from sexuality is excluded."[56] It was the nineteenth century that also saw the shift from pornography locked away in private collections, printed in small, expensive print runs, or in a language accessible only to the enlightened few, to the possibility of being available for purchase by large numbers of the population. Sexually explicit material was no longer confined to elite men but was there to corrupt women and children.[57] However, in the twentieth century the possibilities for production exploded still further with print, photography, film, video, and computer-generated words and images. The Attorney General's Commission on Pornography during 1985–86, discussed by Carole Vance in chapter 16, was a product of this more recent phase. Pornography as a category became separated through the very process of classification and condemnation. The effort to classify and prohibit helped to sharpen the definition of pornographic works—in effect helping to create them and separate them from other literature. Hence pornography has been created by its suppression: a supreme example of the way in which prohibition of sex contributes to its construction. Vance discusses the irony of the "excited repression" of the carefully staged hearings, what Susan Stewart has described as "the impossibility of describing desire without generating desire."[58]

Many of the readers of this volume will not have experienced sexuality as it was before AIDS, that deadly, shorthand, four-letter word that dominates the structure of books and university courses dealing with the history of sex. AIDS is always the last chapter, lurking ominously at the end of the history of twentieth-century sexuality.[59] Jeffrey Weeks once observed that what is remarkable about AIDS is "not simply its virulence, but the weight of symbolic meaning that it carries. . . . [I]t throws into sharp focus the murkier preoccupations of our age."[60] If, as it is often said, the history of sex contains an inexorable pairing of freedom and repression, it is possible to see the cataclysmic impact of AIDS in the early 1980s as a more dramatic intensification of this process. It arrived amid a freeing up of sexual norms, including a challenge to marriage and heterosexuality as compulsory cultural and social requirements. AIDS gave a powerful boost to the forces of conservatism. AIDS is not a gay disease, yet it became one in all the imagery and panic of the 1980s. As Steven Seidman explains in chapter 17—first published in 1988 as AIDS went heterosexual—the casualties of this discourse were not just homosexuals, but they bore the brunt of the backlash. AIDS represented the penalty for homosexual promiscuity.[61]

The medicalizing—and thereby the regulating—of sex has been intriguingly illustrated in some recent inventions of sexual conditions. The sex addict is one such recent construct. Born of a wider culture of self-help and addiction anxiety, promoted by the media, reinforced by the impact of AIDS in the 1980s, and amenable to extremely conservative impulses toward sexual control and correspondingly gendered heterosexual morality, the sex addict tells us much about the sexual anxieties of the late twentieth century. "[T]he invention of the figure of the sex addict does not speak to the discovery of an essential condition or type of person, but is rather the medical product of specific social and political circumstances."[62] In chapter 18, Janice Irvine charts the brief histories and implications of the creation of the sex addict and his/her other, those said to suffer from "inhibited sexual desire" (ISD).

One of the silences in Foucault's sexual histories is the interaction between race and sex. Ann Laura Stoler has argued persuasively for the importance of race and empire in the construction of European sexualities.[63] Abdul R. JanMohamed has highlighted the limitations of a Foucauldian polymorphous view of power in explaining what he terms "racialized sexuality," in which European "positional superiority" is maintained by a discourse of bipolarity: white/black, superior/inferior, rational/sensual, self/other, and so on.[64] In a notorious case of racial and sexual othering in the nineteenth century, Saartje Baartman, the so-called Hottentot Venus, was exhibited for her (perceived) protruding buttocks and the enlarged genitalia and hypersexuality that they were held to represent. "The antithesis of European sexual mores and beauty is embodied in the black," writes Sander Gilman, "and the essential black . . . is the Hottentot. The physical appearance of the Hottentot is, indeed, the central nineteenth-century icon for sexual difference between the European and the black."[65] In chapter 19—employing historical comparison with the othering of Baartman—Magdalena Barrera discusses an example of racialized sexuality in contemporary popular culture involving a famous body part: Jennifer Lopez's butt.

Much recent work on identity has thrown binary certainties into doubt, questioning not only any direct and necessary correspondence between sex and gender, but arguing that sex itself is a gendered category. Gender, in this new conceptual framework, is best considered as performance, "a corporeal style."[66] There are several ways of demonstrating the nonfixity of gender, the possibility, as Judith Butler has expressed it, of becoming a being "whom neither *man* nor *woman* truly describes."[67] The implications for sexualities are of course immense. Figures of cyberfiction, literary invention, and film and video, pop and performance artists, surgically transformed "trans-intersexuals," and a range of practitioners of queer sex have literally fucked with gender and sexuality ("genderfuck") by shattering the link between the body, sex, gender, and desire.[68] Transgender has unleashed the possibility of a social female with a penis and a social male with a vagina. The final chapters, by C. Jacob Hale (chapter 20) and Kay Schaffer (chapter 21), provide two fascinating examples of a postmodern unsettling of sex: leatherdyke boys and leatherdyke daddies, and the fluid cyber-sex bodies and sexualities of the DNA Sluts.

It must have been observed many times that, like whiteness, the power of heterosexuality resides in the combination of its invisibility and assumed naturalness—"dominance by seeming not to be anything in particular."[69] As suggested by the quotation with which we began this introduction, heterosexuality has maintained a hidden power in traditional ways of viewing the past. One of the great contributions of the histories of sexualities has been to demonstrate that heterosexuality—like its other, homosexuality—is a very recent construct. The actual word *heterosexual* did not enter the English language until the 1890s with an article in the *Chicago Medical Recorder* and the translation of Krafft-Ebing's book *Psychopathia sexualis,* but it probably did not become part of more widespread usage until the 1930s.[70] It is interesting that sex researchers and subjects were using the term in a New York survey of 1935.[71] For many, the claim that heterosexuality is a recent construct will still seem a rather bizarre statement. In modern Western culture, whatever our tolerances, heterosexuality is the dominant ideology. It is assumed, a given, portrayed as the natural state of affairs in a myriad of everyday messages, representations, and interactions. The definition of *heterosexual,* according to the *Concise Oxford Dictionary,* as late as the 1960s, was "relating to or characterised by the *normal* relation of the sexes." Its opposite was homosexual (by implication: *abnormal*). Moreover, generations of historians have imposed heterosexual assumptions on the past, and, as they did so, helped to construct the heterosexuality of their own society—just as the early wave of gay historians were using the past to construct their identities, the only difference lying in their respective awarenesses of what they were doing. Historians merely assumed that heterosexuality had always been—because it was "natural"—and that it was only homosexuality that had been constructed.

But Jonathan Ned Katz has argued that heterosexuality is only "one historically specific way of organizing the sexes and their pleasures," and accordingly divides the past into several phases, all of which he terms examples of non-heterosexual societies.[72] The short but complex history of the fashioning of heterosexuality begins with the late-nineteenth-century location, definition, and then separation of homosexuality from heterosexuality, facilitated, as we have seen, by the work of the sexologists. Heterosexuality arose as the other to emerging homosexuality, and that is why it is artificial to separate the histories of the two: Jennifer Terry's brilliant history of American scientific thinking about homosexuality is as much a history of the making of American heterosexuality.[73] But the construction of systematic opposite-sex desire also emerged from the free sexuality of the early part of the twentieth century: the consumer youth culture of the charity girl and the flapper, with its stress on female sexual autonomy and recognition of female desire. Historians have mapped out the construction of what they call a heterosexual masculinity in twentieth-century America, the male equivalent of the new woman. Thus there emerged the "heterosexual mystique." The new sex norm was based on the difference of the sexes; the assumption that this difference was best represented and expressed through opposite-sex attraction, *and* the normality of this. Heterosexuality was thus a strange amalgam of open parading of male-female sexual pleasure and a stress on marriage, the family, and procreation. This combination varied in its emphasis according to the historical period: the pleasure of hetero sex was strong in the 1920s; the hetero family dominated the 1950s.[74]

If this collection has one central aim it is to work toward destabilizing the silent historical hegemony of a unitary heterosexuality.[75] But it should be read as providing analysis of a series of provisional moments and shifting ideals rather than any kind of comprehensive chronology. *Sexualities in History* consists of rethinking fragments toward a variety of sexual histories. It is surely significant that another contributor to this collection, Carole Vance, an anthropologist, once began an account of the development of research on sexuality with the observation that the source of a "more cultural and non-essentialist" approach to the subject was not her own discipline but *history*.[76] To paraphrase Robert Darnton, the history of sex is indeed good to think with.[77]

NOTES

1. Eve Kosofsky Sedgwick, *Tendencies* (Durham, 1994), pp. 10–11.

2. R. C. Lewontin, "Sex, Lies, and Social Science," *New York Review of Books* (April 20, 1995): 24–29 (quote on p. 28); and the reply by Edward O. Laumann and others, *New York Review of Books* (May 25, 1995): 43–44.

3. There were two reports. Edward O. Laumann and others, *The Social Organization of Sexuality* (Chicago, 1994) was for professionals. Robert T. Michael and others, *Sex in America: A Definitive Survey* (Boston, 1994) was aimed at a more popular market. The quotes above come from the latter: see Michael and others, *Sex in America*, pp. 55, 67, 123, 130, 131, 135.

4. Mary Poovey, "Sex in America," *Critical Inquiry* 24 (1998): 366–92 (esp. pp. 375–76).

5. Donald E. Hall and Maria Pramaggiore, eds., *RePresenting Bisexualities: Subjects and Cultures of Fluid Desire* (New York, 1996), esp. chs. by the editors and Michael du Plessis. The quote comes from p. 3.

6. Anthony Giddens, *The Transformation of Intimacy* (Oxford, 1992), pp. 14–15, 27.

7. Lynn Jamieson, *Intimacy: Personal Relationships in Modern Societies* (Cambridge, 1998), esp. ch. 5: "Sex and Intimacy." For an interesting example of heteronormativity in action, see Chrys Ingraham, *White Weddings: Romancing Heterosexuality in Popular Culture* (New York, 1999).

8. Ingraham, *White Weddings*, pp. 15–18.

9. A. L. Rowse provides a biographical survey of "homosexual" men from the Middle Ages to the twentieth century in *Homosexuals in History: A Study of Ambivalence in Society, Literature and the Arts* (London, 1977).

10. See Robert A. Padgug, "Sexual Matters: On Conceptualizing Sexuality in History," *Radical History Review* 20 (1979): 3–23 (reprinted in *Hidden from History: Reclaiming the Gay and Lesbian Past*, ed. Martin Duberman, Martha Vicinus, and George Chauncey [Harmondsworth, 1989], pp. 54–64); Arnold I. Davidson, "Sex and the Emergence of Sexuality," *Critical Inquiry* 14 (1987): 16–48; Jeffrey Weeks, *Sex, Politics, and Society: The Regulation of Sexuality since 1800* (London, 1989), ch. 1; David M. Halperin, John J. Winkler, and Froma I. Zeitlin, "Introduction," in *Before Sexuality: The Construction of Erotic Experience in the Ancient Greek World*, ed. Halperin, Winkler, and Zeitlin (Princeton, 1990), pp. 3–7; Domna C. Stanton, "Introduction: The Subject of Sexuality," in *Discourses of Sexuality from Aristotle to Aids*, ed. Domna C. Stanton (Ann Arbor, 1992), pp. 1–46; Gayle S. Rubin, "Thinking Sex: Notes for a Radical Theory of the Politics of Sexuality," in *The Lesbian and Gay Studies Reader*, ed. Henry Abelove, Michele A. Barale, and David M. Halperin (New York, 1993), ch. 1; David M. Halperin, "Is There a History of Sexuality?" in *The Lesbian and Gay Studies Reader*, ed. Abelove, Barale, and Halperin, ch. 28; Joseph Bristow, *Sexuality* (London, 1997), pp. 1–6; Jeffrey Weeks, *Making Sexual History* (Cambridge, 2000), esp. "Introduction: Making Sexual History."

11. Davidson, "Sex," pp. 41–47.

12. G. Rattray Taylor, *Sex in History* (London, 1953), pp. 19, 48–49.

13. James A. Brundage, *Law, Sex, and Christian Society in Medieval Europe* (Chicago, 1987), p. 1.

14. Vern L. Bullough, *Sex, Society, and History* (New York, 1976), p. ix; (with Bonnie Bullough), *Sin, Sickness, and Sanity: A History of Sexual Attitudes* (New York, 1977), pp. 1–9.

15. Notably, Kate Millett, *Sexual Politics* (London, 1969); Susan Brownmiller, *Against Our Will: Men, Women, and Rape* (New York, 1975); J. [Ned] Katz, *Gay American History: Lesbians and Gay Men in the U.S.A.* (New York, 1976).

16. Michel Foucault, *The History of Sexuality, Volume 1: An Introduction*, trans. Robert Hurley (New York, 1978).

17. Michel Foucault, *The History of Sexuality, Volume 2: The Use of Pleasure*, trans. Robert Hurley (New York, 1985); Michel Foucault, *The History of Sexuality, Volume 3: The Care of the Self*, trans. Robert Hurley (New York, 1986). Classicists are divided over the extent to which these volumes provide useful portrayals of ancient sexualities: see the essays in David H. Larmour, Paul Allen Miller, and Charles Platter, eds., *Rethinking Sexuality: Foucault and Classical Antiquity* (Princeton, 1998).

18. Jonathan Ned Katz, *The Invention of Heterosexuality* (New York, 1995), pp. 6–11; Padgug, "Sexual Matters"; Jeffrey Weeks, *Sexuality* (London, 1986). It is interesting that Foucault's and Weeks's projects were being developed at much the same time. Weeks explains that *Sex, Politics, and Society* (1981 edn.) was "conceived before I encountered Foucault, but completed in full knowledge of Foucault's enterprise." See Weeks, *Making Sexual History*, p. 9.

19. John Boswell, *Christianity, Social Tolerance, and Homosexuality: Gay People in Western Europe from the Beginning of the Christian Era to the Fourteenth Century* (Chicago, 1980); Judith C. Brown, *Immodest Acts: The Life of a Lesbian Nun in Renaissance Italy* (New York, 1986).

20. See John Boswell, "Revolutions, Universals, and Sexual Categories," in *Hidden from History*, ed. Duberman, Vicinus, and Chauncey, pp. 34–36.

21. Edward Stein, "Conclusion: The Essentials of Constructionism and the Construction of Essentialism," in *Forms of Desire: Sexual Orientation and the Social Constructionist Controversy*, ed. Edward Stein (New York, 1990).

22. Weeks, *Sex, Politics, and Society*, p. 12.

23. Esther Newton, "My Best Informant's Dress: The Erotic Equation in Fieldwork," *Cultural Anthropology* 8 (1993): 3–23; Don Kulick and Margaret Willson, eds., *Taboo: Sex, Identity, and Erotic Subjectivity in Anthropological Fieldwork* (London, 1995). Such a stark contrast between enhancement and compromise does an injustice to the purpose of these two publications; we are making a rhetorical point.

24. Jane Gallop, *Feminist Accused of Sexual Harassment* (Durham, 1997).

25. Samuel R. Delany, "Street Talk/Straight Talk," *differences* 3.2 (1991): 21–38 (quote from p. 37).

26. Anne Fausto-Sterling, *Sexing the Body: Gender Politics and the Construction of Sexuality* (New York, 2000), p. 11. It is a very good cartoon.

27. Weeks, *Sexuality*, p. 32. Among the large number of studies now available on ancient sexualities, see David M. Halperin, "Sex before Sexuality: Pederasty, Politics, and Power in Classical Athens," in *Hidden from History*, ed. Duberman, Vicinus, and Chauncey, pp. 37–53; David M. Halperin, *One Hundred Years of Homosexuality and Other Essays on Greek Love* (New York, 1990); Marilyn B. Skinner, "Introduction: *Quod multo fit aliter in Graecia*," in *Roman Sexualities*, ed. Judith P. Hallett and Marilyn B. Skinner (Princeton, 1997); C. A. Williams, *Roman Homosexuality: Ideologies of Masculinity in Classical Antiquity* (New York, 1999).

28. Halperin, "Sex before Sexuality," pp. 48–51.

29. David Cohen, *Law, Sexuality, and Society: The Enforcement of Morals in Classical Athens* (Cambridge, 1991), pp. 171–82.

30. Amy Richlin, "Foucault's *History of Sexuality*: A Useful Theory for Women?" in *Rethinking Sexuality*, ed. Larmour, Miller, and Platter, p. 139.

31. Bernadette J. Brooten, "Response," in the forum "Lesbian Historiography before the Name?" (on Bernadette J. Brooten's *Love between Women: Early Christian Responses to Female Homoeroticism* [Chicago, 1996]) in *GLQ* 4 (1998): 557–630, esp. pp. 615–16.

32. David M. Halperin, contribution to ibid., pp. 565–69.

33. Thomas Laqueur, *Making Sex: Body and Gender from the Greeks to Freud* (Cambridge, Mass., 1990).

34. Ibid., pp. 8, 52, 124–25, 149.

35. Ibid. A shorter version is his "Orgasm, Generation, and the Politics of Reproductive Biology," in *The Making of the Modern Body: Sexuality and Society in the Nineteenth Century*, ed. Catherine Gallagher and Thomas Laqueur (Berkeley, 1987), pp. 1–41. For medieval theories of women's orgasm derived from ancient texts, see Joan Cadden, *Meanings of Sex Difference in the Middle Ages: Medicine, Science, and Culture* (Cambridge, 1993), ch. 4. The dominance of the two-seed theory up to the eighteenth century despite the existence of the Aristotelian one-seed theory (long lost to the West but revived after the twelfth century) reveals a respect for the centrality of women's role in reproduction and the importance of the reproductive matrix for organizing medieval and early modern sexualities.

36. Danielle Jacquart and Claude Thomasset, *Sexuality and Medicine in the Middle Ages*, trans. Matthew Adamson (Princeton, 1988), p. 46. The clitoris had been known of earlier, but its role in female pleasure not fully explored.

37. Jacques Donzelot, *The Policing of Families*, trans. Robert Hurley (New York, 1979), p. 171.

38. Merry E. Wiesner-Hanks, *Christianity and Sexuality in the Early Modern World: Regulating Desire, Reforming Practice* (New York, 2000).

39. Robert A. Nye, ed., *Sexuality* (Oxford, 1999), pp. 51–53.

40. Robert Muchembled, *Popular Culture and Elite Culture in Early Modern France, 1400–1750* (Baton Rouge, 1985); Lawrence Stone, *The Family, Sex, and Marriage in England, 1500–1800* (London, 1977), pp. 631–35.

41. Hitchcock has also written an excellent history of early modern English sexualities: Tim Hitchcock, *English Sexualities, 1700–1800* (London, 1997).

42. Walter Kendrick, *The Secret Museum: Pornography in Modern Culture* (Berkeley, 1996), p. 43. This influential history of pornography was first published in 1987.

43. Ibid., pp. 58–64; Paula Findlen, "Humanism, Politics, and Pornography in Renaissance Italy," in *The Invention of Pornography: Obscenity and the Origins of Modernity, 1500–1800*, ed. Lynn Hunt (New York, 1993), ch. 1.

44. Roy Porter, "The Literature of Sexual Advice before 1800," in *Sexual Knowledge, Sexual Science: The History of Attitudes to Sexuality*, ed. Roy Porter and Mikuláš Teich (Cambridge, 1994), p. 150.

45. See Lynn Hunt, "Introduction: Obscenity and the Origins of Modernity, 1500–1800," in *The Invention of Pornography*, ed. Hunt, pp. 9–45. Quote is from p. 10.

46. Weeks, *Sex, Politics, and Society,* esp. ch. 2.

47. Martha Vicinus, "Lesbian History: All Theory and No Facts or All Facts and No Theory?" *Radical History Review* 60 (1994): 68. See also Lilian Faderman, *Surpassing the Love of Men: Romantic Friendship and Love between Women from the Renaissance to the Present* (New York, 1981); M. Vicinus, " 'They Wonder to Which Sex I Belong': The Historical Roots of the Modern Lesbian Identity," in *The Lesbian and Gay Studies Reader*, ed. Abelove, Barale, and Halperin, ch. 29; and the interesting recent intervention by Judith M. Bennett, " 'Lesbian-Like' and the Social History of Lesbians," *Journal of the History of Sexuality* 9 (2000): 1–24.

48. Terry Castle, "The Diaries of Anne Lister," in her *The Apparitional Lesbian: Female Homosexuality and Modern Culture* (New York, 1993), ch. 5.

49. Bristow, *Sexuality*, p. 4.

50. Ibid., p. 15. Bristow's ch. 1 is the best short introduction to sexology. See also Lucy Bland and Laura Doan, eds., *Sexology in Culture: Labelling Bodies and Desires* (Chicago, 1998).

51. Jennifer Terry, *An American Obsession: Science, Medicine, and Homosexuality in Modern Society* (Chicago, 1999), chs. 6–7.

52. This overly schematic view has most recently been stated in Trumbach's *Sex and the Gender Revolution, Volume One: Heterosexuality and the Third Gender in Enlightenment London* (Chicago, 1998), ch. 1. The same tendency is applied to "heterosexuality" in his analysis. In other words, he sees both "modern homosexuality" and "modern heterosexuality" emerging at the start of the eighteenth century: "By 1880 modern Western homosexuality and heterosexuality had existed for nearly two hundred years" (p. 19). We trust that it will become clear that this is not the approach favored by the editors of this reader.

53. George Chauncey, *Gay New York: Gender, Urban Culture, and the Making of the Gay Male World, 1890–1940* (New York, 1994).

54. For a recent histories of sex surveying, see Janice M. Irvine, *Disorders of Desire: Sex and Gender in Modern American Sexology* (Philadelphia, 1990); Julia A. Ericksen and Sally A. Steffen, *Kiss and Tell: Surveying Sex in the Twentieth Century* (Cambridge, Mass., 1999).

55. See also Terry, *American Obsession*, ch. 9.

56. Steven Marcus, *The Other Victorians: A Study of Sexuality and Pornography in Mid-Nineteenth-Century England* (London, 1966), p. 274.

57. Kendrick, *Secret Museum*. For a recent survey of the history of pornography, based on a UK Channel 4 TV documentary, see Isabel Tang, *Pornography: The Secret History of Civilization* (London, 1999).

58. Susan Stewart, "The Marquis de Meese," *Critical Inquiry* 15 (1988–89): 162–92 (quote is from p. 163).

59. For example, Angus McLaren, *Twentieth-Century Sexuality: A History* (Oxford, 1999), ch. 10: "Backlash" (the last chapter).

60. Jeffrey Weeks, *Against Nature* (London, 1991), p. 133.

61. See also Paula A. Treichler, "AIDS, Gender, and Biomedical Discourse: Current Contests for Meaning," in *AIDS: The Burdens of History*, ed. Elizabeth Fee and Daniel M. Fox (Berkeley, 1988), pp. 190–266; Jeffrey Weeks, "AIDS and the Regulation of Sexuality," in *AIDS and Contemporary History*, ed. Virginia Berridge and Philip Strong (Cambridge, 1993), ch. 1.

62. See Janice M. Irvine, "Reinventing Perversion: Sex Addiction and Cultural Anxieties," *Journal of the History of Sexuality* 5 (1995): 429–50 (quote is from p. 429).

63. Ann Laura Stoler, *Race and the Education of Desire: Foucault's History of Sexuality and the Colonial Order of Things* (Durham, 1995).

64. Abdul R. JanMohamed, "Sexuality on/of the Racial Border: Foucault, Wright, and the Articulation of 'Racialized Sexuality,' " in *Discourses of Sexuality*, ed. Stanton, pp. 94–116.

65. Sander L. Gilman, "Black Bodies, White Bodies: Toward an Iconography of Female Sexuality in Late-Nineteenth-Century Art, Medicine, and Literature," *Critical Inquiry* 12

(1985): 212. See also Anne Fausto-Sterling, "Gender, Race, and Nation: The Comparative Anatomy of 'Hottentot' Women in Europe, 1815–1817," in *Deviant Bodies*, ed. Jennifer Terry and Jacqueline Urla (Bloomington, 1995), ch. 1.

66. Judith Butler, *Gender Trouble: Feminism and the Subversion of Identity* (New York, 1990), pp. 6–7, 17, 25, 139.

67. Ibid, p. 127.

68. For just some examples, see June L. Reich, "Genderfuck: The Law of the Dildo," *Discourse* 15 (1992): 112–27; Laura Doan, ed., *The Lesbian Postmodern* (New York, 1992); Elizabeth Grosz and Elspeth Probyn, eds., *Sexy Bodies: The Strange Carnalities of Feminism* (London, 1995); Chris Straayer, *Deviant Eyes, Deviant Bodies: Sexual Re-Orientations in Film and Video* (New York, 1996), esp. "Postscript: A Graphic Interrogatory—Beyond Dimorphic Sex," pp. 253–87; Stephen Whittle, "Gender Fucking or Fucking Gender?" in *Blending Genders: Social Aspects of Cross-Dressing and Sex-Changing*, ed. Richard Elkins and Dave King (London, 1996), ch. 14; Nadine Hubbs, "Music of the 'Fourth Gender': Morrissey and the Sexual Politics of Melodic Contour," *Genders* 23 (1996): 266–96; Judith Halberstam, *Female Masculinity* (Durham, 1998); Del Lagrace Volcano and Judith "Jack" Halberstam, *The Drag King Book* (London, 1999).

69. Richard Dyer, "White," *Screen* 29.4 (1988): 44. Dyer is referring to whiteness.

70. Katz, *Invention of Heterosexuality*, chs. 2–5. See also his "The Invention of Sexuality," *Socialist Review* 20 (1990): 7–34.

71. See the interviews reported in Terry, *American Obsession*, ch. 7.

72. Katz, *Invention of Heterosexuality*, p. 34.

73. Terry, *American Obsession*.

74. See John D'Emilio and Estelle B. Freedman, *Intimate Matters: A History of Sexuality in America* (Chicago, 1997) (first published in 1988), chs. 8–11; Elaine Tyler May, *Homeward Bound: American Families in the Cold War Era* (New York, 1988); Steven Seidman, *Romantic Longings: Love in America, 1830–1980* (New York, 1991), chs. 3–4; Katz, *Invention of Heterosexuality*, ch. 5; Kevin White, *The First Sexual Revolution: The Emergence of Male Heterosexuality in Modern America* (New York, 1993); Carolyn J. Dean, *Sexuality and Modern Western Culture* (New York, 1996), ch. 3; Sharon R. Ullman, *Sex Seen: The Emergence of Modern Sexuality in America* (Berkeley, 1997).

75. See David Halperin's extremely useful recent genealogical analysis of male homosexuality, in which modern concepts "dissolve" as they are traced historically. There is a strong message here for histories of heterosexuality: D. M. Halperin, "How to Do the History of Male Homosexuality," *GLQ* 6 (2000): 87–124. See also the comments by Calvin Thomas, "Straight with a Twist: Queer Theory and the Subject of Heterosexuality," *Genders* 26 (1997): 83–115.

76. Carole S. Vance, "Anthropology Rediscovers Sexuality: A Theoretical Comment," *Social Science and Medicine* 33 (1991): 875.

77. See chapter 10.

PART 1

RETHINKING SEX

SEXUALITY AND HISTORY REVISITED

JEFFREY WEEKS

WRITING ABOUT SEX

Writing about sex can be dangerous. It makes you, as Ken Plummer put it, "morally suspect."[1] Until recently, in the academic world at least, it marked you also as marginal to the central intellectual preoccupations of the major disciplines.

Nearly forty years ago, the young William Masters felt sufficiently inspired by the example of Alfred Kinsey to want to pursue a career in sex research. He was advised by his obviously more worldly wise supervisor to do three things first: to complete his medical qualifications; to establish his reputation in another field; and to wait until he was forty before venturing into these treacherous waters.

This little anecdote tells us quite a lot about the moral climate in postwar America, and probably about the present too. Here we find, for example, the hegemony of medicine which has dominated most "respectable" discussions of sex over the past century. Then there is the emphasis on reputation and credentials, a positive underlining of the importance of a student in this field demonstrating his or her objective, scholarly interest in the subject before venturing into it. And, of course, reputation, credentials, respectability and objectivity are assumed to come with age.

It has always been possible to write about sexuality. But, to do so and be listened to, it has usually been necessary to work within the confines of an acceptable discourse. The authorized voices have been religious, medical, medico-moral, legal, psychological, pedagogical, and certainly "official." They have rarely been sensitive to the nuances of history or social variability. It is striking that the only social scientific research initiative with a direct relationship to sexual behaviour spontaneously launched by the (British) Economic and Social Research Council has to do with yet another medico-moral problem, that associated with the tragic spread of AIDS.

Needless to say, quite a lot of writing about sexuality has gone on outside these parameters. But it is noticeable how, even today, many of us who venture into this field still feel the need to stress our academic credentials for doing so. If you look at any journal whose main concern is sexuality in some form you will find the title page full of the names of impeccably scholarly advisers, complete with a long list of their academic qualifications, from M.D. to Ph.D. (Candidate). Academic awards permit us to speak with authority; and to make what we say acceptable.

To get back to my anecdote: the young William Masters followed the advice of his mentor absolutely. And who can say he was wrong? Alongside his partner and future wife Virginia he was to become half of the world-famous sex-research and sex-therapy duo, Masters and Johnson. Their popular success has always been underpinned by their "scientific" reputation. The very turgidity of their writing style may be seen as a simulacrum of the scientific text.

Some things at least have changed. Since the early 1970s there has been a major expansion in the study of sexuality in general, and of sexual history in particular. We now know a good deal about marriage and the family, illegitimacy and birth control, prostitution and homosexuality, changing patterns of moral, legal and medical regulation, rape and sexual violence, sexual identities and sexual communities, and oppositional cultures. Historians have interrogated old and discovered new documentary evidence; they have deployed extensive oral history sources; and all but exhausted the records of births, marriages and deaths.[2]

Major scholars, whose reputations were, significantly, made elsewhere, have entered the field. To name just some of the best known: Lawrence Stone has exhaustively chronicled the (largely upper-class) family, sex and marriage in pre-modern England.[3] Peter Gay is venturing into the complexities of the "bourgeois experience."[4] Most influentially of all, Michel Foucault has essayed a genealogy of the Western apparatus of sexuality.[5] The subject has achieved an unprecedented range, depth and, dare I say it, respectability.

This signals an important and welcome shift. But it is vital that we understand its real significance, which lies not in who writes but what they write about. The really noteworthy point about the new sexual history lies in the fact that increasingly it is being recognized that far from being a minor adjunct to the mainstream of history, sexuality in its broadest sense has been at the heart of moral, social and political discourse. We cannot properly understand the past, let alone the present, unless we grasp that simple fact.

Two lessons for the historical enterprise flow from this. First, it is imperative to recognize not only the desirability but the absolute necessity of inter-, multi- and cross-disciplinary approaches to the subject. The new sexual history has in fact been fed not only by new sources and new topics, but also by a multitude of approaches, from psychoanalysis to poststructuralism and semiology, and nurtured by a number of disciplines, from the "new social history" to sociology, philosophy and literature. They go far beyond the conventional intellectual tools of the traditional empirical historian. I would go so far as to say that the study of sexuality as a historical phenomenon fundamentally challenges the existing disciplinary boundaries, illustrating perhaps better than any other topic their contingent natures. Traditional historical methods have proved inadequate to the understanding of sexuality. The history of sexuality should not be studied by historians alone.

The second factor is that sexual history is to a high degree a politicized history, underlined by an energetic grassroots input into the study of sexuality. To an extraordinary degree, much of the most innovative historical work in this field has come from women and men whose initial concern was as much "political" as purely "academic." Many of the pioneering feminist writers about sexuality in the early 1970s are now in often senior academic positions; their work has grown in empirical richness and theoretical sophistication. But their publications, while achieving the highest scholarly standards, are still clearly within a developing tradition of feminist writing.[6] Similarly, within the area of lesbian and gay studies, important historical works have appeared which, though initially stimulated by the moral and political preoccupations of the authors, have begun to transform the wider intellectual debate.[7] In the study of sexuality, it seems, scholarship and politics, broadly defined, are inextricably intertwined.

I want to devote much of the rest of this chapter to exploring the implications of these factors, concentrating on several interrelated questions. What, for example, is the impact of the new sexual history on our understanding of sexuality? Or, to put it another way, what is it we study when we say we are exploring the history of sexuality? What do our studies tell us about the relationship of the sexual to the social, to power and politics? In what ways do they illuminate our understanding of social and moral regulation, and the role of the state? How, in turn, does this affect our perception of the historic present in which we live? Why, in particular, has sexuality become so important in the contemporary political discourse of both left and right? My aim is not to supply the answers, but to sharpen the questions we must ask if we are to rethink the history of sexuality.

THE SUBJECT OF SEXUAL HISTORY

At the heart of the new sexual history is the assumption that sexuality is a social and historical construct. In the famous words of Foucault, "Sexuality must not be thought of as a kind of natural given which power tries to hold in check, or as an obscure domain which knowledge tries gradually to uncover. It is the name that can be given to a historical construct."[8]

Leaving aside the ambiguities of and problems with this statement, I want to emphasize the revolution in the approach to sexuality that this symbolized. Of all social phenomena, sex has been most resistant to social and historical explanations. It seems the most basic, the most natural thing about us, the truth at the heart of our being. This has been reflected until very recently in even the most sophisticated studies of sexuality. As pioneering sexual theorists sought to chronicle the varieties of sexual experience throughout different periods and different cultures they assumed that beating at the centre of all this was a core of natural sexuality, varying in incidence and power, no doubt, as a result of chance historical factors, the weight of moral and physical repression, the patterns of kinship, and so on, but nevertheless basically unchanging in biological and psychological essence.

Such an assumption governed equally the naturalist approaches of the early sexologists and the metatheoretical approaches of such Freudo-Marxists as Reich and Marcuse. It dominated the thoughts of functionalist anthropologists with their commitment to cultural relativism as much as the evolutionists they displaced. It lurked as effortlessly behind the sexual writings of cultural radicals as behind the work of moral conservatives. It was the taken-for-granted of sexual studies.[9]

The new sexual history has changed that. Its origins are disparate, owing, as I have already indicated, something to sociology and anthropology (their emphasis on cultural relativism, social organization and micro-studies),[10] something to psychoanalysis (especially the challenge offered by the theory of the unconscious to fixed gender and sexual positions),[11] something to the new sexual movements of the early 1970s (their critique of existing social and sexual categories),[12] something to the new social history (in as far as these diverse strands can be disentangled from the new history). Foucault's work made such an impact in the early 1980s because, in part at least, it complemented and helped to systematize work already going on. Unifying the new approach were several common themes.

First, there was a general rejection of sex as an autonomous realm, a natural domain with specific effects, a rebellious energy that the social controls.

Once you begin to see sexuality as a "construct," as a series of representations, as an "apparatus" with a history of its own, many of the older certainties dissolve. It is no longer appropriate to state, as Malinowski did, that "Sex really is dangerous," the source of most human trouble from Adam and Eve on.[13] Instead, we are forced to ask: Why is it that sex is regarded as dangerous? We can no longer speculate about the inevitable conflict between the powerful instinct of sex and the demands of culture. Instead, we need to ask why our culture has conceived of sexuality in this way.

Second, it followed that the new sexual history assumed the social variability of sexual forms, beliefs, ideologies and behaviours. Sexuality has not only a history, but many histories, each of which needs to be understood both in its uniqueness and as part of an intricate pattern.

Third, it became necessary to abandon the idea that the history of sexuality can usefully be understood in terms of a dichotomy of pressure and release, repression and liberation. "Sexuality" as a domain of social interest and concern is produced by society in complex ways. It is a result of diverse social practices that give meaning to human activities, of social definitions and self-definitions, of struggles between those who have the power to define, and those who resist. Sexuality is not a given. It is a product of negotiation, struggle and human agency.

The most important outcome of the resulting historical approach to sexuality is that it opens up the whole field to critical analysis and assessment. It becomes possible to relate sexuality to other social phenomena and to ask new types of questions (new at least to the field of sex research). Questions such as the following: How is sexuality shaped, and how is it articulated with economic, social and political structures—in a word, how is it "socially constructed"? Why and how has the domain of sexuality achieved such a critical organizing and symbolic significance? Why do we think it so important? If sexuality is constructed by human agency, to what extent can it be changed?

Questions such as these have produced an impressive flood of new work— and new questions—across a range of issues from the shaping of reproduction[14] to the social organization of disease,[15] from the pre-Christian origins of the Western preoccupation with the association between sex and truth[16] to the making of the modern body.[17]

I'll take a further example from an area which I myself have been particularly interested in—the history of homosexuality. Fifteen years ago there was virtually nothing in the way of serious historical studies of same-sex activity. Such writings as existed assumed an unchanging essence of homosexuality across cultures and over the millennia of human history, as if one could readily identify the experience of the modern gay subcultures with the socially sanctioned male intergenerational sexual patterns of ancient Greece or the institutionalized cross-dressing of certain preindustrial tribal societies.

I became convinced (following McIntosh)[18] that this was an inadequate way of seeing this particular past, and my early researches persuaded me that there had been significant shifts in attitudes to, and the organization of, same-sex erotic activities. In particular, it became clear that the idea that there was such a thing as a homosexual person, and an associated homosexual identity, was of comparatively recent origin, no more, in most Western cultures at least, than two or three hundred years old.[19] Other work carried on at the same time was reaching similar conclusions.[20]

Since the 1970s this approach has been much debated, and has occasioned a great deal of controversy. There is by no means unanimous agreement about it.[21] It has at the same time become the major hypothesis for the study of homosexual history. For example, a conference at the Free University of Amsterdam in December 1987 brought together over five hundred people from all over the world to debate the relevance of "essentialist" versus "constructionist" perspectives in addressing the question "Homosexuality, Which Homosexuality?" The history papers covered a wide range of topics, from Aristotelean philosophy to the sexual and emotional proclivities of Eleanor Roosevelt. But central to the majority of them was a sensitivity to historical context that illumined hitherto obscure issues, and largely confirmed the "constructionist" hypothesis.[22]

But sensitivity to context is one thing; doing away with a unifying concept of sexuality is quite another. One of the problems with the new sexual history is that it is in danger of becoming a history without a proper subject. The history of sexuality is at the same time a history of a category of thought, which, if we follow Foucault, has a delimited history; and a history of changing erotic practices, subjective meanings, social definitions and patterns of regulation whose only unity lies in their common descriptor. "Sexuality" is an unstable category, in constant flux.[23]

It is, nevertheless, a vital one. All societies find it necessary to organize the erotic possibilities of the body in one way or another. They all need, as Plummer suggests, to impose "who restrictions" and "why restrictions" to provide the permissions, prohibitions, limits and possibilities through which erotic life is organized.[24] But they do so in a wide variety of ways. The study of sexuality therefore provides a critical insight into the wider organization of a culture. The important question then becomes not what traditional disciplines such as history or sociology can contribute to our understanding of sexuality, but rather what the study of the sexual can contribute to our grasp of the historical, the social and the political.

SEX, POLITICS AND SOCIETY

This brings me to the second of the major issues I want to explore: What indeed does the new history of sexuality tell us about the relationship of sexuality to other elements of social life, and especially what insights does it give to the nature of power and politics in the modern world?

"To some," the feminist scholar Gayle Rubin has argued, "sexuality may seem to be an unimportant topic, a frivolous diversion from the more critical problems of poverty, war, disease, racism, famine, or nuclear annihilation. But it is precisely at times such as these, when we live with the possibility of unthinkable destruction, that people are likely to become dangerously crazy about sexuality."[25]

Why is this so? Why is sexuality so thoroughly bound up with the modern play of power, as Foucault suggested?[26] What is it about sexuality that makes it so susceptible to anxiety, conflict and moralizing zeal?

The first point to make is that this is not always the case. Although our culture attributes a peculiar significance to the sexual, there is plentiful anthropological and historical evidence to suggest that other cultures interpret the possibilities of the body quite differently.[27] While all societies have to make arrangements for the organization of erotic life, not all do so with the obsessive concern we show in the West. Different cultures have varying responses to childhood sexuality, marriage, homosexuality, even reproduction. Some societies display so little interest in erotic activity that they have been labelled more or less "asexual." Islamic cultures, by contrast, have developed a lyrical view of sex with sustained attempts to integrate the religious and the sexual—as long, that is, as it was heterosexual.[28]

We in the West are heirs of a Christian tradition which has tended to see in sex a focus for moral anguish and conflict, producing an enduring dualism between the spirit and the flesh, the mind and the body. It has produced a culture which simultaneously disavows the body while being obsessively preoccupied with it.

Michel Foucault was centrally concerned with this issue. He abandoned the original scheme for his *History of Sexuality* and went back to the ancient Greeks and Romans in the two volumes published at the very end of his life precisely because of his growing conviction that the Western preoccupation with the relationship between sex and truth was of very ancient lineage, and crucial to the understanding of power and subjectivity.[29] For the ancients, he argued, concern with the pleasures of the body was only one, and not necessarily the most important, of the preoccupations of life, to be set alongside dietary regulations and the organization of household relations. We, on the other hand, seek the truth of our natures in our sexual desires. In the course of that shift, with pre-Christian as well as Christian origins, sexuality has emerged as a domain of danger as well as pleasure, emotional anxiety as well as moral certainty.

I do not wish here to assess the merits and defects of this argument. I cite it because it illustrates the major point I want to make. The new social history takes for granted that sexuality as an historical phenomenon is in fact a consequence of an obsessive social preoccupation with the body and its possibilities for erotic pleasure. As a result, far from being stubbornly resistant to social moulding, it is a peculiarly sensitive conductor of cultural influences, and hence of social and political divisions.

There are five broad categories of social relations which both are constructed around and in turn shape and reshape sex and gender relations.[30] First, there are the kinship and family systems that place individuals in relationship to one another, and constitute them as human subjects with varying needs and desires, conscious and unconscious. Second, there are the economic and social organizations that shape social relations, statuses and class divisions, and provide the basic preconditions and ultimate limits for the organization of sexual life. Third, there are the changing patterns of social regulation and organization, formal and informal, legal and moral, populist and professional, religious and secular, unintended consequences as well as organized and planned responses. Fourth, there are the changing forms of political interest and concern, power and policies. Finally, there are the cultures of resistance which give rise to oppositional subcultures, alternative forms of knowledge and social and sexual movements.

These are quite general categories. They have had different weighting at different historical conjunctures. But their intricate and complex interaction in the West has produced a culture which assigns a critical role to sexuality in the definition of subjectivity and self, morality and sin, normality and abnormality.

Modern sexuality has been shaped and defined at the intersection of two absolutely central concerns: with who and what we are as human subjects and social individuals; and with the nature and direction of the society as a whole. And as the state, as the organizing focus of the social sphere, has become more and more concerned with the lives of its members, for the sake of moral uniformity, economic well-being, national security or hygiene and health, so it has become more and more involved with the sex lives of individuals, providing the rationale for techniques of moral and legal management, detailed intervention into private lives and scientific exploration of the subject of sex.

As a result, sexuality has become an increasingly important political as well as moral issue, condensing a number of critical issues: with the norms of family life, the relations between men and women, adults and children, and the nature of normality and abnormality. These are central issues in any culture. The debate about them has become increasingly heated and bitter in recent years because debates about sexuality are debates about the type of society we want to live in. As sex goes, so goes society.[31]

POWER AND THE STATE

This is another way of restating that issues of sexuality are at the heart of the whole workings of power in modern society. "The state," broadly defined, clearly has a crucial role to play here. Through its role in determining legislation and the legal process it constitutes the categories of the permissible and the impermissible, the pure and the obscene. Through its symbiosis with the forces of moral regulation (from the churches to the medical profession) it can shape the climate of sexual opinion. Through its organization of health and welfare it can help to determine the patterns of marriage, child-bearing, child-rearing, and so on.

Of course, the actual practice of the state varies enormously, depending on a variety of historical factors and contingencies. A would-be theocracy like modern Iran can make adultery a criminal offence, with draconian penalties. An ostensibly secular state might formally eschew a direct role in moral regulation (though all the evidence suggests that it is easier to make the declaration of disinterest than to carry it out when faced by the host of pressures to which the modern state is heir). The state can shape through its prohibitions and punishments. It can also organize and regulate through its positive will and injunctions, and influence through its omissions and contradictions.

But however critical the role of the state, both in the abstract and in real historical situations, it would be wrong to see its functions as either predetermined or necessarily decisive. One of the key achievements of the new sexual history is that it has helped us to understand the mechanisms through which sexuality is organized and produced in and through a host of different social practices. And in this complex process a variety of often interlocking power relationships are at play.

Take, for example, the question of gender and sexual difference. Various feminist writers have argued forcibly that the elaboration of sexual difference has been central to the subordination of women, with sexuality not only reflecting but being constitutive in the construction and maintenance of the power relationship between men and women. Sexuality is fundamentally gendered.

On the one hand, this can lead to an argument that all hitherto existing definitions of female sexuality (at least in recorded history) are male definitions, so that the category of sexuality itself is fundamentally corrupted by male power and the actual practices of "masculinity."[32] On the other, the perception of the symbiosis between definitions of gender and of sexuality can lead to careful analyses of the play of definition and self-definition, power and resistance.[33] In other words, it becomes a sensitizing device which allows us to explore the complexities of practices—theoretical as well as social and political—which have given rise to the relations of domination and subordination that characterize the world of gender.

This has enabled Laqueur, for example, to argue that: "the political, economic, and cultural transformations of the eighteenth century created the context in which the articulation of radical differences between the sexes became culturally imperative."[34] The hierarchical model that held sway from ancient times interpreted the female body as an inferior and inverted version of the male, but stressed nevertheless the generative role of female sexual pleasure. The breakdown of this model, in political as well as medical debates, and its replacement by a reproductive model which stressed the radical opposition of male and female sexualities, the woman's automatic reproductive cycle, and her lack of sexual feeling, was a critical moment in the reshaping of gender relations.

It did not arise straightforwardly from scientific advance. Nor was it the product of a singular effort at social control by and through the state. The emergent discourse about sexual difference allowed a range of separate, and often contradictory, social and political responses to emerge. But this new perception of female sexuality and reproductive biology has been absolutely central to modern social and political discourse. Its effects can be discerned in a vast range of political practices, from the legal regulation of prostitution to the social security structures of the welfare state.[35]

If gender is a key variable in the organization of sexuality, class is another. Class differences in sexual regulation are scarcely unique to the modern world. In the slave societies of the ancient world, moral standards varied enormously with social status. But in the modern world class definitions of appropriate sexual behaviour have been sharply demarcated. It has, in fact, been argued by Foucault that the very idea of sexuality is an essentially bourgeois one, which developed as an aspect of the self-definition of the class against the decadent morals of the aristocracy and the rampant immorality of the lower classes in the course of the eighteenth and nineteenth centuries.[36] It was a colonizing system of beliefs which sought to remould society in its own emerging image.

Undoubtedly, the respectable standards of family and domestic life, with its increased demarcation between male and female roles, a growing ideological distinction between private and public life, and a marked concern with moral and hygienic policing of nonmarital, nonheterosexual sexuality, were increasingly the norm by which all behaviour was judged.[37]

This does not mean, of course, that all or even most behaviour conformed to these norms, or that the state acted in a uniform way to institutionalize acceptable forms of behaviour. There is a great deal of evidence that the sexual lives of the working class remained highly resistant to middle-class mores.[38] What one can say with confidence is that the complex sexual and moral patterns that exist in the twentieth century are the product of social struggles in which class played an important part.

Not surprisingly, the imagery of class has become a key element in sexual fantasy.[39] At the same time, the impact of formal regulation of sexual behaviour through the law and social policy is inevitably coloured by class-bound assumptions. In the 1860s and 1870s the Contagious Diseases Acts, ostensibly directed against prostitutes, were perceived to be aimed at working-class womanhood in general. This fuelled the feminist and labour opposition to them, and helped to shape the new sexual regime that followed their repeal in the 1880s.[40] More recently, it is impossible to understand the significance of the liberal sexual reforms of the 1960s in Britain without relating them to the re-formation of social boundaries, including, crucially, those of class.[41] Class does not determine sexual behaviour, but it provides one of the major lenses through which sexuality is organized and regulated.

Categorizations by class intersect with those of ethnicity and race. Eurocentric concepts of correct sexual behaviour have helped to shape centuries of response to the non-European world. So in the evolutionary model of sexuality dominant until the early twentieth century, the black person was classed as lower down the evolutionary scale, closer to nature than the European. This view has survived even in the culturally relativist work of twentieth-century anthropologists, who in their eagerness to portray the lyrical delights of other cultures take for granted that this is because the natives are somehow more "natural" than modern "civilized" peoples.[42]

One of the most abiding myths is that of the insatiability of the sexual needs of non-European peoples, and the threat they pose to the purity of the white races. This has been constitutive of real effects in shaping sexual codes. A fear of black male sexuality was integral to slave society in the American South, and has continued to shape public stereotypes to the present. In South Africa, fear of intermarriage and miscegenation was at the heart of apartheid legislation. In Britain, immigration policy is shot through with a dense network of assumptions where race, sex and gender are inextricably linked.

As European societies become more ethnically and racially diverse, so dominant racial assumptions shape responses to manifest cultural differences, in family patterns, gender relations and sexual assumptions.[43] Sexuality here, as elsewhere, becomes a battleground for competing notions of what constitutes proper behaviour.

The boundaries of race, gender and class, as of other social divisions like age or disability I could have discussed, inevitably overlap. They are not clear-cut categories. The essential point is that sexuality is constructed and reconstructed through a complex series of interlocking practices, all of which involve relations of power—and of challenges to that power. In this dialectic of power and resistance, definition and self-definition, the formal bodies of the state inevitably play a crucial part. The state can organize the terrain of sexual struggle through its patterns of legal regulation, its political interventions and social policies. But the state is itself a locale of struggle over the meaning of sexuality: its impact can be highly contradictory as its different organs adopt conflicting policies. There is no functional fit between state intention and sexual regulation. On the contrary, the historian of sexuality must stand amazed at the unintended consequences of state action: laws designed to outlaw homosexuality which encourage it; injunctions to parents to bring forth children for the greater good of the community which are followed by a drop in the birth rate; and attempts to limit childbirth (for the greater good . . .) which lead to an exponential increase in live births.

The major lesson we can draw from all this is that there is no simple way to understand the social organization of sexuality. Instead of seeing sexuality as a unified whole, we have to recognize that there are various forms of sexuality, that there are in fact many sexualities: class sexualities and gendered sexualities, racially specific sexualities and sexualities of struggle and choice. The historian of sexuality must try to understand these, both in their distinctiveness and in their complex interactions.

HISTORY AND THE PRESENT

This brings me to the final theme I want to pursue: the implications of the new sexual history for our understanding of the historic present. As I suggested earlier, a major stimulus to the study of our sexual pasts has come from preoccupations that were clearly located in the present. Feminist history is, for example, by definition a history that has current political concerns at its heart. Thus a book produced by the London Feminist History Group, called *The Sexual Dynamics of History*, observes that "Our link with contemporary political struggles gives our work as historians a special edge, because our analysis is constantly being reworked and developed."[44]

At the very least this implies that the questions that are asked of the past are prompted by the concerns of the present. Sometimes these questions can lead to the exploration of new or neglected themes. A good example here is the interest in the history and politics of male violence against women, whose starting point is very much recent experience.[45] Sometimes the result is a reexamination of well-worn but controversial subjects in new ways. For example, Boswell's work on attitudes to homosexuality in the early Christian church is a work of great (traditional) scholarship, but is clearly also part of a fierce debate within both the Roman Catholic Church and the gay community about the real implications of the Christian tradition's attitudes towards homosexuality.[46]

But there is something more at stake than simply finding new or better ways of addressing the past. Sexuality is a highly contentious issue in contemporary society, and at the centre of some highly influential political programmes. I have mentioned feminism and lesbian and gay politics. Perhaps even more important today are the projects of moral regeneration that lie close to the centre of the politics of the New Right in some at least of its manifestations. In the resulting political struggles around sexuality the past is freely raided for its contemporary relevance—as, for example, in the capture by the Thatcher government in Britain of the idea of Victorian values.[47] The new sexual history is important in so far as it contributes to these debates, and to the extent that it illuminates the present.

I do not mean by this that historians should only study the recent past, or concentrate on issues that are of current concern. But at the very least, if the perspectives I have described on the historical construction of sexuality have any merit, the new sexual history should be able to undermine the certainty with which the past is called in to redress the difficulties of the present. As we have seen, sensitive studies of sexual behaviour in other cultures,[48] or at other times within our own, serve to problematize the whole idea of a single history. Instead they direct our attention to the variety of forces and practices that shape sexual categories.

The historic present is a product of many histories, some of very ancient lineage, some very recent. What we can use the new sexual history for is to question the taken-for-granted, challenge our own culturally specific preoccupations, and to try to see whether what we assume is natural is not in fact social and historical. At the same time, we can explore the continuities and the discontinuities of our sexual histories.

Let's take as an example the ways in which our culture is responding to a crisis that is both personal and social, medical and moral, and also highly political—that relating to AIDS. This is a new problem in that it is a new, or at least newly discovered, disease or group of diseases. It is also a phenomenon that is very closely connected with sexuality, both because it can be sexually transmitted and because, at least in the West, the people most affected so far have been gay men.

What is most striking is the degree to which, in reacting to AIDS, people call on preexisting discourses and shape them to the current crisis. As Frank Mort has shown, for example, there is a substantial medico-moral tradition, going back at least to the early nineteenth century, linking beliefs about health and disease to notions of moral and immoral sex, "dangerous sexualities."[49] The linkage of AIDS with homosexual lifestyles evokes a rich tradition that sees homosexuality as itself a disease.[50] Even the question of whether people with AIDS should be segregated and confined refers back to a heated debate in the late nineteenth century about whether the most effective means of controlling the spread of syphilis was by compulsorily testing and confining prostitutes.[51]

These are political and moral debates where more is at stake than mere historical accuracy. But it so happens that all the issues I have just referred to have been the object of investigation by the new sexual historians, who have effectively demonstrated the social conditions for the emergence of these discourses. It is too much to hope, perhaps, that their work would dispel illusions and prejudices. But at the very least it should force us to pause and ask about the conditions which are shaping our interventions. What their work underlines above all is the living nature of the past—and the historical nature of the present.

SOME CONCLUSIONS

To conclude, I want to offer just three brief observations. First, I want to underline my belief that the new sexual history has fundamentally transformed the way we interpret the sexual past and present. It is no longer possible to see sex as caught in the toils of nature, outside the bounds of history. It is a legitimate subject for historical investigation.

Having said that, it is worth stressing that the particular theoretical position I have adopted on the "social construction of sexuality," while influential, is by no means dominant. As Carole Vance put it in the late 1980s, "Social construction theory may be the new orthodoxy in feminist, progressive, and lesbian and gay history circles, but it has made a minimal impact on mainstream authorities and literatures in sexology and biomedicine."[52] What this means in practice is that historians have been much more willing to recognize that homosexuality is "socially constructed" than to examine the historical evolution of heterosexuality. A latent naturalism often survives in even the most advanced history. To my mind the great advantage of the deconstructionist approach outlined here is that it forces us to think beyond the boundaries of existing categories and to explore their historical production.

The second observation I want to make is that deconstruction should also imply reconstruction. There is no point in fragmenting the past into a series of disparate histories unless we deploy them for some purpose. What I have suggested is that an important outcome of the new sexual history is that it contributes to our understanding of the present. Increasingly we can see the present not as the culmination of an unproblematic past but as itself historical: a complex series of interlocking histories whose interactions have to be reconstructed, not assumed.

Finally, I want to suggest that the new sexual history may have a valuable political and ethical outcome. In demonstrating the sexual and moral diversity of the past it may lead us to be a little more accepting of the diversity of the present. Perhaps that is why writing about sex can still be dangerous.

NOTES

1. Ken Plummer, *Sexual Stigma* (London, 1975), p. 4.
2. See Jeffrey Weeks, *Sexuality and Its Discontents* (London, 1985).

3. Lawrence Stone, *The Family, Sex, and Marriage* (London, 1977).

4. Peter Gay, *The Bourgeois Experience*, Vol. 1, *Education of the Senses* (Oxford, 1984); Gay, *The Bourgeois Experience*, Vol. 2, *The Tender Passion* (Oxford, 1986).

5. Michel Foucault, *The History of Sexuality*, Vol. 1, *An Introduction* (London, 1979); Foucault, *The History of Sexuality*, Vol. 2, *The Use of Pleasure* (London, 1987); Foucault, *The History of Sexuality*, Vol. 3, *The Care of the Self* (London, 1988).

6. For example, Judith R. Walkowitz, *Prostitution and Victorian Society* (Cambridge, 1980); Barbara Taylor, *Eve and the New Jerusalem* (London, 1983); Carroll Smith-Rosenberg, *Disorderly Conduct* (Oxford, 1986).

7. For example, John Boswell, *Christianity, Social Tolerance, and Homosexuality* (Chicago, 1980); Alan Bray, *Homosexuality in Renaissance England* (London, 1982); Estelle B. Freedman et al., eds., *The Lesbian Issue* (Chicago, 1985).

8. Foucault, *The History of Sexuality*, Vol. 1, p. 105.

9. See Weeks, *Sexuality and Its Discontents*, part 2.

10. John H. Gagnon and William Simon, *Sexual Conduct* (London, 1974); Plummer, *Sexual Stigma*.

11. Rosalind Coward, *Patriarchal Precedents* (London, 1983).

12. Jeffrey Weeks, *Coming Out* (London, 1977).

13. Bronislaw Malinowski, *Sex, Culture, and Myth* (London, 1963), p. 127.

14. For example, Rosalind P. Petchesky, *Abortion and Women's Choice* (London, 1986).

15. For example, Frank Mort, *Dangerous Sexualities* (London, 1987).

16. Foucault, *The History of Sexuality*, Vols. 2 and 3.

17. Catherine Gallagher and Thomas Laqueur, eds., *The Making of the Modern Body* (Berkeley, 1987).

18. Mary McIntosh, "The Homosexual Role," *Social Problems* 16 (1968): 182–92, republished in *The Making of the Modern Homosexual*, ed. Ken Plummer (London, 1981).

19. Weeks, *Coming Out*.

20. See Carroll Smith-Rosenberg, "The Female World of Love and Ritual," in Smith-Rosenburg, *Disorderly Conduct*; Jonathan Katz, *Gay American History* (New York, 1976); Foucault, *History of Sexuality*, Vol. 1.

21. Boswell, *Christianity, Social Tolerance, and Homosexuality*.

22. D. Altman et al., eds., *Which Homosexuality* (London, 1989); S. Franklin and J. Stacey, "Dyketactics in Difficult Times: A Review of the 'Homosexuality, Which Homosexuality?' Conference," *Feminist Review* 29 (1988): 136–50.

23. Robert Padgug, "Sexual Matters," *Radical History Review* 20 (1979): 3–23.

24. Ken Plummer, "Sexual Diversity," in *Sexual Diversity*, ed. Kevin Howells (Oxford, 1984).

25. Gayle Rubin, "Thinking Sex," in *Pleasure and Danger*, ed. Carole Vance (London, 1984), p. 267.

26. Foucault, *The History of Sexuality*, Vol. 1.

27. Pat Caplan, ed., *The Cultural Construction of Sexuality* (London, 1987).

28. Abdelwahab Bouhdiba, *Sexuality in Islam* (London, 1985); Jeffrey Weeks, *Sexuality* (London, 1986), pp. 25–26.

29. Foucault, *The History of Sexuality*, Vols. 2 and 3.

30. Weeks, *Sexuality*; Weeks, *Sex, Politics, and Society* (London, 1989).

31. Weeks, *Sexuality*, p. 36.

32. Adrienne Rich, "Compulsory Heterosexuality and Lesbian Experience," in *Desire: The Politics of Sexuality*, ed. Ann Snitow, Christine Stansell, and Sharon Thompson (London, 1984); Lal Coveney et al., *The Sexuality Papers* (London, 1984); Andrea Dworkin, *Intercourse* (London, 1987).

33. For example, Rosalind Coward, *Female Desire* (London, 1984).

34. Thomas Laqueur, "Orgasm, Generation, and the Politics of Reproductive Biology," in _The Making of the Modern Body_, ed. Gallagher and Laqueur, p. 35.

35. Weeks, _Sex, Politics, and Society_.

36. Foucault, _The History of Sexuality_, Vol. 1.

37. Leonore Davidoff and Catherine Hall, _Family Fortunes_ (London, 1987).

38. Weeks, _Sex, Politics, and Society_.

39. Leonore Davidoff, "Class and Gender in Victorian England," in _Sex and Class in Women's History_, ed. Judith L. Newton, Mary P. Ryan, and Judith R. Walkowitz (London, 1983); Steven Marcus, _The Other Victorians_ (London, 1967).

40. Walkowitz, _Prostitution and Victorian Society_.

41. Weeks, _Sex, Politics, and Society_.

42. Coward, _Patriarchal Precedents_.

43. V. Amos and P. Parmar, "Challenging Imperial Feminism," _Feminist Review_ 17 (1984): 3–19.

44. London Feminist History Group, _The Sexual Dynamics of History_ (London, 1983), p. 1.

45. For instance, Deborah Cameron and Elizabeth Frazer, _The Lust to Kill_ (Cambridge, 1987); Klaus Theweleit, _Male Fantasies_, Vols. 1 and 2 (Cambridge, 1987, 1990).

46. Boswell, _Christianity, Social Tolerance, and Homosexuality_.

47. James Walvin, _Victorian Values_ (London, 1987); Weeks, _Sex, Politics, and Society_.

48. For example, Caplan, ed., _The Cultural Construction of Sexuality_.

49. Mort, _Dangerous Sexualities_.

50. Weeks, _Coming Out_.

51. Walkowitz, _Prostitution and Victorian Society_.

52. Carole Vance, "Social Construction Theory," in _Which Homosexuality?_ ed. Altman et al., p. 29.

FORGETTING FOUCAULT

Acts, Identities, and the History of Sexuality

DAVID M. HALPERIN

When Jean Baudrillard published his infamous pamphlet *Forget Foucault* in March 1977, "Foucault's intellectual power," as Baudrillard recalled ten years later, "was enormous." After all, the reviews of *La volonté de savoir*, the first volume of Michel Foucault's *History of Sexuality* (published the previous November), had only just started to appear. At that time, according to Baudrillard's belated attempt in *Cool Memories* to redeem his gaffe and to justify himself—by portraying his earlier attack on Foucault as having been inspired, improbably, by sentiments of friendship and generosity—Foucault was being "persecuted," allegedly, by "thousands of disciples and . . . sycophants"; in such circumstances, Baudrillard virtuously insisted, "to forget him was to do him a service; to adulate him was to do him a disservice." Just how far Baudrillard was willing to go in order to render this sort of unsolicited service to Foucault emerges from another remark of his in the same passage: "Foucault's death. Loss of confidence in his own genius. . . . Leaving the sexual aspects aside, the loss of the immune system is no more than the biological transcription of the other process."[1] Foucault was already washed up by the time he died, in other words, and AIDS was merely the outward and visible sign of his inward, moral and intellectual, decay. Leaving the sexual aspects aside, of course.

(Baudrillard freely voices elsewhere what he carefully suppresses here about "the sexual aspects" of AIDS: the epidemic, he suggests, might be considered "a form of viral catharsis" and "a remedy against total sexual liberation, which is sometimes more dangerous than an epidemic, because the latter always ends. Thus AIDS could be understood as a counterforce against the total elimination of structure and the total unfolding of sexuality."[2] Some such New Age moralism obviously provides the subtext of Baudrillard's vengeful remarks in *Cool Memories* on the death of Foucault.)

Baudrillard's injunction to forget Foucault, which was premature at the time it was issued, has since become superfluous. Not that Foucault is neglected; not that his work is ignored. (Quite the contrary, in fact.) Rather, Foucault's continuing prestige, and the almost ritualistic invocation of his name by academic practitioners of cultural theory, has had the effect of reducing the operative range of his thought to a small set of received ideas, slogans, and bits of jargon that have now become so commonplace and so familiar as to make a more direct engagement with Foucault's texts entirely dispensable. As a result, we are so far from remembering Foucault that there is little point in entertaining the possibility of forgetting him.

Take, for example, the title of a recent conference on "Bodies and Pleasures in Pre- and Early Modernity," held from 3 to 5 November 1995 at the University of California, Santa Cruz. "Bodies and pleasures," as that famous phrase occurs in the concluding paragraphs of Foucault's *History of Sexuality, Volume I,* does not in fact describe "Foucault's zero-degree definition of the elements in question in the history of sexuality," as the poster for the conference confidently announces. To be sure, the penultimate sentence of *The History of Sexuality, Volume I,* finds Foucault looking forward to the day, some time in the future, when "a different economy [*une autre économie*] of bodies and pleasures" will have replaced the apparatus of sexuality and when, accordingly, it will become difficult to understand "how the ruses of sexuality . . . were able to subject us to that austere monarchy of sex."[3] An incautious reader might take that phrase, "a different economy of bodies and pleasures," to denote a mere rearrangement of otherwise unchanged and unchanging "bodies and pleasures," a minor modification in the formal design of the sexual "economy" alone, consisting in a revised organization of its perennial "elements" (as the conference poster terms them). But such an interpretation of Foucault's meaning, though superficially plausible, is mistaken—and in fact it runs counter to the entire thrust of his larger argument. The change of which Foucault speaks in the next to last sentence of *The History of Sexuality, Volume I,* and which he seems fondly to anticipate, involves nothing less than the displacement of the current sexual economy by *a different economy* altogether, an economy that will feature "bodies and pleasures" instead of, or at least in addition to, such familiar and overworked entities as "sexuality" and "desire." Foucault makes it very clear that bodies and pleasures, in his conception, are not the eternal building blocks of sexual subjectivity or sexual experience; they are not basic, irreducible, or natural "elements" that different human societies rearrange in different patterns over time—and that our own society has elaborated into the cultural edifice now known as "sexuality." Rather, "bodies" and "pleasures" refer to two entities that modern sexual discourse and practice include but largely ignore, underplay, or pass quickly over, and that accordingly are relatively undercoded, relatively uninvested by the normalizing apparatus of sexuality, especially in comparison to more thoroughly policed and more easily pathologized items such as "sexual desire." (Or so at least it seemed to Foucault at the time he was writing, in the wake of the sexual liberation movement of the late 1960s and early 1970s, which had exhorted us to liberate our "sexuality" and to un-repress or desublimate our "desire.") For that reason, bodies and pleasures represented to Foucault an opportunity for effecting, as he says earlier in the same passage, "a tactical reversal of the various mechanisms of sexuality," a means of resistance to the apparatus of sexuality.[4] In particular, the strategy that Foucault favors consists in asserting, "against the [various] holds of power, the claims of bodies, pleasures, and knowledges in their multiplicity and their possibility of resistance."[5] The very possibility of pursuing such a body- and pleasure-centered strategy of resistance to the apparatus of sexuality disappears, of course, as soon as "bodies" and "pleasures" cease to be understood merely as handy weapons against current technologies of normalization and attain instead to the status of transhistorical components of some natural phenomenon or material substrate underlying "the history of sexuality" itself. Such a notion of "bodies and pleasures," so very familiar and uncontroversial and positivistic has it now become, is indeed nothing if not eminently forgettable.

In what follows I propose to explore another aspect of the oblivion that has engulfed Foucault's thinking about sexuality since his death, one particular "forgetting" that has had important consequences for the practice of both the history of sexuality and lesbian/gay studies. I refer to the reception and deployment of Foucault's distinction between the sodomite and the homosexual—a distinction often taken to be synonymous with the distinction between sexual acts and sexual identities. The passage in *The History of Sexuality, Volume I,* in which Foucault makes this fateful distinction is so well known that it might seem unnecessary to quote it, but what that really means, I am contending, is that the passage is in fact so well forgotten that nothing but direct quotation from it will do. Foucault writes,

> As defined by the ancient civil or canonical codes, sodomy was a category of forbidden acts; their author was nothing more than the juridical subject of them. The nineteenth-century homosexual became a personage—a past, a case history and a childhood, a character, a form of life; also a morphology, with an indiscreet anatomy and possibly a mysterious physiology. Nothing in his total being escapes his sexuality. Everywhere in him it is present: underlying all his actions, because it is their insidious and indefinitely active principle; shamelessly inscribed on his face and on his body, because it is a secret that always gives itself away. It is consubstantial with him, less as a habitual sin than as a singular nature. . . . Homosexuality appeared as one of the forms of sexuality when it was transposed from the practice of sodomy onto a kind of interior androgyny, a hermaphroditism of the soul. The sodomite was a temporary aberration; the homosexual is now a species.

> [La sodomie—celle des anciens droits civil ou canonique—était un type d'actes interdits; leur auteur n'en était que le sujet juridique. L'homosexuel du

XIX siècle est devenu un personnage: un passé, une histoire et une enfance, un caractère, une forme de vie; une morphologie aussi, avec une anatomie indiscrète et peut-être une physiologie mystérieuse. Rien de ce qu'il est au total n'échappe à sa sexualité. Partout en lui, elle est présente: sousjacente à toutes ses conduites parce qu'elle en est le principe insidieux et indéfiniment actif; inscrite sans pudeur sur son visage et sur son corps parce qu'elle est un secret qui se trahit toujours. Elle lui est consubstantielle, moins comme un péché d'habitude que comme une nature singulière. . . . L'homosexualité est apparue comme une des figures de la sexualité lorsqu'elle a été rabattue de la pratique de la sodomie sur une sorte d'androgynie intérieure, un hermaphrodisme de l'âme. Le sodomite était un relaps, l'homosexuel est maintenant une espèce.][6]

Foucault's formulation is routinely taken to authorize the doctrine that before the nineteenth century the categories or classifications typically employed by European cultures to articulate sexual difference did not distinguish among different kinds of sexual actors but only among different kinds of sexual acts. In the premodern and early modern periods, so the claim goes, sexual behavior did not represent a sign or marker of a person's sexual identity; it did not indicate or express some more generalized or holistic feature of the person, such as that person's subjectivity, disposition, or character. The pattern is clearest, we are told, in the case of deviant sexual acts. Sodomy, for example, was a sinful act that anyone of sufficient depravity might commit; it was not a symptom of a type of personality. To perform the act of sodomy was not to manifest a deviant sexual identity, but merely to be the author of a morally objectionable act.[7] Whence the conclusion that before the modern era sexual deviance could be predicated only of acts, not of persons or identities.

There is a good deal of truth in this received view, and Foucault himself may even have subscribed to a version of it at the time he wrote *The History of Sexuality, Volume I*.[8] Although I am about to argue strenuously against it, I want to be very clear that my aim is to revise it, not to reverse it. I do not want to return us to some unreconstructed or reactionary belief in the universal validity and applicability of modern sexual concepts or to promote an uncritical acceptance of the categories and classifications of sexuality as true descriptors of the basic realities of human erotic life—and, therefore, as unproblematic instruments for the historical analysis of human culture in all times and places. It is certainly not my intention to undermine the principles and practices of the new social history, let alone to recant my previous arguments for the historical and cultural constitution of sexual identity (which have sometimes been misinterpreted as providing support for the view I shall be criticizing here). Least of all do I wish to revive an essentialist faith in the unqualified existence of homosexual and heterosexual persons in Western societies before the modern era. I take it as established that a large-scale transformation of social and personal life took place in Europe as part of the massive cultural reorganization that accompanied the transition from a traditional, hierarchical, status-based society to a modern, individualistic, mass society during the period of industrialization and the rise of a cap-italist economy. One symptom of that transformation, as a number of researchers (both before and after Foucault) have pointed out, is that something new happens to the various relations among sexual roles, sexual object-choices, sexual categories, sexual behaviors, and sexual identities in bourgeois Europe between the end of the seventeenth century and the beginning of the twentieth.[9] Sex takes on new social and individual functions, and it assumes a new impor-tance in defining and normalizing the modern self. The conception of the sex-ual instinct as an autonomous human function without an organ appears for the first time in the nineteenth century, and without it our heavily psychologized model of sexual subjectivity—which knits up desire, its objects, sexual behavior, gender identity, reproductive function, mental health, erotic sensibility, personal style, and degrees of normality or deviance into an individuating, normativizing feature of the personality called "sexuality" or "sexual orientation"—is incon-ceivable.[10] Sexuality is indeed, as Foucault claimed, a distinctively modern pro-duction. Nonetheless, the canonical reading of the famous passage in *The History of Sexuality, Volume I,* and the conclusion conventionally based on it— namely, that before the modern era sexual deviance could be predicated only of acts, not of persons or identities—is, I shall contend, as inattentive to Foucault's text as it is heedless of European history.

Such a misreading of Foucault can be constructed only by setting aside and forgetting the decisive qualifying phrase with which his famous pronouncement opens: "*As defined by the ancient civil or canonical codes,*" Foucault begins, "sodomy was a category of forbidden acts."[11] Foucault, in other words, is mak-ing a carefully limited point about the differing styles of disqualification applied to male love by premodern legal definitions of sodomy and by nineteenth-cen-tury psychiatric conceptualizations of homosexuality, respectively. The intended effect of his rhetorical extravagance in this passage is to highlight what in par-ticular was new and distinctive about the modern discursive practices that pro-duced the category of "the homosexual." As almost always in *The History of Sexuality,* Foucault is speaking about discursive and institutional practices, not about what people really did in bed or what they thought about it. He is not attempting to describe popular attitudes or private emotions, much less is he presuming to convey what actually went on in the minds of different historical subjects when they had sex. He is making a contrast between the way something called "sodomy" was typically defined by the laws of various European states and municipalities and by Christian penitentials and canon law, on the one hand, and the way something called "homosexuality" was typically defined by the writ-ings of nineteenth-century and early-twentieth-century sexologists, on the other.

A glance at the larger context of the much-excerpted passage in *The History of Sexuality, Volume I,* is sufficient to make Foucault's meaning clear. Foucault introduces his account of "the nineteenth-century homosexual" in order to illus-trate a more general claim, which he advances in the sentence immediately pre-ceding: the "new persecution of the peripheral sexualities" that occurred in the modern era was accomplished in part through "an *incorporation of perversions* and a new *specification of individuals*"[12] (Earlier efforts to regulate sexual behavior did not feature such tactics, according to Foucault.) The whole discussion of this distinctively modern method of sexual control is embedded, in turn, within a larger argument about a crucial shift in *the nature of sexual prohibitions* as those prohibitions were constructed in *formal discursive practices*, a shift that occurred between the premodern period and the nineteenth century. Comparing medieval moral and legal codifications of sexual relations with nineteenth-century medical and forensic ones, Foucault contrasts various premodern styles of sexual prohibition, which took the form of specifying rules of conduct, making prescriptions and recommendations, and discriminating between the licit and the illicit, with modern styles of sexual prohibition. These latter-day strategies took the form of establishing norms of self-regulation—not by legislating standards of behavior and punishing deviations from them but rather by constructing new species of individuals, discovering and "implanting" perversions, and thereby elaborating more subtle and insidious means of social control. The ultimate purpose of the comparison is to support Foucault's "historico-theoretical" demonstration that power is not only negative but also positive, not only repressive but also productive.

Foucault is analyzing the different modalities of power at work in premodern and modern codifications of sexual prohibition, which is to say in two historical instances of sexual discourse attached to institutional practices. He carefully isolates the formal discursive systems that he will proceed to discuss from popular moral attitudes and behaviors about which he will have nothing to say and that he dismisses from consideration with barely a parenthetical glance: "Up to the end of the eighteenth century, three major explicit codes [*codes*]—*apart from regularities of custom and constraints of opinion*—governed sexual practices: canon law [*droit canonique*], Christian pastoral, and civil law."[13] Foucault goes on to expand this observation in a passage that directly anticipates and lays the groundwork for the famous portrait he will later sketch of the differences between "the sodomy of the old civil and canonical codes" and that novel invention of modern psychiatry, "the nineteenth-century homosexual." Describing the terms in which premodern sexual prohibitions defined the scope of their operation and the nature of their target, he writes,

> What was taken into account in the civil and religious jurisdictions alike was a general unlawfulness. Doubtless acts "contrary to nature" were stamped as especially abominable, but they were perceived simply as an extreme form of acts "against the law"; they, too, were infringements of decrees—decrees which were just as sacred as those of marriage and which had been established in order to rule the order of things and the plan of beings. Prohibitions bearing on sex were basically of a juridical nature [*de nature juridique*].[14]

This passage prepares the reader to gauge the differences between these "juridical" prohibitions against "acts" " 'contrary to nature' " and the nineteenth-century prohibitions against homosexuality, which did not simply criminalize sexual relations between men as illegal but medically disqualified them as pathological and—not content with penalizing the act—constructed the perpetrator as a deviant form of life, a perverse personality, an anomalous species, thereby producing a new specification of individuals whose true nature would be defined from now on by reference to their abnormal "sexuality." The nineteenth-century disciplining of the subject, though it purported to aim at the eradication of "peripheral sexualities," paradoxically required their consolidation and "implantation" or "incorporation" in individuals, for only by that means could the subject's body itself become so deeply, so minutely invaded and colonized by the agencies of normalization. The discursive construction of the new sexual perversions was therefore a ruse of power, no longer simply prohibiting behavior but now also controlling, regulating, and normalizing embodied subjects. As Foucault sums up his argument, "The implantation of perversions is an instrument-effect: it is through the isolation, intensification, and consolidation of peripheral sexualities that the relations of power to sex and pleasure branched out and multiplied, measured the body and penetrated modes of conduct."[15] Want an example? Take the case of homosexuality. "The sodomy of the old civil and canonical codes was a category of forbidden acts; their author was nothing more than the juridical subject of them. The nineteenth-century homosexual became a personage." So that's how the overall argument works.

Foucault narrowly frames his comparison between sodomy and homosexuality with the purpose of this larger argument in mind. The point-by-point contrast between legal discourse (*codes* and *droits*) and psychiatric discourse, between juridical subjects and sexual subjects, between laws and norms, between acts contrary to nature and embodied subjects or species of individuals is ruthlessly schematic: that schematic reduction is in keeping with the general design of the first volume of Foucault's *History,* which merely outlines, in an admittedly preliminary and tentative fashion, the principles intended to guide the remaining five unfinished studies that Foucault projected for his *History* at the time. His schematic opposition between sodomy and homosexuality is first and foremost a discursive analysis, not a social history, let alone an exhaustive one. *It is not an empirical claim about the historical existence or nonexistence of sexually deviant individuals.* It is a claim about the internal logic and systematic functioning of two different discursive styles of sexual disqualification—and, ultimately, it is a heuristic device for foregrounding what is distinctive about modern techniques of social and sexual regulation. As such, it points to a historical development that will need to be properly explored in its own right (as Foucault intended to do in a separate volume) and it dramatizes the larger themes of Foucault's *History*: the historical triumph of normalization over law, the decentralization and dispersion of the mechanisms of regulation, the disciplining of the modern subject, the traversal of sexuality by relations of power, the productivity of power, and the displacement of state coercion by the technical and bureaucratic administration of life ("biopower"). By documenting the existence of both a discursive and a temporal gap between two dissimilar styles of defining, and disqualifying, male same-sex sexual expression, Foucault highlights the historical and political specificity of sexuality, both as a cultural concept and as a tactical device, and so he contributes to the task of "introducing" the history of sexuality as a possible field of study—and as a radical scholarly and political project. Nothing Foucault says about the differences between those two historically distant, and operationally distinct, discursive strategies for regulating and delegitimating forms of male same-sex sexual contacts prohibits us from inquiring into the connections that premodern people may have made between specific sexual acts and the particular ethos, or sexual style, or sexual subjectivity, of those who performed them.

A more explicit argument to this effect was advanced nearly a decade ago by John J. Winkler, in opposition less to Foucault than to the already current dogmatic and careless readings of Foucault. Winkler, a classical scholar, was discussing the ancient Greek and Roman figure of the *kinaidos* or *cinaedus,* a "scare-image" (or phobic construction) of a sexually deviant and gender-deviant male, whose most salient distinguishing feature was a supposedly "feminine" love of being sexually penetrated by other men.[16] "Scholars of recent sex-gender history," Winkler wrote in his 1990 book, *The Constraints of Desire,* "have asserted that pre-modern systems classified not persons but acts and that 'the' homosexual as a person-category is a recent invention." He went on to qualify that assertion as follows:

> The *kinaidos,* to be sure, is not a "homosexual" but neither is he just an ordinary guy who now and then decided to commit a kinaidic act. The conception of a *kinaidos* was of a man socially deviant in his entire being, principally observable in behavior that flagrantly violated or contravened the dominant social definition of masculinity. To this extent, *kinaidos* was a category of person, not just of acts.[17]

Ancient Mediterranean societies, of course, did not exactly have "categories of person," types of blank individuals, in the modern sense, as Winkler himself pointed out. The ancient conception of the *kinaidos,* Winkler explained, depended on indigenous notions of gender. It arose in the context of a belief system in which, first of all, the two genders are conceived as opposite ends of a much-traveled continuum and, second, masculinity is thought to be a difficult accomplishment—one that is achieved only by a constant struggle akin to warfare against enemies both internal and external—and thus requires great fortitude in order to maintain. In a situation where it is so hard, both personally and culturally, to be a man, Winkler observed, "the temptation to desert one's side is very great." The *kinaidos* succumbed to that temptation.

The *kinaidos* could be conceived by the ancients in both universalizing and minoritizing terms—as a potential threat to the masculine identity of every male, that is, and as the disfiguring peculiarity of a small class of deviant individuals.[18] Because ancient Mediterranean discourses of sex and gender featured the notion that "the two sexes are not simply opposite but stand at poles of a continuum which can be traversed," as Winkler pointed out, " 'woman' is not only the opposite of a man; she is also a potentially threatening 'internal émigré' of masculine identity."[19] The prospect of losing one's masculine gender status and being reduced to the social ranks of women therefore represented a universal possibility for all men. In such a context, the figure of the *kinaidos* stands as a warning to men of what can happen to them if they give up the internal struggle to master their desires and if they surrender, in womanly fashion, to the lure of pleasure. The clear implication of this warning is that the only thing that prevents men from allowing other men to use them as objects of sexual degradation, the only thing that enables men to resist the temptation to let other men fuck them like whores, is not the nature of their own desires, or their own capacities for sexual enjoyment, but their hard-won masculine ability to withstand the seductive appeal of pleasure-at-any-price. The *kinaidos,* on this view, is not someone who has a different sexual orientation from other men, or who belongs to some autonomous sexual species. Rather, he is someone who represents what *every* man would be like if he were so shameless as to sacrifice his dignity and masculine gender status for the sake of gratifying the most odious and disgraceful, though no doubt voluptuous, bodily appetites. Such a worthless character is so radical and so complete a failure as a man that he can be understood, at least by the ancients, as wholly reversing the internal gender hierarchy that structures and defines normative masculinity for men and that maintains it against manifold temptations to effeminacy. The catastrophic failure of male self-fashioning that the *kinaidos* represents is so complete, in other words, that it cannot be imagined as merely confined within the sphere of erotic life or restricted to the occasional performance of disreputable sexual acts: it defines and determines a man's social identity in its totality, and it generates a recognizable social *type*—namely, the "scare-image" and phobic stereotype of the *kinaidos,* which Winkler so eloquently described.

As the mere existence of the stereotype implies, the ancients were quite capable of conceptualizing the figure of the *kinaidos,* when they so desired, not only in anxiously universalizing terms but also in comfortably minoritizing ones. Although some normal men might acknowledge that the scandalous pleasures to which the *kinaidos* succumbed, and which normal men properly avoided, were universally pleasurable in and of themselves,[20] still the very fact that the *kinaidos* did succumb to such pleasures, whereas normal men did not, contributed to defining his difference, and it also marked out the vast distance that separated the *kinaidos* from normal men. Just as some moderns may think that, whereas anyone *can* get addicted to drugs, only people who have something fundamentally wrong with them actually *do,* so some ancients evidently thought that, although the pleasures of sexual penetration in themselves might be universally pleasurable, any male who actually pursued them suffered from a specific constitutional defect—namely, a constitutional lack of the masculine capacity to withstand the appeal of pleasure (especially pleasure deemed exceptionally disgraceful or degrading) as well as a constitutional tendency to adopt a specifically feminine attitude of surrender in relations with other men. Hence, the desire to be sexually penetrated by other men, which was the most dramatic and flagrant sign of the *kinaidos*'s constitutional femininity, could be interpreted by the ancients in sharply minoritizing terms as an indication of a physiological anomaly in the *kinaidos* or as the symptom of a moral or mental "disease."[21] Conceived in these terms, the *kinaidos* did not represent the frightening possibility of a failure of nerve on the part of every man, a collapse in the face of the ongoing struggle that all men necessarily waged to maintain and defend their masculinity; he was simply a peculiar, repugnant, and perplexing freak, driven to abandon his sexual and gender identity in pursuit of a pleasure that no one but a woman could possibly enjoy. (And there were even some abominable practices, like fellatio, which a *kinaidos* might relish but no decent woman would so much as contemplate.)

The details in this minoritizing conception of the *kinaidos* have been filled in with great skill and documented at fascinating length by Maud Gleason, most recently in her 1995 book, *Making Men*. "The essential idea here," writes Gleason, corroborating Winkler's emphasis on the gender deviance of the *kinaidos* and calling attention to what she fittingly terms the ancient "semiotics of gender" that produced the *kinaidos* as a visibly deviant kind of being, "is that there exist [according to the axioms of Greek and Roman social life] masculine and feminine 'types' that do not necessarily correspond to the anatomical sex of the person in question."[22] Gleason approaches the figure of the *kinaidos* from an unexpected and original scholarly angle—namely, from a close study of the neglected scientific writings of the ancient physiognomists, experts in the learned technique of deciphering a person's character from his or her appearance. Gleason's analysis of the ancient corpus of physiognomic texts makes clear that the portrait they construct of the figure of the *kinaidos* agrees with the stereotypical features commonly ascribed by the ancients to the general appearance of gender-deviant or "effeminate" men. Like such men, the *kinaidos* could be identified, or so the Greeks thought, by a variety of physical features: weak eyes, knees that knock together, head tilted to the right, hands limply upturned, and hips that either swing from side to side or are held tightly rigid. Latin physiognomy agrees largely with the Greek tradition in its enumeration of the characteristics of the *cinaedus*: "A tilted head, a mincing gait, an enervated voice, a lack of stability in the shoulders, and a feminine way of moving the body." Gleason adds that a *kinaidos* could also be known by certain specific mannerisms:

He shifts his eyes around in sheep-like fashion when he speaks; he touches his fingers to his nose; he compulsively obliterates all traces of spittle he may find—his own or anyone else's—by rubbing it into the dust with his heel; he frequently stops to admire what he considers his own best feature; he smiles furtively while talking; he holds his arms turned outwards; he laughs out loud; and he has an annoying habit of clasping other people by the hand.[23]

The *kinaidos,* in short, is considerably more than the juridical subject of deviant sexual acts. To recur to Foucault's terminology, the *kinaidos* represents at the very least a full-blown morphology. As Gleason observes, "Foucault's description of the nineteenth-century homosexual fits the *cinaedus* remarkably well. . . . The *cinaedus* was a 'life-form' all to himself and his condition was written all over him in signs that could be decoded by those practiced in the art." Gleason hastens to add, however, that "what made [the *cinaedus*] different from normal folk . . . was not simply the fact that his sexual partners included people of the same sex as himself (that, after all, was nothing out of the ordinary), nor was it some kind of psychosexual orientation—a 'sexuality' in the nineteenth-century sense—but rather an inversion or reversal of his gender identity: his abandonment of a 'masculine' role in favor of a 'feminine' one."[24]

Gleason's conclusion has now been massively confirmed by Craig Williams, a specialist in ancient Roman literature, who has undertaken an exhaustive survey of the extant Latin sources. Williams's careful discussion makes clear that the category of *cinaedus* does not map easily onto modern sexual taxonomies: "When a Roman called a man a *cinaedus,*" Williams explains, "he was not ruling out the possibility that the man might play sexual roles other than that of the receptive partner in anal intercourse." Hence,

the *cinaedus* was not the same thing as the "passive homosexual," since it was neither his expression of sexual desire for other males nor his proclivity for playing the receptive role in anal intercourse that gave him his identity or uniquely defined him as a *cinaedus*: he might engage in sexual practices with women and still be a *cinaedus,* and a man did not automatically become a *cinaedus* simply by being penetrated (victims of rape, for example, would not be described as such). A *cinaedus* was, rather, a man who failed to be fully masculine, whose effeminacy showed itself in such symptoms as feminine clothing and mannerisms and a lascivious and oversexed demeanor that was likely to be embodied in a proclivity for playing the receptive role in anal intercourse. *Cinaedi* were, in other words, a prominent subset of the class of effeminate men (*molles*) . . . but hardly identical to that whole class.[25]

Whatever its superficial resemblances to various contemporary sexual life-forms, the ancient figure of the *cinaedus* or *kinaidos* properly belongs in its own cultural universe. It represents an extinct category of social, sexual, and gender deviance.

In fact, the *kinaidos* has not as yet brought us quite into the realm of deviant sexual subjectivity. For whether he was defined in universalizing or minoritizing terms, the *kinaidos* was in any case defined more in terms of gender than in terms of desire. Although he was distinguished from normal men in part by the pleasure he took in being sexually penetrated, his peculiar taste was not sufficient, in and of itself, to individuate him as a sexual subject. Rather, it was *a generic sign of femininity.* Even the *kinaidos*'s desire to play a receptive role in sexual intercourse with other men—which was about as close to manifesting a distinctive sexual orientation as the *kinaidos* ever got—represented to the ancients "merely a symptom of the deeper disorder, his gender deviance," as Williams emphasizes, and so did not imply a different kind of specifically sexual subjectivity. At once a symptom and a consequence of the *kinaidos*'s categorical reversal of his masculine gender identity, the desire to be sexually penetrated identified the *kinaidos* as womanly in both his gender identity and his sexual desire; beyond that it did not distinguish him as the bearer of a unique or distinct sexuality. Neither did his lust for bodily pleasure, since far from being considered a deviant desire, as we have seen, such lust was thought common to all men. Nor was there anything peculiar about the *kinaidos*'s sexual object-choice: as Gleason mentions, it was quite possible in the ancient Mediterranean world for a male to desire and to pursue sexual contact with other males without impugning in the slightest his own masculinity or normative identity as a man—just so long as he played an insertive sexual role, observed all the proper phallocentric protocols in his relations with the objects of his desire, and maintained a normatively masculine style of personal deportment. Unlike the modern homosexual, then, the *kinaidos* was not defined principally by his sexual subjectivity. Even without a sexual subjectivity of his own, however, the *kinaidos*'s betrayal of his masculine gender identity was so spectacular as to brand him a deviant type of person and to inscribe his deviant identity all over his face and body. To put it very schematically, the *kinaidos* represents an instance of deviant sexual morphology *without* deviant sexual subjectivity.

(In an ongoing series of essays, much discussed and generally well received by professional classicists in the United States, Amy Richlin has assailed the historical work of Winkler, myself, and our collaborators [such as Gleason], all of whom she lumps together under the uncomplimentary, not to say phobic, title of "Foucaultians."[26] She faults us in particular for approaching the figure of the *kinaidos* from the standpoint of ancient sexual discourses; she prefers to see in that figure a material embodiment of "homosexuality," which she regards as a useful category for analyzing ancient societies—although she concedes that "there was no ancient word for 'homosexual.'"[27] Much could be said about the gaps in Richlin's argument, about its simplistic treatment of the interpretative issues, or about its unappetizing but evidently highly palatable combination of an old-fashioned positivism with a more fashionable blend of political and professional opportunism.[28] The only point I want to make here about Richlin's critique is that it is doubly ignorant and misinformed—wrong, that is, both about Foucault and about so-called Foucaultians. In the first place, Richlin claims, mistakenly, that in the famous passage from *The History of Sexuality, Volume I,* "Foucault is distinguishing . . . between behavior and essence." In the second place, she maintains that accounts of sex in antiquity by "Foucaultians" such as Winkler and myself "start from this axiom."[29] In fact, as I have tried to show, Foucault was not distinguishing between anything so metaphysical as behavior and essence but simply between two different discursive strategies for disqualifying male love. Winkler and Gleason, moreover, far from adhering uncritically to the erroneous reading of Foucault that Richlin propounds, explicitly *challenged* the misapplication of such a pseudo-Foucauldian "axiom" to the interpretation of the figure of the *kinaidos*. And in *One Hundred Years of Homosexuality* I made a rigorous distinction between a sexual orientation in the modern sense and the kinds of sexual identity current in the ancient Greek world; the latter, I argued, tended to be determined by a person's gender and social status rather than by a personal psychology. Moreover, I was careful to emphasize in a number of passages that it was possible for sexual acts to be linked in various ways with a sexual disposition or sexual subjectivity well before the nineteenth century.[30] Richlin's "Foucaultians," no less than her Foucault, are the product and projection of her own misreadings. Why her misreadings have been so widely, and so uncritically, acclaimed is another question, an interesting one in its own right, but this is not the place to pursue it.)

Let's move on, then, from matters of sexual morphology and gender presentation and take up at last questions of sexual subjectivity. My chief exhibit in this latter department will be an ancient erotic fable told by Apuleius in the second century and retold by Giovanni Boccaccio in the fourteenth. The two texts have been the subject of a trenchant comparative study by Jonathan Walters in a 1993 issue of *Gender and History*; I have taken his analysis as the basis of my own, and my interpretation closely follows his, although I have a somewhat different set of questions to put to the two texts.[31] Here, first of all, in bare outline, is the plot of the erotic fable under scrutiny. A man dining out at the home of a friend finds his dinner interrupted when his host detects an adulterous lover concealed in the house by the host's wife, who had not expected her husband to arrive home for dinner, much less with a guest in tow; the disappointed guest then returns to his own house for dinner ahead of schedule and tells the story to his righteously indignant wife, only to discover that she herself has hidden in his house a young lover of her own. Instead of threatening to kill the youth, however, the husband fucks him and lets him go. The end. This bare summary does little justice to the artistry and wit with which the stories are told by their respective authors, but the point I wish to make is a historical one, not a literary one. I trust it will emerge from the following comparison.

Apuleius's tale of the baker's wife in book 9 of *The Golden Ass* begins with a description of her lover. He is a boy (*puer*), Apuleius's narrator tells us, still notable for the shiny smoothness of his beardless cheeks, and still delighting and attracting the sexual attention of wayward husbands (*adulteros*).[32] According to the erotic postulates of ancient Mediterranean societies, then, there will be nothing out of the ordinary about a normal man finding him sexually desirable. So the first thing to note is that Apuleius explains the sexual motivation of the wronged husband by reference to erotic qualities inherent in the sexual *object,* not by reference to any distinguishing characteristics of the sexual *subject*—not, in other words, by reference to the husband's own erotic subjectivity. The point of specifying the attractiveness of the boy is to prepare for the ending of the story without portraying the husband as different in his sexual tastes from normal men. In fact, as Walters observes, the husband "is not described in any way that marks him out as unusual, let alone reprehensible: he is portrayed as blameless, 'a good man in general and extremely temperate'"; this is in keeping with a story designed, within the larger context of Apuleius's narrative, to illustrate the mischief caused to their husbands by devious, depraved, and adulterous wives.[33] When the baker discovers the boy, he locks up his wife and takes the boy to bed himself thereby (as Apuleius's narrator puts it) enjoying "the most gratifying revenge for his ruined marriage." At daybreak he summons two of his slaves and has them hold the boy up while he flogs his buttocks with a rod, leaving the boy "with his white buttocks the worse for their treatment" both by night and by day. The baker then kicks his wife out of the house and prepares to divorce her (9.28).

Boccaccio's tale of Pietro di Vinciolo of Perugia, the Tenth Story of the Fifth Day of the *Decameron,* is based directly on Apuleius; its departures from its model are therefore especially telling.[34] Boccaccio's narrator begins further back in time, at the point when Pietro takes a wife "more to beguile others and to abate the general suspect [*la generale oppinion*] in which he was held by all the Perugians, than for any desire [*vaghezza*] of his own" (trans. Payne-Singleton). As Walters remarks, "Boccaccio . . . is at pains to tell us from the beginning that something is wrong with the husband."[35] What Boccaccio marks specifically as deviant about Pietro, or so the foregoing quotation from the *Decameron* implies, is his *desire*.[36] This turns out to refer to his sexual object-choice and to comprehend, in particular, two different aspects of it: first, the customary objects of his sexual desire are young men, not the usual objects of desire for a man, and, second, Pietro (unlike the baker in Apuleius) has no desire for the usual objects of male desire—namely, women. So he desires the wrong objects, and he doesn't desire the right objects. Both of these erotic errors are dramatized by the narrative. We are told that his wife's lover is "a youth [*garzone*], who was one of the goodliest and most agreeable of all Perugia," and that when Pietro discovers him, he instantly recognizes him as "one whom he had long pursued for his own lewd ends." Understandably, Pietro "no less rejoiced to have found him than his wife was woeful"; when he confronts her with the lad, "she saw that he was all agog with joy because he held so goodly a stripling [*giovinetto*] by the hand." No wonder that far from punishing his wife Pietro hastens to strike an obscene bargain with her to share the young man between them. As for Pietro's sexual indifference to women, we are told that his lusty, red-haired, highly sexed young wife, "who would liefer have had two husbands than one," is frustrated by her husband's inattention and realizes that she will exhaust herself arguing with him before she will change his disposition. Indeed, he has "a mind far more disposed otherwhat than to her [*molto più ad altro che a lei l'animo avea disposto*]." At the culmination of the story, Pietro's wife reproaches him for being as desirous of women as "a dog of cudgels [*cosí vago di noi come il can delle mazze*]."[37]

Note that Boccaccio's narrator says nothing to indicate that Pietro is effeminate, or in any way deviant in terms of his personal style or sexual morphology.[38]

You wouldn't know he was a pederast or a sodomite by looking at him: nothing about his looks or his behavior gives him away or gives his wife any advance warning about the nature of his sexual peculiarities. As she says, she had supposed he desired what men do and should desire when she married him; otherwise, she would never have done so: "He knew I was a woman," she exclaims to herself; "why, then, did he take me to wife, if women were not to his mind [*contro all'animo*]?" Nothing in his morphology made her suspect he harbored deviant desires. And why in any case should we imagine the husband would exhibit signs of effeminacy? He no more resembles the ancient figure of the *kinaidos* than does his literary forebear in Apuleius: far from displaying a supposedly "feminine" inclination to submit himself to other men to be sexually penetrated by them, the husband in Boccaccio plays a sexually insertive role in intercourse with his wife's lover. That, after all, is the point of the story's punchline: "On the following morning the youth was escorted back to the public square not altogether certain which he had the more been that night, wife or husband"—meaning, obviously, *wife to Pietro* or *husband to Pietro's wife*.[39] What is at issue in Boccaccio's portrait of Pietro di Vinciolo, then, is not gender deviance but sexual deviance.

Finally, in Apuleius's tale the husband's enjoyment of his wife's lover is an incidental component of his revenge and does not express any special or distinctive sexual taste on his part, much less a habitual preference, whereas in Boccaccio's tale the husband is identified as the subject of deviant sexual desires and is only too happy to exploit his wife's infidelity for the purposes of his own pleasure.[40]

A comparison of these two premodern texts indicates that it is possible for sexual acts to be represented in such texts as either *more* or *less* related to sexual dispositions, desires, or subjectivities. Whereas Apuleius's text makes no incriminating association between the baker's sexual enjoyment of the adulterous youth and the baker's character, masculinity, or sexual disposition, Boccaccio's text connects the performance of sodomitical acts with a deviant sexual taste and a deviant sexual subjectivity. In order to update Apuleius's plot it seems to have been necessary for Boccaccio to posit a sodomitical disposition or inclination on the husband's part; he seems to have had no other way of motivating the scandalously witty conclusion of the tale as he had inherited it from Apuleius. Pietro's inclination is not the same thing as a sexual orientation, much less a sexual identity or form of life, to be sure: for one thing, his sexual preference seems contained, compartmentalized, and does not appear to connect to any other feature of his character, such as a sensibility a set of personal mannerisms, a style of gender presentation, or a psychology.[41] Nonetheless, Pietro's sexual taste for young men represents a notable and perhaps even a defining feature of his life as a sexual subject, as well as a distinctive feature of his life as a social and ethical subject. Pietro may not be a deviant life-form, like the ancient Greek or Roman *kinaidos*—a traitor to his gender whose deviance is visibly inscribed in his personal demeanor—but neither is he merely the juridical subject of a sodomitical act. Rather, his sexual preference for youths is a settled feature of his character and a significant fact about his social identity as a moral and sexual agent.[42]

To sum up, I have tried to suggest that the current doctrine that holds that sexual acts were unconnected to sexual identities before the nineteenth century is mistaken in at least two different respects. First, sexual acts could be interpreted as representative expressions of an individual's sexual morphology. Second, sexual acts could be interpreted as representative expressions of an individual's sexual subjectivity. A sexual morphology is not the same thing as a sexual subjectivity: the figure of the *kinaidos,* for example, represents an instance of deviant morphology without subjectivity, whereas Boccaccio's Pietro represents an instance of deviant subjectivity without morphology. Thus, morphology and subjectivity, as I have been using those terms, describe two *different* logics according to which sexual acts can be connected to some more generalized feature of an individual's identity. In particular, I've argued that the ancient figure of the *kinaidos* qualifies as an instance of a sexual life-form or morphology and that the property of *kinaidia* (or being a *kinaidos)* is accordingly a property of social beings, not merely of sexual acts. Nonetheless, what defines the *kinaidos* is not a unique or peculiar subjectivity, but a shameless appetite for pleasure, which is common to all human beings, along with a deviant gender-style, which assimilates him to the cultural definition of woman. The sodomitical character of Boccaccio's Pietro di Vinciolo, by contrast, does not express itself through a deviant morphology but through his sexual tastes, preferences, or desires—that is, through a deviant subjectivity.

Neither the sexual morphology of the *kinaidos* nor the sexual subjectivity of the fourteenth-century Italian sodomite should be understood as a sexual identity, or a sexual orientation in the modern sense—much less as equivalent to the modern formation known as homosexuality. At the very least, modern notions of homosexual identity and homosexual orientation tend to insist on the *conjunction* of sexual morphology and sexual subjectivity: they presume a convergence in the sexual actor of a deviant personal style with a deviant erotic desire.[43] In fact, what historically distinguishes "homosexuality" as a sexual classification is its unprecedented combination of at least three distinct and previously uncorrelated conceptual entities: (1) a psychiatric notion of a perverted or pathological *psychosexual orientation,* derived from nineteenth-century medicine, which applies to the inner life of the individual and does not necessarily entail same-sex sexual behavior or desire; (2) a psychoanalytic notion of same-sex *sexual object-choice* or desire, derived from Sigmund Freud and his coworkers, which is a category of erotic intentionality and does not necessarily imply pathology or deviance (since, according to Freud, most normal individuals make an unconscious homosexual object-choice at some point in their fantasy lives); and (3) a sociological notion of sexually *deviant behavior,* derived from nineteenth- and twentieth-century forensic inquiries into "social problems," which focuses on sexual practice and does not necessarily refer to erotic psychology or psychosexual orientation. Despite their several failures to meet the requirements of the modern definition of the homosexual, both the *kinaidos* and Boccaccio's Pietro, in their quite different and distinctive ways, challenge the orthodox pseudo-Foucauldian doctrine about the supposedly strict separation between sexual acts and sexual identities in European culture before the nineteenth century.

My argument, in short, does not refute Foucault's claim about the different ways male same-sex eroticism was constructed by the discourse of "the ancient civil or canonical codes" and by the discourse of nineteenth-century sexology. Nor does it demolish the absolutely indispensable distinction between sexual acts and sexual identities that historians of homosexuality have extracted from Foucault's text (where the term *identity* nowhere occurs) and that, in any case, antedated it by many years.[44] Least of all does it undermine a rigorously historicizing approach to the study of the social and cultural constitution of sexual subjectivity and sexual identity. (Whatever I may be up to in this paper, a posthumous rapprochement with John Boswell is not it.) What my argument does do, I hope, is to encourage us to inquire into the construction of sexual identities before the emergence of sexual orientations, and to do this *without* recurring to modern notions of sexuality or sexual orientation and thereby contributing to a kind of antihistoricist backlash. Perhaps we need to supplement our notion of sexual identity with a more refined concept of, say, partial identity, emergent identity, transient identity, semi-identity, incomplete identity, proto-identity, or sub-identity.[45] In any case, my intent is not to reinstall a notion of sexual identity as a historical category so much as to indicate *the multiplicity of possible historical connections between sex and identity,* a multiplicity whose existence has been obscured by the necessary but narrowly focused, totalizing critique of sexual identity as a unitary concept. We need to find ways of asking how different historical cultures fashioned different sorts of links between sexual acts, on the one hand, and sexual tastes, styles, dispositions, characters, gender presentations, and forms of subjectivity, on the other.

It is a matter of considerable irony that Foucault's influential distinction between the discursive construction of the sodomite and the discursive construction of the homosexual, which had originally been intended to open up a domain of historical inquiry, has now become a major obstacle blocking further research into the rudiments of sexual identity formation in premodern and early modern European societies. Foucault himself would surely have been astonished. Not only was he much too good a historian ever to have authorized the incautious and implausible claim that no one had ever had a sexual subjectivity, a sexual morphology, or a sexual identity of any kind before the nineteenth century (even if he painstakingly demonstrated that the conditions necessary for having a *sexuality,* a psychosexual orientation in the modern sense, did not in fact obtain until then). His approach to the history of the present was also too searching, too experimental, and too open-ended to tolerate converting a heuristic analytic distinction into an ill-founded historical dogma, as his more forgetful epigones have not hesitated to do.

Of course, the chief thing about Foucault that his self-styled disciples forget is that he did not propound a theory of sexuality. That fact about Foucault is the more easily forgotten as Foucault has become, especially in the United States and Britain, the property of academic critical theorists—the property of those, in other words, whose claim to the professional title of "theorist" derives from the reflected status, authority, and "theoretical" credentials of the thinkers they study. As one of those thinkers whose identity as a "theorist" is necessary to ground the secondary and derived "theoretical" status of others, Foucault is required to have a theory. Theories, after all, are what "theorists" are supposed to have. Now Foucault's *History of Sexuality, Volume I,* is perforce theoretical, inasmuch as it undertakes a far-reaching critical intervention in the realm of theory. It is, more specifically, an effort to dislodge and to thwart the effects of established theories—theories that attempt to tell us the truth about sexuality, to produce true accounts of its nature, to specify what sexuality really is, to inquire into sexuality as a positive thing that has a truth that can be told, and to ground authoritative forms of expertise in an objective knowledge of sexuality. Foucault's radical take on sexuality consists in approaching it from the perspective of the history of discourses, treating it accordingly not as a positive thing but as an instrumental effect, not as a physical or psychological reality but as a social and political device: Foucault is not trying to describe what sexuality is but to specify what it does and how it works in discursive and institutional practice. That approach to sexuality represents *a theoretical intervention* insofar as it engages with already existing theories of sexuality, but the nature of the engagement remains purely tactical: it is part of a larger strategic effort to effect a thoroughgoing *evasion* of theories of sexuality and to devise various means of circumventing their claims to specify the truth of sexuality—not by attempting to refute those claims directly but by attempting to expose and to delegitimate the strategies they employ to construct and to authorize those claims in the first place. It is this deliberate, ardent, and considered resistance to "theory" that defines Foucault's own practice of theory, his distinctive brand of (theoretical) critique.[46]

To undertake such a theoretical critique, to attempt to reorient our understanding of sexuality by approaching the history of sexuality from the perspective of the history of discourses, is obviously not to offer a new theory of sexuality, much less to try to substitute such a theory for those that already exist. Nor is it an attempt to claim, theoretically, that sexuality *is* discourse, or that it is constituted discursively instead of naturally. It is rather an effort to denaturalize, dematerialize, and derealize sexuality so as to prevent it from serving as the positive grounding for a theory of sexuality, to prevent it from answering to "the functional requirements of a discourse that must produce its truth."[47] It is an attempt to destroy the circuitry that connects sexuality, truth, and power. And thus it is an effort to make sexuality available to us as a possible source for a series of scholarly and political counterpratices. *The History of Sexuality, Volume I,* in short, does not contain an original theory of sexuality; if anything, its theoretical originality lies in its refusal of existing theory and its consistent elaboration of a critical antitheory. It offers a model demonstration of how to dismantle theories of sexuality, how to deprive them of their claims to legitimate authority. *The History of Sexuality, Volume I,* is a difficult book to read chiefly because we read it as conveying Foucault's formulation of his theory of sexuality. (There is no easier way to baffle students than by asking them to explain what Foucault's definition of "sexuality" is: it's the worst sort of trick question.) As a theory of sexuality, however, *The History of Sexuality, Volume I,* is unreadable. That may be one of its greatest virtues.

For our hankering after a correct account or theory of sexuality seems scarcely diminished since Foucault's day, least of all among academic practitioners of so-called queer theory.[48] By juxtaposing to this "theoretical" tendency Foucault's example, by contrasting the theorizing of sexuality with the strategic undoing of sexual theory, I am not trying to lend aid and comfort to "the enemies of theory" (who would forget not just Foucault but "theory" itself), nor do I mean to contribute to the phobic totalization and homogenization of "theory"—as if there could possibly be any sense in treating theory as a unitary entity that could then be either praised or disparaged. To argue that *The History of Sexuality, Volume I,* contains not a theory but a critical antitheory is not to argue that the book is "anti" theory, against theory, but rather to indicate that its theoretical enterprise, which is the derealization or desubstantialization of sexuality, militates strenuously against the construction or vindication of any theory *of* sexuality. Moreover, no inquiry into the deficiencies of contemporary work in lesbian and gay studies or the history of sexuality that pretends to be serious can content itself with mere carping at individual scholarly abuses of "theory" (the notion that scholars nowadays have all been corrupted by "theory" is about as plausible as the notion that lesbian and gay academics have seized control of the universities); rather, it must take up such institutional questions as how many professors with qualifications in "queer theory" are tenured at major universities and are actually guiding the work of graduate students intending and able to pursue scholarly careers in the field.

Nonetheless, I find the doctrinaire theoretical tendencies in "queer theory" and in academic "critical theory" to be strikingly at odds with the antidogmatic, critical, and experimental impulses that originally animated a good deal of the work we now consider part of the canon of "theory." Foucault stands out in this context as one of the few canonical theorists whose theoretical work seems calculated to resist theoretical totalization, premature theoretical closure, and thereby to resist the weirdest and most perverse instance of "the resistance to theory": namely, the sort of resistance to theory that expresses itself *through* the now standard academic practice of so-called critical theory itself.[49] Foucault's refusal of a theory of sexuality resists the complacencies of the increasingly dogmatic and reactionary resistance to theory that misleadingly and all too often answers to the name of "theory." I believe it is our resistance to Foucault's resistance to this resistance to theory, our insistence on transforming Foucault's critical antitheory into a theory of sexuality, that has led us to mistake his discursive analysis for a historical assertion—and that has licensed us, on that basis, to remake his strategic distinction between the sodomite and the homosexual into a conceptual distinction between sexual acts and sexual identities, into a bogus theoretical doctrine, and into a patently false set of historical premises. I also believe it is what has led us to convert his strategic appeal to bodies and pleasures as a means of resistance to the apparatus of sexuality into a theoretical specification of the irreducible elements of sexuality. And it is what has made Foucault's intellectual example increasingly, and quite properly, forgettable. If indeed it is as a theorist of sexuality that we remember Foucault, perhaps Baudrillard was right after all: the greatest service we can do to him, and to ourselves, is to forget him as quickly as possible.

Let me give the last word to Foucault, however. In an early essay on Gustave Flaubert, Foucault described an experience of the fantastic that he believed was new in the nineteenth century, "the discovery of a new imaginative space" in the archives of the library.

> This domain of phantasms is no longer the night, the sleep of reason, or the uncertain void that stands before desire, but, on the contrary, wakefulness, untiring attention, zealous erudition, and constant vigilance. Henceforth, the visionary experience arises from the black and white surface of printed signs, from the closed and dusty volume that opens with a flight of forgotten words; fantasies are carefully deployed in the hushed library, with its columns of books, with its titles aligned on shelves to form a tight enclosure, but within confines that also liberate impossible worlds. The imaginary now resides between the book and the lamp. The fantastic is no longer a property of the heart, nor is it found among the incongruities of nature; it evolves from the accuracy of knowledge, and its treasures lie dormant in documents.[50]

The history of sexuality, at its best, should serve as a reminder of the one thing that no one who has been touched by Foucault's writing is likely ever to forget: namely, that the space of imaginative fantasy that the nineteenth century discovered in the library is not yet exhausted, and that it may still prove to be productive—both for academic scholarship and for our ongoing processes of personal and cultural self-transformation.

NOTES

1. For all of the information and the quotations in this paragraph, I am indebted to David Macey, *The Lives of Michel Foucault* (London, 1993), esp. pp. 358–60. See, further, Jean Bau-

drillard, *Cool Memories, I et II. 1980–1990* (Paris, 1993), pp. 139–42, esp. pp. 140 ("L'oublier était lui rendre service, l'aduler était le desservir"), 139 ("Mort de Foucault. Perte de confiance en son propre génie. . . . La perte des systèmes immunitaires, en dehors de tout aspect sexuel, n'est que la transcription biologique de l'autre processus").

For some resumptions of the "forget Foucault" theme, see E. Greblo, "Dimenticare Foucault?" *Aut-Aut* 242 (1991): 79–90; Kate Soper, "Forget Foucault?" *New Formations* 25 (1995): 21–27.

2. Baudrillard delivers himself of this enlightened opinion in the course of an interview with F. Rötzer, "Virtuelle Katastrophen," *Kunstforum* (1990): 266; I reproduce here the quotation and citation provided by Douglas Crimp, "Portraits of People with AIDS," in *Cultural Studies,* ed. Lawrence Grossberg, Cary Nelson, and Paula A. Treichler (New York, 1992), pp. 117–33 (quotation on p. 130).

3. Michel Foucault, *The History of Sexuality, Volume I: An Introduction,* trans. Robert Hurley (New York, 1980), p. 159; cf. Michel Foucault, *La volonté de savoir,* vol. 1 of *Histoire de la sexualité* (1976; reprint, Paris, 1984), p. 211. Wherever possible, I quote the English text of Foucault's *History of Sexuality,* because it is this text that has influenced Foucault's Anglophone disciples, but I have altered the published translation whenever necessary to restore Foucault's original emphasis or meaning.

4. Foucault, *History of Sexuality,* p. 157. See, further, David M. Halperin, *Saint Foucault: Towards a Gay Hagiography* (New York, 1995), pp. 92–97.

5. Foucault, *History of Sexuality,* p. 157 (emended); *La volonté de savoir,* p. 208.

6. Foucault, *History of Sexuality,* p. 43 (translation considerably modified); *La volonté de savoir,* p. 59.

7. This view has recently been contested by Mark D. Jordan, *The Invention of Sodomy in Christian Theology* (Chicago, 1997), esp. pp. 42, 44, 163.

8. In a passage that provides the closest textual and historical parallel in Foucault's writings to the famous passage in *The History of Sexuality, Volume I,* Foucault seems to distinguish between sodomy and homosexuality in much the same terms as do those historians of sexuality whose views I am criticizing here. The passage occurs in a book-length transcript of six taped interviews with a young gay man named Thierry Voeltzel that Foucault recorded during the summer of 1976, just as he was completing *The History of Sexuality, Volume I,* and that he arranged to have published under Voeltzel's name. At one point in the conversation the anonymous interviewer (i.e., Foucault) makes the following observation: "The category of the homosexual was invented lately. It didn't use to exist; what existed was sodomy, that is to say a certain number of sexual practices which, in themselves, were condemned, but the homosexual individual did not exist." ("La catégorie de l'homosexuel a été inventée tardivement. Ça n'existait pas, ce qui existait, c'était la sodomie, c'est-à-dire un certain nombre de pratiques sexuelles qui, elles, étaient condamnées, mais l'individu homosexuel n'existait pas"); Thierry Voeltzel, *Vingt ans et après* (Paris, 1978), p. 33. (I wish to thank Didier Eribon for calling my attention to this important passage.) Here Foucault may sound as if he's saying that once upon a time there were only sexual acts, not sexual actors. Note, however, that Foucault is simplifying matters for the benefit of his decidedly unacademic interlocutor and that even here he stops short of making a formal distinction between acts and identities, nor in fact does he say that before the nineteenth century there were no sexual identities, only sexual acts. What preoccupies him in his exchange with Voeltzel, just as in *The History of Sexuality, Volume I,* is the relatively recent invention of the normalizing "category" of the homosexual, the discursive constitution of a class of deviant individuals as opposed to the mere enumeration of a set of forbidden practices; when he refers to "the homosexual individual," he is referring to the entity constructed by that discursive category. It is only lately, Foucault emphasizes in his interview with Voeltzel, that it has become almost impossible simply to pursue the pleasures of homosexual contact, as Voeltzel appears to have done, "just so, when you felt like it, every once in a while, or in phases" ("comme ça, quand tu en avais envie, par moments, ou

par phases"), without being forced to deduce from one's own behavior that one *is* homosexual, without being interpellated by the culpabilizing category of "the homosexual." Voeltzel's narrative reminds Foucault of an earlier historical period when it was possible to *practice* homosexuality without *being* homosexual. As time went by, and Foucault's thinking about the history of sexuality evolved, he abandoned the contrast between sodomy and homosexuality, along with the implicit opposition between practices and persons, and came up with new strategies for representing the differences between modern and premodern forms of same-sex sexual experience. In 1982, for example, in a review of the French translation of K. J. Dover's 1978 monograph *Greek Homosexuality,* Foucault wrote: "Of course, there will still be some folks disposed to think that, in the final analysis, homosexuality has always existed. . . . To such naive souls Dover gives a good lesson in historical nominalism. [Sexual] relations between two persons of the same sex are one thing. But to love the same sex as oneself, to take one's pleasure in that sex, is quite another thing, it's a whole experience, with its own objects and their meanings, with a specific way of being on the part of the subject and a consciousness which he has of himself. That experience is complex, it is diverse, it takes different forms, it changes." ("Bien sûr, on trouvera encore des esprits aimables pour penser qu'en somme l'homosexualité a toujours existé. . . . A de tels naïfs, Dover donne une bonne leçon de nominalisme historique. Le rapport entre deux individus du même sexe est une chose. Mais aimer le même sexe que soi, prendre avec lui un plaisir, c'est autre chose, c'est toute une expérience, avec ses objets et leurs valeurs, avec la manière d'être du sujet et la conscience qu'il a de lui-même. Cette expérience est complexe, elle est diverse, elle change de formes"); Michel Foucault, "Des caresses d'hommes considérées comme un art," *Libération* (June 1, 1982): 27. Here Foucault inveighs against applying to the Greeks an undifferentiated, ahistorical, and transcendental notion of homosexuality defined in terms of mere sexual *practice* ("sexual relations between two persons of the same sex") in favor of a more nuanced understanding of specific, conscious "ways of being" on the part of different historical and sexual subjects. This is very much in keeping with Foucault's emphasis in his famous 1981 interview in *Le gai pied* on homosexuality as a "way of life" *mode de vie;* Michel Foucault, "De l'amitié comme mode de vie," *Le gai pied* 25 (1981): 38–39, trans. John Johnston, in *Foucault Live (Interviews, 1961–1984),* ed. Sylvère Lotringer (New York, 1989), pp. 308–12. But now it is not so much a question of opposing "sexual practices" to categories of individuals, as Foucault was inclined to do in 1976; rather, it is a question of systematically defining different historical forms of sexual experience—different ways of being, different sets of relations to others and to oneself, different articulations of pleasure and meaning, different forms of consciousness. The exact terms in which such historical discriminations are to be made, however, remain unspecified. Foucault leaves that practical question of historical analysis and methodology to the individual historian. He is content simply to offer a model of how to proceed in the second and third volumes of his own unfinished *History of Sexuality.*

9. See, for example, Mary McIntosh, "The Homosexual Role," *Social Problems* 16 (1968–69): 182–92; Randolph Trumbach, "London's Sodomites: Homosexual Behavior and Western Culture in the Eighteenth Century," *Journal of Social History* 11 (1977): 1–33; Richard Sennett, *The Fall of Public Man: On the Social Psychology of Capitalism* (New York, 1978); Jeffrey Weeks, *Sex, Politics, and Society: The Regulation of Sexuality since 1800* (London, 1981); Arnold I. Davidson, "Sex and the Emergence of Sexuality," *Critical Inquiry* 14 (1987–88): 16–48; John D'Emilio and Estelle D. Freedman, *Intimate Matters: A History of Sexuality in America* (New York, 1988); Thomas Laqueur, *Making Sex: Body and Gender from the Greeks to Freud* (Cambridge, Mass., 1990); George Chauncey, *Gay New York: Gender, Urban Culture, and the Making of the Gay Male World, 1890–1910* (New York, 1994); Jonathan Ned Katz, *The Invention of Heterosexuality* (New York, 1995); Carolyn J. Dean, *Sexuality and Modern Western Culture* (New York, 1996).

10. See the very careful demonstration of this point by Arnold I. Davidson, "Closing up the Corpses: Diseases of Sexuality and the Emergence of the Psychiatric Style of Reasoning,"

in *Meaning and Method: Essays in Honor of Hilary Putnam,* ed. George Boolos (Cambridge, 1990), pp. 295–325.

11. Foucault's French text, ironically, allows more scope for misinterpretation than the English-language version, which explicitly emphasizes that the relevant sense of the term *sodomy* in this passage is determined by the formal discursive context of medieval civil and canon law. In Foucault's original formulation, the unambiguous initial phrase "as defined by" does not occur; instead, we find a more offhand reference to "the sodomy of the old civil and canonical codes." Foucault, it seems, didn't feel the need to be so careful about instructing his readers to understand "sodomy" here as a strictly discursive category rather than as a sexual practice or as a cultural representation; instead, it is Foucault's translator who has expanded the original formulation in order to make its meaning clear. As I am concerned with the misreadings of Foucault by scholars who work largely from the published translation of *The History of Sexuality, Volume I,* and as my exegesis of Foucault is facilitated by (without at all depending on) the greater explicitness of the English-language version, I have not hesitated to cite it in my text for the sake of clarity, jettisoning it later once the interpretative point has been established.

12. Foucault, *History of Sexuality,* pp. 42–43; *La volonté de savoir,* pp. 58–59. Italics in original.

13. Foucault, *History of Sexuality,* p. 37 (translation modified); *La volonté de savoir,* p. 51. Italics added.

14. Foucault, *History of Sexuality,* p. 38 (translation modified); *La volonté de savoir,* pp. 52–53. Foucault explains, in a sentence that follows the conclusion of the passage quoted here, that "the 'nature' on which [sexual prohibitions] were based was still a kind of law."

15. Foucault, *History of Sexuality,* p. 48; *La volonté de savoir,* p. 66.

16. A more complete and systematic definition of this ancient term has now been provided by Craig A. Williams, *Roman Homosexuality: Ideologies of Masculinity in Classical Antiquity* (New York, 1999), pp. 175–76: "[A] cinaedus is a man who fails to live up to traditional standards of masculine comportment, and one way in which he may do so is by seeking to be [anally or orally] penetrated; but that is merely a symptom of the deeper disorder, his gender deviance. Indeed, the word's etymology suggests no direct connection to any sexual practice. Rather, borrowed from Greek *kinaidos* (which may itself have been a borrowing from a language of Asia Minor), it primarily signifies an effeminate dancer who entertained his audiences with a *tympanum* or tambourine in his hand, and adopted a lascivious style, often suggestively wiggling his buttocks in such a way as to suggest anal intercourse. . . . [T]he primary meaning of *cinaedus* never died out; the term never became a dead metaphor."

17. John J. Winkler, *The Constraints of Desire: The Anthropology of Sex and Gender in Ancient Greece* (New York, 1990), pp. 45–46. The formulation is repeated by Winkler, somewhat less emphatically, in "Laying Down the Law: The Oversight of Men's Sexual Behavior in Classical Athens," in *Before Sexuality: The Construction of Erotic Experience in the Ancient Greek World,* ed. David M. Halperin, John J. Winkler, and Froma I. Zeitlin (Princeton, 1990), pp. 171–209, esp. pp. 176–77.

18. I borrow the distinction between universalizing and minoritizing concepts of (homo)sexual identity from Eve Kosofsky Sedgwick, *Epistemology of the Closet* (Berkeley, 1990), pp. 1, 9, 85–86.

19. Winkler, *Constraints of Desire,* p. 50; Winkler, "Laying Down the Law," p. 182.

20. See, for example, Plato, *Gorgias* 494C–E (quoted and discussed by Winkler, *Constraints of Desire,* p. 53).

21. For ancient physiological explanations, see pseudo-Aristotle, *Problems* 4.26; Phaedrus, 4.15 (16). For imputations of mental disease, see Aristotle, *Nicomachean Ethics* 7.5.3–4 (1148b26–35); *Priapea* 46.2; Seneca, *Natural Questions* 1.16.1–3; Dio Cassius, 80.16.1–5; Caelius Aurelianus, *On Chronic Diseases* 4.9. Williams, *Roman Homosexuality,* pp. 180–81, to whom I owe the foregoing citation from the *Priapea,* also provides additional parallels

(Seneca, *Letters* 83.20; Juvenal, *Satires* 2.17 and 2.50), noting however that "a predilection for various kinds of excessive or disgraceful behaviors was capable of being called a 'disease'" by the Romans (he cites a number of compelling instances of such a usage) and therefore "*cinaedi* were not said to be *morbosi* in the way that twentieth-century homosexuals have been pitied or scorned as 'sick.'" The medicalizing language, in other words, does not operate in the two cultures in the same way, nor does it give rise to the same kind of disqualification. The point is an important one: the ancient usage is disapproving, but it is not wholly pathologizing.

22. Maud W. Gleason, "The Semiotics of Gender: Physiognomy and Self-Fashioning in the Second Century C.E.," in *Before Sexuality,* pp. 389–415 (quotation on p. 390); Maud W. Gleason, *Making Men: Sophists and Self-Presentation in Ancient Rome* (Princeton, 1995), p. 58.

23. Gleason, *Making Men,* p. 64; Gleason, "The Semiotics of Gender," p. 396.

24. Gleason, "The Semiotics of Gender," pp. 411–12. Cf. David M. Halperin, *One Hundred Years of Homosexuality and Other Essays on Greek Love* (New York, 1990), pp. 22–24.

25. Williams, *Roman Homosexuality,* p. 178.

26. Amy Richlin, review of Halperin, *One Hundred Years of Homosexuality,* in *Bryn Mawr Classical Review* 2 (1991): 16–18; Amy Richlin, "Zeus and Metis: Foucault, Feminism, Classics," *Helios* 18 (1991): 160–80; Amy Richlin, introduction to *The Garden of Priapus: Sexuality and Aggression in Roman Humor,* rev. ed. (New York, 1992), pp. xiii–xxxiii; Amy Richlin, introduction to *Pornography and Representation in Greece and Rome* (New York, 1992), pp. xi–xxiii; Amy Richlin, "Not before Homosexuality: The Materiality of the *Cinaedus* and the Roman Law against Love between Men," *Journal of the History of Sexuality* 3 (1992–93): 523–73; Amy Richlin, "The Ethnographer's Dilemma and the Dream of a Lost Golden Age," in *Feminist Theory and the Classics,* ed. Nancy Sorkin Rabinowitz and Amy Richlin (New York, 1993), pp. 272–303; Amy Richlin, "Towards a History of Body History," in *Inventing Ancient Culture: Historicism, Periodization, and the Ancient World,* ed. Mark Golden and Peter Toohey (London, 1997), pp. 16–35; Amy Richlin, "Foucault's *History of Sexuality*: A Useful Theory for Women?" in *Rethinking Sexuality: Foucault and Classical Antiquity,* ed. David H. J. Larmour, Paul Allen Miller, and Charles Platter (Princeton, 1998), pp. 138–70.

27. Richlin, "Not before Homosexuality," p. 530 (cf. p. 571, where Richlin describes her work as employing "a model that uses 'homosexuality' as a category for analyzing ancient societies"). See also the revised introduction to *The Garden of Priapus* for Richlin's insistence that her approach is distinguished by its "essentialism" and "materialism" (p. xx).

28. Compare, for example, the following two statements by Richlin, both of them made in the revised introduction to *The Garden of Priapus* "I suggest that Foucault's work on antiquity is so ill-informed that it is not really worth reading" (p. xxix, n. 2), and "Thus *The Garden of Priapus,* though it originated in a different critical space from Foucauldian work, exhibits some similar traits, a true Foucauldian child of its time (what Skinner 1986 calls 'post-classicist'). I accept wholeheartedly the approach that melds anthropology with history; I define humor as a discourse of power; I view texts as artifacts; I am seeking to piece together social norms by juxtaposing different kinds of evidence that seem to describe different realities, and I am examining what produces those disparities" (p. xxvii). In other words: "Everything Foucault said was wrong, and besides I said it first."

The ferocity and tenacity of Richlin's polemics have largely succeeded in intimidating and silencing public expressions of disagreement with her, but see the review of *Pornography and Representation in Greece and Rome* by Earl Jackson Jr., *Bryn Mawr Classical Review* 3 (1992): 387–96, and for a recent (if rather mild) rebuke, see Marilyn B. Skinner, "Zeus and Leda: The Sexuality Wars in Contemporary Classical Scholarship," *Thamyris* 3 (1996): 103–23.

29. Richlin, "Not before Homosexuality," p. 525.

30. See, for example, Halperin, *One Hundred Years of Homosexuality,* pp. 8 ("A certain identification of the self with the sexual self began in late antiquity; it was strengthened by the Christian confessional. Only in the high middle ages did certain kinds of sexual acts start to get identified with certain specifically sexual types of person: a 'sodomite' begins to name not

merely the person who commits an act of sodomy but one distinguished by a certain type of specifically sexual subjectivity"), 26 ("Before the scientific construction of 'sexuality' . . . certain kinds of sexual *acts* could be individually evaluated and categorized, and so could certain sexual tastes or inclinations"), and 48 (the *kinaidos* is a "life-form").

31. Jonathan Walters, " 'No More than a Boy': The Shifting Construction of Masculinity from Ancient Greece to the Middle Ages," *Gender and History* 5 (1993): 20–33.

32. Apuleius, *The Golden Ass* 9.22.

33. Walters, "No More than a Boy," pp. 22–23, quoting Apuleius *The Golden Ass* 9.14.

34. See Walters, "No More than a Boy," p. 22.

35. Ibid., p. 24.

36. Ibid., p. 26: "In Boccaccio's version . . . we find the husband defined wholly in terms of his sexual desire, which marks him as abnormal from the start and indeed sets the plot in motion."

37. Cf. ibid., pp. 24–25. For the common view in Florentine texts of the period that sodomites "had little erotic interest in women," see Michael Rocke, *Forbidden Friendships: Homosexuality and Male Culture in Renaissance Florence* (New York, 1996), pp. 40–41, 123 ff., who also provides a useful survey of other literary portraits of sodomites in contemporary Italian *novelle,* many of which correspond in a number of respects to Boccaccio's portrait of Pietro di Vinciolo (pp. 123 ff. and 295, n. 79). Rocke also points out, however, that many Florentine sources, both literary and judicial, presume that a man with sodomitical desires for boys might equally desire insertive sex with women (pp. 124–27).

38. Walters, "No More than a Boy," p. 27, also emphasizes this point.

39. See, further, ibid., pp. 27–28. Whereas the ancient conception of the *kinaidos* foregrounded his effeminacy and passivity, the fourteenth- and fifteenth-century Florentine definitions of "sodomy" and "sodomite" referred only to the "active" or insertive partner in anal intercourse; see Rocke, *Forbidden Friendships,* pp. 14, 110. Cesare Segre, the editor of my text of Boccaccio, gets this point exactly wrong when he says, in a note, that the Perugians regarded Pietro as *un invertito*; Giovanni Boccaccio, *Opere,* ed. Cesare Segre (Milan, 1966), p. 1280: Pietro is a sodomite but, unlike the *kinaidos,* he is not an invert.

40. An erotic temperament midway between that of Apuleius's baker and Boccaccio's Pietro is represented a century *before* Apuleius in a two-line epigram by the Roman poet Martial, *Epigrams* 2.49: "Uxorem nolo Telesinam ducere: quare? / moecha est. sed pueris dat Telesina. volo" ("I don't want to take Telesina for my wife.—Why not?—She's an adulteress.—But Telesina puts out for boys.—I'll take her!"). As Williams, *Roman Homosexuality,* p. 27, to whom I owe this reference, explains, Martial's joke depends on the background knowledge that a longstanding traditional punishment for adultery in the classical world was anal rape of the male offender. The man imagined in the epigram overcomes his initial reluctance to marry Telesina when it is pointed out to him that her bad character will procure him endless opportunities for enacting a sweet revenge on her youthful partners. Martial's satirical epigram constructs an outlandish scenario in which a man is so fond of insertive anal sex with boys that he is willing to enter into a disgraceful and corrupt marriage merely in order to expand his possibilities for enjoying it. Exaggeration is part of the joke; nonetheless, as Williams, who also cites the passage from Apuleius in this connection, demonstrates with abundant argumentation and evidence, the imaginary husband's preference falls well within the range of acceptable male sexual tastes in Roman culture.

41. Walters, "No More than a Boy," pp. 26–27, overstates the case, I believe, when he writes, "What we see in Boccaccio's version of the story is one of the earliest portrayals in Western culture of a man defined by his sexuality, which is somehow his most deeply defining characteristic, and which tells 'the truth' about him. We witness here an early form of the constitution and demarcation of the field of sexuality." Compare Glenn W. Olsen, "St. Anselm and Homosexuality," *Anselm Studies: An Occasional Journal* 2 (Proceedings of the Fifth International Saint Anselm Conference: St. Anselm and St. Augustine—Episcopi ad

Saecula), ed. Joseph C. Schnaubelt et al. (White Plains, N.Y., 1988), pp. 93–141, esp. pp. 102–3: "If one were to eliminate from Boswell's book [*Christianity, Social Tolerance, and Homosexuality*] all the materials which do not satisfy his definition of 'gay,' one might arguably be left with the truly novel and important observation that, as far as the Middle Ages are concerned, it was about 1100 in certain poems of Marbod of Rennes, and then later in the century in writers like Bernard of Cluny and Walter of Chatillon, and above all in the late twelfth century 'A Debate between Ganymede and Helen,' that we might see the appearance of a clear erotic preference for one's own sex that, by still being called 'sodomy,' began the expansion of that term into the modern 'homosexuality'" (see also pp. 129–30, n. 61, and p. 133, n. 87). Olsen puts the point very clearly, and in fact he might have been speaking of Boccaccio's Pietro di Vinciolo, although Boccaccio never uses the term *sodomy* in reference to Pietro. Nonetheless, I would still want to insist that mere sexual object-choice, even the settled and habitual preference for sexual relations with persons of the same sex as oneself, falls short of the definitional requirements of "(homo)sexuality" or "sexual orientation." After all, such exclusive sexual preferences were not unknown in the ancient world: see my partial list of citations in *One Hundred Years of Homosexuality*, p. 163, n. 53. A "sexuality" in the modern sense would seem to require considerably more than same-sex sexual object-choice, more even than conscious erotic preference. In particular, "homosexuality" requires, first of all, that homosexual object-choice *itself* function as a marker of difference, of social and sexual deviance, independent of the gender identification or sexual role (active or passive) performed or preferred by the individual; it also requires homosexual object-choice to be connected with a psychology, an inner orientation of the individual, not just an aesthetics or a form of erotic connoisseurship. See *One Hundred Years of Homosexuality*, pp. 24–29, esp. pp. 26–27 with notes; and for an expansion of that argument, see my essay "Historicizing the Subject of Desire: Sexual Preferences and Erotic Identities in the Pseudo-Lucianic *Erôtes*," in *Foucault and the Writing of History*, ed. Jan Goldstein (Oxford, 1994), pp. 19–34, 255–61, which documents several instances of same-sex sexual object-choice, and even of conscious erotic preferences for persons of the same sex as oneself, that nonetheless do not satisfy the criteria for homosexuality. In the absence of the distinctively modern set of connections linking sexual object-choice, inner orientation, and deviant personality with notions of identity and difference, the substantive category of "homosexuality" dissolves into the descriptive category of "men who have sex with men" (an artifact of AIDS epidemiology, not a sexuality per se), and homosexually active but otherwise non-gay-identified men escape interpellation by the category of "homosexuality."

42. I have chosen to dwell on the figure of Boccaccio's Pietro di Vinciolo not because I believe he is somehow typical or representative of medieval sodomites in general but because he provides the starkest possible contrast with the ancient figure of the *kinaidos*: the latter represents an instance of morphology without subjectivity, or so at least I am contending for the purposes of my argument, whereas Pietro represents an instance of subjectivity without morphology. I do not mean to imply that constructions of the sodomite in premodern Europe *mostly* or even *typically* emphasized subjectivity at the expense of morphology, or that the sodomite was *never* thought to have a peculiar sensibility or style of gender presentation or appearance (on the gradual expansion of the term *sodomy,* see Olsen, "St. Anselm and Homosexuality," pp. 102–3). It is precisely the aim of this paper to open up such questions for further research.

43. This is not to deny that some lesbians can be conventionally feminine or that some gay men can be conventionally masculine, and that both can pass for straight—some can and some do—but rather to insist that modern concepts and images of homosexuality have never been able to escape being haunted by the specter of gender inversion, gender deviance, or at least some kind of visibly legible difference. For a systematic and brilliant exploration of this issue, see Lee Edelman, *Homographesis: Essays in Gay Literary and Cultural Theory* (New York, 1994); see also Sedgwick, *Epistemology of the Closet.*

44. I wish to thank Carolyn Dinshaw for pointing out the absence of the term *identity* from Foucault's text.

45. Cf. Alan Sinfield, *Cultural Politics—Queer Reading* (Philadelphia, 1994), p. 14, noting that premodern histories of homosexuality by social-constructionist historians "tend to discover ambivalent or partial signs of subjectivity; they catch not the absence of the modern subject, but its emergence." He adds, "I suspect that what we call gay identity has, for a long time, been always in the process of getting constituted." This last remark closes off, rather too glibly, the historiographic and conceptual issues before us.

46. I elaborate further on this point in a forthcoming paper, "The Art of Not Being Governed: Michel Foucault on Critique and Transgression."

47. Foucault, *History of Sexuality,* p. 68.

48. A notable exception is Eve Kosofsky Sedgwick, "Queer Performativity: Henry James's *The Art of the Novel,*" *GLQ: A Journal of Lesbian and Gay Studies* 1 (1993): 1–16, esp. p. 11: "The thing I *least* want to be heard as offering here is a 'theory of homosexuality.' I have none and I want none." See also Jordan, *Invention of Sodomy,* p. 5: "I myself tend to think that we have barely begun to gather [historical] evidence of same-sex desire. We are thus very far from being able to imagine having a finished theory." Statements to this effect in works of so-called queer theory are rather less frequent than one might imagine.

49. For the notion that theory is ultimately "the universal theory of the impossibility of theory" and therefore that "nothing can overcome the resistance to theory since theory *is* itself this resistance," see Paul de Man, "The Resistance to Theory," in *The Resistance to Theory* (Minneapolis, 1986), pp. 3–20 (quotations on p. 19). For a further exploration of these paradoxes, see the scathing remarks of Paul Morrison, "Paul de Man: Resistance and Collaboration," *Representations* 32 (1990): 50–74.

50. Michel Foucault, "Fantasia of the Library," in *Language, Counter-Memory, Practice: Selected Essays and Interviews,* ed. and trans. Donald F. Bouchard (Ithaca, 1977), pp. 87–109 (quotation on p. 90). This passage was originally brought to my attention by James W. Bernauer, *Michel Foucault's Force of Flight: Toward an Ethics for Thought* (Atlantic Highlands, N.J., 1990), p. 183.

PART 2

SEXING THE BODY

BODIES THAT DON'T MATTER

Heterosexuality before Heterosexuality in Gottfried's Tristan

JAMES A. SCHULTZ

Nowadays most of us assume we will feel sexual desire either for men or for women and that we will be able to tell one from the other. This does not seem to be the case in Gottfried von Straßburg's *Tristan und Isold.* To be sure, women only desire men and men only desire women. Yet it's hard to see how they can keep themselves straight, since one can scarcely tell the men's bodies from the women's. When bodies are described as desirable, sex-specific features are not mentioned, and when men or women are described as beautiful, they are said to be beautiful in the same terms. And yet, somehow, the inhabitants of Gottfried's fictional world must be able to tell the men from the women, since they will always desire someone of the other sex. What sort of sexual economy ensures that women and men will always desire the other sex when the anatomy of desire scarcely distinguishes one sex from the other? How does heterosexuality work in a homomorphic world?

My answer to this question falls into three parts. The first is devoted to the bodies that are not differentiated by sex. The second considers the conventions of clothing that create gendered bodies. And the third traces the structures of desire in a world where, although much seems familiar, the relations of sex, gender, and desire are quite different from those to which we are accustomed.

BODIES: THE MORPHOLOGY OF DESIRE

According to Judith Butler, culture produces bodies: "Historically revisable criteria of intelligibility . . . produce and vanquish bodies that matter."[1] Because the criteria change, "morphological possibilities" that are intelligible today would not necessarily have been intelligible in the past, and bodies that were intelligible in the past may not be so today. This is particularly true for the body as an object of desire. In 1928 Stephen Gordon, heroine of the *Well of Loneliness,* looked in a mirror and found her body, with its narrow hips and small breasts, "poor," "desolate," "monstrous"[2]—in other words, unintelligible; but things have changed, as Marjorie Garber notes, and the "monstrous body of 1928" is now "the ideal female body of the fitness generation."[3] What was desolate is now desirable. I want to describe the historically specific "morphological possibilities" represented by the desirable bodies in Gottfried's *Tristan.* In doing so I take seriously Caroline Walker Bynum's caution against assuming that medieval people eroticized the body in the same ways we do.[4] And I also take seriously what I understand to be the implications of Butler's argument: medieval "regulatory schemas" will have produced bodies different from ours, bodies in which morphological features that matter to us may not have been culturally intelligible and, in that sense, simply did not exist.

Although Gottfried is fascinated with the workings of desire, there are in fact only five bodies that he describes in any detail as the objects of desire: the body of Riwalin as he is jousting at Mark's springtime festival and is admired by the ladies of the court (699–719);[5] the body of Blanscheflur as Riwalin contemplates her beauty and falls more deeply in love (921–36); the body of Tristan as he enters Mark's court, just after he has displayed his skills as a hunter (3332–50); the body of Isold when she appears in splendor at her father's court, just before she departs for Cornwall (10885–11020); and the body of Isold again, this time as Mark looks at her through the window of the *Minnegrotte* (17557–607). These are the only passages in which a body is explicitly marked as desirable and is represented in enough detail that one gets some idea of its anatomical specificity. They are, in other words, the only passages in which one can investigate the relation of morphology and desire.

Of course, anatomy is not the only thing that sparks desire: the ladies of Mark's court are drawn to Riwalin not only for the shape of his arms and legs but also for the elegance with which he jousts, while Tristan and Isold, even though they have long been aware of each other's beauty, are only sexually attracted once they drink the fateful potion. And yet, although the body may not always be sufficient, it is nevertheless frequently accorded a crucial role in inciting desire. When Tristan appears at Mark's court, it is "his body" that makes him desirable, since it "was formed as Love required."[6] When Mark looks at Isold through the window of the *Minnegrotte,* it is "the beauty of her body" with which "Love enflamed the man."[7] Mark's reaction will not surprise those who share the assumption attributed to modern sex researchers that "the male body respond[s] to the presence of the female body, as if to a natural sign."[8] Medievals and moderns do agree that the body is important. But it is not the same body. For, as I hope to show, although Mark may be "enflamed" by the sight of Isold, it is not a female body to which he responds, nor is her body a natural sign.

Isold's body is not a female body for the simple reason that the desirable bodies in Gottfried's *Tristan* are not distinguished by sex. When the ladies of Mark's court admire Riwalin they note: "How perfect his body is! How evenly his magnificent legs move together! . . . How the spear becomes his hand! . . . How he carries his head and hair! . . . Fortunate is the woman who will have lasting joy from him!"[9] Although the last lines suggest that the women regard Riwalin as sexually desirable, the only parts of his body they mention are his legs, his hands, his head, and his hair, none of which is unique to males. In this Riwalin is like the knights in the French *Prose Lancelot,* the descriptions of whom, as Jane Burns shows, "do not in any way tie [their] bodies to a gendered anatomy."[10]

It is the same when Isold appears before the Irish court. As she enters, the narrator describes her as "tall, shapely, and slender. . . . Her robe fell in folds around her feet. . . . The beautiful maiden had inserted the thumb of her left hand [in a string of pearls holding her cloak together]. . . . She had brought her right hand down to where the cloak should be closed, where she held it together elegantly with two of her fingers. . . . On her head she wore a small crown of gold. . . . Even the wisest man there, if he had not seen the gems [on the crown], would have insisted that there was no crown at all: so equal and so identical was her hair to the gold."[11] Although the description of Isold is considerably more elaborate than the praise of Riwalin, the elaboration is rhetorical rather than anatomical. In her case, as in his, the desirable body is represented by a limited number of parts that are visible to the public eye and that are common to men and women: head, hair, and the elements of the face; arms, legs, and feet. This is true not only for Riwalin and Isold but also for the other desirable bodies listed earlier.

Of course Gottfried might have mentioned parts of the body that distinguish one sex from the other: he could have given Riwalin a beard or referred to Isold's breasts, anatomical features that do manage to exist in other contexts. We learn, for instance, that when Rual arrives at Mark's court "the hair of his beard was so matted that he seemed to be a wild man"[12] and that when Isold wants to convince Mark of her devotion one night in bed she draws him "extremely close to her soft, smooth breasts."[13] But such anatomical signs of sex difference do not figure in the descriptions of bodies that are said to be beautiful.

There are historical reasons for this. While older men like Rual might have beards, the ideal of youthful male beauty in Middle High German (MHG) courtly texts requires young men to be beardless. Thus Wolfram von Eschenbach calls Parzival "the young man without a beard"[14] long after he has married, fathered children, and become lord of Pelrapeire; and Rudolf von Ems writes of knights who are just getting their very first beard hairs when they are nearly thirty.[15] Since thirteenth-century legal texts take the beginnings of a beard as a sign that a man is at least fourteen,[16] it seems unlikely that MHG writers really believed that men ordinarily remained beardless until they were thirty. Nevertheless, since courtly standards of beauty frowned on beards, these same writers insist that their heroes' faces are still smooth long after they have become adults.[17] Breasts are only slightly more common than beards. Before 1200 they do not figure in any descriptions of beautiful women in MHG texts.[18] In fact, Isold's embrace of Mark, mentioned earlier, and Jeschute's second encounter with the hero of *Parzival*[19] represent the first references by MHG writers to women's breasts in erotic contexts. Between 1200 and 1250 breasts figure in the description of the desirable woman's body in only two other MHG texts.[20] The vernacular writers are not alone in their reticence: according to Joan Cadden, when medieval medical and scientific authors discuss sex differentiation they do not often mention breasts.[21]

The evidence suggests then that Gottfried's omission of the most obvious anatomical signs of sex difference from his descriptions of beautiful bodies reflects more general medieval constructions of the body. According to these, beards are not part of the desirable male body and breasts play only a very occasional role in distinguishing the body as female, so that the standard of beauty for men and women is nearly the same. Thus, when Rennewart sits down next to his sister in Wolfram's *Willehalm,* the two are said to look the same—except that Rennewart's beard *has* begun to grow. This moves the narrator to comment: "I would be happier if [the hairs of his beard] were not there, for then one might have taken the man for the woman, their bodies were so similar."[22] The narrator *wants* to take the young hero for a woman; he thinks a beautiful man and a beautiful woman *should* look the same.

Just because, given the information that Gottfried provides about desirable bodies, it would be difficult to tell men's bodies from women's, that does not mean that all bodies are indistinguishable. When Rual appears at Mark's court, his clothes in tatters, his hair and his beard matted after years of searching for Tristan throughout Europe, Gottfried stops to assure us that, no matter how miserable his clothing, Rual was "in body and bearing, perfectly magnificent. His was a noble body."[23] After noting that Rual had a resonant voice and that he was in the prime of life, Gottfried concludes: "In the true dignity proper to a lord he was the equal of any emperor."[24] Although beautiful bodies do not reveal their sex, lordly bodies, even in hardship, reveal their class.

That, of course, is what Isold learns when she studies Tristan shortly before the famous scene in the bath. After inspecting his hands, face, arms, and legs, she declares: "It would be right and proper for him to have an empire at his service."[25] A bit later she recalls: "How well I have known all along since I have been observing him, and taking careful note of every detail of his body and his bearing and everything about him, that he was a lord by birth!"[26] Looking him over from head to toe—or rather from face to legs—Isold does not say: Great body, we've got to have sex; but: Great body, he's got to be a lord. Of course, she is right: Tristan is of royal blood.

Some have argued that Isold begins to fall in love with Tristan as she studies him in this scene,[27] a view for which I do not think the text gives much support. And yet, if it is true, if Isold really does begin to fall in love here, then the body she desires is one that is marked not as a *male* body but as a *noble* body. What Isold sees in Tristan is not sex but class.

Obviously these are not the bodies that Calvin Klein displayed so relentlessly a few years ago on billboards and buses throughout urban America—worked out, stripped down, lighted, and photographed so that every primary and secondary sexual characteristic leaps out at you and fills you with desire to buy new underwear.[28] Nor are they the bodies represented in a thirteenth-century manuscript of Aldobrandino of Siena's *Régime du corps,* which, as Michael Camille shows, "emphasize and reinscribe the radical difference between male and female bodies."[29] No, these are bodies that, as Gottfried represents them, simply do not have primary or secondary sexual characteristics. They are bodies that, although beautiful and desirable, do not distinguish morphologically between male and female. In this they are like the bodies of Lancelot and Guenevere, in which, according to Jane Burns, one cannot distinguish clearly between the man's mouth and hands and the woman's. And yet Gottfried's bodies can easily be distinguished by class: the body of Rual, travel-weary and filthy, and the body of Tristan, just recovered from nearly fatal wounds, are easily recognized as noble. Noble bodies reveal class more readily than desirable bodies reveal sex—even when the noble bodies look *least* courtly and the desirable bodies look *most* beautiful. Needless to say, in Gottfried's world sex does matter: desire for the other sex is the only possibility. And sex is always known. The point is not that one cannot tell women from men but rather that in the one domain where we think anatomical sex difference is of paramount importance, Gottfried clearly does not. When it comes to eliciting desire, Gottfried's female and male bodies are morphologically indistinguishable.

One should recall that Gottfried was writing before heterosexuality. I mean this not in the trivial sense that the term had not yet been invented, but in the more important sense that the cross-sexual relation between the desiring subject and the desirable object does not constitute either the identity of the subject or the morphology of the object in the profound way it is assumed to under a regime of compulsory heterosexuality. The modern Western organization of sexuality is unusual in that it takes sexual object choice as the primary criterion of sexual classification: if I desire men I am a homosexual, if I desire women I am a heterosexual, and it makes no difference whether I wear a necktie or a dress or who does what to whom in bed. Such a standard is not only unusual among human cultures but is, even in the West, very recent. The word "heterosexual"— along with its longtime companion "homosexual"—was not invented until 1868;[30] it only came to be widely used in its current meaning in the course of the twentieth century,[31] and even at the end of the twentieth century, as sex researchers discovered recently, it is "not well understood by many people."[32]

In earlier times sexual behavior was classified according to other criteria. In classical Athens people involved in sexual relations were divided into those who *did* sex (adult male citizens) and those to whom sex *was done* (women, boys, foreigners, and slaves).[33] In the thirteenth century Thomas Aquinas classified the species of lust according to their relation to reason (children must be raised by married parents) and to nature (the natural end of sex is procreation). Best are those "venereal acts" that respect reason and nature (the union of a married couple desiring children), worse are those that violate reason since they are outside marriage (fornication, seduction, adultery, rape), and worst of all are those that violate nature because conception is impossible (masturbation, sodomy, bestiality).[34] One could say that the ancient boy-lovers and the medieval sodomites were really homosexuals, and that most of the rest were heterosexuals. If one were to make this claim, however, one would blind oneself to the ways in which people in past times understood their sexual behavior. If we "perpetually look for precursors to our categories of sexuality in essentially different domains," writes Arnold Davidson, we will produce "anachronisms at best and unintelligibility at worst."[35]

For us the sex of the object is crucial since it is the primary criterion of sexual classification; it defines the sexual identity of the subject. Writing in a world before heterosexuality, Gottfried did not feel the pressure we feel to proclaim the sex of the object of desire. To be sure, the sex of the desired body does matter and it is always known. But it is not the obsession it is nowadays because less is at stake. Thus Isold can expect a response when she draws Mark to her breasts: she knows that directing her husband's attention to her specifically female body is likely to divert his mind from other matters. But at the same time Gottfried can ignore anatomical signs of sex difference when he describes desirable bodies: they are no more constitutive elements of the desirable body than is hair color, which he notes for Isold but ignores for Riwalin. One knows that this body is female, that one male, but this difference is not so important that it determines the morphology of the object of desire. Class, one of those "other regimes of regulatory production [that] contour the materiality of bodies,"[36] is written on the body more clearly than sex. Bodies differ in visible ways because they are noble or because they are beautiful (for which their nobility is a prerequisite). The nobility and the beauty of the desirable body are culturally visible in the morphology of the body itself. The sex of the desirable body is not.

CLOTHING: INVESTING IN GENDER

While the sex of the desirable body is not culturally visible, the gender of the desirable body is. And of all the means by which gender is made visible in Gottfried's *Tristan,* the one that lies closest to the body is clothing. The human body stands "in a relation of signification with clothing," according to Roland Barthes: "as pure sentience, the body cannot signify; clothing guarantees the passage from sentience to meaning."[37] This is especially true when clothing signifies gender. When clothing signifies class, which it often does, it accomplishes something that, as has just been seen, bodies can also accomplish.[38] But when clothing signifies gender it does something that bodies cannot do, since Gottfried's desirable bodies do not distinguish themselves morphologically as men or women. Clothing, which relates differently to men's and to women's bodies, establishes thereby a difference between men and women: it guarantees the passage to meaning. It creates the gendered body.

Although the basic elements of courtly clothing were the same for men and women in this period,[39] men's and women's clothes were not identical. Women's garments reached to the floor, while men's only extended part of the way down the leg, and since the leg coverings fit very closely, the contours of men's legs were clearly visible. As a result shapely legs came to be regarded as the hallmark of masculine beauty.[40] When Tristan appears at Mark's court Gottfried tells us: "His feet and his legs, in which his beauty was most apparent, were praiseworthy indeed, as such things should be praised in a man."[41] Evidently, beautiful legs are an excellence that is peculiarly masculine. It is not surprising then that Riwalin's legs receive special praise from the ladies who watch him jousting and that Tristan's legs are noted again just after he is armed for the fight with Morold (709–10, 6705–6). Of course, legs in themselves are not peculiarly male. Thus one cannot say that men's clothes reveal a sexed body. Rather, men's clothes create a gendered body. Exposing the legs turns the body into a man's, since the body with visible legs can only be a man's. It is the clothes, not the legs, that make the body masculine.

Clothes reveal the body not only because they leave some parts exposed but because they fit other parts so closely. Like so much else that was prized in German courts of the twelfth and thirteenth centuries, the fashion for clothes that were cut to fit the torso had been imported from France.[42] When Isold appears in splendor before the Irish court, "she wore a robe and a cloak of purple samite, cut in the French style."[43] Close-fitting clothes were also fashionable for men.[44] When Tristan is presented to Mark we learn that "his clothes were very courtly, having been cut to fit his body."[45]

But the close fit does not treat women and men in the same way. When Isold greets the Irish court, the contours of her robe are described as follows: "There, toward the place where the sides join the hips, her robe was fringed and narrowed and pulled close to her body by a sash, which lay precisely where a sash should. The robe was intimate with her and clung to her body; it was nowhere bulky and tried to keep close everywhere from top to bottom."[46] Gottfried's description of Isold's robe invites us to contemplate "the place where the sides join the hips" and to visualize the effect of a garment that was "pulled close to her body," that was "intimate with her," that "clung to her body," and that "tried to keep close everywhere." While Isold's robe clothes her body, it discloses her body at the same time. Of course, "sides" and "hips" are not peculiarly female: the body that is disclosed is not a sexed body. Rather the clothes create a gendered body: if you see through the clothes, then it must be a woman's body.[47]

The close fit of Tristan's garments has a different effect. In preparation for his grand appearance before the Irish court, Tristan dispatches CurveCurvenal to bring him clothes "of the very best cut."[48] Once dressed, Tristan joins Isold, her mother, and Brangaene, and when the three women looked at him, "they thought: 'Truly, this man is a manly creature; his clothes and his figure create the man in him: they suit each other so well.'"[49] When Tristan enters the court a little while later the narrator repeats the women's thoughts in his own voice: Tristan's "body and his clothes harmonized marvelously with each other. Together the two of them formed a knightly man."[50] Gottfried seems to believe that "clothes make the man" in a very concrete way. The clothes cannot do it alone: they need a body with which they harmonize. But that body remains ungendered as long as it is unclothed. Ungendered body and suitable clothes *together* create the gendered man. The vocabulary of construction is Gottfried's, not mine. He is the one who claims that "the manly creature" is *created*, that the "knightly man" is *formed* only when he gets dressed.[51]

Clothes create gender in Gottfried's *Tristan* not because of their materials or their cut or their close fit, nor on account of the sexed body parts they reveal. Gender is created rather by the differential relation that clothes sustain with the body. If they clothe the body and disclose it at the same time, they create a woman. If they harmonize with the body and reveal the leg, they create a man. Through clothing, writes Barthes, "the body is taken 'in charge' by an intelligible system of signs, and sentience is dissolved in the signifier."[52] Gottfried's bodies, which are not differentiated by sex, are "dissolved" into their clothing. The clothing, which distinguishes women from men not so much by its form as by its formal relation to the body, creates difference: an intelligible system of signs. "Dissolved" in their clothing, bodies exist only as feminine or masculine.[53]

Predictably, when clothing creates gendered bodies it does not create them equal. Clothing collaborates with the man's body and confirms its nobility. It turns Tristan into the subject of heroic action, "a knightly man." Clothed, Tristan is admired, first by Isold, her mother, and Brangaene, then by the whole court, "many of whom said: 'Where has God ever created a figure better suited to the order of knighthood?' "[54] The woman's body, on the other hand, is exposed by its clothing and offered to public view. Isold is turned into the object of voyeuristic fantasy. Clothed and thereby disclosed, Isold is desired: when she appears in court, "glances like feathered predators flew thick as snowflakes back and forth, hunting."[55] Through clothing Gottfried's bodies are indeed "taken in charge."[56] Undifferentiated morphologically by sex, they are, through their clothing, invested in a differential hierarchy of gender: Tristan to be admired as a knight, Isold to be desired as quarry.[57]

In making gender visible, clothes can represent many other "marks of gender"[58] that distinguish women and men. It is such signs—pronouns, names, behaviors, clothes—that enable the women and men in Gottfried's *Tristan* to keep themselves straight, even when their bodies seem to be very much the same. Among the marks of gender, however, clothing has a special status because of its proximity to the body. We assume that there is a sexed body underneath the gendered clothes, that the sexed body is prior and relatively stable, and that clothes are superficial and easily changed. For Gottfried, there is no sexed body underneath the gendered clothes. Clothes create gender difference for desirable bodies that do not differ morphologically by sex. Whatever distinction exists between women's and men's bodies results not from any anatomical *sex* differences, of which there are none, but from vestimentary *gender* differentiation. Bodies are understood to be female and male only because they are *already* known to be feminine and masculine.

It is hardly remarkable that, in a world before heterosexuality, gender should take precedence over sex. In nineteenth-century America no one imagined that two women who lived together were anything less than completely respectable—provided they both appeared suitably feminine.[59] Sexual relations, after all, could only take place between a man and a woman. Thus, if two females were sexually involved, one was assumed to have been "the man" (aggressive, sex-driven), the other "the woman" (passive, not interested in sex). Only the former, the "invert," was considered deviant. Not until sexual object choice was established as the crucial determinant of normalcy—not, that is, until the advent of heterosexuality—were both partners in a homosexual relationship considered perverts.[60] Even today, in many parts of the world, two men who have anal intercourse are not thought to belong to the same category: rather, the one who plays the "women's part" is considered deviant, while the one who acts the "man's part" is considered a "normal man."[61] As these examples show, where sexual object choice is not the determining factor in classifying sexual actors, gender often is. Since Gottfried was writing in a world before heterosexuality, one might expect that for him too gender is more important than sex.

DESIRE: THE TYRANNY OF THE OBJECT

If one shifts one's attention from the desired object to the desiring subject, here too gender differences matter a great deal. In Gottfried's *Tristan* women's desire for men is something quite different from men's desire for women. And yet, shifting from Butler's "genealogical efforts" concerning the "materiality of the body"[62] to Foucault's "genealogy . . . of the desiring subject,"[63] one thing does remain constant: like the morphology of bodies and the gender of clothes, the structures of desire are produced by historically contingent "regulatory schemas." Foucault (re)defined his project as "a historical and critical study" of "the forms within which individuals . . . *are obliged* to recognize themselves as . . . subjects of desire."[64] Just as "the matter of bodies [is] a kind of materialization governed by regulatory norms,"[65] so desire can only be recognized when it observes certain obligatory forms. Regulatory norms on the one hand, obligatory forms on the other: desires, like bodies and clothes, are only intelligible when they conform to the regulatory schemas of the culture that produces them.

Since I am concerned with the relation between morphology and desire, I will limit myself to those passages where desire is clearly a response to a body described in some detail and explicitly marked as desirable. I return therefore to the five passages listed earlier.

When the women of Mark's court observe Riwalin jousting, their desire is distant but direct: " 'Look,' they said, 'the youth is a fortunate man: how wonderfully everything he does suits him! How perfect his body is! How his legs, worthy of an emperor, move in and out together! How firmly his shield remains glued to its spot at all times! How the spear becomes his hand! How all his clothes look good on him! How he carries his head and hair! How gracious are all his movements! How excellent he is! Fortunate is the woman who will have lasting joy from him!' "[66] The women remain distant, observing Riwalin from a certain remove but not talking to him. Yet they are direct, showing no hesitation about expressing their admiration, praising various parts of his body and his performance as a knight, and imagining the pleasure that he might bring to some woman. But it will be brought to some unnamed other woman, not to themselves. The ladies' direct but distant stance corresponds nicely to their brisk, declarative language: they list Riwalin's excellences as a series of exclamations, linked by parallel syntax and anaphora.[67]

When a man desires a woman, things are quite different—as is evident in the scene in which Mark observes Isold through the window of the *Minnegrotte*. The passage goes on for sixty lines, three times as many as the ladies get to watch Riwalin, and includes the following: "Her chin, her mouth, her complexion, and her body were so completely delightful, so lovely, and so charming that she pleased Mark: he was overcome with the desire to kiss her. . . . His eyes presented everything to him: he looked very intimately at how her throat and her shoulder, her arms and her hands shone beautifully out of her garments."[68] Mark takes advantage of the fact that Isold is asleep to regard her "very intimately," following the rays of the sun as they play on her face, looking at her chin, mouth, complexion, body; then he returns again to look at her throat and shoulders, her arms and hands. He is so taken by what he sees that he wants to kiss her. Where the women watching Riwalin take note of his good points quickly, one at a time, and then move on, Mark lingers, returning his gaze to things he has already seen, and fantasizes about approaching the body he desires.

The lingering, repetitive, fantasizing gaze engenders a correspondingly expansive rhetoric, one whose figures are the simile, the extended metaphor, and the insinuation. Gottfried begins with similes: "Isold's complexion and her radiance glowed, sweet and lovely as a rose of several colors. . . . Her mouth flamed and burned just like a glowing coal."[69] A few lines later he combines the rays of the sun with the radiance of Isold into an extended metaphor: "Just then two beauties were playing a game with each other, light and light were shining together. The sun and the sun had staged a joyous festival there to the glory of Isold."[70] The metaphor of Isold as the sun is one of Gottfried's great conceits, inciting him to rhetorical bravura on a number of occasions, not only in connection with Isold but also in connection with her mother and Brangaene. Although radiance can be an attribute of male beauty—we know that Tristan's "complexion was radiant,"[71] for instance—the metaphorical elaboration of radiance is peculiar to women.

Gottfried takes time not only to develop the metaphor of Isold as sun but also to play a game of insinuation. At the beginning of the passage, he pretends to be unable to imagine what exertion might have caused Isold to look flushed as she sleeps next to Tristan—only to remember after ten lines that she had been out of doors that morning and that she must have acquired her color then

(17561–75). Before he thinks of this explanation, of course, a different one has already occurred to us.

To judge from these two cases, women's desire is different from men's desire. Where the subject of desire is a woman, she is distant but direct. The language of desire is quick, favoring lists and anaphora. Where the subject of desire is a man he lingers, returns to what has already been seen, and attempts to draw near. The language is elaborate, metaphoric, and insinuating.

Remarkably, this difference does not seem to depend on the gender of the subject but on that of the object, as one can see from the behavior of the narrator. When the narrator sketches the portrait of Tristan as he first appears at Mark's court, he adopts the same spatial and rhetorical stance as the women who watch Riwalin joust. Like them he observes and describes from a distance—in this case from a position outside of the diegetic world. And like the women's praise, the narrator's is structured as a list of excellences held together by parallel syntax and anaphora: "His lips were red as a rose, his complexion radiant, his eyes clear . . . his arms and his hands well formed and white."

When the narrator sketches the portrait of a woman, however, he adopts the spatial and rhetorical stance of Mark at the window of the *Minnegrotte.* When Isold is led ceremonially through the Irish court by her mother before leaving for Cornwall, she is once again offered up to the male gaze under circumstances over which she has little control. Most of the passage is devoted to the description of her clothes—a description in which, like Mark at the *Minnegrotte,* the narrator lingers, moving his eye back and forth across Isold's body and trying to get close. That the narrator lingers is obvious: the passage goes on for 135 lines. As he lingers, his description of Isold's robe repeatedly draws us through the fabric to her body, as was noted in the discussion of her clothing. Gottfried's description is just like the robe: it is "intimate with her," clinging to her body and trying "to keep close everywhere from top to bottom."

The delight in rhetorical elaboration that Gottfried displays when the object of desire is a woman is evident not only in the description of Isold's clothes but also, once again, in the elaborate metaphor of Isold as the sun. The passage opens when the queen mother, the dawn, "led her sun by the hand . . . the radiant maiden Isold,"[72] and concludes by noting that "the joy-bringing sun spread her radiance over all, gladening the people in the hall."[73] Insinuation also plays a large role, not only in suggesting Isold's body beneath her robe but also in the description of her cloak. While the thumb of her left hand clasps a string of pearls holding the cloak together at the top, "she had moved her right hand farther down below, as you well know, to the place where the cloak should be closed, and she brought it together in an elegant manner with two of her fingers: from there it fell further on its own, falling in folds all the way to the bottom, so that you could see this and that—I mean the fur [lining] and the outer covering."[74] Like the passage about Isold's exertions at the *Minnegrotte,* this one also deliberately incites our fantasy—to imagine the place, farther down, that we know so well and to guess what might be revealed by Isold's cloak as it falls to the floor—only to draw a cloak of less titillating information over whatever it was that we had thought of. Here, however, the imagination is incited even further, bringing us even closer to the object of desire. The viewer is invited to shape Isold's body, to form, at least in the imagination, "this and that," the place "farther down," and the way her "robe fell in folds around her feet, just as much as any of you might wish."[75] The viewer is invited to construct the body—just as he might wish.

Desire takes two forms in Gottfried's *Tristan*. When men are desired, the subject is distant but direct; desire is articulated in anaphoric lists. When women are desired, the subject lingers, returns to what has already been seen, and attempts to draw near; the language is elaborate, metaphoric, and insinuating. The women who observe Riwalin desire according to the first paradigm; Mark at the *Minnegrotte* desires according to the second. One might reasonably assume that the choice of paradigm is determined by the gender of the subject: women desire one way, men another. However, the behavior of the narrator shows this not to be the case. When the narrator describes the desirable Tristan he adopts the stance of the women who admire Riwalin, but when he describes the desirable Isold he adopts the stance of Mark at the *Minnegrotte*. If the narrator can, as circumstances require, assume the subject position of Mark or the ladies at Mark's court, then the choice of one paradigm of desire or the other cannot depend on the identity of the subject. It is the gender of the object that determines the structure of desire, whether this is felt by a character or represented by the narrator.

That Gottfried treats desire for women at greater length, with more complex figures and more subtle devices than he treats desire for men, thereby making it a good deal more interesting, surely reflects and reinforces the hegemony of men and of men's desire for women within the culture in which he wrote. That women are held before our eyes, objects of insinuation and voyeuristic display, surely reproduces the position of women as the primary objects of desire in the sexual-political system of that world. That the narrator and the women at Mark's court accommodate themselves to the subordination and distancing that defines the desire for men is hardly surprising: "individuals are obliged" to desire according to the "forms" their culture makes available. By showing that the forms of desire are determined not by the gender of the subject but by the position of the object in the gender-power relations of the larger society, Gottfried demonstrates that the forms of desire are not authentic manifestations of an individual identity but rather cultural paradigms by which patriarchal power reproduces itself.

Again, Gottfried was writing before heterosexuality, which is to say, before our modern understanding of sexuality. We tend to believe "that sexuality comes from within, that it is a feature of the individual,"[76] and that it plays a crucial role in determining who we are: sexuality is "a constitutive principle of the self."[77] Part of the "self" that sexuality constitutes is our sexual identity, "a personal essence defined . . . in specifically sexual terms."[78] Gottfried believes none of this. Although he is committed to exploring the effects of passion on the individual, he does not locate the origin of desire within the individual but outside, in the sight of a beautiful body or in the effects of a love potion. And although Gottfried differentiates kinds of desire, he does not distinguish between heterosexual desire for the other sex and homosexual desire for the same sex, "other" and "same" being defined in relation to the sex of the *subject,* but between desire for the man and desire for the woman, "man" and "woman" describing the gender of the *object.* Of course, in Gottfried's world desire is always for the other sex: Mark cannot look through the window of the *Minnegrotte* and desire Tristan.[79] But the nature of desire does not define the nature of the desiring subject, the "sexual identity" of the subject, in the way that heterosexual and homosexual desire are thought to. Freed from having to define the individual sexual identity, Gottfried's desire for the man and desire for the woman directly and unambiguously reinforce women's and men's positions in the gender hierarchy.

Some will point to the "sex" of Tristan and Isold and insist that, in spite of everything, desire in Gottfried's *Tristan* is "heterosexual." But I believe this is a mistake, even if one takes only the most minimal definition of heterosexual, "attraction to the opposite sex."[80] There are no opposite sexes in *Tristan.* There are no attractions defined simply on the basis of sex. There is no realm of the sexual, independent of gender and class. Even less do these desires conform to the broader meanings we usually attach to "heterosexual": a sexual identity, defined by the opposite sex of the desired object, that is "a constitutive principle of the self." If we use the modern terms "heterosexuality" and "homosexuality" to describe sexual relations in medieval texts, we only make it more difficult to recognize that it is precisely certain familiar aspects of what we call (hetero)sexuality that are *absent* from texts like *Tristan.* In order to trace the relations of sex, gender, and desire in medieval contexts we need to clear a space as free as possible from modern assumptions about these relations. Terms like "heterosexual" and "homosexual" clutter up such a space with modern meanings and make it even more difficult than it would otherwise be to see the medieval relations clearly.[81]

BEFORE HETEROSEXUALITY

There are two striking differences between the sexual organization of Gottfried's world and that of our own. First, sex difference is not visible in the body of the object. Second, sexual desire is not determined by the identity of the subject. These two differences, mediated and thus shaped by culturally specific relations of gender, combine to produce structures of desire quite different from those we might expect. The beautiful human body, gendered by clothing and other markers as masculine, elicits a masculinist cultural desire for the man: distant and admiring. The beautiful human body, gendered by clothing and other markers as feminine, elicits a masculinist cultural desire for the woman: insinuating and possessive. A woman will not experience desire for a body morphologically male but for a beautiful body, made masculine by its clothing, that can therefore be admired from a distance. A man will not experience desire for a body morphologically female but for a beautiful body, made feminine by its clothing, that can therefore be looked at, approached, and possessed. The sex of the body matters not because, readily visible, it sparks desire in the opposite sex by a kind of biologically inevitable combustion but because, merely known, it determines which of two culturally determined kinds of desire will be experienced by someone of the other sex who has been attracted to a beautiful body. Where we assume that a visible difference in the sexed object will attract a desire preformed by the sexual identity of the subject, Gottfried represents a world in which a visible difference in the gendered object elicits a desire preformed by the gender relations of the larger society.

One cannot say that bodies don't matter in Gottfried's *Tristan,* only that they don't matter in the ways we expect them to. In a world "before heterosexuality" the hegemonic desire for the other sex does not exercise its tyranny in the same way it does today—perhaps because there is no competition in sight, perhaps because the identity of the individual is not at stake. The desired body, not required to certify its legitimacy as a heterosexual object, need not proclaim its sex so loudly. Differential desire, not required to certify the heterosexual normalcy of the subject, need not be rooted within the body of that subject. Not pressed into service defending heterosexuality, Gottfried's bodies can be mobilized to uphold other interests—noble precedence or masculine prerogative. It's not that bodies don't matter in Gottfried's *Tristan.* It's that they don't matter heterosexually.

NOTES

1. Judith Butler, *Bodies That Matter: On the Discursive Limits of "Sex"* (New York, 1993), p. 14.

2. Radclyffe Hall, *The Well of Loneliness* (Garden City, N.Y., n.d.), p. 211.

3. Marjorie Garber, *Vested Interests: Cross-Dressing and Cultural Anxiety* (New York, 1992), p. 136.

4. Caroline Walker Bynum, "The Body of Christ in the Later Middle Ages: A Reply to Leo Steinberg," in Caroline Walker Bynum, *Fragmentation and Redemption: Essays on Gender and the Human Body in Medieval Religion* (New York, 1991), p. 85. See also Karin Lützen, *"La mise en discours* and Silences in Research on the History of Sexuality," in *Conceiving Sexuality: Approaches to Sex Research in a Postmodern World,* ed. Richard G. Parker and John H. Gagnon (New York, 1995), p. 27.

5. Parenthetical references in the text and in the notes refer to Gottfried von Straßburg, *Tristan und Isold,* ed. Friedrich Ranke, 15th ed. (Zurich, 1978), by line number.

6. "dar zuo was ime der lip getan, als ez diu Minne gebot" (3332–33).

7. "Minne envlammete den man mit der schœne ir libes" (17594–95).

8. John H. Gagnon and Richard G. Parker, "Conceiving Sexuality," in *Conceiving Sexuality,* ed. Parker and Gagnon, p. 12.

9. "wie gar sin lip ze wunsche stat! wie gant im so geliche in ein diu siniu keiserlichen bein! . . . wie zimet der schaft in siner hant! . . . wie stat sin houbet und sin har! . . . o wol si sæligez wip, der vröude an ime beliben sol!" (708–19).

10. E. Jane Burns, "Refashioning Courtly Love: Lancelot as Ladies' Man or Lady/Man?" in *Constructing Medieval Sexuality,* ed. Karma Lochrie, Peggy McCracken, and James A. Schultz (Minneapolis, 1997), p. 124.

11. "lanc, uf gewollen unde smal. . . . [der roc] nam den valt unde den val under den vüezen. . . . da haete diu schœne in geslagen ir dumen von ir linken hant. die rehten haete si gewant . . . da man den mantel sliezen sol, und sloz in höfschliche in ein mit ir vingere zwein. . . . Si truoc uf ir houbete einen cirkel von golde. . . . dan was kein alse wise man, hæter der steine niht gesehen, daz er iemer hæte verjehen, daz da kein cirkel wære: so gelich und alse einbære was ir har dem golde" (10894–985).

12. "sin har [was] . . . an barte verwalken also harte, als ob er wilde wære" (4004–7).

13. "zir senften linden brusten twanc sin vil harte nahen" (14160–61).

14. "der junge âne bart" (Wolfram von Eschenbach, *Parzival,* in *Wolfram von Eschenbach,* ed. Karl Lachmann, 6th ed. [Berlin, 1926], line 307,7).

15. Rudolf von Ems, *Der guote Gêrhart,* ed. John A. Asher, 2nd ed., Altdeutsche Textbibliothek, 56 (Tübingen, 1971), lines 1540–45.

16. F[riedrich] L. A. von Lassberg, ed., *Der Schwabenspiegel oder schwäbisches Land- und Lehen-Rechtbuch,* (Tübingen, 1840; reprint, Aalen, 1961), Landrecht §27.

17. For a more extended discussion of beards, see James A. Schultz, *The Knowledge of Childhood in the German Middle Ages, 1100–1350* (Philadelphia, 1995), pp. 120–21, and the literature cited there.

18. According to the evidence collected in Anna Köhn, *Das weibliche Schönheitsideal in der ritterlichen Dichtung,* Form und Geist, 14 (Leipzig, 1930), pp. 28–34, 92–93.

19. Wolfram, *Parzival,* lines 258,24–259,4.

20. Konrad Fleck, *Flore und Blanscheflur,* ed. Emil Sommer, Bibliothek der gesammten deutschen National-Literatur, 12 (Quedlinburg, 1846), lines 6395–401, 6904–5; Heinrich von dem Türlin, *Diu Crône,* ed. Gottlob Heinrich Friedrich Scholl, Bibliothek des Litterarischen Vereins in Stuttgart, 27 (Stuttgart, 1852; reprint, Amsterdam, 1966), lines 8213–17. Wolfram mentions the development of Sigune's breasts as a sign that she is maturing: Wolfram von Eschenbach, *Titurel,* in *Wolfram von Eschenbach,* ed. Lachmann, lines 39,2–3.

21. Joan Cadden, *Meanings of Sex Difference in the Middle Ages: Medicine, Science, and Culture* (Cambridge, 1993), p. 180.

22. "mir wær noh liep, wærn die her dan: man ersæhe den man wol für daz wîp: sô gelîche was ir bêder lîp" (Wolfram von Eschenbach, *Willehalm,* in *Wolfram von Eschenbach,* ed. Lachmann, lines 274,24–26).

23. "an libe und an gebare vollekomen unde rich. er was des libes edelich" (4032–34).

24. "er was an rehter herschaft aller keiser genoz" (4044–45).

25. "im solte billich unde wol ein riche dienen" (10020–21).

26. "wie wol ich wiste al dise vart, sit ich in merkende wart, sit ich an ime lip unde gabar und sin dinc allez also gar besunder in min herze las, daz er gebürte ein herre was!" (10127–32).

27. Hugo Bekker, *Gottfried von Strassburg's* Tristan: *Journey through the Realm of Eros* (Columbia, S.C., 1987), p. 147; Bodo Mergell, *Tristan und Isolde: Ursprung und Entwicklung der Tristansage des Mittelalters* (Mainz, 1949), p. 165; Gottfried Weber, *Gottfrieds von Strassburg* Tristan *und die Krise des hochmittelalterlichen Weltbildes um 1200* (Stuttgart, 1953), 1:52, 58–59.

28. For gender and modern men's underwear, see Daniel Harris, "The Current Crisis in Men's Lingerie: Notes on the Belated Commercialization of a Noncommercial Product," *Salmagundi* 199 (1993): 130–39. For gender and medieval underwear, see E. Jane Burns, "Ladies Don't Wear *Braies*: Underwear and Outerwear in the French *Prose Lancelot,*" in *The Lancelot-Grail Cycle: Texts and Transformations,* ed. William W. Kibler (Austin, 1994), pp. 152–74.

29. Michael Camille, "Manuscript Illumination and the Art of Copulation," in *Constructing Medieval Sexuality,* ed. Lochrie, McCracken, and Schultz.

30. Jonathan Ned Katz, *The Invention of Heterosexuality* (New York, 1995), p. 52.

31. Ibid., pp. 83–112.

32. Robert T. Michael, John H. Gagnon, Edward O. Laumann, and Gina Kolata, *Sex in America: A Definitive Survey* (Boston, 1994), p. 31.

33. David M. Halperin, *One Hundred Years of Homosexuality: And Other Essays on Greek Love* (New York, 1990), pp. 29–30.

34. Thomas Aquinas, *Summa theologica*, trans. Fathers of the English Dominican Province, 3 vols. (New York, 1974), 2d part of the 2d part, question 154, articles 1, 12.

35. Arnold Davidson, "Sex and the Emergence of Sexuality," *Critical Inquiry* 14 (1987): 37.

36. Butler, *Bodies That Matter*, p. 17.

37. Roland Barthes, *The Fashion System*, trans. Matthew Ward and Richard Howard (New York, 1983), p. 258.

38. "Clothing was the fundamental medium to distinguish the status and privilege of aristocratic society from all other groups" (John W. Baldwin, *The Language of Sex: Five Voices from Northern France around 1200* [Chicago, 1994], p. 100). See also Elke Brüggen, *Kleidung und Mode in der höfischen Epik des 12. und 13. Jahrhunderts* (Heidelberg, 1989), p. 113; Gabriele Raudszus, *Die Zeichensprache der Kleidung: Untersuchungen zur Symbolik des Gewandes in der deutschen Epik des Mittelalters,* ORDO, Studien zur Literatur und Gesellschaft des Mittelalters und der frühen Neuzeit, 1 (Hildesheim, 1985), p. 156.

39. Brüggen, *Kleidung*, p. 102.

40. Ibid., pp. 104, 114.

41. "sine vüeze und siniu bein, dar an sin schoene almeistic schein, diu stuonden so ze prise wol, als manz an manne prisen sol" (3341–44).

42. Brüggen, *Kleidung*, pp. 42, 72.

43. "si truoc von brunem samit an roc unde mantel, in dem snite von Franze" (10900–2).

44. Brüggen, *Kleidung*, p. 100, n. 299.

45. "sin gewant . . . was mit grozer höfscheit nach sinem libe gesniten" (3345–47). See also 2542. For a discussion of the fit of Tristan's clothes, see Raudszus, *Zeichensprache*, p. 149.

46. "der roc [was] . . . da engegene, da die siten sinket uf ir liten, gefranzet unde genget, nahe an ir lip getwenget mit einem borten, der lac wol, da der borte ligen sol. der roc der was ir heinlich, er tet sich nahen zuo der lich: ern truoc an keiner stat hin dan, er suohte allenthalben an al von obene hin ze tal" (10902–13).

47. Brüggen considers this passage in some detail, although only as a matter of fashion and courtly behavior, which is consistent with her claim that writers before 1250 were concerned only with the description of the color, shape, and material of clothing and not with the revelation of the feminine body beneath (*Kleidung*, pp. 41–44, 76). It seems to me that she underestimates the effect of insinuation, which will be treated in more detail below.

48. "diu von dem allerbesten snite" (10762).

49. "si gedahten . . . 'zeware, dirre man der ist ein menlich creatiure; sin wat und sin figiure si schepfent wol an ime den man: si zement so wol ein ander an' " (10853–59).

50. "sin geschepfede und sin wat die gehullen wunnecliche in ein: si bildeten under in zwein einen ritterlichen man" (11098–101).

51. While Tristan's body harmonizes with his civilian clothing, he is always *superior* to his armor, no matter how spectacular it is. At his knightly investiture Tristan is armed in the same way *externally* as those who will be knighted with him, but *inside* he is said to be much better (4975–5011). The armor that Tristan wears into the battle with Morold is splendid, but the workman who created what is inside the armor had done an even better job (6622–58). See also 6570–77. As a courtier, Tristan's noble body and his fashionable clothing correspond with one another and together turn him into a man. As a knight, Tristan exceeds the splendid armor that he is wearing.

52. Barthes, *The Fashion System*, p. 260.

53. Jochens notes that in Old Norse texts, as in MHG, one's clothes are "important markers of gender" (p. 9), but that these clothes draw attention to "the most apparent sexual distinctions between men's and women's bodies" (penis, breasts) (p. 21), which is not the case in *Tristan* (Jenny Jochens, "Before the Male Gaze: The Absence of the Female Body in Old Norse," in *Sex in the Middle Ages: A Book of Essays*, ed. Joyce E. Salisbury [New York, 1991], pp. 3–29).

54. "ir genuoge sprachen daz: 'wa geschuof ie got figiure baz ze ritterlichem rehte?'" (11203–5).

55. "gevedere schachblicke die vlugen da snedicke schachende dar unde dan" (10957–59).

56. For the role of clothing in securing masculine authority, see Dyan Elliott, "Dress as Mediator between Inner and Outer Self: The Pious Matron of the High and Later Middle Ages," *Mediaeval Studies* 53 (1991): 279–308.

57. This distinction parallels the one Jane Burns discovers in Old French texts between the armor by which a knight is "gendered masculine" and the exposed skin that defines femininity. Burns finds that this "highly polarized" system is actually much "more fluid" than it seems: when knights take off their armor to don the same courtly garments worn by women, perhaps even revealing exposed flesh, they thereby "shift into the hybrid status of lady/knight" (Burns, "Refashioning Courtly Love," p. 122). Burns calls this a " 'feminization,' " an "erasing [of] sexual distinctions between armor and skin" (p. 123). This, it seems to me, would be true only if skin and courtly dress were *not*-masculine in the same way that armor is *not*-feminine. Since gender is constructed not only by prescription but also by proscription—it is "indissociable from relations of discipline, regulation, punishment" (Butler, *Bodies That Matter,* p. 232)—one must consider what is prohibited as carefully as what is recommended. But the unisex courtly chemise is not off limits for men. Burns herself notes that when knights don this garment they suffer "no loss of status," nor can I see anything in the texts to indicate that they are considered less masculine for being desirable. Where is the feminization? The economy of attribution and prohibition in the courtly romances suggests to me that vestimentary masculinity is defined not by armor itself but by the ability to move freely between armor, courtly dress, and exposed skin (knighthood, courtliness, desirability), while femininity is restricted to the last two, courtly dress and skin. Such a definition expresses the asymmetry of gender but is able to accommodate the fact that no one in the texts considers Lancelot and Tristan any less masculine when they exchange their battle gear for civilian dress. In the case of *Tristan,* at least, this may be because courtly clothes for men and women, although they differ little in form, nevertheless differ in function, providing men with something rather like armor while offering women something more like exposure. Nor are Lancelot or Tristan considered any less masculine when they reveal their bare skin. This may be because, as I have argued, the desirable body itself (including its skin) is neither masculine nor feminine.

58. Monique Wittig, "The Mark of Gender," in Monique Wittig, *The Straight Mind and Other Essays* (Boston, 1992), pp. 76–89.

59. Carroll Smith-Rosenberg, "The Female World of Love and Ritual: Relations between Women in Nineteenth-Century America," *Signs* 1 (1975): 1–29.

60. George Chauncey, "From Sexual Inversion to Homosexuality: Medicine and the Changing Conceptualization of Female Deviance," *Salmagundi* 58/59 (1982–83): 114–46.

61. This is the case in much of Latin America. See Tomás Almaguer, "Chicano Men: A Cartography of Homosexual Identity and Behavior," *differences* 3.2 (1991): 76–86.

62. Butler, *Bodies That Matter,* p. 17.

63. Michel Foucault, *The Use of Pleasure,* vol. 2 of *The History of Sexuality,* trans. Robert Hurley (New York, 1985), p. 5.

64. Ibid., pp. 4–5, emphasis added.

65. Butler, *Bodies That Matter,* p. 16.

66. " 'seht' sprachen si 'der jungelinc der ist ein sæliger man: wie sælecliche stet im an allez daz, daz er begat! wie gar sin lip ze wunsche stat! wie gant im so geliche in ein diu siniu keiserlichen bein! wie rehte sin schilt zaller zit an siner stat gelimet lit! wie zimet der schaft in siner hant! wie wol stat allez sin gewant! wie stat sin houbet und sin har! wie süeze ist aller sin gebar! wie sælecliche stat sin lip! o wol si sæligez wip, der vröude an ime beliben sol!' " (704–19).

67. Poag argues that the repetition of words related to *sælde* "implies that there is an underlying connection between sexuality and felicity (at least for these female representatives of Tintagel)" (James F. Poag, "The Onset of Love: The Problem of the Religious Dimension in

Gottfried von Straßburg's *Tristan*," in *Semper idem et novus: Festschrift for Frank Banta*, ed. Francis G. Gentry, Göppinger Arbeiten zur Gemanistik, 481 [Göppingen, 1988], p. 290).

68. "ir kinne, ir munt, ir varwe, ir lich daz was so rehte wunneclich, so lieplich und so muotsam, daz ir Marken gezam: in gelangete unde geluste, daz er si gerne kuste. . . . sin ouge stuont im allez dar: er nam vil innecliche war, wie schone ir uz der wæte schein ir kele unde ir brustbein, ir arme unde ir hende" (17587–603). While at first glance it might seem that Mark, in looking at Isold's *brustbein,* is looking at a peculiarly female body part (Hatto translates the word as "breast"), it becomes apparent at line 18205 that Tristan also has one.

69. "ir varwe unde ir schin [luhte] als suoze und alse lose als ein gemischet rose. . . . ir munt der viurete unde bran reht alse ein glüejender kol" (17564–69).

70. "zwo schœne hæten an der stunt ein spil gemachet under in zwein: da schein lieht unde lieht in ein. Diu sunne und diu sunne die hæten eine wunne und eine hohzit dar geleit Isote zeiner sælekeit" (17580–86).

71. "sin varwe lieht" (3335).

72. "vuorte ir sunnen an ir hant . . . die liehten maget Isote" (10887–89).

73. "diu wunnebernde sunne si breite ir schin über al, si ervröute liute unde sal" (11006–8).

74. "die rehten hæte si gewant hin nider baz, ir wizzet wol, da man den mantel sliezen sol, und sloz in höfschliche in ein mit ir vingere zwein: vürbaz da viel er selbe wider und nam den valt al zende nider, daz man diz unde daz da sach, ich meine vederen unde dach" (10940–48).

75. "er nam den valt unde den val under den vüezen alse vil, als iuwer iegelicher wil" (10914–16). Brüggen treats this passage at length, but sees nothing in it besides clothing and courtly bearing (*Kleidung,* pp. 41–44). Although Raudszus has less to say, she at least recognizes that this is a "sehr suggestive Beschreibung" (*Zeichensprache der Kleidung,* p. 155). Baldwin sees that Gottfried speaks "coyly"—although everything else he says about the passage is wrong (*The Language of Sex,* p. 104). According to Baldwin, "Iseut" holds the mantle together "suggestively" by placing her hand in the string of pearls "lest the opening reveal 'this and that.'" The heroine's name is not Iseut but Isold; the mantle is not held together by her hand but by the string of pearls; there is nothing suggestive about the way she places her hand there; it is *another* hand that holds the mantle closed; it is not closed *lest* something be revealed but falls in a way *so that* "this and that" is revealed. When Baldwin talks about other passages in Gottfried he is no more accurate: Tristan is not "wounded and unconscious" when Isold examines him, and he is not "in the bath" (p. 102).

76. Michael et al., *Sex in America,* p. 16.

77. Halperin, *One Hundred Years,* p. 24.

78. Ibid., p. 25.

79. Krohn's reading of *Tristan,* according to which Mark's homosexual desire for Tristan is meant to defame him, has been rightly criticized by Jaeger: Rüdiger Krohn, "Erotik und Tabu in Gottfrieds 'Tristan': König Marke," in *Stauferzeit: Geschichte, Literatur, Kunst,* ed. Rüdiger Krohn, Bernd Thum, and Peter Wapnewski, Karlsruher Kulturwissenschaftliche Arbeiten, 1 (Stuttgart, 1979), pp. 362–76; C. Stephen Jaeger, "Mark and Tristan: The Love of Medieval Kings and Their Courts," in *in hôhem prîse: A Festschrift in Honor of Ernst S. Dick,* ed. Winder McConnell, Göppinger Arbeiten zur Germanistik, 480 (Göppingen, 1989), pp. 183–97.

80. William Morris, ed., *The American Heritage Dictionary of the English Language* (Boston, 1976), S.V. "heterosexual."

81. Thus it is not surprising that medievalists who use these terms, even those who write thoughtfully about the issues involved, end up discovering that the Middle Ages are more or less like the present. Simon Gaunt, who argues for the use of "homosexuality," discovers that "homophobia" in *Lanval* plays the same role "that Eve Kosofsky Sedgwick attributes to it in modern culture" ("Straight Minds/'Queer' Wishes in Old French Hagiography: *La Vie de Sainte Euphrosine,*" *GLQ: A Journal of Lesbian and Gay Studies* 1 [1995]: 441–42). Carolyn Dinshaw, who argues for the use of "heterosexuality," finds that *Sir Gawain and the Green*

Knight "theorizes heterosexuality in a way that accords with the theoretical articulations of Foucault and, particularly, Butler" ("A Kiss Is Just a Kiss: Heterosexuality and Its Consolations in *Sir Gawain and the Green Knight*," *diacritics* 24.2/3 [1994]: 214). For Dinshaw heterosexuality is a very capacious term, embracing not only marriage, procreation, gender, and the body but also all the binaries in the prologue to the Canterbury Tales—April and March, summer and winter, earth and sky, knowing and unknowing, public and private, and a good deal more ("Chaucer's Queer Touches/A Queer Touches Chaucer," *Exemplaria* 7 [1995]: 80–83). Defined in such generous terms, it is hard to see how heterosexuality could be anything *but* "invisible, cosmic and inevitable" (p. 82). To be sure, Dinshaw insists that modern terms "need historical particularizing" ("A Kiss," p. 206). But while her analysis is rich in particulars from the texts under discussion, the historical particulars of "heterosexuality" are effaced. When *Cleanness* is found to allow sex for pleasure rather than for procreation, Dinshaw concludes: "Heterosexuality is thus subtly reconfigured here; at the same time, crucial structuring principles stay traditional" (pp. 217–18). What is arguably one of the most profound realignments in the construction of European sexuality (procreation to pleasure) is dismissed as a subtle reconfiguration, while the timeless principles of heterosexuality are reaffirmed. What I find missing is the middle ground, the space between the idiosyncrasies of a particular text and the inevitability of male-female relations. It is the space in which one might describe a distinctive historical structure of male-female relations in the context of which the details of a particular text will have been meaningful. If the history of sexuality is to be something more than the collection of idiosyncrasies or the affirmation of universal truths, then we must find a way of generalizing the former somewhere short of the latter.

"UT CUM MULIERE"

A Male Transvestite Prostitute in Fourteenth-Century London

RUTH MAZO KARRAS AND DAVID LORENZO BOYD

Although legal records provide much valuable information on the practice of "sodomy" in late medieval Italy, such evidence is remarkably scant for other parts of Europe.[1] The document presented here stands practically alone for medieval England as a description of same-sex intercourse as well as male transvestism.[2] It thus helps assess how medieval English society viewed such behavior. Medieval ideas about what modern people call "sexuality" cannot be elucidated only from the writings of canonists and theologians,[3] but must also be sought from documents recording social practice. First-person accounts on which scholars might base a reconstruction of an individual's sexual subjectivity are rare in the Middle Ages. When such accounts do appear, they are likely to have arisen in a legal context and to be subject to all sorts of problems of interpretation.[4] Nevertheless, as they reflect both the way individuals saw themselves and the way the legal system interpreted their behavior, such accounts are important avenues into medieval constructions of sexuality.

Read within the context of current understandings of the legal regulation and cultural construction of sexualities in the Middle Ages, this document indicates that gender distinctions, rather than those of sexual behavior or "identity," were most crucial. Recognizing that there is no way of verifying the facticity of Rykener's account, we base our analysis here on the premise that if the account is a fiction, it is a verisimilar one, and that what is important is not the actual behavior of this individual, but the construction of sexuality that his account implies.[5]

The document translated as the appendix to this article (the first case on membrane 2 of Plea and Memoranda Roll A34, Corporation of London Records Office), describes the testimony of John Rykener, "calling himself

Eleanor," who was apprehended in women's clothing having sex with another man in a London street one night in December 1394.[6] Rykener claimed that he had worked as a prostitute in London, having been initiated by women who taught him to cross-dress. He then worked in Oxford as an embroideress, having sex with several students, and in Burford as a tapster, again also practicing prostitution. His partners included priests, Franciscans, and Carmelites. He also reported having sex with many women, including nuns, but not apparently for money.

Unfortunately, the result of the case does not survive, if indeed any formal action was ever taken. It is not entirely clear why the examination of Rykener was entered on the roll, but the maintenance of "public order" may have been a reason, although Rykener's offense was never labeled prostitution (the main sexual offense that the courts treated as a threat to public order). Nothing in the document indicates that any sort of formal legal process was under way. What is clear—from the case's physical placement on the roll and the hand in which it is written—is that it is not a later interpolation.

It was rare indeed for a temporal court in England to deal with cases of sodomy, which is one way Rykener's case could have been legally classified. Sexual matters, in England as elsewhere in Europe, were within the jurisdiction of the church courts, and had been so since at least the twelfth century (although temporal authorities also regulated sexual matters when they deemed them relevant to public order). Though canon lawyers, the theorists of the law applied in the church courts, had a good deal to say about sodomy, in actual cases the charge of sodomy appears most often as a further accusation to hurl at heretics. Even so, it does not appear frequently in English church court records of the later Middle Ages; only one case, for example, turns up among the thousands of cases in the records from the London diocese for the late fifteenth century.[7] As no late-fourteenth-century church court records survive for that jurisdiction, it is not possible to determine whether Rykener and his partner were prosecuted under ecclesiastical jurisdiction.

Despite the general rule that sexual offenses were matters for the church courts, in some cases the city of London took charge of these offenses. Prostitution and procuring, for example, involved public order, and the temporal courts dealt with them for that reason, so that the same people might be prosecuted in both jurisdictions for the same offense. Even a few adultery and fornication cases ended up in the city courts, most involving priests.[8] The city authorities seem to have been particularly eager to bring clerics' sexual transgressions to light, and this may be why they recorded the examination of Rykener. Indeed, awareness of their interest in rooting out clerical offenses may have prompted Rykener's concluding remark that he preferred priests to his other customers. The emphasis on priests does not explain why the authorities were interested in Rykener's cross-dressing in the first place—as we argue below, his gender transgression was the most important factor here—but it does explain why the details of his testimony were so carefully recorded.

Rykener's interrogation raises issues central to our understanding of the role of sexuality in medieval culture. These include the construction, or lack thereof, of specific sexualities; the deployment of the concept of sodomy to impugn the masculinity of a celibate clergy; the relation between the grammatical subject-object relation and the social subject-object relation; and the medieval understanding of gender as performative and the issues of "passing" that arise from it. These questions are a heavy burden for John/Eleanor Rykener to bear alone, but the document is at least a starting point for considering them.

Before discussing the information the document brings to bear on these questions, we need first to consider the discursive context in which the case was situated. In modern terms, Rykener would be described as a transvestite (because he cross-dressed) and a prostitute (because he took money for sex), and probably a bisexual. The relevance of the last term is the most problematic. According to his account, Rykener had sex with both men and women, but all his sexual encounters with men were for money, while those with women were not. This raises the question of whether his motivation for sex with men was more financial than libidinal; he may have been bisexual in his choice of partners but not in his desires. In medieval terms the question of bisexuality would not even have arisen. While people would certainly have been aware that there were some men who had sexual desire for both males and females, this was not seen as a fixed orientation, and did not define a particular type of individual.[9]

For that matter, transvestism would not have been seen as a sexual orientation. Medieval culture is full of stories of women who cross-dressed, but few such stories concern men, and when they did medieval authors did not see cross-dressing as a sexual preference, but rather as a means of gaining access to women.[10] Rykener's case gives no indication that cross-dressing brought him any sexual gratification. We have no idea how he felt about it himself, although the fact that he named the woman who "first dressed him as a woman" indicates that someone else may have suggested the cross-dressing because of the earning opportunities it presented.

In medieval terms, then, what was Rykener? How would medieval culture have viewed his sexuality? Medieval texts, legal and literary, suggest two common cultural categories into which he might have fallen. First, he might have been a prostitute. That is certainly what the man with whom he was arrested took him for. Second, he might have been a sodomite, the common medieval term for a man who had sex with another man (although Rykener was apparently the "passive" partner and this term was sometimes used only for the active one).[11]

Perhaps surprisingly, Rykener does not seem to have been treated under either of these two categories. The language used in the confession itself suggests that Rykener might have been seen as a woman, and that it was the gender-crossing, rather than the sexual behavior, that constituted his identity. The following discussion of the cultural categories of prostitution and sodomy will indicate why Rykener did not really fit into them, and we will then turn to an analysis of the document's focus on gender transgression.

It may seem somewhat strange to speak of prostitution in terms of a sexual identity or sexual orientation, because, to a modern sensibility, prostitution is an act, the exchange of sex for money. Prostitution was until relatively recently a status offense (that is, one could be arrested for *being* a prostitute), but now—legally and in most people's minds—it is defined in terms of specific behavior.[12] In the Middle Ages, however, although prostitution was never clearly defined in the law, the offense for which women were presented and prosecuted in both church and temporal courts was that of being a prostitute (*meretrix, feme publique, gemeine fraw,* common woman, and so on), rather than soliciting sex.[13] Prostitutes in many towns had to wear distinguishing clothing.[14] Some municipalities had officially recognized brothels in order strictly to demarcate prostitutes from other women. Under these circumstances, it may not be pushing the evidence too far to argue that a prostitute was seen as a certain type of person rather than as a person who did certain things. In this sense, prostitution was a sexual orientation, an important component of personal identity.

The way prostitution was defined, when medieval writers did go to the trouble to define it, also indicates that it involved being a certain type of person, rather than engaging in sex for money. Medieval people were certainly aware that those they called "*meretrix*" commonly did engage in sex for money, but it was not that which distinguished them as a category. Indeed, "whore" is probably a better translation of "*meretrix*" than "prostitute," because the term had a wider meaning. Although canonists certainly recognized that those they called "*meretrices*" operated commercially, they did not consider that this was what made them *meretrices*; rather it was the public nature of their sexual activity, or the fact that they did not refuse any partner, or the number of partners they had, that placed them in that category.[15] The practice of the church courts followed the canonists' analysis: while the fact of taking money was occasionally alleged as evidence that a given woman is a whore, the fact of her having sex with several men, or with one man who was a priest, could also be cited as evidence.[16]

It is true that other medieval writers recognized financial exchange as one of the factors defining the category "whore," but only one among many, and not the defining one. The early-thirteenth-century moral theologian Thomas of Chobham, for example, cites several different meanings of "*meretrix*": a woman who has sex outside marriage; a woman who has sex with many men; a woman who denies herself to none; a woman whose sin is public; and a woman who sells herself.[17] The fourteenth-century English handbook for preachers, *Fasciculus Morum,* in discussing the types of lust, defined fornication as follows:

> While fornication is any forbidden sexual intercourse, it particularly refers to intercourse with widows, prostitutes (*meretrices*), or concubines. But the term "prostitute" (*meretrix*) must be applied only to those women who give themselves to anyone and will refuse none, and that for monetary gain.[18]

Here the author seems to have an understanding similar to the modern understanding of the prostitute. Yet it is noteworthy that this text does not have a category for single women who fornicate, other than widows, whores or concubines. Any sexually active woman who is not attached to a particular man is defined as a *meretrix*. The category of prostitute included more than just women who took money for sex.

This terminological conflation of all women who had sex with multiple partners and commercial prostitutes is the key to understanding the deployment of the concept of *meretrix* in medieval society. Those who had sex for money were a recognized group; but because of the way whoredom or prostitution was defined, any woman who was sexually deviant, or any woman who was not under the control of a man, could be placed in that group as well. The classification of sexually independent women as *meretrices* could thus be used as a warning, a tool to control all women.[19]

In this way, prostitution was intimately tied up with femininity. The whore was the extreme case of what all women could be, and any woman risked classification as a whore if she stepped out of line. For a man to be considered a prostitute, then, would have been an oxymoron. A whore was first and foremost a sinful woman, although probably one who happened to take money for her sin. A man who took money for sex did not fall into the same category. This may explain why Rykener was not accused of prostitution in the London court.

Men could, of course, be prosecuted for sexual offenses in the same way women could; they were also accused and convicted of fornication and adultery. There is, however, no case extant from the medieval English ecclesiastical courts (or in fact from any other medieval courts, as far as we know) in which a man was accused, let alone convicted, of prostitution. Men's other sexual offenses typically involved their control over women: they were pimps or procurers. Even if we look at common sexual defamations or insults directed at men and women, men are rarely called sodomites and never prostitutes; the sexual insults involved women under their control, as they were called cuckolds or whoremongers.[20] Little wonder that once Rykener's biological sex had been determined, he was not accused of prostitution. He may have operated in the same way and in the same milieu as women who were accused of prostitution, but in medieval terms his offense was not the same as theirs.[21]

If Rykener cannot be considered a prostitute in terms of medieval understandings of the concept, then, to what extent can he be considered a sodomite? It is telling that he never referred to himself as a sodomite, or to his activities as sodomy, in his confession. The phrases "detestable, unmentionable, and ignominious vice," "libidinous and unspeakable act" and "abominable vice" were used, however, and "unmentionable" and "unspeakable" are often connected with sodomy in medieval discourses about sex. These words may have been spoken by Rykener, who would have been familiar with them from the confessional (Rykener, who was not a cleric, almost certainly did not give his deposition in Latin, so the phrases must be the scribe's interpretation of what he said). Other European jurisdictions in this period were not afraid to use the term "sodomy," and the hesitancy to do so here may signify indecision or confusion about the nature of Rykener's activity and, indeed, of sodomy itself.[22]

It is important to note that the legal crime of sodomy did not mean "having the status of being a homosexual" or "being attracted to men." Legally, it was an act, usually though apparently not always, the act of anal intercourse.[23] In discussing here whether or not Rykener was a sodomite, we are not discussing whether or not he was exclusively attracted to men; a sodomite convicted because of a sex act with a man could also have had sex with women, and in fact Rykener testified that this was so in his case.

But not every act of anal intercourse was necessarily considered sodomy. Alan Bray has argued that, in Renaissance England, routine sex between men was taken more or less for granted and was not equated with sodomy, a vice connected mainly with the debauched court.[24] If Bray is correct, it is also possible that this was true at an earlier period as well, and it may account for the lack of visible enforcement of the anti-sodomy law in England. This renders problematic any attempt to determine whether Rykener would have been considered a "sodomite."

The logic behind the condemnation of sodomy also problematizes Rykener's case. Is the problem of the unmentionable vice the vice itself or, rather, the disruption of social norms it represents? The more one reads medieval texts concerning sodomy, the more apparent it becomes that it was not the act of sodomy *per se* that constituted wrongdoing. Sodomy was only one of the manifestations of a more important issue subtending the denunciation of male homosexual contact in medieval culture: gender transgression and conflation.[25] As we shall see, this gender transgression is precisely what is at issue in Rykener's case. The concern with homosexual behavior as gender disruption surfaces constantly throughout both Latin and vernacular writing, beginning as early as Ennodius' epigrams, which mark the way that sodomy disrupts a stable sex/gender system:

Vir facie, mulier gestu, sed crure quod ambo,
jurgia naturae nullo discrimine solvens,
es lepus, et tanti conculcas colla leonis.

Respice portentum permixtu jure creatum,
communis generis, satius sed dicitur omnis.

Ludit in ancipiti constans fallacia sexu:
femina cum patitue, peragit cum turpia, mas est.

[Your face is masculine, your gestures feminine, but your thighs are both
You resolve an opposition in nature by negating the difference.
You are a rabbit and trample the neck of a great lion.

Look at this monster created by promiscuous rule
Of common gender or, rather, of all genders.

There is a constant deception at play in his double sex:
He's a woman when passive, but when active in shameful deeds, he's a man.][26]

That man can couple with man as with a woman threatens to obscure sharp distinctions between gendered bodies—and gendered orifices. From this perspective, it is little wonder that theologians such as Peter Damian found the flexibility of gender identity dangerous and in need of immediate disciplinary action: the male body under no circumstances should be feminized.[27] Vernacular literary texts such as the *Romance of the Rose* and *Eneas* treat the issue of sodomy in similar fashion.

Similar concerns over sodomy as part of a larger issue of gender transgression also surface in fourteenth-century English poems, literary productions close to Rykener's cultural situation and to the textualization of his confession as a written document. Here the literary constructions of sodomy emphasize not the act itself but the feminizing subversiveness of the activity. In both *Sir Gawain and the Green Knight* and *The Miller's Tale,* the substitution of the male for the female (or a male orifice for a female one) becomes the focal point of transgression.[28] The concern with gender arises perhaps most clearly in *Cleanness,* also written by the author of *Sir Gawain.* Speaking to Abraham in *Cleanness,* God describes the activities of the Sodomites and condemns homosexual sodomy as both unclean and antithetical to heterosexual intercourse:

> Þay han lerned a lyst þat lykez me ille,
> Þat þay han founden in her flesch of fautez þe werst:
> Vch male matz his mach a man as hymseluen,
> And fylter folyly in fere on femmalez wyse.
> I compast hem a kynde crafte and kende hit hem derne,
> And amed hit in Myn ordenaunce oddely dere,
> And dyȝt drwry þerinne, doole alþer-swettest,
> And þe play of paramorez I portrayed Myseluen,
> And made þerto a maner myriest of oþer:
> When two true togeder had tyȝed hemseluen,
> Bytwene a male and his make such merþe schulde come,
> Welnyȝe pure paradys moȝt preue no better;
> Ellez þay moȝt honestly ayþer oþer welde,
> At a stylle stollen steuen, vnstered wyth syȝt,
> Luf-lowe hem bytwene lasched so hote
> Þat alle þe meschefez on mold moȝt hit not sleke.
> Now haf þay skyfted My skyl and scorned natwre,
> And henttez hem in heþyng an vsage vnclene.

(II. 693–710).

[They have learned a lust [pleasure] that ill-pleases me,
That they have founded in their flesh the worst of faults:
Each male takes for a mate a man as himself,
And they join together lewdly as [a man] with a woman.
I devised for them a natural [lawful] craft and taught it to them in secret,
And esteemed it as singularly precious in my ordinaunce,
And ordained lovemaking therein, intercourse as the sweetest of all

96

And the play of paramours I fashioned myself,
And made the manner of it the merriest of all:
When two people joined themselves together,
Pure paradise might prove itself no better;
If they would honestly possess one another
At a private, secret rendezvous, undisturbed by sight,
The love-flame between them would burn so hotly
That all the mischief in the world might not quench it.
Now they have altered my devising and scorned nature
And contemptuously founded [in themselves] an unclean custom.][29]

As an unclean usage of male bodies that feminizes one of them, homosexual activity scorns the sweet heteronormativity sanctioned by Nature and God, and disregards the proper, gendered use of male bodies. They, much like Rykener, act *"ut muliere"* ("as a woman").

Finally, the portrait of Chaucer's much-discussed Pardoner in the *General Prologue* to *The Canterbury Tales* also privileges gender transgression over sodomy. When Chaucer describes this ambiguous and effeminate character, he expresses confusion over whether the Pardoner is a gelding or a mare ("mare" probably being slang for one who engages in homosexual activity while taking the passive role).[30] But the Pardoner's uninterpretability does not dominate the description; rather, it appears as a way of proving, of explaining, the effeminacy already described in the Pardoner's features and the gender instability already expressed amply throughout the text. Perhaps even more telling is that the greatest hint of the Pardoner's sodomitical behavior comes in the Summoner's portrait, where we learn that the Summoner supplies the Pardoner with a stiff "burdoun"—a double entendre possibly meaning both musical accompaniment and penis. By focusing on the ambiguous gender of the Pardoner—and on the ambiguity of his (male?) body—the *General Prologue* succeeds in highlighting the disruptive influence that gender transgression might have had on medieval culture's systems of order and interpretation.[31]

In light of this medieval focus on gender, it is less surprising that the account of Rykener's confession makes no explicit mention of sodomy, but rather employs words such as "unmentionable," "nefarious," and "vice"; focusing on sodomy itself might have taken away from the larger issue about gender that Rykener's case shares with the literature discussed above. We are thus left with a fascinating scenario: while Rykener might have engaged in prostitution, he was not identified as a prostitute; while he might have practiced sodomy, he was not clearly identified as a sodomite. He was identified as a man who had forsaken his gendered identity and had become a woman, engaging in sexual intercourse with men "as a woman." This is why his "confession" of what could have been called, but were not called, sodomy and prostitution, does not seem to be of primary interest to the authorities in this case. That he prostituted himself and engaged in sodomy only confirm his gender loss and conflation. While "sodomite" is largely (though not entirely) a question of choice of orifice, "effeminate" is a question of transgression of gender roles. Hence, not only did his clients think that Rykener was a woman (at least he dressed as one, and never said that his clients knew otherwise), but he had in effect become a woman, allowing them to have sex with him "as with a woman." His "error," to use a medieval phrase, was not primarily, then, that he committed these "sins," but, rather, that he renounced his male body and the privilege that masculine morphology entailed, a renunciation that allowed these sins subsequently to take place.

Not surprisingly, then, the document repeatedly treats Rykener as a woman. He commits the sex act "*modo muliebri*" ("in a womanish manner") and men have sex with him "*ut cum muliere*" ("as with a woman") or "*ut cum femina*" ("as with a female"), while when he has sex with women, he does it "*ut vir*" ("as a man") or "*modo virili*" ("in a manly fashion"). It is not object choice that affects his sexual identity, but the role he plays. When he acts as a man, he is the subject of the verb "*concubo*" ("to lie with, to have sex with"), but when he acts as a woman, he is its object; his sexual passivity is inscribed in the Latin verbal construction. The text does not persistently stress the sinful or criminal nature of his behavior: on several occasions when he acts "as a woman," his partners alone are said to "commit that vice," as though the feminine partner has disappeared. A male who dressed as a woman provided the extreme case for the medieval habit of gendering any "passive" partner (the one who is penetrated) as feminine.[32]

Rykener's case suggests that gender was seen as performative, that it was behavior and not intrinsic nature that made one a man or a woman. As Judith Butler has argued, gender "is always a doing . . . [gender] identity is performatively constituted by the very 'expressions' that are said to be its results."[33] That gender is constituted by behavior can clearly be seen in this medieval case. The male-dominated medieval social order, built upon clearly delineated and constantly reenforced gender roles, naturalized and maintained these roles through a variety of practices: differences in dress, mannerisms, sexual positions and activities, social pastimes, occupations, familial roles, legal rights, and duties all functioned to distinguish the masculine from the feminine.[34] Male cross-dressing undermined the male dominance and status that these practices created, exposing gender roles as performative and constructed. It is also for this reason, among others, that sodomy, disrupting the "natural" order and use of male and female bodies and orifices, was condemned, for it turned men into women through the *performance* of sexual acts.[35] Thus, this disruption of masculine and feminine gender differences becomes an offence not only against nature but against the "natural" social order as well.

John Rykener, by describing himself in the terminology of gender transgression rather than sodomy or prostitution, represents such disruption in two interrelated ways. First, by dressing as female and naming himself Eleanor, Rykener's performance as a woman marks him *as a woman,* so much so that periodically he is linguistically gendered feminine in the Latin document.[36] Second, as a male adopting a passive or feminine function with men during sex, he undermines the use of sexual performance and activity to construct masculine and feminine gender roles, and blurs the distinction between the male and the female. These roles are emphasized in the text as constructed behaviors: he learns his sexual behavior from a prostitute named Anna, and his transvestism from Elizabeth Brouderer. Hence, performatively gendered both through sexual activity and dress, Rykener is doubly feminized and disempowered through being perceived as a woman and used sexually by other males. What makes Rykener's case so interesting theoretically is not that he practiced transvestism or the unspeakable vice, but rather that he did both simultaneously. It is in the relationship between the two performances that the politics of medieval gender emerge.

Rykener's position as a male who is gendered feminine cannot be taken as typical of all men at the time who engaged in same-sex relations; the fact that he dressed in women's clothing and that at least some of his partners thought he was a woman certainly contributed to his gendering as feminine. The medieval understanding of Rykener's behavior is much closer to a nineteenth-century concept of "sexual inversion" (a person born into the wrong sexed body) than a modern concept of "homosexuality" focused mainly on object choice.[37] Yet it cannot be concluded that this would have been the way medieval culture understood all or most men who were involved in sexual relations with other men.

What, then, was Rykener in medieval terms? He was feminine, if not literally a woman; but this was not a crime. He was not a prostitute as medieval people understood that concept, and it was unclear whether he was a sodomite. Our perplexity as to where medieval culture would have classified him may well parallel that of the London civic officials. If, in fact, they did not prosecute him, but took his statement and released him, this may have been because they did not know quite what to make of him. He disrupted the traditional boundaries. There may not have been a category in medieval England for Rykener; as a gender-crosser, he was strange, unusual, queer.

Although arguing from negative evidence is always dangerous, it is interesting to speculate on why no further information about Rykener's case appears in the record. Was further action taken and recorded elsewhere, in a document that does not survive? Did the authorities release Rykener without any further action because they did not find his behavior criminal, at least not according to any of the established categories of criminal behavior? Did they not record any further information about him because his crime was so abominable and unmentionable it could not be publicly discussed? Or did they abandon the case out of confusion about what to do? What we can say for certain is that Rykener did not fit the expectations of normal masculine behavior (or even criminal behavior) in fourteenth-century English society and culture.

APPENDIX
Corporation of London Records Office,
Plea and Memoranda Roll A34, m. 2 (1395)

This case is found at the top of the membrane, and is followed by several unrelated cases in the same hand.[38] A transcription of the original Latin of this document can be found in *GLQ* 1 (1994): 461–62.

On 11 December, 18 Richard II, were brought in the presence of John Fressh, Mayor, and the Aldermen of the City of London John Britby of the county of York and John Rykener, calling [himself][39] Eleanor, having been detected in women's clothing, who were found last Sunday night between the hours of 8 and 9 by certain officials of the city lying by a certain stall in Soper's Lane[40] committing that detestable, unmentionable, and ignominious vice.[41] In a separate examination held before the Mayor and Aldermen about the occurrence, John Britby confessed that he was passing through the high road of Cheap on Sunday between the above-mentioned hours and accosted John Rykener, dressed up as a woman, thinking he was a woman, asking him as he would a woman if he could commit a libidinous act with her. Requesting money for [his] labor, Rykener consented, and they went together to the aforesaid stall to complete the act, and were captured there during these detestable wrongdoings by the officials and taken to prison. And John Rykener, brought here in woman's clothing and questioned about this matter, acknowledged [himself] to have done everything just as John Britby had confessed. Rykener was also asked who had taught him to exercise this vice, and for how long and in what places and with what persons, masculine or feminine, [he] had committed that libidinous and unspeakable act. [He] swore willingly on [his] soul that a certain Anna, the whore of a former servant of Sir Thomas Blount, first taught him to practice this detestable vice in the manner of a woman. [He] further said that a certain Elizabeth Brouderer[42] first dressed him in women's clothing; she also brought her daughter Alice to diverse men for the sake of lust, placing her with those men in their beds at night without light, making her leave early in the morning and showing them the said John Rykener dressed up in women's clothing, calling him Eleanor and saying that they had misbehaved with her. [He] further said that a certain Phillip, rector of Theydon Garnon,[43] had sex with him as with a woman in Elizabeth Brouderer's house outside Bishopsgate, at which time Rykener took away two gowns of Phillip's, and when Phillip requested them from Rykener he said that [he] was the wife of a certain man and that if Phillip wished to ask for them back [he] would make [his] husband bring suit against him. Rykener further confessed that for five weeks before the feast of St. Michael's last [he] was staying at Oxford and there, in women's clothing and calling himself Eleanor, worked as an embroideress; and there in the marsh three unsuspecting scholars—of whom one was named Sir William Foxlee,[44] another Sir John, and the third Sir Walter—practiced the abominable vice with him often. John Rykener further confessed that on Friday before the feast of St. Michael [he] came to Burford in Oxfordshire and there dwelt with a certain John Clerk at the Swan in the capacity of tapster for the next six weeks,[45] during which time two Franciscans, one named Brother Michael and the other Brother John, who gave [him] a gold ring, and one Carmelite friar and six foreign men committed the above-said vice with him, of whom one gave Rykener twelve pence, one twenty pence, and one two shillings. Rykener further confessed that [he] went to Beaconsfield[46] and there, as a man, had sex with a certain Joan, daughter of John Matthew, and also there two foreign Franciscans had sex with him as with a woman. John Rykener also confessed that after [his] last return to London a certain Sir John, once chaplain at the Church of St. Margaret Pattens,[47] and two other chaplains committed with him the aforementioned vice in the lanes behind St. Katherine's Church by the Tower of London. Rykener further said that he often had sex as a man with many nuns and also had sex as a man with many women both married and otherwise, how many [he] did not know. Rykener further confessed that many priests had committed that vice with him as with a woman, how many [he] did not know, and said that [he] accommodated priests more readily than other people because they wished to give [him] more than others.

NOTES

The authors thank Sheila Lindenbaum for drawing their attention to the existence of the document, and the Corporation of London Records Office for permission to publish it in *GLQ*.

1. Michael J. Rocke, "Male Homosexuality and Its Regulation in Late Medieval Florence" (Ph.D. diss., State University of New York, Binghamton, 1987); [see also his *Forbidden Friendships: Homosexuality and Male Culture in Renaissance Florence* (New York, 1996); Guido Ruggiero, *The Boundaries of Eros: Sex, Crime, and Sexuality in Renaissance Venice* (New York, 1985), pp. 109–45.

2. John Boswell provides the most thorough treatment of the general subject: *Christianity, Homosexuality, and Social Tolerance: Gay People in Western Europe from the Beginning of the Christian Era to the Fourteenth Century* (Chicago, 1980). See also Michael Goodich, *The Unmentionable Vice: Homosexuality in the Later Medieval Period* (Santa Barbara, 1979). Bullough and Bullough, in their chapter on the medieval period, generally do not associate male transvestism with homosexuality. They adduce instances of ritual transvestism but none of prostitution: Vern L. Bullough and Bonnie Bullough, *Cross Dressing, Sex, and Gender* (Philadelphia, 1993), pp. 45–73.

3. James A. Brundage, *Law, Sex, and Christian Society in Medieval Europe* (Chicago, 1987); Pierre J. Payer, *The Bridling of Desire* (Toronto, 1993).

4. Such legal accounts may reflect the kinds of questions that were put and therefore the way the legal system constructed sexuality, rather than the way the individual experienced it subjectively. See the interrogation of Arnold of Vernioulles, translated in Goodich, *Unmentionable Vice*, pp. 89–123.

5. Paul Strohm, *Hochon's Arrow: The Social Imagination of Fourteenth-Century Texts* (Princeton, 1992), p. 4.

6. The modern editor of the Plea and Memoranda Rolls suppressed this case by omitting the details from the published calendar, which is in most cases very detailed and reliable. To describe this case he wrote just a single sentence: "Examination of two men charged with immorality, of whom one implicated several persons, male and female, in religious orders" (A. H. Thomas, *Calendar of Select Pleas and Memoranda of the City of London, A.D. 1381–1412*, 3 vols. [Cambridge, 1924–32], vol. 3, p. 228). He thus made invisible the nature of the "immorality" with which they were charged, although he claimed that "care has been taken . . . to include all passages which seem to add in any way to our knowledge of the times" (p. vii). For fuller discussion, see the earlier version of this article in *GLQ*, pp. 459–60.

7. Richard Wunderli, *London Church Courts and Society on the Eve of the Reformation, Speculum* Anniversary Monographs, 7 (Cambridge, Mass., 1981), pp. 83–84. For another

example, see York Minster Library, MS M2(1)f (Dean and Chapter, Court of Audience Register of Comperta 1357–1420 with Chapter act material 1359–1485), fol. 32r.

8. See, for example, Corporation of London Records Office, Letter-Book I, fols. 286r–290r. These date from the early fifteenth century.

9. A great many medieval writers assumed that males and females were in some ways fungible as sex partners. David Lorenzo Boyd, "Disrupting the Norm: Sodomy, Culture, and the Male Body in Peter Damian's *Liber Gomorrhianus*," in *Essays in Medieval Studies*, Vol. 11, ed. Allen J. Frantzen and David J. Robertson (Chicago, 1994), pp. 63–74; Ruth Mazo Karras, "Sexuality and Marginality," in *Peripheral Visions: Reading the Margins in the Middle Ages*, ed. James W. Earl, forthcoming.

10. Bullough and Bullough, *Cross Dressing*, pp. 45–73.

11. Boyd, "Disrupting the Norm," pp. 69–70.

12. For example, Pennsylvania Consolidated Statutes §5902 provides that "A person is guilty of prostitution; a misdemeanor of the third degree, if he or she: (1) is an inmate of a house of prostitution or otherwise engages in sexual activity as a business; or (2) loiters in or within view of any public place for the purpose of being hired to engage in sexual activity." The statute goes on to define several other terms ("inmate," "house of prostitution," "sexual activity"). See B. J. George, "Legal, Medical, and Psychiatric Considerations in the Control of Prostitution," *Michigan Law Review* 60 (1962): 720, on the use of "common prostitute" in U.S. law; for popular understandings of the term see William H. Swatos and Judith A. Klein, "The Lady Is Not a Whore: Labeling the Promiscuous Woman," *International Journal of Women's Studies* 1 (1978): 159–66.

13. In some jurisdictions—York, for example—the ecclesiastical courts did not prosecute women as *meretrices*; rather, they charged them with multiple acts of fornication or adultery, focusing on acts rather than on status but ignoring the issue of money. See Borthwick Institute for Historical Research, MS D/C AB (Dean and Chapter Act Book) 1 (1387–1494).

14. Brundage, *Law, Sex, and Christian Society*, pp. 346, 351–52; Peter Schuster, *Das Frauenhaus: Städtische Bordelle in Deutschland, 1350–1600* (Paderborn, 1992), pp. 145–53; Ruth Mazo Karras, *Common Women: Prostitution and Sexuality in Medieval England* (New York, 1996).

15. Brundage, *Law, Sex, and Christian Society*, pp. 248, 389–90.

16. Ruth Mazo Karras, "The Latin Vocabulary of Illicit Sex in English Ecclesiastical Court Records," *Journal of Medieval Latin* 2 (1992): 6–8.

17. *Thomae de Chobham Summa Confessorum*, ed. F. Broomfield, Analecta Mediaevalia Namurcensia, 25 (Louvain, 1968), pp. 346–47.

18. Siegfried Wenzel, ed., *Fasciculus Morum: A Fourteenth-Century Preacher's Handbook*, (Philadelphia, 1989), p. 669.

19. Ruth Mazo Karras, "The Regulation of Brothels in Later Medieval England," *Signs: Journal of Women in Culture and Society* 14 (1989): 425–26; Karras, *Common Women*.

20. L. R. Poos, "Sex, Lies, and the Church Courts of Pre-Reformation England," *Journal of Interdisciplinary History* 25 (1995): 585–607; Karras, *Common Women*.

21. The case of Rolandino Ronchaia, from fourteenth-century Venice, suggests the same thing: he was a male transvestite working as a prostitute, but he was accused of sodomy, not prostitution (Ruggiero, *Boundaries of Eros*, p. 136).

22. The confusion about whether Rykener's activity amounted to sodomy cannot be entirely resolved by modern scholars, for we do not know what the law of sodomy actually was. Thirteenth-century lawbooks prescribed the death penalty for it, but these are textbooks, not law codes, and actual legislation does not survive, nor do any examples of enforcement of such legislation. See H. G. Richardson and G. O. Sayles, eds., *Fleta*, Selden Society, Vol. 72 (London, 1955), 2:90; Francis Morgan Nichols, ed., *Britton* (Oxford, 1865), 1:42; Boswell, *Christianity, Social Tolerance, and Homosexuality*, pp. 292–93. Examples do, however, survive from other parts of Europe of the harsh punishment of sodomy in the fourteenth and fifteenth centuries, including castration and death. See Goodich, *Unmentionable Vice*, pp.

71–88; Rocke, *Forbidden Friendships*; Ruggiero, *Boundaries of Eros*, pp. 109–45; Elisabeth Pavan, "Police des mœurs, société politique à Venise à la fin du Moyen Age," *Revue Historique* 264 (1980): 241–88; Jacques Chiffoleau, *Les Justices du Pape: délinquance et criminalité dans la région d'Avignon au quatorzième siècle,* Histoire ancienne et médiévale, 14 (Paris, 1984), pp. 191–95; Bariša Krekić, "Abominandum Crimen: Punishment of Homosexuals in Renaissance Dubrovnik," *Viator* 19 (1987): 337–45; Patricia H. Labalme, "Sodomy and Venetian Justice in the Renaissance," *Tijdschrift voor rechtsgeschiedenis/Revue d'histoire du droit* 52 (1984): 217–54. For a slightly later period, cf. Mary Elizabeth Perry, "The 'Nefarious Sin' in Early Modern Seville," in *The Pursuit of Sodomy: Male Homosexuality in Renaissance and Enlightenment Europe,* ed. Kent Gerard and Gert Hekma (New York, 1989), pp. 67–89 (where the *pecado nefando* was clearly anal intercourse); E. William Monter, "Sodomy and Heresy in Early Modern Switzerland," in *Historical Perspectives on Homosexuality,* ed. Salvatore J. Licata and Robert P. Petersen (New York, 1981), pp. 42–55.

23. This is not to say that there was in late medieval Europe no category of "sodomite" based on sexual preference rather than on discrete acts; this is not an issue that legal discourse alone can resolve. See Simon Gaunt, "Straight Minds/'Queer' Wishes in Old French Hagiography: *La Vie de Sainte Euphrosine,*" in *Premodern Sexualities,* ed. Louise Fradenburg and Carla Freccero (New York, 1996), pp. 155–73.

24. Alan Bray, *Homosexuality in Renaissance England* (London, 1982), pp. 67–69.

25. Boyd, "Disrupting the Norm."

26. Thomas Stehling, ed. and trans., *Medieval Latin Poems of Male Love and Friendship* (New York, 1984), pp. 6–7.

27. Boyd, "Disrupting the Norms."

28. Sir Gawain in particular has recently been subject of such analyses. See Carolyn Dinshaw, "A Kiss Is Just a Kiss: Heterosexuality and Its Consolations in *Sir Gawain and the Green Knight,*" *diacritics* 24 (1994): 205–26.

29. Malcolm Andrew and Ronald Waldron, eds., *The Poems of the Pearl Manuscript* (Berkeley, 1978).

30. Monica McAlpine, "The Pardoner's Homosexuality and How It Matters," *PMLA* 95 (1980): 8–22.

31. Glen Burger, "Kissing the Pardoner," *PMLA* 107 (1992): 1143–56.

32. John Boswell, "Revolutions, Universals, and Sexual Categories," in *Hidden from History: Reclaiming the Gay and Lesbian Past,* ed. Martin Duberman, Martha Vicinus, and George Chauncey (New York, 1989), pp. 33–34. See David Halperin, "Sex before Sexuality: Pederasty, Politics, and Power in Classical Athens," in the same volume, on the ancient period, esp. pp. 46–47. For a similar phenomenon in a rather different period see Preben Meulengracht Sørenson, *The Unmanly Man: Concepts of Sexual Defamation in Early Northern Society,* trans. Joan Turville-Petre (Odense, 1983).

33. Judith Butler, *Gender Trouble: Feminism and the Subversion of Identity* (New York, 1990), p. 25. On the applicability of this notion to the Middle Ages, see the essays in *Medieval Feminist Newsletter* 13 (1992).

34. Medieval misogyny also enforced this distinction. See Laura Kendrick, "Transgression, Contamination, and Women in Eustache Deschamps's *Miroir de Mariage,*" *Stanford French Review* 14 (1990): 211–30; Barbara Hanawalt, "Golden Ages for the History of Medieval English Women," in *Women in Medieval History and Historiography,* ed. Susan Mosher Stuard (Philadelphia, 1987), pp. 1–24.

35. On sodomy as "unnatural," see Boswell, *Christianity, Social Tolerance, and Homosexuality,* pp. 303–32. The passive role was typically understood as a type of "gender switch," or inversion from masculine to feminine, throughout the Middle Ages, as well as before and after the period.

36. For example, when Rykener describes being shown to his alleged customers by Elizabeth Brouderer, the record describes him as "*ipsa*" ("she").

37. George Chauncey, "From Sexual Inversion to Homosexuality: Medicine and the Changing Conceptualization of Female Deviance," *Salmagundi* 58/59 (1982–83): 114–46.

38. For the cases that precede and follow, see Thomas, *Calendar of Select Pleas and Memoranda*, Vol. 3, pp. 228–30.

39. We have put in brackets the places where the Latin pronoun used for Rykener is of indeterminate gender, or where we supply a pronoun that the Latin omits. Where we use an unbracketed masculine or feminine pronoun to refer to Rykener, this is because the Latin so specifies. The feminine is only used twice to refer to Rykener, both in indirect speech, so it seems reasonable and consistent to translate the indeterminate pronouns as masculine. We have indicated, however, where we have thus disambiguated the text.

40. Soper's Lane, in Cheap and Cordwainer Wards, ran south from Cheapside. The name probably comes from *soparii,* shopkeepers, not soapmakers. See Mary D. Lobel, ed., *The City of London from Prehistoric Times to c. 1520,* Vol. 3 of *The British Atlas of Historic Towns* (Oxford, 1989), p. 94.

41. Since this language is stronger than that used to refer to prostitution in the legal records, it probably refers to sodomy here. See Karras, *Common Women,* ch. 3, for the legal language employed in reference to prostitutes. On the unmentionability of sodomy, see David Lorenzo Boyd, *Sodomy, Silence, and Social Control: Queer Theory and Medieval Texts,* n.d.

42. This may not be a surname but a byname for an embroideress. She may be the same woman as Elizabeth, wife of Henry Moryng, who was convicted in 1385 of bawdry for taking on young women as apprentice embroideresses and then prostituting them. Elizabeth Moryng lived in Broad Street Ward, in the parish of All Hallows Next the Wall, and Elizabeth Brouderer ten years later lived nearby, outside Bishopsgate. Corporation of London Records Office, Letter-Book H, fol. 194; English translation in H. T. Riley, *Memorials of London and London Life* (London, 1868), p. 484.

43. In Essex, near Epping.

44. The title "Dominus" or "Sir" was commonly used for priests. No William Foxlee (or any other Foxlee at that date) is found in A. B. Emden, *A Biographical Register of the University of Oxford to A.D. 1500* (Oxford, 1957–59).

45. Tapsters were often connected with prostitution, and indeed taverns were suspect places for this reason. See P. J. P. Goldberg, "Women in Fifteenth-Century Town Life," in *Towns and Townspeople in the Fifteenth Century,* ed. J. A. F. Thompson (Gloucester, 1988), p. 118.

46. Beaconsfield in Berkshire.

47. St. Margaret Pattens in Tower Ward, between Fanchurch Street and East Cheap.

GENDER AND GENERATION

Representing Reproduction in Early Modern England

MARY FISSELL

The human body has been an almost infinitely flexible symbolic resource; historians and anthropologists analyse the multitude of ways in which the body has been construed in terms of politics, religion, sexuality and social structure. The body is at once both intensely individual and a collective representation, an image of the social world shared by its inhabitants.[1] However, these representations are not fixed or stable; they are made and remade in response to specific circumstances and are often contested across multiple realms. The act of imagining one's body is a kind of drawing together of these kinds of representations, negotiating amongst images and meanings particular to one's historical circumstance. By asking questions about the processes by which people came to understand and interpret their bodies, about the cultural materials from which bodies were constructed, we can begin to develop a history of the body which accounts for multiple meanings, which illuminates the ways in which the body is always being remade.

Attention to cultural materials which provide a repertoire for making bodies might enable early modern historians to develop interpretations which avoid some of the totalizing impulses of pioneering work on *the* history of *the* body. The scholarship of Bakhtin, Elias and Foucault invented "the body" as a topic for historical study, but a desire to emphasize the alien qualities and strangeness of early modern bodies (an emphasis explicable in terms of the need to historicize the previously ahistorical human body) created a very general and implicitly male early modern body. One of the aims of this paper is to explore how we might understand cultural constructions of female bodies in a specific historical context, that of seventeenth- and early-eighteenth-century England. Nor should we see constructions of those bodies as simply products or outcomes of historical change; the relationship is a more dynamic one. Discussions of female bodies were important sites for reimagining and renegotiating not just the bodies themselves but the social and cultural worlds in which bodies were constituted.

The materials from which seventeenth- and eighteenth-century English women and men made their views of bodies were probably extensive: devotional works and religious practices, ballads, exhibits of monsters, public executions, and a host of others. Among these were popular health texts: manuals of medicine specifically addressed to a lay audience. Hundreds of these books were published in the later seventeenth and eighteenth centuries, propelled into print in the 1640s as a part of a revolutionary anti-monopoly movement, and sustained, it seems, by emerging middle-class patterns of consumption.[2]

These texts provide us with a set of discourses about bodies which claimed to be for a broad audience.[3] As I will argue, these bodies are both natural and social; the childbearing guides I analyse connect sex and gender in complex ways. An analysis of these texts provides a vernacular counterpoint to studies such as that of Thomas Laqueur, which focus largely on texts produced by and for a social elite. Laqueur argues that very long continuities in a "one-sex" model of the body persist from classical antiquity until the late eighteenth century. In this model, the burden of sexual difference rests not in the body (male and female bodies are only slight variants of each other), but in society. However, any analysis which seeks to go from the Greeks to Freud must choose continuity over complexity and contest.[4]

Descriptions of bodies in childbearing guides suggest a more complex interpretation of sex and gender in early modern England than Laqueur's synoptic vision permits. The ways in which these texts inscribe power relationships on the body are related to other forms of prescriptive literature, such as the conduct book. Indeed, conduct books of the later seventeenth century make explicit the prescriptions implicit in popular health texts. In other words, rather than reading popular medical books as some kind of watered-down science or medicine, they can be understood as parallel to other domestic works such as conduct books and works of household devotion. It is in these domestic discourses of difference that significant shifts in gender roles and relations were rehearsed and articulated in late seventeenth- and early-eighteenth-century England.

Childbearing guides are a part of a set of discourses about womanhood which have been somewhat overlooked.[5] The functions of such prescriptive literature—works of popular devotion, conduct books, and popular health guides—are still poorly understood, but these are the works which seem to have enjoyed great popularity in their own day. In order to understand how gender functioned politically and culturally, we need to explore what made these discourses so compelling.

One of the ways in which popular health texts talked about gender relations in an indirect but powerful way was in their use of elaborate systems of metaphor in discussions of sex and reproduction. Emily Martin's *The Woman in the Body* provides a model for looking at the ways in which reproduction is imagined through systems of metaphor and analogy today.[6] For a historian, however, understanding the meanings of metaphorical systems presents interpretive problems different from those facing an anthropologist studying her own culture. I use other kinds of evidence, such as proverbs and dictionaries of slang, which seventeenth- and eighteenth-century writers labelled as common or popular knowledge, in order to contextualize and make sense of metaphors in popular health texts.[7] Such a strategy, of course, runs the risk of seeming to reify a category of "popular culture," but without context, these metaphors remain opaque or seemingly timeless.[8] Although some late-seventeenth-century scientific and medical writers criticized the use of metaphor, claiming that figurative language was imprecise, childbearing guides use a great deal of metaphor and analogy.[9]

In post-1650 English childbearing guides, three overlapping sets of metaphors dominate discussions of reproduction. Figures of speech are drawn from arable farming, from orchard keeping, and from craft work. Many popular health manuals are quite derivative, so that certain patterns of metaphor are repeated and repeated from text to text.

Both grain-growing and fruit-growing metaphors often employed a two-seed (male and female seeds) model of conception, although one seed was usually predominant. From classical antiquity through the seventeenth century, two different theories of generation were common. Some medical writers argued that both parents contributed seeds for conception (the two-seed model) while other writers claimed that only males contributed seed (the one-seed model).[10]

Both Jane Sharp and Nicholas Culpeper employed the grain metaphor. Sharp said, "The Yard [the penis] is as it were the Plow wherewith the ground is tilled, and made fit for production." Culpeper deployed another layer of metaphor, comparing the active female seed to the Moon, which made the earth fertile.[11] Culpeper's Paracelsian and astrological style of thought imbued the Moon with these special powers. However, his seed analogies had many other resonances, and I doubt that the Paracelsian aspects of his work were significant to many of his readers.

Other writers emphasized male seed. John Maubray put it this way: "as the SEED of plants requires the Matrix of the Earth, to nourish it well, and safely defend it; so doth that SEMINAL Virtue of Men, [require] the Womb."[12] These male-seed metaphors depicted the infertile womb as infertile ground: Henry Bracken referred to "wet marshy moist ground, which rots the seed"; John Maubray compared scarred wombs to stony ground, and Jane Sharp made the analogy of a barren womb to a quagmire or dry sand.[13]

This agrarian metaphor moved from the world of the imagination to that of action. Both Sharp and Culpeper advocated diagnostic procedures which made an analogy between grain and fertility. For example, if a woman wanted to know if she were pregnant, she was to water a kernel of grain with her urine; if it grew, she was pregnant.[14] Determining infertility was accomplished similarly: grain was watered with the man's and the woman's urine, and whoever's grain did not sprout was the infertile one.[15]

Making an analogy between human reproduction and seeds or grain goes back to antiquity. However, metaphors such as these are reconstrued over time. For instance, the meanings of "seed" are different for me, a twentieth-century urban gardener who buys flower and vegetable seeds in colorful packets, than for an individual living in the largely agrarian economy of seventeenth-century England, an economy only recently free of subsistence crises.

In reconstructing some of the potential meanings of "seed" for a seventeenth-century man or woman, two areas are particularly significant: Biblical references and agricultural commonplaces. For example, the parables of the mustard seed and of the sower who cast his seed upon different kinds of ground might be recognized by churchgoers or Bible-readers. The agrarian analogies also drew upon a common store of agricultural knowledge, expressed in proverbs, almanacs, directions for planting, and the like. Contemporary proverbs include "He that sows good seed shall reap good corn"; "he that sows thistles shall reap prickles"; "Such seed such harvest," and the Biblical "as they sow so let them reap."[16] These analogies stressed the close relation between seed and plant, or parent and offspring, rendering pregnancy and gestation an ordinary and predictable process.

Another set of agricultural metaphors made analogies to fruit trees, comparing gestation to fruiting. John Maubray used this fruit metaphor to structure most of his discussion. In early months of pregnancy, women were to take care of themselves because the embryo was delicate: "the *Fruit* of her *WOMB*; especially in the *First Months*, . . . may be justly compar'd to the tender BLOSSOMS of *Trees,* which are easily blasted, or shaken-off."[17] Many aspects of generation lent themselves to this set of analogies, and often there are so many kinds of relationships between parts of the body and parts of trees, fruit and flowers, that no fully coherent and consistent analogy was developed; rather a range of images could be invoked. The tip of the penis, the glans, was said to resemble a nut or acorn. As Jane Sharp put it, "The Nut of the Yard, when it is half covered with the foreskin, looks like an Acorn in the Cup, and therefore some call it Glans, which in Latin signifies an Acorn."[18] This acorn was compared to the mouth of the womb in a slightly imperfect Galenic inside/outside analogy.[19]

Metaphors of trees, flowers, and fruit played upon anatomical names. The testicles were widely referred to as "stones," which then as now might mean the pits of fruit such as peaches and plums. Some writers noted that women's terms, or menstruation, were known as flowers because fruit followed.[20] The entrance to the vagina was frequently described in floral terms. Both Culpeper and Sharp refer to it as like "a rose half-blown"; Sharp adds that it is like a clove-gilliflower (a pink or carnation). Both note that this anatomical detail is why the loss of virginity is called deflowering.[21]

This network of metaphors and allusions to trees, flowers and fruit alluded to figures of speech already in common parlance. Proverbs include: "an evil tree brings forth ill fruit"; "the tree is known by the fruit"; "such as the tree is such as the fruit."[22] Indeed, Jane Sharp used a variant of the proverb "such as the tree is such as the fruit" to persuade her readers of the truth of her remarks. In a discussion on the care of infants and the selection of a wet nurse, she said, "If a Nurse be well-complexioned her milk cannot be ill; for a Fig-Tree bears not Thistles: a good Tree will bring forth good Fruit."[23] Satirical or parodic writers referred to the penis as "arbor vitae" or trees of life, and the expression "to be tied to the sowre-apple tree" meant to be married to a bad husband.[24]

Aside from proverbs, and the biblical resonances of being fruitful and multi-plying, not to mention the tree of knowledge, there is another cultural referent which gave this set of metaphors a special edge. The tree of life was also the tree of death; in dictionaries of slang, proverbs and jokes, the tree is emblematic of Tyburn Tree and death by hanging. Many expressions allude to the connections between life's beginning and life's end on the gallows, making connections between sexuality and death. "Marriage and hanging go by destiny." "Better half-hanged than ill-wed" went two proverbs.[25] The many punning ways of referring to hanging, such as "you'll ride a horse that was foaled of an acorn," underline these connections.[26]

Both the tree and the grain metaphors make women's bodies into landscapes. The histories of "mother nature," "mother earth," the feminizing of landscape which Annette Kolodny called "the lay of the land," are long and complex.[27] Carole Fabricant has analyzed how Augustan gardens played upon images of the female, making landscape highly gendered. The land was a woman, a woman tamed and controlled, alluring and erotic. Men planted, constructed, and enclosed her in ways congruent with cultural expectations of women's behav-ior.[28] It is difficult to know how this set of metaphors, based upon aristocratic practices, related directly to views of the body held by other groups. These metaphors which linked women's bodies to landscapes can also be found in pornography; Charles Cotton's *Erotopolis,* published in 1684, is the first erotic cartography in English. Again, however, this literature was composed for a lim-ited readership, and making connections to wider audiences is problematic.[29]

The third set of analogies related generation to craft processes. These com-parisons varied from building to alchemy, but tended to center on a vaguely defined sequence of concoction, storage, and construction. Various analogies were made to explain the actual process by which seed was made from blood. Most writers understood this as a process of concoction, the seed "being per-fected and thoroughly concocted by the heat and force of the Stones."[30] Jane Sharp compared seed making to alchemy: "by which means they (the stones) draw as a Limbeck the matter of seed from the whole body."[31] In other words, seed was distilled from blood in an alembic.

Once the seed was made, it was stored up in the carrying vessels. In Sharp's explanation, it was kept in "storehouses" so that "the whole should not be wasted in one act."[32] Even Pierre Dionis, a French writer translated into English, who explicitly criticized this craft-process analogy, found himself employing it when he discussed seed. When it came to storing seed, he called the *vesiculae seminales* "Conservatories of Seed" in which "this part of the Seed is laid up for use." When a man was sexually excited, passion made the seed "frisk up and down in their Reservatories."[33] These commercial metaphors for male seed carry a different value than those describing female reproduction. A common slang term for women's genitals was the word "commodity," conveying a very different image to that of the thrifty male saving up his seed in warehouses.[34]

The craft analogy also became more elaborate when applied to the inside of women's bodies. The very word used to describe the womb—the matrix—had resonances of this explanation of generation. Sharp described how male and female seeds mix: "the Matrix contracts itself and so closely embraceth it, being greedy to perfect this work, that by succession of time she stirs up the formative faculty which lieth in the seed and brings it into act, which was before but in possibility, this is the natural property of the womb to make prolifick seed fruitful."[35] The word "matrix" played upon both craft and agriculture. A matrix was a place where something was produced, either minerals in rocks or new plants in the earth. A matrix was also a mould used for casting or shaping metal; in printing, it referred to the piece of metal punched with a letter which served as a mould for type. In some of these meanings, the matrix does not have creative powers itself—it forms a substance or causes a seed to sprout, but as a kind of faculty. In others, such as the above quote from Sharp, the matrix assumes a greater role, "being greedy to perfect this work."

John Maubray, in his discussion of how monsters are formed, employed a rich and detailed version of the craft metaphor:

> such as have been in Glass-Works and have seen Glasses made, may readily comprehend how Monsters are formed in the Womb: For in modeling the Glass, if the Work-Man blow the Pipe too much or too strongly, the Stuff is so extended, that the Glass becomes both longer and wider than its due proportionable Form; and so it may also happen in the Womb, by an immoderate Action, or too great an Extension or Diffusion of the Seminal Spirit.[36]

Here the phallic actions of the glassblower are center stage; the womb is merely the background.[37]

What kinds of concerns, beliefs, practices were articulated through these discussions of craft, flowers and grain? How do body and culture fit? Part of the answer to these questions lies in the fact that the agricultural and manufacturing processes by which generation was understood were masculine ones in early modern England. Plowing and sowing grain was male work, although women harvested and gleaned. Generation was not compared to, for example, gardening.[38] Women gardened, growing vegetables and herbs for family and market. The care of orchards, again, was by and large a male activity. In the realm of manufacture, most processes still took place within the home, but childbearing guides usually characterize the workers as male. Processes such as casting metal and glassblowing were likely to be male preserves.[39]

However, these systems of male-thematized metaphor were not timeless.[40] In general, pre-1650 childbearing guides are quite varied in their format and contents; male-work analogies common to post-1650 health texts were not necessarily predominant in earlier texts, nor were a few systems of metaphor clearly dominant.[41] Eucharius Roeslin's *The Birth of Man-Kinde* was published in German in 1513, translated into English in 1540 and reprinted frequently up to the 1630s; it appears to have been the most reprinted childbearing guide in English before the 1650s.[42] Its format is similar to later guides, but the metaphorical systems it employs to explain reproduction are different. Three examples illustrate how Roeslin, aided by his English translator, employed a more female-based imagery.

First, activities within a mother's body are often characterized in terms of a female Nature. In discussing the functions of menstruation, Roeslin says, "prudent Lady nature full wisely hath provided, that there should always be present and ready a continuall course and resort of bloud in the vaynes of the matrix, as a very natural course, spring, fountaine or well, ready to arrouse, water and nourish." [43] Even if a woman never conceives, "yet there is no fault in Nature, who hath prepared a place and food to be at all times in readinesse."[44] In other words, a woman's reproductive functions are a kind of synecdoche for her social role; in reproduction, as in a household, women are responsible for preparing food and drink and providing hospitality.

Second, rather than comparing seed-making to agricultural or commercial processes, Roeslin employs a mining metaphor. This mine, however, is very much a female domain: "And heere yee shall understand, that most commonly alwayes when nature is disposed to make a transmutation of any matter, that can shee not do, unlesse she have a mine, shop or a workhouse, wherein continual circulation of the matter transmutable, shee may bring her purpose to passe."[45] Thus, just as metals are formed in mines in the earth, seeds are formed in men and women.

Third, Roeslin compares reproduction with other bodily processes. For example, making seeds is not the only "mine" in the body: the liver, heart and brain also act as mines, making blood and spirits.[46] So too, making seed is rather like digestion, where the juices of food are somehow transmuted into blood.[47] Digestion is neither male nor female work; in this instance, by equating reproduction with other body functions, Roeslin makes reproduction gender-neutral.

By making processes within women's bodies un-mysterious, just like processes which happened every day in every English village or town, the later sets of metaphors diminished women's unique and quasi-magical powers of reproduction. In the seventeenth century, childbirth was still associated with various kinds of supernatural powers. For example, women were "churched" after they got up from their month's lying-in after childbirth. Although the Anglican church understood this ceremony as one of thanksgiving, it is clear that there were connotations of powerful pollution connected with the new mother, who might cause grass to die if she stepped on it in her un-churched state. So too, some childbirth products, such as the caul, had supernatural powers associated with them. Systems of male-thematized metaphors about reproduction suppressed female connotations of power and mystery.[48]

These systems also denied the femaleness of reproduction, recasting it as a male process. There was nothing that special about planting seeds or orchard keeping or concoction. Female anatomy and physiology was not just an inferior version of male, as the Galenic model indicated.[49] Women's bodies were spaces in which masculine activity reigned. As Culpeper described it, a scarred womb was like a ill workman: "you know a Man that is sick or wounded, cannot Work, tho' his Work be beside him."[50] Finally, of course, these sets of metaphors made women passive in reproductive terms. They were the ground, the earth, the raw material, which male action transformed into life itself.

Masculinist metaphors shaded into misogyny. Pierre Dionis compared a childless woman "to a dry Tree which bears no Fruit, but is pull'd up by the Roots, and cast into the Fire."[51] Within the churchgoing population, this metaphor called up visions of being cast into the flames of hell itself as a punishment for not reproducing. As a proverb had it, "Old maids would lead apes in hell" because they had not had children since they had refused to marry.[52] The infertile woman's lot on earth was no better. Where a woman had no children, "the Husband (like a Gard'ner) is at no pains to cultivate the Tree which yields him no Fruit."[53] Metaphors of women's passive role in reproduction thus shaded into claims that women existed to make men's children.

Another example of the ways in which the female body was reimagined in terms of male activity lies in the story of the vagina. Before 1682, English child-bearing guides do not refer to the vagina at all. Instead, they conceptualize women's interior parts of reproduction as the womb, the mouth of the womb (which we would call the cervix) and the neck of the womb (which we would call the vagina).[54] For example, Roeslin describes reproductive anatomy thus: "The necke of this wombe, otherwise called the woman's privitie, we call the wombe passage, or the privie passage."[55] However, the neck of the womb was gradually reconceptualized as a sheath whose function was to receive the penis. The word "vagina" was used in English for the first time in 1682, taken directly from the Latin word for sheath. In the words of Dionis' translator (1719), it "receives the Sword of the Male, and becomes a case to it, and therefore is call'd the Vagina, that is to say, its sheath."[56] By 1740, *The Ladies Dispensatory* recasts "the neck of the womb" in solely sexual terms: "The Sheath is so called because it receives the virile member like a sheath . . . it embraces the Yard . . . the Sheath is so artificially made, that it can suit with Virile member of any Man."[57] This shift in terminology was thus part of the gradual reconstruction of an anatomical part, from the neck of the womb, an important part of women's reproductive anatomy, to the vagina or sheath, the part of women anatomically constructed for men's pleasure.

In dictionaries of slang, expressions for women's private parts echo this construction of the female body for male pleasure. Among the many terms for women's genitals, a dictionary of slang recorded "cock alley" or "cock lane," "mantrap" and "Miss Laycock."[58] The male construction of the female body is revealed in other expressions. For example, "to be in a man's beef" meant to stab him with a sword; "to be in a woman's beef" meant to have sex with her.[59] This complex connection of swords and sheaths, sex and violence, suggests to me some darker implications of male-thematized metaphors used to describe the female body.

Thus the invention of the vagina *per se* is part of the larger process by which the insides of women's bodies are reimagined through masculine activities. This type of representation of reproductive processes is a way in which childbearing guides can be interpreted as discussions of gender relations. These representations of reproduction were read in the context of the explicit directives concerning gender roles, family, and household contained in conduct books. In order to trace how a system of gender assignment worked, how social and cultural prescriptions about male and female were encoded in imaginings of the body itself, we need to turn to those prescriptions.

Conduct books are a form of didactic literature which lacks a modern equivalent. They addressed a wide range of behaviour—far greater than a modern book on etiquette or manners—prescribing appropriate conduct for children and parents, husbands and wives, masters and apprentices.[60] They were also, it seems, very popular: many different ones survive, and the bestsellers among them were printed, pirated and reprinted. Of course, like popular health texts, they are prescriptive. We cannot directly read actual behaviour from their advice.

Conduct books and popular health texts shared a number of conventions of prescriptive literature. Often their titles indicate this relationship: John Sadler's *The Sicke Womans Private Looking-Glasse* (1636) employs one of the most common rhetorical devices of conduct literature, the "mirror" or "looking-glass" figure of speech. Conversely, the title of John Shirley's conduct book, *The Accomplisht Ladies Rich Closet,* draws upon household advice and health literature and contains recipes as well as precepts for behaviour. Robert Codrington's *Decency in Conversation Amongst Women* (1664) has a similar overlap, containing recipes for domestic remedies, advice on surgery, chapters on conduct, and sample letters for specific social situations.

In conduct books from the 1640s to the 1710s, three related themes are repeated. First, a woman's sexuality is made central to her virtue: any failing of a woman is a sexual failing. Second, women's virtue, linked to sexuality, is central to the nation's political stability. Finally, women are repeatedly counselled about their appearance, told that they should avoid cosmetics and rich clothing: that the appearance of vice was vice itself. These preoccupations were to become significant to a religious revival in the later seventeenth century, which took institutionalized form in the 1690s (the reformation of manners movement), but they date from at least the 1650s.[61] Of course, chastity is a sempiternal theme in advice directed to women.[62] The crucial shift involves the consequences of women's sexuality: where once individual men were at risk because of women's sexual rapacity, here women's sexuality threatens all men because it harbors potential unrest.

Any female fault could be cast in sexual terms. Drunkenness: "she who is first a prostitute to wine, will soon be to lust also."[63] Gossip: "revealing secrets . . . is a kind of incontinence of the mind."[64] Curiosity: "Every indecent curiosity, or impure fancy, is a deflowering of the mind and the least corruption of them gives some degrees of defilement to the body, too."[65] Fearlessness: "it is requisite for them [women] to stand upon their Guard continually . . . since they carry a Treasure . . . she that is without fear, is as a Town without a Wall, as easie to take, as it is hard to keep."[66] If all female sins were sexualized, then all of women's virtue depended upon chastity. A 1707 text summed it up for women: "chastity, above all, is so Essential and Natural to our Sex, that every Declination from it, is a proportionable receding from Womanhood."[67]

In comparison, conduct manuals from the early seventeenth century do not emphasize the dangers of female sexuality in the same way. For instance, William Gouge's *Of Domesticall Duties* takes as its central theme the importance of wives' submission to their husbands. For Gouge, the failings of a wife were almost always failures of submission. Refusing to join one's husband when called for, or journeying abroad against his will, or ordering servants to perform tasks he had forbidden, or fulfilling a wife's duty to be obedient but doing so in a sullen manner—these were the dangers women posed to men and to marriage.[68]

If Gouge's central theme is submission, William Whately's *A Bride-Bush: Or Directions for Married Persons* repeatedly alludes to themes of adultery and fornication. Whately's first duty of marriage is chastity, a mutual responsibility of husband and wife, and Whately often focuses upon male sexuality. For instance, when Whately discusses temperance as essential to chastity, he only discusses husbands and states that, "Fulness of bread will make a man a Sodomite."[69] Whately's text illustrates that early-seventeenth-century conduct books which emphasized the dangers of sexuality might focus on men or women.

In contrast, after midcentury, the emphasis was on female sexuality. Indeed, women's sexual sins struck at the nation itself in a way that men's did not. Adultery, according to A. M., was not only a contravention of one of the ten commandments, "but maliciously strikes at the Root, and aims at the destruction of the Society to which you belong."[70] A. M. set out to discuss the sins of the nation and then confined himself to fornication, adultery, incest and rape.[71] For A. M., as for other authors, political stability rested upon women's sexual virtue, because adultery created wrongful heirs.[72] Comments such as these had powerful resonances in the late seventeenth century. Inheritance and legitimate succession had been troubled issues since the execution of Charles I, if not earlier. Charles II was succeeded by his brother since he and his wife had had no children. Subsequently, the Glorious Revolution involved deposing the ruling monarch, replacing him with his daughter and her husband. As Rachel Weil has analyzed, the controversy surrounding the so-called warming-pan baby rehearsed these themes with specific reference to the Queen's sexual virtue; political discourse employed metaphors of family relations and vice versa.[73] More generally, these issues about legitimate succession were played out in a context where the specter of political instability raised its head again and again, in incidents such as the Popish Plot, the Exclusion Crisis, and Monmouth's Rebellion.

If the nation's fate rested upon its women's virtue, that virtue depended upon appearances. Conduct-book writers claimed that a woman's appearance was an infallible guide to her moral status: in the words of John Shirley, "by the Motion of the Body, the Thoughts of the Mind may be discovered."[74] Again and again, conduct books chided women on their use of makeup and their fondness for fancy clothing.[75] Women's attention to their own appearances was linked to their desires to be outside the home, in some kind of public space.[76] Robert Codrington allowed that a few women might do some good by appearing in public, but then he continued by faulting others:

> they give too much and too loose Reins to Liberty, making Pleasure their Vocation, as if they were created for no other ends, than to dedicate the first fruits of the Morning to their Looking-glass, and the Remainder of it to the Exchange. The Artificial Colour is no sooner laid on their faces, but the Play-Bills for that Day must be brought unto her by her Pensioner whom she keeps in Constant pay for that Purpose; her Eye views it and reviews it, and out of her Female Judgement, she makes choice of one which she is resolved to see, purposely to be seen.[77]

Here a woman's toilette was directly linked to her desire to appear in public, and conduct writers instructed that women should not desire to be in public places. One observed that if women were not allowed "sumptuous attire" they would shun the public realm: "Truly if we take away from most Women their precious Ornaments, they will voluntarily and willingly stay at home."[78] Nor should they enjoy the pleasures of spectatorship. As Nancy Armstrong has noted, it is not that women were faulted for their modes of recreation; they were faulted for pursuing that recreation outside the home, in public.[79]

Another conduct writer compared women to bees, reiterating the idea that women's place was in the home:

> I would have Wives to imitate the Ringleaders of Bees, who know, receive and preserve whatsoever is placed within their Hives, and, until the necessity of their concerns shall otherwise require, they are always present with their Honey-combs, that they may be exquisitely and maturely perfected: Wives may send abroad their men and maide-servants if they perceive it will be advantageous to them.[80]

By 1705, William Fleetwood was able to argue that women's sole function in civilized countries was, "for the solace of mankind, the care of some domestick Matters, and the continuance of the World." In other words, women's functions were purely domestic and reproductive.[81]

Nor was this attack on women in public a timeless feature of conduct literature. Richard Brathwait, author of one of the most influential conduct books of the early seventeenth century, advised wives that it was not "sufficient to bee onely an Housekeeper, or Snaile-like, to bee still under roofe."[82] Brathwait, although condemning women's attendance at theaters and other idle amusements, encouraged worthy women to take a public role: "in my Judgement . . . a modest and wellbehaved woman may by her frequent resort to publike places conferre no less benefit to such as observe her behaviour; than occasion a profit to her private family."[83] But by the latter half of the century, virtuous women did not belong in public places; modest and chaste women were not supposed to care about their personal appearances or desire to appear in public.

Thus, both popular childbearing guides and conduct books share certain crucial features. In different ways, both discourses hinge upon male assertions of control over female sexuality. In imagining reproduction as a simple male process, popular health texts attempted to diminish women's unique reproductive powers and define the female body around male pleasure. Conduct books explicitly circumscribed women's activities, making political stability dependent upon female sexual virtue and forbidding women to enter public spaces. In other words, these are parallel recastings of gender relationships in post–civil war England.

Much remains to be written of seventeenth-century women's history; what follows is suggestive rather than specific. In general terms, there is a something of a consensus that "things got worse" for women over the course of the seventeenth and eighteenth centuries. Whether we follow Hilda Smith and Katherine Rogers in looking at elite women who articulated (or did not articulate) various kinds of feminisms, or we take the well-travelled but not fully superseded path of Alice Clark in exploring women's waged work, the picture is one of fewer options and declining status for the female sex.[84] My analysis of the languages of sex and reproduction in the late seventeenth century can be understood in part as an exploration of this "decline." However, I want to find ways to move beyond a general (and problematic) assessment of female status to look more closely at specific kinds of gender relations, which have their own chronologies and patterns.[85] In particular, I want to suggest some contexts for the reconstruction of gender relations which I have outlined in conduct books and childbearing guides.

Three related contexts suggest potential sources of tensions or concerns which fostered a reshaping of gender relations. First, events during the English civil war abolished parts of the customary framework which sustained family life at the village level. Church courts, which provided some regulation of sexual behaviour, were closed. For three years, marriages were no longer solemnized in churches, but were performed by a civil functionary; nor were women churched after they had borne children. In other words, institutions and practices which underwrote certain kinds of family structures were shaken up.[86] Historians have focused upon affective relationships within the seventeenth-century family. Here I am more interested in social modes of representation of the family, of the moments and ceremonies which embodied and reproduced "the family" as a cultural institution (and, of course, reproduced certain kinds of gendered authority within the family which historians who focus on questions about emotional relationships within the family tend to overlook).

Second, gender roles were contested in the context of religion. As Phyllis Mack, Diane Purkiss, Christine Berg, Phillippa Berry and others have explored, in the 1640s and 1650s women began to preach and prophesy all over the country. Such public transgressions of usual gender roles represented, as these historians have variously argued, a powerful questioning of traditional hierarchy. Many small independent congregations which flourished in the 1640s allowed women to debate and to vote. In the 1650s, the new sect of the Quakers accorded women and men equal status in church government. These religious movements granted women a form of authority outside the usual sphere of the household, one which transcended fathers, husbands and brothers.[87]

Third, women took direct political action in ways largely unprecedented in early modern England. Although women had long participated in local food riots and the like, in 1642 and 1643 a group of women petitioned Parliament, arguing that the war had destroyed trade and hence their livelihoods. Thousands of women held the members of the House of Commons virtual prisoners for several hours until dispersed by force of arms. In 1649, wives of the Levellers petitioned, claiming ten thousand women's signatures and denying that they were represented by their husbands who had already attempted to negotiate with Parliament. They defended their actions citing a Biblical precedent in Esther and a historical one in medieval British women who had helped defeat the Danes.[88] The profusion of pamphlet literature in the 1640s and 1650s made actions like these nationwide spectacles rather than local disturbances.

In other words, the world turned upside down was not without its significances for gender relations.[89] Perhaps the term "backlash" is too freighted with contemporary meaning, but some of the ways in which male authority was reinscribed upon female bodies in the later seventeenth century were, I suggest, related to the experiences of the 1640s and 1650s.[90] Similarly, a new concern about women in public places can be read as a reassertion of men's governance of a public realm. In other words, the trends I see in conduct books and childbearing guides can be partly understood in terms of a desire, identified in other realms by other historians, to bury the past, to subdue faction and dissent of all kinds.

However, the creation of male-centered representations of reproduction was not uncontested or monolithic. On the most basic level, women who were literate were still reading copies of Roeslin's *The Birth of Mankind*.[91] Women, literate or not, were still chuckling at ballads which portrayed men as ignorant of basic facts of reproduction.[92] Nor can we assume that female or male readers of childbearing guides read those texts in the ways their authors intended.[93]

A closer look at the work of Jane Sharp, the only known female author of an English midwifery guide before the 1730s, suggests some of the potential for contest and resistance. The power of a male-thematized metaphorical system for representing the female body is underlined by Sharp's reliance upon it. However, her use of metaphor suggests that she was not unaware of the multiple meanings of this female body. She plays with this model, using it for purposes unlike those of male writers. Sharp's work is all the more interesting because she based most of her text upon Culpeper's *Directory for Midwives,* first published two decades earlier.

First, Sharp takes the languages of agriculture and craft and makes them serve to praise women's bodies. She says explicitly that women have nothing to be ashamed about in their own bodies and then reinforces her message in her poetic descriptions. She compares women's nipples to strawberries and women's genitals to classical landscapes.[94] She writes, "therefore these wings are called Nymphs, because they joyn the passage of the Urine, and the neck of the Womb, out of which as out of Fountains, whereof the Nymphs were called Goddesses, waters and humours do flow, and besides in them is all the joy and delight of Venus."[95] At times, these descriptions seem to verge on parody, but whether they are intended to be read straightforwardly or with a tinge of irony, women's anatomy is praiseworthy.

Next, in a deft rhetorical move, Sharp subverts the craft metaphor by changing the sex of the craft worker. First she says that "the seed is the workmaster which makes the infant." Six pages later, the workman has become a female nature: "nature is not a minute idle in her work" and the fetus is once again the product of female capacity.[96]

In addition, Sharp occasionally employs humor to deflate male definitions of the female body. She describes the neck of the womb as "a fit sheath to receive the Yard," following Culpeper and others in making this analogy, but retaining the concept of the neck of the womb. She goes on to make fun of men's thoughts about the sheath analogy. A Frenchman, she tells us, complained because when he was young, his wife's sheath was tight-fitting, but now it was as capacious as a sack. Sharp counters, "Perhaps the fault was not the woman but his own, his weapon shrunk and was too little for the scabbard."[97] Such comments afforded a female reader an occasional snicker at the expense of the male-thematized model of the female body.

Finally, Sharp provides the only analogy for reproduction based on female work. She compares conception to milk coagulating. In doing so, she is utilizing a widespread metaphor which dated back to Aristotle, who compared conception to cheese making.[98] In Sharp's time, dairying and cheese making were very largely female work.[99] Although Sharp does not elaborate this figure of speech, it is suggestive that she is the only writer to provide an analogy for conception drawn from women's work.

In the way that she reworks Culpeper's images, it seems to me that Jane Sharp provides us with hints of a woman's response to the construction of a particular female body. Sharp's humour and self-conscious parody hint that she saw some of the implications of writing about reproduction as though it were a male process. Given the paucity of women's writing on the mechanics of generation, these suggestions about the spaces for resistance must remain possibilities rather than fully realized alternate perceptions.

Popular health texts purveyed a natural knowledge which was rich in meaning, which drew upon cultural commonplaces and played with everyday expressions. Both popular health texts and conduct books explored questions about the relationships of women and men within the family. Where conduct books were explicit about the proper roles for mothers and fathers, husbands and wives, popular health texts described male and female bodies in ways that made social categories into natural ones. While nature is always being made into culture and vice versa, the ways in which body and society or sex and gender are connected are historically specific. Here I have argued that social and political turmoil in seventeenth-century England helped to produce a female body which could be imagined in ways that defined gender relationships that underwrote the stability of family and polity.

However, this female body was not universal or hegemonic. First, metaphors which related agriculture to pregnancy were age-old; I have argued that these metaphors had particular resonances in the seventeenth and eighteenth centuries. But metaphor is always a comparison which works both ways, and it is always unstable. Nor can we be certain that the kinds of contextual readings I have made here had much purchase in their own time. Second, as I noted at the outset, imagining one's own body is both an intensely personal and a social act. This paper has explored one set of materials available to early modern English men and women when they envisioned the processes of reproduction. Although childbearing guides were a significant resource, they were by no means the only source. Finally, Jane Sharp's work reminds us that, even within a coherent set of images, multiple readings and interpretations were always possible.

Seeing the female body in this specific historical context, however contested and problematic, also makes the early modern relationship between sex and gender more complicated and perhaps more interesting than some historians have suggested. The relationship between sex and gender rehearsed in these childbearing guides was neither that which we recognize today nor was it that which Laqueur has outlined as the "one-sex" model. The sex/gender system we often employ today implies a distinction between biological sexual difference and the cultural elaboration of that difference; biology and culture are separate domains, but cultural difference is grounded in biological difference.[100] The system which Laqueur has postulated for the early modern period puts the burden of sexual difference squarely on society; he argues that biological sexual difference was a matter of degree rather than kind and that therefore it could not serve as the foundation for gender relations.

This exploration of childbearing guides suggests that the relationship between sex and gender was not fixed but was being negotiated and worked out. The ways in which bodily difference could be connected to culture were multiple. Medical discourses could be read as moral discourses, making the body into an exemplum of social relations, or vice versa. Characterizing this relationship is difficult, but perhaps we can understand sex and gender as mutually constitutive, rather than as different domains. Perhaps body and society were far more interlocked, far harder to tease apart, for early modern English men and women than they seem for twentieth-century historians.

1. I draw on Roger Chartier's resuscitation of Marcel Mauss's formulation, which emphasizes the connections between representation and power: "Even the highest collective representations have existence and are truly what they are only to the extent that they command acts." It also, at least in theory, accounts for the ways in which individuals define themselves and others in the process of imagining their social world. Roger Chartier, *Cultural History: Between Practices and Representations* (Ithaca, 1988), p. 6.

2. By and large historians have studied individual examples of popular health texts rather than the production of these texts as a historical phenomenon in its own right. See, for example, Ludmilla Jordanova, "The Popularization of Medicine: Tissot on Onanism," *Textual Practice* 1 (1987): 68–79; Charles Rosenberg, "Medical Text and Social Context: William Buchan's *Domestic Medicine*," *Bulletin of the History of Medicine* 57 (1983): 22–42; Christopher Lawrence, "William Buchan: Medicine Laid Open," *Medical History* 19 (1975): 20–35.

3. I am not pursuing here the many and complex questions about the potential readership of these books. See Charles Webster, *The Great Instauration: Science, Medicine, and Reform, 1628–1660* (London, 1975), pp. 264–73, 488–90, for discussions of the quantities of medical works in English, 1600–60.

4. Thomas Laqueur, *Making Sex: Body and Gender from the Greeks to Freud* (Cambridge, Mass., 1990).

5. But see Hilda Smith's pioneering article, "Gynaecology and Ideology in Seventeenth-Century England," in *Liberating Women's History*, ed. Berenice Carroll (Urbana, 1976). See also Robert A. Erickson, " 'The Books of Generation': Some Observations on the Style of the English Midwife Books," in *Sexuality in Eighteenth-Century Britain*, ed. Paul-Gabriel Boucé (Manchester, 1982).

6. Emily Martin, *The Woman in the Body* (Boston, 1987).

7. In citing proverbs and dictionaries of slang, I am not implying such texts offer us unproblematic access to some kind of unwritten popular culture. Instead, I am looking at another set of texts which purport to be about some kind of common knowledge in order to see how certain metaphors might have worked within and across these genres. On proverbs, see Natalie Zemon Davis, *Society and Culture in Early Modern France* (Stanford, 1975), pp. 227–67; James Obelkevich, "Proverbs and Social History," in *The Social History of Language*, ed. Peter Burke and Roy Porter (Cambridge, 1987); Françoise Loux, *Sagesse du Corps: La santé et la maladie dans les proverbes régionaux français* (Paris, 1978). See also Wolfgang Mieder, *Proverbs Are Never Out of Season* (Oxford, 1993). Thanks to Suzanne Yang for this last reference.

8. I found the following historical explorations of metaphors especially helpful: Helen King, "Sacrificial Blood," *Helios* 13 (1987): 117–26; Marie-Christine Pouchelle, *The Body and Surgery in the Middle Ages* (New Brunswick, 1990). See also JoAnne Brown, *The Definition of a Profession: The Authority of Metaphor in the History of Intelligence Testing, 1890–1930* (Princeton, 1992), esp. pp. 3–17 and 22–34.

9. Brian Vickers, "Analogy versus Identity: The Rejection of Occult Symbolism, 1580–1680," in *Occult and Scientific Mentalities in the Renaissance*, ed. Brian Vickers (Cambridge, 1984).

10. Joan Cadden, *Meanings of Sex Difference in the Middle Ages: Medicine, Science, and Culture* (Cambridge, 1992).

11. Jane Sharp, *The Midwives Book* (London, 1671), p. 18. Nicholas Culpeper, *A Directory for Midwives: Or a Guide for Women* (London, 1681), p. 30. Books such as these, although entitled "Midwife" are usually specifically intended for all childbearing women rather than solely for midwives.

12. John Maubray, *The Female Physician* (London, 1724), pp. 196–97.

13. Henry Bracken, *The Midwife's Companion* (London, 1737), p. 19; Maubray, *Female Physician*, p. 371; Sharp, *Midwives Book*, pp. 313–14.

14. Sharp, *Midwives Book,* p. 104.

15. Ibid., p. 164; Nicholas Culpeper, *A Directory for Midwives: Or a Guide for Women, in Their Conception, Bearing and Suckling of Their Children* (London, 1651), p. 90.

16. Morris Tilley, *A Dictionary of Proverbs in English in the Sixteenth and Seventeenth Centuries* (Ann Arbor, 1950), p. 591; G. L. Apperson, *English Proverbs and Proverbial Phrases: A Historical Dictionary* (London, 1929), pp. 591–92; John Ray, *A Collection of English Proverbs* (Cambridge, 1670), p. 210. See the invaluable Gordon Williams, *A Dictionary of Sexual Language and Imagery in Shakespearean and Stuart Literature* (London, 1994), pp. 11–13, 517, 598, 966, 1058, 1170, 1214, for discussions of agricultural imagery.

17. Maubray, *Female Physician,* p. 74.

18. Sharp, *Midwives Book,* p. 32.

19. Maubray, *Female Physician,* p. 187.

20. Sharp, *Midwives Book,* p. 288. See Patricia Crawford, "Attitudes to Menstruation in Sixteenth and Seventeenth Century England," *Past and Present* 91 (1981): 47–73.

21. Sharp, *Midwives Book,* p. 48; Culpeper, *Directory,* p. 19.

22. Tilley, *Dictionary,* pp. 680–82; Apperson, *Proverbs,* pp. 607, 645; [Nathan Bailey], *Old English Proverbs Collected by Nathan Bailey, 1736,* ed. John Ettlinger and Ruby Day (Metuchen, N.J., 1992), p. 24.

23. Sharp, *Midwives Book,* pp. 362–63.

24. Francis Grose, *A Classical Dictionary of the Vulgar Tongue,* ed. Eric Partridge (from the 3rd edn. of Grose, 1796; 1st edn. is 1785) (New York, 1963), p. 18; Ray, *Collection,* p. 210. On fruit and flower sexual imagery see Williams, *Dictionary,* pp. 28–31, 34, 517, 560–62, 1170.

25. Ray, *Collection,* p. 44; Bailey, *Old English Proverbs,* p. 67; Apperson, *Proverbs,* p. 403.

26. Ray, *Collection,* p. 197.

27. Annette Kolodny, *The Lay of the Land: Metaphor as Experience and History in American Life and Letters* (Chapel Hill, 1975).

28. Carole Fabricant, "Binding and Dressing Nature's Loose Tresses: The Ideology of Augustan Landscape Design," *Eighteenth-Century Culture* 8 (1979): 109–35.

29. Bridget Orr, "Whores' Rhetoric and the Maps of Love: Constructing the Feminine in Restoration Erotica," in *Women, Texts and Histories 1575–1760,* ed. Clare Brant and Diane Purkiss (London, 1992), pp. 195–216; Paul-Gabriel Boucé, "Chthonic and Pelagic Metaphorization in Eighteenth-Century English Erotica," *Eighteenth-Century Life* 9 (1985): 202–16.

30. Culpeper, *Directory* (1651), p. 13.

31. Sharp, *Midwives Book,* p. 11.

32. Ibid., p. 15.

33. Pierre Dionis, *A General Treatise of Midwifery* (London, 1719), pp. 51, 5, 13. Some figures of speech are taken directly from the French text, while others are made more commercial in translation. Pierre Dionis, *Traité General des Accouchemens* (Paris, 1718).

34. Grose, *Dictionary,* p. 95. What this system of metaphor might mean in reverse, where money/commerce is figured as some sort of female sexuality, is intriguing. For approaches to this intersection, see Thomas Laqueur, "Sexual Desire and the Market Economy during the Industrial Revolution," in *Discourses of Sexuality: From Aristotle to AIDS,* ed. Domna Stanton (Ann Arbor, 1992), pp. 185–215; Laura Mandell, "Bawds and Merchants: Engendering Capitalist Desires," *English Literary History* 59 (1992): 107–24.

35. Sharp, *Midwives Book,* p. 93.

36. Maubray, *Female Physician,* pp. 369–70.

37. On commercial and manufacturing images more generally, see Williams, *Dictionary,* pp. 179, 236, 282–5, 813, 856, 913, 1116.

38. This lack of gardening metaphors is striking since Williams, *Dictionary,* pp. 580–82, documents many uses of gardening metaphors for sex and reproduction.

39. Michael Roberts, "Sickles and Scythes: Women's Work and Men's Work at Harvest Time," *History Workshop Journal* 7 (1979): 3–28; A. Hassell Smith, "Labourers in Late Six-

teenth-Century England: A Case Study from North Norfolk, parts 1 and 2," *Continuity and Change* 4 (1989): 11–52, 367–94. More generally, see Bridget Hill, *Women, Work and Sexual Politics in Eighteenth-Century England* (Oxford, 1989); Keith Snell, *Annals of the Labouring Poor: Social Change and Agrarian England, 1660–1900* (Cambridge, 1985).

40. Nor are the changes I discuss based upon changes in physicians' ideas about reproduction. Although "generation" was the focus of sustained inquiry in the later seventeenth century, I see few links between those discussions and what is happening in popular texts. Elizabeth Gasking, *Investigations into Generation 1651–1828* (Baltimore, 1967); Estelle Cohen, "The Body as a Historical Category: Science and Imagination, 1660–1760," in *The Good Body: Asceticism in Contemporary Culture,* ed. Mary G. Winkler and Letha B. Cole (New Haven, 1994), pp. 67–90.

41. Pre-1650 texts vary considerably. For instance, James Guillimeau, *Childbirth, or the Happy Deliverie of Women* (London, 1612) discusses labor and delivery but does not describe reproductive anatomy. John Sadler, *The Sicke Woman's Private Looking-Glasse* (London, 1636) does not use much imagery but briefly describes the womb as a room with a door, and the menses as nourishment or hospitality.

42. Eucharius Roeslin, *The Birth of Man-kinde, Otherwise the Woman's Book* (London, 1626). The work was first published as *Der swangern Frauwen und Hebammen Rosegarten,* translated into Latin in 1532, and into Dutch in 1555. STC and Wing list over a dozen English editions up to 1634. Although there were Dutch editions in the 1670s and 1680s, the last English one seems to have been that of 1654. D'Arcy Power, "The Birth of Mankind or the Woman's Book: A Bibliographical Study," *The Library* 8 (1927): 1–58.

43. Roeslin, *Birth,* p. 48.

44. Ibid., p. 48.

45. Ibid., p. 34.

46. Ibid., p. 34.

47. Ibid., p. 37.

48. Keith Thomas, *Religion and the Decline of Magic* (New York, 1971), pp. 38–9, 188. See also Angus McLaren, *Reproductive Rituals* (London, 1984), esp. ch. 2, although this deals more with midwifery magic than with magical properties associated with childbearing. The long and somewhat tedious historiographic controversy about whether midwives were really witches also points to the ways in which magic, if not specific witchcraft, could be linked with midwifery. For the most recent of these discussions, see David Harley, "Historians as Demonologists: The Myth of the Midwife-witch," *Social History of Medicine* 3 (1990): 1–26. Adrian Wilson's analyses of the rituals of childbirth could be read as suggestive of the magical powers associated with childbirth: Adrian Wilson, "The Ceremony of Childbirth and Its Interpretation," in *Women as Mothers in Pre-Industrial England,* ed. Valerie Fildes (London, 1990), pp. 68–107.

49. Laqueur, *Making Sex.*

50. Culpeper, *Directory* (1681 ed.), p. 27.

51. Dionis, *General Treatise,* p. 61.

52. Williams, *Dictionary,* pp. 24–25.

53. Dionis, *General Treatise,* p. 56.

54. Laqueur suggests that the use of the word vagina only entered European vernacular languages around 1700; prior to that the word had long been used as a simile in Latin texts. Gradually the use of the comparison became literal. Laqueur, *Making Sex,* pp. 96, 158–59.

55. Roeslin, *Birth,* pp. 24–25.

56. Dionis, *General Treatise,* p. 43.

57. *The Ladies Dispensatory, or Every Woman Her Own Physician,* 2nd ed. (London, 1740), pp. 164, 167. See also Williams, *Dictionary,* pp. 1199, 1228.

58. Grose, *Classical Dictionary,* pp. 89, 229, 233; Williams, *Dictionary,* p. 894.

59. Grose, *Classical Dictionary,* p. 30; Williams, *Dictionary,* pp. 92–93.

60. We lack a cultural history of English conduct literature. Older studies such as J. E. Mason, *Gentlefolk in the Making: Studies in the History of English Courtesy Literature and Related Topics from 1531 to 1774* (Philadelphia, 1935) remain useful. See also K. M. Davies, "The Sacred Condition of Equality—How Original Were Puritan Doctrines of Marriage?" *Social History* 2 (1977): 563–80; Michael Curtin, "A Question of Manners: Status and Gender in Etiquette and Courtsey," *Journal of Modern History* 57 (1985): 395–423; Fenella Childs, "Prescriptions for Manners in English Courtesy Literature 1690–1760 and Their Social Implications" (D.Phil. diss., Oxford University, 1984); Susan Amussen, *An Ordered Society: Family and Village in England, 1560–1725* (Oxford, 1988) esp. pp. 34–46. More generally, see Nancy Armstrong and Leonard Tennenhouse, eds., *The Ideology of Conduct* (London, 1987).

61. Robert B. Shoemaker, "Reforming the City: The Reformation of Manners Campaign in London, 1690–1738," in *Stilling the Grumbling Hive: The Response to Social and Economic Problems in England, 1689–1750*, ed. Lee Davison et al. (Stroud, 1992), pp. 99–120; A. G. Craig, "The Movement for the Reformation of Manners, 1688–1715" (Ph.D. diss., Edinburgh University, 1980); T. C. Curtis and W. A. Speck, "The Societies for the Reformation of Manners: A Case Study in the Theory and Practice of Moral Reform," *Literature and History* 3 (1976): 45–64; John Spurr, " 'Virtue, Religion and Government': The Anglican Uses of Providence," in *The Politics of Religion in Restoration England*, ed. Tim Harris, Paul Seaward and Mark Goldie (Oxford, 1990), pp. 29–47.

62. More generally, see Suzanne Hull, *Chaste, Silent and Obedient: English Books for Women 1475–1640* (San Marino, Calif., 1982); Margaret Ezell, *The Patriarch's Wife: Literary Evidence and the History of the Family* (Chapel Hill, 1987); Kathleen M. Davies, "Continuity and Change in Literary Advice on Marriage," in *Marriage and Society: Studies in the Social History of Marriage*, ed. R. B. Outhwaite (London, 1981), pp. 58–80.

63. Richard Allestree, *The Ladies Calling* (Oxford, 1673), p. 14.

64. Ibid., p. 11.

65. Ibid., p. 148.

66. Robert Codrington, *The Second Part of Youth's Behavior, or Decency in Conversation Amongst Women* (London, 1664), p. 54. See also p. 78 where he suggests that "love of bravery" is equivalent to original sin in women.

67. A Lady, *The Whole Duty of a Woman by a Lady*, 4th ed. (London, 1707), p. 15. Female sexuality is so dangerous, says "A Lady," that "between the State of Pure Unspotted Virginity, and Prostitution, there are not many intermediate steps" (pp. 32–33). Allestree's *Ladies Calling*, upon which this text is based, went further. He said that if a woman is falsely accused of infidelity by her husband, she must examine her heart because she is probably guilty of disloyalties to God, and therefore should accept whatever punishments her husband doles out (pp. 27–28). By 1744, *The Virgin's Nosegay* made the lack of chastity the source of other failings. The lack of chastity, "like the Loadstone, attracts and draws after it all other Crimes; Pride, Insolence, Avarice, and theft, perjury and Perfidy, Hypocrisy and Sacrilege, Impiety and Irreligion." *The Virgin's Nosegay, or, the Duties of Christian Virgins* (London, 1744), p. 29.

68. William Gouge, *Of Domesticall Duties, Eight Treatises*, 3rd ed. (London, 1634), pp. 320, 314, 313, 338.

69. William Whately, *A Bride-Bush. Or, Directions for Married Persons* (London, 1623), pp. 8–12; quote is from p. 10. See also Whately's use of figurative language, such as his analogy between a stingy husband and an ungracious whore-master, for concerns about male sexuality, p. 183.

70. A. M., *The Reformed Gentleman* (London, 1693), p. 67.

71. Ibid., p. 58.

72. Ibid., p. 69. An anonymous author of a conduct book noted that the sexual double standard might be unjust, but "The Root and Excuse of this Injustice is the preservation of Families from any Mixture which may bring a Blemish to them." Any unfairness in this inequality "is more than recompens'd, by having the Honour of Families in their [i.e.,

women's] Keeping." A Lady, *Whole Duty of a Woman* (London, 1737), p. 121. This book is based on Allestree, *Ladies Calling,* and is not the same as either the 1707 *Whole Duty of a Woman* or William Kenrick's 1753 *Whole Duty of Woman.*

73. Rachel Weil, "The Politics of Legitimacy: Women and the Warming-Pan Scandal," in *The Revolution of 1688–1689: Changing Perspectives,* ed. Lois Schwoerer (Cambridge, 1992), pp. 65–82. More generally, see Rachel Weil, "Sexual Ideology and Political Propaganda in England 1680–1714" (Ph.D. diss., Princeton University, 1991).

74. John Shirley, *The Accomplished Ladies Rich Closet of Rarities,* 7th ed. (London, [1715?]), p. 176. See also Francisco Barbaro, *Directions for Love and Marriage* (London, 1677), p. 79; and William Fleetwood, *The Relative Duties of Parents and Children, Husbands and Wives, Masters and Servants Considered in Sixteen Sermons* (London, 1705), pp. 180–81: "But it is not refraining from adulterous practice only, that is enough to denominate a Conversation chast: The outward carriage must also be honest and inoffensive, void of Suspicion as well as Blame."

75. Earlier in the century, both Gouge and Whately discussed clothing, but their concerns focused on the importance of dressing according to one's station in life—and warnings were addressed to men as well as women. Whately, *Bride-Bush,* p. 181; Gouge, *Domesticall Duties,* pp. 282–83.

76. Nancy Armstrong places this critique in the context of a reshaping of the female middle-class body. She argues that the Renaissance aristocratic body, based upon display, was displaced in conduct literature for women by a body which denied its own materiality and emphasized that a woman's significance lay inside, beneath the surface of her body. Thus such works could advocate women's education and the development of women's moral qualities. At the same time, laboring women's value in their working bodies was displaced by this denial of the material aspects of female bodies. Nancy Armstrong, *Desire and Domestic Fiction: A Political History of the Novel* (Oxford, 1987), pp. 75–76. See also Allestree, *Ladies Calling,* pp. 150–55.

77. Codrington, *Decency,* pp. 38–39. This passage, where Codrington initially suggests that there is an appropriate public role for modest women, and then shifts to a stronger critique of women's pleasures in public, is a kind of microcosm of the larger change in conduct literature which increasingly restricted women to the home. In general, Codrington is a moderate in terms of the extent to which women's natures are irredeemably sinful. He says that some of his contemporaries cannot see a woman laugh without construing the behavior as "vicious," but that he believes in women's "innocency" (p. 57).

78. Barbaro, *Directions,* p. 90; see also p. 82 and Codrington, *Decency,* p. 21.

79. Armstrong, *Desire and Domestic Fiction,* p. 77.

80. Barbaro, *Directions,* p. 105.

81. Fleetwood, *Relative Duties,* p. 170.

82. Richard Brathwait, *The English Gentleman and the English Gentlewoman* (London, 1641; 1st ed. 1631), p. 269. William Gouge's anxieties about women distributing goods, and about women's property, is couched in terms of submission to husbands, not the dangers of the marketplace in which goods and property circulated. *Domesticall Duties,* pp. 292–303, 328.

83. Brathwait, *English Gentleman,* p. 298. However, Brathwait's message is sometimes contradictory, since some pages later he advises married women not to gad about: "These walking Burses and moveable exchanges, sort not with the constansie of your Condition. You must now intend the growth and proficience of those Olive branches around your table" (p. 331).

84. Hilda L. Smith, *Reason's Disciples: Seventeenth-Century English Feminists* (Urbana, 1982); Katherine M. Rogers, *Feminism in Eighteenth-Century England* (Urbana, 1982); Alice Clark, *The Working Life of Women in Seventeenth Century England* (London, 1919); on women's work in London, see Peter Earle, *A City Full of People: Men and Women of London 1650–1750* (London, 1994), esp. ch. 4; Hill, *Women, Work and Sexual Politics;* Mary Prior, ed., *Women in English Society 1500–1800* (London, 1985). See also Margaret Hunt, et al., *Women and the Enlightenment,* special issue of *Women and History* 9 (1984). In construing the historiography

this way, I owe much to Phyllis Mack, "The History of Women in Early Modern Britain. A Review Article," *Comparative Studies in History and Society* 28 (1986): 715–23.

I do not want to imply that historians of the late sixteenth and early seventeenth centuries should be understood as painting a particularly rosy picture of women's lives. For example, both Susan Amussen and David Underdown analyse how gender relations in small communities were structured: Susan Amussen, "Gender, Family and the Social Order," and David Underdown, "The Taming of the Scold: The Enforcement of Patriarchal Authority in Early Modern England," both in *Order and Disorder in Early Modern England,* ed. Anthony Fletcher and John Stevenson (Cambridge, 1985), pp. 196–217, 116–36.

85. For discussions of the limitations of "decline" arguments, see Underdown, "Taming of the Scold," pp. 135–36; Judith M. Bennett, "Medieval Women, Modern Women: Across the Great Divide," in *Culture and History 1350–1600,* ed. David Aers (Hemel Hampstead, 1992), pp. 147–76; Amanda Vickery, "Golden Age to Separate Spheres? A Review of the Categories and Chronology of English Women's History," *Historical Journal* 36 (1993): 383–414.

86. For discussions of these institutions in local communities, see Amussen, *Ordered Society;* Martin Ingram, *Church Courts, Sex and Marriage in England, 1570–1640* (Cambridge, 1988); and the somewhat limited treatment in Christopher Durston, *The Family in the English Revolution* (Oxford, 1989).

87. Phyllis Mack, *Visionary Women: Ecstatic Prophecy in Seventeenth-Century England* (Berkeley, 1992); Christina Berg and Phillipa Berry, "Spiritual Whoredom: An Essay on Female Prophets in the Seventeenth Century," in *1642: Literature and Power in the Seventeenth Century,* ed. Francis Barker et al. (Colchester, 1981), pp. 37–54; Elaine Hobby, "Discourses So Unsavoury: Women's Published Writings of the 1650s," and Diane Purkiss, "Producing the Voice, Consuming the Body: Women Prophets of Seventeenth Century," both in *Women, Writing, History 1640–1740,* ed. Isobel Grundy and Susan Wiseman (Athens, GA, 1992); Keith Thomas, "Women and the Civil War Sects," *Past and Present* 13 (1958): 42–62; Patricia Crawford, *Women and Religion in Seventeenth-Century England* (London, 1993).

88. Patricia Higgins, "The Reactions of Women, with Special Reference to Women Petitioners," in *Politics, Religion and the Civil War,* ed. Brian Manning (London, 1973), pp. 179–222. See also the more impressionistic treatment in Margaret George, *Women in the First Capitalist Society* (Brighton, 1988), pp. 37–68.

89. I don't wish to suggest that the civil war was the only cause of tensions in gender relations. However, in the context of a kind of midlevel shift in representing female sexuality, the civil war seems especially significant. I have no doubt that other longer-term changes in economy and society also contributed to various reshapings of the body.

90. My argument here parallels that of Patricia Crawford, "The Challenges to Patriarchalism: How Did the Revolution Affect Women?" in *Revolution and Restoration: England in the 1650s,* ed. John Morrill (London, 1992), pp. 112–28.

91. However, the values accorded written texts changed as well. Patricia Crawford, "Sexual Knowledge in England, 1500–1750," in *Sexual Knowledge, Sexual Science: The History of Attitudes to Sexuality,* ed. Roy Porter and Mikulas Teich (Cambridge, 1994) pp. 82–106, argues that there was a change over the sixteenth and seventeenth centuries in the mode of transmission of sexual knowledge, a shift away from women's orally shared sexual knowledge towards a privileging of textual forms of that knowledge. Drawing upon different materials, Robert Martenson also suggests a shift away from women's knowledge, in this case a privileging of anatomical textual knowledge. Robert Martenson, "The Transformation of Eve," in *Sexual Knowledge,* ed. Porter and Teich, pp. 107–33.

92. See, for example, "The Lass of Lynn's New Joy" [ca. 1680] in *The Bagford Ballads,* ed. J. W. Ebsworth (New York, 1968), pp. 466–68, in which a midwife assures a man that the child born to his wife five months after their wedding day is in fact his by explaining that five months of days and five months of nights add up to ten months of pregnancy. Helen Weinstein's work on the gender relations represented in the Pepys ballads provides rich evidence of

the complexities of these kinds of representations. Helen Weinstein, "Doing It by the Book: Representing Sex in the Seventeenth-Century English Ballad" (forthcoming).

93. One adolescent male reader borrowed his mother's copy of Culpeper's *Directory for Midwives* in search of hidden knowledge about sex and pursued his researches by spying on the family's maidservant. John Cannon diary, Somerset Record Office, DD/SAS C/1193/4, p. 41.

94. Sharp, *Midwives Book,* p. 360.

95. Ibid., pp. 33–34, 43.

96. Ibid., pp. 86, 92.

97. Ibid., p. 53.

98. See Sandra Ott, "Aristotle among the Basques: The 'Cheese Analogy' of Conception," *Man* 14 (1979): 699–711, for this analogy as it has been developed in a Basque community.

99. On dairying as women's work, see Deborah Valenze, " 'The Art of Women, the Business of Men': Women's Work and the Dairy Industry c. 1740–1840," *Past and Present* 130 (1991): 142–69. Primary sources include Brathwait, *English Gentleman,* suppl. p. 9; Codrington, *Decency,* p. 103.

100. Of course, this relationship is far more complicated than this formulation permits; at the very least, "biology" is socially constructed in very gendered ways.

PART 3

CONTROLLING SEX

BODIES AND MINDS

Sexuality and Renunciation in Early Christianity

PETER BROWN

Toward the end of the second century, the doctor Galen had come to know of Christians. A remark preserved in an Arabic source, if authentic, shows that he may have been prepared to be impressed by them: "Their contempt of death is patent to us every day, and likewise their restraint in intercourse. For they include not only men but also women who refrain from intercourse all through their lives."[1] For reasons which Michel Foucault has elucidated with rare perceptiveness in his *Le souci de soi*, Galen and a small but articulate circle of his peers were prepared to admire those whose fine-tuned lives had come to include a measure of sexual austerity.[2]

A generation before Galen arrived in the city, the Christian Justin had taught in Rome. He always made a point of wearing the somber *pallium* of the philosopher.[3] He knew what such men wished to hear. Christianity, he asserted in his *First Apology*, was a religion distinguished by stringent sexual codes for the many, and proud of the sexual heroism of the few. With deceptive ease, Justin organized the random and potentially conflicting statements of Jesus on sexuality, which are scattered throughout the Gospels, into a neat, high-pitched pyramid. We begin with the challenge to the unruly heart of the unmarried man: "*But I say unto you, that whosoever looketh on a woman to lust after her committeth adultery with her already in his heart*"; and we ascend, with the irrefutable smoothness of an a fortiori argument, to those "*who have made themselves eunuchs for the sake of the Kingdom of Heaven.*"[4] "Nay, many, both men and women of the age of sixty or seventy years, who have been disciples of Christ from their youth, continue in immaculate purity. . . . It is our boast to be able to display such before the human race."[5]

By the time of Justin and Galen, in the middle years of the second century, we can already notice the creation of one of the most enduring misperceptions of European history. Until this century, it was assumed that Christianity had rendered more coherent, more stringent because more internalized and truly "spiritual," codes of sexual discipline that had already been canvassed, in a less consequential manner, by the finest minds of paganism. The life of continence for men, and the life of virginity for women, were regarded as no more than the logical culmination of these codes. Nowadays, of course, the enthusiasm for such a development has evaporated. But the story remains the same. The Christian church is made to bear the odium of having succeeded only too well in what our ancestors once acclaimed as its eminently desirable, because providential, mission in the Roman world. Christianity "overtuned" the sexual austerity of earlier ages.[6] From the fourth century onward, the combined authority of church and state imposed on the populations of the Mediterranean world principles of sexual restraint and of sexual abstinence, whose origins lay in that dark streak of discomfort with the life of the body, based on the Greek dualism of body and mind, which had lurked like a virus in the classical world since the days of Plato.[7]

I would like to step aside from this interpretation. I wish, rather, to draw attention to certain folds in the immense landscape of the Christian church. I use the word "immense" advisedly. We are not dealing with the fiery dwarf star of a Greek city-state, but with a veritable galaxy: we are speaking of experiences in Christian communities that stretched from the Rhone Valley to the Zagros Mountains, over a period of four hundred years, preserved for us in documents in at least five major languages—Greek, Latin, Hebrew, Syriac and Coptic.[8] Some of the most prominent folds in this wide landscape seem to me to owe their distinctive, abrupt contours to the continued pressure exerted by three major tectonic plates, whose sheer mass and momentum would have escaped the notice of a man such as Galen and the readers to whom Justin addressed his *Apology*.

First: a muted but tenacious tendency to treat sexuality as a privileged ideogram of all that was most irreducible in the human will. Second: a marked tendency, vociferously advocated in radical groups but widely accepted outside those groups, to herald sexual renunciation as a privileged emblem of human freedom. Third: by the late third century, a widespread tendency to regard the body itself, by reason of its sexual components, as a highly charged locus of choice, of admiration in its virgin state and of avoidance in its sexually active state—with all that such attitudes implied for the structuring of a post-classical community.

Many Jewish and early Christian texts bring us up against a distinctive map of the human heart. It is a map drawn from the outside in, as it were, by fellow members of a group, as they peer anxiously at each other. For the "heart" is what lies hidden behind the surface of the "face." And even the "heart" itself is partly hidden: at the very back of the heart there lies a zone of negative privacy, a closed chamber of secret intent that no human eye can pierce. The ideal was that the hidden heart of the believer might become transparent to the demands placed upon it from the outside, by the law of God and by the claims of one's neighbor. The reality was different: in the depths of the self, the "evil heart," the "evil inclination," the "heart of stone," "murmured" ceaselessly. Transparency was for another age.

God spoke to Israel (said the rabbinic commentary on *Numbers*): "In this age, you are separated by reason of your evil inclination from fulfilling the commandments. But in the world to come, I will tear that evil heart out of you, as it is written: *A new heart also will I give you.*"[9] As on an X-ray photograph, therefore, a patch of disquieting opacity lay at the center of the human heart. What is distinctive is the speed and the tenacity with which that dark spot came to be identified, in Christian circles, with specifically sexual desires, with unavowed sexual stratagems, and, as we shall see, with the lingering power of sexual fantasy. Only a comparative history of Christianity and early rabbinic Judaism in the first, formative centuries of both movements can explain this subtle parting of the ways. The *yezer ha-raᶜ*, the "evil inclination," of the rabbis was never so thoroughly sexualized as related notions came to be in Christian circles.[10] Among Christians, the "demon of fornication" was perceived as a lurking, mute presence in the heart. It came to function as a symbol of quite exceptional absorptive power. It drained into its own texture the equally diffuse and weighty anxieties aroused in ancient men by the many other forms of faceless malice associated with the untamed self, such as hypocrisy, guile, and sorcery.[11] For a Christian prophet, Hermas, who was active in Rome in the generation before that of Justin, to adopt a life of continence meant more than to make his body "pure" in order to receive the Spirit: it was to untwist a sinew of peculiarly private motivation in his own heart. Only from such a person would the word of God fall among the saints, as heavy, because as unfissured by double-hearted guile of any kind, as the clear, solid crystal of a hailstone.[12]

The momentum of this particular tectonic plate—that is, the tendency to allow sexuality to condense all that was least transparent in the human will—continued to build up pressure along the line of an equally massive concern, whose thrust lay at a tangent to it. "What new thing did the Lord bring, by coming down to earth?"[13] This was a question that preoccupied many Christian groups in the age of Justin and Galen. The answer was clear: "One mighty deed alone was sufficient for our God—to bring freedom to the human person."[14]

What was far from clear was how that freedom could be shown. The coming of Christ to earth, his mighty Resurrection and his glorious Ascension, had brought the "present age" to an end. This "present age" was perceived in terms of an overriding tyranny, of a crushing flow of irreversible, negative processes. How, then, could ordinary men and women find, in their own cramped circumstances, the outward, visible sign of the huge inward mutation associated with the triumph of Christ over the powers of the "present age"? As Tertullian asked, with pertinent sarcasm: "How can you possibly think that you are freed from the Ruler of this age, when even his flies still crawl all over you?"[15]

There was, however, one potentially reversible process shared by all human beings. Sexuality was based on a drive that was widely spoken of as irresistible: the current Greek euphemism for the penis was "the necessity."[16] The drive, furthermore, was the cause of the one irrefutably unidirectional process to which human beings freely contributed—procreation. Without human collaboration, this layer, at least, of the overpowering landslip of the "present age" would not happen. "Jordan" would "roll backwards": the booming cascade of the human race from copulation, through birth, to the grave would come to a halt.[17] It was the perfect answer to Tertullian's challenge. The "present age" might be a vast engine, too immense to be seen, its faceless energy too dangerously impalpable to control. But one part of its mighty current could be symbolically concretized in the sexual urge and in the processes manifestly connected with that urge—the endlessly repeated cycle of birth and death. In a world seemingly governed by iron constraints, the human body was thought able to stand out as a clearly marked locus of free choice. To renounce sexual intercourse was to throw a switch located in the depths of the human body itself; and to throw that precise switch was to cut the current that sustained the sinister *perpetuum mobile* of the "present age." By their uncanny "singleness," their studied isolation from marriage and childbirth, groups of Christians, scattered throughout the eastern Mediterranean and as far as the foothills of Iran, strove to render audible the vast hush of the imminent end of the "present age."

It is easy enough to place appropriate labels on this way of thinking—to speak of "realized eschatology," to itemize the groups as "Encratites," as "withholders" from the physical actions that marked the "present age," and to place them in their correct niche among the movements of the second and third centuries.[18] It is harder to step back a little, in order to register the profound implications of this structure of thought, and of the role that sexuality played in it.

For the first time in ancient Christian thought, sexuality replaced mortality as the magnetic pole to which all reflection on the extent of mankind's frailty must turn. In the Encratite exegesis of the fall of Adam and Eve, death was intimately associated with a sexual act: it was either caused by such an act, or, in a less radical version of the exegesis of the fall and its consequences, the fall of Adam and Eve into mortality made sexual acts necessary, if the human race was to survive. The free abandonment of sexuality, in turn, was thought to have brought a halt to the chill contagion of the grave. Seen in this way, sexuality could be viewed as an area in the human person that offered both the clue to present human bondage, and its renunciation, the key to future human liberation.[19]

Furthermore, the sexuality that held this clue was a sexuality now perceived as common to all human beings. One cannot emphasize strongly enough the effect of Encratite thought in stirring the myth of Adam and Eve from its long lethargy. From the second century onward, the meaning of sexuality in the human person was usually debated, in Christian circles, in terms of the fall of Adam and Eve—that is, in terms of a prototypical human couple. In practice, of course, the inflexible compartmentalizations of a Mediterranean and Near

Eastern society ensured that sexuality continued to be viewed through narrow slits. The average Christian continued to regard it as a problem raised for the self by the other. Seen by the aged, the intensity of sexual feeling was dismissed as a problem for the hot-blooded young. Seen by men, sexual desire was feared as a source of disruption, only too frequently brought upon them by the wiles of women.[20] But in theory at least, if not in practice, the shift to a universal paradigm tended to flatten these neat divisions. Our first tectonic plate—sexuality as a darkened ideogram of the untamed self—still presupposed the privileged viewing-point of the old and the male. The notion survived most vehemently, as far as we can tell, in villages of morose misogynists, gathered into the church through marriage and organized in sober households. Austere patriarchs, they chose to express their nagging discontents in terms of fear of the covert ravages of fornication among their young and of the ever-present possibility of adultery on the part of their wives.[21] With the Encratite model, by contrast, men and women, young and old were joined in the catastrophe of a shared sexuality that admitted as few gradations as did the grave.

It is, indeed, in Encratite sources, especially in the brilliant third-century novel, the *Acts of Judas Thomas*, that we can see the beginnings of a crucial shift in Christian sensibility. The female body came to be presented as the condensed essence of all human bondage and of all human vulnerability.[22] For the female body was the precise place where the terrible unidirectional flow that passed directly from the womb, through birth, to the grave, first began. It is on the surface of the female body, therefore, that it was possible to measure most clearly the gigantic, impalpable weight with which the atmosphere of the "present age" bore down on all humanity. It is to the wives of the powerful that Judas Thomas addressed his message. For it was the boycott of the womb by women, and not simply male control of the unruly heart, that was the most stunningly appropriate gesture with which to halt the mindless flow of the "present age."[23] The life of the young girl was marked by poignant discontinuities: her untouched body was taken from the tranquility of the women's quarters; she was joined to her husband beneath the heavy cloth of gold of the marriage bed; she first put on her veil, as a sign of the novel wrench of sexual shame. Even the eventual dispersal of the good cheer of the wedding feast was a premonition of the long years of bondage to the "present age," through her body, as the bearer and nurturer of children destined to the grave. It was from the viewing-point of the young bride that it was possible to glimpse the sheer extent of the chasm that separated the eternal kingdom of Christ from a humanity devoured by time, by the pains of childbirth, and by the corruption of death: "[for] marriage passeth away with much contempt, Jesus alone abideth."[24]

In the decisive century that stretched between the death of Galen and the conversion of Constantine, the pressure of the third tectonic plate was registered, so insistently that its effects on Christians could be observed even by pagans. Among Christians, a mystique came to surround the physical body of the continent. It was seen to rest in its most intense form on the body of the virgin girl. Porphyry, the pagan Neoplatonic philosopher, knew his Christians. He reminded them that Paul had said, *"concerning virgins I have no commandment of the Lord"*:

> For it is clear that a young girl does not do well by remaining a virgin, or a married person by renouncing marriage . . . how then can it be that some who practice the virgin state make so great a thing of it, and say that they are *Filled with the Holy Spirit,* for all the world like she who gave birth to Jesus?[25]

The concern with the preservation of a virgin body and the sense of the body as a *temple of the Holy Spirit* are ideals so well known through later Christian thought that it is easy to lose a sense of the first, sharp contours of these notions. It is important to recapture their first meaning, as they impinged on the non-Christian world.

Christian concern with virginity meant, above all, that the tension between the individual and society tended to be seen in terms of a defiance made, through the body itself, to the demands placed upon the individual by the "present age." As a result, a decisive shift of emphasis occurred. A new dualism emerged in Christian circles. It was a "horizontal" dualism. It laid its main emphasis on the individual in relation to society, and no longer on the more "vertical" relation of man to the cosmos. What defined the body was not its role as a link between the mind and the physical world—at once a "muddy vesture" that trapped the star-bound soul and the soul's own watch post on the frontier of spirit and matter. The body was now seen as a bridge between self and society. It was on the body that the "present age" made its most terrible demands and rested its most insistent pressure. In the age of the martyrs, society rained pain on the unflinching bodies of the faithful. Less demonstratively, but equally insistently and at all times, society demanded that the intact body of the young girl be made, through marriage, "an instrument for the furtherance of death's domain."[26]

In Christian thought, society tended to lose its organic cohesion. It would not flower, ever and again, by means of the body, in the measured satisfaction of eros among the young. That ancient bedrock could no longer be taken for granted. For conventional society lay in the shadow of the "present age." It had resulted from the sin of Adam. It was maintained by an unspoken sexual social contract. Since Adam's fatal slip, society had been built up by free acts of the body; and it was by free acts of the body, namely by sexual renunciation, that it would be dismantled, so that humanity might regain the majestic state from which Adam and Eve had fallen. With this, a chasm opened up between the pagan heirs of the traditions that Galen had once represented and to whom Justin had appealed, and the cultivated Christian listeners of an Origen, a Methodios of Olympos, and a Gregory of Nyssa.

The scenarios of renunciation relished by Christians came to differ dramatically from those appreciated by pagans. The disciples of Plotinos liked to linger on scenes of public life refused by the wise and the middle-aged. Rogatianus, a senator "on the point of taking up the praetorship, the lictors already at the door, refused to come out or to have anything to do with the office."[27] Rogatianus' exact contemporaries were Christian readers of the *Acts of Judas Thomas* and of countless similar narratives. They thrilled to a different, more elemental act: the high drama of sexuality renounced by the young on their own wedding night.[28] Shepherded into marriage by his kinsfolk, escorted through the city by acclaiming crowds, the young man was urged, in the bridal speech, to "fight in a manner worthy of your fathers . . . so that you can provide children for our city".[29] In the bridal chamber, the young couple would have found themselves alone with each other, possibly for the first time in their courtship. They now had nothing but their own bodies, and were free to use them as they wished. True freedom was to do nothing. "And our Lord [looking like Judas Thomas] sat down on the bed, and let the young people sit down on the chairs [on each side of the bed] . . . and so they passed their night in separate places."[30] Seldom have the unquestioned solidarities of the ancient city been exploded, by the young body itself, with such imaginative verve.

Such things were deeply shocking to Porphyry and to all later Platonists. Men of known austerity, their asceticism had been resonant with very different meanings. By dislodging young persons from the organic unity of the city, Christian asceticism prised the human race loose, also, from the comforting embrace of a timeless universe.

Even for a man as much a Platonist as was Gregory of Nyssa, the time of the "present age" was a hurried time. It was an eminently human, social time, its relentless passing measured off by the social device of marriage, as mankind sought frantically to soften the somber tick of the clock of death by marriage and the begetting of children. For Gregory, the cosmos had no other time: it raced from Adam's fall to the final resurrection of the dead. All that its solemn rhythms spoke of was of "that time which is necessary for the unfolding of the human race."[31]

Gregory's sister, Macrina, made the clock of human time stop in her heart by abandoning marriage. She had placed as little distance as possible between herself and the immense silence that would precede the cry "*The Bridegroom cometh!*" She and her unmarried companions already stood "on the frontier" of another world.[32] Sosipatra, by contrast, a pagan peer and contemporary of Macrina, was a woman quite as austere as was Macrina. From childhood up, she had been fostered, as Macrina had been, by rustling invisible presences. But Sosipatra could, in the course of a long life, bear three children to a husband whose exact moment of death and precise future location of his soul among the stars she confidently told him on the day of their betrothal.[33] Unlike Macrina, Sosipatra could bide her time. For her, traditional society, and her role within it as a bearer of children, did not lie in the swiftly passing shadow of the "present age." It rested in the bosom of a universe whose time was not measured by the clock of human marriage. The cosmos as a whole would continue forever. "Misty and dim" to human souls caught in the body, it was, at the same time, "sacred and pleasing" in its harmonious immensity. In that cosmos, souls were destined to descend into matter ceaselessly, as they must learn to rise again from matter; and for that to be so, the gods of "generative love" must continue to weave "sea-purple garments" of human flesh and blood, as Sosipatra and her husband had done, all in its due time, upon the ancient, well-tried loom of the marriage bed.[34]

It was with these sharp contours already in evidence that Christianity came to dominance in the fourth-century Roman Empire. Let us end by looking at what this could mean. I will take one theme only: the new implications of the body.

In Christian circles, the body was stripped of its ancient, civic associations; it was stripped by means of an increased emphasis on its intrinsic sexuality. Marriage, for instance, was no longer held to belong to the city. The frank eroticism associated with the marriage procession to the bridegroom's house and the subsequent jollity, even licensed obscenity, of the marriage feast had expressed the interest of the city in the high-spirited and, it was hoped, delightful sexual act that would produce a further generation of little civic notables. The gates of the sober Christian household must close against such exuberant demonstrations of civic hope. Such things, said John Chrysostom, were "the Devil's garbage." The city was full enough with this garbage; it had no place within the courtyards of a well-ordered Christian household.[35] When the young couple retired to bed (assuming that no Apostle had intervened), they made love no longer so as to "build a wall for the city," through personal concord and well-begotten progeny.[36] They were put to bed *dia tas porneias*, to "avoid fornication," to "bring down the high temperature" of a sexual drive that was assumed to know nothing of the higher purposes of civic procreation.[37]

Nudity, also, ceased to be a form of civic dress. The ease with which the great ladies of Antioch would strip down in the baths, their white, well-nurtured flesh, draped with golden chains and jewels, conveying, to their male retinue, a message of a social distance so secure as to admit no flicker of sexual shame — this must cease.[38] So must the public nudity of the games. The naked bodies that splashed in the great artificial pools created in the circus, acting the role of the shining Nereids who brought *apolausis*, in the form of the sensual, civic delight of sparkling water in the midst of a sweltering Near Eastern city, were no longer viewed from across a social precipice. These were no longer the bodies of *atimoi*, of civic nonpersons whose sexual shame meant nothing: "For say not this, that she that is stripped is a harlot; but that the nature is the same, and they are bodies alike, both that of the harlot and that of the free woman."[39]

Like an overgrown rosebush pruned down to its last bud, the Christian city that emerged, if in theory only, in the sermons of John Chrysostom, was a collection of bodies, each carrying within itself the inescapable marks of its sexual nature. The new sense of sexuality had the immediate effect of flattening the ancient, civic compartmentalizations of the urban community. For this reason, it was closely linked, in the Christian rhetoric of the fourth and early fifth centuries, to the notion of poverty. Here also the ancient screen that had separated citizen from noncitizen was bluntly pushed aside by a new sense of the human body at risk. Joined together in the somber democracy of sexual shame, the Christian civic community that John and others hoped to build was to be a community cemented by shared compassion for the frail bodies of the poor.[40] Owners of bodies now insistently presented as equal, in that all were equally vulnerable to sexual shame, were urged to see in the poor no longer faceless, noncivic persons, living in a world apart from the city, but common bodies—bodies like their own, because bodies placed at risk by Adam's fall, gnawed by desire, and, in the case of the poor, ravaged also by the bite of famine, disease, and destitution.[41]

One cannot but sense the weight that had come to press down upon the body as the Christian church struggled to find a language with which to express its new position in the Roman world. By the start of the fifth century, sexuality had been swept into a new debate on the limitations of the human person. The outcome of the Pelagian controversy in the Latin West and the extensive writings of Augustine of Hippo on the fallen state of the sexual drive were but one mighty downpour in a weather front that swept from one end of the Mediterranean to the other.[42]

All over the Christian world, forms of ascetic radicalism that had once hinted at the possibility of the transcendence of sexual desire, even of sexual differences, were condemned by bishops and by Imperial laws. Debates on the resurrection, sparked off by the works of Origen, now emphasized the survival of the physical body, and hence validated the lasting, untransformable distinction of men from women.[43] By the end of the fourth century, our second great tectonic plate—sexuality as a symbol of reversibility—had lost much of its momentum. John Chrysostom noticed that a high wooden railing now stood between the men and the women in the great church of Antioch; it had not been there in earlier generations. It was no longer a world where men and women could be safely allowed to be *one in Christ Jesus.*[44] Women were women, and men must remain men. A chilling Imperial edict of 390 reveals, in the very incoherence of its official anger, the slow turning of an age. Male prostitutes in Rome—that is, those who played a passive role, by allowing themselves to be penetrated in the male brothels of the city—must be burned. The very thought that males could adopt such practices "sapped the rude rural vigor of the Roman people"; then, the edict goes on—with a new, Christian certainty—it was unpardonable that a soul allotted in perpetuity to the "sacrosanct dwelling place" of a recognizable male body should force that body into female poses.[45]

The upshot of that vehement debate was to fix the human body and its sexual components: a sense of the inflexible differentiation of men and women went hand in hand with a sense of the untranscendable power of the sexual urge. Only in the desert did a few, still voices continue to speak to small circles of monastic disciples of the hope of transformation. Writing in Lérins, around 425, John Cassian returns us to our first tectonic plate—sexuality as an ideogram of the unopened heart. For the monks of Egypt, whose leisurely and singularly candid reminiscences on sexual temptation Cassian recorded in his *Institutes* and *Conferences*, the aim of the ascetic life had always been "purity of heart."[46] The heart of the just must be all of one piece. It must be as unfissured by the knotted grain of private, unshared thoughts and of private, covert motivations as was the solid, milk-white heart of the date palm.[47]

Precisely because sexual fantasy lingered so tenaciously in the heart of the monk, it stood for all that the monk could not share with others. But Cassian insisted that its presence in the heart was largely symptomatic. Sexual temptation, sexual dreams, and night emissions were deeply disturbing to him and his monastic readers: they were as closely observed by Cassian as they were by Augustine. But Cassian did not draw from them so bleak a conclusion as had Augustine. God had placed sexual desire in the very depths of the human body, so as to render mercifully concrete the deeper processes of the impalpable soul. Sexuality acted as an alarm system. Unwelcome onsets of sexual temptation and the shame of night emissions warned the monk of the tread of more terrible beasts within his soul—egotism, hard pride, and icy rage.[48]

Only when the clenched heart had opened in its very depths would the monk come to feel, in the palpable, physical form of a change in his imaginative life and a decrease in the frequency and intensity of his night emissions, that he had gained the crowning gift of "purity of heart." The cessation of sexuality signaled a victory in a more distant, and far more bitterly contested, theater of war. It showed that the last fissure between the self and others, and between the self and God, had closed: "And so he shall be found in the night as he is in the day, in bed as when at prayer, alone as when surrounded by a crowd. *For you have possessed my inward parts.*"[49]

Quia tu possedisti renes meas. Let us end by lingering a little on the image—*renes meas*, my kidneys. Galen would have known what Cassian meant. The kidneys are "exciters of sexual desire . . . for the veins which empty into the testicles . . . pass directly through the kidneys, deriving thence a certain pungency provocative of lust."[50] For Cassian, these kidneys are stilled. The place where the shadows lingered longest in the private self, the place of sexual desire, has become transparent to the will of God.

All of three centuries have passed since Galen. The body is no longer treated as a self-contained system, whose smooth functioning (due to an austere regime) enabled the wise man to put his body "in brackets," as it were, in order to concentrate, undisturbed, on the long labor of self-formation through the mind.[51] For good or ill—and frequently in a manner that the monks felt ill-equipped to express in terms of the "fixed components" of their inherited thought—body and mind had become compacted. The one was now watched with an entirely new circumstantiality as a sensor to the other. Among the Desert Fathers, in the *Sayings of the Fathers*, through Euagrios of Pontos and John Cassian, to the *Spiritual Ladder* of John Climacus, the physical and imaginative manifestations of sexuality came to be scanned with a sophistication that takes a modern reader by surprise. Why was it, Philoxenos of Mabbug would ask, that night emissions seem to increase when the novices grow in the love of God, so that their love appears to take forms "akin to the passion of fornication?" "Oh how difficult this is to understand! How the knowledge of the scholar is tried!"[52] For it was precisely the intimacy of sexuality, and its apparent position on the shadowy borderline of body and mind, that enabled men such as John Cassian to look to it for the first, unmistakable signs of the mighty works of deliverance wrought by God in the recesses of the soul: "*And I will give to thee the treasures of darkness, and hidden riches of secret places.*"[53] Body and mind, now sensed as mysteriously interconnected through sexuality, had sunk together since the time of Galen, receding into the depths of the half-charted and, from now onward, everfascinating unity of the self. Therein, perhaps, lies the true novelty associated with the sexual revolution brought about by the rise of Christianity in the Roman world.

NOTES

1. Cited in R. Walzer, *Galen on Jews and Christians* (Oxford, 1947), p. 15.

2. M. Foucault, *Le souci de soi* (Paris, 1984), pp. 101–69. English translation, *The Care of the Self: The History of Sexuality*, Vol. 2, trans. Robert Hurley (New York, 1985).

3. Jerome, *De viris illustribus* 23.

4. *Matthew* 5:32 and 19:12.

5. Justin, *Apologia 1* 15.

6. Foucault, *Le souci de soi*, pp. 269–71.

7. E. R. Dodds, *Pagan and Christian in an Age of Anxiety* (Cambridge, 1964), pp. 5–36.

8. I have dealt with the themes touched on here in considerably greater detail in P. Brown, *The Body and Society: Men, Women, and Sexual Renunciation in Early Christianity* (New York, 1988), to which I must refer the reader for fuller references.

9. *Midrash Rabba: Numbers* 17:6, trans. J. Slotki (London, 1939), 2:707.

10. E. E. Urbach, *The Sages: Their Concepts and Beliefs* (Jerusalem, 1975), pp. 471–83.

11. *Testaments of the Twelve Patriarchs: Reuben*: 2.8–4.2.

12. Hermas, *Pastor*, Mandatum 11.43.20.

13. Irenaeus, *Adversus Haereses* 4.34.1

14. Tertullian, *Adversus Marcionem* 1.17.

15. Tertullian, *Adversus Marcionem* 1.24.6.

16. Artemidoros, *Oneirokritika* 1.79.

17. Hippolytos, *Refutatio* 5.2 and *The Testimony of Truth: N.H.C. 9.3*, 30.19ff., in *The Nag Hammadi Library in English*, trans. J. M. Robinson (New York, 1977), p. 407.

18. F. Beatrice, "Continenza e matrimonio nel cristianesimo primitivo," in *Etica sessuale e matrimonio nel Cristianesimo delle origini*, ed. R. Cantalamassa (Milan, 1976), pp. 3–68; and D. E. Aune, *The Cultic Setting of Realized Eschatology in Early Christianity*, Supplements to Novum Testamentum 28 (Leiden, 1977), pp. 195–212, do this as well as any.

19. Ton H. J. Van Eijk, "Marriage and Virginity, Death and Immortality," in *Epektasis: Mélanges offerts au cardinal J. Daniélou*, ed. J. Fontaine and C. Kannengiesser (Paris, 1972), pp. 209–35.

20. *Testaments of the Patriarchs: Reuben* 5.1–4.

21. Pseudo-Clement, *Homiliae* 13.14–18.

22. J. Perkins, "The Apocryphal Acts and Early Christian Martyrdom," *Arethusa* 18 (1985): 211–30.

23. E. Peterson, *Frühkirche, Judentum und Gnosis* (Rome, 1959), p. 219.

24. A. F. J. Klijn, trans., *The Acts of Judas Thomas*, Supplements to Novum Testamentum, 5 (Leiden, 1962), p. III.

25. A. von Harnack, "Porphyrios, 'Gegen die Christen,'" *Abhandlungen der königlichen preussischen Akademie der Wissenschaften*, Philologische-historische Klasse (Berlin, 1916), p. 60.

26. Gregory of Nyssa, *De virginitate* 14.1; see P. Brown, "The Notion of Virginity in the Early Church," in *Christian Spirituality*, ed. B. McGinn, J. Meyendorff, and J. Leclercq (New York, 1985), pp. 428–31.

27. Porphyry, *Vita Plotini* 7.

28. B. de Gaiffier, "'*Intactam sponsam relinquens*,'" *Analecta Bollandiana* 65 (1947): 157–95.

29. Menandor Rhetor, *Epideiktika* 406–8.

30. Klijn, *Acts of Judas Thomas* 11 and 13, pp. 70, 71.

31. Gregory of Nyssa, *De hominis opificio* 22.7.

32. Gregory of Nyssa, *Vita Macrinae* 11.33.45.

33. Eunapios, *Vitae sophistarum* 467–70.

34. Porphyry, *De antro nympharum* 14.

35. John Chrysostom, *Homilia 12 in Coloss.* 4; *Patrologia Graeca* 62:387.

36. Musonius Rufus, fr. 14.

37. John Chrysostom, *De virginitate* 19.1.1–2.

38. John Chrysostom, *Homilia 28 in Hebr.* 6; *Patrologia Graeca* 63:199.

39. John Chrysostom, *Homilia 6 in Matth.* 8; *Patrologia Graeca* 57:72.

40. E. Patlagean, *Pauvreté économique et pauvreté sociale à Byzance* (Paris and The Hague, 1977), remains the indispensable statement of this change of sentiment.

41. Jerome, *Epp.* 76.6, 79.10.

42. Now studied by P. Brown, "Sexuality and Society in the Fifth Century A.D.: Augustine and Julian of Eclanum," in *Tria Corda: Studi in onore di Arnaldo Momigliano*, ed. E. Gabba (Como, 1983), pp. 49–70, and E. A. Clark, "'Adam's Only Companion': Augustine and the Early Christian Debate on Marriage," *Recherches augustiniennes* 21 (1986): 139–62.

43. Jerome, *Epp.* 75.2, 84.6.

44. John Chrysostom, *Homilia 73 in Matth.* 3; *Patrologia Graeca* 57:677.

45. *Mosaicarum et Romanarum Legum Collatio* 5.3.

46. M. Foucault, "Le combat de la chasteté," *Communications* 35 (1982): 15–25.

47. *Anonymous Apophthegmata* 362, in F. Nau, "Histoires des solitaires Egyptiens," *Revue de l'Orient chrétien* 18 (1913): 138.

48. Cassian, *Collationes* 1.22.

49. Cassian, *Collationes* 12.8.

50. Galen, *De usu partium* 14.9; compare Nemesios of Emesa, *De natura hominis* 28:45; *Patrologia Graeca* 40:716.

51. P. Hadot, *Exercices spirituels et philosophie antique* (Paris, 1981), pp. 25–70; and G. Lardreau, *Discours philosophique et science spirituelle: Autour de la philosophie spirituelle de Philoxène de Mabboug* (Paris, 1985), p. 39.

52. Philoxenus of Mabbug, *Letter Sent to a Friend* 13, in G. Olinder, "Philoxenus of Mabbug: Letter Sent to a Friend," *Acta Universitatis Gotoburgensis* 51.1 (1950): 9*.

53. John Cassian, *Institutiones* 5.2.

FAMILY LIFE AND THE REGULATION
OF DEVIANCE

JOHN D'EMILIO AND ESTELLE B. FREEDMAN

In 1650, young Samuel Terry of Springfield, Massachusetts distressed his neighbors when, during the Sabbath sermon, he stood outside the meetinghouse "chafing his yard to provoak lust." Several lashes on the back may have dissuaded him from masturbating in public again, but in 1661 Samuel Terry endured another punishment for sexual misconduct. Now married, his bride of five months gave birth to their first child, clear evidence that the pair had indulged in premarital intercourse. A four-pound fine was not the last Terry would pay for defying the moral standards of his community. In 1673 the court fined Terry and eight other men who had performed an "immodest and beastly" play. Despite this history of sexual offenses, however, a sinner like Samuel Terry could command respect among his peers. Terry not only served as a town constable, but, in addition, the court entrusted him with the custody of another man's infant son.[1] In short, as long as he accepted punishment for his transgressions, Samuel Terry remained a citizen in good standing.

The case of Samuel Terry allows us to refine the stereotype of the American colonists as prudish, ascetic, and antisexual. This view has enjoyed so much popularity in modern America that the term *puritanical* has come to mean sexually repressive. Not all colonists were Puritans, those nonconforming, largely middle-class English men and women who attempted to establish a community of saints in seventeenth-century New England. Members of the Anglican and Quaker churches, and migrants from the Netherlands, Germany, and northern Ireland settled in the southern and middle colonies, especially during the eighteenth century. Even among the Puritans and their Yankee descendants, sexuality exhibited more complexity than modern assumptions about their repressiveness suggest.

An accurate portrait of sexuality in the colonial era both incorporates and challenges the puritanical stereotype. Early Americans did indeed pay close attention to the sexual behavior of individuals, as the case of Samuel Terry and numerous church and court records confirm. They did so, however, not in order to squelch sexual expression, but rather to channel it into what they considered to be its proper setting and purpose: as a duty and a joy within marriage, and for the purpose of procreation. Both religious beliefs and economic interests supported this family-centered sexual system. A close look at sexuality in colonial America reveals that, despite gender differences in the meaning of sexuality, for both women and men the organizing principle of sexual relations was reproduction. An examination of, first, the family and, second, the treatment of deviance illustrates the main contours of this reproductive matrix from the mid-seventeenth to the mid-eighteenth centuries.

SEXUALITY IN THE FAMILY LIFE CYCLE

Despite initial regional variations, the family quickly became the central economic unit in every American colony. As in other preindustrial societies, the family both produced and consumed almost all goods and services. Reproduction and production went hand in hand, for family survival in an agricultural economy depended on the labor of children, both in the fields and in the household. Moreover, English inheritance practices supported parental authority, for fathers bequeathed to their sons the land that was necessary for establishing new families. For all of these reasons, colonial laws and customs strongly supported family formation. New England colonies forbade "solitary living" in order to insure that everyone resided within a family, either their own or, as in the case of servants and apprentices, in another household. Even in colonies without such laws, economic survival demanded family living. Thus the life of the individual was integrally connected with that of the family. To understand the meaning and practice of sexuality in colonial America, then, we look first at the life cycle of the individual within the family, beginning with attempts to socialize children to channel sexual desire toward marriage, and turning next to the experiences of courtship, marriage, and childbearing.

A young person growing up in colonial America learned about sexuality from two primary sources: observation within the family and moral instruction from parent and church. A small minority of colonists were also exposed to medical advice literature published in London and reprinted in America during the eighteenth century. Although these various sources of information might conflict on specific points, overall they transmitted the expectation that sexuality within marriage, aimed toward reproduction, would become a part of normal adult life.

Childhood observation of sexual activity is common in agricultural societies, and all regions remained agricultural throughout the colonial period. "Procreation was everywhere, in the barnyard as well as in the house," one historian has written of seventeenth-century New England.[2] Colonial laws against bestiality, and scattered prosecutions for buggery with farm animals, attest to one influence of the barnyard. In Connecticut, for example, a man confessed to having had sexual relations with a variety of animals since the age of ten; Massachusetts executed several teenage boys for buggery. Sexual relations with animals required harsh punishment, for colonists believed that these unions could have reproductive consequences. The mating of humans and animals, they feared, would produce monstrous offspring. For this reason, colonists insisted on punishing not only the man but also the beast, who might bear such monsters. Thus William Hacketts, "found in buggery with a cow, upon the Lord's day," had to witness the execution of the cow before his own hanging took place. Sixteen-year-old Thomas Grazer of Plymouth confessed to buggery "with a mare, a cow, two goats, five sheep, two calves and a turkey." The court ordered a lineup of sheep at which Grazer identified his sexual partners, who were "killed before his face," and then "he himself was executed."[3] Although executions were rare, sexual observation or experimentation with animals was no doubt as widespread in colonial America as in other agricultural societies.

Children also learned about sex in the home. The small size of colonial dwellings allowed children quite early in their lives to hear or see sexual activity among adults. Although curtains might isolate the parental bed, all family members commonly slept in the same room, especially during winters, when a single fireplace provided the heat. Thus a four-year-old girl reported to a servant that she saw a man "lay on the bed with her mamma," and heard him instruct the mother to "lay up higher." Furthermore, the practice of sharing beds exposed some young people to adult sexuality. In one home, three adults and a child were sleeping together when one of the men unbuttoned his breeches and had "carnal knowledge" with a female bedmate. One woman got into bed with her children, and when a man joined them, her daughter recalled, the mother instructed the children to "lie further or else she would kick us out of bed." Even couples who sought greater privacy had difficulty finding it, for loosely constructed houses allowed neighbors and kin to observe what happened behind closed doors.[4]

Whatever they observed, children learned early on that sexual behavior ought to be limited to marriage. The harsh language directed at those who defied this model provided one kind of moral lesson. Neighbors cursed women with epithets such as whore, adulteress, slut, or "brasen-faced bawd." While women's illicit sexual relations evoked scorn, for men the equivalent slander was to be accused of cuckoldry, that is, ignorance or tolerance of a wife's infidelity. For example, a Massachusetts woman hurled a slanderous comment at a couple, claiming that "the wife was a whore and that shee had severall children by other men, and that Cuckoldlay old Rogue her husband owned [acknowledged] them." In an extreme insult, a Maryland man declared that "Mis [Alice] Hatches Cunt would make Souse Enough for all the doogs in the Toune." In at least one instance, a man was ridiculed for monitoring too closely the sexual morality of women. In 1664, after an investigation into a morals case near the town of Concord, Massachusetts, neighbors posted a satiric verse outside the meetinghouse charging "cunstable" Thomas Pinion of unseemly behavior. To keep Pinion from prying further, one verse read: "If natures purll bag does burn / Then quickly send for they pinion. / If sick though art and like to die / Get pinon to fuck thee quickly."[5] Such scornful or satiric speech encouraged youth and adults alike to limit sexuality to the marriage bed.

Formal moral teaching confirmed what popular speech implied. Clergy and lawmakers warned that sex ought to be limited to marriage and aimed at procreation rather than mere physical gratification. Ministers throughout the colonies invoked biblical injunctions against extramarital and nonprocreative sexual acts, while colonial statutes in both New England and the Chesapeake outlawed fornication, rape, sodomy, adultery, and sometimes incest, prescribing corporal or capital punishment, fines, and, in some cases, banishment for sexual transgressors. Together these moral authorities attempted to socialize youth to channel sexual desires toward marriage.

The best known of the colonial authorities, the New England Puritan clergy, were extremists among Protestants on issues of church doctrine and sexual morality. These ministers left abundant evidence that they considered sexuality itself "uncleane," and lust a danger to body and soul. Spiritual leaders such as Thomas Shephard and Cotton Mather advised youth and adults alike to avoid sexual stimulation and to control the desires that "lie lurking in thy heart." As Mather wrote, extramarital sexuality would "bloodily Disturb the Frame of our Bodies, and Exhaust and Poison the Spirits, in our Bodies, until an Incurable Consumption at last, shall cut us down, Out of Time." Puritan clergy emphasized marriage as the only suitable outlet for sexual desire and warned against both masturbation and premarital sex. Their ideas reflected age-old gender distinctions about proper sexual behavior. To young women they directed a particular message about the importance of chastity. According to Mather, it was scandalous for a woman to exhibit "sensual lusts, wantonness and impurity, boldness and rudeness, in Look, Word or Gesture." New England ministers chastised women for wearing immodest dress and blamed them for enticing men into sexual sin.[6] Men, considered more rational and better able to control their passions than women, were raised with warnings to resist their carnal desires by concentrating on their love of God.

Puritan clergy, however, were not the only moral authorities in early America. Youths growing up in the middle colonies or the Chesapeake might be exposed to the religious advice of Quaker and Anglican ministers or Catholic priests. Equally important, both secular advice and the model of adults around them influenced the sexual values of the young. Although all adults agreed on an ideal of marital, reproductive sex, some permitted greater acceptance of sexual desire than did the early Puritans. Describing early American childrearing practices, historian Philip Greven identified three categories of Protestant "temperaments," each of which had a different attitude toward sexuality. Unlike Puritan "evangelicals," who emphasized the suppression of lust, "moderate Protestants" placed less emphasis on sexual control. Thus John Adams acknowledged to his children that he was "of an amorous disposition," even as he assured them that he had sired no illegitimate offspring. A third temperament allowed the open expression of sexual desires and approximated the European libertine ideal, represented by three young rakes who frequented New York coffeehouses and indulged in a "good deal of polite smutt then went out whoring." This "genteel" model, which appeared more frequently after 1740, characterized many upper-class southern men, such as William Byrd of Virginia, whose diary recorded numerous sexual conquests. Even though church and court in this region upheld the ideal of marital, reproductive sexuality, young white males of the planter class learned that they did not necessarily have to exert sexual control around female servants and slaves.[7]

Although church and court remained the most important sources of sexual standards, in the eighteenth century a limited medical advice literature appeared in America. It is impossible to know whether these books about reproduction and sexuality were read by youth, but if so, young men were far more likely than young women to have access to them, for women's literacy rates lagged behind those of men. Only a few gynecological or marital advice texts could be found in early America, including *The Oeconomy of Love* (1736) and *The Art of Preserving Health* (1744), both reprinted from British editions. The eighteenth-century anti-masturbation tract *Onania* had only two or three editions in America.[8]

Aristotle's Masterpiece, first published in London in 1684, did become highly popular in America. Largely a compendium of reproductive lore, *Aristotle's Masterpiece* also contained a prescriptive message about sexuality. It repeated early modern English beliefs that sexual pleasure for both male and female was not only desirable but also necessary for conception. That reproduction was the primary goal of sexuality recurred as a theme throughout its various editions. Offering no information about contraception, the book stressed means to insure conception. It admonished couples to chain the imagination to melodious airs, rather than to sadness, during intercourse, and to avoid withdrawal too soon after "they have done what nature requires," lest they lose "the fruit of the labor." Moreover, the language of *Aristotle's Masterpiece* underscored the association of pleasure and procreation. Thus an explanation of sexual desire stated that "nature has implanted in every creature a mutual desire of copulation, for the increase and propagation of its kind."[9]

It is difficult to know to what extent colonial youth internalized either religious or medical views about sexuality. Most personal testimony about youthful sexual feelings comes from Puritan clergy, who were most likely to have left introspective written accounts and to have accepted the evangelical view that emphasized the suppression of lust. In their diaries, young Puritan men recorded their efforts to contain the desires that rose up in them and to subordinate sexual desire to the love of God. Michael Wigglesworth's diary recounted his dismay over frequent "unresistable torments of carnal lusts"—masturbation and seminal emissions—that were provoked when he read, dreamed, or felt "fond affection" for his pupils at Harvard College. He prayed to God to deliver him from his lusts: "The last night some filthiness in a vile dream escaped me for which I loathe myself and desire to abase myself before my God." Only marriage, Wigglesworth concluded, could save him from temptation. Similarly, Cotton Mather prayed and fasted for fear that as "a Young Man in my single *Estate*" he might fall into "lascivious violations of the *Seventh Commandment.*" Although no such personal accounts exist for young women, one kind of evidence, conversion narratives recorded during the religious revivals of the mid-eighteenth century, suggests that New England women who joined the church accepted the evangelical view of sexuality. Women, even more than men, interpreted their past sinfulness in sexual terms. References to improper dress signified mere wastefulness in men's narratives but represented "Harlotry" in women's accounts.[10]

Not all young people were as devout as the clergy and the newly converted. Court records attest to the sexual escapades of those youths who, rather than struggling against their lusts in private, attempted to express them in public. Recall Samuel Terry of Springfield, whose first sexual offense involved public masturbation. Similarly, a group of "sundrie youthes" in New Haven "committed much wickedness in a filthy corrupting way one with another"—so filthy, in fact, that the court refused to record the acts. In Middlesex County, Massachusetts, a "girl and youth" partied until two in the morning one Thanksgiving by singing dirty songs. Harvard students often engaged in "youthful lusts, speculative wantonness and secret filthiness," according to Thomas Shepard, Jr., who warned his son that "there are and will be such in every scholastic society, for the most part, as will teach you how to be filthy." One group of Harvard students, for example, spent their evenings drinking, singing, and dancing with Negroes and maids, for which several were fined or whipped. Furthermore, servants in all colonies defied proscriptions on premarital sex. Indentured servant Elizabeth Storkey committed fornication and adultery in Virginia. In Massachusetts, a female servant confessed to fornicating with two men "when all in the house were in bed" and a black maid and servant held secret rendezvous in the attic of the home in which she worked.[11]

For those young people who accepted the primacy of marital sexuality, courtship provided a transitional period in which they might begin to express their sexual desires. In the colonial system of courtship, parents did not arrange marriages. Nonetheless, parental opinion played a large role in the selection or approval of a future spouse, for as long as sons expected to inherit land from their fathers, they tended to heed parental advice. Furthermore, although a young man courted the daughter, he proposed marriage to her parents. According to a popular British advice book available in the colonies, "Children are so much the goods, the possessions of their Parents, that they cannot without a kind of theft, give away themselves without the allowance of those that have the right in them." Thus, for example, William Byrd of Virginia spoke first to Lucy Parkes's father about marrying her, and in turn Byrd threatened to disown his own daughter if she married a particular gentleman who did not meet with his approval.[12]

Within the confines of parental approval, formal courtship between young men and women took place unhampered by the supervision of a chaperon but often in public view. In New England, courtship included visits by a young man to a young woman's home or meetings after church. In the Chesapeake, within the planter class, family connections played an important role in introducing couples. Young people met at social affairs such as barbecues, dances, and, in the late eighteenth century, elaborate balls. When a couple did form, their choice rested largely upon a sense of compatibility rather than on notions of romantic love. Couples hoped to develop loving relationships, and courtship gave them an opportunity to begin the process.[13]

That courting couples sought to explore their sexual desires is clear from their efforts to circumvent community surveillance. During warm weather a couple might wander off into the barn or fields in search of the privacy unobtainable in small colonial homes. According to one moralist, during harvest time, with its abundant opportunities for outdoor meetings, New England youth were filled "with folly and lewdness." In 1644, a New England couple left a party but were soon "seen upon the ground together, a little from the house." The cold winters necessitated greater ingenuity. One daring young man crept through the window of his beloved's home, only to wind up in court charged with "incivility and immodesty" for courting without her parents' consent. Some young men tried to exploit opportunities for premarital sexual encounters. After three years of courting Elizabeth Gary of Maryland, Robert Hawood cornered her in a garden and forced her "to yield to lie with him" in an attempt to ruin her for any man but himself.[14]

In the eighteenth century, and probably earlier, courting couples in New England and the middle colonies had the opportunity for physical intimacy with parental approval through the custom of bundling. This practice, which had antecedents among Welsh, Dutch, and German peasants, allowed a couple to spend the night together in bed as long as they remained fully clothed or, in some cases, kept a "bundling board" between them. Bundling served the needs of suitors who traveled long distances and called in small houses that offered neither privacy nor much heat. Parents and youth shared the expectation that sexual intercourse would not take place, but if it did, and pregnancy resulted, the couple would certainly marry.[15]

The treatment of premarital pregnancy suggests that, as in England, engagement might include the right to have sexual intercourse. As one young woman explained, "He promised marriage or I never would have yielded." As long as a couple's sexual relations were channeled toward marriage, colonial society could forgive them. Although church and civil authorities officially condemned fornication and prosecuted offenders, they showed greater leniency toward betrothed couples. In addition, in both New England and the Chesapeake, those who had sex and then married could remain respectable members of the community as long as they participated in the rituals of punishment affirming that marriage provided the only appropriate locus for sexual relations.[16]

Fornication carried heavy penalties, including fines, whipping, or both. In Maryland, where laws were less likely to be enforced, unmarried couples who had sex could receive up to twenty lashes and be fined as much as five hundred pounds of tobacco. In Plymouth Colony, civil penalties for fornication included a ten-pound fine—reduced to only fifty shillings for a betrothed couple—several lashes on the back, or both. Throughout New England, a fine of nine lashes awaited both parents of a child born too soon after marriage. Thus, when Lawrence Clenton and Mary Woodin of Massachusetts confessed to fornication, he was sentenced to be severely whipped and fined forty shillings plus court fees, and she too received a whipping and a fine.[17]

Prenuptial pregnancy rates varied by region and over time. The high rates of up to 30 percent of all brides for the mid-seventeenth-century Chesapeake declined in the eighteenth century, while the low 10 percent rate of early New England rose significantly during the same period. There is little data for the middle colonies, but in one eighteenth-century community, Germantown, Pennsylvania, one-fourth of all first births occurred under nine months after marriage, a pattern that reflected in part the premarital pregnancy rates in the settlers' German homeland.[18]

Through confession and repentance, colonial society offered a means of clearing the stigma associated with premarital pregnancy. In New England, couples whom the church court found guilty of fornication had to repent publicly before their child could be baptized. They stood before their congregation, confessed to premarital sex, and often wept, as did a Plymouth woman who in 1689 "manifested much sorrow and heavyness by words and tears." Having confessed, and if truly repentant, sinners were welcomed back into good standing in the church. Even in Maryland, where there was less church discipline, marriage and repentance could reduce the punishment. In 1663, for example, Thomas Hynson, Jr., came into court "very sorrowfull" for having committed fornication with Ann Gaine. Since Hynson had "now made her his Lawfull Wife," the magistrate ordered no fine or whipping, but merely suspended him from sitting in the county court for a year and a day. His wife, Ann, later appeared in court, as ordered. For "submissively tendering her selfe . . . and Acknowlidgeing her faulte with Extreame Sorrow," the court remitted her punishment.[19] That Thomas Hynson, Jr., could resume his seat at the county court after a year and a day reflects the ease with which Chesapeake society reintegrated sinners. Similarly, New Englanders accepted the penitent fully. Like Samuel Terry, who became a Springfield town constable, New England men convicted of fornication later served as town clerks, selectmen, and even as representatives to the General Court. Women convicted of fornication could marry and join the church.[20] In contrast, those who refused to undergo public confession could be excommunicated from their congregation.

Whatever ambivalence colonists had toward premarital sexual relations, they agreed that husbands and wives ought to have sex. For New England Puritans, conjugal union was a duty; if unfulfilled, the neglected spouse might be tempted to commit adultery. So important was marital sex that a bride could leave a marriage if her husband proved to be impotent. At least one church excommunicated a husband because he denied conjugal relations to his wife for two years. Sexual attraction was valued within marriage only in moderation, however, and sexual intercourse as an act necessary to propagate the family. The Puritans admonished married couples not to allow their affections for one another to compete with their love for God. Cotton Mather warned of the "Inexpressible *Uncleannesses* in the married State," including "*Inordinate Affection.*" Michael Wigglesworth decided to marry as a way of channeling his lusts, but then feared that his conjugal relations were excessive. "Lord, forgive my intemperance in the use of marriage," he prayed.[21] Some authorities believed that too-frequent marital sex could be physically dangerous as well as impious, warning that "satiaty gluts the Womb and renders it unfit for its office."[22]

In spite of these fears of sexual excess, affectionate and even passionate relations developed between husbands and wives. The Puritan Edward Taylor valued spiritual union with his savior over physical union in marriage, yet he wrote of his relationship with his wife as "the True-Love knot, more Sweet than Spice." Similarly, John Winthrop wrote to his "sweet wife," Margaret, that her "love is such to me and so great is the bond between us." "I Kisse and love Thee," he closed, "with the Kindest affection." The correspondence between married couples in the southern colonies included expressions of affection and desire. "How is it possible for me to live without my only Joy & comfort?" wrote the southerner Thomas Jones to his wife, Elizabeth, in 1728. Margaret Parlor wrote to her husband that she longed to go to bed with him, while Theodore Bland, Jr., assured his "dearest Patsy" that on his return she would feel her "husband's lips flowing with love and affection warmth."[23]

Explicit discussions of physical relations in marriage were much less common than references to affection, and so we have few clues about the nature of marital sex. Mary Knight of Massachusetts threw some light on the subject when she forgave her lover for having climaxed too soon. "That is no strange thing," she said, "for my Husband has done so often when he has been gone a few Nights."[24] Her admission suggests both an ideal of mutual pleasure and the difficulty of achieving it. We know that couples sometimes had sex during pregnancy, for women cautioned their husbands to be gentle at such times. The Virginian William Byrd had sex with his wife, Lucy, during her frequent pregnancies, even in the later months. Byrd's "secret diary" provides a rare, though probably atypical, record of marital intimacy among southern planters. Lucy and William Byrd quarreled often, and sexual union provided an important means of resolving their differences. According to Byrd's accounts of his sexual prowess, both husband and wife enjoyed these unions. "I gave my wife a powerful flourish and gave her great ecstasy and refreshment," he wrote in 1711. Another time, after a quarrel, the couple reconciled with a "flourish" performed on the billiard table.[25] Unfortunately, Lucy Parkes Byrd did not record her version of these events.

Sexual complaints from both husbands and wives appeared in divorce cases heard in New England in the eighteenth century. Dissatisfaction did not necessarily result from physical disappointment but rather when one partner believed that the other had stepped outside the bounds of the marital, reproductive sexual system. The Puritan Benjamen Keayne sought a divorce because of "the insatiable desire and lust" of his wife, Sara, whom he accused of adultery and of exposing him to "the french pox," or venereal disease. Abigail Bailey, mother of ten, filed for divorce after her husband not only had sexual relations with a servant but also began to "court" their eldest daughter. The importance of maintaining marriage, despite sexual conflicts, is illustrated by the case of Stephen Temple's wife. Although she went to court to accuse her husband of sexually violating their fourteen-year-old daughter, Mrs. Temple did not seek a divorce. Rather, she wanted to force her husband to change his behavior. When he apologized and promised to reform, the couple reconciled.[26]

Whether sexuality was a source of comfort or conflict, married couples engaged in intercourse with the knowledge and hope that it would lead to children. Among free, white colonists, the availability of land and the need for laborers in the New World encouraged reproduction. They welcomed the birth of a child and, within most families, had little reason to think about preventing conception. For Puritans, theological principles supported the emphasis on procreation, including the biblical injunction to "be fruitful and multiply" and the view that childbearing was woman's "calling." So important was reproduction to marriage that failure to participate in marital sexual relations could be grounds for divorce. A Plymouth wife testified in a 1686 divorce case that her husband was "always unable to perform the act of generation."[27] Her choice of a reproductive term to describe male impotence reflected the understanding that the duty to engage in marital relations meant the duty to procreate, and not simply to provide mutual comfort. For similar reasons, a woman who was past her childbearing years was less likely to gain a divorce on the grounds of her husband's impotence.[28]

The need to produce children, along with the risk that a child would not live to adulthood, required that married women endure repeated pregnancies. In addition to the risk of death in childbirth—which in some regions of the colonies accounted for as many as 20 percent of maternal deaths—the physical labors of pregnancy, childbirth, and nursing preoccupied married women. For good reason, women feared childbirth, or in one woman's terms, "the Dreaded apperation."[29] Mary Clap, who bore six children and buried four before she died at the age of twenty-four, recognized that "Bearing tending and Burying Children was Hard work." At the same time, however, most women assumed that childbearing was their natural "calling." Mary Clap believed "it was the work she was made for and what god in his providence Had Called Her to." After six childless years of marriage, the Puritan poet Anne Bradstreet expressed a longing for pregnancy: "It please God," she wrote, "to keep me a long time without a child, which was a great grief to me and cost me many prayers and tears before

I obtained one." Bradstreet knew that lying-in carried the possibility that she would "see not half my day's that's due." She herself survived the births of eight children, seven of whom outlived her. Less fortunate was her daughter-in-law Mercy Bradstreet, who lost three infants and died herself after childbirth at the age of twenty-eight. After each of these deaths, Anne Bradstreet wrote not only of her grief, but also of her resignation to God's will. She consoled herself that the dead "with thy Saviour art in endless bliss."[30]

Although colonists knew about contraceptive methods such as withdrawal or prolonged nursing, demographic evidence from New England and Pennsylvania reveals that few married women limited family size. Women commonly spaced pregnancies by breastfeeding their infants for a year, during which time many couples refrained from intercourse. Throughout the colonies, however, other means to impede conception or terminate pregnancy were rarely employed. Women turned to folk remedies and fertility medicines to encourage conception and avoid miscarriage rather than to avoid pregnancy.[31] Contraceptive practice could lead to divorce, as in the case of Abigail Emery, who in 1710 complained that her husband practiced the "abominable" sin of Onan (withdrawal) because "he feared the charge of children." The Plymouth Pilgrims banished an adulterous minister not only because he "satisfied his lust" on women, but because he did so while he "endeavored to hinder conception." Cases of attempted abortion usually involved illicit lovers, not married couples. "When a single woman," Margaret Lakes later confessed, she "used means to destroy the fruit of her body to conceal her sin and shame." Elizabeth Robins of Maryland confessed that she had twice taken savin, an abortifacient; her husband suspected that she had an incestuous relationship with her brother.[32] In contrast, married couples had little motive to prevent or terminate pregnancy.

Once sex ratios had balanced in the late seventeenth century, this emphasis on reproduction contributed to the rapid increase of the colonial population, which doubled itself every generation. Natural increase, rather than immigration, accounted for this remarkable growth rate. A lower average marriage age than was prevalent in England allowed native-born women to begin childbearing early; many bore a child every two to three years, an interval determined in part by breastfeeding practices. Some white women had as many as ten pregnancies and bore up to eight live children. They could expect from three to seven of these to survive. Completed families could include from six to eight children.[33] In the eighteenth century, early marriage and high fertility contributed to population growth in the South as well, and among the planter class, women bore as many as seven to eight children, of whom five to six survived into adulthood. Slave fertility rates also rose by the mid-eighteenth century. Married black women bore an average of six children. Their lower fertility rates no doubt resulted from the poorer health and more strenuous labor performed by slaves.[34]

The high fertility rates of the colonial period, along with qualitative evidence about both religious beliefs and personal behavior, all point toward the importance of marital, reproductive sexuality in early America. Over the course of the life cycle, youths expected to marry and couples expected to engage in mutually pleasurable marital sex that would lead to procreation. The goals of reproduction and sexual pleasure did not necessarily clash, as long as they were combined within marriage. Even premarital intercourse could be accommodated if a couple wed and affirmed that marriage was the rightful place for sexual relations. When the primacy of marital, reproductive sexuality was challenged, however, colonists took strong steps to maintain their sexual institutions.

REGULATING THE BOUNDARIES: THE TREATMENT OF DEVIANCE

Although colonial society upheld an ideal of marital, reproductive sexuality, and many individuals attempted to put it into practice, a significant minority deviated from the norm when they committed adultery, sodomy, incest, or rape, or when women bore bastard children. Church and court records reveal the extensive efforts colonists made to identify, outlaw, and punish such practices. New Englanders enforced their laws against sexual deviance more thoroughly, but all English colonists inherited a legacy in which the state played a role in the regulation of personal life. From the founding of each colony, community members, churches, and the courts mobilized to impose sanctions in response to sexual offenses—that is, sexual relations that took place outside of marriage and, especially in the South, those that threatened the racial dominance of whites over blacks. In doing so, they revealed the extent of community involvement in the sexual lives of others.

Through their response to sexual transgressions, colonists reaffirmed the boundaries of acceptable behavior. Courts in New England and the Chesapeake typically sentenced offenders to some form of public humiliation, such as whipping at the post or sitting in the stocks. Thus a Maryland court sent Agnes Taylor to the whipping post to receive twelve lashes "in the Publick Vew of the People" for having borne a bastard child. Hugh Davis of Virginia was whipped "before an assembly of Negroes and others for . . . defiling his body in lying with a negro."[35] In New England, public confession and repentance both restored the individual to the congregation and at the same time confirmed the propriety of sexual rules. When someone was convicted of a capital crime, such as rape or infanticide, clergy preached execution sermons, elaborating on the wages of sexual sin and the need to resist temptation. The regulation of deviance served the larger function of reminding the community at large that sexuality belonged within marriage, for the purpose of producing legitimate children.

The gender of offenders shaped the treatment of deviance. Sodomy and rape were men's crimes. Although adultery, fornication, and bastardy involved couples, women in both northern and southern colonies were more likely than men to be prosecuted and convicted for these sexual offenses.[36] The fact that pregnancy made a woman's participation in these acts apparent helps account for the disparity. In addition, Western culture had traditionally feared the sexual voraciousness of women. As the "weaker vessell," woman supposedly had less mastery over her passions and had to be carefully controlled. Penalties also differed. Men more often had to pay fines and court costs, while women, who had less access to property, had to accept whipping. Despite these distinctions, both women and men participated fully in the regulation of deviance. Both kept a close watch on neighbors and testified in court about illicit activities; both faced fines, whipping, public humiliation, or execution; both could repent and be reinstated in the community.

For men and women, laws against extramarital sexuality carried harsh penalties. Even behaviors that might lead to sex outside marriage required punishment. The relatively minor offense of being a "person of Lude Life and conversation" earned a fine of fifty pounds sterling in Virginia, while one man paid twenty pounds for "profainly" drinking and dancing with a married woman. In 1631, Massachusetts enacted the death penalty for adultery—a crime defined as sexual relations between a man and a married woman. (Sex between a married man and a single woman, or between a single man and woman, would have been charged as fornication.) Most other colonies adopted the death penalty for adultery, although it was rarely enforced. After 1660, New England courts usually imposed fines of ten to twenty pounds, along with public whipping or the wearing of the letters *AD* on a garment or burned onto the forehead. In 1736, Thomas Clarke of Dorchester, Massachusetts, had to choose between a five-pound fine or ten stripes for having "in a wanton and Lascivious Manner had the use and Carnal Knowledge of the Body of Susannah the Wife of Joseph Browne . . . with her consent." Maryland law condemned adultery whether the man or woman was married. Southern courts often sentenced whipping and sometimes used the threat of banishment to punish adulterers; they might also require a bond of up to one hundred pounds sterling to prevent an adulterous couple from seeing each other.[37]

In some cases, adultery could lead to divorce, separation, or violence. In New England, over half the divorce cases in the seventeenth century cited adultery as a cause. One woman sought a divorce when her husband acknowledged "that he had Rog[e]red other women and meant to Roger Every Likely Woman He Could and as many as would Let Him."[38] Husbands sometimes physically attacked adulterous partners. After Stephen Willey found his wife, Abigail, in bed with one man and saw her sitting on the lap of another, he struck her and threatened to kill her.[39]

The regulation of adultery, like all forms of nonmarital sexuality, depended upon the extensive involvement of community members in each other's lives. Intrusiveness characterized the attitude toward sexuality, especially in the closely knit settlements of New England, where individuals could not easily engage in illicit sexual activities without being noticed.[40] Among Puritans, each community member had responsibility for upholding the morality of all lest God punish the group as a whole. Acting on these precepts, Clement Coldom of Gloucester, Massachusetts, "heaved the door off the hinges" to see what his neighbor John Pearce was doing with "the widow Stannard" at night. So clear was the responsibility of family and neighbors to help regulate sexuality that a New England father who allowed his son to live with an unmarried woman was charged as an "accessory to fornication."[41] Even without the Puritan religious obligation to oversee the behavior of others, men and women in other colonies testified about the sexual crimes of neighbors, illustrating an acceptance of intrusiveness in what would later come to be considered purely private matters.

The testimony of observant neighbors was essential for convicting adulterers in court. In Maryland, for example, several people witnessed John Nevill having sexual relations with Susan Attcheson, a married woman; they testified that they had seen her hand in his breeches and his "in Susan's placket" (a slit in her skirt). The court fined Nevill and ordered Attcheson whipped. When Susanna Kennett and John Tully of Virginia heard snoring in the next room, they stood on a hogshead of tobacco and peered over the wall to see that "Richard Jones Laye snoring in her plackett and Mary West put her hand in his Codpis." Kennett then pried loose a board to observe Mary West "with her Coates upp above her middle and Richard Jones with his Breeches down Lying upon her." In 1732, a New England woman testified to having "look'ed in at a hole in the End of the house," where she saw her neighbor's wife and another man "on the bed in the act of Adultery." Similarly, a widowed lodger testified in the 1760s that he "heard a Man and woman discoursing in the Chamber over the Room" and looked in to find the mistress of the house having sex with a male friend.[42]

In addition to testifying in court, neighbors zealously guarded moral standards in the community. The comments of two Massachusetts women who observed a man "in Act of Copulation" attest to the sense of community responsibility for regulating morality. Interrupting the act, the women asked "if he was not Ashamed to Act so when he had a Wife at home." An incident in Maryland further suggests how even in a less settled area, the community could mobilize against adultery. Several travelers lodged overnight at the residence of Captain Fleet, who became "verie angerie" when he realized that one lodger, Mr. Carline, was committing adultery on the premises. Fleet had the couple turned out-of-doors. The court subsequently banished Carline for disowning his wife; when he tried to return home, Carline's neighbors would not allow him to show his face. Finally, in the fishing town of Marblehead, Massachusetts, neighbors wielding clubs attacked the home of William Beale, whose wife, Martha, was suspect for having a previous marriage annulled and an intimate relationship with a servant. "Come out, you cuckolly cur," they called to William, "we are come to beat thee. Thou livest in adultery."[43]

Because they so clearly defied the norm of reproductive sexuality, the crimes of sodomy, buggery, and bestiality carried the death penalty. As the founder of Massachusetts Bay Colony, John Winthrop, explained in the case of William Plaine, who was executed for sodomy and corrupting youths "by masturbations," these acts were "dreadful" because they "tended to the frustrating of the ordinance of marriage and the hindering [of] the generation of mankind." The narrow legal definition of sodomy, which required proof of penetration, along with the requirement of two witnesses for capital punishment, limited the application of the death penalty. At least five men were executed for sodomy or buggery during the seventeenth century—one by the Spanish in Florida, one in Virginia, one in New Haven, and two in New York. No one was executed for sodomy in the eighteenth century, but men convicted of "sodomitical acts," such as "spending their seed upon one another," received severe and repeated whipping, burning with a hot iron, or banishment. As in other morals cases, the higher the status of the accused, the less likely was severe punishment. Despite his thirty-year history of attempted sodomy with servants and neighbors, the wealthy Nicholas Sension of Connecticut merely had his estate held as bond to insure his future good behavior.[44]

It is important to note that the crime of sodomy was not equivalent to the modern concept of homosexuality. Sodomy referred to "unnatural"—that is, nonprocreative—sexual acts, which could be performed between two men, a man and an animal (technically considered buggery or bestiality), or between a man and a woman. When a Maryland woman sued her husband for divorce, charging that he had committed "diverse inhumane usages and beastly crimes," she could have meant anal intercourse in marriage or with another man. Although the term *sodomy* was not applied to sexual relations between women, one colony, New Haven, listed among its capital offenses women's acts "against nature." The few surviving cases that refer to "lewd behavior" between women record punishments of whipping or admonishments, rather than execution. In 1642, for example, a Massachusetts court severely whipped a servant and fined her for "unseemly practices btwixt her and another maid."[45]

Unlike many native American tribes in which the male *berdache* might live as a woman and marry a man, colonial society had no permanent cultural category for those who engaged in sexual relations with members of their own gender. Like other sinners, women or men who were punished for unnatural sexual acts did not acquire a lifetime identity as "homosexuals," and they could be reintegrated into the fold. In 1732, for example, Ebenezer Knight of Marblehead confessed and repented "a long series of Uncleanness with Mankind." His church suspended Knight, but after he returned from a six-year sojourn in Boston, the congregation reinstated him.[46]

As in the case of sodomy, conviction for rape carried the death penalty, but lesser punishments usually applied. Rape was the only sexual offense that did not involve consensual acts, and much of the testimony by a rape victim and the required witnesses focused on proving that the woman did not consent to the act. Accounts of rape and attempted rape emphasize the extent to which women resisted their assailants. Nonetheless, conviction and sentencing patterns disclose a reluctance to prosecute men fully for this crime. Out of seventy-two rape accusations in seventeenth-century New England, only six resulted in executions, though more than half the men were convicted. That Massachusetts courts were more likely to convict when a child or a married woman had been raped suggests that single, adult women were often perceived as willing sexual partners. The rape of a daughter or wife could be seen as an attack on the "property" of a father or husband, rather than a crime against the woman herself. Indeed, the death penalty for rape applied only if a woman was married, engaged, or under the age of ten.[47]

The disposition of rape cases depended strongly upon the status of both victim and assailant. Men of higher social standing—farm owners and artisans, for example—were less likely to be brought to trial for rape or attempted rape, while lower-class and nonwhite men accused of rape could expect harsher treatment by the courts. In 1685, a servant convicted of attempted rape upon a married woman received the severe punishment of thirty-five lashes. In eighteenth-century Massachusetts, three of the five executions for rape involved blacks or Indians, even though nonwhite men represented only 14 percent of those accused of rape. The other two executed were white laborers.[48] The harshest penalties for sexual assault applied to blacks who attacked white women. In New York, a free black convicted of two attempted rapes of white women was burned alive. Another free black in Virginia received twenty-nine lashes, an hour in the pillory, and a sentence of temporary servitude for attempted assault on a seven-year-old white girl. In several colonies, the laws prescribed castration for blacks who attempted to rape white women.[49]

Neighbors were especially important as witnesses in rape cases, for it was incumbent upon the victim to call out in order to notify others of an attack; otherwise, the court might consider her a willing partner. When Elizabeth Goodell of Salem accused her brother-in-law of frequent "assaults" and "affronts," her neighbors stated that she should have called out for help. Even nine-year-old Ruth Parsons testified that she had cried out when Edward Sanders forcibly abused her by "enteringe her body with his pisseinge place (as shee called it)," but no one was near the house to hear her, except "little children wch he put out of doores."[50] In some cases, women were punished for not having called out when assaulted. When a victim of unwanted sexual advances was afraid to call out or press charges, neighbors might step in to bring the case to light. The testimony of other members of the community was also important in determining whether a rape had actually occurred. Midwives and other women who examined the victims of assault helped the court determine whether to prosecute for rape or a lesser charge.[51] As in the response to adultery, the entire community mobilized to ferret out those who engaged in sexual acts outside of marriage.

Bastardy, like adultery, sodomy, and rape, threatened the centrality of marital, reproductive sexuality, but it also posed a particularly troubling economic problem for the colonists: Who would provide for children born out of wedlock in a society in which the family was the central economic unit? Lest the cost fall upon other members of the community, colonies passed bastardy laws, patterned upon English antecedents, that severely punished the parents of bastards and attempted to hold the purported father responsible for the child's care. In order to establish paternity, midwives questioned an unmarried woman during labor, "the time of her travell [travail]," when they believed she would be incapable of lying about the father's identity. The court then accused the father and meted out punishment to both parents in the form of fines or whipping, along with an effort to enforce marriage. Maryland courts, for example, doled out thirty-nine lashes to parents of bastards, while Connecticut courts sentenced five pounds and ten stripes of the lash. By the mid-eighteenth century, many courts ceased to punish the parents for their sexual transgressions and concentrated entirely on obtaining support for the child. It was then left to the churches to enforce morality and try to pressure the parents of bastards into marrying.[52]

The mechanism by which colonists attempted to determine paternity was extremely vulnerable to manipulation by either the mother or the father of a bastard. For one, no matter how coercive they might be, midwives could not always force an unwilling mother—like Nathaniel Hawthorne's fictional Hester Prynne—to reveal the name of her child's father. The Quakers, as an added sanction, disowned from their church congregations a woman who did not name the father. Or, a woman might calculatingly decide to follow the course of the servant Elizabeth Wells, who told another servant that "[i]f shee should bee with child shee would bee sure to lay it un to won who was rich enough abell to mayntayne it weather it wear his or no." A pattern of false paternity accusations is revealed by another woman, who wrote to her illicit lover: "der loue [love] . . . i am a child by you and i will ether kil it or lay it to an other . . . I have had many children and none [of the fathers] have none of them [to support]."[53]

At the same time, fathers could refuse to acknowledge paternity. The wealthy George Hammond of Maine, cited by Lydia Spinney as father of her child, refuted the charge and would not pay child support. Some men attempted to deny responsibility by claiming that the mother had been promiscuous; others claimed economic inability to support a child. In New Amsterdam, Geleyn Verplank admitted "to have had carnal conversation" with Geertruyd Wingres, but he denied that he promised to marry her and failed to pay the lying-in charges and child maintenance ordered by the court.[54] John Harrington denied paternity in a 1771 bastardy case by claiming that he could not possibly be the father of the child. In the process, he inadvertently revealed what was probably the predominant method for avoiding conception: "I f—d her once," he admitted, "but I minded my pullbacks. I sware I did not get it." The court did not share his faith in coitus interruptus, and Harrington was convicted.[55]

The female servant could have an especially hard time sustaining a paternity charge. If a man denied her claim, she had to produce witnesses to support her in court. If a free man, and particularly a master, denied paternity, the court might well accept his word over that of a servant. In Maryland, servant Jane Palldin bore an illegitimate child by her married master, John Norton. Afraid of the consequences of revealing the father, she first claimed that a stranger "gott her with Child." Indeed, after she confessed the truth, Norton's wife "began to raile at her" and a brawl broke out among the three of them.[56] Masters could abuse the law by impregnating a servant and enjoying not only sexual privilege but an extra year of servitude as well. To prevent this practice, courts began to remove female servants from households if their masters allowed them to become pregnant.[57]

Despite the difficulties of enforcement, colonial society did maintain a low rate of illegitimacy. Historical demographer Robert Wells has estimated that prior to 1750, between 1 and 3 percent of all births occurred outside of marriage. The seventeenth-century Chesapeake, with its large number of indentured servants, had a much higher rate, while some regions had even lower ones. In the middle colonies, Quaker congregations recorded no bastardy cases until 1780, and in Germantown, Pennsylvania, illegitimate children accounted for under 1 percent of all colonial-era baptismal certificates. Persistent regional variation is clear from the ratios of illegitimate births per thousand live births at the beginning of the eighteenth century. These ranged from a low of one in a New York Dutch Reformed church, to between thirteen and eighteen in several Connecticut, Massachusetts, and Virginia counties, to a high of twenty-six in one Maryland county.[58]

Both the stigma and the cost of bearing an illegitimate child led some unwed mothers, whether free or servant, to commit infanticide. In Massachusetts, Grace, a "Negro single woman servant," murdered her bastard son in 1692, and Elizabeth Emerson, an unwed mother who lived with her parents, buried her illegitimate children in the garden. Lucy Stratton of Maryland received thirty lashes for having "unnaturally dried up her milk," a neglectful action that the court believed had put her infant's life in danger.[59] Because unwed mothers, attempting to avoid prosecution, sometimes claimed that their children had been stillborn or had died of natural causes, colonial, like English, law assumed maternal guilt if a bastard child was found dead. Therefore it was a crime to conceal the death of a bastard child. Widespread concern about infanticide led the colonies by the eighteenth century to enact laws providing that unless sworn witnesses could testify that a child was stillborn, the mother of a dead bastard was presumed to be guilty of murder. Nonetheless, New England courts charged only thirty-two women with infanticide in the seventeenth century. Although the overall indictment rate was over twice as high in the Chesapeake, conviction rates were lower in the South. As in other criminal prosecutions, black servants and slaves had a higher conviction rate than all whites, free or servant.[60]

Even though infanticide rates remained low throughout the colonies, this crime provided a particularly frightening symbol of the wages of sexual sin. Since so many infanticide victims were newborn bastard children, the crime represented the ultimate destructiveness wrought by illicit sexual union. The clergy did not miss the opportunity to bring this message home to their flock. As Cotton Mather expounded in his sermon on the execution of Sarah Smith, who had murdered her newborn infant, "an *Unchaste Life*" had brought Smith to the gallows, for the "*Fires of Lust*" had baked her heart into "Insensible Hardness."[61] Lust, unchecked, could lead not only to illegitimacy, but worse, to the death of both child and sinner as well.

In the late seventeenth century, the prohibition of interracial sex and marriage emerged as an additional sexual boundary. In the early years of settlement, before slavery became entrenched, interracial unions, though unpopular, did not necessarily elicit harsh punishment. In cases of fornication, adultery, or bastardy, the offenders received punishments similar to those white couples endured. In 1640, for example, a Virginia gentleman had "to do penance in church . . . for getting a negroe woman with child," while the woman received a whipping—not an extraordinary punishment.[62] In many areas of the South, the white sex ratio remained so unbalanced that white men sometimes sought black mates in the absence of white women. By the late seventeenth century, however, the white sex ratio began to even out. More importantly, large numbers of Africans were being imported as slaves, and slavery began to supplant indentured servitude as the major source of labor. Colonial assemblies soon enacted an array of statutes—including laws punishing interracial sexual relations—to strengthen the race line by reinforcing the unequal status of blacks and whites.

As with native American Indians, sexual stereotyping provided one means by which the English colonists justified their domination of Africans. English colonists brought to America a set of stereotypes that differentiated Europeans from Africans by assigning to the latter a sexual nature that was more sensual, aggressive, and beastlike than that of whites. Influenced by the Elizabethan image of "the lusty Moor," colonists accepted the notion that Africans were "lewd, lascivious and wanton people." With the growing reliance on slavery, colonists drew upon these English stereotypes to help justify their economic and social control of blacks. Not only their dark color, but also their allegedly animal-like sexuality, whites argued, proved that blacks were of a different breed than whites; it was thus "natural" that the two races should not mix, and that whites should dominate blacks. Throughout the American colonies, a caste system based on race took hold by the eighteenth century. From New Englander Samuel Sewall to Virginian Thomas Jefferson, white colonists, regardless of their views on slavery, opposed interracial mixing. But in the southern colonies, where slavery grew in economic importance, the racial boundary became more deeply institutionalized.[63] Individuals who transgressed this racial boundary challenged not only a set of cultural values but also the basis of an emerging system of racial control.

As African slaves came to dominate the labor force, slavery required legal support. Colonial legislatures acted to outlaw and penalize individuals who practiced what would later be termed miscegenation. Legislation to regulate interracial unions first appeared in the 1660s. The Virginia legislature in 1662 doubled the fines for fornication in the case of interracial couples, and in 1691 it outlawed "that abominable mixture" of interracial union, ordering banishment from the colony for any white man or woman who married or fornicated with a Negro, mulatto, or Indian. In 1705, the Assembly strengthened the law by ordering six months' imprisonment and a ten-pound fine for interracial marriage or fornication, and fined the minister who performed an interracial marriage ten thousand pounds of tobacco. Maryland banned such marriages in 1664, ordering a white woman who married a slave to serve her husband's master. Between 1705 and 1750, all of the southern colonies, as well as Pennsylvania and Massachusetts, passed laws prohibiting interracial marriages and any other "unnatural and inordinate Copulations" between whites and blacks. Discriminatory treatment of interracial children further supported the institution of slavery. Delaware enacted heavier fines in interracial than white bastardy cases, and the 1664 Maryland anti-miscegenation law defined the children of mixed marriages as slaves. In most colonies, bastard children of mixed unions had to spend up to thirty-one years in servitude.[64]

The laws against miscegenation did not entirely prevent the formation of interracial unions. Where French, Spanish, and West Indian influences remained strong, as in Louisiana and coastal South Carolina, the taboos on amalgamation were weaker, and interracial unions might be discussed in public. In all of the English colonies, however, some forms of miscegenation persisted. In New England, where few blacks lived and slavery failed to take root, some interracial marriages survived social and legal proscription. More typical, however, were illicit unions formed between southern whites and blacks. Male planters, by virtue of their class, were not bound by the prohibitions against interracial sex. Thus relationships between white planters and black women often formed. Some southern men acknowledged these unions when they manumitted or left property to their mulatto children.[65]

In addition to ongoing interracial relations, brief sexual encounters took place frequently in the South. As a Boston traveler to South Carolina observed in 1773, "The enjoyment of a negro or mulatto woman is spoken of as quite a common thing." Given the prevailing stereotype of African sensuality, white men assumed that black women were willing to have sexual relationships with them. In fact, female slaves had little choice about whether to respond to white men's sexual advances, whatever their actual desires. Interracial unions between white women and black men were least frequent and usually confined to the rural backcountry of the South, where the status difference between poor whites and slaves was narrower. One Maryland husband banished his wife from his sight and refused financial responsibility for her because she "polluted my Bed, by taking to her in my stead, her own Negro slave, by whom she hath a child." As in this case, a woman's adultery with a slave or free black male might lead to divorce.[66]

Probably the rarest form of interracial union, but the most symbolically charged, was the rape of a white woman by a black man. So frightening was the specter of this inversion of the racial hierarchy that colonial legislatures devised a uniquely American criminal penalty, castration, as a means of deterrence. Laws in Pennsylvania, New Jersey, and Virginia allowed castration for blacks who attempted to rape white women. Even when this literally emasculating punishment was dropped from other criminal codes, it could still be applied in cases of assaults on white women by slaves. That assaults on black women provoked no such reaction confirms the racial character of this legislation. At least one eighteenth-century Virginia slave was formally sentenced to castration. Blacks convicted of rape were usually hanged.[67] Nonetheless, the law set a precedent that could be followed by extralegal means. Thus in 1718, when a white man in Connecticut observed a black man lying with a white woman, he attacked the black and castrated him. Whites particularly feared that when slaves revolted against their masters, as they did on several occasions during the eighteenth century, the men would assault white women to retaliate for white assaults on black women. However, there is no evidence that black men sexually assaulted white women during the slave uprisings of the colonial period.[68]

White attitudes toward interracial sexual relations reflected complex psychological, economic, and legal dynamics. That white men of the planter class could have casual sexual relations with slave women, but reserved the most brutal corporal punishment for black men who slept with white women, clearly illustrates the ways that sexual rules reinforced a system of racial dominance. That enormous scorn was heaped upon a white woman who had sex with a black man—even if they were married—while black women were expected to service the sexual needs of white men, reveals the combined forces of gender and racial hierarchy. As Winthrop Jordan has convincingly argued, white men desired sexual union with blacks, but given their culture's aversion to racial mixing they refused to acknowledge that desire and those unions. Thus white men projected sexual desire onto black women, viewing them as lustful and available, and onto black men, fearing them as potential rapists. Finally, white men refused to acknowledge the products of interracial union by systematically relegating mulatto children to the status of slaves. Unlike Spanish and Portuguese colonies, with their elaborate racial hierarchies in which mulatto children were often considered to be free rather than enslaved, the English colonies allowed no gradation of color. They condemned the child of mixed unions to the status of slave.[69] The different sex ratios of Latin and North American colonies contributed to this divergent practice, but so did the colonists' psychological conflicts about interracial union. "Sexual intimacy," Jordan has written of the white man, "strikingly symbolized a union he wished to avoid. If he could not restrain his sexual nature, he could at least reject its fruits and thus solace himself that he had done no harm. . . . By classifying the mulatto as a Negro he was in effect denying that intermixture had occurred at all."[70]

The regulation of deviance in the American colonies, from the mid-seventeenth to the mid-eighteenth centuries, helped to enforce the system of marital, reproductive sexuality and to maintain white dominance over blacks. Just as the socialization of youth channeled sexuality into marriage, so too did church, court, and community join forces to identify sexual crime and publicly affirm the proper place of sex. Selective enforcement led to the prosecution of more women than men, and to lesser penalties for free, white, and wealthier individuals. For all colonists, however, a clear message surrounded the public pronouncements about sexual crime: the family provided the only acceptable outlet for sex, with the primary goal of producing legitimate children.

Paralleling the growth of colonial society and the decline of Puritanism, the regulation of morality changed over time. In the eighteenth century, the sexual boundary between white and black intensified. In contrast, the enforcement of marital, reproductive sexuality among whites lessened. Even New Englanders, with their religious obligation to create a godly community, meted out fewer, and less severe, punishments for adultery, sodomy, rape, and infanticide in the eighteenth century. The middle and southern colonies traditionally had lower rates of enforcement for morals offenses, but there, too, convictions declined after 1720. As white colonists turned their attention to the pursuit of the secular goal of a prosperous community, sexual transgressions elicited less public concern, while state regulation of morality weakened. After 1750, even more rapid social changes would begin to transform the American family and with it sexual norms and their regulation.

NOTES

1. Stephen Innes, *Labor in a New Land: Economy and Society in Seventeenth-Century Springfield* (Princeton, 1983), pp. 132–33.

2. Laurel Thatcher Ulrich, *Goodwives: Image and Reality in the Lives of Women in Northern New England, 1650–1750* (New York, 1983), p. 95.

3. Robert Oaks, " 'Things Fearful to Name': Sodomy and Buggery in Seventeenth-Century New England," in *The American Man*, ed. Joseph Pleck and Elizabeth Pleck (Englewood Cliffs, N.J., 1980), pp. 66–69. See also Jonathan Ned Katz, ed., *Gay/Lesbian Almanac: A New Documentary* (New York, 1983), pp. 87, 111. Bestiality persisted in rural areas long after the colonial period. In 1867, for example, a sixteen-year-old white boy had "carnal intercourse with one of his ewes" (Herbert G. Gutman, *The Black Family in Slavery and Freedom, 1750–1925* [New York, 1976], p. 394).

4. David H. Flaherty, *Privacy in Colonial New England* (Charlottesville, 1972), esp. pp. 42–43, 76, 78; Nancy Cott, "Eighteenth-Century Family and Social Life Revealed in Massachusetts Divorce Records," in *A Heritage of Her Own*, ed. Nancy F. Cott and Elizabeth H. Pleck (New York, 1979), p. 119; Linda K. Kerber, *Women of the Republic: Intellect and Ideology in Revolutionary America* (Chapel Hill, 1980), p. 166; and Manuscript Court Records, New Hampshire State Archives, Concord, N.H, vol. 7, p. 225 (1683).

5. Roger Thompson, *Women in Stuart England and America* (London, 1974), p. 244; Mary Beth Norton, "Gender and Defamation in Seventeenth-Century Maryland," *William and Mary Quarterly* 44 (1987): 3–39; Roger Thompson, *Sex in Middlesex: Popular Mores in a Massachusetts County, 1649–1699* (Amherst, 1986), pp. 180–81. See also Ulrich, *Goodwives*, p. 96; and Robert B. St. George, "Heated Speech and Literacy in Seventeenth-Century New England," in *Seventeenth-Century New England*, ed. David D. Hall et al. (Publications of the Colonial Society of Massachusetts Collections, 1984), pp. lxiii, 275–322.

6. Katz, *Gay/Lesbian Almanac*, p. 83; Lyle Koehler, *A Search for Power: The "Weaker Sex" in Seventeenth-Century New England* (Champaign, Ill., 1980), pp. 73, 76. See also Kathleen Verduin, " 'Our Cursed Natures': Sexuality and the Puritan Conscience," *New England Quarterly* 56 (1983). On women, see Barbara Epstein, *The Politics of Domesticity: Women, Evangelism, and Temperance in Nineteenth-Century America* (Middletown, Conn., 1981), pp. 42–43.

7. Philip Greven, *The Protestant Temperament: Patterns of Child-Rearing, Religious Experience, and Self in Early America* (New York, 1977), esp. pp. 248, 314, 316.

8. Otto T. Beall, "Aristotle's Master Piece in America: A Landmark in the Folklore of Medicine," *William and Mary Quarterly* 20 (1963): 208–10; Steven Nissenbaum, *Sex, Diet, and Debility in Jacksonian America: Sylvester Graham and Health Reform* (Westport, Conn., 1980), ch. 2.

9. *Aristotle's Compleat Masterpiece* (New York, 1788), p. 58.

10. Edmund S. Morgan, ed., *The Diary of Michael Wigglesworth, 1653–1657: The Conscience of a Puritan* (reprint, New York, 1965), pp. 4, 30–31, 50, 80; Verduin, "'Cursed Natures,'" p. 225. On women's conversions, see Epstein, *Politics of Domesticity*, p. 42.

11. Franklin B. Dexter, ed., *Ancient Town Records* (New Haven, 1917), vol. 1, *New Haven Town Records, 1649–1662*, pp. 178–79; Thompson, *Sex in Middlesex*, pp. 72–73, 87–88; Susie M. Ames, ed., *Country Court Record of Accomack-Northampton, Virginia, 1640–1645* (Charlottesville, 1973), p. 117; Edmund S. Morgan, *The Puritan Family: Religion and Domestic Relations in Seventeenth-Century New England* (New York, 1944), pp. 128–29; Eli Faber, "Puritan Criminals: The Economic, Social, and Intellectual Background to Crime in Seventeenth-Century Massachusetts," *Perspectives in American History* 11 (1977–78): 101, 116–17.

12. Daniel Blake Smith, *Inside the Great House: Planter Life in Eighteenth-Century Chesapeake Society* (Ithaca, 1980), pp. 140–41.

13. Ibid., pp. 130–34; Morgan, *Puritan Family*, pp. 54–57.

14. Koehler, *Search*, p. 424; Flaherty, *Privacy*, pp. 82, 156, 73; William Hand Browne et al., eds., *Archives of Maryland* (Baltimore, 1891–1936), vol. 10, p. 499 (hereafter *Arch. Md.*).

15. Henry Reed Stiles, *Bundling: Its Origins, Progress and Decline in America* (Albany, 1869), pp. 13, 66; Dana Doten, *The Art of Bundling* (New York, 1938), p. 66; Flaherty, *Privacy*, p. 78.

16. Koehler, *Search*, pp. 80, 434; Morgan, *Puritan Family*, p. 33; John Demos, *A Little Commonwealth: Family Life in Plymouth Colony* (New York, 1970), p. 158, n. 35.

17. Ralph Semmes, *Crime and Punishment in Early Maryland* (Baltimore, 1938), pp. 182–83; Demos, *Little Commonwealth*, 152–58; Ulrich, *Goodwives*, p. 31; Massachusetts State Archives, Boston, Mass. (hereafter cited as Mass. Arch.), vol. 9, p. 104a (Sept. 25, 1677) (Mary Woodin). See also vol. 9, p. 378 (March 13, 1749).

18. Lorena S. Walsh, "'Till Death Do Us Part': Marriage and Family in Seventeenth-Century Maryland," in *The Chesapeake in the Seventeenth Century: Essays in Anglo-American Society*, ed. Thad W. Tate and David L. Ammerman (Chapel Hill, 1979), pp. 126–52; Stephanie Grauman Wolf, *Urban Village: Population, Community, and Family Structure in Germantown, Pennsylvania, 1683–1800* (Princeton, 1976), p. 259; Daniel Scott Smith, "The Long Cycle in American Illegitimacy and Prenuptial Pregnancy," in *Bastardy and Its Comparative History*, ed. Peter Laslett et al. (Cambridge, Mass., 1980), p. 369; Daniel Scott Smith and Michael Hindus, "Premarital Pregnancy in America, 1640–1971: An Overview and an Interpretation," *Journal of Interdisciplinary History* 5 (1975): 537–70.

19. On New England, see Flaherty, *Privacy*, p. 160. See also Emil Oberholzer, *Delinquent Saints: Disciplinary Actions in the Early Congregational Churches of Massachusetts* (New York, 1956), ch. 8; and *Arch. Md.* 54: 366, 371.

20. Faber, "Puritan Criminals," pp. 140–43.

21. Morgan, *Wigglesworth*, p. 88. See also Ulrich, *Goodwives*, p. 109; and Morgan, *Puritan Family*, p. 141.

22. Koehler, *Search*, pp. 78–79.

23. Ibid., p. 37; Smith, *Great House*, pp. 155–56, 162.

24. Cott, "Massachusetts Divorce," p. 126.

25. William Byrd, *The Secret Diary of William Byrd of Westover, 1709–1712*, ed. Louis B. Wright and Marion Tinling (Richmond, Va., 1941), p. 337. See also Smith, *Great House*, p. 162; and Catherine M. Scholten, *Childrearing in American Society: 1650–1850* (New York, 1985), p. 19.

26. Ulrich, *Goodwives*, p. 112; Ethan Smith, ed., *Memoirs of Mrs. Abigail Bailey* (reprint, New York, 1980); Cott, "Massachusetts Divorce," pp. 119–20.

27. Demos, *Little Commonwealth*, p. 95. See also Kerber, *Women of the Republic*, p. 172.

28. Koehler, *Search*, pp. 78–79.

29. Mary Beth Norton, *Liberty's Daughters: The Revolutionary Experience of American Women, 1750–1800* (Boston, 1980), p. 77. See also Mary P. Ryan, *Womanhood in America, from*

Colonial Times to the Present (New York, 1975), pp. 54, 57; and Demos, *Little Commonwealth,* p. 66.

30. Scholten, *Childrearing,* p. 13. On Bradstreet, see Koehler, *Search,* p. 56; and Jeannine Hensley, ed., *The Works of Anne Bradstreet* (Cambridge, Mass., 1967), pp. 236ff.

31. Daniel Scott Smith, "The Demographic History of Colonial New England," in *The American Family in Social-Historical Perspective,* ed. Michael Gordon (New York, 1973), p. 410; Wolf, *Urban Village,* p. 262; Scholten, *Childrearing,* pp. 72–73; Koehler, *Search,* pp. 56–57.

32. Cott, "Massachusetts Divorce," p. 119; Michael Zuckerman, "Pilgrims in the Wilderness: Community, Modernity, and the Maypole at Merry Mount," *New England Quarterly* 50 (1977): 266; Carol F. Karlsen, "The Devil in the Shape of a Woman: The Witch in Seventeenth-Century New England" (Ph.D. diss., Yale University, 1980), p. 218; *Arch. Md.* 10: 503–4, 41: 20.

33. Wilson H. Grabill et al., "A Long View," in *American Family,* ed. Gordon, pp. 377–78; Norton, *Liberty's Daughters,* pp. 72–75; Nancy Osterud and J. Fulton, "Family Limitation and Age at Marriage: Fertility Decline in Sturbridge, Massachusetts, 1730–1850," *Population Studies* 30 (1976): 483.

34. Smith, *Great House,* pp. 27–28; Allan Kulikoff, "A 'Prolifick' People: Black Population Growth in the Chesapeake Colonies, 1700–1790," *Southern Studies* 16 (1977): 408.

35. *Arch. Md.* 53: xxix, 54: 518, 30: 560; Edmund S. Morgan, *American Slavery, American Freedom* (New York, 1975), p. 333.

36. Donna J. Spindel and Stuart W. Thomas, "Crime and Society in North Carolina, 1633–1740," *Journal of Southern History* 49 (1983): 223–44. Witchcraft was one offense in which women predominated—up to 80 percent of accused witches were women—but it is not clear that American witchcraft charges had much to do with sexuality, as opposed to gender. According to John Demos, colonial women accused as witches were less likely to have had a prior record of sexual offenses than were other women. Property relations seem to have been more important than sexual behavior in determining witchcraft accusations in seventeenth-century New England. John Demos, *Entertaining Satan: Witchcraft and the Culture of Early New England* (New York, 1982), pp. 77–78; Karlsen, "The Devil," pp. 214–19, 333–34.

37. Peter C. Hoffer and William B. Scott, eds., *Criminal Proceedings in Colonial Virginia* (Athens, Ga., 1984), pp. 19–20, 71, 77; e.g., *Arch Md.* 10: 112; Betty B. Rosenbaum, "The Sociological Bases of the Laws Relating to Women Sex Offenders in Massachusetts, 1620–1860," *Journal of Criminal Law and Criminology* 27 (1938): 820–21; Mass. Arch. 9: 221–22 (January 31, 1736) (Thomas Clarke) (see also 9: 265 [July 16, 1742]).

38. Cott, "Massachusetts Divorce," p. 126. On the seventeenth century, see Koehler, *Search,* pp. 147–52.

39. Manuscript Court Records, New Hampshire State Archive, Concord, N.H., vol. 7 (1683), pp. 225, 233, 241, 245; Semmes, *Crime,* pp. 178–79, cites attacks on men.

40. Flaherty, *Privacy,* p. 176.

41. Christine Heyrman, *Commerce and Culture: The Maritime Communities of Colonial Massachusetts* (New York, 1984), pp. 49–50; Flaherty, *Privacy,* p. 207.

42. Semmes, *Crime,* pp. 182–83; Ames, *Accomack* (record for July 4, 1643), p. 290; Flaherty, *Privacy,* p. 43.

43. Cott, "Massachusetts Divorce," p. 110 (see also Mass. Arch. 9: 265); *Arch. Md.* 54: 55 (see also 53: 225); Heyrman, *Commerce,* p. 216.

44. Katz, *Gay/Lesbian Almanac,* pp. 90–91, 111–18; and Katz, *Gay American History* (New York, 1976), pp. 12–13; Robert S. Oaks, "Defining Sodomy in Seventeenth-Century Massachusetts," *Journal of Homosexuality* 6.1–2 (1980–81): 82. Katz has found twenty legal cases concerning homosexual relations in the period 1607 to 1740. See also Mass. Arch. 38b: 41, 41a (n.d.).

45. Semmes, *Crime,* p. 204; Katz, *Gay/Lesbian Almanac,* pp. 54–55, 84–85; Koehler, *Search,* p. 82.

46. Heyrman, *Commerce,* p. 286.

47. Thompson, *Sex in Middlesex,* p. 75; Koehler, *Search,* p. 95; Barbara S. Lindemann, " 'To Ravish and Carnally Know': Rape in Eighteenth-Century Massachusetts," *Signs* 10 (1984): 80.

48. Lindemann, " 'To Ravish,' " p. 80.

49. Winthrop D. Jordan, *White over Black: American Attitudes towards the Negro, 1550–1812* (Baltimore, 1969), pp. 157 and n. 44. See also D'Emilio and Freedman, *Intimate Matters,* for discussion of interracial sex.

50. Lindemann, " 'To Ravish,' " p. 68; Ulrich, *Goodwives,* pp. 99–102; Mass. Arch. 38B: 189 (September–October 1654).

51. Flaherty, *Privacy,* p. 207; Ulrich, *Goodwives,* pp. 90–92. For examples of midwives' role, see Elizabeth Taylor's affidavit in James Otis papers, August 18, 1681, Massachusetts Historical Society, Boston; and *Arch. Md.* 41: 20.

52. Robert V. Wells, "Illegitimacy and Bridal Pregnancy in Colonial America," in *Bastardy,* ed. Laslett et al., p. 358; Morgan, *Puritan Family,* pp. 130–31; Ulrich, *Goodwives,* pp. 102–3; Koehler, *Search,* p. 354.

53. Morgan, *Puritan Family,* pp. 130–31. On Quakers, see Jack Donald Marietta, "Ecclesiastical Discipline in the Society of Friends, 1662–1776" (Ph.D. diss., Stanford University, 1968).

54. Neal W. Allen, ed., *Province and Court Records of Maine,* vol. 7 (Portland, Maine, 1975), pp. 121–23 (April 2, 1723). Berthold Fernow, ed., *The Records of New Amsterdam, 1653 to 1674,* vol. 3 (Baltimore, 1976), p. 370.

55. Quoted in Wells, "Illegitimacy," p. 361.

56. *Arch. Md.* 41: 14–16. See also Wolf, *Urban Village,* p. 298.

57. Robert V. Wells, *Revolutions in Americans' Lives: A Demographic Perspective on the History of Americans, Their Families, and Their Society* (Westport, Conn., 1982), p. 59.

58. Wells, *Revolutions,* p. 40, and "Illegitimacy," pp. 354ff; Wolf, *Urban Village,* p. 261.

59. Misc. bound ms., April 25, 1693, Massachusetts Historical Society, Boston; Ulrich, *Goodwives,* p. 198; Semmes, *Crime,* p. 195.

60. Wells, "Illegitimacy," p. 360; Koehler, *Search,* pp. 200–1; Peter C. Hoffer and N. E. H. Hull, *Murdering Mothers: Infanticide in England and New England, 1558–1803* (New York, 1981), pp. 45–48, 53, 58, 63.

61. Verduin, " 'Cursed Natures,' " p. 227.

62. Jordan, *White over Black,* p. 78.

63. Ibid., pp. 30–32, 196–97, 459; David Brion Davis, *The Problem of Slavery in Western Culture* (Ithaca, 1966), pp. 468–70.

64. Morgan, *American Slavery,* pp. 335–36; Letitia Woods Brown, *Free Negroes in the District of Columbia, 1790–1846* (New York, 1972), pp. 25–29; Jordan, *White over Black,* pp. 77–80, 139–41, 164; Wells, "Illegitimacy," p. 358; Peter H. Wood, *Black Majority: Negroes in Colonial South Carolina, from 1670 to the Stono Rebellion* (New York, 1974), pp. 233–35.

65. Jordan, *White over Black,* pp. 137–38, 473, n. 80; Davis, *Problem of Slavery,* p. 281.

66. Jordan, *White over Black,* pp. 139, 145, and 473, n. 81.

67. When Pennsylvania lawmakers substituted life imprisonment for the death penalty from 1700 to 1718, they did so only for whites. For blacks, rape of a white (but not black) woman—along with buggery, burglary, and murder—remained capital offenses (Katz, *Gay/Lesbian Almanac,* p. 61).

68. Jordan, *White over Black,* pp. 158, 398.

69. Davis, *Problem of Slavery,* pp. 274–75; Carl N. Degler, *Neither Black nor White: Slavery and Race Relations in Brazil and the United States* (New York, 1971).

70. Jordan, *White over Black,* p. 178.

SEXUALITY IN CALIFORNIA'S FRANCISCAN MISSIONS

Cultural Perceptions and Historical Realities

ALBERT HURTADO

At one of these Indian villages near this mission of San Diego the gentiles therein many times have been on the point of coming here to kill us all, [because] some soldiers went there and raped their women, and other soldiers who were carrying mail to Monterey turned their animals into their fields and they ate up their crops. Three other Indian villages about a league or a league and a half from here have reported the same thing to me several times. For this reason on several occasions when Father Francisco Dumetz or I have gone to see these Indian villages, as soon as they saw us they fled from their villages and fled to the woods or other remote places, and the only ones who remained in the village were some men and some very old women. The Christians here have told me that many of the gentiles of the aforesaid villages leave their huts and the crops which they gather from the lands around their villages, and go to the woods and experience hunger: They do this so the soldiers will not rape their women as they have already done so many times in the past.[1]

—Father Luís Jayme, 1772

Before Father Junípero Serra founded California's Franciscan missions, he led a religious revival in Mexico's Oaxaca region. Francisco Palóu, Serra's companion and biographer, approvingly reported that Serra's religious work produced concrete results. He reformed an adulteress who at the tender age of fourteen had begun to cohabit with a married man whose wife lived in Spain. This sinful arrangement had lasted for fourteen years, but on Serra's order she left the house of her lover. The man was desolate. He threatened and begged, but to no avail. Then "one night in desperation," Palóu related, "he got a halter, took it with him to the house where she was staying, and hung himself on an iron gate, giving over his soul to the demons." At the same moment a great earthquake shook the town, whose inhabitants trembled with fear. Thereafter, the woman donned haircloth and penitential garb and walked the streets begging forgiveness for her shameful past. "All were edified and touched at seeing such an unusual conversion and subsequent penance," the friar wrote. "Nor were they less fearful of divine Justice," he added, "recalling the chastisement of that unfortunate man." Thus, Palóu believed, the tragedy brought "innumerable conversions . . . and great spiritual fruit" to Serra's Oaxaca mission.[2]

This story was a kind of parable that prefaced Palóu's glowing account of Serra's missionary work in California. It demonstrated not only the presence of sexual sin in Spain's American colonies—which is not especially surprising—but that priestly intervention could break perverse habits, and that public exposure and sincere repentance could save souls. This incident is especially important because Palóu linked Serra's Mexican missionary triumph with the rectification of sexual behavior on the eve of his expedition to California. Thus, a discussion of sexuality in the California missions is not merely a prurient exercise, but goes to the heart of missionaries' intentions. While errant sexuality was not the only concern of priests, the reformation of Indian sexual behavior was an important part of their endeavor to Christianize and Hispanicize native Californians. Their task was fraught with difficulty, peril, and tragedy for Indians and Spaniards alike.

Native people, of course, already behaved according to sexual norms that, from their point of view, worked perfectly well. From north of San Francisco Bay to the present Mexican border, tribes regulated sexual life so as to promote productive family relationships that varied by tribe and locality. Everywhere the conjugal couple and their children formed a basic household unit, sometimes augmented by aged relatives and unmarried siblings. Indian families, however, were not merely a series of nuclear units, but were knit into sets of associations that comprised native society. Kinship defined the individual's place within the cultural community, and family associations suffused every aspect of life.

Indian marriages usually occurred within economic and social ranks and tended to stabilize economic and power relationships. Chiefs (who were occasionally women) were usually from wealthy families and inherited their positions. Since secure links with other groups provided insurance against occasional food shortages, chiefs frequently married several elite women from other *rancherías* (a Spanish term for small Indian communities). Diplomatic polygyny provided kinship links that maintained prosperity and limited warfare that could result from poaching or blood feuds. In the event of war, kinship considerations helped to determine who would be attacked, as well as the duration and intensity of conflict.[3]

Given the significance and intricacy of kinship, marriage was an extremely important institution, governed according to strict rules. Parents or respected *ranchería* elders often arranged marriages of young people and even infants. California Indians regarded incest—defined according to strict consanguinial and affinal rules—as a bar that prohibited marriage if a couple was related within three to five generations, depending on tribal affiliation. Consequently, men had to look for eligible wives outside their tribelet. Since most groups had patrilocal residence customs, women usually left their home communities, thus strengthening the system of reciprocity that girded native California.

The bride price symbolized women's place in this scheme. The groom gave his parents-in-law a gift to recognize the status of the bride's family, demonstrate the groom's worth, and compensate her family for the loss of her labor. The bride price did not signify that the wife was a chattel. No husband could sell his spouse, and an unhappy wife could divorce her husband. Even so, men were considered to be family heads, descent was usually through the male line, and residence in the groom's *rancheria*.[4]

California's native household economy was based on hunting and gathering according to a sexual division of labor. Men hunted and fished, and—after the advent of white settlement—raided livestock herds. Women gathered the plant foods that comprised the bulk of the Indian diet—acorns, seeds, roots, pine nuts, berries, and other staples. All California tribes prized hardworking, productive women.[5] Women's material and subsistence production was of basic importance to Indian society, but they made another crucial contribution as well—they bore children, thus creating the human resources needed to sustain native communities. When populations suffered significant reductions, the lack of fertile women meant that the capacity to recover was limited.

Re-creating the sexual behavior of any people is a difficult task, but it is especially difficult in societies that lacked a written record. Still, modern anthropology and historical testimony make possible a plausible—if partial—reconstruction of intimate native life. California Indians regulated sexual behavior in and out of marriage. Premarital sex does not seem to have been regarded as a matter of great importance, so virginity was not a precondition in a respectable mate. After marriage spouses expected fidelity from their husbands and wives, possibly because of the importance of status inheritance. Consequently, adultery was a legitimate cause for divorce and husbands could sometimes exact other punishments for the sexual misbehavior of their wives. Chumash husbands sometimes whipped errant wives. An Esselin man could repudiate his wandering wife, or turn her over to her new lover who had to pay the cuckold an indemnity, usually the cost of acquiring a new bride. A wronged Gabrielino husband could retaliate by claiming the wife of his wife's lover, and could even go so far as to kill an adulterous spouse, but such executions were probably rare.

Women were not altogether at the mercy of jealous and sadistic spouses, for they could divorce husbands who mistreated them, a circumstance that probably meant they could leave if their husband committed a sexual indiscretion. In Chumash oral narratives, women often initiated sex and ridiculed inadequate partners. Some women even killed their husbands. It is impossible to know how frequently adulterous liaisons and subsequent divorces took place, but anthropologists characterize the common Gabrielino marital pattern as serial monogamy with occasional polygyny, indicating that separations were common. It is not unreasonable to suppose that because so many marriages were arranged in youth some California Indians subsequently took lovers after meeting someone who struck deeper emotional chords than their initial partners had. Nor is it implausible to speculate that some grievances were overlooked completely in the interest of maintaining family harmony and keeping intact the economic and diplomatic advantages that marriage ties were meant to bind. Prostitution was extremely rare in California, and was noted only among the Salinan Indians before the arrival of the Spanish. The lack of a flesh trade may indicate that such outlets were simply not needed because marital, premarital, and extramarital associations provided sufficient sexual opportunities.[6]

There was one other sexual practice common among California Indians — male homosexual transvestism, or the so-called *berdache* tradition which was evident in many North American tribes. The *berdache* dressed and acted like women, but they were not thought of as homosexuals. Instead, Indians believed that they belonged to a third gender that combined both male and female aspects. In sex they took the female role, and they often married men who were regarded as perfectly ordinary heterosexual males. Sometimes a chief took a *berdache* for a second wife because it was believed that they worked harder. Moreover, the *berdache* were thought to have special spiritual gifts that made them especially attractive spouses.[7]

Serra and the secular colonizers of Spain's northern frontier based their familial concepts on a narrower Spanish model that was in some respects contradictory. The state regarded marriage as a contract that — among other things — transferred property and guaranteed rights to sexual service. On the other hand, the church regarded marriage as a sacrament before God and sought to regulate alliances according to religious principles.[8]

In theory, although not always in practice, Spanish society forbade premarital sex and required marital fidelity. Marriages were monogamous and lasted for life; the church granted divorces only in the most extraordinary cases, although remarriage of widows and widowers was permitted. The church regarded all sexual transgressions with a jaundiced eye, but held some acts in special horror. By medieval times Christian theologians had worked out a scheme of acceptable sexual behavior that also reflected their abhorrence of certain practices. Of course, fornication, adultery, incest, seduction, rape, and polygamy were sins, but far worse than any of these were the execrable sins "against nature," which included masturbation, bestiality, and homosexual copulation. The church allowed marital intercourse only in the missionary position; other postures were unnatural because they made the woman superior to her husband, thus thwarting God's universal plan. Procreation, not pleasure, was God's purpose in creating the human sexual apparatus in the first place. Therefore, to misuse the instruments of man's procreative destiny was to subvert the will of God. Medieval constraints on intimate behavior began to erode in the early modern period, but Catholic proscriptions against what the church defined as unnatural sexual behavior remained a part of canon law when Spain occupied California.[9]

This was the formal sexual ideology that Franciscans, soldiers, and *pobladores* brought to California. They also brought sinful lust. Maintaining sexual orthodoxy in the remotest reaches of the empire proved to be a greater task than Franciscan missionaries and secular officials could accomplish. Spaniards also brought to California an informal sexual ideology rooted in Mediterranean folkways that often ran counter to the teachings of the church. In this informal scheme, honor was an important element in determining family and individual social ranking and male status was linked to sexual prowess. To seduce a woman was to shame her and to dishonor her family while her consort acquired honor and asserted his dominant place in the social hierarchy. Women were thought to be sexually powerful creatures who could lead men astray, and more importantly, dishonor their own families. Society controlled female sexual power by segregating women, sometimes going so far as to sequester them behind locked doors to assure that they would not sully the family escutcheon with lewd conduct.[10] Catholic priests labored to restrict sexual activity in a world of philanderers, concubines, prostitutes, and lovers.

Thus California's Spanish colonizers brought with them formal and informal ideas about sexuality that were riven with contradictions. The conquest of the New World and its alien sexual conventions made the situation even more complicated, but did not keep Spaniards from intimate encounters with native people. From the time of Cortés the crown and the church encouraged intermarriage with native people, and informal sexual amalgamation occurred with great regularity. Throughout the empire interracial sex resulted in a large mixed-race, *mestizo* population. Ordinarily, the progeny of these meetings attached themselves firmly to the religion and society of their Spanish fathers. Thus, sexual amalgamation was an integral part of the Spanish colonial experience that served to disable native society and strengthen the Hispanic population as it drew Indians and their children into the colonial orbit.[11] This was the world that Serra had tried to reform in Oaxaca; it was a world that he and fellow Spaniards would unwittingly replicate in California.

In 1775 Father Serra wrote thoughtfully to the viceroy of New Spain about interracial marriages in California. Three Catalán soldiers had already married neophyte women and three more were "making up their minds to marry soon."[12] Serra approved of new Spanish regulations that subsidized such marriages with a seaman's salary for two years, and provided rations for the mixed-race couple for five years. Such families should be attached permanently to the wife's mission and receive some livestock and a piece of land from the royal patrimony, provided the husband had "nothing else to fall back upon."[13] To Father Serra, these marriages symbolized the foundation of Spanish society. The new families formed "the beginnings of a town" because all the families lived in "houses so placed so as to form two streets." The little town of Monterey, Serra observed, also included the mission buildings and "all together make up a square of their own, in front of our little residence and church."[14] Happily, children were already beginning to appear in Monterey, thus assuring that the community would have a future.

Serra's idealistic vision of colonization incorporated Spanish town building and Catholic marriages that tamed the sinful natures of Spaniards and Indians and harnessed them to Spanish imperial goals.[15] If he could have had his way, the only sexual activity in California would have occurred in the few sanctified marriage beds that were under the watchful eye of the friars. But that was not to be.

Serra recognized that Spanish and Indian sexual transgressions occurred, and they troubled him. Common Indian sexual behavior amounted to serious sins that merited the friars' solemn condemnation. Perhaps the worst cases were the *berdache*, who seemed ubiquitous in California. Their so-called sins against nature challenged religious and military leaders alike. While Serra extolled the virtues of marriages, Captain Pedro Fages, in 1775, reported that Chumash Indians were "addicted to the unspeakable vice of sinning against nature," and that each *ranchería* had a transvestite "for common use."[16] Fages, reflecting Spanish and Catholic values, apologized for even mentioning homosexuality because it was "an excess so criminal that it seems even forbidden to speak its name."[17] The missionary Pedro Font observed "sodomites addicted to nefarious practices" among the Yuma and concluded that "there will be much to do when the Holy Faith and the Christian religion are established among them."[18]

Civil and church officials agreed on the need to eradicate homosexuality as an affront to God and Spanish men alike. At the Mission Santa Clara the fathers noticed an unconverted Indian who, though dressed like a woman and working among women, seemed to have undeveloped breasts, an observation that was made easier because Indian women traditionally wore only necklaces above the waist. The curious friars conspired with the corporal of the guard to take this questionable person into custody, where he was completely disrobed confirming that he was indeed a man. The poor fellow was "more embarrassed than if he had been a woman," said one friar. For three days the soldiers kept him nude— stripped of his sexual identity—and made him sweep the plaza near the guardhouse. He remained "sad and ashamed" until he was released under orders to abjure feminine clothes and stay out of women's company.[19] Instead, he fled from the mission and reestablished a *berdache* identity among gentiles.[20]

The Spanish soldiers thoroughly misconstrued what they were seeing and what they had done. The soldiers no doubt thought they had exposed an impostor who was embarrassed because his ruse had been discovered. They did not realize that their captive—and his people—regarded himself as a woman and reacted accordingly when stripped and tormented by men.

Humiliated beyond endurance and required to renounce a sexual orientation that had never raised an eyebrow in Indian society, the Santa Clara transvestite was forced to flee, but perhaps he was more fortunate than he knew. Father Francisco Palóu reported a similar incident at the Mission San Antonio, where a *berdache* and another man were discovered "in an unspeakably sinful act." A priest, a corporal, and a soldier "punished them," Palóu revealed, "although not as much as they deserved."[21] When the horrified priest tried to explain how terrible this sin was, the puzzled Indians told him that it was all right because they were married. Palóu's reaction to this news was not recorded, but it is doubtful that he accepted it with equanimity. After getting a severe scolding the homosexual couple left the mission vicinity. Palóu hoped that "these accursed persons will decrease, and such an abominable vice will be eradicated," as the Catholic faith increases "for the greater Glory of God and the good of those pitiful, ignorant people."[22]

The revulsion and violence that ordinary Indian sexual relations inspired in the newcomers must have puzzled and frightened native people. Formerly accepted as an unremarkable part of social life, *berdache* faced persecution at the hands of friars and soldiers. To the Spaniards homosexual behavior was loathsome, one of the many traits that marked California Indians as a backward race. In a word, they were "incomprehensible" to Father Gerónimo Boscana. The "affirmative with them, is negative," he thought, "and the negative, the affirmative," a perversity that in the priest's mind was clearly reflected in Indian homosexuality. In frustration, Boscana compared the California Indians "to a species of monkey."[23]

For Spaniards and California Indians alike, the early days of colonization created a confused sexual landscape, but Spanish intolerance of homosexuality was not the only cause of this. In order to convert Indians, the Franciscans had to uproot other aspects of the normative social system that regulated Indian sexuality and marriage. At the very least, missionaries meant to restructure Indian marriage to conform to orthodox Catholic standards of monogamy, permanence, and fidelity, changes in intimate conduct that engendered conflict on the California frontier.

At the outset, friars had to decide what to do about married Indians who became mission neophytes. Even the acerbic Father Boscana believed that monogamous Indian marriages were lawful and should be permanently binding on neophytes, except for couples who were united against their will.[24] But what about marriages where one partner became a Christian while the other remained a heathen? And what should be done about polygynous unions? Missionaries worked out the answers according to canon law and its application to Indian converts in Mexico. Neophyte couples remarried in the Catholic Church, and when indigenous marriages were divided by religious beliefs the Christian partner was permitted to take a new Christian spouse. Plural marriages presented a knottier problem for married Indians because the church required the husband to recognize only his first wife while renouncing the others, a decision that necessarily depended solely on Indian testimony. This requirement sometimes led to convoluted explanations from a husband who claimed to have married his youngest wife first. The desire to retain a particular wife among several may have reflected economic as well as sexual preferences since a young wife would probably produce more children than her older counterpart, work longer, and be able to care for her husband in his old age.[25]

Franciscans applied these Christian marriage rules to California. Records from seven missions in northern California show that between 1769 and 1834 the church remarried 2,374 Indian couples.[26] This practice was wise, for it permitted thousands of native couples to retain family and emotional attachments while taking up Catholic and Spanish life. The retention of conjugal connections eased the Indian transition to mission authority and no doubt encouraged some Indians to convert.

Not all Indian marriage customs were admissible under Catholic scrutiny, however. Father Francisco Palóu, generally sympathetic to Indian marriage customs, unfortunately found that the Chumash were inclined to wed "their sisters-in-law, and even their mothers-in-law," thus adding incest to the sin of polygamy.[27] Chumash widows and widowers remarried within their deceased spouse's family, a practice that the church prohibited. Indian spouses with such ties who wished to enter the mission had to abandon established marriages, lie about their relationships, or reject conversion.[28]

The road to imposing a new sexual orthodoxy in California was a hard one. Christian ceremonies did not automatically eliminate older cultural meanings of Indian marriage, nor did they necessarily engender Catholic values in the Indian participants. Dissident neophyte runaways sometimes abandoned their old wives and took new ones according to tribal custom.[29] When the fathers forbade specific neophyte marriages, unhappy Indians found ways to insist on having the relationship that they preferred. In 1816, for example, an Indian man, probably Chumash, left the Mission San Buenaventura to be with the woman he wanted at Santa Barbara. "This happens," Father José Señan revealed, "every time his shackles are removed."[30] It is not clear if the missionaries had shackled the man for previously running off to his lover or for some other offense, but Señan allowed that it would be best to permit the couple to wed quietly. If, however, the Indian made mischief, "send him back to us."

Not all Christian marriages, of course, were blissful, nor did they all reflect the wifely obedience that Hispanic society celebrated. Sometimes, dissatisfied Indian wives used traditional kinship links to solve domestic problems. The inherent possibilities of such arrangements were revealed in 1795, after a skirmish between unconverted Chumash Indians near Mission San Buenaventura. Almost immediately after the fight—and perhaps related to it—the priests found a dead neophyte in the mission garden. His Christian wife, her neophyte brother, and two other neophytes had decapitated him.[31] Their motives are not known, but it is clear that neophytes who wanted to violate Christian precepts—or observe Indian concepts of justice—could enlist traditional kin to do so.

Spanish attempts to reform Indian behavior caused many problems among the tribes of California. Costanoans near Mission Santa Cruz became restive because of Spanish interference with Indian marriages. In 1794, a traditional Costanoan man organized some Christian and gentile Indians who attacked the mission guards, wounded two soldiers, and burned two buildings. The motive for this assault, Father Fermin Francisco de Lasuén explained, was that the soldiers had taken the Costanoan leader's wife to the San Francisco presidio along with some other neophyte runaways.[32] Evidently, the Spaniards ran risks when they separated Indian couples. A few years later the Santa Cruz friars claimed that sexual restrictions caused Costanoan neophytes to flee from the mission. Indians who could not "entirely gratify their lust because of the vigilance of the missionaries," they reckoned, decamped "in order to give full sway to their carnal desires."[33]

The missionaries simply could not accept that Indians adhered to a different set of sexual rules than did Spanish Catholics. Nor did they understand Indians' kinship practices. Instead, Franciscans like Father Lasuén thought of California Indians as people utterly without "government, religion, or respect for authority" who "shamelessly pursue without restraint whatever their brutal appetites suggest to them." They were "people of vicious and ferocious habits who knew no law but force, no superior but their own free will, and no reason but their own caprice." Father Lasuén evidently believed that sex was high on the list of brutal native appetites for he thought that Indians were inclined to "lewdness."[34]

What is lewd in one culture, however, is not necessarily lewd in another. Conflicting Indian and missionary attitudes about the human body are a case in point. California Indian men were customarily nude, and the women wore only skirts of bark or skins. Missionaries wondered that nudity did not embarrass the Indians, who "showed not the least trace of shame" even though the natives saw that Spaniards wore clothes.[35] A Spaniard who went about naked would not have been allowed to run loose in Spanish society for very long, and the Franciscans regarded undress as a mark of uncivility and paganism. Consequently, missionaries devoted much time and energy to clothing the neophytes. Indians and missionaries were caught in a classic case of cultural misunderstanding. The missionaries could not accept Indian sexual attitudes and practices because they contravened a sacred sexual ideology and Spanish cultural norms. Indians could not comprehend the need for such strict rules.

Caught in this conflict, missionaries demanded that Christian Indians adopt formal Spanish attitudes about sex and punished them when they did not. Within the mission they tried to achieve this goal by segregating the Indians by sex at night, a policy that—as we shall see—was not altogether successful.[36] Neophytes who failed to live up to Catholic standards ran afoul of the missionaries who imposed corporal punishment. When, for example, Chumash neophytes at Mission Santa Barbara reverted to polygyny—which the friars evidently regarded as concubinage after Christian conversion—Father Esteban Tapis first admonished the offenders. On the second offense Tapis laid on the whip, and when this did not convince the Indians of the error of their ways he put them in shackles.[37]

Franciscans believed they had a right to use corporal punishment to correct unruly Indians. Indeed, the lash was used throughout Spanish society. Eighteenth-century Spanish parents whipped children; teachers whipped pupils; magistrates whipped civil offenders; pious Catholics whipped themselves as penance. Neophytes accepted the lash as a fact of mission life when their sexual transgressions caught the watchful eyes of the friars, but the Spanish and Catholic understanding of the whip as an instrument of correction, teaching, mortification, and purification probably eluded them.[38] In Indian society, corporal punishment as a means of social control was rare. Some tribes permitted husbands to physically punish adulterous wives, but Indians saw punishment as a husband's right because adultery threatened the economic and diplomatic role of the family, not because sex was wrong or sinful.[39]

Indian sexuality was not the only carnal problem that the fathers had to contend with in California. Civilians and soldiers brought to California sexual attitudes and behavior that were at odds with Catholic and Indian values. Rape was a special concern of friars, who monitored Spanish deviant sexual behavior in California.[40] As early as 1772 Father Luís Jayme complained about some of the soldiers, who deserved to be hanged for "continuous outrages" on the Kumeyaay women near the Mission San Diego.[41] "Many times," he asserted, the Indians were on the verge of attacking the mission because "some soldiers went there and raped their women." The situation was so bad that the Indians fled from the priests, even risking hunger "so the soldiers will not rape their women as they have already done so many times in the past."

Father Jayme thought Spaniards' assaults were all the worse because the Kumeyaay Indians had become Christians and given up polygyny and incestuous marriages. Married neophytes did not commit adultery and bachelors were celibate. Kumeyaay sexual behavior was not only the result of the missionaries' teaching, but a reflection of their traditional belief that adultery was bad. "If a man plays with a woman who is not his wife," Jayme explained, "he is scolded and punished by his captains."[42] An unconverted Indian told Jayme, "although we did not know that God would punish us in Hell, [we] considered [adultery] to be very bad, and we did not do it, and even less now that we know that God will punish us if we do so." When the missionary heard this, he "burst into tears to see how these gentiles were setting an example for us Christians."

Jayme's version of the Kumeyaay statement seems to confuse rape and adultery, a problem that may have stemmed from linguistic and cultural misunderstanding. In any case, Jayme described two rapes and their consequences. In one instance, three soldiers had raped an unmarried woman who became pregnant. She was ashamed of her condition and ultimately killed the newborn infant, an act that horrified and saddened Father Jayme. The second incident occurred when four soldiers and a sailor went to a *ranchería* and dragged off two women. The sailor refused to take part and left the four to complete the assault. Afterward, the soldiers tried to convert the act from rape to prostitution by paying the women with some ribbon and a few tortillas. They also paid a neophyte man who had witnessed the assault and warned him not to divulge the incident. Insulted and angry, the Indians were not overawed by the rapists' threats and told Jayme. In retaliation, the soldiers locked the neophyte man in the stocks, an injustice that outraged Jayme who personally released him.[43]

The situation at San Diego was not unique. "There is not a single mission where all the gentiles have not been scandalized," Jayme wrote, "and even on the road, so I have been told."[44] Spaniards' sexual behavior did not escape the eye of Father Serra, who asserted that "a plague of immorality had broken out." He had heard the bitter complaints of the friars who wrote to him of disorders at all of the missions. Serra worried especially about the muleteers who traversed the vast distances between missions with their pack trains. Serra feared the consequences of allowing these unbridled characters among the Indians. There were so many Indian women along the road that Serra expected sexual transgressions, for "it would be a great miracle, yes, a whole series of miracles, if it did not provoke so many men of such low character to disorders which we have to lament in all our missions; they occur every day." Serra came perilously close to blaming the women for the sexual assaults that they suffered. Nevertheless, he believed rapes could imperil the entire mission enterprise by alienating the Indians who would "turn on us like tigers."[45]

Serra was right. In 1775, some eight hundred neophyte and non-Christian Kumeyaays, fed up with sexual assaults and chafing under missionary supervision, attacked Mission San Diego. They burned the mission and killed three Spaniards, including Father Jayme, beating his face beyond recognition.[46] Rapes were not the sole cause of the attack, but as Jayme and Serra had predicted, sexual abuse made California a perilous place. Still, the revolt did not dissuade some Spaniards from sexual involvement with Indian women. In 1779, Serra was still criticizing the government for "unconcern in the matter of shameful conduct between the soldiers and Indian women," a complaint that may have included mutual as well as rapacious liaisons.[47]

Serra's argument implied that without supervision some Spaniards acted without sexual restraints. Spaniards believed in a code of honor that rewarded sexual conquests, and soldiers may have asserted their ideas about honor and status by seducing California Indian women. There was no honor in rape. Honorable sexual conquest required a willing partner who was overcome by the man's sensuality, masculinity, and magnetism, not merely his brute ability to overpower her. Recall the San Diego rapists who tried to mitigate their actions by making a payment to their victims.[48] Serra argued that there were men of bad character who could not control their urges, but rape is a complex act that requires more than opportunity and a supposedly super-heightened state of sexual tension. Recent research shows that rape is an act of domination carried out by men who despise their victims because of their race or gender. Stress, anger, and fear also motivate some rapists.[49] It should not be forgotten that Spaniards were fearful of California Indians—outnumbered and surrounded by Indians who seemed capable of overwhelming them at any moment.[50] There were frequent minor skirmishes, livestock thefts, and occasional murders that reinforced the Spanish conception of the Indian enemy. As late as 1822 one missionary thought that it was impossible to know how many troops were necessary to defend the Mission San Buenaventura because there were so many un-Christianized Indians in the interior. "May God keep our neophytes peaceful and submissive," he wrote, "for they would not want for allies if they should rise against our Saint and our charity!"[51] It is not difficult to imagine that some men, sent to a dangerous frontier outpost, violently and subconsciously used Indian women as objects to ward off fear and dominate the numerous native population that the Spanish crown and Catholic Church sought to subdue, colonize, and convert.

Sexuality, unsanctioned and perversely construed as a way to control native people, actually threatened Spain's weak hold on California by angering the Indians and insulting their ideas about sexuality, rectitude, and justice. It is impossible to know how many rapes occurred in Spanish California, but sexual assaults affected Indian society beyond their absolute numbers. Moreover, Indian rape victims likely displayed some of the somatic and emotional symptoms of rape-trauma syndrome, including physical wounds, tension, sleeplessness, gastrointestinal irritations, and genitourinary disturbances. In our own time raped women are often stricken with fear, guilt, anger, and humiliation, and some raped women develop a fear of normal sexual activity.[52] There is no reason to believe that Indian women did not react to rape in similar ways. Fear of assault may have affected many women who were not themselves victims as they tried to help friends and relatives cope with the consequences of rape. Sexual assaults echoed in the Indian social world even as they frightened friars who feared the consequences of an outraged Indian population.

It is impossible to know how many free-will assignations occurred in California during the mission period, but it is safe to assume that such cross-cultural trysts were fraught with misunderstanding. Indian women, accustomed to looking outside of their communities for husbands, likely viewed Spaniards as potential mates who could bring them and their families increased power, wealth, and status. Some women may have hoped that sex would lead to marriage, but it seldom did.[53]

Indians responded to Spanish sexual importunities in several ways. Physical resistance to missions, as at San Diego in 1775 and on the Colorado River in 1781, was one way to deal with rapists and other unwanted intruders. Marriage to a Spaniard was another strategy that could protect women, but evidently only a few dozen Indians were able to use this tactic. Other Indians, like the transvestites mentioned above, withdrew from Spanish-controlled areas to avoid any infringement on their social life and values. On the other hand, some women might have entered the missions for protection that the mission setting provided from sexual abuse by Spanish soldiers. There is also reason to believe that Indians altered their sexual practices as a result of meeting the Spanish. Prostitution, which had formerly been rare among the Indians, became common. In 1780 Father Serra complained about Nicolas, a neophyte who procured women for the soldiers at San Gabriel.[54] A few years later a Spanish naturalist observed that the Chumash men had "become pimps, even for their own wives, for any miserable profit."[55]

Nicolas and other Indians had several reasons to resort to prostitution. Spanish men seduced and raped the Indians' female kinfolk but did not marry them. Perhaps Indians were recovering lost bride prices through prostitution. Since there were Hispanic men who were willing to pay for sex, prostitution might have seemed a logical way to enhance the economic value of wives and daughters who were expected to be productive. How women felt about being so used is not known, but the missions would have been one avenue of escape for those who were unhappy with these new conditions. In the early years of colonization, Indian women outnumbered male neophytes, indicating that females found the mission especially attractive in a rapidly changing world.[56]

Another California Indian reaction to a new sexual world was physiological: they contracted syphilis and other venereal diseases, maladies to which they had not previously been exposed. So rapidly did syphilis spread among Indians that, in 1792, a Spanish naturalist traveling in California believed the disease was endemic among the Chumash.[57] Twenty years later the friars recorded it as the most prevalent and destructive disease in the missions.[58] Syphilis was particularly deadly among the Indians because its weakened victims became easy prey for epidemic diseases that periodically swept the missions. In addition, stillbirths increased and infected women died more frequently in childbirth. If they bore live children the infants were likely to have congenital syphilis.[59]

Despite the intentions of Serra and other friars, mission life did not necessarily provide neophytes with a respite from sexual activity. Friars declared almost unanimously that mission Indians committed a variety of sexual sins. Between 1813 and 1815 missionaries recorded that the neophytes were guilty of "impurity," "unchastity," "fornication," "lust," "immorality," "incontinence," and so forth, indicating that the mission experience had not fully inculcated Catholic sexual values in the neophytes.[60]

How could the fathers have known about the intimate lives of mission Indians? The Indians confessed their sins at least once a year, and suspicious priests questioned the neophytes closely about their sexual behavior. Franciscan *confesionarios* with lists of questions in California Indian languages provide some idea of the level of priests' interest in neophyte sex. Have you ever sinned with a woman, a man, an animal? Do you have carnal dreams? Did you think about the dream later? What is your relationship with the people with whom you sin? Have you given your wife or husband to someone else? Do you become aroused when you watch them or when you see animals having intercourse? What did you think? Do you play with yourself? Have you tried to prevent pregnancy? Have you ever *not* had sex with your wife when she wanted to? So the questions continued for many pages.[61] The investigation of Indians' sexual lives was thorough and relentless. And so missionaries knew that men and women fell short of ideal sexual behavior. The friars' frank words about Indian sexuality betray disappointment born of the unspoken realization that their best missionary efforts had not reformed Indian sexuality.

The combination of virulent endemic syphilis and sexual promiscuity created a fatal environment that killed thousands of mission Indians and inhibited the ability of survivors to recover population losses through reproduction. Franciscans—and some of their critics—believed that the carnal disintegration of the California missions occurred because the Indians simply continued to observe the sexual customs of native society.[62] The Indians were unrestrained libertines who had learned nothing of Catholic moral behavior in the missions, and were incapable of realizing that syphilis was killing them. This view is incomplete because it assumes that sexuality was unregulated in native society and that Indian sexual behavior was unchanged during sixty-five years of mission experience.

Perhaps mission Indian sexuality was a response to new conditions. Who would have understood desperate demographic conditions at the missions better than the neophytes themselves? Locked into a system that assured their ultimate destruction, dying rapidly from unheard-of diseases, perhaps neophytes chose procreation as a means of group survival. Sadly, they failed, but it was not for want of trying.

It should not be assumed that neophyte sexual behavior was monolithic. Rather, it was influenced by both ethnic and gender considerations. By the end of the mission period missionaries had recruited substantial numbers of interior Indians to replace the neophytes who were rapidly dying. Many of the new converts were Indians from the interior, who formerly had fought against the coastal Indians.[63] In the missions, long-standing animosities could have released interethnic sexual aggression that was meant to assert dominance in this new setting. Priests reported that mission women who became pregnant resorted to abortion and infanticide, and these acts may have been based in Indian customs, especially in the case of the Chumash, who believed that unless the first child died the mother would not conceive again. But women had other reasons, too. Unwed mothers would be subjected to close questioning and punishment by priests. What if the father were a soldier who did not want his identity revealed, what then? Thus, Indian women who attempted to apply old norms to assure fertility contributed to the destruction of the Indian population.[64]

Whatever the causes of mission sexuality, neophytes relied on old ways and new ones to solve difficult problems in a new setting. In the end, efficacious solutions eluded them, but it is not accurate to say that Indians were immoral, amoral, or incapable of assimilating the message that the missionaries brought them. The mission experience demonstrates that Indians were simultaneously resolute and unsure, conservative and radical, forward looking and bound to tradition. They exemplified, in other words, the human condition.

Ultimately, the history of California's missions is a sad one that elucidates a series of human misunderstandings, failures, and terrible, unintended consequences. That Spaniards and Indians were often incapable of comprehending each other should hardly be surprising, because they came from radically different cultures. As was so often the case in the history of the Western Hemisphere, Indians and newcomers talked past each other, not with each other. This was true even of their most personal contacts in California. Sacred and profane, intimate, carnal, spiritual, ecstatic, bringing life and death—Indian and Spanish sexuality embodied the paradox and identity of their all too human encounter.

NOTES

1. Maynard J. Geiger, *Letter of Luís Jayme, O.F.M. San Diego, October 17, 1772* (Los Angeles, 1970), pp. 38–39.

2. Francisco Palóu, *Palóu's Life of Fray Junípero Serra,* ed. and trans. Maynard J. Geiger (Washington, D.C., 1955), p. 49.

3. Alfred L. Kroeber, *Handbook of Indians of California* (1925; reprint, Berkeley, 1953), pp. 647, 748, 803; Lowell John Bean, "Social Organization in Native California," in *Native Californians: A Theoretical Retrospective,* ed. Lowell John Bean and Thomas C. Blackburn (Socorro, N.M., 1976), pp. 105–12; Robert F. Heizer and Albert B. Elsasser, *Natural World of the California Indians* (Berkeley, 1980), pp. 28–56.

4. Bean, "Social Organization," pp. 106–10; John Bushnell and Donna Bushnell, "Wealth, Work, and World View in Native Northwest California: Sacred Significance and Psychoanalytic Symbolism," in *Flowers of the Wind: Papers on Ritual, Myth, and Symbolism in California and the Southwest,* ed. Thomas C. Blackburn (Socorro, N.M., 1977), p. 133.

5. Robert F. Heizer, "The California Indians: Archaeology, Varieties of Culture, and Arts of Life," *California Historical Society Quarterly* 41 (1962): 5–6, 10–12; Nona C. Willoughby, "Division of Labor among the Indians of California," in *California Indians,* Garland American Indian Ethnohistory Series, 6 vols. (New York, 1974), 2: 60–68.

6. Robert F. Heizer, ed., *Handbook of North American Indians,* vol. 8, *California* (Washington, D.C., 1978), pp. 498, 502, 511, 523, 544–45, 556, 566, 602, 684–85; Thomas Blackburn, ed., *December's Child: A Book of Chumash Oral Narratives* (Berkeley, 1975), pp. 56–58, 137–38, 154–55.

7. Several recent works examine the *berdache* tradition in North America. Cf. Walter L. Williams, *The Spirit and the Flesh: Sexual Diversity in American Indian Culture* (Boston, 1986), pp. 17–127; Will Roscoe, *The Zuni Man Woman* (Albuquerque, 1991), pp. 123–46, and passim; Ramón A. Gutiérrez, *When Jesus Came the Corn Mothers Went Away: Marriage, Sexuality, and Power in New Mexico, 1500–1846* (Stanford, 1991), pp. 33–35. For references to *berdache* in California, see Heizer, *Handbook,* vol. 8, pp. 131, 134, 159, 466, 502, 512, 689; Kroeber, *Handbook,* pp. 46, 180, 497, 500, 647, 748, 803.

8. Gutiérrez, *When Jesus Came,* pp. 176–240; Ramón A. Gutiérrez, "Honor Ideology, Marriage Negotiation, and Class-Gender Domination in New Mexico, 1690–1846," *Latin American Perspectives* 12 (1985): 81–104; Ramón A. Gutiérrez, "From Honor to Love: Transformations of the Meaning of Sexuality in Colonial New Mexico," in *Kinship Ideology and Practice in Latin America,* ed. Raymond T. Smith (Chapel Hill, 1984), pp. 237–63.

9. Vern L. Bullough, *Sexual Variance in Society and History* (Chicago, 1980), pp. 347–457; on sins against nature, see pp. 378–89. An instructive essay on how actual behavior could vary from church teachings is Jean-Louis Flandrin, "Sex in Married Life in the Early Middle Ages: The Church's Teaching and Behavioural Reality," in *Western Sexuality: Practice and Precept in Past and Present Times,* ed. Philippe Ariès and André Béjin, trans. Anthony Forster (Oxford, 1985), pp. 114–29.

10. See especially Ramón A. Gutiérrez, "Honor-Ideology and Sexual Inversion in Colonial New Mexico," paper presented at the Annual Meeting of the Western History Association, St. Paul, Minn., October 1983. No one has applied Gutiérrez's suggestive ideas to California. See also Janet Lecompte, "The Independent Women of Hispanic New Mexico, 1821–1846," *Western Historical Quarterly* 12 (1981): 17–36. On honor and seduction, see Verena Martínez-Alier, *Marriage, Class, and Colour in Nineteenth-Century Cuba: A Study of Racial Attitudes and Sexual Values in a Slave Society* (Cambridge, 1974), pp. 109–12. For a sinister analysis of Mexican machismo and its role in sexual behavior, see Octavio Paz, *The Labyrinth of Solitude,* trans. Lysander Kemp, Yara Milos, and Rachel Phillips Belash (New York, 1985), pp. 73–88. On women in other parts of Spanish America, see Guillermo Céspedes, *Latin America in the Early Years* (New York, 1974), pp. 56–62; James Lockhart, *Spanish Colonial Peru, 1532–1560: A Colonial Society* (Madison, 1968), pp. 150–62.

11. Céspedes, *Latin America,* pp. 56–62. For data on racial amalgamation on the northern frontier, see Henry F. Dobyns, *Spanish Colonial Tucson: A Demographic History* (Tucson, 1976), pp. 133–80; Alicia V. Tjarks, "Comparative Demographic Analysis of Texas, 1777–1793," in *New Spain's Far Northern Frontier: Essays in the American West, 1540–1821,* ed. David J. Weber (Albuquerque, 1979), pp. 135–69.

12. Serra to Antonio María de Bucareli y Ursua, August 24, 1775, in *Writings of Junípero Serra,* 4 vols., ed. Antonine Tibesar (Washington, D.C., 1955–66), 2: 149.

13. Serra to Antonio María de Bucareli y Ursua, March 13, 1773, in Tibesar, *Writings of Junípero Serra,* 1: 325.

14. Serra to Bucareli, August 24, 1775, in Tibesar, *Writings of Junípero Serra,* 2: 149. While Serra approved of handsome subsidies for marriages of Catalán men and Indian women, he also made it clear that he did not want to apply such liberal rewards to the mixed-blood leather jackets who manned the presidio. Evidently Serra, like many other Hispanos on the

northern frontier, accepted as a matter of course the social superiority of *peninsulares*, who should receive preferential treatment. On marriage, ethnicity, and race in California and the Southwest, see Gloria E. Miranda, "Gente de Razón Marriage Patterns in Spanish and Mexican California: A Case Study of Santa Barbara and Los Angeles," *Southern California Quarterly* 63 (1981): 1–21; Jack D. Forbes, "Hispano-Mexican Pioneers of the San Francisco Bay Region: An Analysis of Racial Origins," *Aztlán* 14 (1983): 175–89; Gutiérrez, "Honor Ideology, Marriage Negotiation, and Class-Gender Domination," pp. 81–104; Oakah L. Jones, *Los Paisanos: Spanish Settlers on the Northern Frontier of New Spain* (Norman, Ok., 1979), p. 246.

15. Jones, *Los Paisanos,* pp. 12–13, 252–53.

16. Pedro Fages, *A Historical, Political, and Natural Description of California by Pedro Fages,* trans. Herbert Ingram Priestly (1937; reprint, Ramona, Calif., 1972), p. 48.

17. Ibid., p. 33.

18. Herbert E. Bolton, trans. and ed., *Font's Complete Diary: A Chronicle of the Founding of San Francsico* (Berkeley, 1931), p. 105.

19. Palóu, *Palóu's Life of Fray Junípero Serra,* p. 198.

20. Ibid., p. 199.

21. Ibid.

22. Ibid.

23. Boscana, quoted in Alfred Robinson, *Life in California during a Residence of Several Years in that Territory* (1846; New York, 1969), pp. 334–35. Boscana also noted transvestism and homosexual marriage, which he regarded as a "horrible custom" (pp. 283–84).

24. Ibid., p. 282.

25. Sherburne F. Cook and Woodrow Borah produced a remarkable range of demographic data and analysis for eight northern California missions in *Essays in Population History,* vol. 3, *Mexico and California* (Berkeley, 1979), pp. 177–311. For Catholic policy on remarriage, see pp. 278–80.

26. Cook and Borah, "Table 3.9: Marriages of Converts Who Had Previously Been Married by Indian Custom," in *Essays in Population History,* vol. 3, p. 282.

27. Palóu, *Palóu's Life of Fray Junípero Serra,* p. 194.

28. Cook and Borah, "Table 3.9," *Essays in Population History,* vol. 3, p. 282

29. Serra to Felipe de Neve, January 7, 1780, in Tibesar, *Writings of Junípero Serra,* 3: 409–13; responses of the Indians Leopoldo, Senen, and Fernando Huililiaset to *interogatorio,* June 1, 1824, in S. F. Cook, ed., "Expeditions to the Interior of California: Central Valley, 1820–1840," *University of California Anthropological Records* 20 (1962): 153–54.

30. Señán to José de la Guerra, June 19, 1816, in José Señán, *The Letters of José Señán, O.F.M.: Mission San Buenaventura, 1796–1823,* ed. Leslie Byrd Simpson, trans. Paul D. Nathan (San Francisco, 1962), p. 87.

31. Lasuén to Antonio Nogueyra, November 28, 1795, in Fermin Francisco de Lasuén, *Writings of Fermin Francisco de Lasuén,* trans. and ed. Finbar Kenneally, 2 vols. (Washington, D.C., 1965), 1: 363.

32. Lasuén to Tomás Pangua, February 3, 1794, in Lasuén, *Writings,* 1: 363.

33. Francis F. Guest, *Fermín Francisco de Lasuén (1736–1803): A Biography* (Washington, D.C., 1973), p. 207.

34. Lasuén, "Refutation of Charges," June 19, 1801, in Lasuén, *Writings,* 2: 220.

35. Palóu, *Life of Fray Junípero Serra,* p. 66.

36. Lasuén, *Writings,* 2: 206–7.

37. Guest, *Fermín Francisco de Lasuén,* p. 201.

38. Ibid.; and Francis F. Guest, "Cultural Perspectives on California Mission Life," *Southern California Quarterly* 65 (1985): 6–22.

39. Heizer, *Handbook,* vol. 8, pp. 511, 544–45.

40. Daniel J. Garr, "Rare and Desolate Land: Population and Race in Hispanic California," *Western Historical Quarterly* 6 (1975): 135–37.

41. Jayme, in Geiger, *Letter of Luís Jayme,* pp. 38, 39.

42. Ibid., pp. 40, 41.

43. Ibid., pp. 44–46.

44. Serra to Antonio María de Bucareli y Ursua, April 22, 1773, in Tibesar, *Writings of Junípero Serra,* 1: 341.

45. Ibid.

46. Hubert Howe Bancroft, *History of California,* 7 vols. (San Francisco, 1886–90), vol. 1, pp. 249–54. Franciscan historian Maynard J. Geiger attributes rape as a principal cause of the San Diego revolt in Geiger, *Letter of Luís Jayme,* p. xxx.

47. Serra to Rafael Verger, August 8, 1779, in Tibesar, *Writings of Junípero Serra,* 3: 349–51.

48. Gutiérrez, "Honor-Ideology and Sexual Inversion."

49. A. Nicholas Groth, *Men Who Rape: The Psychology of the Offender* (New York, 1979), pp. 60–61; Julia R. Schwendinger and Herman Schwendinger, *Rape and Inequality* (Beverly Hills, 1983), pp. 202–4; P. Robert et al., quoted in E. A. Fatah, "The Use of the Victim as an Agent of Self-Legitimization: Toward a Dynamic Explanation of Criminal Behavior," in *Victims and Society,* ed. E. C. Viano (Washington, D.C., 1976), p. 108; Suzanne Ageton, *Sexual Assault among Adolescents* (Lexington, Mass., 1983), pp. 111–12.

50. Bancroft, *History of California,* vol. 1, pp. 362–64. Soldiers' fears of native people were no doubt augmented by the Diegueño attack on Mission San Diego and the Yuma destruction of the Colorado River missions in 1781.

51. José Señam to the Commissioner, November 9, 1822, in Señán, *Letters,* p. 165.

52. Ann Wolbert Burgess and Lynda Lytle Holstrom, "Rape Trauma Syndrome," *American Journal of Psychiatry* 131 (1974): 981–86.

53. Lasuén, *Writings,* 2: 212; Cook and Borah, *Essays in Population History,* vol. 3, pp. 267–78, 304–10. See also Garr, "Rare and Desolate Land," pp. 134–37.

54. Serra to Felipe de Neve, January 7, 1780, in Tibesar, *Writings of Junípero Serra,* 3: 409–13.

55. José Longinos, *Journal of José Longinos Martínez: Notes and Observations of the Naturalist of the Botanical Expedition in Old and New California and the South Coast, 1791–1792,* ed. and trans. Lesley Byrd Simpson (San Francisco, 1961), p. 55.

56. Sherburne F. Cook, "Population Trends among the California Mission Indians," *Ibero-Americana* 17 (1940): 29–34.

57. Longinos, *Journal,* p. 44. While prehistoric Californians suffered from numerous health problems, like other Indians in the Western Hemisphere, they had not been exposed to the infectious crowd diseases, nor is there evidence for syphilis in precontact times. Phillip L. Walker, Patricia Lambert, and Michael J. DeNiro, "The Effects of European Contact on the Health of Alta California Indians," in *Columbian Consequences, Volume I: Archaeological and Historical Perspectives on the Spanish Borderlands West,* ed. David Hurst Thomas (Washington, D.C., 1989), pp. 349–64. See also Brenda J. Baker and George J. Armelagos, "The Origin and Antiquity of Syphilis: Paleopathological Diagnosis and Interpretation," *Current Anthropology* 29 (1988): 703–37.

58. Maynard J. Geiger, trans. and ed., and Clement Meighan, ed., *As the Padres Saw Them: California Mission Life and Customs as Reported by the Franciscan Missionaries, 1813–1815* (Santa Barbara, 1976), pp. 71–80.

59. Sherburne F. Cook, "The Indian versus the Spanish Mission," *Ibero-Americana* 21 (1943): 22–30.

60. Geiger and Meighan, *As the Padres Saw Them,* pp. 105–6.

61. Madison S. Beeler, ed., *The Ventureño Confesionario of José Señan, O.F.M.* (Berkeley, 1967), pp. 37–63; Harry Kelsey, ed., *The Doctrina and Confesionario of Juan Cortés* (Altadena, Calif., 1979), pp. 113–16, 120–23.

62. Cook, "Indian versus the Spanish Mission," pp. 101–13.

63. Sherburne F. Cook, "The Physical and Demographic Reaction of the Non-mission Indians in Colonial and Provincial California," *Ibero-Americana* 22 (1943): 1–55.

64. Longinos, *Journal,* p. 56; Lasuén, "Refutation of Charges," May 28, 1801, in Lasuén, *Writings,* p. 210.

PART 4

REDEFINING SEX

REDEFINING SEX IN
EIGHTEENTH-CENTURY ENGLAND

TIM HITCHCOCK

In 1705 John Cannon, a Somerset farm labourer of twenty-one years, began "a love intrigue" with his uncle's servant, Mary Rose. Some forty years later he described this event in his memoir:

> our jesting complements began to burn up to a fervent ardour & earnest, she by her sweet singing & syrene notes alured me so that I never for a long time after could think of any other. . . . This beginning accompanied with amorous talks & quaint glances, kissing & toying when together in private . . . brought on by degrees a more close familiarity even to a plane discovery of such matters & concerns wch modesty teaches me to omit. Seldom a night passed but she passing through my bedchamber to her own came to my bedside & after some amorous whisperings we bid each other good night by tender and loving kisses. This I confess to be odd doings & somewhat difficult to be kept long a secret by reason of ye boy my bedfellow although we never acted any other than above mentioned wch might bring us disgrace.[1]

John and Mary continued their liaison for a further twelve years. They never had full penetrative sex, and throughout his memoir Cannon congratulates himself on his studious avoidance of the sins of fornication and adultery. But, he, Mary, and the two other young women John courted at the same time did have very active sex lives. Mutual masturbation, long-drawn-out sessions of kissing and fondling, and sincere promises of future marriage characterised all these relationships. None of the three women involved became pregnant, and each was, by Cannon's account at least, considered a virgin on marriage. While unusual in being recorded, there is nothing to suggest that the experiences of these people were other than typical of popular sexual activity at the turn of the eighteenth century.[2]

Some eighty or ninety years later, during a period described in Francis Place's autobiography, a very different sexual culture existed, at least among the artisanal classes of London. Place believed that most young people in the 1780s and 1790s were having penetrative sex; that lack of sexual probity in this regard was felt to be no barrier to marriage; and that both women and men considered their sexual lives essentially outside of a moral framework. While claiming that "want of chastity in girls was common," the songs and sayings he quotes leave little doubt as to the penetrative nature of the sexual activity with which he was familiar:

> First he niggled her, then he tiggled her
> Then with his two balls he began to batter her
> At every thrust, I thought she'd have burst
> with the terrible size of his Morgan Rattler.[3]

While Place wrote in order to condemn the lack of sexual control he saw around him, contemporary bastardy and prenuptial pregnancy figures support his conclusions about the sexual proclivities of his contemporaries.

The experience of these two men, and their partners, fit tremendously well with the evidence adduced by demographic historians. According to the Cambridge Group for the History of Population and Social Structure there does seem to have been a transition in the prevalence of sexual activity that could lead to pregnancy. The timing and content of this transition also seem to be supported by the work of writers on a range of other eighteenth-century topics. The histories of pornography and the novel, some cultural histories, and perhaps most obviously the histories of the family, all seem to point in the same direction. Indeed, the work of the best-known historian of sexuality, Michel Foucault, would likewise suggest an eighteenth-century transition towards greater sexual activity.[4]

At the same time this transition from relative probity to dangerous sexualities is seriously at odds with a range of other historiographies. In particular, the literature concerned with the history of gender and women which charts the rise of a separate-spheres ideology, as well as the recently developed histories of the body, suggest that just the opposite transition should have been occurring during this period. The maternalization of women's bodies, the creation of homosocial worlds of home and work, the denial of the existence of the female orgasm and the general increase in the policing of particularly middling sort social interaction all suggest that the barriers to greater sexual activity were growing, just as the demographic evidence for an increase of that sexual activity, in the form of more babies, was becoming more certain.

This paper is an attempt to describe the ways in which these various literatures seem to contradict each other, and to then suggest an alternative way of thinking about sexual behaviour, which, I hope, will allow us to fit these dichotomous perspectives into a single understanding.

The most developed literature on eighteenth-century sex describes itself as being about populations. Demographic historians have demonstrated, to almost everyone's satisfaction, that a number of things changed over the course of the eighteenth century. The age at first marriage dropped significantly. The percentage of bastards born increased three-fold over the course of the century, while the percentage of marriages celebrated while the female partner was pregnant grew to a third of the total. And finally, the percentage of the population remaining unmarried (and presumably celibate) dropped precipitately.[5] The result was, of course, a huge increase in population, and a transition in the nature of the demographic regime. These changes almost necessarily reflect a situation in which more people were having more sex leading to the birth of a child, both inside and outside marriage.[6]

The explanations adduced for this transition have been numerous, but most writers have viewed the transition as a response to economic change. E. A. Wrigley has suggested it resulted from a rise in real wages during the late seventeenth century, while other historians associated with the Cambridge Group have examined the roles of proto-industrialisation, urbanisation, the decline in apprenticeship and the changing nature of rural employments. All have suggested that greater economic opportunities encouraged young people to enter courtship, marriage and sexual activity sooner. Wrigley's explanation, however, has fallen on the implausibility of the influence of rising real wages only being felt nearly half a century later, while the others have generally been criticised on the grounds that the perceived changes occurred throughout the country (and indeed, were common to much of western Europe) and hence cannot be aligned with economic changes which were regional or sectoral in their nature. An excellent article by David Levine concludes, after examining each of the possible explanations put forward, that we really have no good idea of why people started marrying and having children at a greater rate during the eighteenth century.[7]

One set of explanations has come from various family and cultural historians. Writers such as Edward Shorter, Lawrence Stone, and, most recently, Thomas Laqueur and Henry Abelove have examined the content of the transition, with a sharp eye for the rise of "sentiment" and desire in sexual activity. Edward Shorter, for instance, argued in the mid-1970s that rising fertility and bastardy rates reflected a new attitude towards sex on the part of plebeian women. He suggested that with the growth of urbanisation and the increasing incorporation of young women into the moneyed economy, they chose to participate in penetrative sex more frequently—that, in other words, there was a "sexual revolution" in female desire which was made possible by economic change. Shorter has been roundly condemned by a number of commentators, and his argument was largely vitiated by the discovery that changes in sexual behaviour were equally apparent in rural and urban areas.[8]

A more measured case was made by Lawrence Stone. He argued that the period between 1660 and 1800 witnessed the rise of a "companionate" model of marriage in which love and affection became more significant, replacing the more austere puritan family of the previous century. Romance and the rise of the novel, the ability of children to choose their own partners, and the influence of the law, in Stone's view, all ensured that a new pattern of marriage would become established.[9] Stone's chronology has been questioned, and the rather unfocused relationship he suggests between these changes and the demographic transition has been criticised. Likewise, he has been taken to task for concentrating on the experiences of the elite at the expense of the poor majority of the population.[10] But, nevertheless, most historians would accept Stone's view that some form of change in sentiment occurred, even if they cannot agree as to its actual content or timing.

More recently, cultural historians Henry Abelove and Thomas Laqueur have each suggested a link between sentiment and desire, as it relates to sex, and broader cultural and economic shifts which characterised the eighteenth century. While each studiously avoided the reductionism of Edward Shorter, both agreed that there was a change in the fundamental experience of sexual activity which owed its content to changing patterns and discourses of consumption and production. Abelove, for instance, suggested that just as the reality of, or discourses associated with, production grew in cultural force as part of the industrial revolution, so the popularity of penetrative sex grew.[11] In a similar, if more complex way, Laqueur sought to locate the changing pattern of sexual behaviour within a wide variety of eighteenth-century discourses—those about reading, medicine, gender and capitalism in particular; and further hinted that the transition in sexual behaviour must be seen as an integral part of the cultural and production revolutions associated with the eighteenth century.[12]

All of these historians saw a transition moving in essentially the same direction—from a sexual culture characterised by repression and a relative lack of emotion to one in which love, friendship, sexual pleasure, and increased sexual activity all played a growing role. And if we look at another historiography the same developmental line can be drawn. The histories associated with the rise of pornography, the novel, and the Enlightenment derive much of their intellectual vigour from literary criticism, but in many ways reinforce the historical demographers. In the works of Paul-Gabriel Boucé, Roy Porter, G. S. Rousseau, Peter Wagner and Lynn Hunt, we find again a story of change towards greater sexual activity. The libertinism of many Enlightenment figures, as well as the publication of works such as *Fanny Hill*, and more significantly the novels of De Sade, when combined with the activities of popular sex therapists such as James Graham, are all used to suggest that discourses around sex in general were becoming more widely distributed, more explicit, and most importantly, more modern. In this scenario the heroes of the "sexual revolution" are John Wilkes and his libertine friends, the radical pornographers of the London underworld, and perhaps most importantly, the romantic poets of the early nineteenth century. In apparent agreement with Abelove and Laqueur, they argue that the notion of desire is re-created in the imagination of the population at large, resulting in more sex and more babies. The Enlightenment, therefore, became an intellectual justification for free love, which justification associated sophistication with the power relationships inherent in pornography, and created a taxonomy of sexual pleasure which reified the male orgasm. While this account of the Enlightenment contains some ambivalence, its overall implication is that sex is good and more sex is bet-ter, and that the Enlightenment itself contributed to the creation of more sex.[13]

These various bodies of work seem to provide a coherent analysis of change, but at the same time they are completely at odds with two other equally impor-tant historical literatures. From Alice Clark onwards, women's history, and lat-terly the history of gender, has emphasised an early modern transition from greater openness and possibility for women, to a situation in which women are increasingly controlled by a powerful patriarchal ideology. And while the depic-tion of the sixteenth and seventeenth centuries as a period of relative gender equality has been replaced by a more nuanced view, most historians would still agree that authority within the household was increasingly transferred to men, while women's ability to participate in the public sphere was increasingly restricted. The apparently easygoing heterosocial world of a domestic economy which characterised the sixteenth and seventeenth centuries was replaced by more and more homosocial worlds of home and work. Whereas seventeenth-century gender relationships, although marked by a frequently vicious misog-yny,[14] have been characterised as generally negotiated within the household, and open to variation depending on personality and situation, by the end of the eighteenth century, those possibilities were slipping away, and greater defini-tional rigour was imposed on gender roles.[15] The rise of single-sex professions and of professional training, the closing down of traditional female occupations, such as midwifery, and the increasing denigration of traditional forms of female knowledge, such as those associated with magic and healing, all contributed to a set of circumstances which undermined the negotiated nature of women's power and position.[16] Davidoff and Hall have described this as an ongoing process of repression starting with the rise of religious dissent in the eighteenth century.[17] And while some historians, such as Amanda Vickery, have questioned the impact of the discourses Davidoff and Hall describe to affect the intimate lives of individuals, there is little doubt that the nature of the ideological framework within which women acted was changing, and that the expectations contained in advice books and conduct manuals were growing more restrictive.[18]

Unless one stretches one's credulity beyond the breaking point, and imagines that this transition was restricted to a tiny middling sort, or that it represented a backlash to the sexual liberalism thought to exist at the end of the eighteenth century, we must accept the apparent contradiction between this literature and that surveyed above.

Indeed, the components of this literature amply confirm this contradiction. One need only think of the extensive literature on the rise of the maternalization of women in the late eighteenth century. Works on breastfeeding, child care, and general social advice, all suggest that women's roles were being increasingly restricted to that of mother and homemaker—increasingly restricting their ability to act as independent social beings, and likewise, tying them physically to the bawling demands of a growing number of infants. The recent work of Ruth Perry, for instance, has brilliantly laid out the importance and impact of these changes.[19]

At the very least this suggests an apparent contradiction. On the one hand we find more sex, both inside and outside of marriage, and sex which we must assume was largely consensual. On the other we find the greater repression of women. Nor can we ignore the range of subsidiary literatures which support this story of greater gender definition and control. The histories of medicine and the body are cases in point.

Historians of the body Londa Shiebinger, Catherine Gallagher and Thomas Laqueur, whose work I have mentioned in a different context, have each suggested that the eighteenth century saw a quite dramatic transition from what they call a "one-body" model of gender differentiation, to a "two-body" model. Londa Shiebinger has demonstrated that it was only at the end of the century that anatomists identified different male and female skeletons, while Laqueur has convincingly argued that the same period saw the redefinition of women's genitalia.[20] Up until the eighteenth century, it had been argued that both men and women needed to reach an orgasm in order to conceive, and that the process of generation involved essentially the same process for both sexes. During the course of the century, new theories of generation (not supported by anatomical observation) suggested that women did not ejaculate at orgasm, and that the active element in the process was male sperm.[21] In terms of the definition of gender, this suggested that women could be seen as different to, and it is important to note, less important to reproduction than men. This began a process whereby gender distinctions became "natural."[22] At least for those familiar with elite medical discourses it ceased to be the case that men and women were perceived to be on a continuum from hot and dry to wet and cold characteristics as they had been in the seventeenth century, and instead became simply men and women—a distinction which could then be used in both law and usage to debar women from an increasing number of public activities.[23]

In terms of the history of sexuality, this transition resulted in the perception of increasing female passivity. From being perceived as sexually aggressive— hungry for the hot and dry essence they consumed in sex—women became sexually passive, their bodies a receptacle for the newly important sperm. The female orgasm, the belief in aggressive female sexuality and indeed the role of the clitoris, were only re-created in popular texts at the end of the nineteenth century with the rise of sexology and psychoanalysis.[24]

From the perspective of the historian of sexuality, the question which all of these literatures would seem to ask is whether there was a "sexual revolution" in the eighteenth century or else a closing down of sexual experience, and a new sexual

McCarthyism directed specifically at women. But this strikes me as an inappropriately dichotomous approach. The questions these literatures address are the result of the extreme polarities of modern gender politics, and as such lead to unilluminating answers. A more appropriate question to ask is what changed about sex that would allow it to create the new demographic regime, to be viewed by some as a liberation, and by others as a denigration?

The answer has to lie in the definition of sex itself. What the demographers are measuring and the historians of the Enlightenment are celebrating is heterosexual penetration and ejaculation. But what the experience of someone like John Cannon and his friends should demonstrate, is that this is only one minor variation in sexual practice. If we think about sex more broadly, if we start the definition at the kiss rather than at the point of mutual genital contact, the way in which these various literatures fit together becomes more apparent.

My suggestion is that sex changed. At the beginning of the century it was an activity characterised by mutual masturbation, much kissing and fondling, and long hours spent in mutual touching, but very little penal/vaginal penetration — at least before marriage. If penetration did occur, coitus interruptus was likely to be practised, and if this failed and a pregnancy resulted, there was always recourse to abortion.[25] But the important thing is that there was an equality of emphasis on a wide range of different parts of the body.

By the end of the century sex had become increasingly phallocentric. Putting a penis in a vagina became the dominant sexual activity — all other forms of sex becoming literally foreplay. Indeed, it is little wonder that use of the word "play" without its prefix, as a term for sexual activity, died out in our period.[26] But, more significantly, it was the penis that became the active member. What the eighteenth century saw was the development of an obsession with the penis, and of an assumption that there was only one thing to do with it.[27]

This transition fits well with the literatures discussed above. Redefining or changing the nature of sex towards penetration would have the effect of increasing the bastardy rate, and indeed the rate of population growth overall, both within and without marriage. And would likewise ensure that the proportion of the population who never married would fall. Pregnancy was a significant cue for marriage. Forms of courting which involved penetrative sex leading to pregnancy were more likely to result in marriage than nonpenetrative forms.

The literatures associating sex with productivity and the industrial revolution would likewise be satisfied — after all, the transition to penetrative sex is fundamentally about a change from nonproductive, antinatal to productive, pronatal, activities. Finally, the literature on the Enlightenment and pornography can be explained. The demands of narrative structure, if nothing else, ensure that, while erotica may be about fondling, pornography is generally about penetration. While the narrator in a work such as *Fanny Hill* may be female, the action always revolves around putting a penis somewhere. This transition also fits well with the literature on the history of the body. If women were seen to be increasingly passive, then the necessity of sexually satisfying anyone other than the male participant was obviated, and penetration became the quickest way of doing this.

The apparent creation of a phallocentric sexual economy also fits well the story of change in gender relations and the development of separate spheres. The active male actor on the world stage becomes the active inserter on the petit stage of the bedroom. Forms of sexual activity which dramatically increased the risk of pregnancy generally reflected the interest of men over those of women. Mutual masturbation and antinatal forms of sex reflected instead a set of gender relations in which women's interests were more likely to be taken into account, and in which negotiation between partners was more equal. This seems to parallel the more open and apparently negotiated relations associated with the seventeenth century. The increasingly phallocentric and penetrative sexual culture of the late eighteenth century both encouraged and made possible the denigration of female sexuality and perceived passivity. In the process it also reflected and contributed to women's increasingly restricted role in society as a whole.[28]

What all of this suggests is that there was indeed, as Shorter *et al.* have suggested, a "sexual revolution" in the eighteenth century. It suggests this revolution resulted in more penetrative sex: not more sex overall, but rather a different type of sex. In other words, it resulted in a transition from a form of sex in which the interests of both individuals played a substantive part, to a form where the male orgasm became the all-important outcome. In the process two things happened simultaneously. Men, newly concerned about their penises, were in a very restricted sense, liberated; while women, biologically redefined in order to deny them a sexual role, were repressed and their sexual activity was more heavily policed.

This is, of course, a bald assertion, which while providing a useful way of squaring a range of historical literatures, is hardly open to empirical testing. We simply do not know what most people did with each other at different times. And while one can collect the scattered evidence of diaries and court cases, and in the process trace a balance of change in the direction I have suggested, this hardly provides a demonstrable proof. The hit-or-miss nature of these sources, as well as the fact that most of them come from men, all ensure that any argument made on this basis would be profoundly problematic. Likewise, the demographic record provides few ways forward. It responds only to procreative sex. And while this measure may be significant in determining the timing of change, it gives us no proof of the existence or otherwise of nonprocreative sex.[29]

Perhaps an easier way forward lies in the existence of prescriptive literatures on specific types of sexual activity. These literatures cannot demonstrate the case, but they are highly suggestive. There are two forms of popular literature which are important here—the widely read anti-masturbation literature, in particular, *Onania* and Tissot's *Onanism*, and the equally popular sex manuals, *Aristotle's Masterpiece* and Venette's *Secrets of Conjugal Love Revealed*. Both of these literatures were increasingly popular over the course of the eighteenth century, and both provide a perspective on what people read, if not direct evidence of what they did.

Up until the beginning of the eighteenth century the sin of Onan was generally associated with coitus interruptus. Masturbation, when it was mentioned at all, was considered a lesser sin, and while it was expected to have some ill effects, was but a sin among many others. As the century progressed there was increasing and vociferous concern about the masturbatory habits of both men and women, and by the end of the eighteenth century male masturbation in particular had been transformed for both elite and popular audiences into a serious medical and social concern, on which many of the social problems of the day could be heaped.

The earliest condemnatory pamphlet was Josiah Woodward's *Rebuke of the Sin of Uncleanness* published by the Society for Promoting Christian Knowledge in 1704.[30] But the popular breakthrough for anti-masturbatory literature came in 1708 with the publication of the enormously successful, *Onania, or the Heinous Sin of Self-Pollution, and All Its Frightful Consequences in Both Sexes, Considered.* Anonymously produced, but the work of a clergyman-cum-quack named Beckers or Bekkers, *Onania* was a pseudomedical account of the horrible consequences of masturbation.[31] Within an essentially Galenic framework, *Onania* warned of the debilitating effects of loss of vigour for both men and women. Merely to list some of the consequences adduced by the author gives a flavour of the whole volume. Male masturbators could suffer from stunted growth, priapisms, gonorrhoeas, and stranguries. Their seed could become waterish, and they could experience frequent fainting fits. Women might expect hysteria, barrenness, and imbecility and a "total ineptitude to the Act of Generation itself."[32] The dangers for both the individual and society were continually stressed, and a course of pills, available from a London publisher by mail-order, was recommended as the surest remedy.

This book went through some nineteen editions and sold almost forty thousand copies, and in the process helped to create what has been described as a "general neurosis."[33] What started as a pamphlet of some 60 pages rapidly grew to 194 pages and later received a 142-page supplement—most of the additional material being composed of lurid accounts of the masturbatory habits of various men and women.[34] This was followed in 1758, by the Swiss doctor Samuel Tissot's *L'Onanisme, ou Dissertation physique sur les maladies produites par la masturbation* which was translated into English as *Onanism: or a Treatise upon the Disorders Produced by Masturbation.* It remained in print until 1905, and formed the basis for a respectable medical theory of the debilitating consequences of masturbation.[35]

Tissot's theories were based on the assumption of the importance of sperm, and in many ways stood within a solidly Galenic tradition. What is significant, however, is first, that he places greater emphasis on a spermatic economy of health than previous writers, and second, that his work was and remained so popular. From the publication of *Onanism* onward, it became almost impossible to write a popular health text without roundly condemning the likely consequences of masturbation for both men and women. By the nineteenth century, the process of medicalization had progressed so far that hospital deaths were regularly being ascribed to excessive masturbation.[36]

Historians have treated the popularity of *Onania* and Tissot's *Onanism* in a number of different ways. *Onania* has been seen largely in the context of the development of eighteenth-century pornography, while Tissot's emphasis on the spermatic economy has been associated with mercantilism. The eighteenth century emphasis on masturbation in general has been associated with the redefinition of childhood identified by Philippe Ariès, and the search for new "scientific" explanations for madness during an age of growing rationality.[37]

All of these analyses provide useful perspectives on the rise of a literature of masturbation. But the importance of this material in the context of the history of sexuality is its role in policing heterosexual, penetrative and procreative sex. Here we have a literature which is specifically and explicitly opposed to forms of sexual behaviour which can be satisfying and nonpenetrative. It seems to me that by denigrating perhaps the single most common sexual practice, this literature valorises a crude, phallocentric emphasis on penetration, over all else. One way in which to view this material is to see it as a strongly didactic literature concerned to ensure that penetrative, heterosexual sex became increasingly the only form of sexual activity which could be countenanced. And while this literature is not, for the most part, directed at courting couples, its pronatal and penetrative lessons would be equally applicable to them, as to individual masturbators.

A similar role in the regulation of popular sexual activity can be ascribed to the popular sex manuals of the eighteenth century. The most common was *Aristotle's Master-piece: or, the Secrets of Generation Displayed in All the Parts Thereof.* First published in 1684, the anonymous *Masterpiece* went through at least forty-three editions by 1800, and became, if anything, more popular during the nineteenth century.[38] Its popularity was rivalled only by Dr. Nicholas Venette's *Tableau de l'amour conjugal* (1696) which was first published in an English translation in 1703 as the *Mysteries of Conjugal Love Revealed*. It too went through numerous editions, and was still in print in the 1950s.[39]

What has emerged from the growing body of historical literature on this genre is the sheer confusion, and the ad hoc nature of much of this writing. The content of these manuals changes from edition to edition, apparently depending on the energy, or lack of it, of the particular compiler or publisher. They mix, in what at first sight seems almost a random order, magical and Galenic understandings of sexual processes, juxtaposing apparently commonsensical advice with detailed directions on appropriate sexual positions and the course of foetal development. Roy Porter has described the content of the *Masterpiece* as a "codification of sexual folklore" directed at the readers of ballads and almanacs.[40] But, more significantly, what the analysis of these works has revealed is their pronatalist content.

In a series of articles Roy Porter has argued that these works were guides to having babies, rather than to having good sex. He argues that they were predicated on the assumption that having babies was a good thing and that the boundaries these works created were those between reproductive and sterile forms of sex. Hence, the sexual positions recommended by both the *Masterpiece* and Nicholas Venette were those thought to produce conception, with what would later be dubbed the missionary position being the most highly recommended. Variations from this recommendation were only allowed where factors such as obesity made them imperative. The time of the month during which sex was most appropriate, and the diet of both the hopeful parents and the pregnant mother, were all matters these works felt it reasonable to comment upon, as was the frequency of sexual activity in marriage.[41]

At the same time they were concerned with sexual dysfunction. Dietary advice designed to encourage greater sexual appetite in men was provided, as were discussions of love sickness and infertility. In *Aristotle's Masterpiece* in particular, it was generation rather than sexual technique which formed the fundamental focus of the work.

What these works most certainly did not include were instructions on how to have nonpenetrative sex. While sexual pleasure, and the necessity of "fore-play" were certainly emphasised, penetration and procreation were the defining characteristics of the sex these manuals advocated, while fondling and mutual masturbation as ends in themselves were entirely absent.

In the late seventeenth century most sexual knowledge would have been transmitted through word of mouth. John Cannon, along with a group of his school fellows, for example, learned how to masturbate from a seventeen-year-old cousin. As literacy and urbanisation progressed over the course of the century, the availability of the ever popular eighteenth-century sex manual grew as well. If these manuals emphasised putting penises in vaginas, it would be little wonder if a larger and larger proportion of young people followed their advice.

Both of these literatures, in their different ways, spoke to the same concern— the creation of a body of sexual knowledge in which the point of sex was penetration. In the process, they equally emphasised the penis as the all-important organ of generation, and together created and reflected a profound shift in sexual practice.

I want to end this paper with a brief examination of two bodies of historical literature—those on male homosexuality and lesbianism. The rise of urban gay subcultures in eighteenth-century Europe is now well attested. While the Netherlands had the greatest numbers of prosecutions, there is little doubt that London had one of the largest and most organised communities.[42] What the historians of this community have noted is both an increasingly homophobic attitude on the part of the population as a whole, and an increasing association of gay men with effeminacy. At least two historians, Randolph Trumbach and Antony Simpson, have suggested that these changes reflect a profound shift in the construction of masculinity, a shift in which penetrative, heterosexual sex became increasingly significant as a talisman of normal, i.e. heterosexual, masculinity.[43] The decline of male kissing, and physical signs of affection, and the apparently increasing desire on the part of both the courts and the crowds that surrounded the pillories to vilify sodomites as both a social danger and an "other" are used to suggest the development of a well-defined and phallocentric masculine identity shared by both urban working people and the middling sort.[44] The use of female clothing and forms of speech by many gay men within the London subculture is likewise noted to suggest the existence of an increasingly strident heterosexual identity, against which these men are reacting.

What this literature implies is that men increasingly felt the need to participate in penetrative, heterosexual sex in order to demonstrate their "normality." Simply to fondle and masturbate, even in a heterosexual context, could increasingly cast doubt on the heterosexual identity of courting men. And while women were not under the same pressures, they likewise must have played a role in ensuring (if only to satisfy themselves about a prospective partner) that men toed the line in this regard. All of which suggests, again, the existence of a profound shift in sexual attitudes and forms of sexual behaviour.

Similarly, if one looks at the history of lesbianism, what appears to be a marked transition can be identified. Recent historians of eighteenth-century lesbian culture, most notably Emma Donaghue, have argued for the existence of a series of essentially unchanging identities, but the decline in female cross-dressing at the end of the eighteenth century, when combined with the rise of romantic friendship around the middle of the century, argues for the existence of a developmental process intimately intertwined with the history of heterosexuality.[45] Rudolf Dekker and Lotte van de Pol have convincingly argued that in many cases when women took on a male guise as part of a lesbian relationship, they likewise adopted a male persona as a way of legitimising and imagining love between two women. While strap-on dildos and penetration of various sorts formed an element of the behavioural pattern associated with cross-dressing, its popularity as a lesbian strategy must likewise reflect the extent to which heterosexual behaviour in the first half of the eighteenth century comprised a wide enough variety of activities to form a reasonable model for women who loved other women.[46]

The rise of romantic friendship from midcentury can likewise be seen as part of the process of redefining all forms of sex. As heterosexuality became more and more dominated by the phallus, new and different definitions and categories were needed to accommodate lesbian love. In part the rise of romantic friendship simply reflects the development of a new ideology of femininity. Emotional sensitivity and a separate sphere of homosocial relationships are characteristics shared between a broader female culture, and the elements of that culture which can be described as lesbian.[47] Perhaps ironically, the development of lesbian culture seems to suggest a transition from the occasional use of penetrative sexual activities to more mutual masturbation, but the timing and changing categories of lesbian identity available to eighteenth-century women, likewise reflect, affect and are intertwined with the story of changing heterosexualities. And while there are certainly more identities available to eighteenth-century lesbians than that of cross-dresser or romantic friend, the changing nature of the social perception of these two most common lesbian strategies is highly indicative.

What we are left with is, in Edward Shorter's term, a "sexual revolution." What I hope I have suggested is that sexual practice changed, and that in a heterosexual context people increasingly restricted their behaviour to forms of phallocentric, penetrative sex which could be countenanced as procreative. In the process the definitions of both masculinity and femininity changed. Both men and women were created as "naturally" and biologically sexed, with an increasing onus, and this was particularly true for men, to find the other and now "opposite" sex attractive. What occurred was not a liberation. For women it heralded a period of intense patriarchal oppression, but for men as well, it reflected an increasingly restrictive form of masculinity, which was policed by a highly effective public and print culture.

NOTES

1. Somerset Record Office, MS DD/SAS C/1193/4, "Memoirs of the Birth, Education, Life and Death of: Mr John Cannon. Sometime Officer of the Excise & Writing Master at Mere Glastenbury & West Lydford in the County of Somerset," p. 57.

2. For a discussion of early modern courtship, see John R. Gillis, *For Better, For Worse: British Marriages, 1600 to the Present* (Oxford, 1985), pp. 11–54.

3. British Library, Add. MS 27825, fs. 165. Quoted in *The Autobiography of Francis Place (1771–1854)*, ed. Mary Thale (Cambridge, 1972), p. 59.

4. Foucault argues in his *The History of Sexuality, vol. 1, An Introduction* (London, 1979), that the eighteenth century witnessed a growing discourse around sexuality, and that while much of this was condemnatory, the very existence of more discussion was itself the significant transition. For a recent critique of Foucault's approach, see Roy Porter, "Is Foucault Useful for Understanding Eighteenth and Nineteenth Century Sexuality?" *Contention* 1 (1991): 61–82.

5. For material on eighteenth-century demography, see Peter Laslett, Karla Oosterveen, and Richard Smith, eds., *Bastardy and Its Comparative History* (London, 1980); David Levine, *Family Formation in an Age of Nascent Capitalism* (New York, 1977); David Levine, " 'For Their Own Reasons': Individual Marriage Decisions and Family Life," *Journal of Family History* 7 (1982): 255–64; Roger Schofield, "English Marriage Patterns Revisited," *Journal of Family History* 10 (1985): 2–20; Pamela Sharpe, "Locating the 'Missing Marryers' in Colyton, 1660–1750," *Local Population Studies* 48 (1992): 49–59; Pamela Sharpe, "Marital Separation in the Eighteenth and Early Nineteenth Centuries," *Local Population Studies* 45 (1990): 66–70; Richard Wall, "Leaving Home and the Process of Household Formation in Pre-Industrial England," *Continuity and Change* 2 (1987): 77–101; David R. Weir, "Rather Never than Late: Celibacy and Age at Marriage in English Cohort Fertility, 1541–1871," *Journal of Family History* 9 (1984): 340–54; Adrian Wilson, "Illegitimacy and Its Implications in Mid-Eighteenth Century London: The Evidence of the Foundling Hospital," *Continuity and Change* 4 (1989): 103–64; E. A. Wrigley and R. S. Schofield, *The Population History of England, 1541–1871* (Cambridge 1981); E. A. Wrigley, "The Growth of Population in Eighteenth Century England: A Conundrum Resolved," *Past and Present* 98 (1983): 121–50; E. A. Wrigley, "Marriage, Fertility and Population Growth in Eighteenth Century England," in *Marriage and Society: Studies in the Social History of Marriage,* ed. R. B. Outhwaite (New York, 1982), pp. 137–85; Grace Wyatt, "Bastardy and Prenuptial Pregnancy in a Cheshire Town during the Eighteenth Century," *Local Population Studies* 49 (1992): 38–50. For a powerful critique of the overall methodological approach contained in the above volumes, see Bridget Hill, "The Marriage Age of Women and the Demographers," *History Workshop Journal* 28 (1989): 129–47.

6. It has been pointed out that many of the phenomena mentioned here can be found at different times in English history. The bastardy rate, for instance, reached similar levels around 1600. But the collective impact of all the changes noticed in the eighteenth century does suggest a fundamental transition. Also, to say that more people are having penetrative sex in 1750 than they were in 1700, does not preclude the existence of a higher rate of penetrative sex in 1600 than in 1700.

7. Levine, "'For Their Own Reasons,'" pp. 255–64.

8. Edward Shorter, *The Making of the Modern Family* (New York, 1975); for critiques of Shorter's analysis, see Cissie Fairchilds, "Female Sexual Attitudes and the Rise of Illegitimacy: A Case Study," *Journal of Interdisciplinary History* 4 (1978): 627–67; Peter Laslett, "Introduction: Comparing Illegitimacy over Time and between Cultures," in *Bastardy*, ed. Laslett, Oosterveen, and Smith, pp. 26–29.

9. See Lawrence Stone, *The Family, Sex, and Marriage in England, 1500–1800,* 1st ed. (London, 1977); for a more recent rendition of Stone's views, see Lawrence Stone, *Road to Divorce: England, 1530–1987* (Oxford, 1990).

10. For a critique of Stone's early work on the family, see Richard T. Vann, "Review Essay," *Journal of Family History* 4 (1979): 308–15.

11. Henry Abelove, "Some Speculations on the History of Sexual Intercourse during the Long Eighteenth Century in England," *Genders* 6 (1989): 125–30.

12. Thomas Laqueur, "Sex and Desire in the Industrial Revolution," in *The Industrial Revolution and British Society*, ed. Patrick O'Brien and Roland Quinault (Cambridge, 1993), pp. 100–23.

13. For a selection of some recent works on pornography, see Jan Bremmer, *From Sappho to De Sade: Moments in the History of Sexuality* (London, 1989); Louis Crompton, "*Don Leon*, Byron, and Homosexual Law Reform," *Journal of Homosexuality* 8.3–4 (1983): 53–72; Lynn Hunt, ed., *The Invention of Pornography, 1500–1800* (New York, 1994); Dorelies Kraakman, "Reading Pornography Anew: A Critical History of Sexual Knowledge for Girls in French Erotic Fiction, 1750–1840," *Journal of the History of Sexuality* 4 (1994): 517–48; Iain McCalman, "Unrespectable Radicalism, Infidels and Pornography in Early Nineteenth Century London," *Past and Present* 104 (1984): 74–110; Iain McCalman, *Radical Underworlds: Prophets, Revolutionaries and Pornographers in London, 1795–1840* (Cambridge, 1988); Donald H. Mengay, "The Sodomitical Muse: *Fanny Hill* and the Rhetoric of Crossdressing," *Journal of Homosexuality* 23.1–2 (1991): 185–98; G. S. Rousseau and Roy Porter, eds., *Sexual Underworlds of the Enlightenment* (Manchester, 1987); Roy Roussel, *The Conversation of the Sexes: Seduction and Equality in Selected Seventeenth- and Eighteenth-Century Texts* (New York, 1986), ch. 2, "Fanny Hill and the Androgynous Reader"; Lawrence Stone, "Libertine Sexuality in Post-Restoration England: Group Sex and Flagellation among the Middling Sort in Norwich in 1706–07," *Journal of the History of Sexuality* 2 (1992): 511–26; Roger Thompson, *Unfit for Modest Ears: A Study of Pornographic, Obscene, and Bawdy Works Written or Published in England in the Second Half of the Seventeenth Century* (Totowa, N.J., 1979); Peter Wagner, "The Veil of Medicine and Mortality: Some Pornographic Aspects of the *Onania*," *British Journal for Eighteenth-Century Studies* 6 (1983): 179–84; Peter Wagner, "Trial Reports as a Genre of Eighteenth-Century Erotica," *British Journal for Eighteenth-Century Studies* 5 (1982): 117–23; Peter Wagner, *Eros Revived: Erotica of the Enlightenment in England and America* (London, 1987); Peter Wagner, ed., *Erotica and the Enlightenment* (London, 1990).

14. For a recent account of literary attacks on women in the late seventeenth and early eighteenth centuries, see Felicity Nussbaum, *The Brink of All We Hate* (Lexington, 1984).

15. For some work on the histories of women and gender, see Susan Amussen, *An Ordered Society: Gender and Class in Early Modern England* (Oxford, 1988); Maxine Berg, *The Age of Manufactures* (London, 1985): esp. chs. 6 and 7; Alice Clark, *The Working Life of Women in the Seventeenth Century* (London, 1992); Anna Clark, *Struggle for the Breeches: Gender and the Making of the British Working Class* (London, 1995); Leonore Davidoff and Catherine Hall,

Family Fortunes: Men and Women of the English Middle Class, 1780–1850 (London, 1987); Valerie Fildes, *Women as Mothers in Pre-Industrial England* (London, 1990); Jacques Gélis, *History of Childbirth: Fertility, Pregnancy and Birth in Early Modern Europe* (London, 1991); Margaret George, *Women in the First Capitalist Society: Experiences in Seventeenth Century England* (London, 1988); Bridget Hill, *Women, Work and Sexual Politics in Eighteenth-Century England* (London, 1989); Olwen Hufton, "Survey Articles: Women in History: Early Modern Europe," *Past and Present* 101 (1983): 125–41; Ilana Krausman Ben-Amos, "Women Apprentices in the Trades and Crafts of Early Modern Bristol," *Continuity and Change* 2 (1991): 227–52; Anne Laurence, *Women in England, 1500–1760: A Social History* (London, 1994); Sherrin Marshall, ed., *Women in Reformation and Counter-Reformation Europe: Public and Private Worlds* (London, 1989); Ivy Pinchbeck, *Women Workers and the Industrial Revolution*, 3rd ed. (London, 1981); Mary Prior, ed., *Women in English Society, 1500–1800* (London, 1985); Eric Richards, "Women in the British Economy since about 1700: An Interpretation," *History* 59 (1974): 337–57; K. D. M. Snell, *Annals of the Labouring Poor* (Cambridge, 1985), esp. ch. 3; W. Thwaites, "Women in the Market Place: Oxfordshire c. 1690–1800," *Midland History* 9 (1984): 23–24.

16. For an account of this transition in one industry, see Deborah Valenze, "The Art of Women and the Business of Men: Women's Work and the Dairy Industry, c. 1740–1840," *Past and Present* 130 (1991): 142–70. For examples of the extensive literature on midwifery, see J. Donnison, *Midwives and Medical Men: A History of Interprofessional Rivalries and Women's Rights* (New York, 1977); Audrey Eccles, *Obstetrics and Gynaecology in Tudor and Stuart England* (Kent, Ohio, 1982); Thomas Forbes, "The Regulation of English Midwives in the Sixteenth and Seventeenth Centuries," *Medical History* 8 (1964): 235–44; Roy Porter, "A Touch of Danger: The Man-Midwife as Sexual Predator," in *Sexual Underworlds,* ed. Rousseau and Porter, pp. 206–32.

17. Davidoff and Hall, *Family Fortunes.*

18. Amanda Vickery, "Golden Age to Separate Spheres? A Review of the Categories and Chronology of English Women's History," *Historical Journal* 32 (1993): 383–414.

19. Ruth Perry, "Colonizing the Breast: Sexuality and Maternity in Eighteenth-Century England," *Journal of the History of Sexuality* 2 (1991): 204–34.

20. Londa Schiebinger, "Skeletons in the Closet: The First Illustrations of the Female Skeleton in Eighteenth-Century Anatomy," in *The Making of the Modern Body: Sexuality and Society in the Nineteenth Century,* ed. Catherine Gallagher and Thomas Laqueur (Berkeley, 1987), pp. 42–82; Thomas Laqueur, *Making Sex: Body and Gender from the Greeks to Freud* (Cambridge, Mass., 1990).

21. For an excellent account of the competing theories of generation, see Angus McLaren, *Reproductive Rituals: The Perception of Fertility in England from the Sixteenth Century to the Nineteenth Century* (London, 1984).

22. Thomas Laqueur, "Amor Veneris, vel Dulcedo Appeletur," in *Fragments for a History of the Human Body,* vol. 3, ed. M. Feher (New York, 1989), pp. 90–131; Thomas Laqueur, "Bodies of the Past," *Bulletin of the History of Medicine* 67 (1993): 155–61; Laqueur, *Making Sex*; Thomas Laqueur, "Orgasm, Generation, and the Politics of Reproductive Biology," in *Making of the Modern Body,* ed. Gallagher and Laqueur, pp. 1–41.

23. For a recent critique of this literature and of Thomas Laqueur's work in particular, see Lyndal Roper, *Oedipus and the Devil: Witchcraft, Sexuality and Religion in Early Modern Europe* (London, 1994). Roper argues that too much emphasis has been placed on the role of discourses surrounding the body, and insufficient allowance made for the shared experience of inhabiting a physical form.

24. For a specific treatment of the history of the clitoris, see Laqueur, "Amor Veneris."

25. For an excellent discussion of family limitation in this period, see McLaren, *Reproductive Rituals.*

26. The most recent use of the term in this sense recorded in the *OED* is dated 1667.

27. There is a significant literature on phallocentrism in late-eighteenth-century English culture, although it has been largely concerned with issues associated with homosexual desire. See, for example, G. S. Rousseau, "The Sorrows of Priapus: Anticlericalism, Homosocial Desire, and Richard Payne Knight," in *Sexual Underworlds,* ed. Rousseau and Porter, pp. 101–53.

28. It is important to note that what is being suggested here is a shift in emphasis, rather than a cataclysmic change in behaviour. Penises appear quite regularly in the popular literature of the seventeenth century, and interest in and writings related to penetrative sex are reasonably common throughout the early modern period. For an account of the sexual assumptions and content of chapbooks and ballads, see Margaret Spufford, *Small Books and Pleasant Histories: Popular Fiction and Its Readership in Seventeenth-Century England* (Cambridge, 1981).

29. The demographic transition seems to be centred around the 1730s and 1740s. See Wrigley and Schofield, *Population History of England.*

30. For accounts of the publishing activities of the SPCK, see Leonard W. Cowie, *Henry Newman: An American in London, 1708–1743* (London, 1956); and M. G. Jones, *The Charity School Movement: A Study of Eighteenth Century Puritanism in Action* (Cambridge, 1938). For the Societies for the Reformation of Manners, see Robert Shoemaker, "Reforming the City: The Reformation of Manners Campaign in London, 1690–1738," in *Stilling the Grumbling Hive: The Response to Social and Economic Problems in England, 1688–1750,* ed. Lee Davison et al. (Stroud, 1992), pp. 99–120; D. W. R. Bahlman, *The Moral Revolution of 1688* (New Haven, 1957); T. C. Curtis and W. A. Speck, "The Societies for the Reformation of Manners: A Case Study in the Theory and Practice of Moral Reform," *Literature and History* 3 (1976): 45–47; A. G. Craig, "The Movement for the Reformation of Manners, 1688–1715" (Ph.D. diss., Edinburgh University, 1980); Tina Beth Isaacs, "Moral Crime, Moral Reform, and the State in Eighteenth-Century England: A Study of Piety and Politics" (Ph.D. diss., University of Rochester, 1979); John Spurr, " 'Virtue, Religion, and Government': The Anglican Uses of Providence," in *The Politics of Religion in Restoration England,* ed. Tim Harris et al. (Oxford, 1990), pp. 29–47.

31. Wagner, "Veil of Medicine and Mortality," p. 179.

32. Robert H. MacDonald, "The Frightful Consequences of Onanism: Notes on the History of a Delusion," *Journal of the History of Ideas* 28 (1967): 425.

33. Wagner, "Veil of Medicine," p. 179.

34. Ibid., pp. 179–84.

35. R. P. Neuman, "Masturbation, Madness, and the Modern Concepts of Childhood and Adolescence," *Journal of Social History* 8 (1975): 2.

36. E. H. Hare, "Masturbatory Insanity: The History of an Idea," *Journal of Mental Science* 108 (1962): 2–25.

37. See, respectively, Neuman, "Masturbation, Madness"; Ludmilla Jordanova, "The Popularisation of Medicine: Tissot on Onanism," *Textual Practice* 1 (1987): 68–79.

38. The ascription of the work of Aristotle was entirely apocryphal. For an account of the publishing history of the *Masterpiece,* see Roy Porter, "The Literature of Sexual Advice before 1800," in *Sexual Knowledge, Sexual Science: The History of Attitudes to Sexuality,* ed. Roy Porter and Mikulas Teich (Cambridge, 1994), p. 136.

39. Roy Porter, "Spreading Carnal Knowledge or Selling Dirt Cheap? Nicholas Venette's *Tableau de l'Amour Conjugal* in Eighteenth-Century England," *Journal of European Studies* 14 (1984): 237.

40. Porter, "Sexual Advice before 1800," p. 136.

41. For material on this topic in general, see Otho T. Beall, "*Aristotle's Masterpiece* in America: A Landmark in the Folklore of Medicine," *William and Mary Quarterly* 20 (1963): 207–22; Patricia Crawford, "Sexual Knowledge in England, 1500–1750," in *Sexual Knowledge, Sexual Science,* ed. Porter and Teich, pp. 82–106; Mary Fissell, "Readers, Texts, and Contexts: Vernacular Medical Works in Early Modern England," in *The Popularization of Medicine,*

1650–1850, ed. Roy Porter (London, 1992), pp. 72–96; Roy Porter, " 'The Secrets of Generation Display'd': *Aristotle's Masterpiece* in Eighteenth-Century England," in *'Tis Nature's Fault: Unauthorized Sexualities during the Enlightenment,* ed. Robert P. Maccubbin (New York, 1985), pp. 1–21; Roy Porter, "The Sexual Politics of James Graham," *British Journal for Eighteenth-Century Studies* 5 (1982): 199–206; Porter, "Sexual Advice before 1800"; Roy Porter, "Love, Sex and Medicine: Nicolas Venette and His *Tableau de l'Amour Conjugal,*" in *Erotica and the Enlightenment,* ed. Wagner, pp. 90–122; Porter, "Spreading Carnal Knowledge"; Roy Porter, " 'The Whole Secret of Health': Mind, Body and Medicine in *Tristram Shandy,*" in *Nature Transfigured,* ed. John Christie and Sally Shuttleworth (Manchester, 1989), pp. 61–84. Roy Porter has recently synthesized much of his earlier work on this topic in Roy Porter and Lesley Hall, *The Facts of Life: The Creation of Sexual Knowledge in Britain, 1650–1950* (New Haven, 1995).

42. For some recent work on this subject, see L. J. Boon, "Those Damned Sodomites: Public Images of Sodomy in the Eighteenth-Century Netherlands," *Journal of Homosexuality* 16.1–2 (1989): 237–48; Alan Bray, *Homosexuality in Renaissance England* (London, 1982); B. R. Burg, "Ho Hum, Another Work of the Devil: Buggery and Sodomy in Early Stuart England," *Journal of Homosexuality* 6.1–2 (1980–81): 69–78; Arend H. Huusen, "Sodomy in the Dutch Republic during the Eighteenth Century," in *'Tis Nature's Fault,* ed. Maccubbin, pp. 169–78; Stephen O. Murray, "Homosexual Acts and Selves in Early Modern Europe," *Journal of Homosexuality* 16.1–2 (1989): 457–77; Dirk Jaap Noordam, "Sodomy in the Dutch Republic, 1600–1725," *Journal of Homosexuality* 16.1–2 (1989): 207–28; Rictor Norton, *Mother Clap's Molly House: The Gay Subculture in England, 1700–1830* (London, 1992); Michel Rey, "Police and Sodomy in Eighteenth-Century Paris: From Sin to Disorder," *Journal of Homosexuality* 16.1–2 (1989): 129–46; Michel Rey, "Parisian Homosexuals Create a Lifestyle, 1700–1750: The Police Archives," in *'Tis Nature's Fault,* ed. Maccubbin, pp. 179–91; G. S. Rousseau, "The Pursuit of Homosexuality in the Eighteenth Century: 'Utterly Confused Category' and/or Rich Repository?" in *'Tis Nature's Fault,* ed. Maccubbin, pp. 132–68; G. S. Rousseau, " 'In the House of Madam Van der Tasse, on the Long Bridge': A Homosocial University Club in Early Modern Europe," *Journal of Homosexuality* 16.1–2 (1989): 311–47; Laurence Senelick, "Mollies or Men of Mode? Sodomy and the Eighteenth-Century London Stage," *Journal of the History of Sexuality* 1 (1990): 33–67; Antony Simpson, "Masculinity and Control: The Prosecution of Sex Offences in Eighteenth-Century London" (Ph.D. diss., New York University, 1984); Randolph Trumbach, "Sodomitical Subcultures, Sodomitical Roles, and the Gender Revolution of the Eighteenth Century: The Recent Historiography," in *'Tis Nature's Fault,* ed. Maccubbin, pp. 109–21; Randolph Trumbach, "London's Sodomites: Homosexual Behaviour and Western Culture in the Eighteenth Century," *Journal of Social History* 11 (1977): 1–33; Randolph Trumbach, "Sex, Gender, and Sexual Identity in Modern Culture: Male Sodomy and Female Prostitution in Enlightenment London," *Journal of the History of Sexuality* 2 (1991): 186–203; Randolph Trumbach, "The Birth of the Queen: Sodomy and the Emergence of Gender Equality in Modern Culture, 1660–1750," in *Hidden from History: Reclaiming the Gay and Lesbian Past,* ed. Martin Duberman, Martha Vicinus, and George Chauncey (London, 1991), pp. 129–40; Randolph Trumbach, "Sodomitical Assaults, Gender Roles, and Sexual Development in Eighteenth-Century London," *Journal of Homosexuality* 16.1–2 (1989): 407–29; Theo van der Meer, "The Persecution of Sodomites in Eighteenth-Century Amsterdam: Changing Perceptions of Sodomy," *Journal of Homosexuality* 16.1–2 (1989): 263–307.

43. See Simpson, "Masculinity and Control"; Trumbach, "Sodomitical Subcultures, Sodomitical Roles"; Trumbach, "London's Sodomites"; Trumbach, "Sex, Gender, and Sexual Identity in Modern Culture"; Trumbach, "The Birth of the Queen"; Trumbach, "Sodomitical Assaults, Gender Roles, and Sexual Development." For a recent piece which clearly lays out Trumbach's views and which is particularly valuable for its emphasis on the relationship between the development of the homosexual subculture and the broader creation of new forms of gender definition, see Randolph Trumbach, "Erotic Fantasy and Male Libertinism in Enlightenment England," in *Invention of Pornography,* ed. Hunt, pp. 253–82.

44. For an excellent recent work on the history of the role of kissing and gestures in male friendship, see Alan Bray, "Homosexuality and the Signs of Male Friendship in Elizabethan England," *History Workshop Journal* 29 (1990): 1–19. For an accessible account of changing attitudes to homosexuals exposed on the pillory, see Norton, *Mother Clap's Molly House,* pp. 128–33.

45. Emma Donaghue, *Passions between Women: British Lesbian Culture, 1668–1801* (London, 1993).

46. Rudolf Dekker and Lotte van de Pol, *The Tradition of Female Transvestism in Early Modern Europe* (London, 1989). For further material on female cross-dressing, see Dianne Dugaw, *Warrior Women and Popular Balladry, 1650–1850* (Cambridge, 1989); Lynne Friedli, "'Passing Women': A Study of Gender Boundaries in the Eighteenth Century," in *Sexual Underworlds,* ed. Rousseau and Porter, pp. 234–60; Marjorie Garber, *Vested Interests: Cross-Dressing and Cultural Anxiety* (London, 1992); Pat Rogers, "The Breeches Part," in *Sexuality in Eighteenth-Century Britain*, ed. Paul-Gabriel Boucé (Manchester, 1982), pp. 244–58; Kristina Straub, "The Guilty Pleasures of Female Theatrical Cross-Dressing and the Autobiography of Charlotte Charke," in *Body Guards: The Cultural Politics of Gender Ambiguity,* ed. Julia Epstein and Kristina Straub (New York, 1991), pp. 142–46; Julie Wheelwright, *Amazons and Military Maids: Women Who Dressed as Men in Pursuit of Life, Liberty and Happiness* (London, 1989). For a detailed account of the life of one lesbian for whom cross-dressing seems to have formed an important part of her identity, see Brigitte Eriksson, "A Lesbian Execution in Germany, 1721: The Trial Records," *Journal of Homosexuality* 16.1–2 (1980–81): 27–40.

47. For a selection of literature on romantic friendship, see Lillian Faderman, *Surpassing the Love of Men* (London, 1981); George Haggerty, "'Romantic Friendship' and Patriarchal Narrative in Sarah Scott's *Millennium Hall,*" *Genders* 13 (1992): 108–22; Elizabeth Mavor, *The Ladies of Llangollen: A Study in Romantic Friendship* (London, 1973). For an excellent discussion of the relationship between romantic friendship and other types of lesbian identity as they relate to the history of Anne Lister, see Terry Castle, *The Apparitional Lesbian: Female Homosexuality and Modern Culture* (New York, 1993), ch. 5. For a more general discussion of the same issues in a Dutch context see Myriam Everard, "Lesbian History: A History of Change and Disparity," in *Historical, Literary, and Erotic Aspects of Lesbianism*, ed. Monika Kehoe (New York, 1986).

SEX FOR THOUGHT

ROBERT DARNTON

The missing element in the current debate about pornography can be put as a proposition derived from Claude Lévi-Strauss: sex is good for thinking. In *La Pensée sauvage* and other works, Lévi-Strauss argues that many peoples do not think in the manner of philosophers, by manipulating abstractions. Instead, they think with things—concrete things from everyday life, like housing arrangements and tattoos, or imaginary things from myth and folklore, like Brer Rabbit and his briar patch. Just as some materials are particularly good to work with, some things are especially good to think about (*bonnes à penser*). They can be arranged in patterns, which bring out unsuspected relationships and define unclear boundaries.

Sex, I submit, is one of them. As carnal knowledge works its way into cultural patterns, it supplies endless material for thought, especially when it appears in narratives—dirty jokes, male braggadocio, female gossip, bawdy songs, and erotic novels. In all these forms, sex is not simply a subject but also a tool used to pry the top off things and explore their inner works. It does for ordinary people what logic does for philosophers: it helps make sense of things. And it did so with greatest effect during the golden age of pornography, from 1650 to 1800, primarily in France.

1

Fortunately, this proposition can be tested, because for the last ten years French publishers have been reprinting whole shelf-loads of the most illegal and most erotic works from the Old Regime. They have capitalized on the freer attitudes toward sex among the public and the police, and they have drawn on an endless supply of copy in the famous "Enfer" ("Hell") section of the Bibliothèque Nationale.

The librarians created "l'Enfer" sometime between 1836 and 1844 in order to cope with a contradiction. On the one hand, they needed to preserve the fullest possible record of the printed word; on the other, they wanted to prevent readers from being corrupted by bad books. The answer was to cull all the most offensive erotic works from the library's various collections and shut them up in one spot, which was declared off limits to ordinary readers.

This policy belonged to the bowdlerization of the world that took place in the nineteenth century. As part of the general buttoning-up and locking-away, the librarians everywhere put certain kinds of books beyond the reach of readers and invented codes to classify them: the "Private Case" of the British Museum, the Delta call-mark of the Library of Congress, the ***** of the New York Public Library, and the Bodleian's Greek letter φ which when pronounced in Oxford English sounded like "Fie!"

The greatest collection of them all was generally believed to be in the Bibliothèque Nationale, because Paris—the naughty Paris of the Regency and the Rococo—passed as the capital of pornography. Downstairs in the Nationale's cavernous Salle des Imprimés readers sometimes allowed their thoughts to wander upstairs, where, curiously, "Hell" was located. Instead of trudging through the sermons of Bourdaloue or the histories of Rollin, they imagined themselves climbing up two flights into a Baudelairean realm of *luxe, calme, et volupté.* "Hell" therefore became something more than a storage space defined by call numbers—the D2 series devised in 1702 and the extraordinary Y2, which goes back to 1750. "Hell" was heaven, an escape fantasy charged with poetic energy.

One of France's greatest poets, Guillaume Apollinaire, visited it and catalogued its holdings in 1911: 930 works, one apparently more delicious than another. A more scholarly catalog produced by Pascal Pia in 1978 lists 1,730 titles, although many are modern reprints, the originals having disappeared from the stacks at various times since the seventeenth century. Evidently "Hell" contained a huge supply of forbidden fruit, but most of it remained beyond the reach of ordinary readers until 1980, when the Enfer was abolished and the publishers began to reprint its contents.

Now all this literature has fallen into the public domain. You can pick some up in any Parisian bookstore and sample vast amounts in the seven-volume selection from the Enfer published by Fayard: twenty-nine novels complete with scholarly introductions and illustrations. The Fayard series does not include many of the most important works, such as *Margot la ravaudeuse, Les Lauriers ecclésiastiques,* and *La Chandelle d'Arras,* which were bestsellers in the clandestine book trade of the Old Regime. But some of them can be found in an excellent anthology published last year by Raymond Trousson, *Romans libertins du*

XVIIIe siècle: a dozen novels and stories crammed into one volume of 1,300 pages. So now at last one can take a fairly complete tour of France's literary Hell. What does it reveal about the history of pornography and pornography's place in the history of thought?

The word, like the thing, is a matter of dispute. For some, "pornography" should be restricted to its etymological root, meaning writing about prostitutes, as distinct from eroticism in general. For others, it involves descriptions of sexual activity that are meant to arouse the reader or beholder and that violate conventional morality. A postmodernist might argue that the thing did not come into existence until the word was coined—that is, not until the first half of the nineteenth century (the earliest use of a related term seems to be in Restif de la Bretonne's tract about public prostitution, *Le Pornographe,* of 1769). Only then, through measures like the creation of the Enfer, did the public discourse on sex define a category of erotica as peculiarly worthy of repression.

The difficulty with such definitions is that sexual practices and cultural taboos keep shifting. Indeed, it is their very shiftiness that made sex so good for thinking, because it served as a way to explore ambiguities and establish boundaries. No one in the sixteenth and early seventeenth centuries thought of banning books because of bawdiness that might be considered pornographic today. Religion, not sex, determined the main boundary lines of illicitness. But it is impossible to separate sex from religion in the earliest works of modern pornography: Aretino's *Ragionamenti* (1536), where the most lascivious scenes are set in a convent; *L'Ecole des filles* (1655) and *L'Académie des dames* (1680), which adapt Aretino's themes to French anticlericalism; and *Vénus dans le cloître* (c. 1682), where free love promotes free thinking. At the high tide of pornography in the eighteenth century, bestselling works like *Thérèse philosophe* (1748) employed eroticism in the cause of Enlightenment. And on the eve of the Revolution, sex books such as *Correspondance d'Eulalie* (1784) served above all as vehicles of social criticism.

After 1789, pornography provided a whole arsenal of weapons for bashing aristocrats, clergymen, and the monarchy. But after turning political (for example, *Dom Bougre aux Etats-Généraux,* an indictment of deputies in the Estates General), it became trivial (*Les Quarante manières de foutre,* a pseudo–sex manual that reads like a recipe book, most of it for fast food: "Take a thigh, add butter, cover, heat to simmering . . ."). True, the century ended with the Marquis de Sade, whom some have hailed as a prophet of the modern avant-garde. But the endless permutation of copulating bodies in the work of a more typical author, André-Robert Andréa de Nerciat, suggests a genre that had exhausted itself. In the nineteenth and twentieth centuries, Baudelaire and Bataille made sex good for thinking in new ways; and the new era of mass literacy and mass production turned pornography into a phenomenon of mass consumption.[1]

In short, pornography has a history. It grew within a body of literature whose contours kept changing but which maintained a certain coherence. The works in the Enfer constantly refer back to the same sources, especially Aretino and the ancient phallic cult of Priapus. They cite one another, sometimes by describing "gallant libraries" that are used as sexual props. They exploit the same devices, above all voyeurism (the reader is made to look over the shoulder of someone looking through a keyhole at a couple copulating in front of a mirror or under pictures of copulating couples on the wall). They use the same narrative strategies: first-person autobiographies by courtesans, dialogues between sexual veterans and innocent beginners, pseudo–sex manuals, and tours of convents and brothels (which are always presented as two versions of the same thing, a usage preserved in the slang expression *abbaye* for whorehouse). In many cases, they even give their characters the same names—Nana, Agnès, Suzon were favorites—and advertise their wares by means of the same false addresses on their title pages: "à Rome, de l'imprimerie du Saint Père," "à Gratte-mon-con, chez Henri Branle-Motte," "à Tribaldis, de l'imprimerie de Priape," "à Cythère, au Temple de la Volupté," "à Lèchecon, et se trouve dans les coulisses de tous les théâtres."

Yet despite these conventions, which cast the reader in the role of a voyeur and oriented his expectations toward an erotic experience, early modern pornography did not stand out in the eyes of its contemporaries as a clear and distinct genre of literature. Instead, it belonged to a general category, known at the time as "philosophical." Eighteenth-century publishers and booksellers used the term "philosophical books" to designate illegal merchandise, whether it was irreligious, seditious, or obscene. They did not bother about finer distinctions, because most forbidden books gave offense in several ways. *Libre* in the jargon of their trade sometimes meant lascivious, but it invoked the libertinism of the seventeenth century—that is, free thinking. By 1750, libertinism had become a matter of the body and the mind, of pornography and philosophy. Readers could recognize a sex book when they saw one, but they expected sex to serve as a vehicle for attacks on the church, the crown, and all sorts of social abuses.

Consider *Thérèse philosophe,* one of the two or three most important pornographic works of the eighteenth century. It begins with a fictitious version of a notorious scandal in which a Jesuit priest seduced a young woman who had come to him for spiritual guidance. In the novel, the Jesuit preaches a radical variety of Cartesianism. He expounds Descartes's dichotomy between spirit and matter by instructing his pupil, Mlle. Eradice, to detach her soul from her body through spiritual exercises, such as lifting her skirts while he flagellates her buttocks and she concentrates on the Holy Ghost. If she concentrates hard enough, he assures her, she won't feel any pain. Instead, her soul will abandon her body and soar to heaven on a wave of spiritual ecstasy.

After an adequate flogging, Eradice is ready for the ultimate spiritual exercise: sexual intercourse. The Jesuit explains that thanks to the use of a relic—stiff remnant of the rope that Saint Francis wore around his habit—she will undergo a pure form of spiritual penetration. Then, as she prays from a nearly prostrate position, he mounts her from behind. The scene is described by Thérèse, the heroine and narrator of the novel, as she witnessed it from a hiding place:

"Oh, father!" cried Eradice. "Such pleasure is penetrating me! Oh, yes, I'm feeling celestial happiness; I sense that my mind is completely detached from matter. Further, father, further! Root out all that is impure in me. I see . . . the . . . an . . . gels. Push forward . . . push now . . . Ah! . . . Ah! . . . Good . . . Saint Francis! Don't abandon me! I feel the cord . . . the cord . . . the cord . . . I can't stand it any more . . . I'm dying!"

This episode provides Thérèse with more than a lesson in the dangers of priestcraft. It is the first step in her education. Having learned to throw off the authority of the church, she pursues the pleasure principle, which leads through physics, metaphysics, and ethics to a happy ending in the bed of a philosophic count. Strange as it may seem to a modern reader, the sex and the philosophy go hand in hand throughout the novel. The characters masturbate and copulate, then discuss ontology and morality, while restoring their forces for the next round of pleasure. This narrative strategy made perfect sense in 1748, because it showed how carnal knowledge could open the way to enlightenment — the radical enlightenment of La Mettrie, Helvétius, Diderot, and d'Holbach.

In the end, Thérèse becomes a *philosophe* of their stripe. She learns that everything can be reduced to matter in motion, that all knowledge derives from the senses, and that all behavior should be governed by a hedonistic calculus: maximize pleasure and minimize pain. But she is a female *philosophe*. The greatest pain she can imagine is childbirth, all the more so as her mother and her female mentor almost died in labor. Therefore, much as she enjoys sex and wants to make love with a count who is courting her, she decides that intercourse is not worth the risk. Given the character of eighteenth-century demography and obstetrics, her calculation makes perfect sense, and so does her answer: masturbation at first, and contraception by means of coitus interruptus in the end.

Because Thérèse is a poor commoner and her lover a count, she cannot expect to marry him. But she strikes a good bargain: a generous annuity of 2,000 livres a year and the run of his chateau. She even calls the tune in their lovemaking — and in an earlier episode repulses a rapist by seizing him by the throat. Instead of accepting her lot in life, Thérèse refuses the role of wife and mother and pursues her own happiness on her own terms — as a materialistic, atheistic, and liberated woman.

She was also a figment of a male imagination, because, like most pornography, *Thérèse philosophe* was written by a man — probably Jean-Baptiste de Boyer, Marquis d'Argens, possibly a certain D'Arles de Montigny, or perhaps even Diderot. Thérèse herself belongs to a long line of female narrators that stretches back to Aretino's Nanna. They express men's fantasies, not the long-lost voice of early modern feminism. As prostitutes, kept women, and nuns, they perpetuate the myth of the female voluptuary who accepts her subjection in order to give full rein to her lasciviousness. Nothing could be further from the horrors of prostitution than the fiction of the happy whore.

But the fictitious females represented a challenge to the subordination of women under the Old Regime. Above all, they challenged the authority of the church, which did more than any other institution to keep women in their place. The pornography is so shot through with anticlericalism that it often seems more a matter of religion than obscenity—it is more irreligious, in fact, than the impieties scattered through some standard works of the Enlightenment such as Montesquieu's *De l'Esprit des lois* and Diderot's *Encyclopédie*. Priests are always abusing the confessional to seduce their parishioners. Monks are always turning convents into harems. Country curates always abuse the peasantry, deflowering, cuckolding, and shipping their victims off to cities, where they become the prey of prelates. Bishops and abbots have their own pimps and houses of pleasure. Even so, they fail to protect themselves from venereal disease, which is consuming the upper clergy along with the upper nobility.

These themes can be put abstractly as a matter of corruption and exploitation, but the pornography makes them effective by embodying them in sex stories. The heroine of *Vénus en rut, ou vie d'une célèbre libertine* (1771?) cites Mme. de Pompadour's famous remark about the Bishop of Condom (no less), who had contracted syphilis: "Why didn't he stay in his diocese?" And then she reveals what she did with a bishop of her own when she got him between the sheets. In order to make him believe that he was a great lover, she called out as he humped away, "Ah! Monseigneur, what voluptuousness!" "Shut up!" he replied, "or I won't be able to come." After limping to an orgasm, he explained that any reference to his title, Monseigneur, was enough to spoil his erection for the rest of the evening. "A Monsieur would be too much."

In *Correspondance d'Eulalie* a bishop buys a few nights with the kept woman of a marquis. Tipped off by a spy, the marquis surprises them in bed. But instead of flying into a rage, he presents the bishop with a bill for 15,000 livres, the sum he has spent on the woman for the last three months (and the equivalent of three hundred years' wages for a skilled artisan), threatening to expose his conduct if he refuses to pay. The bishop coughs up the blackmail, but is made a laughing-stock in the Paris rumor mill and therefore is obliged to retreat to his see. Margot in *Margot la ravaudeuse* soaks a prelate for even more: 24,000 livres in two weeks, and sends him back to his parishioners with a case of venereal disease—his just reward, she claims, for having extorted the money from the common people in the first place.

True, one could find similar anecdotes in earlier anticlericalism, especially the bawdy variety of Boccacio, Rabelais, and Aretino. But those authors remained fundamentally Christian—Aretino nearly became a cardinal and wrote saints' lives as well as pornography—while the pornographers of the eighteenth century used sex to express all the key ideas of the Enlightenment: nature, happiness, liberty, equality. Like Margot, the courtesan narrator of *Vénus en rut* exposes the artificiality of social distinctions by sleeping her way from the bottom of society to the top. She learns that all men are equal, once you get them in bed—or, rather, that they vary according to the gifts they have received from nature: "temperament" (but the lower classes always outdo the upper; three orgasms of a servant are worth more than eight of a count) and physique (but penises should not be rated according to their length; "seven to eight inches should amuse any woman of taste"). The conclusion is clear: "In the state of nature, all men are equal; that assuredly is the state of the courtesan." As a proposition, the idea was common enough; but it came across with uncommon force, because it was embodied in narratives with a strong story line: that is how sex helped readers to think about equality in a deeply inegalitarian society.

The same line of thought applied to the relations between men and women. By stripping everyone of their social distinctions, pornography exposed similarities and differences in the sexuality of the sexes, at least as they were understood by male authors writing as female narrators. At their most basic, in *Thérèse philosophe,* for example, the differences came down to little or nothing, because all humans were "machines" composed of the same tiny particles of matter. Pleasure simply set the matter in motion, first as a stimulus of the sense organs, then as a sensation transmitted through the nervous system, and finally as an idea to be stored and combined in the brain.

The differences between men and women were also minimal in seventeenth-century pornography, which drew on Galen and Descartes to advance a physiological view of sex. In *L'Ecole des filles,* the vagina is an inverted penis, complete with "testicles" and "spermatic canals," and women ejaculate the same "thick, white liquor" in the same way as men. Fecundation occurs by means of mutual orgasm, when the two liquors meet; so the woman's pleasure is crucial to reproduction. She can also prevent conception by controlling "the combat of semen against semen" through movements of her thighs and buttocks. She should direct the action and mount the man when she pleases, both to maximize pleasure and to develop his "humility." By bestriding her lover, the heroine of *Histoire de Marguerite* (1784) "ejaculated so amply that she drowned me with her delicious semen from my belly button to the middle of my thighs."

Behind the mechanics and hydraulics of this sexology was a utopian notion of men and women copulating and ejaculating endlessly, in perfect synchrony. *L'Ecole des filles* even revived the ancient myth that men and women are divided halves of the same androgynous whole, which seeks forever to reunite. It dismissed the sexual doctrines of the Catholic Church as so much nonsense, invented by men in order to dominate women, despite the self-evident truths of the order of nature. A century and a half later, *Eléonore, ou l'heureuse personne* (1798) pursued the same theme in a fable about the hermaphrodite who switched sexes once a year, moving back and forth between monasteries and nunneries while experimenting with every conceivable sexual combination. In its wildest fantasies as well as its most scientific fictions, early modern pornography therefore made it possible to think about sexual equality in ways that challenged the basic values of the Old Regime.

In some cases, the thought experiments came close to themes in modern feminism. In 1680, *L'Académie des dames* protested against the skewed social code that subjected women to "the inhumanity of men." Although women had greater capacity for sexual pleasure, men were given greater freedom to indulge in it. Therefore, it argued, women should avenge themselves by pretending to honor society's absurd conventions in public while giving full vent to their natural instincts in secret—in a word, by cuckolding their husbands. Tullie, the wordly-wise matron, warns Octavie, the naive bride-to-be, that in marriage, "Civil laws are contrary to those of nature." But a wife can find justice by sexually doing unto her lover what her husband does unto her: "The former [the husband] commands me; I command the other. My husband has the enjoyment of my body, and I the body of my lover."

In 1740, *Histoire de Dom B . . .* condemned "the captivity in which [the female] sex is kept." The hero's mother delivered a remarkable sermon on courtship and marriage, denouncing conventional morality as a way of subjecting women to men. And in 1784, *Correspondance d'Eulalie* played with a fanciful solution to the problem of male dominance: women could withdraw to self-sufficient lesbian communities in the country. It repeated the well-worn theme of women's superior capacity for multiple orgasms, and celebrated their general superiority in verse:

Par des raisons, prouvons aux hommes
Combien au-dessus d'eux nous sommes
Et quel est leur triste destin.
Nargue du genre masculin.
Démontrons quel est leur caprice,
Leur trahison, leur injustice.
Chantons et répétons sans fin:
Honneur au sexe féminin.[2]

2

After reading through 150 years of early modern pornography, I found it difficult to resist the conclusion that some feminists have got it wrong. Instead of condemning all pornography outright, they could use some of it to advance their cause. Catharine MacKinnon may be correct in associating modern pornographers with the proposition that "having sex is antithetical to thinking." But that claim flies in the face of arguments developed in "philosophical books" three centuries ago that sex is "an inexhaustible source of thought."[3] And Andrea Dworkin's indictment of pornography rests on a breathlessly ahistorical view of culture:

In the intimate world of men and women, there is no mid-twentieth century distinct from any other century. There are only the old values, women there for the taking, the means of taking determined by the male. It is ancient and it is modern; it is feudal, capitalist, socialist; it is caveman and astronaut, agricultural and industrial, urban and rural. For men, the right to abuse women is elemental, the first principle. . . . In pornography, men express the tenets of their unchanging faith, what they must believe is true of women and of themselves to sustain themselves as they are.[4]

Instead of refusing historical reflection and restricting their arguments to culture-bound notions of gender, feminists could draw on the history of pornography to show how male dominance has been exerted and resisted over time. While asserting the right of women to defend themselves against men, early modern pornography frequently portrayed the male animal as a predator, who pawed every female within reach and felt no compunctions about rape. Dom B . . . masturbates while taking confession, then rapes his most succulent parishioner. His violence and her resistance is described in excruciating detail. But as soon as he penetrates her, she responds passionately and outdoes him in lasciviousness. By fighting him off she had really been trying to turn him on—that is, she had meant yes by saying no, another stock theme in the literature. When the heroine's first lover in *La Cauchoise* catches her with another man, he avenges himself by arranging for her to be gang-raped by eight of his friends while he urges them on. The women in the prostitute narratives are frequently raped; and one of them, Mlle. Rosalie in *Correspondance d'Eulalie,* is found dangling from a noose in the Bois de Boulogne with her breasts cut off.

Some of these episodes seem to have been inspired by the sensationalist fiction of penny dreadfuls (*canards, feuilles volantes,* and chapbooks). One should not take them literally, just as one should not read *Fanny Hill* (*La Fille de joie* in the inadequate French translation) as a clinical account of female sexuality. But taken as literature, the pornography expressed the assumption that women were in constant danger of rape, especially when exposed to men of superior power and status. It favored violent metaphors. A bride's virginity was a fortress to be stormed, the bed a battlefield, the deflowering a slaughter. *L'Académie des dames* describes the hymen as "a victim . . . which must be sacrificed or massacred and torn to pieces with plenty of bloodshed." A groom instructs his bride to surrender "that part of your body that is no longer yours but mine"; and by entering her vagina he "takes possession of a thing that belongs to me."

Male dominance could hardly be put more bluntly. True, the sex books often seem to condone as well as to condemn the brutal treatment of women. It would be silly to read a modern argument for women's liberation into ancient texts designed primarily to arouse men. Yet the texts also advance ideas that undercut simplistic notions of phallocracy. After losing their virginity, the heroines of early modern pornography often gain a kind of independence—not legal or professional or social autonomy: that was virtually impossible under the conditions of the Old Regime; but self-reliance of an intellectual sort, because once they discover that sex is good for thinking, they learn to think for themselves. In *L'Ecole des filles* Fanchon remains silly and servile until she makes love. Then she awakens to a new power in herself:

> Formerly I was only good for sewing and holding my tongue, but now I can do all sorts of things. When I speak with my mother, I now find reasons to support what I say; I hold forth as if I were another person, instead of fearing to open my mouth as I used to do. I am beginning to be clever and to stick my nose into things that were almost unknown to me before.

L'Académie des dames equates the opening of the vulva with the opening of the mind and describes the loss of virginity as the first step toward the acquisition of intellectual independence. For the next hundred years, pornographic writing continued to develop variations on this master theme.

In *Vénus dans le cloître*, Sister Dosithée, a religious fanatic, flagellates herself so violently that she ejaculates, bursting her hymen with a discharge released from deep within her womb. Then suddenly her mind clears, she recognizes the superstition at the core of Catholicism, and she converts to deism. In *Histoire de Dom B . . .*, Sister Monique frees herself of ignorance and opens her mind to the light of reason by means of masturbation. Dom B . . . himself first becomes aware of the rational order of nature by watching a couple copulate. And in *Thérèse philosophe*, voyeurism and masturbation clear a way through the claptrap of religion, making it possible for Thérèse to become a philosopher.

The theme appears everywhere in early modern pornography. In fact, the literature of the Enfer uses a special verb to convey it: *déniaiser*, to lose one's silliness by gaining carnal knowledge. At the other end of the process, the heroines in the sexual success stories become *savantes*—not the kind of *femmes savantes* satirized by Molière and not necessarily learned, but critical and intellectually independent. "I became *savante*," declares the narrator of *La Cauchoise* after an account of her initiation in the mysteries of sex. She therefore rejects religion and refuses to accept "any authority other than nature itself."

The narrator of *Vénus en rut* pursues the knowledge of nature even further by seducing a doctor and compelling him to give her lessons in physiology, complete with wax models of the inner workings of the sexual organs. The heroines of *Margot la ravaudeuse* and *La Correspondance d'Eulalie* set up salons and rule over the literary world. They do not all embrace the cause of the Enlightenment, but all of them pursue enlightened self-interest and fight their way to the top of the Old Regime by refusing to accept its prejudices and by exploiting its corruption.

In the end, therefore, sex turns out to be good for thinking not merely in order to resist the exploitation of women by men but to oppose exploitation in general. The pornography provides a general indictment of the Old Regime, its courtiers, manor lords, financiers, tax collectors, and judges, as well as its priests.

Everyone who lives off the labor of the common people receives a drubbing at one point or another. Not that the sex books call for a revolution. Some of them, *Lucette ou les progrès du libertinage,* for example, even satirize free thinkers and philosophers. But by pursuing standard themes like a harlot's progress and the corruption of country youth, they expose the web of wealth and influence that constituted *le monde,* France's all-powerful elite. *La Correspondance d'Eulalie* can be read as a map of *le monde* and also as a *chronique scandaleuse* or underground journal. It provides a running commentary on plays and operas, exhibitions of paintings, ministerial intrigues, foreign affairs, and all sorts of current events along with the sex lives of the rich and powerful. The sex merely serves as a vehicle for social criticism, and the criticism runs in many directions, not merely along the Great Divide separating men and women.

By concentrating exclusively on the victimization of women, feminist critics of pornography fail to recognize the part it played in exposing other kinds of social abuses. But its history also confirms some of their central arguments, notably their claim that "pornography is masturbation material."[5] Not only did works like *Thérèse philosophe* take masturbation as a major theme, they also encouraged the reader to masturbate along with the characters in the stories. The Comte de Mirabeau put it at its crudest in the introduction to *Ma conversion ou le libertin de qualité* (1783): "May the reading [of this book] make the whole universe beat off."

Such remarks seem to assume a male audience, although they did not necessarily exclude women. In claiming to be written for the edification of girls, *L'Ecole des filles* and *Lucette ou les progrès du libertinage* were trying to tickle the imagination of men. But *La Cauchoise* included women servants in a more straightforward description of the reading public; and the narrator of *Eléonore ou l'heureuse personne* referred casually to "my women readers," as if she expected to have some. Iconographic evidence such as Emmanuel de Ghendt's notorious "Le Midi" shows women using books for stimulation while masturbating. And the texts themselves stressed female masturbation, often in connection with reading. The nuns in *Vénus dans le cloître* excite themselves by reading *L'A-cadémie des dames*; the prostitutes in *Correspondance d'Eulalie* by reading Aretino; the female philosophers in *Thérèse philosophe* by reading *Histoire de Dom B . . .*; and the lesbians in *Les Progrès du libertinage* by reading *Thérèse philosophe.* "Gallant libraries" are often described in the novels. The references back and forth between texts are so thick and so shot through with autoeroticism that it can be sensed on every page, but it cannot be identified exclusively with men.

3

The issue is not whether pornography was meant to arouse sexual desire or meant to arouse only males, but rather whether it can be reduced to its function as masturbation material. In order to argue their case more effectively, the feminists could find some unexpected allies in the camp of literary theory. Above all, they could draw on the work of Jean Marie Goulemot, which represents the best in the current scholarship on pornography.

Goulemot argues that eighteenth-century pornography came closer than any other genre to realizing the aim of all literature before Mallarmé—namely, to create a "reality effect," one so powerful that it seemed to obliterate the distinction between literature and life.[6] In pornographic novels, unlike other kinds of narrative, the words printed on paper produced an unmediated, involuntary response in the body of the reader. The fiction worked physically, as if it could insinuate itself into flesh and blood, abolishing time and language and everything else that separated reading from reality. Goulemot's argument fits perfectly with Catharine MacKinnon's contention that "pornography is often more sexually compelling than the realities it presents, more sexually real than reality."[7] But the thesis has drawbacks.

It combines theories of reader-response and of genre to advance the notion of an ideal type, something that might be called "pure" pornography, because it operates exclusively on the reader's libido. Any disruption (*brouillage*)—in the form of plot development, psychological complexity, philosophy, humor, sentiment, or social comment—will mitigate the effect and detract from the pornography's pureness. Unfortunately for the theory, however, early modern pornography consisted mainly of *brouillage*—that is, of the very ingredients that created impurities. Its greatest successes, *Histoire de Dom B . . .* and *Thérèse philosophe,* went to the furthest extremes in steering the reader through narrative and philosophical complexities. And its founding father, Aretino, shifted from sex to social criticism in the course of his *Ragionamenti.*

True, Aretino was famous for the explicit description of copulating techniques in his *Sonetti lussuriosi.* But it seems unlikely that the sonnets were widely read in France; and it is inaccurate to claim, as Goulemot does, that Aretino was "tirelessly translated and retranslated" into French under the Old Regime. Aside from some of his religious writings and one fragment of the *Ragionamenti,* the French did not publish a single translation of his work between 1660 and 1800.[8] Instead, they printed and reprinted *L'Arrétin moderne* by Henri-Joseph Du Laurens (first edition, 1763; at least thirteen others before 1789), a scandal sheet that was three parts gossip to one part sex. The "modern Aretino" of eighteenth-century France actually had a lot in common with his Italian ancestor from the sixteenth century. But he was above all a *libelliste*—that is, a specialist in slandering eminent figures of the church and state. Libel, like irreligion, can hardly be distinguished from pornography in the "philosophical" works of the Old Regime. If pornography was a genre, it was such a mixed genre that it defies any attempt to isolate a pure variety. Its impurities provided the very elements that made its sex so good for thinking.

In the end, then, literary theory fails to account for the defining characteristics of early modern pornography. Jean Marie Goulemot comes close to acknowledging this failure in the conclusion of his book, where he toys with the fantasy of a "golden age of reading." He locates it in eighteenth-century France, a time when readers could plunge into texts like adolescents, free of the inhibitions produced by training in literary criticism. Thanks to their passionate primitivism, he fancies, they may have used pornography as a way of abandoning themselves to the call of the wild. Indeed, some librarians are said to have found spermatic traces, possibly from the eighteenth century, on the leaves of the eighteenth-century sex books. Could a modern researcher follow in the steps of those long-forgotten readers and, by divesting himself of enough sophistication, respond in the same way? The proof of his success would be, to put it bluntly (but Goulemot steers his argument around all such coarseness), an orgasm. In that case, the books from "Hell" could function as time machines, propelling their readers into sensations that burned out two centuries ago; and pornography could provide historians with an experience that has hitherto eluded them: direct access to passions in the past.

4

This fantasy should not be taken too seriously, but it illustrates a serious impediment to understanding the history of pornography: the illusion of immunity from anachronism. No matter how erotic a text may be, it can hardly affect readers today in the same way that it affected them centuries earlier; for reading now takes place in a mental world that differs fundamentally in its assumptions, values, and cultural codes from the world of the Old Regime. Instead of searching through early modern pornography for parallels to modern varieties of male dominance, one could therefore take the opposite tack and read it for what it says about mentalities that no longer exist. Take one step into an obscene novel from seventeenth- or eighteenth-century France, and you enter an unfamiliar landscape. Read through several shelves, and you find yourself on an ethnographic journey through a vast museum of foreign folkways. In this way, too, sex is good for thinking—not just for primitives from the Old Regime but for anyone who wants to understand them.

Consider the question of beauty. Like natives in many developing countries, the characters in early modern pornography fancied fat, fat in general and fat in particular places—on arms, for example, and in the small of the back. Back fat produced dimples at the *chute de reins,* a sensuous spot just above the buttocks immortalized by Boucher in paintings of his famous model, Mademoiselle O'Murphy. It was Eradice's "admirable *chute de reins*" that made her so irresistible to her Jesuit confessor in *Thérèse philosophe* and Lucette's arms that made her fortune as a courtesan in *Les progrès du libertinage*: "Her chubby arms make Cupid smile; one longs to fix one's mouth to them and to be squeezed in their soft bondage." Women used their arms more than their legs as means of seduction. "No doubt Monsieur likes to see the movement of a naked arm," Mme. C

. . . says to arouse her lover in *Thérèse philosophe*. But legs mattered, too, especially on men, because men's breeches left their calves exposed, and spindly calves disgusted women. Thus Margot's populist scorn for the leg of one of her clients in *Margot la ravaudeuse*: "He had the leg of a man of breeding—that is to say, skinny and meatless." Men were also repelled by "hideous thinness." They found breasts and buttocks alluring, but only if abundantly upholstered: the more meat, the better, although they preferred Boucher-like fleshiness (*embonpoint*) to Rubenesque obesity. The heroine of *Vénus en rut* put the ideal succinctly when she described herself as "a little ball of fat."

Of course, one must allow for literary conventions in the descriptions of beautiful women. So it is not surprising that the narrator of *Vénus en rut* presents herself to the reader as having "the freshness of a new rose." But she immediately goes on to praise her teeth. Teeth stand out everywhere in the descriptions, probably because of the prevalence of rotting jaws and stinking breath in early modern society. In *Le Rut ou la pudeur éteinte* (1676), Dorimène has skin like a lily, a mouth like a rose, and "Her teeth were white, so equal and perfectly aligned that this part of her alone would have sufficed to inspire love in a soul less sensitive than his [Celadon's]."

What do they do, these two sensitive souls, when they get past the self-presentation and the foreplay? They organize an orgy with two other couples in a prison, where the hero, Celadon, holds court after being locked up by a nasty attorney. In order to hump more effectively, one of the gallants props his feet against a cupboard. But he thrusts so hard that he knocks it over onto one of the ladies, Hiante, who is copulating on the floor—and having some difficulty because her lover, Le Rocher, cannot sustain an erection, and she is enormously pregnant. The blow causes her to have a still birth on the spot. The ladies then withdraw, and the cavaliers give themselves over to a poetry contest.

Le Rocher wins the contest by improvising all sorts of verse, including a sonnet on the poor performance of his penis. It went limp, he explains in perfect Petrarchian style, because after penetrating Hiante it found Death waiting for it at the far end of her womb. While the poets woo their muse, the guard dog of the prison eats the body of the baby, all except its head, and promptly dies of indigestion. The poets realize what has happened when they spot the prison cat playing with the head as if it were a ball. "This spectacle gave them great pleasure," the narrator observes. It stimulates their appetites and also their creativity; so they sit down to a hearty meal and produce epitaphs for the dog, improvising rhymes around the theme of birth and death. Then they send a lackey to nail the baby's head on the front door of the attorney's house.

When the attorney looks out his window the next morning, he sees a crowd gathered in front of his door. Assuming they are a lynch mob, he confesses all the crimes he has committed at the expense of the local peasants. But then he notices the head and realizes that the crowd is a collection of bumpkins venting its "joy" at the sight of something strange. So he retracts his confession and explains that the head came from a monkey that his brother killed in the forest—a creature that had been unaccountably swinging through the trees outside Alençon. The bumpkins then disperse, delighted at having seen, for free, the kind of curiosity that would have cost them a penny at a village fair.

What makes this episode so strange for the modern reader is not its violence—we have more than enough of that in pornography today—but its humor. It is clearly meant to be funny. While stringing one horror after another, the text describes the incidents as "comic," "funny," and "buffoonish." If we have absorbed an adequate supply of picaresque novels we might recognize some themes. If we have mastered enough Shakespeare and Cervantes, we might begin to get our bearings. But none of us today can laugh at those jokes. Our inability to get them should tip us off to the difficulty of "getting" a culture that was fundamentally different from ours, although it might have some specious familiarity if it appeared under the heading "Renaissance" or "Baroque" in a textbook of Western civilization.

Early modern pornography grew out of a culture that seems unthinkable today, just as the car crashes and shoot-outs of our television will look baffling to researchers three centuries from now. In the seventeenth century, works like *Le Rut ou la pudeur éteinte* belonged to a Rabelaisian world, which combined the rough and tumble of the street with the sophistication of the court. In the eighteenth century, the street culture continued to leave its mark on bawdy books, but it changed in character. It became concentrated in the boulevards that had replaced the medieval walls of Paris, providing a setting for a new kind of popular theater and a new kind of prostitute: the *grisette* who graduated from clothes shops along the rue Saint-Honoré to fancy apartments behind the boulevards in the rue de Cléry and the rue Tiquetonne.

All of the prostitute narratives after 1750 take their readers on tours of this territory, describing the food in the bistros, the furniture in the *bordels*, the music in the dance halls, the gestures in the pantomimes, and the farces in the theaters. *La Correspondance d'Eulalie* reads in places like a guidebook, complete with footnotes for the edification of ignorant provincials. At one point, Mlle. Julie, a high-class courtesan, amuses herself by picking up a man from the lowlife in Nicolet's vaudeville theater. She lets him think "that I was one of those girls who is willing to accept a supper in a good boulevard bistro as the price of their favors." So she sends him off to order a meal chez Bancelin and then disappears. A footnote explains that Bancelin's is the most famous tavern on the boulevard and that to spice up a meal one can order bawdy songs from *joueuses de veille* (girl street-singers who accompany themselves on a hurdy-gurdy), who also provide sexual services. At another point, Julie goes dining on the boulevard and orders an evening's worth of off-color ballads, which she then transcribes into the text; so the prostitute's memoirs briefly turn into an anthology of street music.

This is the milieu that would later evolve into the Balzacian world of *Splendeurs et misères des courtisanes,* the bohemian world of *La Bohème,* and the poetic world of *Les Enfants du Paradis*. But in the eighteenth century it remained far removed from sentiments that still resonate today. Suzon in the *Mémoires de Suzon* becomes a dancer in a boulevard cabaret. One night on her way home, she comes across two soldiers, who carry her off to a field on the road to Montmartre and rape her. It is quite an ordinary occurrence, except for the fact that one soldier has such a monstrous penis that he cannot get inside her. On their way back, they spot a grindstone in a wheelbarrow left outside a tavern by an itinerant knife sharpener, and Suzon suggests a solution to the soldier's problem. She climbs on the wheelbarrow and urinates on the grindstone to reduce the friction while he grinds his penis down to a usable size. This "funny scene," as Suzon calls it, amuses the crowd of two hundred onlookers, but it doesn't look funny to the modern reader. Nor do Suzon's other experiences on the boulevards: gymnastic group sex with some Spanish acrobats and "comic" copulating backstage with the Harlequin and Pierrot of a pantomime.

Equally unfunny are the deflowerings that bring comic relief to the sexual tension throughout the literature. The whores often joke about how they use astringents to fake virginity and thereby dupe their clients into paying supplements. One of them, Mlle. Felmé in *Correspondance d'Eulalie*, retires to the provinces under a false name, marries a magistrate, and describes her burlesque wedding night with professional expertise: the tiny packet of blood slipped up her vagina, the vinegar treatment, the hiding under the covers, the insistence on blowing out the candles, the faked resistance, the faked frigidity, and the groom's triumphal cry the morning after, when he finds the fake blood on the bedclothes: "Ah! My wife was a virgin! How happy I am!"

One can see the joke, but one cannot really get it—any more than one can laugh at cuckolding and transmission of venereal disease, two other inexhaustible subjects of hilarity in the sex books. To see deeper into the humor it is crucial to know more about the serious scenarios for wedding nights, and they, too, are available in the pornography. The best of many examples comes in *L'Académie des dames*. It takes place in the house of the bride's parents. Her mother undresses her in front of the groom, puts her to bed naked, and joins the rest of the family in the next room, locking the door behind her. After stripping, the groom turns back the covers and checks the bride's virginity by sticking his finger up her vagina. She freezes, then resists as he fondles and kisses; so he forces open her thighs and mounts her. While he batters his way into her, she screams in pain and terror, much to the satisfaction of her family listening next door.

A preliminary orgasm slows the groom down before he can penetrate her. But his second "attack" strikes deeper, and the third breaks through the hymen so that the "fortress" is taken. The groom demands that the vagina, "all broken and torn," acknowledge his penis "as its sovereign." Then he attacks again, making the bed groan and the bride scream so loudly that when at last the room falls silent her mother reenters it. She presents the groom with some perfumed wine and acknowledges him formally as her son: "My son, she says, how valiantly you fought! You are a hero! The screams of my daughter bear irrevocable witness to her defeat. I congratulate you on your victory."

Another wedding night later in the book follows the same scenario, which is described with the same profusion of military metaphors. When the mother arrives with the drink, she says, "Brave soldier . . . I now recognize you as my son and my son-in-law." And still later, a third groom deflowers his bride according to the identical ritual, but this time it is parodied. She is a simple peasant girl, he a servant of an aristocratic lady, who uses him as a stud. In order to exert her power and enjoy a practical joke, the lady indoctrinates the girl with the wrong information about how to behave. So instead of freezing, the bride grabs the groom's penis, moves her buttocks wildly, and lifts her legs in the air. She gives off all the wrong signals, as if she were a prostitute rather than a virgin: that is the joke, but it is funny only to those who share the cultural code.

To be sure, *L'Académie des dames* is a sex book, not the field notes of an ethnographer. It provides a literary version of an ideal wedding night as imagined in the seventeenth century, not a reliable account of how people actually behaved in bed. But that ideal still served as a foil for jokes a hundred years later. Even if it did not correspond closely to actual behavior, it defined a certain mentality—that is, a world we have (fortunately) lost, lost so completely that we must consult pornography in order to catch a glimpse of it.

As a final example of the strangeness of this literature, consider *Histoire de Dom B . . .*, the greatest and most outrageous of all the books in "Hell." This time, exceptionally, the narrator is a man, the monk Dom B . . . (the B . . . stands for bugger, but his name is actually Saturnin). As an oversexed adolescent peering through a hole in his bedroom wall, Saturnin spots his mother copulating with a monk. He wants to do the same with his sister, Suzon. (It turns out later that none of them is a blood relative, but the text plays with every variety of the incest taboo.) In order to excite Suzon, he leads her to his peephole; and while she observes the next round of copulation, he slides to the floor and looks up her skirt. Then he slips his hand up her leg, higher and higher, following the rhythm of her thighs, which tighten and loosen in response to the humping in the next room. At last he pushes into her vagina: "I've got you, Suzon; I've got you?"

While Suzon remains glued to the peephole, Saturnin masturbates her and pulls off her clothes. She spreads her legs, and he tries to take her from behind. But the position is impossible, so he spins her around and pulls her to the bed. He penetrates, she pushes, and just as they begin to heave with abandon the bed collapses under them. Their mother rushes in, furious; but when she spots Saturnin's erection, she changes her tune and drags him to the bed in the other room, while the monk takes Saturnin's place with Suzon. Thus, after violating his sister's virginity, Saturnin cuckolds his father and concludes with a defiant address to the reader:

> Here is plenty of food for thought for readers whose glacial temperament has never felt the furies of love! Go ahead, Messieurs, think away, give full vent to your moralizing! I abandon the field to you, and want to say just one thing: if you had a hard-on as unbearable as mine, who would you fuck? The devil himself.

Today's reader might reply: Very well, here we have some eighteenth-century hard-core; what makes it so surprising? The rest of the novel continues in the same manner, at a breathless pace, piling social criticism on anticlericalism as one orgy leads to another. Each episode tops the previous one, until all inhibition seems to be destroyed. The sexual escalation sweeps everything before it, and in the end it deposits the hero in a particularly crapulous whorehouse. There, after years of separation, he meets Suzon again. Having been seduced and dumped in the road by a priest, she has survived a near-fatal miscarriage, a term in a pestilential poorhouse, and a horrific career as a hooker. Now she is in the terminal stage of a vicious case of syphilis.

Yet Saturnin loves her. He has always loved her, with a visceral passion that has never loosened its grip on his soul. So he wants to make love with her once more. She refuses, knowing that she would kill him with her disease. But he insists, and they unite their bodies for the last time, all through the night, deep in the dark of a decrepit brothel. Not a foul word in the text. Not a hint of lasciviousness.

Suddenly the police burst in. They seize upon Suzon. Saturnin fells one of them with a blow from an andiron, but the others drag him down the stairs, knocking him unconscious. Suzon disappears into one prison, where she immediately dies of her disease. Saturnin wakes up in another, feverish from the onset of syphilis. He passes out again. Again he regains consciousness, this time awakened by a pain between his legs. He reaches down with his hand, and discovers he has been castrated. From deep within his bowels, a sound forms, rises through his throat, and breaks out as a scream, beating at the ceiling: Saturnin has ceased to be a man; he has nothing more to live for.

The surgery saves him, although he wants to die, having learned of Suzon's death. He does not know where to turn or what to do with his new freedom. So he takes to the road, abandoning himself to Providence. He comes upon a Carthusian monastery, and suddenly has a vision of a life to be lived outside the agony of passion. After hearing his story, the superior takes him in; and Saturnin becomes Dom B . . ., gatekeeper to the Carthusians:

> I am waiting here for death, without fearing or desiring it. After it releases me from the world of the living, they will carve in golden letters on my tomb: *Hic situs est Dom Bougre, fututus, futuit.* [Here lies Dom Bugger, fucked, he fucked.]

It is an astounding story, one that deserves a place beside *Manon Lescaut* and *La Nouvelle Héloïse*. In it, eroticism is swallowed up in asceticism, pornography in religiosity. Of course, the burlesque epitaph leaves everything unsettled. The note of passion at the end could be one more trick of priestcraft: the moralizing could be specious. But the unsettling character of the story is part of its point. Sex may lead to love, love to salvation, and salvation to closure in a narrative of escalating surprises. Or everything could be a joke. The novel is so rich that it permits many readings. But if it is a joke, it cannot be grasped by anyone who has never had a brush with Augustinian piety, especially the kind known as Jansenism in the seventeenth and eighteenth centuries.

Seen in this light, the entire story leads to a spectacular non sequitur: the monastery, instead of being a brothel, turns out to be a genuine refuge from the torments of the flesh; and Saturnin, after working through every conceivable kind of sexual sin, finds his true vocation as a monk. Is he saved, or is he, as his epitaph says, merely fucked? Whether a send-up of religion or a confirmation of it, his story illustrates the precariousness of the struggle to find some solid meaning in life in the mid-eighteenth century, when Jansenism and the Enlightenment threatened to cancel each other out, and also today; for one cannot close a pornographic masterpiece like *L'Histoire de Dom B . . .* without thinking that sex is good for thought.

NOTES

This essay deals with *L'Enfer de la Bibliothèque Nationale,* 7 vols. (Paris, 1984–88); Raymond Trousson, ed., *Romans libertins du XVIIIe siècle* (Paris, 1993); Jean Marie Goulemot, *Ces Livres qu'on ne lit que d'une main: Lecture et lecteurs de livres pornographiques au XVIIIe siècle* (Paris, 1991).

1. The best general history of erotic literature is still Paul Englisch, *Geschichte der erotischen Literatur* (Stuttgart, 1927). As an example of current scholarship, see Lynn Hunt, ed., *The Invention of Pornography: Obscenity and the Origins of Modernity, 1500–1800* (New York, 1993), especially the excellent chapters by Lynn Hunt and Paul Findlen.

2. Literally: "By reasons, let us prove to men / How superior we are to them / And what is their sad fate. / Phooey to the male gender. / Let us demonstrate their capriciousness, / Their treason, their injustice. / Sing and repeat endlessly: / Honor to the female sex."

3. Catharine MacKinnon, *Only Words* (Cambridge, Mass., 1993), p. 17; and *L'Ecole des filles* (1655), reprinted in *L'Enfer de la Bibliothèque Nationale,* vol. 7, p. 274.

4. Andrea Dworkin, *Pornography: Men Possessing Women* (New York, 1981), p. 68.

5. MacKinnon, *Only Words,* p. 17.

6. Goulemot, *Ces Livres qu'on ne lit que d'une main,* pp. 134, 153–55.

7. MacKinnon, *Only Words,* p. 24.

8. Carolin Fischer, "Die Erotik der Aufklärung. Pietro Aretinos 'Ragionamenti' als Hypotext des libertinen Romans in Frankreich" (Ph.D. diss., Freie Universität Berlin, 1993).

PARASEXUALITY AND GLAMOUR

The Victorian Barmaid as Cultural Prototype

PETER BAILEY

Sexuality, we are now told, plausibly enough, is everywhere.[1] Yet recent scholarship, for all its advances, has done little to register or interpret this ubiquity. The history of sexuality which sees the nineteenth century as the crucial era in creating its modern sensibility has concentrated on certain areas: the submerged histories of "deviant" groups; the ideology of written texts; controversies over regulation; and individual cases of that remarkable phenomenon, closet *hetero-sexuality*.[2] These emphases on the wilder and more esoteric reaches of sexuality reinforce the construct of separate terrains by focusing on the (unacceptable) public face and the (secretive) private face in civil society. What is missing is an illumination of the "middle" ground of sexuality, not as another exclusive territory, but as an extensive ensemble of sites, practices and occasions that mediate across the frontiers of the putative public/private divide.[3] Arguably it is here — in such everyday settings as the pub, the expanding apparatus of the service industries, and a commercialised popular culture — that capitalism and its patriarchal managers construct a new form of open yet licit sexuality that I propose to term *parasexuality,* a form whose visual code is known to us as the familiar but largely unexamined phenomenon of glamour.

Parasexuality? The prefix combines two otherwise discrete meanings: first, in the sense of "almost" or "beside," denoting a secondary, or modified form of sexuality (cf. paramedic); second, the counter sense of being "against," denoting a form of protection from, or prevention of sexuality (cf. parachute). However here the function argued is conceived somewhat differently, as an inoculation in which a little sexuality is encouraged as an antidote to its subversive properties. Parasexuality then is sexuality that is deployed but contained, carefully channelled rather than fully discharged; in vulgar terms it might be represented as "everything but."

Everything but what? What is the prime form of sexuality for which parasexuality is taken to offer a modification or antidote? The language of discharge bespeaks a fundamentally male or phallocentric concept of sexuality—the hydraulic model—in which sex is a limited but powerful energy system, a spermatic economy whose force must always be either fully released or suppressed, its prime expression being the male orgasm. While the upheaval in sexual politics in our own day has taught us to recognise other less oppressive forms, this was a powerful model of sexuality in nineteenth-century Britain and, however rebarbative it may be, it remains on the historical agenda.[4] The objectification of women as spectacle and commodity examined below is now understood as a projection of male hegemony and has been further defined in the pathologies of scopophilia and fetishism; yet while we recognise the saliency of such features in modern capitalism their formation is still underexplored.[5]

Parasexuality identifies a significant historical initiative as a *managed* version of the fraught imperatives of release or suppression in orthodox bourgeois sexuality. Management is an appropriate term in the increasingly rationalised operations of an emergent leisure industry in the nineteenth century, and is taken here to denote not only systematic direction, but also the proper utilisation of resources. In the pub, the music hall and the popular theatre, unlike the home, the courts and legislature, sexuality was a natural resource rather than a natural enemy. Thus while parasexuality was certainly a form of control, it started from a point of acknowledgment and accommodation rather than denial and punishment—in this sense it might be said to reverse Foucault's couplet of regulation as production.

Of course, management of any kind is rarely as efficient a process as the word implies, and this was certainly true of the business of pleasure which was in any case marked by its own distinctive practices. Paradoxically, if unsurprisingly, the normalisation of sexuality that was parasexuality proved to be controversial and was much contested by vigilante groups as a threat to established values. In exploring the limits of normative tolerance a new breed of capitalist cultural managers could therefore be represented as challenging the dominant ideology, yet the impression remains that whatever the charges made against them, these men were interested only in flexing not transgressing such limits. Parasexuality may be understood therefore as an exercise in framed liminality or contained licence that constituted a reworking rather than a dismantling of hegemony.[6] At the same time, the definition of limits was not just an issue between an industry and its critics, but a matter of everyday negotiation among front-line participants, whose exchanges constituted an informal process of management that made its own contribution to the repatterning of nineteenth-century sexuality. History is also made by the people in pubs.

And so to the barmaid, a seemingly unproblematical social type, and an unlikely subject for any kind of historical theorising. For the unreconstructed male she is an instant cue for the knowing smile; for the feminist she is the classic token woman.[7] Both perspectives register the barmaid's role with its obvious but safely anchored sexuality as a timelessly familiar feature of the British pub. This essay is concerned to show that the barmaid was not always taken for granted, but has a specific and indeed sensational history of her own in the Victorian era, one of whose important themes is her glamorous embodiment of a distinct form of modernity—parasexuality.

What follows is an attempt to locate this specific strategy of cultural management within the popular discourse of pub sexuality by relating rather than merely juxtaposing the modes of social history and cultural or critical studies. The history of the barmaid is examined first in relation to the modernisation of the Victorian pub. The concept of glamour is then discussed as a preliminary to a reading of contemporary graphic texts and what they suggest of male subjectivities in relationship to the barmaid. In the light of this evidence the essay then situates pub sexuality and its controversies in the material context of female bar work. It concludes with a brief speculative reconnaissance of the barmaid's membership in the larger constituency of young women service workers, notes some further representations of their type, and considers the implications for sexual politics in the critical years of the late Victorian period.

1

The modern barmaid was a product of the transformation of the urban public house from the 1830s, when the tavern was superseded by the so-called gin palace with its dramatic innovations of scale, plan, management and style.[8] The new pub was devised to service the increasing volume of custom in the expanding towns, and to hold its market share in the face of heightened competition in the licensed trade. Many old pubs were little more than the parlours or kitchens of private houses catering to a familiar neighbourhood clientele. In catering to the more numerous, transitory and anonymous urban crowd, the new pubs were much bigger, and sales were made across a bar counter which separated customers from the drink supply and made for a more efficient and secure operation. Capacity was maximised by doing away with chairs and tables which also ensured a more rapid turnover in customers. Any feeling of congestion was relieved by the upward spaciousness of high ceilings and the illusory roominess contrived by the generous use of mirrors and plate glass, for the gin palace sought to attract the new generation of "perpendicular drinkers" by the lavishness of its amenities. The new pubs needed the barmaid both as staff behind the counters of its enlarged premises and as a further item of allurement among its mirrors and mahogany, its brassware and coloured tile.[9]

There was, of course, nothing new in the employment of women and their attractions in the serving of drink. The older alehouse had commonly been a family enterprise wherein the service of wives and daughters was routinely exploited as an extension of their domestic duties. The alewife who ran the business in the absence of her husband was variously rough or motherly, but dependent upon an outgoing manner as a social stock in trade, while daughters or maidservants often added a fresher allure.[10] What was new about the barmaid of the 1830s was the redefinition of her traditional role brought by changes in the social logistics of the pub. Most importantly, she was now physically separated from the public by the novel device of the bar counter, part of the pub's duplication of the apparatus of the retail shop which formalised selling and began the conversion of its clientele from guests to customers.[11] The bar was now also a boundary or cordon sanitaire which kept the barmaid almost literally out of reach of the customer (or vice versa), and met the publican's new concern for respectability to protect his licence and greater business investment in a time of tighter licensing controls and reform hostility.

Yet if the roaming wanton of the alehouse had now become contained within the closed territory of the serving area, the configuration that secured her separation from the public house made her role there more conspicuous and seductive. The bar counter with its newly sumptuous fittings was the visual as well as transactional focus of the pub–gin palace and provided a framing effect that gave it the dramatic properties of a stage, thus heightening the presence of its attendants as social actors and objects of display. This theatrical aura was amplified by the flaring quality of the new gas lighting and the reflections of the pub's numerous mirrors. Moreover, the new barmaid shared her stage with a concentration of the commodities that the pub sold, suggesting that she herself might be an article for purchase and consumption.

The impact of the barmaid as spectacle was registered in significant terms from her earliest appearance in the new setting. Thus in the 1820s Thompsons, of Holborn Hill, London, was "particularly noted" for retaining "four handsome, sprightly and neatly dressed young females, but of modest deportment. . . . An opportunity of casting a scrutinising glance at the so-highly spoken of barmaids operated as a spell, and myriads . . . were drawn in thither."[12] There was renewed attention to the modern barmaid during the Crimean War, when a fashionable pub in the City hired women to make good the loss of men to the services. Such was the reported sensation at their appearance that other houses rapidly copied the practice, while barmaids had also been noted in the 1840s serving behind the refreshment counters of railway stations.[13]

The number of pubs grew steadily from the 1830s, but there was also growth in other forms of catering as well as the railway system; thus music halls, theatres, hotels, restaurants, and exhibitions provided more newly conspicuous jobs in bar work from the third quarter of the century. Of the Oxford music hall that opened in 1861 as the first purpose-built hall in the West End, it was recorded that "the brightest, most glittering, and most attractive thing about the bars was the barmaids," and Billy Holland's barmaid contests at various other London venues provided steady publicity in the 1860s and 1870s.[14]

Most renowned of London barmaids were the nine hundred or so employed by Spiers and Pond, pioneers of large-scale commercial catering, with extensive interests that included the sumptuous Criterion in Piccadilly where the barmaids operated in shifts: "one corps would march out from behind the bars and others would walk in and relieve them like soldiers relieving the sentry." Kaiser William II was said to have insisted on an incognito trip to a branch of Spiers and Pond on his first London visit, and was delighted by its spectacle of well-drilled pretty women.[15]

Foreigners were particularly impressed by the English barmaid, for her occupation and setting were virtually unique to Britain and the colonies of Australia and New Zealand.[16] English barmaids excited great attention in the English pub-restaurant at the Paris Exhibition in 1867.[17] The story was told of the American visitor to England who, on being asked what had struck him most, replied without hesitation, "Barmaids!," an exclamation that reformers took to be one of horror.[18] Some of his more enthusiastic countrymen sought to exploit such a novelty by replicating an English bar and its barmaids in New York in the 1890s, but fell foul of legislation prohibiting the employment of women in public saloons.[19] Thus the barmaid attracted controversy and attention both at home and abroad.

As these accounts suggest, much of the impact of the barmaid lay in her enhanced public visibility, her staged openness to the "scrutinizing glance." What is significant here is not just, as we now conventionally say, the woman as sex object, but the woman as bearer of *glamour,* arguably a distinctively modern visual property, and central to parasexuality in its practice of managed arousal.

The most familiar usage of the word is in its description of the Hollywood stars of the 1930s and after—the "glamour girls" of screen and pin-ups—and a film historian defines glamour in this context as "alluring charm or fascination, often based on illusion, that transforms or glorifies a person or thing."[20] Previous usage in the nineteenth century was confined to a poetic vocabulary, as introduced by Sir Walter Scott to denote a magical or fictitious beauty.[21] There is considerable significance in the word's debut in Scott's novels, for in its application to the world of the past that was the setting for his work, we can identify a further property of glamour, implicit but unacknowledged in other definitions yet crucial to its operation as parasexuality—that of distance. Distance not only sustains and protects the magical property that is commonly recognised in glamour, but also heightens desire through the tension generated by the separation of the glamour object and the beholder, a separation that also functions to limit the expression or consummation of desire. Distance may be secured in a variety of ways: by time and history as in Scott's usage; by putting the loved one up a tower as in the conventions of courtly love; by the traditional device of the stage; more recently by the shop window or the distance inherent in the mechanical representations of photography, film and television; or, by a bar. Thus it is the bar that constitutes the necessary material and symbolic distance that simultaneously heightens and contains the sexual attractiveness of the barmaid and qualifies her as a glamour figure. It may be that something of the enigmatic property of glamour lies in its asexuality, but glamour here is conceived as a dramatically enhanced yet distanced style of sexual representation, display or address, primarily visual in appeal.[22]

The operation and meaning of glamour as embodied in the Victorian barmaid can be read from contemporary illustrations. The point of departure, however, is not Victorian Britain, but Paris and the Folies Bergères whose barmaid was immortalised in Manet's famous painting of 1881. This needs acknowledgment not only as probably the most familiar image already in readers' minds (which excuses its nonreproduction here), but as the subject of a suggestive recent interpretation. In general, Manet's picture exemplifies points made previously. Together with the richly rendered fruit and bottles on the counter before her, the barmaid here is plainly on display, her presence dramatised by the reflections of chandeliers and mirrors in what seems a particularly luscious but unproblematic still life. For the art historian T. J. Clark, however, the picture is a tissue of uncertainties, whose formal symmetry disguises disjunctions of planes and surfaces that correspond to the disjunctions of *modernité*—the unsettling mobility, the shifting and elusive nature of identity, the emphasis on externals, the ennui. In Clark's reading of Manet, the emptiness of the barmaid's face is the emptiness of alienation, for she herself is no more than a glamorous article, seller and commodity in one, as "the whore appraising the client while offering herself for appraisal."[23] My concern is not to challenge this interpretation, but to use it as a point of reference in reading other graphic texts, to the rear of the artistic avant-garde, that offer more palatable significations of modernity and its subjects.

In figure 1, we are back in London in the confidences of J. Stirling Coyne, who contributed "The Barmaid," with illustration by Gavarni, to a collection edited by Albert Smith, *Sketches of London Life and Character,* in 1849.[24] Gavarni was a celebrated French illustrator and Bohemian, just then in the middle of an extended trip to London. Smith was a journalist whose book is of a familiar type as a guided tour of the exotic world on or under our own doorstep, an insider's look at London's terra incognita. Coyne was both journalist and dramatist whose specialty was the world of the lower middle and working classes. Coyne's text is a fulsome tribute to the barmaid as priestess of the night amid the gaslights of the temple of Bacchus; she is "the modern Hebe, whose champagne is not more intoxicating than her *oeillades."* What is conveyed is both the intensity of the sexual focus on the barmaid and her immunity from its dangers. Her smiles, her banter, her various marks of favour are, we are assured, "a mere matter of business with which the heart has nothing to do," for "the Barmaid seems to be a kind of moral salamander, living unharmed in the midst of the amorous furnace in which Destiny has placed her."

In Gavarni's illustration, the barmaid's presence is central and dramatic. The sexual charge is strong but mediated by convention, idealisation and displacement. On the first count, the glamour is softened by the conventional prettiness of the ringlets, the oval face, and rosebud mouth. Although a daughter of the people, the barmaid is rendered in the style of the drawing-room belle, a traditional solution in coming to terms with working-class sexuality. The idealisation

Figure 1   Garvani, "The Barmaid," from Alfred Smith, ed., *Sketches of London Life and Character* (1849).

comes in the quasi-sanctification of her beauty through the aura of light and its halo effect. Here now is the woman as the ministering angel, a role central to the Victorian conception of the ideal wife. Light also reinforces the written text's assertion of the barmaid's fundamental purity, her resistance to the defilement of the pub as "the amorous furnace." This receives further symbolic emphasis in the contrast between her representation and that of her most visible admirer, who wears the soiled working dress of the London coal-heaver. For the rest, the Freudian will note the displaced symbolism of the beer engine: the phallic pump, the spurting tap and the ready receptacle—the hydraulic model indeed. (An admirer of the barmaid heroine in a play of the 1890s noted in particular "that divine poise of the arm as she draws the handle,"[25] and there is also the vulgar legend of the publican's daughter "who pulled the wrong knob and got stout.")

Arguably, however, the greatest impact of the picture would have come from the privileged access it affords the male beholder, for whom the frustrations of

Figure 2   "Bar and Saloon London," from George Sims, ed., *Living London* (1901–3).

distance have been collapsed.[26] If the bar was the barmaid's stage, then the spectator has here been allowed backstage. The bar—a solid structure indeed—now serves to keep other admirers out, enhancing the sense of privileged inclusion. The woman's turned head and tender expression clearly signal favour, but the basic power of the picture to suggest a personal and private intimacy in a *public* house would seem to depend on its magical suspension of the normal barriers to its fulfilment. It is by antithesis a considerable testimony to the cultural effectiveness of their everyday operation. The commentary also carries the strong presumption that the invisible male observer will be middle class, so that while Coyne emphasises the barmaid's unyielding heart in business hours and records her courtship with a young man of her own class, the picture encourages interest in a cross-class liaison which adds to its sexual charge.

The other contemporary representation of the barmaid at work (figure 2) is significantly later, being the illustration accompanying a contribution on "Bar and Saloon London" to George Sims' encyclopaedic three-volume *Living London,* 1901–3.[27] Sims was a popular journalist, novelist, and latter-day Bohemian. Since this is now imperial London, the editorial style is correspondingly grander than Smith's, promising a panoramic vision of the world city while emphasising the accuracy as well as the range of the compilation. To this end these volumes rely heavily on the photographic record, and though the scene reproduced here was considered, because of its particular animation, to be more suitably rendered by a drawing, the (anonymous) graphic artist has clearly aimed for a high degree of photographic realism. The written text is unadorned reportage, with none of the Bohemian poetics of Coyne's sensational if cosy exoticism of fifty years previous.

It seems therefore at first acquaintance that the documentary has superseded the artistic mode. Certainly the picture offers us a finely detailed rendition of the pub, its fittings and inmates: the island bar and the compartmentalised division of the drinking area, each with its own distinctive clientele, are well observed and typical of the development of the large urban pub by this date; the debris on the floor, including a cast-off shoe from one of the bar staff further suggests the naturalistic intention of the artist. In such a setting we may conclude that the barmaid herself has become no more than a workaday matter of fact.

Yet together with its documentary content, this illustration offers its own mythical interpretation and significant continuities with Gavarni. If the gin-palace glitter is a little muted, the barmaids are nonetheless glamorised in the style of the conventional fin-de-siècle beauty. More notably, the beholder is again afforded a privileged access to the scene; of course the perspective meets the artist's need for a panoramic comprehensiveness, but he exploits it beyond its necessary visual function. The invisible observer—the male stranger—has again circumvented the bar, and penetrated backstage (Victorian journalists had called the inner reaches of the new pubs the "penetralia"). He is thus privy to the dramatic incident in the foreground where the barmaid coolly hears out the overtures of the soldier; whereas the soldier must surely be disappointed, the onlooker is encouraged by the complicit glance of favour from the other barmaid, and the admiration of the pot-boy. Thus this "modern" documentary slice of life has a traditional hero-protagonist and a story line: the invisible spectator, in echoes of an older genre style, is on the brink of romantic success, to be achieved no doubt at the gratifying expense of a virile rival—"the wild colonial boy" or Boer War veteran—and played out before an appreciative audience of his own sex, albeit only of one.

So, unlike Manet's barmaid of Clark's reading, the women in these two more popular treatments do not simply return the stare of the beholder, but confer recognition and identity. In this context, the beholder is less the voyeur or predator than the ultimate participant in a flattering drama of opportunity and inclusion in the press and rush of big-city life. Should we then say that the vision of the avant-garde is disturbing yet probably more accurate, while that of a more popular aesthetic is reassuring yet ultimately deceitful? Maybe; but it should be noted that whatever the element of fantasy and manipulation in the latter, there is a considerable grounding in reality. It is the particular genius loci of the pub, as it was with the popular theatre and music hall, to be an intermediate institution that combines the properties of both public and private domains. Its internal space is in part firmly ordered between the open and closed, but much of it remains negotiable, including that across the bar counter—and from both sides.[28]

Yet the bar as separator remains a crucial feature of the pub as predominantly male territory. It allows flirtation and the rehearsal of sexual exploit, yet also provides an alibi for the novice or the insecure who are relieved of putting their prowess to the test. Moreover, though the pictures we have seen suggest an opportunity for closer encounter, they remain only images, constituting in effect a doubly distanced view of their subject, perhaps confirming the feminist suspicion that sex at a distance is the only completely secure relationship that a modern man can have with a woman.[29]

A further point is that the bar concealed the lower half of the female body with its attendant risks, thus focusing the male gaze on the breasts which became an exaggerated feature of vernacular representations. This may have reinforced associations of maternal nourishment and the oral appeal of drinking.[30] There is some correspondence here with an upward shift in erogenous focus in the conventions of the carte de visite, the personalised photographic miniature that proliferated from the 1860s and became a requisite item in job applications for female bar workers. Unbeknown to sitters, extra copies of these cards were sometimes sold as early pin-ups.[31]

Of course, the two book illustrations tell us less about the barmaid herself than about a male positioning of her. They do, however, confirm her high visibility—compare the background role assigned to the traditionally dominant figure of mine host the publican in the Sims sketch—and the power of glamour in the force field of a reworked everyday sexuality.

3

Who was the Victorian barmaid? What were the actualities of bar work, and how did they sustain or confound the glamorous images examined above? What else can we learn of sexuality in the subculture of the pub and the perceptions of drink sellers, customers and reform critics?[32]

In England the greatest concentration of women bar workers was in London, but they were common enough in the big provincial cities and larger towns. They were much less common in Scotland and Ireland where employment was restricted to big-city hotels. (In Scotland, as a type, they were referred to with suspicion as "London barmaids.") Reliable numbers cannot be established, but in the improved categories of the 1901 census the number of barmaids was returned as 27,707 for England and Wales, of whom 7,632 were employed in London; the licensed trade habitually claimed higher figures, and argued for a count of 100,000 barmaids in England's public houses during the reform agitation of 1907–8.[33] On the most generous arithmetic, the barmaid was a minor calling compared with the nearly one and a half million female domestic servants enumerated in 1901, but her distribution as well as her setting made her a significant minority.

A wide variety of conditions obtained in the licensed trade and its numerous outlets, but by the 1890s, if not before, a broad distinction was recognised between the "mere" or "old-fashioned barmaid," and the "young lady in the public line of business" or "modern barmaid." Recruitment, remuneration, duties and prospects differed accordingly.[34] The first category was a daughter of the working class who started work early as a housemaid in a small working-class pub before graduating to service at the bar. Though not found in the roughest of houses, she was likely to spend her career in working-class pubs and might keep in employment into her late thirties. The second category came from a higher social background, entering the business in the late teens and passing immediately to work behind the bar in a public house catering predominantly to the upper and middle class. As a saloon or lounge barmaid she could also find employment in theatre, music hall, railway and restaurant bars. From the start she was paid more than her working-class sister, proceeded more quickly to a full wage and had some prospects of advancement to a supervisory post with a big company. In general, however, the career of the saloon barmaid was finished by her mid-twenties.

There were far many more women seeking employment than there were placements. Recruits were said to come from every grade of the working and lower middle class, while the majority of entrants to the London trade enlisted from "the country." At all levels of entry, there was a substantial number of women already socialised in the trade as daughters or relatives of publicans. Yet even the publican's daughter, for whom choice was so obviously predetermined by family, seemed anxious to use her insider's knowledge to break away from family. In this she conformed to a common characterisation of newcomers to the trade as free spirits, for while some were undoubtedly outcasts and casualties to start with, the majority were said to be impatient to escape from the monotony of more conventional jobs and locations, and were drawn to bar work as an avenue to the big city and a fuller life. By the 1890s, too, it seems that the trade was drawing more entrants from a higher social class. There are cases of women who preferred bar work to clerking or governessing, occupations which had disappointed in either remuneration or social interest, and Spiers and Pond were said to receive numerous applications from parents in the clergy and professional classes seeking employment for their daughters. With allowance for status inflation and the defensiveness of the trade, there does seem some plausibility, if a dubious exactitude, to the claim that 1,178 of the barmaids working in London in 1892 were the "daughters of gentlemen."[35]

In turn-of-the-century London, the basic wage for a barmaid was eight to ten shillings a week. In addition the employer provided board and lodging, though deductions for laundry and breakages (a controversial item) chopped as much as two shillings off, and the maintenance of a smart appearance could be expensive. Extra income from tips was mostly prohibited. A full weekly wage for the experienced saloon barmaid in a thriving pub might reach fifteen shillings, though the big London music halls, followed by the theatres, paid more. Wages and terms of work were notably inferior in the provinces, but in general, taking into account the provision of board and lodging, the barmaid's earnings were high compared to other semi-skilled female occupations.[36]

Whatever the sector of the trade, barmaid's work was long and demanding. London pubs were licensed to be open for 123 $\frac{1}{2}$ hours per week in the 1890s and a barmaid might be on duty for more than a hundred of those, but the most reliable report of the period recorded a standard working day of some twelve hours or so, making up a seventy-to-eighty-hour week.[37] The day ran from early morning to past midnight with four or five hours off for meals, dressing and rest. Opening hours were shorter on Sunday, the usual day off for the barmaid; after a year she might take a week's holiday, and up to a month thereafter, in some cases with pay. During working hours a barmaid was habitually on her feet, and though male staff did the heavier work, the physical regimen of the bar was punishing. In addition to serving drink and food—and remaining civil—there was cleaning up after closing time, which could be particularly onerous on Saturday night. At the end of such a demanding schedule, few barmaids can have resembled the refulgent creature of the Gavarni print.

Although the division into old-fashioned and modern or saloon barmaids indicates a clear distinction in status and function, attention to the particular circumstances of bar work suggests a more complex picture. In single-handed berths at the cheap end of the market a barmaid was little better than a maid of all work, with dismal food and accommodation, yet it was in the smaller establishments that a barmaid might find herself welcomed as one of the family.[38] The best conditions were found with the big companies, notably Spiers and Pond who were widely respected as model employers. Employees here lived in company dormitories, and visitors pronounced them well housed, well fed and well looked after. Yet there were complaints from one branch of bad food on the table and dead rats under the floor, and the paternalist regime could be irksome.[39] A further variable in the trade was the high rate of turnover and mobility among women bar workers. One unavoidable constant was a working environment heavily polluted by gas and tobacco fumes, conditions found at their worst in the underground railway bars.

The sense of the evidence is that the barmaid maintained a considerable degree of self-respect and independence in the often testing conditions of her trade. In working-class pubs, she was low caste even in her own class,[40] but the saloon barmaid had a high regard for her status and considered herself superior to other service workers such as domestics and shop clerks.[41] Though she was also subordinate and in some cases closely regulated, it was no requirement of her job that she be either deferential, anonymous, or invisible. Indeed on her own territory the barmaid enjoyed a certain authority: "behind the bar," said one observer, "she is the mistress of the situation . . . and an absolute despot."[42] There was considerable social contact on the job, if much of it was conventionalised and almost exclusively male. In big establishments there was the company of other working women, while in the single-handed berth, which probably accounted for the majority of situations, there was the presence, if not always the support, of the publican's wife. Gossip across the bar provided a bush-telegraph that kept even the solitary barmaid aware of conditions elsewhere in the trade and made her a stubborn defender of her basic terms of employment.[43] The rapid turnover was in part an index to the publican's hunger for fresh faces but may have also been a further expression of the barmaid's confidence in pursuit of her calling.

If the level of earnings and the common requirement of living-in disallowed complete independence, barmaids were reputedly among those best placed to take the traditional avenue to supposed escape and fulfilment, for it was the popular myth that barmaids always married, and almost always married well. Premises in the centre of London afforded a high concentration of wealthy upper-class males, and there were many tales of erstwhile barmaids transported by marriage from some West End bar to a suburban mansion. Furthermore, barmaids were said to prosper in marriage; not only were they sociable creatures but, as the myth went, their schooling behind the bar made them shrewd judges of men.[44]

Such a benign account of the barmaid's expectations of living happily ever after was dismissed by a growing lobby of reformers for whom the barmaid constituted a most serious problem of physical and moral welfare. Dating from the mid-1880s, the reform campaign was part of the more general movement for social purity. Its impetus came from various evangelical rescue organisations and branches of the temperance movement. Its membership was predominantly that of churchmen and middle-class women, with the support of a number of politicians, mostly Labour MPs and Progressive members of the London County Council. The reformers were particularly active in London, but there were organised campaigns in other big cities, notably Manchester and Glasgow. The earliest initiatives sought to provide social centres and services for those out of work, or who wished to live off licensed premises, and a series of Parliamentary bills were introduced (unsuccessfully) from 1890 on, calling for a reduction in hours and the improvement of working conditions.[45] The campaign then moved to call for an end to the employment of women in the bar, and recorded some success in the Licensing Act of 1904, which gave Justices of the Peace discretionary power to forbid such employment in granting new licences. A new licensing bill in 1908 required the phased but ultimately total prohibition of bar work for women (other than members of the publican's family), but the measure failed.[46]

Though the references are obscure, barmaids were reported to have gone on strike in 1889, and they made further attempts to organise themselves in the early 1890s,[47] but in a trade that was difficult to unionise, most active worker participation there was supported the employers' counterattack against the reformers and their demand for the elimination of the barmaid. In this highly controversial issue, the reform proposals of the 1908 bill were also contested by the radical suffragists, Esther Roper and Eva Gore-Booth, who rallied support from the trade in their Manchester-based Barmaids' Political Defence League, which defended the women's right to work.[48]

In their attack on "the Moloch of the drink trade," reformers cast the barmaid as the physical victim of a sweated industry, but they were often more exercised by her plight as a moral casualty, fatally vulnerable to drink, seduction and worse. Drink was the very raison d'être of the barmaid's occupation, but formal constraints upon her personal consumption were well advertised by the trade. House regulations commonly forbade treating by customers, and the larger businesses often demanded abstinence during working hours. Private opinion in the trade varied considerably on the extent of the barmaid's temperance or otherwise, but two of them interviewed by the Parliamentary investigator Eliza Orme in 1892 maintained that "the variety and amusement of the life lessens the propensity to drink."[49] For reformers, however, the bar automatically constituted a permanent temptation; they remained convinced that regulations were habitually set at nought by surreptitious drinking to counter fatigue, and quoted rising insurance premiums as evidence of general intemperance in a trade they pronounced more hazardous than that of filemakers and lead workers.[50] In reform logic, drink also inevitably increased the moral risks of bar work by softening resistance to seduction.

Reformers conceded that the women drawn to bar work were not themselves necessarily of a low character, but maintained that the pub environment was inevitably corrupting. In their view, "the variety and amusement" of bar life meant the inescapable sexualisation of social encounter; accordingly, the "banter" and "chaff" of conventional account translated in reform terms to "bad language . . . [that] tends to the insidious weakening of the barrier of modest and maidenly shame in which her [the barmaid's] strength resides."[51] Reformers were convinced of the publican's sexual as well as economic exploitation of young women. For evidence they referred to the advertisements for vacancies in the trade which targeted the under-twenties and commonly called for photographs (the carte de visite) of applicants. The reform conclusion was that the barmaid "is employed by the publican as a decoy for men, and her very existence depends on her ability to attract."[52] When her novelty as the siren of the bar wore off, she was likely to be dismissed, and numerous personal testimonies to prison chaplains and police court missionaries were adduced to demonstrate how easy was the subsequent descent to prostitution.[53]

As it managed the flow of drink, the trade also managed the flow of sexuality, though this was territory harder to police. Some house rules expressly forbade the shaking of hands across the bar as part of a general prohibition on physical contact between server and customer, and reform investigators found the relative broadness of bar counters worth report.[54] Dress was also formally regulated. By the 1890s "except in very small houses the rule is universal that barmaids . . . must wear black dresses . . . and a large apron of the same material." With this occupational uniform went white collars and cuffs, but no further relief or distraction was allowed, and employers proscribed false hair and busts.[55] It was and has remained a truism in the trade that the plain rather than the showy barmaid was the better choice. In any case, where trade was habitually brisk there was little time for dalliance. A French visitor in the 1860s who noted the prettiness of English barmaids suggested that they were "protected from all human seductions behind the imposing serenity and the Olympian majesty of business."[56] Thus the ritualisation of the task as well as its busyness may have reinforced the sexual controls of pub protocol.

Who were typical customers, and what were their likely perceptions of the barmaid and her glamorised sexuality? It was the saloon or lounge barmaid who was most obviously meant to be attractive. Her customers were middle to lower middle class and, of course, almost exclusively male. Most reports from City and West End premises suggest two broad though overlapping categories of clientele: the habitual "lounger," from the leisured man about town to the more raffish "horsey" type; and the "business man" of varying rank, from the banker down to the clerk and the shop man.[57] Whatever the actual provenance of its customers, the saloon preserved the fiction of catering to gentlemen.

It seems plausible enough that the erotic charge for the male habitue derived in part from the piquant inflections of the conventional gentleman-maidservant relationship, restaged away from home in the liminoid space and time of the pub.[58] Thus the businesslike, even officious manner of the barmaid noted above reversed the normal roles of authority relationships for the middle-class male to whom most women, and certainly those in service, were habitually deferential. It is a commonplace that watching other people work is fascinating, but how much more so would this have been for middle-class males who did so little of it themselves, and for whom the extensive female labour and service that supported their lifestyle was usually either honorific or invisible? There seems to be little need to argue at length for the attractions of the austere livery of the dress uniform. Here, practises meant to register distance exercised their own fascination. At the same time enduring associations of the nurturing role of the nanny or nursemaid could make the barmaid a figure of comfort as well as power, particularly in the case of the older woman who survived in suburban public houses and was plainly valued for her maternal-confessional role.[59]

What the graphic texts also demonstrate is the vital role men ascribed to the barmaid in the bidding for, and bestowal of, recognition. The considerable emotional investment in the winning of the woman's gaze that these attempts signify, strongly suggests the degree of anonymity and competition in the pub crowd that had to be bid against. In consequence men, too, put themselves on display. The hunger for a privileged acknowledgment from the woman behind the bar also suggests a further prize for the male ego, given the intimate terrain of the pub, its eroticised associations of drink and the night, and the fascination the barmaid might hold as the stranger of uncertain background. She was respectable, yes; she was the girl whom a chap might just marry, by Jove; she was also the girl who just might . . . without one having to marry her—perhaps the typical male reading of parasexuality. It may be then that together with perhaps nobler sentiments there was another male perception at play, half fantasy and half calculation—that of the barmaid as potential mistress or "kept woman." Indeed, she may have functioned as a collectively kept woman in the male social psyche. With all these attractions in play, the wonder is not that men had to be lured into pubs, but that they were ever persuaded to leave.

Spokesmen for the licensed trade habitually disclaimed any intentions of even the mildest sexual exploitation of women workers. They preferred women over men not because they were "attractive," but because they were less expensive, less clumsy, less wasteful and less corruptible. Such valued workers were necessarily treated well by their employers, while the presence of women in licensed premises was said to have a civilising influence, an argument made by the barmaids themselves in defending their occupation against elimination in 1908.[60] The licensed victuallers proclaimed the respectability of their trade, their barmaids, and their customers who, according to one spokesman in 1906 "are the fathers and brothers of other respectable middle class girls."[61] The trade thus addressed the world from a moving escalator of respectability such that the gaudy temptress of reformers' accounts was always dismissed as a figure from the periphery of the trade or its unimproved past.[62]

Some employers, however, did manifestly stoke the fires of the "amorous furnace." "In many houses in the West End and the City used by clerks, lawyers and shopmen," according to an account of the mid-1870s, "landlords find it greatly to their interest to have handsome, fine, showy, attractive and talkative young ladies behind the bar." These women were dressed by their employers, served only in peak hours, and were most likely to be trapped as mistresses.[63] Neither adventures nor misadventures were necessarily resolved in marriage— "men in pubs," observed one commentator tartly, "are not the marrying kind"— and a combination of low wages and sweet talk undoubtedly led some barmaids into destructive relationships. Muriel Perry, the mistress but never the wife of J. R. Ackerley's businessman father—was seduced by the latter when a barmaid at the Tavistock in Covent Garden in 1909.[64] Whatever the various controls at work, barmaids were women at risk.

In all of this there remains the important but elusive matter of the barmaid's perception of her role and its sexual dimension—the view from behind. There is little direct testimony but the foregoing evidence does strongly suggest that young women were partly drawn to bar work by its promise of excitement, in which sexual opportunity was a strong element as a prelude to marriage. And while employers denied that the barmaid was as a decoy, it was an acknowledged part of her job that she make herself "agreeable."[65]

But how did the barmaid comply with this requirement? There is some significant indication that the barmaid protected herself from the beeriness and leeriness of the pub's sexual culture by her own manipulation of its particular parameters of distance and intimacy. George Moore catches this in his characterisation of Lizzie Baker, the Spiers and Pond heroine in *Spring Days: A Realistic Novel* (1888):

> Lizzie had her bar manners and her town manners, and she slipped on the former as she would an article of clothing, when she lifted the slab and passed behind. They consisted principally of cordial smiles, personal observations, and a look of vacancy which she assumed when the conversation became coarse. From behind the bar she spoke authoritatively, she was secure, it was different—it was behind the bar; and she spoke with a cheek and a raciness that at other times were quite foreign to her . . . what she heard and said in the bar remained not a moment on her mind, she appeared to accept it all as part of the business of the place.[66]

The crucial function of the bar comes across plainly here, as does Lizzie's modern consciousness of bar work as role-playing, and there is corroborative testimony in the words of some of Miss Orme's barmaid-respondents who ridiculed any idea that they were flattered by the customers' chat: "If they only knew it," they said, "we regard them no more than a set of bottles."[67]

Parasexuality in the Victorian pub was very much the product of a male agenda and male management, yet its women subjects were accomplished managers too. Certainly the anti-barmaid reformers had a case, for bar work could be squalid drudgery and its rewards disappointing. There were also real dangers of sexual corruption. Yet compared with prostitution, parasexuality was mostly safe sex, and the evidence suggests that in general the Victorian barmaid was not, like Clark's reading of Manet's subject, an alienated whore, but an assertive and competent modernist; there may in fact have been more alienation on the other side of the bar.

4

Claiming cultural "firsts" is always likely to be a dubious exercise. It could be argued that there is an earlier and more obvious case than the barmaid of the woman as parasexual and modern glamour object; that is the actress, who made her appearance at the Restoration and functioned as what Tracy Davis terms "a kind of sexual wage earner."[68] The actress was a key figure in the promotion of glamour, but the particular novelty of the Victorian barmaid remains in her relative ubiquity and approachability. She was an everyday phenomenon, marginally distant yet more proximate than the actress; it was, as we have seen, in this sense of normality that the barmaid proved so sensational. Yet while the particular circumstances of her employment kept her a controversial figure into the 1914–18 war, she was by then much less singularly conspicuous, for her visual impact had been diminished by the more general glamorisation of women, of which she had been such a notable prototype.[69]

From the last quarter of the nineteenth century, the barmaid's role in this larger process was shared not only with the actress (and from the 1890s, the chorus girl), but with other young women workers from an expanding new service sector whose more numerous incursion into public life brought further dramatic changes to the sexual landscape.[70] At work, at large, and in representation, these women played an important role in the late-century crisis in sexual politics.

While the licensed trade downplayed her sexual role and reformers cast her as the victimised temptress, the barmaid was elsewhere being celebrated as one of a new type of popular heroine. From the 1870s the popular stage conspired with everyday life to sing the praises not only of the barmaid but of her sister workers in telegraph offices, department stores and multiple tea shops. This new group, too, held court from behind a counter, though their adventures were also set in the street, the omnibus and the various new leisure resorts of the big city. In music hall song they are adept manipulators of the class marginal "gent,"[71] but in the 1890s a new stage genre offered a more idealised representation of these young working women as partners in male exploit and more exalted cross-class romances.

This was musical comedy, a lavish and fashionably popular entertainment whose dramatists, as noted at the opening of *The New Barmaid* in 1896, were "working steadily through the list of female occupations."[72] As the titles of its hit productions testify, musical comedy celebrated its heroines in the rhetoric of the "girl": *The Gaiety Girl* (from the chorus), *The Shop Girl,* and *The Earl and the Girl,* pointing to the typical musical comedy resolution (and some dramatic examples from real life) of the society marriage. Max Beerbohm caught the essentials of the genre. "All the classes mingle on the easiest terms. Everyone wants everyone else to have a good time and tries to make everything easy and simple all round. This good time, as I need hardly say, is of a wholly sexual order. And yet everyone from the highest to the lowest is thoroughly good." It portrayed "an innocent libertinism," at which, he concluded, "all the Tory in me rejoices."[73]

What, more generally, might Beerbohm have been applauding? We may speculate that the blooming of musical comedy represents a reassuring response to several contemporary challenges to male domination and sexual identity. Thus the cosmetic gloss on cross-class relationships shifted attention away from the "Maiden Tribute" case of 1885 and the exposé of upper-class males as vicious predators on working-class girls. Presumably too, musical comedy's sunny heterosexuality helped to dispel the unease brought by Oscar Wilde's conviction in 1895. The parasexual construct of the "girl" evoked a more agreeable romantic companion than the "new woman" who made her troublesome debut in the 1890s, and in general it provided a defensive counter-image to the emergent challenge of feminism signalled in the campaign against the Contagious Diseases Acts and the demands of young professional women in the period.[74] Though the musical comedy heroine was a spirited character, she was no threat to male primacy.

At the same time, the glamorous fantasy of the musical comedy girl was derived from the palpable social reality of a large new group of women who did not fit the exclusive categories of madonna or magdalen. Out of hours, away from the social markers of the workplace, the class and status of the new working woman were harder to read. The young aristocratic protagonist in Moore's *Spring Days* first meets his barmaid-lover at the theatre as one of two girls he cannot readily place: "They were evidently not prostitutes, and they did not seem to be quite ladies." An account from 1880 noted "Strange Women" abroad, "neither ladies nor common," who, it concluded, were "respectable women copying the dress and manners of 'unfortunates' for mere excitement; but they don't want gentlemen to go too far."[75]

This phenomenon may have contributed a more unspecified disquiet to the protests of the more conservative middle-class women who addressed the barmaid problem and other social purity issues. The dilemmas of identification reduced the defences of respectability for women in general, while the expanded field of licit sexual encounter increased the threat to class endogamy at a time when the independence of the "new woman" would have been thought to reduce the pool of eligible young middle-class females. Suddenly, it must have seemed, other young women were everywhere, and the reformers were fearful for the integrity of their class as well as their sex.

The barmaid and the pub were thus part of a larger nexus of people and institutions that stood athwart the public-private line and provided the social space within which a more democratised, heterosocial world of sex and sociability was being constituted, a world that is still inadequately mapped by historians.[76] It is on this distinctive terrain that the less august branches of capitalism converted sexuality from anathema to resource, from resource to commodity, in the development of a modern sexualised consumerism.

Parasexuality, with its safely sensational pattern of stimulation and containment, was a significant mode of cultural management in the construction of this new regime and the sexualisation of everyday life. It is plain from its operation and such self-serving fictions as Beerbohm's "innocent libertinism," that it worked primarily to valorise male pleasures. Yet the making of this world was undertaken not just by a cadre of male managers—who were neither wholly in control nor always trying to be so—but by the members of this cultural complex at large, in a self-conscious and mutual (if structurally and ideologically asymmetrical) working out of new modes of relationship between men and women.[77]

In a society where the collective licence of carnival had been largely outlawed, and ritualised practices such as "bundling" (premodern parasexuality with its equivalent of a bar) had lapsed, determination of the informal rules and boundaries of sexual encounter was now pursued in a more fragmented and inchmeal manner, in the individual transactions of a continuously recomposing leisure crowd—London after work, reported Sims, had become "one vast Lovers' Walk."[78] Thus the mechanistic formula of parasexuality that positioned the barmaid in the Victorian pub dissolved in practice into a more popular discourse, the elasticity of whose rules was scrutinised in a vernacular "knowingness" that informs music-hall song and other popular idioms.[79]

If it is to have any further utility, parasexuality may best serve not as another reified term in the often dismal maze of critspeak, but as an exploratory concept in the examination of other examples and dimensions of this process.[80] Glamour, and the sexual stimulation produced by looking (scopophilia) plainly gave a new emphasis to the visual element in the changing sexual economy, but the reformers' concern with what pub people termed "banter" or "chaff" points to the complementary significance of language and spoken codes, which could be as potent yet as contradictory and unstable as the gaze. The rules against physical contact between barmaid and customer are a reminder that through its very repression, touch took on a new expressive charge, witness the furtive but enraptured holding of hands across the bar depicted in some illustrations. The historical reanimation of this popular discourse in all its sensory dynamics—talking and touching as well as looking ("glotto-" and "frottophilia"?)—would seem a necessary exercise in charting experience along the moving social frontier that was the sexualisation of everyday life, and in understanding its implications for the sexual politics of gender.

1. Jeff Hearn and Wendy Parkin, *"Sex" at "Work": The Power and Paradox of Organisation Sexuality* (Brighton, 1987), p. 3.

2. See R. A. Padgug, "Sexual Matters: On Conceptualising Sexuality in History," *Radical History Review* 20 (1979): 3–23; M. Vicinus, "Sexuality and Power: A Review of Current Work in the History of Sexuality," *Feminist Studies* 8 (1982): 133–56; Jeffrey Weeks, *Sex, Politics, and Society: The Regulation of Sexuality since 1800* (London, 1981 and 1989) offers an admirable synthesis. Of more recent work, note P. Gay, *The Bourgeois Experience: Victoria to Freud,* vol. 1, *Education of the Senses* (New York, 1985); Gay, *The Bourgeois Experience: Victoria to Freud,* vol. 2, *The Tender Passion* (New York, 1986); Catherine Gallagher and Thomas Laqueur, eds., *The Making of the Modern Body: Sexuality and Society in the Nineteenth Century* (Berkeley, 1987); Michael Mason, *The Making of Victorian Sexuality* (Oxford, 1994).

3. On the complexities of this divide, see Janet Wolff, "The Culture of Separate Spheres: The Role of Culture in Nineteenth Century Public and Private Life," in *The Culture of Capital: Art, Power, and the Nineteenth Century Middle Class,* ed. Janet Wolff and John Seed (Manchester, 1988), pp. 117–34.

4. For critiques, see Carroll Smith-Rosenberg, "The Female World of Love and Ritual: Relations between Women in Nineteenth Century America," *Signs* 1 (1975): 1–29; Vicinus, "Sexuality and Power," pp. 136–37.

5. Colin Mercer, "A Poverty of Desire: Pleasure and Popular Politics," in *Formations of Pleasure* (London, 1983), p. 97.

6. Bernice Martin, *A Sociology of Contemporary Cultural Change* (Oxford, 1981), p. 243; Victor Turner, "Comment," in *The Reversible World: Symbolic Inversion in Art and Society,* ed. B. A. Babcock (Ithaca, 1978), pp. 286–87.

7. Cf. M. Cleave, "The Greater British Barmaid," in *The Pub: A Celebration,* ed. A. McGill (London, 1969), pp. 131–48; Valerie Hey, *Patriarchy and Pub Culture* (London, 1986), pp. 43–44, who is valuable on contemporary pub sexuality.

8. Peter Clark, *The English Alehouse: A Social History, 1200–1830* (London, 1983), ch. 12; Brian Harrison, *Drink and the Victorians: The Temperance Question in England, 1815–1872* (London, 1975), pp. 45, 66; Mark Girouard, *Victorian Pubs* (New Haven, 1975), pp. 19–32.

9. For photographic illustrations of typical interiors which can also be compared with the graphic texts considered below, see Girouard, *Victorian Pubs.*

10. On women as proprietors and servants, see Clark, *English Alehouse,* pp. 83–86, 206; Leonore Davidoff and Catherine Hall, *Family Fortunes: Men and Women of the English Middle Class, 1780–1850* (London, 1987), pp. 299–301; *Notes and Queries* 7 (March 21, 1914).

11. Girouard, *Victorian Pubs,* p. 26; Clark, *English Alehouse,* pp. 275–76.

12. Observer, *The Gin Shop: History of Inherent Evils, Special Influences, Deceptive Allurements and Demoralising Nature of the Worship of the Ginshop* (London, 1837).

13. *Notes and Queries* (February 21, 1914); Barbara Drake, "The Barmaid," *Women's Industrial News* 65 (1914): 221–38; Francis Bond Head, *Stokers and Pokers, or the London North Western Railway* ([1849] Newton Abbott, 1968), pp. 86–87.

14. Emily Soldene, *My Theatrical and Musical Recollections* (London, 1897), pp. 41–42; M. Willson Disher, *The Pleasures of London* (London, 1950), pp. 296–97.

15. On Spiers and Pond, see Robert Thorne, "Places of Refreshment in the Nineteenth-Century City," in *Buildings and Society,* ed. A. D. King (London, 1980), pp. 240–43. The quote is from Royal Commission on the Employment of Women, *Parliamentary Papers (PP)* (Victoria, Australia), 2 (1983), vol. 1, p. 1382. For the Kaiser, see *The Barmaid* (December 17, 1891).

16. For Australia, see also Royal Commission on the Employment of Women; Report of Inquiry into Intoxicating Drink to New South Wales Legislative Council (1887); John Freeman, *Lights and Shadows of Melbourne Life* (London, 1888), pp. 46–53; [C. A. Wright], *Caddie: The Autobiography of a Sydney Barmaid* (London, 1953); Keith Dunstan, *Wowsers* (Melbourne, 1968), pp. 72–84. For New Zealand, see Jock Phillips, *A Man's Country? The*

Image of the Pakeha Male: A History (Auckland, 1988), pp. 65–66. A cross-cultural study of the barmaid would be useful.

17. *Era* (April 12, 1867).

18. Joint Committee on the Employment of Barmaids, *The Barmaid Problem* (London, 1904).

19. Final report of Royal Commission on Liquor Licensing Laws, *PP* 36 (1898), q. 31807.

20. Larry Carr, *Four Fabulous Faces* (New York, 1970), p. 3.

21. *Oxford English Dictionary,* 1933.

22. For historical distance in legitimising Victorian erotic art, see Gay, *Education of the Senses,* pp. 379–402; for the shop window as barrier and transparency, see Rachel Bowlby, *Just Looking: Consumer Culture in Dreiser, Gissing and Zola* (London, 1985), pp. 332–34.

23. T. J. Clark, "The Bar at the Folies Bergères," in *Popular Culture in France,* ed. J. Beauroy, M. Bertrand, and E. Gargan (Saratoga, 1977), pp. 233–52; T. J. Clark, *The Painting of Modern Life: Paris in the Art of Manet and His Followers* (London, 1985), pp. 205–58. As noted above, the barmaid was exceptional for France.

24. Originally published by Bogue, the collection was reissued by Dean and Son in 1859.

25. H. A. Jones, *The Masqueraders: A New and Original Modern Play* (London, 1979), first performed 1894. I thank Joel Kaplan for this.

26. This reading is influenced by John Berger, *Ways of Seeing* (London, 1972).

27. "Bar and Saloon London," in *Living London,* ed. George Sims (London, 1901–3), vol. 2, pp. 286–92. Thanks to David Cheshire for this.

28. Michael A. Smith, "Social Usages of the Public Drinking House," *British Journal of Sociology* 34 (1983): 367–85.

29. Rosalind Coward, *Female Desire: Women's Sexuality Today* (London, 1984), p. 76; see also Hey, *Patriarchy and Pub Culture,* p. 43.

30. Antony Easthope, *What a Man's Gotta Do: The Masculine Myth in Popular Culture* (London, 1986), pp. 75–76.

31. *Barman and Barmaid* (July 12, 1879); Avril Lansdell, *Fashion à la Carte, 1860–1900: A Study of Fashion through Cartes de Visite* (Aylesbury, 1985).

32. The evidence for such considerations is sketchy and diffuse. The most authoritative and systematic source, including interview material, is that of Eliza Orme, "Report on Conditions of Work of Barmaids," to Royal Commission on Labour, *PP* 37 (1893–4), pp. 197–229. For Orme, a prominent Liberal, feminist, and middle-class professional woman (who liked a good cigar), see Leslie Howsam, " 'Sound-Minded Women': Eliza Orme and the Study and Practice of Law in Late-Victorian England," *Atlantis* 15 (1989): 44–55. Later pamphlet and periodical treatments drew heavily on Orme while often ignoring her judicious approach. For material on bar*men,* see Booth MS B135, London School of Economics; Dr. V. Padmavathy of Miami University, Oxford, Ohio has completed her thesis on the politics of the barmaid question, and Professor David Gutzke of Southwest Missouri State University, is working on a much-needed history of the licensed trade, 1840–1940. I am grateful to both for sharing references and ideas.

33. National British Women's Temperance Association, *Facts about Barmaids* (December 1907); Eva Gore-Booth, Sarah Dickenson and Esther Roper, *Barmaids Political Defence League* (Manchester, n.d.), for the higher counter estimate.

34. Barbara Drake, "The Barmaid," *Women's Industrial News* (1914): 222–38; "The Girl Workers of London II: The Barmaid," *The Young Woman: An Illustrated Monthly Magazine* 6 (1897–8): 52–54.

35. *Women and Work* (December 19, 1874); *Barmaid* (December 17, 1891); Orme, "Report on Conditions," pp. 205, 208–10; W. H. Wilkins, "A Plea for the Barmaid," *Humanitarian* (1896): 423–34; cutting, February 5, 1898, in the Philip Norman Collection, London Inns and Taverns, Guildhall Library; Drake, "The Barmaid."

36. Orme, "Report on Conditions," pp. 200, 204; Norman Collection cutting, February 5, 1898. For Birmingham, see "Prisoners at the Bar," *Cassell's Saturday Journal* (March 4, 1911).

37. Orme, "Report on Conditions," pp. 198–203.

38. Ibid., pp. 200, 204.

39. Report of Select Committee of House of Commons on the Shop Hours Bill, *PP* 17 (1892), qq. 5453, 5375–82, 5485.

40. George Gissing, *The Nether World* (London, 1903), p. 23; M. Powell, *My Mother and I* (London, 1972), p. 107.

41. Orme, "Report on Conditions," p. 207.

42. *Entr'acte* (October 27, 1877).

43. Drake, "The Barmaid."

44. Among many references, see F. Freeman, "Barmaids," *Weekly Despatch* 4 (February 4, 1883).

45. For an early note of the issue, see Select Committee of the House of Lords on Intemperance, *PP* (1878), qq. 118–19. See also *Toilers in London: An Enquiry concerning Female Labour in the Metropolis* (London, 1889), pp. 205–14; *Barmaid* (January 14, 1892). Joint Committee, *The Barmaid Problem*, details the later, more concerted campaign and its legislative proposals.

46. On the campaign for prohibition, see *The Times* (December 19, 21, 28, 1903); correspondence with the Home Secretary, Herbert Gladstone, from the Countess Carlisle, President of the British Women's Temperance Association, and from Ramsay MacDonald, British Museum Additional MS 46065 f. 208 (April 1, 1908), and Add. MS 45986 f. 102 (April 8, 1908), respectively. For the LCC, see also George Foster, *The Spice of Life: Sixty Five Years in the Glamour World* (London, 1939), pp. 172–77. For the defence, see below.

47. *Ally Sloper's Half-Holiday* (May 11, 1889; October 24, 1891).

48. See Gore-Booth et al., *Barmaids Defence League*; Gifford Lewis, *Eva Gore-Booth and Esther Roper: A Biography* (London, 1988), pp. 103–6; *Licensing World* (March 16, 1907, April 4, 1908); *Brewing Trade Review* (July 1, 1908).

49. Orme, "Report on Conditions," pp. 207–8.

50. *Manchester Guardian* (July 11, 1906).

51. Joint Committee, *The Barmaid Problem*.

52. "The Prisoner at the Bar," *Cassell's Saturday Journal* (January 7, 1911); Carlisle to Gladstone, Add. MS.

53. Drake, "The Barmaid."

54. Norman Collection cutting, February 5, 1898; Orme, "Report on Conditions," p. 197.

55. *Barman and Barmaid* (July 12, 1879); A. B. Deane, ed., *Licensed Victuallers Official Annual for the Year 1895* (London, 1895), pp. 159–60.

56. A. Esquiros, *The English at Home* (London, 1861–3), vol. 1, p. 272.

57. Representative evidence in *Toilers in London*, pp. 209–10; "The Girl Workers of London," p. 54; *Young Girls in Drinking Bars: A Narrative of the Facts*, pamphlet reprinted from Church of England Temperance Chronicle (n.d.); *Licensed World* (September 17, 1904).

58. Leonore Davidoff, "Class and Gender in Victorian England: The Diaries of Arthur J. Munby and Hannah Cullwick," *Feminist Studies* 5 (1979): 89–141; Peter Stallybrass and Allon White, *The Politics and Poetics of Transgression* (London, 1986), pp. 149–70.

59. *Barman and Barmaid* (July 12, 1879); Frederick Willis, *101 Jubilee Road: A Book of London Yesterdays* (London, 1948), p. 57; Frederick Willis, *London General* (London, 1953), pp. 50–57; Hey, *Patriarchy and Pub Culture*, p. 44.

60. Select Committee on Shop Hours (1892), q. 3276; *Licensed World* (March 16, 1907). Cf. Davidoff and Hall, *Family Fortunes*, p. 301.

61. *Manchester Guardian* (July 13, 1906).

62. Deane, *Licensed Victuallers Annual*, p. 159.

63. *Women and Work* (December 19, 1874). See also *Rosa Grey: The Life of a Barmaid* (London, n.d.), Lilly Collection, University of Indiana.

64. Diana Petre, *The Secret Orchard of Roger Ackerley* (London, 1985), pp. 38–39.

65. Report of Royal Commission on Liquor Licensing Laws, *PP* 36 (1898), p. 308.

66. George Moore, *Spring Days: A Realistic Novel* (London, 1888), p. 308.

67. Orme, "Report on Conditions," p. 209.

68. I am grateful for discussions with Tracy Davis on her research on actresses. See Tracy Davis, *Actresses as Working Women: Their Social Identity in Victorian Culture* (London, 1991). See also Juliet Blair, "Private Parts in Public Places: The Case of Actresses," in *Woman and Space: Ground Rules and Social Maps,* ed. Shirley Ardener (New York, 1981), pp. 205–28.

69. Later commentators spoke of "the eclipse of the barmaid" as a consequence of wartime when "sex, as far as it concerned the public house, was abolished." See M. Gorham, *The Local* (London, 1939), pp. 5–7; Disher, *Pleasures of London,* p. 297, but cf. *The Pub and the People by Mass Observation* (London, 1987), pp. 56–57.

70. For this "white blouse revolution" in general, see Jane Lewis, *Women in England, 1870–1950* (Brighton, 1984), pp. 145–58. For accounts from parallel societies of women's work and culture in this sector, see Michael B. Miller, *The Bon Marché: Bourgeois Culture and the Department Store, 1869–1920* (Princeton, 1981); Susan Porter Benson, *Counter Cultures: Saleswomen, Managers, and Customers in American Department Stores, 1890–1940* (Urbana, 1986); Kathy Peiss, *Cheap Amusements: Working Women and Leisure in Turn of the Century New York* (Philadelphia, 1986).

71. Jane Traies, "Jones and the Working Girl: Class Marginality in Music Hall Song, 1860–1900," in *Music Hall: Performance and Style,* ed. J. S. Bratton (Milton Keynes, 1986), pp. 23–48.

72. William Archer, *The Theatrical World of 1896* (London, 1897), pp. 35–38. On musical comedy, see George Rowell, *The Victorian Theatre* (Cambridge, 1978), pp. 143–44; Andrew Lamb, "Music of the Popular Theatre," in *The Romantic Age: Music in Britain, 1800–1914,* ed. Nicholas Temperley (London, 1981), pp. 97–104; Bailey, *Popular Culture,* ch. 8.

73. *Saturday Review* (October 30, 1909).

74. For context and the sense of crisis, see Judith Walkowitz, "Male Vice and Female Virtue: Feminism and the Politics of Prostitution in Nineteenth-Century Britain," *History Workshop Journal* 13 (1982): 79–83; Frank Mort, "Purity, Feminism and the State: Sexuality and Moral Politics, 1880–1914," in *Crisis in the British State 1880–1930,* ed. Mary Langan and Bill Schwarz (London, 1985), pp. 209–25; David Rubinstein, *Before the Suffragettes: Women's Emancipation in the 1890s* (Brighton, 1986); Susan Kingsley Kent, *Sex and Suffrage in Britain, 1860–1914* (Princeton, 1987).

75. Moore, *Spring Days,* pp. 54–55; *Barman and Barmaid* (May 29, 1880). Problems of identification were noted from the 1860s, see Lynda Nead, *Myths of Sexuality: Representations of Women in Victorian Britain* (Oxford, 1988), pp. 180–81.

76. For a persuasive model of another overlapping cultural nexus, though it lacks people, see Tony Bennett, "The Exhibitionary Complex," *New Formations* 4 (1988): 73–102, reprinted in his *The Birth of the Museum: History, Theory, Politics* (London, 1995).

77. For America, see, notably, Peiss, *Cheap Amusements*; Lewis A. Erenberg, *Steppin' Out: New York Night Life and the Transformation of American Culture* (Westport, 1981). In a study of "adult entertainment" in New York since 1900 Laurence Senelick identifies a phenomenon similar to parasexuality in what he terms "spectation"; see "Private Parts in Public Places," in *Inventing Times Square: Commerce and Culture at the Crossroads of the World,* ed. William R. Taylor (New York, 1991), p. 332.

78. "London Sweethearts," in *Living London,* ed. Sims, vol. 2, pp. 15–21.

79. J. S. Bratton, *The Victorian Popular Ballad* (London, 1975), ch. 6; Bailey, *Popular Culture,* chs. 3 and 6.

80. E.g., the female flight attendant invites attention as a latter-day bearer of parasexuality; for details of the occupational training in the United States, see the sociological study by Arlie Hochschild, *The Managed Heart: The Commercialization of Human Feelings* (Berkeley, 1983).

PART 5

CONSTRUCTING SEX

ANNE LISTER'S CONSTRUCTION OF LESBIAN IDENTITY

ANNA CLARK

Anne Lister was a Yorkshire gentlewoman who resided in a manor house called Shibden Hall in the early nineteenth century. An heiress, she was able to educate herself in the classics, she expressed no interest in men, and she did not have to marry. In coded portions of her extensive diaries, Anne Lister wrote of her passionate relationships with women, noting every "kiss" (her term for orgasm) she experienced. Although she did not use the word lesbian, at age thirty, she wrote, "I love and only love the fairer sex and thus, beloved by them in turn my heart revolts from any other love but theirs."[1]

Anne Lister illuminates not only lesbian history but questions of representation and agency in the larger field of the history of sexuality as well. Until recently, historians of homosexuality have followed the social constructionist paradigm that our sexual identities are shaped, even determined, by discourses rather than by our own desires. For instance, women who loved women in the eighteenth and nineteenth centuries were thought to have followed the model of "passionate friendship."[2] Nineteenth-century women, it was thought, could not even conceive of sexual desire for each other, having no words for such feelings. Instead, they kissed, embraced, and exchanged intensely romantic letters, but rarely if ever progressed to genital sex. As a result, society regarded such friendships as perfectly respectable, even touching. In 1811, two schoolteachers won damages against a pupil's relative who accused them of lesbianism, because the judges believed such behavior was impossible between women.[3] Women, therefore, could not develop a lesbian identity, because no such notion existed in their culture.

Similarly, Michel Foucault posited that until the late nineteenth century a man who engaged in sodomy was punished for committing an act regarded as sinful and/or criminal, but he was not regarded as having a homosexual personality. The homosexual identity only arose when sexologists and psychiatrists began to define those who committed certain acts as effeminate homosexual men or masculine lesbians.[4] Passionate friendships that were previously regarded as respectable then became stigmatized as perverted.[5] Yet many lesbians and gay men believed that such theories explained their desires and gave them an identity as biologically different rather than criminally deviant. Drawn together by this new sense of self, gay men, and to a lesser extent lesbians, created subcultures in urban, bohemian areas.

Foucault stressed that homosexuals and other "deviants" could subvert, resist, and manipulate these identities; for instance, a gay man could take a doctor's definition of him as congenitally mentally ill and assert that he was born with these desires so there was nothing wrong with him. Similarly, a lesbian could take the notion that she was a member of a "third sex," incorporating a masculine personality in a feminine body, to take pride in her "butch" identity.[6] Nonetheless, according to the Foucaultian paradigm, there was little room for individual agency. Despite the ability of homosexuals to twist expert definitions, they were never seen to originate their own sexual identity.[7]

This Foucaultian paradigm has been breaking down in the last few years. On an empirical level, Foucault's chronology has been shown to be false. Randolph Trumbach, Theo van der Meer, and George Chauncey have extensively documented gay male subcultures that flourished in eighteenth- and nineteenth-century cities, long before sexologists and psychiatrists invented "the homosexual."[8] Anne Lister's diaries made clear that women who engaged in passionate friendships could be quite aware of their sexual feelings—and act on them, as Martha Vicinus, Terry Castle, Trumbach, and Lisa Moore point out.[9] By discovering Sapphic references in eighteenth-century English diaries, letters, dramas, and pamphlet literature, Emma Donoghue has shown that contemporaries could potentially conceive of lesbian desire, although they continued to perceive it as a sin. Trumbach has also argued that in late-eighteenth-century England, a Sapphic role developed for masculine, lesbian women.[10]

The theory that individuals could only acquire a "homosexual identity" when it was invented by sexologists—that they are inserted into discourses—does not hold water historically. An alternative would be the theory of "sexual scripts," which holds that sexual desires are learned, rather than innate.[11] Men who had sex with other men may have been socialized into their subcultures through mock rituals of gender inversion in their pubs and learned the codes necessary to pick each other up in the street. But the notion of sexual scripts is complicated by the intensely negative attitudes toward sodomy and masculine women in late-eighteenth- and early-nineteenth-century society. Of course, the notion of "stigma" helps us understand that people can take up even a rather negative role, for any identity is better than none.[12] Men who had not been initiated into urban subcultures would hear about the "mollies" or "sodomites" and know that, however hated, their kind did exist. However, people isolated from subcultures sometimes formulated their own more positive sexual identities. For instance, Theo van der Meer discovered the case of an eighteenth-century rural Dutch preacher who asserted that his desires for young men were "proper to his nature."[13]

These theoretical problems become even more pressing when considering the case of early-nineteenth-century lesbianism in England. Although lesbian subcultures probably existed among dancers and prostitutes in eighteenth- and nineteenth-century Paris, no evidence for such subcultures has been found in England so far.[14] Anne Lister therefore could not have been socialized into a subculture. While knowledge about male sodomy was widespread, Sapphic references seem to have been largely confined to sophisticated and cosmopolitan circles of intellectuals and theater people in London and Bath. Anne only moved in these circles after she had several intense sexual relationships with women, and after she had begun trying to develop her own sense of a lesbian self.

To understand Anne, we must therefore construct a model of the individual acquisition of a sexual identity that is more nuanced than simply acquiring a pre-given role.[15] This is not, as Judith Butler fears, to assert that "there is one who arrives in the world, in discourse, without a history."[16] Instead, I want to restore agency to the process by which some individuals attempt to create a sense of self as "something that has to be worked on, invented, and reinvented . . . the modern self . . . is a reflexive process, made and remade by the person in terms of his or her own experience," to quote Jeffrey Weeks.[17] I will take Anne Lister as an example of how some individuals deliberately construct their own identities with three elements: their own temperaments and inherent desires; their material circumstances; and the cultural representations available to them.[18] While many people in the nineteenth century probably passively accepted conventional socialization, an individual whose desires and circumstances dissonantly clashed with his or her cultural role may have been more likely to forge a singular sense of self.

Anne Lister recorded her quest for self-identity in her extensive diaries and notes on her readings.[19] She apparently kept notes for her journal every day and then copied them into bound volumes both in regular script and in code.[20] This code, based on Greek, originated in the context of her first love affair as a young girl. She and Eliza Raine, and later she and Marianna Belcombe, used the code to write love letters to each other, which Anne often copied down in her journals. The code, of course, was used for sexual matters (she also put a cross in the margins to indicate she had an orgasm), but also recorded private thoughts and discussions about her relationships with her family and neighbors. Although her descendant John Lister cracked the diary's code in the late nineteenth century, he and subsequent archivists were horrified at her sexual explicitness, and they concealed the key to the code for generations.[21] In 1988, however, local historian Helena Whitbread, with the help of more modern archivists, transcribed and published a volume of excerpts from the diaries, publishing another in 1992. I have also read and transcribed selections from the diaries and her extracts from her readings. The diaries reveal that Anne was extremely strong-minded, self-willed, opinionated, energetic, intelligent, iconoclastic, curious, and manipulative.

Material circumstances both enabled Anne to pursue her lesbian desires and constrained their open expression. The oldest daughter of a retired captain turned gentleman farmer, Anne Lister conventionally would have married and become a genteel wife according to the influential ideology of separate spheres. However, she engaged in her first lesbian sexual relationship in boarding school and determined never to wed. Fortunately, her money allowed her the eccentricity of spinsterhood and the opportunity to educate herself in the classics and to travel abroad. Yet Anne also owed her wealth, in part, to the force of her personality. Her aunt and uncle bequeathed Shibden Hall to her to keep it in the family after her brother had died but also because she proved to her aunt and uncle that she could run the estate more capably than her ne'er-do-well father.[22]

Waiting for her inheritance, she lacked the funds for most of her life to support a female lover in style. Her first lover was Eliza Raine, a young woman of color who stood to inherit from her West Indian planter father. Next, Anne took up with Isabella Norcliffe, daughter of a wealthy family, but soon fell in love with Marianna Belcombe. Unfortunately, Marianna married for money—being the penniless daughter of a doctor—yet Anne and she continued as lovers for years. Frustrated at this state of affairs, Anne spent some time in Paris, where she had affairs with Maria Barlow and Madame de Rosny. However, what she really wanted was a life-partner who could match her socially and financially; Lister attained this goal, although not true love, with neighboring heiress Anne Walker in 1832 and lived and traveled with Walker until her own death in 1840.[23]

The flux of sexual morality characteristic of the late eighteenth century still flavored Anne's cultural milieu. Anne read about and discussed Queen Caroline's 1820 trial for adultery, which also exposed George IV's much more extensive sexual shenanigans.[24] She knew Byron's poetry, and his bad reputation. The father of one of her friends kept a mistress fairly openly. She also noted in her journal the arrest of the Bishop of Clogher for having sex with a guardsman.[25] Because she belonged to an old landed family (though one rather obscure and reduced) she faced fewer constraints on her behavior than she would as the daughter of a father engaged in commercial or industrial occupations. Such men's credit depended, in part, on the conventional behavior of their daughters and wives.[26] Anne only had to please her uncle and aunt. Anne therefore knew that upper-class, especially aristocratic and royal, people engaged in libertine behavior, but she also realized that such antics had to be concealed.

Anne's diaries reveal that despite her public probity as a genteel heiress, she knew she was a renegade at heart. Like many eighteenth- and nineteenth-century diarists in this era of the "invention of the self,"[27] Anne tried to create a coherent identity while at the same time recording herself playing many different roles. The diary is a way of constructing a private sense of self, but since it is written day by day, rather than invented as a self-conscious whole (as an autobiography would be) the tensions and contradictions between identity and behavior become more apparent. As Irving Howe writes, "Once perceived or imagined, the self implies doubleness, multiplicity. . . . I may be fixed in social rank, but that does not exhaust, it may not even quite define, who I am or what I mean."[28] The eighteenth-century fascination with the masquerade and the era's acceptance of hypocrisy meant that one could create several different selves to suit public and private identities. Like many eighteenth-century politicians, for instance, Boswell publicly spoke with the rhetoric of virtue, presenting himself as a respectable gentleman, but privately confided to his diary his liaisons with prostitutes.[29] Later nineteenth-century diarists such as the anonymous author of *My Secret Life* and Arthur Munby, who was fascinated with working-class women, also recounted their illicit sexual or romantic adventures.[30] Similarly, Anne Lister appeared to be a genteel, Anglican landed heiress, albeit a touch eccentric, while secretly recording her sexual adventures and speculations in code.

The repertoire of available selves, however, was much more restricted for women, let alone lesbians, than for heterosexual men. As Felicity Nussbaum points out, Boswell could try out diverse masculine roles from a variety of cultural sources—the rogue from the theater, the hero from the classics, the patriarch from the Bible.[31] Women could respectably acquire only one role: that of marriage and motherhood. Of course, many apparently conforming women could express covert, perhaps unconscious, discontent, as in the novels of Elizabeth Gaskell and Fanny Burney. Yet, as Patricia Meyer Spacks notes, they consciously conformed to femininity in their diaries, while Anne explicitly wrote about her masculine persona and lesbian activities.[32]

The only potential role in which Anne might have imagined herself was that of a partner in a passionate friendship, such as the Ladies of Llangollen. Anne was fascinated with the Ladies of Llangollen, two Irish gentlewomen who had run off to live with each other in Wales. They provided a celebrated exemplar of feminine, yet respectable romance, rarely seen as sexual.[33] But passionate friendship was of limited use as a paradigm for Anne's relationships. First, she and her great love did not have the financial means to live together; marriage or dependence on relatives were their only options.[34] Second, it is unclear how totally acceptable passionate friendship was in their time.[35] The Ladies of Llangollen were occasionally subtly stigmatized as masculine and lesbian. Anne herself felt she could communicate her dream of taking a woman as a life-partner only to her dear uncle and aunt and to a close friend of radical opinions. Finally, Anne found passionate friendship insufficiently sexual as an ideal. She was convinced the Ladies of Llangollen were lovers.[36] What Anne sought was a notion of the self that could integrate her sexuality with other aspects of her life.

Anne therefore could not simply take up roles already existing in the culture, but instead, creatively put together the fragmentary cultural materials available to her to understand her desires for women. As Teresa de Lauretis describes this process, individuals absorb "external representations" and then "rework the fantasy in their internal world" of the self.[37] Anne's internal reworking of external representations was particularly difficult because depictions of lesbianism were so forbidden and few. Much of her search for lesbianism involved reading between the lines for subtle hints of desire between women and imaginatively reworking heterosexual sources to fit lesbian relationships. The lesbian reader, as Jean Kennard points out, can don and doff masks of consciousness at will, rummaging through representations for her own costumes.[38]

Anne formed her sexual identity by creatively reading two main sources: the classics and Romantic writers. Men of Anne Lister's class who desired sex with other men could find in the classics an alternative sexual identity.[39] Byron and his friends, for example, read the poetry of Catullus and Martial, which praised the beauty of youths as well as women, pondered elements of Plato's Symposium, which celebrated the spiritual aspects of love between men, and enjoyed Juvenal's bawdy, explicit humor when he satirically asked why a man should marry when he could enjoy the pleasures of a boy. Anne copied Byron's quip in *Don Juan* that editors of Martial segregated all his "indecent" poems together in the end of a volume, ostensibly to warn against their obscenity but conveniently collecting them for the curious.[40] Anne would have realized that Byron's poem "To Ellen"—"Oh, might I kiss those eyes of fire, A million scarce would quench desire"—imitated Catullus's verse addressed to the boy Juventius and, hence, conveyed a powerful homoerotic charge.[41] The explicitly homosexual versions of these works, however, were only available in Greek and Latin, and translators increasingly bowdlerized and "straightened" them out. The classics therefore provided a hidden, subterranean circuit of sexuality unknown or little known to the general public. At the same time, the classics were the visible pillar of masculine and aristocratic power.[42]

There is no evidence, however, that Anne imagined herself as a Greek or Roman male lover. Like Byron, Anne found representations of her desires in classical texts, but the task of excavating them was much more difficult for a nineteenth-century woman than it would have been for an upper-class educated man. Classical knowledge was usually unavailable to women, deprived of university educations. Anne herself had a private tutor. Yet with typical duplicity, she publicly stated that classical learning was improper for ladies because it "undrew a curtain better for them not to peep behind."[43] When Anne herself peeped behind this curtain, she had to deploy her own imagination and self-regard to cope with the misogyny she found in such classical authors. In Greek and Roman society, citizen males exhibited their virility through sex with "inferiors," whether boys, women, foreigners, or slaves. At the same time, any sign of "effeminacy" was seen as humiliating to the individual and a dangerous indication of societal decadence.[44] But references to lesbianism were few, oblique, and usually scornful.[45] Anne therefore had to summon all her considerable scholarly and monetary resources to track down rare editions and read in French and Latin to find any references to sexuality between women.

On the most basic level, the classics provided her with the names and concepts of her desires, unavailable to most women of her time and class. At age twenty-three, when she embarked on her first serious sexual relationship with a woman, she made notes on a detailed sexual vocabulary through her extensive reading, writing in coded Latin definitions of the clitoris, tribadism, eunuchs, pederasts, and so on.[46]

Words for sexual acts and organs were not enough; what Anne sought was an identity. Sappho may have been a precedent. However, during Anne Lister's time, classical scholars generally bowdlerized Sappho's poems into heterosexual versions.[47] So she turned to Pierre Bayle's dictionary entry on Sappho. Bayle portrayed Sappho as a brilliant, learned woman whose "amorous passion extended even to the persons of her own sex." Bayle's Sappho thus bears a close resemblance to the character of Anne Lister herself. Bayle wonders why she was called "masculine Sappho" by Horace, citing several sources that conclude that it was because "she was tribas [tribade, or lesbian], and that it denotes the inclination she had for the sciences, instead of handling the spindle and the distaff." But this dictionary entry, replete with footnotes and contending interpretations about every fact of her life, also indicated the difficulty of finding a coherent "truth" about Sappho.[48] Similarly, Anne did not take on a "Sapphic" identity wholesale, but creatively pieced together fragments from many sources to form her own sense of a lesbian self. After noting "most interesting" (but nothing else) regarding her reading of Bayle, Anne Lister set about tracking down his references to Sapphic allusions in Juvenal, Martial, and Horace.[49]

Juvenal, whom Anne studied extensively, used obscene language to satirize Roman society as populated by effeminate men, drunkards, and adulterous women—the aristocratic vices of his age. One of the commentators Anne read on Juvenal, the Reverend D. H. Urquhart, excused the poet as a great republican spirit whose frank verses simply attacked the immorality of his time.[50] Nonetheless, most contemporary translations of Juvenal were highly censored. But perspicacious Anne found a seventeenth-century Latin commentator, Lubinus, who revealed another layer of Juvenal to her: a mine of information about homosexuality, both male and female. Anne definitely read Juvenal for prurient reasons, but she had to read between the lines.[51]

When Juvenal refers to lesbian behavior, it is in oblique and negative terms: for instance, when Tullia and her foster sister Maura

> pass the ancient shrine of Chastity,
>   It's here
> They stop their litters at night and
> piss on the goddess' form,
> Squirting like siphons, and ride each
> other like horses, warm
> And excited, with only the moon as
> witness. Then home they fly.[52]

In commenting on such passages, Lubinus not only defined fellatio, pederasty, and tribadism, he also explained that Juvenal borrowed his image from an epigram of Martial, who much more explicitly referred to "tribadism," that is, women rubbing each other.[53] Martial's epigrams, which Anne knew, are even more negative than Juvenal about lesbianism. He attacks a woman named Bassa for appearing to be chaste and doing without men, but in reality "fucking" women.[54] Philaenis works out with dumbbells, guzzles wine, steak, and girl's "juicy quims," in the words of one late Victorian translator; but the poet attacks her for transgressing her sex and wishing she would "learn to suck a penis," a vicious insult in Roman culture.[55]

As Judith Roof notes, lesbian readings of cultural texts produce the "split, self-contradictory, desiring subject"—both taken in by and refusing negative images.[56] For Anne, although Martial's depictions of lesbian women were intended to be negative, they at least gave evidence that lesbianism existed. Furthermore, she may have enjoyed Martial's depiction of Philaenis's pursuit of athletic workouts, wine, and women, a lusty, vigorous image of womanhood quite different from those available to her in early-nineteenth-century England.[57] In fact, she seems to have found reading Juvenal in Latin sexually stimulating.[58] When Anne read these poems, she did not react with shock, horror, and self-disgust but, rather, learnedly speculated as to whether Bassa used a dildo or not, based on philological evidence.[59]

Even as classical and romantic texts structured the possibilities for her own sexual identity, her own lesbian desire provided the lens through which she read these texts. Anne Lister was able to insert her desire in the absent spaces of these readings. While desire between men was extensively depicted in these texts, presented in a range of ways from the scornful to the heroic, lesbianism was almost invisible, just fragments, traces, fantasies. Therefore, she had more freedom to flesh out her sense of self.

Anne's quest for a self, however, combined many disparate elements in tension. As Foucault has written, the classical and Christian notions of the self differed in several key respects. The Greeks and Romans tended to concentrate on the "care of the self," on discipline, moderation, and self-discovery; for the most part, philosophers cared much more about the danger of excessive indulgence in sex rather than the sex of one's partner. In contrast, Christians espoused the renunciation of the self for the higher love of God.[60] Anne Lister's journal reveals the ethical dilemma she found herself in as she tried to draw upon the classical and Christian traditions in developing her sense of self. The classics provided both a pattern of a disciplined, open-minded quest for knowledge and sexual knowledge itself; Protestantism set a tradition of spiritual self-examination, in which diaries charted the writer's progress from sin to devotion through "meditative dialogues between the body and the soul."[61]

Anne often faced the problem of reconciling her strong Anglican religious beliefs with her powerful sexual desires. The same day she masturbated thinking of another woman and reading Juvenal, she wrote, "There is no comfort but in god oh that my heart were right with him and then I should have peace—lord have mercy on me and not justice."[62] It is significant that she stressed mercy rather than justice. If she had been an Evangelical, she would have been much more tormented by thoughts of sin. Instead, her faith accommodated both a devout Anglicanism and iconoclastic researches into comparative religion. In her notes on readings, she observed the motifs of the cross and the Trinity in different religions and studied the worship of the phallus in India and other cultures. She also copied Edward Gibbon's statement that of all the great Roman emperors only one was "entirely correct"—that is, heterosexual—in his sexual tastes.[63] It is possible that her scholarship enabled her to see that Christianity's strict hostility to sexuality was atypical among religions and to develop her own, more flexible morality. For instance, in struggling with the question of whether her affair with a married woman was "fornication" and therefore sinful, she concluded that her lover's marriage for money was "legalized prostitution."[64] At another moment, however, she feared that her connection with the married Marianna was "adultery."[65] Similarly, when her uncle died, she lamented, "if only my heart were clean."[66] Her religion gave her solace through prayers rather than guilt; for instance, saddened by a letter from her mistress Mrs. Barlow, she cried and prayed to God "to cleanse the thoughts of my heart by the inspiration of his Holy Spirit," and then "felt a little relieved."[67] But she also wanted to cement her relationship with Marianna, and later with Anne Walker, by taking the sacrament together.[68] She declared to Mrs. Barlow, echoing Rousseau, that they had "no priest but love."[69]

Anne exhibited a similar ambivalence in her attitude toward Romantic texts such as novels.[70] On the one hand, she wanted to engage in a quest for self-improvement, of disciplined reading in science, the classics and history, avoiding frivolous activities and discussion. In conversation with acquaintances, she denounced Lady Caroline Lamb's *Glenarvon*—a roman à clef about the author's affair with Byron—as an example of the immorality of novels.[71] On the other hand, she enjoyed the decadent power of novels to overwhelm her sense of discipline and propriety—to her diary, she repudiated novel-reading as "stirring her emotions," lamenting that it had "got her into scrapes," that is, an affair with Marianna Belcombe's sister. But she obviously savored being bad, lacerating herself (figuratively) for delicious, wicked, indulgences.

The Romantic tradition was most important to Anne in allowing her to create a sense of self that could begin to reconcile her ethical and sexual concerns. The Romantics' strength of character came not from their self-control but from the uncontainable force of their passions. While the eighteenth century could accept the duplicity of self as part of the masquerade, the Romantic diarists wanted to strip down to the "essential" inner core that had to be hidden from the world.[72] Anne Lister wrote to her friend Sibella Maclean that "I rarely meet with those who interest me, who have the charm that brings me back to that disguised, and hidden nature, that suits not with the world."[73]

Rousseau was key for the Romantic notion of the hidden inner self defined by passionate, forbidden desires, very suited to the production of lesbian identity. Anne Lister quoted in her diaries the beginning of Rousseau's *Confessions,* in which he declares "I know the feelings of my heart. . . . I am not made like any of those I have seen. I venture to believe that I am not made like any of those who are in existence. Whether Nature had acted rightly or wrongly in destroying the mould in which she cast me, can only be decided after I have been read."

Rousseau defined his singular nature through confessing his adventures in masturbation, masochism, unhappy love affairs, and describing himself as "so effeminate but yet indomitable."[74] Yet Anne, like Mary Wollstonecraft, had to read Rousseau against the grain, emulating the way he used sexual frankness and androgyny to create a unique notion of the self, but rejecting his rigid attitudes toward women and homosexuality.[75] As Charles Taylor points out, Rousseau rejected the notion of original sin. Instead, "the first impulse of nature is always right," and it is "social opinion" that is "perverted." The Romantic self, therefore, allowed the transgression of social norms, and indeed, the quest of originality and uniqueness impelled such nonconformity.[76]

Byron, as Castle observes, was another key Romantic figure whose libertinism may have inspired Anne.[77] At the same time, the fact that Byron masked his homoerotic desires also meant that Anne had to read him with perspicacity and imagination, inspiring her to emulate both his romantic heroism and his duplicity. Anne publicly denounced Byron's poem *Don Juan* as indecent; in private she loved his verses and mourned his death bitterly.[78] His theme of forbidden love may have appealed to her, the "unhallowed bliss," "The smile none else might understand."[79] Byron's romantic orientalism also hinted at transgressive sexuality. In an incident of his most famous poem, for instance, the aggressively heterosexual Don Juan is disguised as a woman and sold as a slave girl to a Sultan's harem, where concubines vie for "her" sexual attentions.[80] Similarly, Anne loved the humid sentimentality of Thomas Moore's poem "Lallah Rookh," which was perfumed with the orientalist sensuality of slave girls chasing each other "Too eloquently like love's pursuit."[81]

Romantic texts allowed Anne to convey lesbian passion. For instance, Anne gave Miss Browne, a "sweet interesting creature" who lived in the neighborhood, a copy of Byron's poem "Cornelian" as a veiled token of her feelings.[82] This poem was about a poor young man who gave a cornelian ring to the poet, a gentleman, as a token of his affection. Although the ring was not a precious gem, the poet valued it above all else; and Anne seemed to have understood that the poem referred to a love affair, not just a friendship.[83] At the same time, the poem conveyed Anne's understanding that Miss Browne was not genteel enough to become Anne's romantic partner. On her part, Miss Browne seems to have felt repelled by Anne's advances and married a local young man. While Anne had kissed Miss Browne, she never openly expressed her intentions but safely veiled them through her romantic allusions.

Anne's use of Byron's poem to communicate romantic interest obliquely is a good example of the way in which she, to use de Lauretis's terms, "rearticulated" cultural materials through her "self-representation—in speech, gesture, costume, body stance and so on."[84] In fact, Anne developed her lesbian sense of self most explicitly in discussions with other women. Yet Anne had to convey her intentions, and her knowledge, in coded terms that enabled her to control interactions with potential friends and lovers. Concealment, of course, was necessary, to survive as a lesbian in a hostile world.[85] However, Anne was also a manipulative person who wanted to control every situation, and often played off lovers against each other, reading aloud one lover's letter to her to another, and deceiving friends about her lesbian nature.[86] Anne typically at first denied her lesbian inclinations and then revealed and justified her feelings only when the other woman had made herself vulnerable. Once she had, Anne justified lesbianism as "natural."

Anne used classical texts to inquire more openly about lesbian sexual knowledge. For instance, she asked Miss Pickford, another learned lady she suspected of being a lesbian, if she had read the Sixth Satire of Juvenal, and Miss Pickford's positive answer confirmed her hunch.[87] But Anne was not attracted to Miss Pickford, despite her classical erudition, for Anne was not "an admirer of learned ladies . . . [who are] not the sweet, interesting creatures that I love."[88] When Miss Pickford discussed her own relationship with a Miss Threlfall, Anne said she did not "censure" them, since their feelings were guided by nature and "mutual affection," rather than artificially learned. For herself, she told Miss Pickford, "I am taught by books, you by nature. I am very warm in friendship, perhaps few or none more so. My manners might mislead you but I don't, in reality, go beyond the utmost verge of friendship."[89] Anne was quite aware that she was deliberately misleading Miss Pickford about her own nature: she wrote, "The success of my deceit almost smote me."[90] A few months later, when the love of her life, Marianna Lawton, felt horrified at the "unnatural" nature of their connection, Anne "observed upon my conduct & feelings being surely natural to me inasmuch as they were not taught, not fictitious but instinctive."[91]

A few years later, in France, Anne again used learning to hint a little more frankly at her predilections. Discussing various Latin poets with a Madame Galvani, she began by observing how indecent they were—ostensibly to disapprove of them—but in actuality to convey her knowledge of sexuality. Observing Anne flirting with Mrs. Barlow, her fellow lodger Miss Mack asked her "Etes-vous Achilles?" Clearly, she referred here to the story of Achilles being dressed as a girl and his later passionate love for Patroclus.[92] Only a woman with classical learning would understand this as a coded reference to homosexuality. In response, Anne "laughed and said she made me blush." Her future mistress Mrs. Barlow then asked her if she had heard of the rumors of Marie Antoinette's lesbian affairs, but Anne typically denied that women could do such things. In similar language as she used with Miss Pickford, Anne declared that "she went to the utmost extent of friendship but that was enough." Clearly, Anne had to sound out another woman before she believed she could safely reveal her desires; she wanted other women to incriminate themselves first by stating their own knowledge. Once she had started to make love with Mrs. Barlow, she declared again that her attraction to women was "all nature," in words reminiscent of her earlier conversation with Marianna.[93]

Anne Lister's notion of her "nature" combined classical sexual knowledge with the romantic sense of inner passions whose truth derived from their transgression of society's laws. For her, her sexual desires for other women were natural and, therefore, justifiable. Furthermore, they composed her "nature" as an individual.

Anne also tried to explain her nature as biological. In Paris, she began to study anatomy in an effort to discern her own nature, attending dissections and discovering the similarities between male and female embryos. Finding no external signs of her own peculiar nature, as she thought of it, she "alluded to there being an internal correspondence or likeness of some of the male or female organs of generation." She derived this theory from reading the popular sex manual, *Aristotle's Masterpiece,* which depicted the female genitals as like the male's turned outside-in—that is, the penis analogous to the vagina, and the testicles resembling the ovaries.[94] She did not, therefore, regard herself as a man trapped in a woman's body or a woman with biologically masculine attributes; rather, she seemed to think that since males and females were not that physically different, she could express her unique nature as she wished.

She seems to have been fascinated with androgynous beings, such as learned, masculine women of antiquity, or effeminate, even homosexual men. In her notes on readings, she quoted excerpts on Pope Joan, hermaphrodites, and eunuchs.[95] Some further clues to Anne's androgyny can be found in her borrowings from Ovid's *Metamorphoses.* For instance, when she told Miss Pickford stories from Ovid, another way in which she hinted at knowledge of lesbianism, Anne chose to mention the tale of Tiresias.[96] Observing the moon one evening, she "smiled and said the moon had tried both sexes, like old Tiresias, but that one could not make such an observation to everyone."[97] Tiresias was a seer who had been transformed from a man to a woman for seven years after striking two mating snakes. Having experienced life and love as both a man and woman, he agreed with the god Jove that women "received more pleasure out of love."[98] By choosing to cite Tiresias, Lister selectively read the messages of Ovid. She enjoyed the thought of switching from masculinity to femininity but implied that women have more pleasure than men. Instead of regarding her love as unnatural and doomed, she read in Ovid a sense of human nature as fluid, as constantly metamorphizing. Significantly, she did not cite the only tale in his *Metamorphoses* in which a woman turned into a man to love another woman. In this story, Iphis, a woman who is brought up as a boy, becomes betrothed to her female beloved. In agony at her feelings, which she knows to be unnatural, for among animals "a female never fires a female's love," she prays to the goddess Isis for help, who obliges by turning her into a male on her wedding night.[99] Anne did not want to turn into a male; she simply took male privileges.

Ovid also provided Anne with other myths of metamorphosis that could help her conceptualize her relationships. Anne referred to Miss Browne as "Kallista" in her diaries; *Kallista* is Greek for "most beautiful" but also refers to the myth, retold by Ovid, of the nymph Callisto, beloved of Diana, chaste leader of the hunt who rejected male company.[100] When Callisto rests while hunting, Jove comes upon her, and in order to seduce her, disguises himself as Diana. When Callisto becomes pregnant, Diana turns her into a bear in disgust and anger at her betrayal.[101] If Miss Browne was Callisto, who did Anne see herself as: Jove or Diana, or one in the disguise of the other? As Jove, Anne could inflame her fantasies of "taking" lower-class young women in a masculine guise. As Diana, Anne could imagine a comradeship of free, virginal young women hunting and loving in the forest and identify with her rage when Jove raped Callisto, just as she resented the marriages of the young women she admired.

This duality between female companionship and masculine sexual predation permeated Anne's relationship with women. As she wrote to her friend Sibella Maclean, she sought "the rational union of two amiable persons . . . a mind in unison with my own."[102] She continuously yearned for a true companion, a love who would be only hers.[103] The model, a sexual version of passionate friendship, was flexible in terms of gender. She referred to her first lover from boarding school days as her "husband," and Isabella Norcliffe, the second significant woman in her life, seems to have been rather gruff and masculine.[104] In contrast, her great love, Marianna Lawton (née Belcombe), referred to her as Fred. After she left boarding school, Anne was able, with a private tutor, to pursue the "masculine" tasks of classical learning and to develop a personal style flavored by masculinity. She liked to stride about the Yorkshire moors, her short hair tousled by the wind, and decided to wear all black bodices, which resembled men's coats, to save money (leaving more for books) and also to conceal her less than voluptuous figure.[105] Yet Marianna, who had married a man for money, felt ashamed at her sexual relationship with the increasingly masculine Anne. In 1820, Marianna was already uneasy about Anne's flirtatious ways: in one session of pillowtalk, she "owned that [Anne's manners] were not masculine but such as my form, voice, & style of conversation, such a peculiar flattery & attraction did I shew, that if this sort of thing was not carried off by my talents & cleverness, I should be disgusting."[106] Anne managed to mollify Marianna's anxieties that night with a "good kiss," but a later incident marred their relationship forever. In 1823, Anne strode across the moors for miles to meet Marianna as she came from York, leaping over "three steps" to bound into the coach with wild hair and sweaty clothes. Marianna recoiled with horror, and Anne felt irrevocably hurt.[107]

Frustrated with her relationship with Marianna, Anne turned her masculine persona from a stigma into a way of appropriating masculine sexual privilege for herself, pursuing mistresses as well as potential "wives." Anne's masculinity signaled to lovers that a woman could sexually desire other women, in a way both threatening and alluring. Flirting with Marianna's sisters, she wrote, "my manners are certainly peculiar, not all masculine but rather softly gentleman-like. I know how to please girls."[108] Anne here differentiated among different kinds of masculinity, choosing an upper-class manner rather than a crudely lower-class approach. Mrs. Kelly (her former inamorata Miss Browne) refuted people who thought Anne should wear a bonnet. "She contended I should not, and said my whole style of dress suited myself and my manner & was consistent & becoming to me. I was more masculine, she said, She meant in understanding."[109] In Paris, some of her new acquaintances even wondered if she were a man, but Mrs. Barlow "herself thought I wished to imitate the manners of a gentleman but now she knows me better, it was not put on."[110] Back in Yorkshire, Anne, frustrated in her relationship with Marianna, began an avid flirtation with Marianna's sister Mrs. Harriet Milne, who was notorious for her heterosexual affairs. After church one day, Mrs. Milne responded to Anne's "marked attention" by admitting "she liked me in my greatcoat and hat," flushing as she spoke. It is possible that Mrs. Milne could conceive of an affair with Anne in libertine terms, another thrill much like a heterosexual affair. She wrote to Anne, "Is it possible that I can have feelings which have never yet been roused to action? Affections that were dormant until you called them forth?" Although Mrs. Milne may be referring to experiencing desire for a woman for the first time, it is more likely she meant that although she had known Anne for years, she had never before felt sexually attracted to her.[111]

On Anne's part, Mrs. Milne's letter made her think, "Tis well I have not a penis. I might never have been continent."[112] Anne also sometimes imagined sexual desire herself in masculine, phallic terms. At one point, she wrote, "All this work and ordering and exercise seem to excite my manly feelings. I saw a pretty girl go up the lane and desire rather came over me."[113] Noting a fantasy of taking a young woman of her acquaintance into a shed and being "connected" with her (having sex) she recounts her "foolish fancying" "supposing myself in men's clothes and having a penis, tho' nothing more."[114] It's quite important that she says, "Tho' nothing more." The phallus was a sign of her desire *for* a woman, rather than of her desire to *be* a man. As de Lauretis observes, "masculinity alone carries a strong connotation of sexual desire for the female body." When a woman imagines having a phallus, the phallus becomes a "fetish," or a signifier, for what she is normally denied: the female body.[115] For Lister, therefore, imagining having a phallus was a way of representing her desire for a woman (and for male privilege) in a culture that gave her almost no other ways of representing a *sexual* lesbian desire.

While she fantasized about having a penis, in lovemaking she does not seem to have used a dildo. To Mrs. Barlow, she repudiated "Sapphic" love as "artifice," by which she seems to have meant the use of a dildo.[116] Of course, she may have been lying, and she was certainly fascinated by such practices.[117] Yet Anne preferred the active role in lovemaking. When Mrs. Barlow felt inside Anne's bosom, Anne "let her do it, observing I should hope to do the same," but added that "I do what I like but never permit them to do so." She also reacted negatively when Mrs. Barlow tried to touch her "queer" (genitals) because it was "womanizing me too much."[118] However, it is interesting that Mrs. Barlow expected to be able to touch Anne, perhaps having experienced or desiring more reciprocal lovemaking. Anne certainly "received" as well as "gave" many orgasms in her other relationships. Yet Anne preferred Marianna because Marianna did not "see her as a woman too much," not only sexually but in terms of observing the intimate details of her life such as menstruation. Marianna knew how to "manage" Anne's temper, which was quite difficult; Anne was also "sensitive" to "anything that reminded me of my petticoats."[119]

This sensitivity in part derived from the fact that Anne's petticoats prevented her from her goal: marrying Marianna openly. Her phallic obsession should be seen in the context of the privilege maleness gave one in her society. For instance, Mrs. Barlow and she carried on protracted negotiations about the nature of their sexual relationship, which were often put in phallic terms. As Anne recorded in her diary, when she made advances, Mrs. Barlow "began joking, saying I had nothing to give; meaning I had no penis." But she went on to make clear that the male organ was not the issue, for she "then declared she was the last to care for my having one. If I only wore breeches it would be enough." Mrs. Barlow really wanted Anne to be like a husband to her, to support her and acknowledge her. "But if, in fact, I would really claim her as my own she would be satisfied." Anne responded that "I often felt the want of breeches—the want of being a proper protector to her."[120] Clearly, the breeches—a phallic symbol—symbolized the male social role of being able to marry a woman, to protect her, and to support her.

Did Anne ever imagine passing as a man? Indeed, a number of women of her time lived as men, including one intellectual, Mary Diana Dods, who passed as another woman's husband.[121] Miss Pickford also enjoyed flirting with young women when she passed as a captain.[122] Yet passing as a man would have meant that Anne would give up her respectable position as an heiress, and with that, any possibility of an independent livelihood. Furthermore, Anne never declared that she felt like a man trapped in a woman's body. She enjoyed the company of women too much to pass as a man. Her negotiations with Mrs. Barlow are quite revealing on this subject. Mrs. Barlow lamented they could not marry, sighing, "It would have been better had you been brought up as your father's son," implying they could then marry. But Anne replied, "No, you mistake me. It would not have done at all. I could not have married & should have been shut out from ladies' society. I could not have been with you as I am."[123]

To use Butler's notion of "performativity," Anne Lister's combination of femininity and masculinity undermined and threatened conventional gender dichotomies during a period of great anxiety about the blurring of boundaries between the genders. During the era of the Napoleonic Wars, ballads celebrated female sailors while caricaturists mocked dandies who wore stays.[124] While public awareness of sodomy and the subculture of effeminate male homosexuals was high at this time (certainly reaching Anne), the linkage of lesbianism and female cross-dressing was much more occluded. Female sailors and soldiers were generally presented as heterosexual, donning male garb only to search for their lovers. To be sure, tales and supposed autobiographies of cross-dressing women sometimes presented them as flirting with young girls who mistook them for men, and occasional "female husband" cases appeared in the newspapers and ballad literature.[125] Cross-dressing actresses such as Madame Vestris, who performed in York before at least one of Anne's friends, were openly thought to allure women as they performed in breeches roles. A poem about Madame Vestris proclaimed, "Her very hair and style would corrupt with a smile—/ Let a virgin resist if she can." These accounts both acknowledged that a woman could attract another woman sexually and evaded the possibility of lesbianism; first, they could only conceive of a woman attracting another woman if she were passing as a man, and second, they denied that this attraction could be fulfilled without a penis. The poem about Madame Vestris goes on to undercut the possibility of this lesbian allure: "Her ambrosial kisses seem heavenly blisses— / What a pity she is not a man."[126] Similarly, an 1816 caricature entitled "My Brother's Breeches—or not quite the thing" portrayed a young woman wearing breeches, telling her friend, "There Maria I think I make as good a Man as my Brother." Maria retorts, "No indeed Cousin! I should think not *Quite*."[127]

Anne's androgynous appearance—she was obviously a woman in skirts, yet she walked like a man—threatened contemporaries because she did not completely cross-dress but still took male freedoms. While for Anne, the lack of a penis symbolized her lack of social power, her very success with women also undercut the assumption that a penis was necessary at all. As Butler argues, when a lesbian "has" a phallus she exposes the "phantasmatic status" of the seemingly natural link between maleness and power and exploits the eroticism of a phallus that does not need to be attached to a man, although at the same time she also signifies the phallus as a traditional masculine symbol.[128] Perhaps this is why men reacted to Anne with such hostility. For instance, when Anne was walking in her own neighborhood, a male passerby asked, "Does your cock stand?"[129] This insult hinted that even if she was a masculine woman, she did not have the real signifier of masculinity. Despite Anne's notoriously masculine appearance, she was often sexually harassed when walking in her neighborhood.[130]

Rumors spread in York about her seductive ways: a Mr. Lally had apparently said, "He would as soon turn a man loose in his house as me." He also joked that Anne's relationship with Isabella Norcliffe failed because "two Jacks" could not go together.[131] In the neighborhood, she was known as "Gentleman Jack," an epithet which may have evoked "Jack Whore," a term for a "large masculine overgrown wench."[132] While Donoghue and Trumbach find several references to "Tommies" as an epithet for masculine lesbians, this usage does not appear in the Anne Lister materials, and the only contemporaneous reference I have found is that the male habitues of a gay pub scornfully referred to their wives as "tommies."[133] "Jack Whore" probably did not have lesbian connotations; "masculine" women were often referred to in newspapers of the time but without any hint that they desired women.[134] However, Anne's masculine appearance seems to have confused and enraged passers-by. As Marianna and she walked through the fields, a countryman asked them if they were man and wife.[135] Waiting for a carriage in York, "several prostitutes . . . would have it that I was a man & one of them gave me a familiar knock on the left breast and would have persisted in following me" but for the manservant.[136] It is more likely that English prostitutes would think that Anne was a hermaphrodite than that they would have a word for lesbian, according to examples I have found in contemporary popular literature.[137]

Masculinity, of course, had many different residual meanings during this period and was often contested. It was not just about sexuality, but also connoted economic and political power. The first three decades of the nineteenth century were a time when rakish aristocratic libertinism was challenged by middle-class respectability.[138] Anne often emulated the first ideal, especially during the 1820s when she embarked on foreign adventures of seduction; but she also knew the real foundation of aristocratic power—landowning—remained, and she wanted access to that power. Despite the 1832 Reform Act, which gave the vote to middle-class men, as Anne knew, landowners still controlled their tenants' votes. In her diary, she secretly leaned toward supporting the Reform Bill to grant middle-class men the suffrage. Although, with typical duplicity, she denounced the Reform Act publicly; she realized that with Halifax's new members of Parliament she could exercise great power as a landowner, and openly pressured her tenants to vote Tory.[139] Since she became a landowner, even her neighbors, who may have expressed hostility toward her masculinity, had to acknowledge her economic and political power.

Yet Anne also became frustrated by the contradiction between her status as the proprietor of Shibden Hall and her lack of political power as a woman. Although she ridiculed the idea of female suffrage at the time of Peterloo in 1819, she started thinking differently during the Reform Act debates of 1831–32. Confiding to her diary that she believed ladies ought to be admitted to the new Literary and Philosophical Society of Halifax (as long as they did not wear large bonnets!) led her to "my old thought and wish for ladies under certain restrictions to be restored to certain political rights, voting for members. . . . Why should [civil and political rights] be withheld from any persons of sufficient property interest in the state and education to be fairly presumed to know how to make a good use of it."[140]

In the 1830s Anne also devoted more energy to finding a respectable romantic partnership with a social equal commensurate with her social status, rather than rakishly pursuing mistresses in Paris. She found Miss Anne Walker, a neighboring heiress, but it was not a happy romantic relationship. Miss Walker felt quite uneasy about their sexual interactions, perhaps regarding it as sinful as had Marianna. To reassure her, Anne wished to sanctify it as a marriage by taking the sacraments together—and by establishing a partnership as equals to validate their sexual relationship. However, she continued her duplicity with Anne Walker. Although occasionally she fancied herself in love with her, she also knew she was playing a romantic part in order to seduce her and became impatient with Anne Walker's evasive coyness. To her journal, she wrote, "She likes me but my affections are not so fearfully and irretrievably hers as she thinks and I shall manage well enough."[141] She did not want a wife in Anne Walker, or a mistress, but an equal partner who could match her money, who could lobby politically her tenants, and who could travel with her. Anne Walker carried out these activities with her, despite a spoiled, melancholy temperament, but Anne never seemed truly in love with her. And she yearned for adventure beyond Yorkshire. Eventually, the two Annes traveled all over Europe and finally to Russia, but Anne Lister died of a fever in a remote area of the Caucasus and Miss Walker went insane upon her return.[142]

What does Anne Lister's story tell us about the prevalence of the Sapphic role in early-nineteenth-century England? Anne Lister's readings and diaries give little evidence that she stepped into a preexisting Sapphic role. Despite occasional references in pamphlets or correspondence, the Sapphic role was not a consistent, well-known cultural motif, unlike the "molly" or sodomite. Rather, it was something to be hidden, to be hinted at, barely imaginable. Instead, Anne, and probably others such as Miss Pickford, had to invent and reinvent their own lesbian identity. Anne did not find hers in the libertine world of the eighteenth-century Sapphic role; rather, she created her lesbian self out of romanticism and classical knowledge.

By writing a secret diary, and behaving as duplicitously as she often did, the self Anne Lister created was not unified but deliberately compartmentalized and contradictory. Anne also reinflected her gendered persona over time. As a young woman, she found that the model of passionate friendship was inadequate to express her sexual feelings and actions and unrealistic in an era when her lovers had to marry for money. Masculinity signaled for her the social power and sexual desire for women she sought, imagining herself as a libertine rake with a wife and a mistress. But she did not want to be a man, only to enjoy male privilege, and simply took the freedoms she desired when wealth enabled her to do so.

Anne Lister did not become part of a lesbian subculture, only a fragile network of lovers, ex-lovers, and friends. The fact that Anne seduced so many women reveals how much lesbian potential lurked among the unhappy wives and proud spinsters of middle- and upper-class Yorkshire. There may have been many other women whose lesbian relationships have gone unrecorded. At the same time, seducing such women required careful, protracted campaigns in which Anne had to explain and justify her lesbian nature. And Anne Lister was not able to create a lesbian network, let alone a subculture, because of her chronic concealment, and duplicity tangled her love relationships into webs of deceit and competition. Romanticism justified her lesbianism as part of her nature, but its focus on the unique individual also hampered her ability to support other lesbians. Meeting the masculine and learned Miss Pickford helped Anne realize that there were other women such as herself in the world, but her scornful treatment of her friend prevented them from developing more solidarity.

While some of this behavior was due to her manipulative and controlling personality, it was also necessary camouflage. As Anne strode about the moors around her home and seduced the women of her social circle, her acquaintances and neighbors had to devise epithets to describe this incongruous, proud woman. Anne Lister's case therefore impels us to reassess our theoretical notions of the creation of a sexual self. Anne Lister did not step into a Sapphic role or assume a stigma; instead, she invented her own fragmented lesbian identity and confused the categories of masculinity and femininity.

NOTES

1. Helena Whitbread, ed., *I Know My Own Heart: The Diaries of Anne Lister, 1791–1840* (London, 1988), p. 145.

2. For a pioneering exploration of this theme, see Leila Rupp, "Imagine My Surprise: Women's Relationships in Historical Perspective," *Frontiers* 5 (1980): 61–70.

3. Lilian Faderman, *Surpassing the Love of Men* (New York, 1981); and *Scotch Verdict* (New York, 1983), p. 281.

4. Michel Foucault, *The History of Sexuality: An Introduction,* vol. 1 of *The History of Sexuality,* trans. Robert Hurley (New York, 1978).

5. Carroll Smith-Rosenberg, *Disorderly Conduct: Visions of Gender in Victorian America* (New York, 1985), p. 265.

6. Jennifer Terry, "Theorizing Deviant Historiography," *differences* 5 (1991): 55–74.

7. As in Joan Scott, "Experience," in *Feminists Theorize the Political,* ed. Judith Butler and Joan W. Scott (New York, 1992), p. 34. To be sure, Scott acknowledges agency, but concentrates on the discursive construction of the subject. See also Judith Butler, *Bodies That Matter: On the Discursive Limits of "Sex"* (New York, 1993), pp. 6–8.

8. For instance, see Randolph Trumbach, "London's Sodomites: Homosexual Behavior and Western Culture in the Eighteenth Century," *Journal of Social History* 11 (1977): 1–33, "Sodomitical Subcultures, Sodomitical Roles, and the Gender Revolution of the Eighteenth Century: The Recent Historiography," *Eighteenth-Century Life* 9 (1985): 109–21, and "Sex, Gender, and Sexual Identity in Modern Culture: Male Sodomy and Female Prostitution in Enlightenment London," *Journal of the History of Sexuality* 2 (1991): 186–203; George Chauncey, *Gay New York* (New York, 1995); Theo van der Meer, "Sodomy and the Pursuit of a Third Sex in the Early Modern Period," in *Third Sex, Third Gender: Beyond Sexual Dimorphism in Culture and History,* ed. Gilbert Herdt (New York, 1994), pp. 137–88; and Gert Hekma, "'A Female Soul in a Male Body': Sexual Inversion as Gender Inversion in Nineteenth-Century Sexology," in *Third Sex, Third Gender,* ed. Herdt, pp. 189–240.

9. Martha Vicinus, "'They Wonder to Which Sex I Belong': The Historical Roots of the Modern Lesbian Identity," *Feminist Studies* 18 (1992): 481; Terry Castle, *The Apparitional Lesbian* (New York, 1993), p. 93; Randolph Trumbach, "The Origins and Development of the Modern Lesbian Role in the Western Gender System: Northwestern Europe and the United States, 1750–1990," *Historical Reflections/Reflexions Historiques* 20 (1994): 289; Lisa Moore, "'Something More Still Tender Still than Friendship': Romantic Friendship in Early Nineteenth-Century England," *Feminist Studies* 18 (1992): 511.

10. Emma Donoghue, *Passions between Women: British Lesbian Culture, 1668–1801* (London, 1993); see also Randolph Trumbach, "London's Sapphists: From Three Sexes to Four Genders in the Making of Modern Culture," in *Body Guards: The Cultural Politics of Gender Ambiguity,* ed. Julia Epstein and Kristina Straub (New York, 1991), pp. 112–41—a revised version can be found in *Third Sex, Third Gender,* ed. Herdt, pp. 111–36, 518–28. For an earlier example, see Patricia Crawford and Sara Mendelson, "Sexual Identities in Early Modern England: The Marriage of Two Women in 1680," *Gender and History* 7 (1995): 362–77.

11. For a recent discussion, see Edward O. Laumann and John H. Gagnon, "A Sociological Perspective on Sexual Action," in *Conceiving Sexuality: Approaches to Sex Research in a Postmodern World,* ed. Richard G. Parker and John H. Gagnon (New York, 1995), pp. 183–214.

12. Erving Goffman, *Stigma* (New York, 1986); Ken Plummer, *Sexual Stigma* (London, 1973).

13. Van der Meer, "Sodomy and the Pursuit of a Third Sex in the Early Modern Period," p. 200.

14. Emma Donoghue and Randolph Trumbach suggest that we simply have not found such evidence because we have not been looking in the right way. That is possible, but in the course of extensive research on other projects into popular literature, prostitution, cross-dressing, police court records, newspapers, and trials in the late eighteenth and early nineteenth centuries in London, Glasgow, Yorkshire, and Manchester I actively looked for such evidence and found none. It is possible that lesbian networks or subcultures did not exist in England in the way they existed in France and Amsterdam. I hope further research proves me wrong!

Such subcultures existed in Paris among dancers, actresses, and prostitutes, as Michael Ryan, a doctor, noted in his *Prostitution in London* (London, 1839), pp. 56, 179. Ryan said he had seen no evidence of such women in London. For Paris, see D. A. Coward, "Attitudes to Homosexuality in Eighteenth Century France," *Journal of European Studies* 10 (1980): 246–47; Marie-Jo Bonnet, *Un choix sans equivoque: Recherches historiques sur les relations amoureuses entre les femmes, XVIe–XXe siècle* (Paris, 1981), p. 65. For Amsterdam, see Theo van der Meer, "Tribades on Trial: Female Same-Sex Offenders in Late Eighteenth-Century Amsterdam," in *Forbidden History: The State, Society, and the Regulation of Sexuality in Modern Europe,* ed. John C. Fout (Chicago, 1992), pp. 189–210.

15. For a discussion of the "incoherence" of binary oppositions in terms of the development of the identity "homosexual," but also how gay people have developed a sense of identity, see Eve Kosofsky Sedgwick, *Epistemology of the Closet* (Berkeley, 1990), p. 9.

16. Butler, *Bodies That Matter*, p. 228.

17. Jeffrey Weeks, "History, Desire, and Identities," in *Conceiving Sexuality*, ed. Parker and Gagnon, p. 38. For further discussions of the self, see Steve Pile and Nigel Thrift, eds., *Mapping the Subject: Geographies of Cultural Transformation* (New York, 1995), pp. 5–35; and Charles Taylor, *Sources of the Self* (Cambridge, Mass., 1989), p. 289. Foucault himself became more interested in the process of self-construction in the last years of his life. See Luther H. Martin et al., eds., *Technologies of the Self: A Seminar with Michel Foucault* (Amherst, Mass., 1988); and Michel Foucault, *The Care of the Self*, vol. 3 of *The History of Sexuality*, trans. Robert Hurley (New York, 1986).

18. For a similar discussion of a materialist approach to working-class autobiographies, see Regenia Gagnier, *Subjectivities: A History of Self-Representation in Britain, 1832–1920* (Oxford, 1991), p. 7.

19. For a study of diaries in general, see Robert A. Fothergill, *Private Chronicles: A Study of English Diaries* (London, 1974), p. 30.

20. Jill Liddington, "Anne Lister of Shibden Hall, Halifax (1791–1840): Her Diaries and the Historians," *History Workshop Journal* 35 (1995): 61.

21. Ibid., p. 52.

22. Anne Lister Manuscript Diaries, July 21, 1820, SH/7/ML/E/4, Calderdale Archives, Halifax. Henceforth referred to as Manuscript Diaries.

23. Helena Whitbread, ed., *No Priest but Love: The Journals of Anne Lister, 1824–1828* (Otley, 1992), pp. 4–5, 204–6.

24. Manuscript Diaries, September 5, 1820.

25. Whitbread, ed., *I Know My Own Heart*, p. 212.

26. Leonore Davidoff and Catherine Hall, *Family Fortunes: Men and Women of the English Middle Class* (London, 1987), p. 208.

27. John O. Lyons, *The Invention of the Self: The Hinge of Consciousness in the Eighteenth Century* (Carbondale, 1978), p. 8.

28. Irving Howe, "The Self in Literature," in *Constructions of the Self*, ed. George Levine (New Brunswick, 1992), p. 249.

29. Felicity Nussbaum, *The Autobiographical Subject* (Baltimore, 1989), p. 25.

30. For *My Secret Life,* see Steven Marcus, *The Other Victorians* (New York, 1966), pp. 91–92; for Munby, Leonore Davidoff, "Class and Gender in Victorian Britain: Arthur J. Munby and Hannah Cullwick," *Feminist Studies* 5 (1979): 87–133.

31. Nussbaum, *Autobiographical Subject*, p. 36.

32. Ibid.; Patricia Meyer Spacks, *Imagining a Self* (Cambridge, Mass., 1976), p. 191.

33. Donoghue, *Passions between Women*, pp. 124, 150; Elizabeth Mavor, *The Ladies of Llangollen* (Harmondsworth, 1973).

34. Similarly, Anne's contemporaries and fellow Yorkshire residents Charlotte Brontë and Ellen Nussey wrote passionate letters to each other and yearned to live out their lives together, unmarried, in a little cottage. See Elaine Miller, "Through All Changes and Through All

Chances: The Relationship of Ellen Nussey and Charlotte Brontë," in *Not a Passing Phase: Reclaiming Lesbians in History*, ed. Lesbian History Group (London, 1989), p. 36.

35. See Marylynne Diggs, "Romantic Friends or 'A Different Race of Creatures': The Representation of Lesbian Pathology in Nineteenth-Century America," *Feminist Studies* 21 (1995): 317–40.

36. Whitbread, ed., *I Know My Own Heart*, p. 210.

37. Teresa de Lauretis, *The Practice of Love: Lesbian Sexuality and Perverse Desire* (Bloomington, 1994), p. 308.

38. For a theory of lesbian reading, see Jean Kennard, "Ourselves Behind Ourself: A Theory for Lesbian Readers," in *Gender and Reading*, ed. Elizabeth Flynn and Patrocinio Schweickart (Baltimore, 1986), pp. 63–77, quoted in Judith Roof, *A Lure of Knowledge: Lesbian Sexuality and Theory* (New York, 1991), p. 162.

39. Louis Crompton, *Byron and Greek Love* (Berkeley, 1985), pp. 89–98; Joan DeJean, *Fictions of Sappho, 1546–1937* (Chicago, 1989), p. 210; Linda Dowling, *Hellenism and Homosexuality in Victorian Oxford* (Ithaca, 1994).

40. Extracts from Readings, vol. 6, fol. 41 (1819), SH 7/ML/EX 1, Calderdale Archives, Halifax. Henceforth referred to as Extracts from Readings.

41. *The Poetical Works of Byron* (Boston, 1975), p. 88, lines 1–2. Christine Battersby, *Gender and Genius: Towards a Feminist Aesthetics* (Bloomington, 1989), pp. 13–14.

42. Richard Jenkyns, *The Victorians and Ancient* Greece (Cambridge, Mass., 1980), pp. 63–64, 169, 280–81.

43. Whitbread, ed., *No Priest but Love*, p. 20.

44. Eva Keuls, *The Reign of the Phallus: Sexual Politics in Ancient Athens* (Berkeley, 1993); Amy Richlin, *The Garden of Priapus: Sexuality and Aggression in Roman Humor* (New York, 1992).

45. Judith P. Hallett, "Female Homoeroticism and the Denial of Reality in Latin Literature," *Yale Journal of Criticism* 3 (1989): 209–27.

46. Extracts from Readings, vol. 6, fol. 33.

47. DeJean, "Fictions of Sappho," pp. 116–98.

48. Pierre Bayle, *Historical and Critical Dictionary*, 2nd ed., edited, revised, and corrected by Mr. Des Maizeaux (London, 1738), vol. 5, p. 44.

49. Manuscript Diaries, March 16, 1820.

50. D. H. Urquhart, *Commentaries on Classical Learning* (London, 1803), p. 332.

51. For instance, Donoghue, *Passions between Women*, notes that Mrs. Thrale was not able to detect the lesbian allusions in Juvenal, although she was looking for them (p. 267).

52. Juvenal, *The Sixteen Satires* (London, 1975), satire 6, lines 306 ff.

53. Extracts from Readings, vol. 6, fol. 33.

54. Martial, *Epigrammes*, translated into French prose by Michel de Marolles (Paris, 1655), bk. 1, no. 91.

55. Martial, bk. 7, no. 67, in J. P. Sullivan and Peter Whigham, *Epigrams of Martial Englished by Divers Hands* (Berkeley, 1977); the translator for no. 67 is George Augustus Sala.

56. Roof, *Lure of Knowledge*, pp. 162, 172.

57. For instance, feminist classicists have argued that other Roman authors, such as Propertius, might be read as providing more varied and vigorous images of women than usually available, even if their intent was sexist. As Barbara K. Gold notes, the feminist reader can try to hear "voices speaking against the text" ("But Ariadne Was Never There in the First Place: Finding the Female in Roman Poetry," in *Feminist Theory and the Classics,* ed. Nancy Sorkin Rabinowitz and Amy Richlin [New York, 1993], p. 89). See also Judith P. Hallett, "Feminist Theory, Historical Periods, Literary Canons, and the Study of Graeco-Roman Antiquity," in *Feminist Theory and the Classics*, ed. Rabinowitz and Richlin, p. 63.

58. Manuscript Diaries, July 21, 1820.

59. Fragment in Extracts from Readings, October 3, 1814, in code.

60. Michel Foucault, "Technologies of the Self," in *Technologies of the Self*, ed. Martin et al., pp. 27–48.

61. Lyons, *Invention of the Self*, p. 88.

62. Manuscript Diaries, July 21, 1820.

63. Extracts from Readings, vol. 4, fol. 103, 104, 138, and vol. 6, fol. 25 (1819). Also Manuscript Diaries, February 3, 1831. She read an article called "Phallic Worship" in *Modern Antiquities* vol. 5, p. 31, and seems to have read Richard Payne Knight's work on phallicism, the cross, and the Trinity. For Richard Payne Knight, see Randolph Trumbach, "Erotic Fantasy and Male Libertinism in Enlightenment England," in *The Invention of Pornography*, ed. Lynn Hunt (New York, 1993), pp. 279–80; and G. S. Rousseau, "The Sorrows of Priapus: Anticlericalism, Homosocial Desire, and Richard Payne Knight," in *Sexual Underworlds of the Enlightenment*, ed. G. S. Rousseau and Roy Porter (Chapel Hill, 1988), pp. 101–55.

64. Whitbread, ed., *I Know My Own Heart*, p. 281.

65. Whitbread, ed., *No Priest but Love*, p. 168.

66. Ibid., p. 156.

67. Ibid., p. 143.

68. Trumbach, "The Origins and Development of the Modern Lesbian Role in the Western Gender System," p. 292; and Whitbread, ed., *No Priest but Love*, p. 281.

69. Whitbread, ed., *No Priest but Love*, p. 49.

70. Of course, many other people of her class and time enjoyed Byron while trying to be very respectable (see Davidoff and Hall, *Family Fortunes*, p. 259).

71. Moore, " 'Something More Still Tender Still than Friendship,' " p. 512.

72. Lyons, *Invention of the Self*, p. 199; Fothergill, *Private Chronicles*, pp. 30, 151.

73. Muriel Green, ed., *Miss Lister of Shibden Hall: Selected Letters (1800–1840)* (n.p., 1992), p. 77.

74. *The Confessions of Jean-Jacques Rousseau* (New York, 1947), p. 3.

75. Similar to Barbara Taylor's discussion of how Rousseau inspired and angered Mary Wollstonecraft ("Mary Wollstonecraft and the Wild Wish of Early Feminism," *History Workshop Journal* 33 [1992]: 209).

76. Taylor, *Sources of the Self*, p. 357.

77. Castle, *Apparitional Lesbian*, p. 104.

78. Manuscript Diaries, July 25, 1820, also Whitbread, ed., *I Know My Own Heart*, p. 344.

79. Byron, "To Thyrza," quoted in Crompton, *Byron and Greek Love*, p. 178.

80. Susan J. Wolfson, " 'Their She Condition': Cross-Dressing and the Politics of Gender in *Don Juan*," *English Literary History* 54 (1987): 606.

81. Thomas Moore, *Lalla Rookh*, 8th ed. (London, 1818), p. 65.

82. Whitbread, ed., *I Know My Own Heart*, p. 78.

83. Crompton, *Byron and Greek Love*, pp. 98–102. Interestingly enough, Byron had tried to suppress this poem when Edlestone, his beloved, was arrested for homosexual acts. Anne therefore may have had a very rare copy.

84. De Lauretis, *Practice of Love*, p. 308.

85. For contemporary concealment, see David Bell and Gill Valentine, "The Sexed Self: Strategies of Performance, Sites of Resistance," in *Mapping the Subject*, ed. Pile and Thrift, p. 148.

86. Whitbread, ed., *No Priest but Love*, pp. 42, 53, 124, 165.

87. Liddington, "Anne Lister of Shibden Hall," p. 61.

88. Whitbread, ed., *I Know My Own Heart*, p. 237.

89. Ibid., p. 273.

90. Ibid., p. 281.

91. Ibid., p. 297.

92. Whitbread, ed., *No Priest but Love*, pp. 26, 29.

93. Ibid., p. 49.

94. Ibid., p. 49. For such theories, which were common medically until the eighteenth century and persisted after that in popular culture, see Thomas Laqueur, *Making Sex* (Cambridge, Mass., 1990).

95. Extracts from Readings, vol. 2, fol. 133.

96. Interestingly enough, "Michael Field" (Katherine Bradley and Edith Cooper, poets who lived, loved, and wrote together) also cited the tale of Tiresias in their oeuvre applying classical precedents to same-sex love (Chris White, "Poets and Lovers Evermore: The Poetry and Journals of Michael Field," in *Sexual Sameness: Textual Differences in Lesbian and Gay Writing*, ed. Joseph Bristow [New York, 1992], p. 30).

97. Whitbread, ed., *I Know My Own Heart*, pp. 235–36.

98. Ovid, *Metamorphoses*, trans. A. D. Melville (Oxford, 1986), pp. 60–61.

99. Ibid., p. 222.

100. Castle, *Apparitional Lesbian*, p. 104, also notes that Anne may be referring to this Callisto but does not develop the interpretation.

101. Ovid, *Metamorphoses*, pp. 36–40.

102. Green, ed., *Miss Lister of Shibden Hall*, p. 87.

103. Manuscript Diaries, July 21, 1820, and January 3, 1831.

104. Liddington, "Anne Lister of Shibden Hall," p. 62; Whitbread, ed., *No Priest but Love*, p. 127.

105. Whitbread, ed., *I Know My Own Heart*, pp. 1, 14, 167, 223.

106. Ibid., p. 116.

107. Ibid., p. 277.

108. Ibid., p. 136.

109. Ibid., p. 342.

110. Whitbread, ed., *No Priest but Love*, pp. 37, 198.

111. Ibid., p. 152.

112. Ibid., p. 153.

113. Whitbread, ed., *I Know My Own Heart*, p. 267.

114. Ibid., p. 151.

115. De Lauretis, *Practice of Love*, p. 228.

116. Whitbread, ed., *No Priest but Love*, p. 49.

117. Whitbread, ed., *I Know My Own Heart*, p. 291, and *No Priest but Love*, p. 32.

118. Whitbread, ed., *No Priest but Love*, p. 85.

119. Ibid., p. 173.

120. Ibid., p. 81.

121. Betty T. Bennett, *Mary Diana Dods: A Gentleman and a Scholar* (New York, 1991); for another intellectual woman who passed as a man, see the case of Theodora de Verdion, the daughter of a Berlin architect who passed in England as a man. She was often rumored to be a woman, but her eccentricity, swearing, and heavy drinking kept such rumors at bay. She died in 1802. See *Kirby's Wonderful and Eccentric Museum* (London, 1820), vol. 7, p. 48; J. T. Smith, *Antient [sic] Topography of London* (London, 1817), p. 20.

122. Whitbread, ed., *No Priest but Love*, p. 290.

123. Ibid., p. 36.

124. Judith Butler, *Gender Trouble: Feminism and the Subversion of Identity* (New York, 1990), p. 136. For discussion of gender images in the early nineteenth century, see my "Womanhood and Manhood in the Transition from Plebeian to Working Class Culture" (Ph.D. diss., Rutgers University, 1987), pp. 165–222. For examples, see *Tegg's Caricatures* (London, 1819), vol. 5, pp. 312, 323, 331–32.

125. For example, the story of Helen Oliver, a journeyman plasterer who seems to have gotten the idea for cross-dressing from a ploughman, actually a woman in disguise, who was thought to be her male lover. See "Helen Oliver," in Miscellaneous Collection of Broadsides, 1875, b. 30 (4), British Library; *London Times*, April 20, 1822. For flirtation, see "The Life and

Extraordinary Adventures of Mary Lacy, the Female Sailor," in C. D. Donald, *Collection of Broadsides* (Glasgow, 1890), Mitchell Library, Glasgow. For female husband, see Michael Ryan, *Medical Jurisprudence* (London, 1836), p. 227. For a general discussion and more examples, see Clark, "Womanhood and Manhood," pp. 196–213; Julie Wheelwright, *Amazons and Military Maids* (London, 1989), p. 59; Rudolf M. Dekker and Lotte C. van de Pol, *The Tradition of Female Transvestism in Early Modern Europe* (New York, 1989).

126. *Memoirs of the Life, Public and Private Adventures of Madame Vestris* (London, 1839), p. 54; see also C. E. Pearce, *Life of Madame Vestris* (London, 1923), p. 56.

127. M. Dorothy George, *Catalogue of Political and Personal Satires in the British Museum* (London, 1978), no. 12843.

128. Butler, *Bodies That Matter*, p. 89.

129. Whitbread, ed., *I Know My Own Heart*, p. 49.

130. Ibid., p. 113.

131. Whitbread, ed., *No Priest but Love*, p. 127.

132. *Dictionary of the Vulgar Tongue* (London, 1811; reprint, London, 1981).

133. Robert Holloway, *The Phoenix of Sodom, or the Vere Street Coterie* (London, 1813), pp. 10, 30.

134. For example, *Weekly Dispatch*, April 11, 1841, May 18, 1845; *Daily News*, July 12, 1846.

135. Whitbread, ed., *No Priest but Love*, p. 171.

136. Whitbread, ed., *I Know My Own Heart*, p. 65.

137. In 1811, a woman severely beat a male neighbor for supposing she was a "hermaphrodite" (*Morning Herald*, January 10, 1811); a violent, large, masculine woman with a low voice was supposed to be a "hermaphrodite" (*Weekly Dispatch*, March 27, 1831); in a no doubt apocryphal anecdote about Madame Vestris, which may nonetheless indicate popular attitudes, Madame Vestris and her sister Miss Bartolozzi "sallied out after dusk in man's apparel, and made love to the ladies," when a prostitute suspected their true sex and declared, "I'll find out whether you are Moffrydites or men" (*New Rambler's Magazine* 2 [c. 1830]: 112). See Donoghue, *Passions between Women*, pp. 25–57, for hermaphrodites.

138. Davidoff and Hall, *Family Fortunes*, p. 110.

139. Manuscript Diaries, March 5, 1831; Liddington, "Anne Lister of Shibden Hall," pp. 68–69.

140. Manuscript Diaries, February 27, 1831.

141. Ibid., November 12, 1832.

142. Whitbread, ed., *No Priest but Love*, p. 206; Manuscript Diaries, November 5, 1832, for her equivocal courtship.

RICHARD VON KRAFFT-EBING'S "STEP-CHILDREN OF NATURE"

Psychiatry and the Making of Homosexual Identity

HARRY OOSTERHUIS

> Although I fear to pester you, Sir, with my letter—after all, in the preface of your *Psychopathia sexualis*, you mention the "innumerable letters by such step-children of nature"—I still trustingly turn to you, hoping that a layman might report something to the scholar that is not entirely without interest: even the most inconspicuous thing may gain importance in the right place and may be worth the researcher's scrutiny.
>
> —Freiherr von R. to Richard von Krafft-Ebing, July 1900[1]

In 1900 a young nobleman, Von R., addressed himself in this manner to the renowned German-Austrian psychiatrist Richard von Krafft-Ebing (1840–1902), author of *Psychopathia sexualis* and one of the founders of scientific sexology. For the most part, Von R.'s letter is an elaborate introspection on his problematic sexuality. When he was ten years old, Von R. ascertained retrospectively, his "contrary sexual feeling" and "masochistic" impulses had already revealed themselves in his fantasies, reading habits, and games. The lust he experienced as a boy when he made a ceremony out of decapitating flowers was a clear symptom of his deep-seated proclivities. His urge to be humiliated by his male subordinates especially caused inward conflict. Torn between his irresistible sexual desire and his class prejudice, Von R. was weighed down by shame and guilt. He meticulously explored and evaluated every circumstance that might shed light on his anomaly: his particular way of acting and feeling, his childhood and puberty, his upbringing in an exclusively female environment, the fantasies and the moral conflicts that accompanied his self-abuse, his failure to copulate with a prostitute, his character and intellectual faculties, his state of health (he detected a slight "nervousness" in his behavior), and his family background, especially possible hereditary taints.

The way Von R. framed his autobiographical account is noteworthy. As if to underline its structure and to add an objective comment to his intimate confession, he took notes in the margins of the pages. The composition of his life story and his marginal notes are reminiscent of many handwritten case histories I found in the Krafft-Ebing archives.[2] After Krafft-Ebing's assistants had written down the patient's biography, symptoms, and anamnesis, Krafft-Ebing added the diagnosis and other remarks in the margins. Thus the individual case was likened to others, classified, and fitted into Krafft-Ebing's taxonomy. One of the leading clinically oriented psychiatrists of his time, he had a reputation for extensive case histories. Although he was influenced by the natural-scientific approach in psychiatry that sought to classify mental diseases on the basis of anatomical pathology, Krafft-Ebing focused not so much on the specific characteristics of a particular illness as on the detailed histories of individuals. In his *Lehrbuch der Psychiatrie auf klinischer Grundlage* (Textbook of Clinically Based Psychiatry) (1879–80), which was widely used by medical students, he laid down a standard for the taking of psychiatric case histories and listed the elements of what was characterized as the individual case approach. Next to the patient's name, age, occupation, dates of admission and consultation, there should be information about his or her ancestry, family medical and mental health history, childhood and puberty history, onset and development of mental disorders, and subjective condition: moods, imaginative powers, dreams, fantasies, perceptiveness, intellectual capacities, decisiveness, and moral awareness.

Much of Krafft-Ebing's work was descriptive and consisted primarily of case histories and sometimes autobiographies written by his patients. The contents and the form of Von R.'s own writing mirror the psychiatric model of the individual case description. Krafft-Ebing's *Psychopathia sexualis*, which contained many case reports and autobiographies, must have inspired Von R. to write his own case history and to diagnose himself. Using the language of psychiatry, his autobiography reflects medical explanations of sexuality. Offering his life story as grist for the interpretative mill, Von R. seems to have placed his fate into the hands of the psychiatrist and his confession appears to be typical of what Michel Foucault has designated as the medical construction of sexuality.[3] Foucault argues that the modern idea of sexuality was historically constituted by medical science, which delimited deviance. Before medical theories emerged that lumped together behavior, physical characteristics, and the emotional makeup of individuals, there was no entity that could be delineated as sexuality. Thus, by differentiating between the normal and the abnormal, and by stigmatizing sexual variance as sickly deviation, physicians, as exponents of an anonymous "biopower," were controlling free and easy pleasures of the body.

Although Foucault himself stressed that sexuality was shaped rather than repressed by the scientific will to know, several historians have associated the emergence of a science of sexuality with a deplorable medical colonization, replacing religious and judicial authority with a new form of medico-moral tyranny. Therefore, Krafft-Ebing's work has been damned as "an unmitigated disaster," and he has been blamed for "the confusion which continues to surround the subject of sexual variation today."[4] For the prophet of antipsychiatry, Thomas Szasz, it is clear that "Krafft-Ebing was not interested in liberating men and women from the shackles of sexual prejudice or the constraints of antisexual legislation. On the contrary, he was interested in supplanting the waning power of the church with the waxing power of medicine." Adding that "*Psychopathia sexualis* is full of falsehoods pretentiously presented as if they were the fruits of hard-won scientific discoveries," Szasz's opinion is typical of the way historians have viewed Krafft-Ebing's work from a presentist perspective.[5]

Contemporaries like Von R., however, experienced it in a different way. Reading *Psychopathia sexualis* had made him aware of the fact that:

> I am not the only "step-child of nature." . . . I would never have believed that my pride could convince me to make such confessions. Only your work has opened my eyes. It made the world and myself not appear in the gray light of disdain any longer, and, reassuring and rehabilitating, it inspired my confidence.[6]

For Von R., Krafft-Ebing's work was a revelation. Von R. was not the only one who made references to the salutary effects of *Psychopathia sexualis.* "A heavily suffering person turns to the benign and great help of your science," another man wrote. "It is incredibly hard for me to expose myself. And I can only do it to you, to you alone in the entire world, because I know from your book *Psychopathia sexualis* that I wouldn't be saying totally strange things."[7] Especially homosexuals who addressed themselves to Krafft-Ebing and sent him their autobiographies expressed themselves in a similar tone. "I read your essay in the *Zeitschrift für Psychiatrie* [Journal of Psychiatry]," a man reported to Krafft-Ebing in 1882.

> Through it, I and certainly thousands with me are revindicated in the eyes of every thinking and halfway honest man and I thank you warmly for it. You yourself probably know to what degree our subject is being frowned on, despised, and persecuted.[8]

Also typical was a man who made clear that recognizing himself in *Psychopathia sexualis* had brought him great relief:

> Your book *Psychopathia sexualis* brought me much comfort. It contains passages that I might have written myself; they seem to be unconsciously taken from my own life.—My heart has been considerably lightened, since I learned from your book of your benevolent interest in our disreputable class. It was the first time that I met someone who showed me that we are not entirely as

bad as we are usually portrayed. Anyway, I feel a great burden has been lifted from me.[9]

How should such expressions be qualified? Are these individuals, as the Foucaultian interpretation would have it, trapped in a medical discourse that constitutes not only power relations and social control of deviant sexualities, but also sexual subjects themselves? The radical implication of Foucault's reasoning is that before 1870 there did not exist "perverts" like homosexuals, fetishists, and masochists, nor their counterparts, "normal" heterosexuals. This contention might be defended, but the problem is that the conclusion has been drawn too readily that new sexual categories and identities were merely medical constructions. As far as the individuals who are labeled as "perverts" are concerned, they have mainly been presented as passive victims of a medical juggernaut, having no other choice than to conform to medical stereotypes.

The emphasis on medical labeling in the creation of "deviants," such as homosexuals, presents a social-deterministic model in which individuals are pawns of social forces with no will of their own. To explain how sexual "perversion" in general and homosexuality in particular were constructed,[10] it is necessary to enter the subjective world of individuals who read Krafft-Ebing's work and responded to it, and to take their intentions, purposes, and meanings seriously on their own terms. How was Krafft-Ebing's work read and used by contemporaries? Who were his patients and informants? What were their social and cultural backgrounds? How did they interpret medical theories, and how did they come into contact with psychiatrists? In what way did medical theories and individual experiences interact, and how did these interferences between scientific and autobiographical constructions of meaning develop?

MORAL OFFENDERS AND DEGENERATES

Although Richard Freiherr von Krafft-Ebing was one of the most prominent psychiatrists of his time in Central Europe and worked in numerous fields of psychiatry, he is remembered today as the author of *Psychopathia sexualis* and as one of the founding fathers of scientific sexology. The first edition of his much quoted book appeared in 1886, followed soon by several new and expanded editions—seventeen in German between 1886 and 1924—and by translations in several languages. Krafft-Ebing revised it several times, especially by adding new categories and case histories. By naming and classifying virtually all nonprocreative sexuality, he was one of the first to synthesize medical knowledge of what was then labeled "sexual perversion." Although in retrospect *Psychopathia sexualis* can be considered an important milestone in the development of what later became sexology, Krafft-Ebing probably did not intend to establish a new medical discipline. His interest in the broader aspects of sexual deviance emerged from experience in asylum psychiatry, which viewed disorders such as masturbation as symptoms of preexisting mental diseases, and he was even more influenced by the preoccupation of forensic medicine with criminal acts such as sodomy. Before the 1890s, his interest in sexual pathology was intrinsically linked to forensic psychiatry, an area in which he was a pioneer and leading expert.[11]

Psychopathia sexualis was therefore written for lawyers and doctors discussing sexual crimes in court. Krafft-Ebing's main point was that in many cases perversion was not a sin or a crime, but a disease—a common position of liberal physicians of the period from 1870 to 1900. "Deviant," nonprocreative sexual acts, traditionally considered immoral and criminal, increasingly came under psychiatric evaluation, as they were regarded not simply as sins and crimes, but as symptoms of an illness caused by natural laws. Since mental disease often diminished responsibility, Krafft-Ebing argued that most sex offenders should not be punished, but treated as patients suffering from mental diseases. Although perversion left reason intact, as a form of "moral insanity" it selectively damaged the moral faculties. Unable to control their strong, irresistible, sexual drives and obsessions, "perverts" could not be held personally responsible for their inclinations because their free will was impaired. Only those who possessed insight into their actions were responsible in a legal sense. Krafft-Ebing distinguished between immoral "perversity," on the one hand, and sickly "perversion" on the other, and he stressed that neither lawyers nor common sense, but only professional psychiatrists were qualified in court to distinguish mental illness. Judgment had to be geared toward a medical diagnosis. Although it was debated whether perversion was inborn or acquired, psychiatrists such as Krafft-Ebing shifted the focus from immoral and criminal acts, a temporary deviation of the norm, to a pathological condition.

In the second half of the nineteenth century, neuropathology and theories of degeneration played an important part in psychiatric explanations of mental illness in general and sexual disorders in particular. Krafft-Ebing was influenced by Charles Darwin (1809–1882) and especially by the French alienist Bénédict Auguste Morel (1809–1873). Morel focused on heredity as the underlying cause of mental diseases, and claimed that these got progressively worse over generations. Following in the wake of Morel, Krafft-Ebing believed that the extraordinary demands of modern civilization on the nervous system were responsible for a rise in mental disturbances, and that acquired disorders could be inherited from "tainted" relatives. Although he believed that perversion might be acquired through bad environmental agents, seduction, and corrupt habits such as masturbation, he increasingly stressed that many sexual disorders were inborn.

Krafft-Ebing's first systematic work on sexual pathology was published in 1877 in a leading German psychiatric journal. Following the dominant clinical-anatomical approach in psychiatry that situated mental disorders in the nervous system and particularly the brain, and adopting Morel's preoccupation with "pathological family," Krafft-Ebing supposed that degeneration was the underlying cause of inborn perversion. His initial classification distinguished between classes of sexual abnormalities that were of a quantitative and qualitative nature.

The first group comprised absence and pathological increase of the sexual drive, and sexual activity during an abnormal period, that is, childhood or old age. The second covered the perversions proper. As far as the last category was concerned, he discussed three subgroups: lust murder, necrophilia, and contrary sexual feeling.[12] Same-sex attraction, which was associated with an inverted gender identity, figured prominently in the last group, but that group also included various biological and psychological fusions of manliness and femininity that would gradually be reclassified in the twentieth century as radically separate phenomena, such as hermaphroditism, androgyny, and transvestitism.

Krafft-Ebing and other physicians such as Karl Westphal (1833–1890) (who published the first psychiatric study of contrary sexual feeling in 1869) were influenced by the writings of the Hannoverian lawyer, Karl Heinrich Ulrichs (1825–1895), who introduced the concept of "Uranism" in 1864.[13] In his dozen brochures (published 1864–79), Ulrichs advocated the decriminalization of the "vice against nature" on the grounds that "Uranism" was a natural phenomenon of "migration of the soul": a woman's soul in a man's body and vice versa. Ulrichs's and Krafft-Ebing's explanations of homosexuality as a form of inversion demonstrates how, in the nineteenth century, sexual attraction was not conceivable without a physical or psychological polarization and matching of male and female elements. Although Ulrichs argued that Urnings' love was natural because it consisted of an attraction between male and female elements, psychiatrists like Krafft-Ebing identified inversion with degeneration and its associated "inverse tendency" toward dedifferentiation.

Krafft-Ebing premised his initial theory of sexual pathology on a comparatively small number of generally severe cases, such as lust murder and necrophilia, often derived from criminal proceedings. New categories of perversion were created and underpinned more or less by systematically collecting and publishing new case histories. In the 1880s, Krafft-Ebing published several articles on contrary sexual feeling, containing extensive case studies and autobiographies. Relabeling already collected cases and assembling new ones, he expanded his taxonomy, and new perversions entered *Psychopathia sexualis* around 1890. Along with "contrary sexual feeling," he introduced "fetishism" (the erotic obsession with certain parts of the body, hair, shoes, nightcaps, handkerchiefs, gloves, ladies' underwear, fur, and silk), and he coined "sadism" and "masochism" as the most fundamental forms of psychosexual perversion. In the last decades of the nineteenth century, especially in France and Germany, several prominent psychiatrists were classifying and explaining the wide range of deviant sexual behaviors they discovered.[14] Several taxonomies were proposed, but the one developed in *Psychopathia sexualis* around 1890 eventually set the tone. Although he also paid attention to voyeurism, exhibitionism, pedophilia, gerontophilia, bestiality, necrophilia, urolagnia, coprolagnia, and other sexual behaviors, Krafft-Ebing distinguished four main perversions: sadism, masochism, fetishism, and contrary sexual feeling (or inversion).

Psychopathia sexualis has been characterized as the climax of the medicalization of sexuality and a typical expression of Victorian hypocrisy. True, there are elements that would substantiate such a judgment, but a close reading of this work makes clear that it cannot be regarded only as a medical and moral disqualification of sexual aberration. Krafft-Ebing's views were far from static or coherent, and in several ways his scientific approach to sexuality was ambivalent. The differentiation of pathological and healthy sexuality—reproduction being the touchstone—was the basic assumption in his taxonomy; at the same time, the barriers between the normal and abnormal were subverted in his discussion of the main perversions. Sadism, masochism, and fetishism were not only disease categories, but also terms that described extremes on a graded scale of health and illness, and explained aspects of "normal" sexuality. He construed sadism as a pathological extension of the normal sexual psychology of males, and masochism as an exaggeration of the female sexual nature. Sadism and masochism were inherent in normal male and female sexuality, the first being of an aggressive and the second of a submissive nature. (However, most of Krafft-Ebing's cases were of male masochists, and therefore he assumed that masochism in males was related to inversion.) In his view, the distinction between sadomasochism and "normal" heterosexuality was quantitative rather than qualitative. Fetishism was also defined by Krafft-Ebing as part and parcel of normal sexuality, because the individual character of sexual attraction and monogamous love was grounded in a distinct preference for particular physical and mental characteristics of one's partner. "Normal" sexuality appeared to have features of perverted desire. In addition, the boundary between masculinity and femininity was blurred. Inversion, spanning the gulf between the masculine and the feminine, occupied a major place in Krafft-Ebing's sexual pathology. The extensive discussion of several forms of physical and mental inversion highlighted the idiosyncratic and chance character of sex differentiation, and hinted that exclusive masculinity and femininity might be mere abstractions. Despite the effort to distinguish perversion from normalcy, there was a clear tendency in *Psychopathia sexualis* to undercut distinctions between divergent desires and to make various forms of normal and abnormal sexuality equivalent and interchangeable, thus abolishing a clear boundary between health and perversion.

Krafft-Ebing's psychiatric theorization of sexuality opened up a new continent of knowledge, not only because it treated sexual abnormality as disease instead of sin, crime, or decadence, but, more importantly, because he made it clear that sexuality deserved serious study since it was central to the existence of the individual and society. He pointed to the danger of the sexual instinct threatening civilization, but at the same time he also drew attention to its constructive role in culture and society, religion, social ethics, and esthetics. For him, love as a social bond was inherently sexual. "Ethical surroundings are necessary in order to elevate love to its true and pure form, but nevertheless, sensuality remains its strongest root. Platonic love is an absurdity, a self-deception, a misnomer for kindred spirits."[15] The longing for physical and psychological union with a partner was valued as a purpose in itself. His discussion of same-sex love indicates that procreation was no longer considered to be an unshakable norm—notably, Krafft-Ebing did not mention contraception in his discussion of abnormality. In fact, he assigned primacy to the satisfaction of desire and psychological matters.

Krafft-Ebing's biological approach to sexuality has often been contrasted with Freud's psychological one.[16] However, in *Psychopathia sexualis* there is a striking inconsistency between organic explanations and clinical descriptions. Although in his case histories he often mentioned physical examinations of his patient's sexual organs, and sometimes even anatomies of the brain if they died while still under medical supervision, these were not very relevant for his classification and definition of perversion. The introduction of fetishism, sadism, and masochism was not only an important broadening of terminology, but also a significant step from a predominantly forensic focus and a physiological explanation to a psychological approach to human sexuality. Not so much bodily characteristics nor actual behavior were decisive in the diagnosis of perversion, but functional disorders, individual character, personal history and emotional life, dreams and fantasies. Although the underlying causes of perversion remained degeneration and heredity, Krafft-Ebing shifted the medical discussion away from explaining sexuality as a series of interrelated physiological events to a more psychological understanding. In this way, he foreshadowed Freud: like Freud, Krafft-Ebing viewed human sexuality as distinct from animal instincts. His analysis primarily had to rely on what "perverts" were telling him; therefore, (auto)biographical accounts were most important to his work. Especially because his case histories displayed an individualization and psychologization of sexuality, his approach marks a central moment in the constitution of the modern concept of sexuality in general and of homosexuality in particular.

"PLATO WAS NOT A FILTHY SWINE"

As indicated before, *Psychopathia sexualis* was illustrated with hundreds of case histories and autobiographical accounts. The twelfth edition (1903), the last to be edited by Krafft-Ebing himself, contained almost 250 of these. In his earlier work, many of them were borrowed from colleagues, or were based on cases of "moral offenders" whom he examined in his capacity as an expert witness. Each new edition presented larger numbers of patients hospitalized in the asylums or university clinics where he was a medical superintendent. Also represented were individuals who contacted Krafft-Ebing of their own accord as private patients, or who corresponded with him because they had recognized themselves in published case histories. Some of them sent in their autobiographies hoping to have them published in a subsequent edition of *Psychopathia sexualis*. Although most cases in his early work were rather short and factual, later editions contained more extensive ones. In publishing autobiographies and quoting his patients, many case studies focused especially on the patient's subjective experiences.

The subjects of Krafft-Ebing's case histories were drawn from various social groups. This was closely connected to his endeavor to expand the boundaries of his psychiatric practice by changing its institutional setting and recruiting new types of patients.[17] When Krafft-Ebing started his career as an Extraordinary Professor of Psychiatry in Graz, his professional élan must have been severely challenged. In the overcrowded Feldhof Asylum, where he was a medical superintendent, he was faced with generally poor, uneducated, chronic, and sometimes violent inmates, who were barely treatable and with whom it was difficult to sympathize. In such an institution, psychiatry consisted mainly of custodial care, and offered few gratifying professional and scientific experiences. For teaching and publishing purposes and for successful treatments, he needed greater variety and a higher turnover of acute cases. His successful struggle for a clinical ward in the university hospital was not only a strategic move to strengthen his position in academia, but was also important for the shaping of psychiatry as a respectable medical specialty. The founding of a private sanatorium for an elite, wealthy clientele suffering from relatively mild disorders like "nervousness" and "neurasthenia" may have been inspired by similar considerations. In asylums and clinical wards, Krafft-Ebing treated mainly lower-class patients, while in the commodious sanatorium and his private practice he catered to men and women from the higher ranks of society, for whom hospitalization was undesirable. Among them were several members of the German, Austrian, and Hungarian aristocracy, and affluent patients from all over Europe. While hospitalized patients and suspected moral offenders had no other choice than to conform to standard medical procedures and have their stories recorded, many of his aristocratic and bourgeois patients, who generally had contacted him of their own accord, were given ample opportunity to speak for themselves. Homosexual men particularly seized this opportunity.

The autobiographies Krafft-Ebing received from Urnings were by members of the upper and educated classes, who often were familiar with his work on sexual pathology and eager to reveal their lives to him. In his early articles on contrary sexual feeling, he had made it clear that he needed more cases to substantiate empirically his taxonomy, and he encouraged Urnings to contact him. They responded with letters and autobiographies. "You ask for biographies of several Urnings," one university graduate wrote in 1885. "In the interest of science I won't make a fuss about giving you an autobiography that is as detailed as possible, and in which I will attempt to give all data as objectively as possible."[18] The almost exclusively male cases he collected in the 1880s, either by direct contact or through letters, were of merchants, civil servants, aristocrats, scholars, writers, artists, and, remarkably, of medical students and physicians.[19] Generally, they were economically independent and, in most cases, living apart from the traditional family. Krafft-Ebing probably had expected them to be nervous and effeminate "degenerates"; however, they argued convincingly that they enjoyed perfect health and that they were physically indistinguishable from their fellow men. The case of G., Ph.D. published in 1882, is typical of this group. This man, who had been arrested in Graz on immorality charges while traveling from Italy to Vienna, and who ended up in Krafft-Ebing's clinic, made clear that he did not consider himself a sinner or a patient. On the contrary, he was perfectly happy, especially because he often stayed in Italy where homosexuality was not punishable. "He reports," Krafft-Ebing wrote in G.'s case history, "with great contentment and remarkable cynicism that he has an innate contrary sexual sensitivity. . . . G. refers to his poetic works with great confidence and asserts that people of his mold, without exception, are talented at poetry." Referring to famous predecessors, like Plato, who, according to G., "certainly was not a filthy swine," he even stated that same-sex love was elevating.[20] Similar statements were made by others: "Our love also sprouts the most beautiful, precious blooms, develops all the more precious drives and encourages the mind, as much as the love of a young man for his girl."[21] Count Z., whose case history also appeared in 1882, was characterized by Krafft-Ebing as "intellectually well-talented . . . , an open, generous character," and

> neither unhappy about the inversion of his sexual sensitivity, nor capable of recognizing it as unhealthy. He is even less capable of doing so, since he feels morally dignified, happy, and relieved because of the contact with men. How could it be unhealthy, that which makes a man happy and inspires in him beautiful and lofty things! His only misfortune is that social barriers and penal codes stand in the way of "naturally" expressing his drive. This would be a great hardship.[22]

Written by educated and often cosmopolitan men, some of the autobiographies were full of learned and literary references, philosophical and medical speculations, and detailed self-analysis. The letters also vividly demonstrated a considerable degree of subjective suffering, not so much because of the author's sexual orientation as such, but because of social condemnation, legal persecution, the need to disguise their real nature, and fear of blackmail and loss of social status. Several men stressed that their sexual behavior could not be immoral or pathological because they experienced their sexual desire as "natural." "Since I gave way to my Urning nature, I am happier, healthier, and more productive!" a forty-eight-year-old academic wrote to Krafft-Ebing.[23] Another man, who had been convicted for "unnatural vice," was of the opinion that in a moral sense he was not guilty at all: "I did not offend against nature, a thousand times no, therefore a part of the other guilt falls away from me and onto an antiquated law."[24] Krafft-Ebing reported that Count Y., first interviewed in 1882, also "does not feel unhappy with his perverse sexual sensitivity, but the fact that the highest sexual pleasure is denied to him because of social reasons often makes him entirely sad, unhappy, embittered, and increases his neurasthenic troubles."[25]

These stories must have touched Krafft-Ebing. In 1884 he introduced an article containing six case histories on contrary sexual feeling with the statement that the task of science was to differentiate disease from immorality. "Scientific research would hereby contribute to the vindication and betterment of the social lot of so many unhappy [men]."[26] In the introduction to the second edition of *Psychopathia sexualis* (1887), which was newly subtitled "With Especial Reference to the Contrary Sexual Feeling,"[27] he stated that some lawsuits in which the accused had been treated unjustly, had given him occasion to draw special attention to these unhappy "step-children of nature."[28] In the chapter on the legal aspects of same-sex behavior, he included a long letter of a highly placed man from London, who criticized Krafft-Ebing for sticking to the opinion that it was an illness:

> Your opinion that the ultimate origin of the phenomenon in question must be attributed in most cases to a congenital "unhealthy" disposition, may, perhaps, make it possible very soon to overcome existing prejudices and to arouse compassion rather than abhorrence and contempt for us poor "sick" men.
>
> Much as I believe that your perspective is most advantageous for us, I am notwithstanding, in the interest of science, unable to accept the word "unhealthy" just like that, and I indulge in giving you some more relevant explications.[29]

Psychological suffering was indeed widespread among Urnings, the man continued, but experience had taught him that the cause was not so much their inborn disposition as the legal and social obstacles with which they contended:

> Such a forcible repression of a deeply implanted drive primarily causes, in my humble opinion, the unhealthy phenomena that we can observe in many Urnings, but it is not necessarily a consequence of the Urning's disposition.[30]

Similar statements could be found in other case histories and autobiographies. For example, a fifty-year-old Belgian Urning wrote to Krafft-Ebing,

> Even though I am an Urning, I cannot admit that my nature is an "unhealthy" [one], otherwise you would also have to classify as unhealthy other entire categories of men who are usually considered normal. . . . Unfortunately, we are considered sick for a completely valid reason, namely, that we really became sick and that one then confuses cause and effect. . . . We certainly become sick, as animals are stricken by rabies if they are prevented from engaging in the sexual act which is adequate to their nature.[31]

By publishing such arguments without any additional medical comment, but instead remarking that they strikingly typified the feelings and suffering of Urnings, Krafft-Ebing made a powerful statement for those concerned. In new editions of *Psychopathia sexualis,* he included more and more extensive autobiographies in which Urnings made clear that they did not seek a cure, since it was not their disposition that made them unhappy, but the social condemnation. "He does not want to become another person nor to lose the sweet memories," reported Krafft-Ebing on the outlook of the forty-two-year-old C. v. Z. "If one suggested he give up men, he would be unhappy. He could not and would not want to 'switch,' because his whole ethics, etc. are developed around this peculiar sexuality."[32] In his elaborate autobiography, a thirty-six-year-old cosmopolitan man insisted:

> I cannot imagine that my condition might appear unnatural, because as far back as I can think I have always felt the same way. . . . I morally suffered a lot, quite a lot, not because I recognized my drive as unhealthy, but because of the common contempt we encounter all around us.[33]

Another man, who had found many sexual partners while traveling all over Europe, indicated that the positive points of his experiences—"the mysterious and enchanting temptations this matter offers"—amply outweighed the prohibitions.[34] Emphasizing that many of his sexual partners were in perfect health and with nerves of steel, he hoped that his confession would give others courage. Some correspondents criticized Krafft-Ebing in no uncertain way for surrounding Uranism with the stigma of pathology. The letter of a thirty-three-year-old man, who had contacted Krafft-Ebing in 1889, was very clear in this regard.

> Your essay "Die conträre Sexualempfindung vor dem Forum" [Considering Contrary Sexual Sensitivity], which I just put down, greatly aroused my interest. It is but a poor attempt at making the abnormal phenomenon (which occurs more often than you know) clear to wider circles and at proving that the actions of the natural drive, even if different from the conventional form, are impossible to punish.
>
> One should not consider the Urning an inferior being, that would be erroneous. Under circumstances, he is the most perfect creation of nature. I know some whose disposition of mind is so noble—unlike that of normal men I have observed.[35]

Between 1882 and 1900, Krafft-Ebing published a series of articles on the legal aspects of homosexuality.[36] At first he did not attack the German and Austrian laws criminalizing "unnatural vice" (§ 175 and 129), but only stressed the need to distinguish crime from disease. Although in 1882 he declared that one of his patients, G., Ph.D. (who criticized German and Austrian legislation) showed "incredible cynicism" and was mentally deranged,[37] a few years later—after having published several autobiographies which showed the harmful effects of penalization—he himself would begin to favor judicial reform. In the early 1890s, Krafft-Ebing put his name to petitions for the abolition of § 175, and he added to *Psychopathia sexualis* that the book should contribute towards changing the law, thus ending the errors and hardships of many centuries. When, at the end of the nineteenth century, homosexuals began to organize protest movements, they referred to Krafft-Ebing as a scientific authority who was on their side,[38] and he indeed supported the homosexual rights movement that was founded in 1897 in Berlin by Magnus Hirschfeld (1868–1935). After he had signed Hirschfeld's petition advocating the abolition of § 175, he admitted in his last article on homosexuality, published in Hirschfeld's *Jahrbuch für sexuelle Zwischenstufen* (Yearbook for Sexual Intermediaries), that the scientific conception of Uranism had been one-sided, and that there was truth to the opinion of many of his homosexual correspondents.[39] Having referred earlier to the decline of Greece and Rome as warning examples from the past, he now believed that Uranism was not incompatible with mental health or even with intellectual superiority. It was not a pathological phenomenon, but a biological and psychological condition that had to be accepted as a more or less deplorable but natural fate. Focusing less on the sexual acts and more on the relational aspects of sexuality, he also attributed an equal ethical value to same-sex and heterosexual loves.

SCIENCE AND HUMANITY

The case histories and autobiographies of Urnings make clear that so-called "perverts" did not play a passive role vis-à-vis the psychiatrist. On the contrary, there is no doubt that Krafft-Ebing's views were influenced by his patients and informants. Not only did Krafft-Ebing delight in scrupulous analysis and in the invention of new categories and subcategories, but also some of his patients were eager to confess the truth about their inner self, and they displayed great diagnostic and classificatory zeal. "I tell everything here, because I want to write only the truth and the whole truth," one of the autobiographers assured Krafft-Ebing. "I hand over these lines to you in the interest of future fellow-sufferers. Publish from it whatever you feel suits the interests of science, truth, and justice."[40] A thirty-four-year-old merchant also made clear that in his autobiography he strove for absolute truth:

> Permeated by the conviction that the mystery of our existence can only be solved or at least examined by unprejudiced, thinking men of science, I describe my life solely with the intention that I may contribute to elucidating this cruel error of nature and hereby be useful to comrades in fate of later generations. . . . I will strive for the most severe objectivity . . . in my communications. And I note concerning my drastic, often even cynical style, that I want to be true above all and, therefore, I do not avoid strong statements because they characterize the matter I am discussing most strikingly.[41]

A man who sent in an elaborate life history and who, with the help of *Psychopathia sexualis,* had come to the painful conclusion that his anomaly was "a mixture of sadism and masochism, complicated by homosexuality, with fetishistic concomitants," underlined that his confession originated from scrupulous and objective self-observation. "I am always capable of fully imagining myself in the situation and feelings of another as well as I myself can judge accurately and mercilessly from an impartial perspective."[42]

The active role of several subjects of Krafft-Ebing's case studies in the genesis of his theories suggests that psychiatry enabled the individuals concerned to speak out and be recognized. While Krafft-Ebing's work has been regarded as a cultural defense against the corruption of morals and "decadence" in fin-de-siè-cle society—and he may have intended it as such—it nevertheless failed to conceal its own tendency to make sexual variance imaginable and to enlarge the sphere allotted to idiosyncratic desires. Although a scientific work intended for physicians and lawyers, *Psychopathia sexualis* probably became a best-seller thanks to laymen interested in the case histories and its pornographic qualities (even if the "offensive" passages were in Latin). In addition to scientific expositions, there were extensive descriptions of sexual experiences, fantasies, erotic temptations and amusements in big cities, examples from history and literature, fragments of semipornographic writings, candid advertisements, and journalistic descriptions of events such as "the Woman-haters Ball" for Urnings in Berlin. Some subjects of case histories made perfectly clear that they knew just where to go to satisfy the perverse desires catalogued by Krafft-Ebing. Specialized forms of prostitution and meeting places had developed in response to new desires. Subcultural pursuits entailed certain roles and a sense of community—"the comfort of belonging together and not being alone anymore"—as one of Krafft-Ebing's correspondents wrote.[43] A thirty-one-year-old homosexual man, who made clear to Krafft-Ebing that he did not want a cure for his leanings, because they had given him so many "unforgettably lovely hours," claimed: "I could write volumes about my acquaintances, which are over 500."[44] A German physician who had written a novel about the life of Urnings was, like others, familiar with the homosexual underground in several cities. "Since I am aware of my abnormal drive, I have come in contact with far more than a thousand men of the same kind. Almost every larger city has some meeting place, as well as a so-called cruising area."[45]

By publishing letters and autobiographies and by quoting statements of his patients ad verbatim, Krafft-Ebing enabled voices to be heard that were usually silenced. Therefore, medical discourse as represented in his work is characterized by multivocality: one can find different, even contradictory, sets of values in *Psychopathia sexualis,* and the book was open to dialogue and divergent meanings. Evidently, contemporary readers interpreted Krafft-Ebing's work in various ways, and, to a large extent, "perverts" gave their own meaning to their sexual feelings and experiences. For several of them the book was clearly the impetus to self-awareness and self-expression. Some of the autobiographers took the opportunity to give expression to their criticism of current social norms and even those of the medical profession. For example, a highly placed German civil servant—who sent in not only an autobiography but also a carefully detailed criticism of § 175—concluded that this law was based on prejudice and ignorance.

Same-sex love was no sin or crime, but part of nature, and medical scientists had the duty to enlighten the general public.[46] Even more self-assured and militant was a twenty-two-year-old medical student whose autobiography appeared in 1890:

> I intentionally and consciously condemn contemporary moral standards, which force sexually abnormal people to offend against arbitrary laws. And I think that sexual contact between two people of the same sex is at their individual discretion, without the legislator having any right to object. . . . I only yearn for a time, when I can pursue the same [sexual contact] in a more comfortable way and with less danger of being discovered, in order to give myself a pleasure that does not harm anyone."[47]

A forty-eight-year-old doctor's autobiography—thirteen pages of small print regularly republished in *Psychopathia sexualis*—was also outstanding because of its criticism of the medical profession. Through his life story this man explained that he had always felt like a woman. In a letter accompanying his autobiography, he advocated that women should be allowed to study medicine, because they showed more intuition than men:

> Finally, I wanted to present you with the results of my recollections and reflections to prove that one can be a doctor given female feeling and thinking. I think it a great injustice that medicine is closed to women. A woman discovers the traces of many maladies through her intuition, while a man gropes in the dark despite diagnostics, at least for women's and children's diseases. If I could make it happen, every doctor would have to undergo a quarter year of femininity. He would have more understanding and more respect for the side of humanity, from which he descended. He would respect women's greatness of mind, and at the same time also the hardness of their fate.[48]

The impact of Krafft-Ebing's medical work was multifaceted: it served not only as a guide for professionals, but also as a mouthpiece and panel for the individuals concerned. To a certain extent, they used psychiatry for their own purposes; for example, the psychiatric concept of hereditary causes was used by homosexual men to argue that their leanings were part of nature, and therefore immutable. The medical model of drives (*Triebe*) suggested that (male) sexuality was a forceful instinct, that had to be released in some way; therefore, many of them argued that their sexual behavior was inevitable and had to be condoned. "Perverts" began to speak for themselves, and they were looking for models with which to identify. Despite the medical bias, many case histories in *Psychopathia sexualis* served as go-betweens, linking painful individual introspection—the self-conscious recognition that one is a deviant kind of person—and social identification—the comforting sense of belonging to a community of like-minded people.[49] Because Krafft-Ebing distinguished himself as an expert who had taken a stand against traditional moral-religious and legal denunciations of sexual deviance, individuals approached him to find understanding, acceptance, and support—as a fragment from a letter by a Belgian Urning to Krafft-Ebing clearly illustrates:

> You will be able to appreciate what it means to lock forever within myself that which touches me by far the deepest, and of not being able to confide in anybody. . . . You are the first to whom I open my heart. Use this letter in any way; maybe one day it will help lighten the fate of future men to whom nature gives the same feelings.[50]

Another Urning, who regretted that he had not read *Psychopathia sexualis* earlier in his life, because this would have prevented a lot of misery, confided to Krafft-Ebing:

> Nobody knows my true nature,—only you, a stranger, you alone know me now, indeed in a more detailed way than father or mother, friend, wife, or [male] lover. It is a real comfort to me to expose, this once, the heavy secret of my own nature.[51]

Krafft-Ebing's humanitarian rhetoric had some real effect. Letters indicate that he had a good relationship with many of his upper-class patients. In a way, they cooperated: "perverts" who wanted to make their voices heard in public depended on sympathetic physicians like Krafft-Ebing because medical science was the only respectable forum available. In turn, Krafft-Ebing had to rely on the confessions of the individuals concerned to validate empirically his theory of sexual pathology. Within the moral climate of his time, Krafft-Ebing showed some open-mindedness and pragmatism. It is true that he experimented with hypnosis to cure perversion, but in general he seems to have applied this remedy only when patients asked for it. Moreover, the endeavor to find a cure for perversions was still of marginal importance in psychiatry then, and Krafft-Ebing made clear that in the case of inborn perversions a cure was not likely.[52] In fact, many patients did not need a medical cure, because pouring out one's heart was therapeutic in itself. Writing their life history, giving coherence and intelligibility to their torn self, might result in a "catharsis" of comprehension. Evidently, many homosexuals viewed Krafft-Ebing not simply as a doctor treating diseases, but also as an ally embodying an ideal of science as a means for improving their lot. "I recently saw . . . your book *Psychopathia sexualis*," one of them informed Krafft-Ebing:

> I saw from it that you ponder and research without prejudice in the interest of science and humanity. Although I cannot convey much new material to you, I still want to talk about some matters, that you may kindly accept as another contribution to your work, and which I trustingly lay in your hands for our social preservation.[53]

Medical theories such as Krafft-Ebing's have played an important role in the making of sexual categories and identities. However, his sexual pathology was not shaped systematically by the logic of medical science exclusively, and neither was it simply a means of stigmatizing and controlling deviants. Medicalization has to be viewed as a process in which new meanings were attached to existing behaviors and feelings. These new meanings were developed with the collaboration of some of the people concerned as they furnished psychiatrists with the life stories and experiences upon which medical interpretations were grounded. Many of the case reports and autobiographies suggest that new ways of understanding sexuality emerged from a confrontation of medical thinking and individual self-definition. By facilitating greater recognition and discussion of homosexuals, psychiatric accounts did not simply encourage medical treatment, restraint, and repression, but also offered a space in which sexual desire could be articulated in the form of autobiographical narrative. A self-conscious homosexual identity and a sense of community clearly evolved in well-educated, urban, and often cosmopolitan bourgeois and aristocratic circles. Medical knowledge of sexuality could only be successful because it was embedded in society: psychiatrists like Krafft-Ebing and his patients shared the same cultural background and the same bourgeois values.

Both Krafft-Ebing's psychiatric explanations and the (auto)biographical case reports he used as empirical material reflected as well as shaped sexual experiences. In his work, sexuality was not just a biological instinct unmediated by experience. On the contrary, because sexuality played a core part in the narration of self, and because perverse desire was linked to individual identity, it was burdened with significance. The interpretation of the self, as narrated by patients and informants in the form of life histories, was crucial in the development of Krafft-Ebing's sexual pathology. The scientific "will to know" moved forward at the same pace as concern for the authentic and voluble self in late-nineteenth-century bourgeois society, particularly in Austria.[54] With the differentiation of the public from the domestic, a sphere of intimacy and privacy had emerged: individual authenticity became a preeminent value and a framework for introspection, self-contemplation, and self-expression. The rise of sexual pathology in psychiatry only magnified the effects of this need for self-comprehension.

It is difficult to ascertain whether the autobiographical accounts of Krafft-Ebing's patients and correspondents are "true" pictures of their lives, in the sense that their stories correspond to the actual events in their lives. Rather than viewing autobiographies as representations of lives as they have been lived, these life stories should be seen as a particular way people gave meaning to their condition and (re)constructed their selves. They appealed to ideals of authenticity and sincerity to bestow moral value on their sexual identity. However, what was presented as an intricate process of self-discovery was in fact a process of self-creation. Neither scientific nor individual meanings of the sexual self should be considered as reflections of an internal, psychological reality. The way people experienced sexuality and gave meaning to it was determined not so much by given natural or psychological facts, but by cultural codes and symbols as they functioned in social life. Above all, homosexual identity as expressed in Krafft-Ebing's work presumed reflexive awareness, an ability to interrogate the past from the perspective of the present, and to tell a coherent story about one's life history in the light of what might be anticipated for the future. The order auto-biographers gave to the facts of their lives is not inherent in them but necessarily of their own devising in order to serve certain needs in the present. Many of Krafft-Ebing's patients had fully developed a sense of themselves as objects of introspection, the more so because they were obliged to keep up appearances in a society in which they felt not well suited, and because they suffered from their inability to communicate with others about their inner nature—their real self.

Homosexual identity crystallized in patterned narratives, and as such, its content and form were of a social rather than of a psychological origin. It did not appear as a distinctive personal trait or essence, but as a script on which individuals modeled their life history. The psychiatric case history preeminently offered a fitting model for self-understanding. In case reports and autobiographies published by Krafft-Ebing, the same elements recur of what was to become a standard "coming out" narrative: ancestry, family background, the retrospective discovery of a peculiar way of feeling and acting during childhood and puberty, the conviction that one has always felt the same, the first sexual experiences, the struggle with masturbation (which often raised more anxieties than sexual contacts with other individuals did), details about sexual fantasies, dreams, and behavior, the exploration of one's health condition and gender identity in the past and present, the sense of being overwhelmed by irresistible and "natural" drives for which one is not responsible, the (mostly failed) attempts to have "normal" sexual intercourse (usually with a prostitute) in order to "test" the constitutional character of one's sexual preference, the painful knowledge of being different and in conflict with society, the comforting discovery of not being alone, and the endeavor for moral self-justification.[55]

The linking of sexuality with privacy and intimacy and the constitution of desire as the clue to the inner self were not so much a concealment from public view as a reconstitution of the function of sexuality. Anthony Giddens and Niklas Luhmann have explained this change in the experience of sexuality as a consequence of modernity, which Luhmann associates with "functional differentiation" and Giddens with, among other characteristics, increasing "institutional reflexivity," "the regularized use of knowledge about circumstances of social life as a constitutive element in its organization and transformation."[56] While sexuality as a function of social behavior hardly had a distinct existence before the nineteenth century, the "sequestration of experience" in modern society entailed the increasing dissociation of sexuality from fixed, putatively "natural" patterns of behavior. As a consequence of the rise of the ideal of romantic love, sexuality was gradually differentiated from a transcendental moral order and from its traditional instrumental integration with reproduction, kinship, and social and economic necessities. In the context of romantic love and privacy, sexuality became a separate sphere in human life. To explain changes in (homo)sexual practices and experiences, not only must developments in medical science be taken into account but also changes in the wider social context. Homosexuality as an individual property is only conceivable in a society in which same-sex bonding is not taken for granted any longer, and more or less casual sexuality between men or between women are viewed as short-term diversions from family roles. With the upgrading of romantic love as the foundation of marriage, physical as well as emotional intimacy were exclusively associated with heterosexual bonds. However, the emergence of "perversions" reveals that, in modern experience, human purposes of sexuality began to spread across alternative meanings. The emergence of a separate sexual domain in society, in turn, created the possibility for medical science to define sexuality as a distinct impulse—the sixth, genital sense, as Krafft-Ebing named this instinct—and to discover its internal physical and psychological laws.

Medical explanations of sexuality took shape at the same time as the experience of sexuality in society was transformed and it became a subject for introspection and obsessive self-scrutiny in bourgeois milieux. "The dull drive became conscious perversity," Krafft-Ebing cited one of his female patients as saying;[57] such self-consciousness—shared by many individuals who read his work—was not only facilitated by his psychiatry, but also presumed a "modern" reflexive awareness among individuals in society. Since the modern reflexive project of the self had to be undertaken in the absence of traditional social routines or moral certainties, self-contemplation was a cause for anxiety and uneasiness. Nevertheless, as many of Krafft-Ebing's case histories illustrate, it also created some space for individuality and self-expression.

Krafft-Ebing's sexual pathology reflected the anxieties and the inconsistencies around sexuality in fin-de-siècle culture, especially the bourgeois preoccupation with its dangers and pleasures.[58] His approach fluctuated between the stigmatization of sexual variations as mental illness and the recognition of individuals' particular and unique desires. The way several of his patients and informants read his work illustrates that the sexual domain became a contested field and that it was but one step from the admission of the individual's right to sexual fulfillment. Krafft-Ebing's model of sexuality tended to center on desire instead of reproduction, and many subjects of his case histories appeared as sexual consumers: they were more or less able to pursue their sexual desires as part of a lifestyle. Marking a transition in the urban bourgeois milieu from an ethos of Christianity and productivity (which dictated self-discipline and control of the passions) to a consumerist culture of abundance (which valued the satisfaction of individual desire), *Psychopathia sexualis* was caught in its own contradictory structure. Modern sexuality was suspended between the absolutism of the dichotomy separating the normal and the abnormal on the one hand, and the increasing relativization of variance on the other.

1. Krafft-Ebing Estate. All original German quotations have been translated by Robert Grimm and Vernon Rosario.

2. Krafft-Ebing's estate is part of the private archive of the Krafft-Ebing family in Graz, Austria.

3. Michel Foucault, *Histoire de la sexualité I. La volunté de savoir* (Paris, 1976).

4. E. M. Brecher, *The Sex Researchers* (Boston, 1969), p. 56.

5. Thomas Szasz, *Sex by Prescription* (Garden City, N.Y., 1980), pp. 19–20.

6. Freiherr von R. to Krafft-Ebing, July 1900. Krafft-Ebing Estate.

7. G. P. to Krafft-Ebing, March 10, 1899. Krafft-Ebing Estate.

8. Richard von Krafft-Ebing, "Zur Lehre von der conträren Sexualempfindung," *Irrenfreund* 26 (1884): 2.

9. Richard von Krafft-Ebing, *Neue Forschungen auf dem Gebiete der Psychopathia sexualis. Eine medizinisch-psychologische Studie* (Stuttgart, 1890), p. 55.

10. For the so-called essentialist-constructionist controversy, see Edward Stein, ed., *Forms of Desire: Sexual Orientation and the Social Constructionist Controversy* (New York, 1990); Jeffrey Weeks, *Sexuality and Its Discontents: Meaning, Myths, and Modern Sexualities* (London, 1985); and David F. Greenberg, *The Construction of Homosexuality* (Chicago, 1988).

11. Richard von Krafft-Ebing, *Lehrbuch der gerichtlichen Psychopathologie mit Berücksichtigung der Gesetzgebung von Österreich, Deutschland und Frankreich* (Stuttgart, 1879).

12. Richard von Krafft-Ebing, "Über gewisse Anomalien des Geschlechtstriebs und die klinisch-forensische Verwerthung derselben als eines wahrscheinlich functionellen Degenerationszeichens des centralen Nervensystems," *Archiv für Psychiatrie und Nervenkrankheiten* 7 (1877): 291–312.

13. See Hubert Kennedy, "Karl Heinrich Ulrichs, First Theorist of Homosexuality," in *Science and Homosexualities*, ed. Vernon A. Rosario (London, 1997), pp. 26–45.

14. On the development of medical sexology, see Annemarie Wettley and Werner Leibbrand, *Von der "Psychopathia sexualis" zur Sexualwissenschaft* (Stuttgart, 1959); Foucault, *Histoire de la sexualité*; Georges Lanteri-Laura, *La lecture des perversions: Histoire de leur appropriation médicale* (Paris, 1979); Frank J. Sulloway, *Freud, Biologist of the Mind: Beyond the Psychoanalytic Legend* (New York, 1979), pp. 277–319; Jeffrey Weeks, *Sex, Politics and Society: The Regulation of Sexuality since 1800* (London, 1981); Weeks, *Sexuality and Its Discontents*; Arnold Davidson, "Sex and the Emergence of Sexuality," *Critical Inquiry* 14 (1987): 16–48; Davidson, "Closing up the Corpses: Diseases of Sexuality and the Emergence of the Psychiatric Style of Reasoning," in *Meaning and Method: Essays in Honor of Hilary Putnam*, ed. G. Boolos (Cambridge, 1990); Lawrence Birken, *Consuming Desire: Sexual Science and the Emergence of a Culture of Abundance, 1871–1914* (Ithaca, 1988); Greenberg, *Construction of Homosexuality*, pp. 397–433; Gert Hekma, *Homoseksualiteit, een medische reputatie. De uitdoktering van de homoseksueel in negentiende-eeuws Nederland* (Amsterdam, 1987); Hekma, "A History of Sexology: Social and Historical Aspects of Sexuality," in *From Sappho to De Sade: Moments in the History of Sexuality*, ed. Jan Bremmer (London, 1989), pp. 173–93; Vern L. Bullough, *Science in the Bedroom: A History of Sex Research* (New York, 1994).

15. Richard von Krafft-Ebing, *Psychopathia sexualis. Mit besonderer Berücksichtigung der konträren Sexualempfindung: Eine medizinisch-gerichtliche Studie für Ärzte und Juristen*, 14th ed. (Stuttgart, 1912; photo-reprint, Munich, 1984), pp. 11–12.

16. Peter Gay, *Freud: A Life for Our Time* (New York, 1988), p. 120.

17. Renate Hauser, "Sexuality, Neurasthenia and the Law: Richard von Krafft-Ebing (1840–1902)" (Ph.D. diss., University of London, 1992), pp. 85–132.

18. Richard von Krafft-Ebing, "Die conträre Sexualempfindung vor dem Forum," *Jahrbücher für Psychiatrie und forensische Psychologie* 6 (1885): 42–43.

19. The relative invisibility of women's voices might be explained by the fact that in Germany and Austria a self-defined lesbian identity and subculture did not emerge until the

1920s. See Hanna Hacker and Manfred Lang, "Jenseits der Geschlechter, zwischen ihnen," in *Das lila Wien um 1900*, ed. Neda Bei et al. (Vienna, 1986), pp. 13–17.

20. Richard von Krafft-Ebing, "Zur 'conträren Sexualempfindung' in klinisch-forensischer Hinsicht," *Allgemeine Zeitschrift für Psychiatrie* 38 (1882): 215–16.

21. Krafft-Ebing, "Zur Lehre von der conträren Sexualempfindung," p. 5.

22. Krafft-Ebing, "Zur 'conträren Sexualemfindung' in klinisch-forensischer Hinsicht," pp. 213–14.

23. Krafft-Ebing, "Die conträre Sexualempfindung vor dem Forum," p. 46.

24. Krafft-Ebing, "Zur Lehre von der conträren Sexualempfindung," p. 4.

25. Ibid., p. 7.

26. Ibid., pp. 1–2.

27. The original German subtitle is "Mit besonderer Berücksichtigung der konträren Sexualempfindung," which was rendered in the English translation of *Psychopathia sexualis* as "With Especial Reference to the Antipathic Sexual Instinct" (trans. Franklin S. Klaf, from the 12th ed. [1903] [New York, 1965]).

28. Richard von Krafft-Ebing, *Psychopathia sexualis. Mit besonderer Berücksichtigung der konträren Sexualempfindung*, 2nd ed. (Stuttgart, 1887), pp. vi, 139.

29. Krafft-Ebing, *Psychopathia sexualis*, 14th ed. (1912), p. 430. (Robert Grimm's translation note: It is difficult to convey the connotative difference between *krank/Krankheit* versus *krankhaft/Krankhaftigkeit*. The former indicates the state of sickness or disease, while the latter suggests the *mental state* of illness—see Friedrich Köhler's *Dictionary of the English and German Languages*, 3rd ed. [Leipzig, 1865]. While this distinction is important in the German nineteenth-century literature on sexual perversions, it is difficult to translate; therefore, I have used *sick* or *ill* for *krank*, and *unhealthy* for *krankhaft*.)

30. Krafft-Ebing, *Psychopathia sexualis*, 14th ed. (1912), p. 430.

31. Kraft-Ebing, *Psychopathia sexualis*, 5th ed. (1890), pp. 129–30.

32. Krafft-Ebing, *Neue Forschungen auf dem Gebiete der Psychopathia sexualis*, p. 58.

33. Ibid., p. 55.

34. Ibid., pp. 60–61.

35. Krafft-Ebing, *Psychopathia sexualis*, 5th ed. (1890), pp. 113–14.

36. Krafft-Ebing: "Zur 'conträren Sexualempfindung' in klinisch-forensicher Hinsicht"; "Zur Lehre von der conträren Sexualempfindung"; "Die conträre Sexualempfindung vor dem Forum"; "Epilogue zu: Par. 175 des deutschen Strafgesetzbuches und die Urningsliebe Von Dr. iur. xxx," *Zeitshcrift für die gesammte Strafrechtswissenschaft* 12 (1892): 34–54; "Zur conträren Sexualempfindung. Autobiographie und strafrechtliche Betrachtungen von einem conträr Sexualen," *Wiener Medizinische Blätter* 15/1 (1892): 7–9; 15/3 (1892): 42–44; *Der Conträrsexuale vor dem Strafrichter. De sodomia ratione sexus punienda. De lege lata et de lege ferenda: Eine Denkschrift* (Leipzig and Vienna, 1894); "Drei Conträrsexuale vor Gericht," *Jahrbücher für Psychiatrie und Neurologie* 19 (1900): 262–82.

37. Krafft-Ebing, "Zur 'conträren Sexualempfindung' in klinisch-forensicher Hinsicht," p. 216.

38. See *Aufruf an alle gebildeten und edelgesinnten Menschen!*, published in 1899 by the Berlin-based "Comité für Befreiung der Homosexualen vom Strafgesetz." Krafft-Ebing Estate.

39. Richard von Krafft-Ebing, "Neue Studien auf dem Gebiete der Homosexualität," *Jahrbuch für sexuelle Zwischenstufen* 3 (1901): 1–36.

40. Krafft-Ebing, *Psychopathia sexualis*, 5th ed. (1890), pp. 162–64.

41. Ibid., p. 189.

42. Krafft-Ebing, *Psychopathia sexualis*, 14th ed. (1912), pp. 165–66.

43. Krafft-Ebing, "Zur Lehre von der conträren Sexualempfindung," p. 4.

44. Krafft-Ebing, *Psychopathia sexualis*, 14th ed. (1912), pp. 279–80.

45. Ibid., p. 288.

46. Krafft-Ebing, "Zur conträren Sexualempfindung: Autobiographie."

47. Krafft-Ebing, *Neue Forschungen auf dem Gebiete der Psychopathia sexualis*, pp. 63, 66.

48. Ibid., p. 79.

49. See Bert Hanson, "American Physicians' 'Discovery' of Homosexuals, 1880–1900: A New Diagnosis in a Changing Society," in *Framing Disease: Studies in Cultural History,* ed. Charles E. Rosenberg and Janet Golden (New Brunswick, 1992), p. 109.

50. Krafft-Ebing, *Psychopathia sexualis,* 5th ed. (1890), p. 135.

51. Krafft-Ebing, *Neue Forshungen auf dem Gebiete der Psychopathia sexualis,* p. 152.

52. Richard von Krafft-Ebing, "Introduction" to Alfred Fuchs, *Therapie der Anomalien Vita sexualis bei Männern. Mit specieller Berüchsichtigung der Suggestivbehandlung* (Stuttgart, 1899).

53. Krafft-Ebing, *Psychopathia sexualis,* 5th ed. (1890), p. 161.

54. Compare Michelle Perrot, ed., *A History of Private Life,* vol. 4, *From the Fires of Revolution to the Great War* (Cambridge, Mass., 1990), pp. 453–667; Jacques Le Rider, *Modernity and the Crisis of Identity: Culture and Society in Fin-de-Siècle Vienna* (Cambridge, 1993); Carl Schorske, *Fin-de-Siècle Vienna: Politics and Culture* (New York, 1981); Michael Worbs, *Nervenkuns. Literatur und Psychoanalyse im Wien der Jahrhundertwende* (Frankfurt, 1983).

55. Compare with Klaus Müller, *Aber in meinem Herzen sprach eine Stimme so laut: Homosexuelle Autobiographien und medizinische Pathographien im neunzehnten Jahrhundert* (Berlin, 1991), pp. 208–30.

56. Anthony Giddens, *Modernity and Self-Identity: Self and Society in the Late Modern Age* (Cambridge, 1991), p. 20; compare Giddens, *The Transformation of Intimacy: Sexuality, Love, and Eroticism in Modern Times* (Cambridge, 1992); Niklas Luhmann, *Liebe als Passion. Zur Codierung von Intimität* (Frankfurt, 1982).

57. Krafft-Ebing, *Psychopathia sexualis,* 12th ed. (1912), p. 314.

58. Compare Birken, *Consuming Desire*; Elaine Showalter, *Sexual Anarchy: Gender and Culture at the Fin de Siècle* (London, 1991); Franz X. Eder, "Erotisierendes Wissen. Zur Geschichte der 'Sexualisierung' im Wiener Fin de Siècle," in *Erotik, Versuch einer Annäherung. Ausstellungskatalog des Historischen Museums der Stadt Wien* (Vienna, 1990).

TRADE, WOLVES, AND THE BOUNDARIES OF NORMAL MANHOOD

GEORGE CHAUNCEY

The most striking difference between the dominant sexual culture of the early twentieth century and that of our own era is the degree to which the earlier culture permitted men to engage in sexual relations with other men, often on a regular basis, without requiring them to regard themselves—or to be regarded by others—as gay. If sexual abnormality was defined in different terms in prewar culture, then so, too, necessarily, was sexual normality. The centrality of the fairy to the popular representation of sexual abnormality allowed other men to engage in casual sexual relations with other men, with boys, and, above all, with the fairies themselves without imagining that they themselves were abnormal. Many men alternated between male and female sexual partners without believing that interest in one precluded interest in the other, or that their occasional recourse to male sexual partners, in particular, indicated an abnormal, "homosexual," or even "bisexual" disposition, for they neither understood nor organized their sexual practices along a hetero–homosexual axis.

This sexual ideology, far more than the other erotic systems with which it coexisted, predominated in working-class culture. It had particular efficacy in organizing the sexual practices of men in the social milieu in which it might be least expected: in the highly aggressive and quintessentially "masculine" subculture of young and usually unmarried sailors, common laborers, hoboes, and other transient workers, who were a ubiquitous presence in early-twentieth-century American cities. After demonstrating how widely it was assumed that "normal" men could engage in sexual relations with other men and the role of this sexual ideology in organizing the sexual world of "rough" working-class men, this chapter explores the basis of that ideology in working-class gender ideology and in the deeper logic of the association of fairies with prostitutes. For the complex conventions governing the social interactions of fairies and normal workingmen established the terms of their sexual relations as well, and reveal much about the organization of gender, sex, and sexuality in working-class culture.

THE SISTERS AND THEIR MEN: TRADE AND THE CONCEPTUALIZATION OF MALE SEXUAL RELATIONS IN WORKING-CLASS CULTURE

The strongest evidence that the relationship between "men" and fairies was represented symbolically as a male–female relationship and that gender behavior rather than homosexual behavior per se was the primary determinant of a man's classification as a fairy was that it enabled other men to engage in sexual activity with the fairies—and even to express publicly a strong interest in such contacts—without risking stigmatization and the undermining of their status as "normal." So long as they maintained a masculine demeanor and played (or claimed to play) only the "masculine," or insertive, role in the sexual encounter—so long, that is, as they eschewed the style of the fairy and did not allow their bodies to be sexually penetrated—neither they, the fairies, nor the working-class public considered *them* to be queer. Thus a private investigator reported in 1927 that a Mr. Farley, owner of a newsstand in the basement of the Times Square Building at Forty-second Street and Broadway, complained to him that "whenever the fleet comes into town, every sailor who wants his d— licked comes to the Times Square Building. It seems to be common knowledge among the sailors that the Times Square Building is the place to go if they want to meet any fairies." He was unhappy about the commotion so many unruly sailors caused around his newsstand and disapproved of their actions. In no way, however, did he indicate that he thought the sailors looking for sex with the fairies were themselves fairies or otherwise different from most sailors. The investigator himself observed "two sailors . . . in the company of three men who were acting in an effeminate manner." He labeled the effeminate men "fairies" even though it was the sailors who were "making overtures to these men to go to their apartments [and the men] declined to go."[1]

Even men working for state policing agencies categorized men in these terms. New York State Liquor Authority agents investigating a sailors' bar in Brooklyn in October 1938 reported that shortly after midnight, "several males who were apparently 'fags' enter[ed] the premises in groups of twos and threes." They later observed "sailors leaving with some girls, and some men in uniform leaving with the fags." To make it clear that they thought the sailors were leaving with the fags for the same sexual reason that other sailors left with female prostitutes, they added: "In particular it was observed that two marines left with two of the fags and remained in the dark street under the railroad trestle." The investigators did not regard the marines who left with the "fags" as "fags" themselves, nor did they otherwise question the marines' status as men. Indeed, their final report recommended that the state close the bar precisely because it "permitt[ed] prostitutes to congregate with male customers . . . [and] permitt[ed] 'fags' to congregate on the premises and solicit males for immoral purposes."[2] They gave no indication that they found it shocking or unusual that the "fags" should have as much success picking up sailors as female prostitutes did. On the contrary, they regarded the sailors' response to the solicitations of "fags" as no different in kind from their responses to those of female prostitutes.

The acceptance of men's relations with fairies as proper manifestations of the male quest for pleasure and power was indicated even more strikingly by the structure of male prostitution in the late nineteenth and early twentieth centuries. By the 1910s and 1920s, it was increasingly common for both gay- and straight-identified men to sell sexual services to gay-identified men. But at the turn of the century the predominant form of male prostitution seems to have involved fairies selling sex to men who, despite the declaration of desire made by their willingness to pay for the encounters, identified themselves as normal. Indeed, while the term *fairy* generally denoted any flamboyantly effeminate homosexual man (whose self-presentation resembled that of a female prostitute), numerous references in the early twentieth century make it clear that the word was sometimes used specifically to denote men who actually worked as prostitutes selling sexual services to "normal" men.[3] Fairies still appeared in this role in several novels published in the 1930s about New York-based homosexual characters. One 1933 novel, for instance, referred to "the street corner 'fairy' of Times Square" as a "street-walker," invariably "rouged, lisping, [and] mincing." And in Kennilworth Bruce's *Goldie,* also published in 1933, a working-class youth from New Jersey explained "the ways and wiles of the twilight world in New York" to the protagonist, whom the youth had identified as a fairy: "He told him about the 'fairies' and the 'wolves' that frequent the streets of New York . . . around the Times Square section. . . . 'The fairies pull down big dough, too. . . . There's the actors and musicians when the shows break; there's the gamblers and guys with small-time rackets; and there's the highbrow sots when they leave the speakeasies in the wee hours. Fairies work up a regular trade.' "[4]

Numerous accounts of turn-of-the-century homosexual prostitution confirm that it commonly involved men paying fairies for sex, while still considering themselves to be the "men" in the encounter. This, after all, was the premise of the Lower East Side resorts, such as Paresis Hall and the Slide, where female prostitutes also gathered and where many of the fairies were not only called "male prostitutes" but (in the language of the day) "sat for company," having the men who joined their tables buy them drinks, just as female prostitutes did. Significantly, in prostitutes' slang a "slide" denoted an "establishment where male homosexuals dress[ed] as women and solicit[ed] men," a meaning apparently known to the officials involved in a state investigation of police corruption in 1894. A Captain Ryan testified he had "closed up every disorderly-house, every gambling-house and policy office, and every slide and dives [*sic*] in the precinct [within] three months [of taking command]." When asked if he were sure he knew what a slide was, he reminded his questioner that "we had one of the most notorious slides in the world in Bleecker street when I had command of that precinct." His comment both confirms the fame of the Slide, which he had shut down in 1892, and suggests that the resort's management had deliberately used the slang term in naming the club in order to announce its character (even though, in fact, the fairies there did not dress as women).[5] Moreover, the very existence of the slang term suggests that other such resorts existed, as indeed they did.

There were also brothels where men could meet fairies more privately, as the Reverend Charles Parkhurst discovered in 1892 when he took his famous tour of New York's underworld (his own form of slumming) to gather evidence for his assault on Tammany Hall corruption. His guide took him to a brothel on West Third Street, the Golden Rule Pleasure Club, where the basement was divided into cubicles, each occupied by "a youth, whose face was painted, eye-brows blackened, and whose airs were those of a young girl, . . . [who] talked in a high falsetto voice, and called the others by women's names," each youth waiting for a man to hire his services.[6] It should be remembered that neither the fairies at the Slide nor those at the Pleasure Club were dressed as women; no customer seeking their services could have mistaken them for "normal" women.

This pattern was not restricted to such brothels and saloons. Fairy prostitutes, usually dressed as men but using their hair, makeup, and demeanor to signal their character, worked along the Bowery, Riverside Drive, Fourteenth Street, and Forty-second Street, and in Bryant Park and Prospect Park, as well as in the back rooms of saloons on Elizabeth Street and Third Avenue. One fairy, for instance, a female impersonator from a poor neighborhood in Brooklyn where he was known as Loop-the-loop, a suggestive play on the name of a popular ride at Coney Island, reported to a doctor in 1906 that he regularly plied his trade "chiefly for the money there is in it." Loop-the-loop often worked in his neighborhood as well as in Prospect Park, where, he reported, he and the other prostitutes paid off the patrolmen so that they could wear dresses. His efforts at female impersonation would not have persuaded any of his clients that they were having sex with a woman, given the inartfulness of his costume and the heavy growth of hair on his legs and arms (he complained of the hair himself, but added that "most of the boys don't mind it").[7] But his costume and demeanor, like those of the fairies at Paresis Hall, *did* signify to "the boys" that he was not a normal man, either, but rather a third-sexer, with whom they could have sex without complicating their understanding of their own sexual character.

The relationship between a fairy prostitute and his male customers emblematized the central model governing the interpretation of male–male sexual relationships. The term *trade* originally referred to the customer of a fairy prostitute, a meaning analogous to and derived from its usage in the slang of female prostitutes; by the 1910s, it referred to any "straight" man who responded to a gay man's advances. As one fairy put it in 1919, a man was trade if he "would stand to have 'queer' persons fool around [with] him in any way, shape or manner."[8] *Trade* was also increasingly used in the middle third of the century to refer to straight-identified men who worked as prostitutes serving gay-identified men, reversing the dynamic of economic exchange and desire implied by the original meaning. Thus the term *trade* sometimes referred specifically to "straight" male prostitutes, but it also continued to be used to refer to "straight" men who had sex with queers or fairies for pleasure rather than money. The sailors eagerly seeking the sexual services of fairies at the Times Square Building, like those who left the Happy Hour Bar & Grill with the "fags," were considered trade, whether or not money was part of the transaction. So long as the men abided by the conventions of masculinity, they ran little risk of undermining their status as "normal" men.

Although it is impossible to determine just how common such interactions were in the early twentieth century or precisely how many men were prepared to engage in homosexual behavior on these or any other terms, Alfred Kinsey's research suggests that the number may have been large. Published in 1948, *Sexual Behavior in the Human Male* was based on the sexual life histories Kinsey and his associates gathered from men in the 1930s and 1940s, and thus offers an overview of sexual patterns among men in the half-century preceding World War II. Although most recent commentary on the Kinsey Report has focused on (and criticized) its supposed estimate that 10 percent of the population were homosexuals, Kinsey himself never made such an estimate and argued explicitly that such estimates could not be based on his findings. His research is much more helpful if used, as Kinsey intended, to examine the extent of occasional homosexual behavior among men who may or may not have identified themselves as "homosexual." Only 4 percent of the men he interviewed reported having been exclusively homosexual in their behavior throughout their lives, but 37 percent acknowledged having engaged in at least one postadolescent homosexual encounter to the point of orgasm, and fully a quarter of them acknowledged having had "more than incidental homosexual experience or reactions" for at least three years between the ages sixteen and fifty-five.[9] Clearly some cultural mechanism was at work that allowed men to engage in sexual relations with other men without thinking of themselves as abnormal.

Kinsey's own remarks about the proper interpretation of his findings suggest the prevalence at the time of the interpretation of homosexual relations outlined here. They indicate that many of the men he interviewed believed their sexual activity with other men did not mean they were homosexual so long as they restricted that behavior to the "masculine" role. (Indeed, his commentary is probably more useful to historical analysis than his statistical claims.) He presumably singled out for comment those notions that his interviews had revealed to be particularly widespread in the culture. His comments are not now generally noted, since the hetero–homosexual binarism has become hegemonic and the ideas against which he argued no longer have credibility. But it is significant that in the 1940s he still believed he needed to take special care to dispute interpretations of homosexual relations that regarded only one of the men involved in them as "genuinely homosexual" (and possibly not genuinely a man) and the other as not homosexual at all. It was absurd to believe, he argued, that "individuals engaging in homosexual activity are neither male nor female, but persons of mixed sex," or that "inversion [by which he meant a man playing the roles culturally ascribed to women] is an invariable accompaniment of homosexuality."[10] Equally untenable (and, apparently, common), he thought, were the claims of men who allowed themselves to be fellated but never performed fellation on other men that they were really "heterosexual," and the popular belief that "the active male in an anal relation is essentially heterosexual in his behavior, and [only] the passive male . . . homosexual."[11]

To argue that the fairy and his man emblematized the dominant conceptual schema by which homosexual relations were understood is not to argue, however, that it was the only schema or that all men were equally prepared to engage in sexual relations with other men on those terms. The image of the fairy was so powerful culturally that it influenced the self-understanding of all sexually active men, but men socialized into different class and ethnic systems of gender, family life, and sexual mores nonetheless tended to understand and organize their sexual practices in significantly different ways. Several sexual cultures coexisted in New York's divergent neighborhoods, and the social locus of the sexual culture just described needs to be specified more precisely. Middle-class Anglo-American men were less likely to accept the fairy–trade interpretive schema Kinsey reported, and even their limited acceptance of it declined during the first half of the century. It was, above all, a working-class way of making sense of sexual relations.

Among working-class men there were also ethnic differences in the social organization and tolerance of homosexual relations. Unfortunately, the evidence is too fragmentary to support a carefully delineated or "definitive" characterization of the predominant sexual culture of any of the city's immigrant or ethnic groups, and, in any case, no single sexual culture existed in any such group since each of them was divided internally along lines of gender, class, and regional origin. Nonetheless, the limited evidence available suggests that African Americans and Irish and Italian immigrants interacted with "fairies" more extensively than Jewish immigrants did, and that they were more likely to engage in homosexual activity organized in different terms as well. Certainly, many Anglo-American, Jewish, and African-American gay men thought that "straight" Italian and Irish men were more likely to respond to their sexual advances than straight Jewish men were, and police records tend to support the conclusions of gay folklore.[12]

The contrast between Italians and Jews, the two newest and largest groups of immigrants in New York at the turn of the century, is particularly striking. A 1921 study of men arrested for homosexual "disorderly conduct," for instance, reported that "the Italians lead" in the number of arrests; at a time when the numbers of Italians and Jews in New York were roughly equal, almost twice as many Italians were arrested on homosexual charges.[13] More significant is that turn-of-the-century investigators found a more institutionalized fairy subculture in Italian neighborhoods than in Jewish ones. The Italian neighborhood of the Lower East Side had numerous saloons where fairies gathered interspersed among the saloons where female prostitutes worked. In 1908, Vito Lorenzo's saloon, located at 207 Canal Street (near Baxter), was charged by the police with being a "fairy place."[14] In 1901, agents conducting a systematic survey of "vice conditions" on the Lower East Side found male prostitutes working in two Italian saloons on the block of Elizabeth Street between Hester and Grand, the same block where the Hotel Zaza's manager hired rooms to female prostitutes who stood at the windows in "loose dresses and call[ed] the men upstairs."[15] One investigator noted that the Union Hall saloon was crowded with old Italian men and several young fairies on the night of March 5; a few doors up the street, at 97 Elizabeth, stood a saloon where the fairies, aged fourteen to sixteen, could "do their business right in [the] back room." A month later the same saloon was said to have "5 boys known as [*finocchio,* or fairies] about 17 to 25 years of age."[16]

Strikingly, the same investigators found no such open "fairy resorts" in the Lower East Side's Jewish section, located just a few blocks to the east, even though they discovered numerous tenements and street corners where female prostitutes worked. The police periodically discovered men soliciting other men in a less organized fashion in the Jewish neighborhood's streets, tenements, and even synagogues, to be sure. Two policemen, for instance, arrested a twenty-two-year-old Jewish immigrant for soliciting men from the window of 186 Suffolk Street, at Houston, in 1900.[17] But they arrested far fewer Jews than Italians on such charges, and the sites of homosexual rendezvous were less stable and commercialized, less well known, and thus, presumably, less tolerated in the Jewish neighborhood than in the Italian.

It is difficult to assess the reasons for the apparent differences in the social organization of and larger community's tolerance of male homosexual relations in Italian versus Jewish immigrant enclaves, particularly given the absence of more extensive ethnographic studies of the overall sexual culture of either group. But three interrelated factors seem particularly crucial: the sexual cultures the Jews and Italians brought with them to the States from Europe, the different circumstances of their immigration, and the ways gender relations were organized in their communities.

The sexual cultures of immigrants in the United States were clearly shaped in large part by the gender and sexual cultures of their homelands, each of which was, in turn, significantly differentiated internally along regional and class lines. Northern Italians brought to the United States a set of cultural assumptions about sex different from those of Sicilians, for instance; middle-class Italians were likely to organize gender relations differently from peasants or workers.[18]

Although both Catholic and Jewish religious authorities condemned homosexual relations, Catholic teaching, especially, focused on the moral dangers posed by sexual contact between men and women to such a degree that it may implicitly have made sexual contact between men seem relatively harmless. One man who grew up in an Italian neighborhood recalled that "homosexuality just wasn't regarded as a mortal sin, it wasn't seen as that bad." Perhaps more significant is that immigrant Italians were well known for their rejection of church teaching on a wide range of moral matters, and the anti-gay religious injunction was much less effective among them than among Jewish men. Kinsey singled out Orthodox Jewish men for their "phenomenally low" rates of homosexual activity.[19]

By the late nineteenth century, southern Italian men had a reputation in northern Italy and in the northern European gay world for their supposed willingness to engage in homosexual relations. Although this reputation doubtless resulted in part from the propensity of dominant cultural groups to try to differentiate and stigmatize subordinate groups by attributing "immoral" or "bizarre" sexual practices to them, considerable evidence nonetheless suggests that such practices were both more common and more accepted in southern Italy than in the north. Numerous British and German gay men traveled to southern Italy at the turn of the century in search of a more tolerant climate; forty years later, during World War II, many gay American soldiers were startled to discover the frequency and overtness of homosexual solicitation there. On the basis of his own observations during a research trip to Europe in 1955 and the reports he received from several of his most trusted informants, Alfred Kinsey also concluded that southern Italian men were considerably more open to homosexual relations than northern Europeans were. Many Italian youths adopted an instrumental attitude toward their bodies before marriage and did not consider it shameful to use them to secure cash or advancement, observers reported, and even many married men were willing to engage in homosexual relations so long as they took the "manly part." Only the adult male who took the "woman's part" was stigmatized.

The patterns of homosexual behavior noted in Sicily appear to have persisted in modified form in the Italian enclaves on the Lower East Side, in Greenwich Village, and in East Harlem. Although more research would need to be done to substantiate the point, it seems likely that an important part of the homosexual culture of fairies and their sex partners visible in turn-of-the-century New York represented the flowering in this country of a transplanted Mediterranean sexual culture.[20]

The relative acceptance of homosexual relations in Italian immigrant communities was related as well to the demographics of Italian immigration to the United States, which were strikingly different from those of eastern European Jews. Given the escalation of anti-Semitic violence and the draconian restrictions placed on Jewish economic and social activities in eastern Europe in the late nineteenth century, most Jewish immigrants to New York had decided to leave their villages for good with as many of their family members as possible. But the great majority of the city's Italian immigrants were single men or married men unaccompanied by their families who planned to return to Italy after earning funds to invest there. Eighty percent of the Italians who entered the United States from 1880 to 1910 were males, and the great majority of them were in their prime working years, from fourteen to forty-four years old. So many of them came to work on a seasonal basis or for only a year or two that 43 Italians left the United States for every 100 who arrived in the mid-1890s, and 73 left for every 100 who arrived in the peak immigration years of 1907–11. By contrast, only 21,000 Jews left the United States in 1908–12, while 295,000 arrived; 42 percent of Jewish immigrants were females in the 1890s—twice the proportion of Italian females—and a quarter were children under fourteen, compared to only 11 percent of the Italians.[21] Italian men may have been more responsive to homosexual overtures than Jewish men in part simply because far fewer of them were living with their wives.

Italian men also tended to have less contact with women than Jewish men did because of the greater gender segregation of Italian neighborhoods, a cultural difference only accentuated by the demographics of southern Italian immigration. Not only did more Jewish men live with their families, they centered their social lives in their apartments as well as in their synagogues, union halls, and other communal meeting places. Young Jewish men and women had their own gender-segregated groups and young women bore heavy responsibilities at home, but they were also likely to socialize in mixed-gender groups and at the dance halls, movie theaters, and other commercial amusements that abounded in their neighborhoods. Although they expected to be asked for permission, Jewish parents tended to allow their daughters to go to dances or take walks with young men. The high degree of interaction between young Jewish men and women stood in sharp contrast to the gender segregation of Italian neighborhoods, as many contemporary observers noted. The social investigator Sophonisba Breckinridge commented in 1921, "Most immigrant parents, except those from southern Italy, recognize the impossibility of maintaining the old rules of chaperonage and guardianship of the girls . . . [but] Italian parents . . . try to guard their girls almost as closely as they did in Italy."[22]

Although many Italian men in New York also lived with their families and many others boarded with families, a large number of them lived in rooming houses, where they organized surrogate, all-male families with other Italian men. Even those men who boarded with families spent much of their time outside their cramped accommodations, in the neighborhood's streets, poolrooms, and saloons; young men living with their parents spent most of their time in similar locales. As the historian Robert Orsi notes, "Men significantly outnumbered women in the first decades of Italian Harlem . . . [and] they lived in a largely male world."[23]

In this all-male social world, clubs or "gangs" of various sorts formed, usually with loosely defined memberships that fluctuated as people moved in and out of the neighborhood. Walking down four short blocks of Mulberry Street, the chief thoroughfare of the Italian Lower East Side, around 1920, John Mariano counted signs announcing the existence of at least thirty such clubs, each of them drawing young men from the immediate neighborhood, often a single block. He described the members of one of them as American-born truckers, dockworkers, and the like, who ranged in age from twenty to thirty. Employed irregularly in seasonal labor markets that made it impossible for most of them to establish even a modicum of economic security, they prided themselves on their rejection of the unrealizable "American" work ethic. "When they desire to be facetious," he noted disapprovingly, "they call themselves 'the Sons of Rest.'" Not only were two-thirds of these men in their twenties unmarried, but the third who were married nonetheless spent a great deal of their leisure time in the all-male group.[24]

THE BACHELOR SUBCULTURE

As men who (whether married or not) spent most of their time in a largely male social world, these first- and second-generation Italian immigrants were proto-typical members of what several historians and sociologists have rather ambiguously termed a "bachelor subculture." This subculture was the primary locus of the sexual dyad of fairies and trade, and its dynamics help explain the sexual culture not only of Italian immigrants but also of many Irish, African-American, and Anglo-American working-class men. The bachelor subculture played a significant (though relatively little studied) role in American cities from the mid-nineteenth century until the mid-twentieth, when about 40 percent of the men over fifteen years old were unmarried at any given time. It was really a series of distinct but overlapping subcultures centered in the poolrooms and saloons where many workingmen spent their time, in the cellar clubrooms and streets where gangs of boys and young men were a ubiquitous presence, and in the lodging houses that crowded the Bowery and the waterfront.[25] It was a highly gender-segregated social world of young, unmarried, and often transient laborers, seamen, and the like, the "rough" working-class men, that is, whom we have already seen at the Times Square newsstand and the Brooklyn sailors' bar and whom Ralph Werther, for one, identified as particularly receptive to his advances.

Many of the young men of the bachelor subculture would later go on to marry. Many were immigrants (such as the Italians) planning to work in the States only a short while before returning to their families in Europe. The Irish contributed disproportionate numbers of men to this subculture as well. Irish-American men, like their compatriots in Ireland itself, tended to marry only in their early thirties, if at all, and much of their social life was consequentially organized around all-male groups. Indeed, the high rates of lifelong bachelor-hood among the Irish provoked periodic discussions in the Irish and Catholic press of the danger of Irish "race suicide."[26] The bachelor subculture also included native-born Anglo-Americans who either had not yet married or planned never to do so, as well as immigrants who had left home precisely in order to escape the pressure to marry. It also included married men from many backgrounds who chose to spend most of their time in the company of other men and moved regularly between the bachelor world of "rough" workingmen and the more family-oriented world of "respectable" workingmen.

The working-class bachelor subculture drew heavily from three sometimes overlapping occupational cultures: sailors, merchant marines, and other seamen; transient workers who spent time in the city between stints in the countryside as agricultural laborers, lumberjacks, construction workers, and ice cutters; and common laborers based in New York, who worked on the waterfront, in construction, and in other heavy manual-labor jobs. The highly irregular and unpredictable work of many of them on shipboard, in agriculture, or in construction often took them out of the city on a seasonal basis and made it difficult for them to support or maintain regular ties with a family. The native-born among them, especially, were part of the immense army of migrant laborers, usually known as hoboes or tramps, who constituted a significant part of the American workforce in the decades before the 1920s.

The sailor, seen as young and manly, unattached, and unconstrained by conventional morality, epitomized the bachelor subculture in the gay cultural imagination. He served for generations as the central masculine icon in gay pornography, as the paintings of Charles Demuth and Paul Cadmus from the early decades of the century and the photographs produced by gay pornographers in its middle decades attest.[27] But as the records of anti-vice investigators show, his role in the gay subculture was not simply as an object of fantasy. He was a central figure in the subculture, and his haunts became the haunts of gay men as well. He was, however, usually not "of" that culture, since he typically declined to identify himself as other than normal and in sexual encounters almost always took the role of the "man."

The members of the bachelor subculture were a ubiquitous presence in New York in 1900, when two of every five men in Manhattan aged fifteen years or older were unmarried. They were especially evident in parts of Harlem, in the Italian and Irish districts, along the bustling waterfront, and along the Bowery, long known as the "main stem," or center, of the city's "Hobohemia." Their world began to disappear in the 1920s, when the sex ratios of immigrant communities started to stabilize after the strict new federal immigration laws passed in that decade made it difficult for immigrant workers to enter the United States for brief periods of work. The number of seamen in the city began to decline as New York's port declined, and the number of transient workers (or hoboes) dropped throughout the country in the 1920s, as economic and technological developments, such as refrigeration, the mechanization of agricultural production, and the expansion of auto transport, reduced the need for them.[28] The men of the working-class bachelor subculture continued to play a significant role in the city's life throughout the half-century before World War II, however, and it was in their social world that the interaction of fairies and trade took its most visible and highly developed form.

The bachelor subculture, as several historians have shown, shared many of the characteristics of working-class male culture as a whole, but it also had certain distinctive elements that made it particularly amenable to the presence of fairies.[29] The dominant working-class ideology made the ability and willingness to undertake the responsibility of supporting a family two of the defining characteristics of both manliness and male "respectability." But many of the men of the bachelor subculture, either because their irregular and poorly paid work made supporting a family difficult or because they had deliberately chosen to avoid such family encumbrances, forged an alternative definition of manliness that was predicated on a rejection of family obligations. Although many of the men would eventually marry, they tended to remain isolated from women and hostile to the constraints of marriage during the many years they were involved in the bachelor subculture. (They were also considerably more open to advances of fairies before their marriages; Ralph Werther, for instance, noted that most of his young Italian and Irish sex partners went on to marry women.[30]) Indeed, not only their disengagement from the conventions of family life and domesticity but their decided rejection of them were central elements of their culture; they were considered "rough" not simply because many of them rejected family life per se, but more precisely because they scorned the manners associated with the domesticating and moralizing influence of women.

Some of the descriptions of "rough" working-class life provided by hostile middle-class observers in the 1900s and 1910s suggest the extent to which the observers considered the rejection of the feminine domestication of male behavior, the casual mingling of men and fairies, and open displays of homosexuality to be characteristic of such life. An agent investigating the Subway Cabaret on East Fourteenth Street for a moral-reform society in 1917 cited such mingling, along with men refusing to doff their hats (a sign of their lack of domestication), in order to illustrate the "lowergrade" character of the place to his supervisor:

> For instance, at one table one sees three or four tough looking fellows . . . who have to be requested to keep their hats off. At another table one sees a sailor, sitting drinking with two other fellows in civilian clothes, the sailor with his arm around the other fellows neck. The proprietor had to make the sailor behave himself. The sailor was constantly going out with one of the other fellows to the lavatory. I went out also a couple of times but they would just stand there and talk while I was there, and thus I was cheated out of witnessing a little homosexuality.[31]

Embodying a rejection of domesticity and of bourgeois acquisitivism alike, the bachelor subculture was based on a shared code of manliness and an ethic of male solidarity. The solidarity it celebrated was expressed in the everyday ties built at work on the waterfront or in construction; it was symbolized by the rituals of saloon conviviality that expressed mutual regard and reciprocity, perhaps most commonly through the custom of treating one's fellows to rounds of drinks. A man's "manliness" was signaled in part by his participation in such rituals and by his behavior on the job, but it was demonstrated as well by his besting of other men in contests of strength and skill in all-male arenas such as the boxing ring, poolroom, and gambling den. Sexual prowess with women was another important sign of manliness, but such prowess was significant not only as an indication of a man's ability to dominate women but also as evidence of his *relative* virility compared to other men's; manliness in this world was confirmed by other men and in relation to other men, not by women.[32]

The way the men in this social milieu constructed their manliness allowed other men to construct themselves as something other than men. The men in this culture regarded manhood as a hard-won accomplishment, not a given, and as a continuum, not an absolute value or characteristic. Even as they celebrated their masculine camaraderie and commitment to fraternity, they constantly had to prove their manhood and often sought to demonstrate that they were more manly than their rivals. To be called a "man" or a "regular guy" was both the highest compliment in this world and the most common. But the very repetitiveness of such praise implied that men were in danger of being called something else: unmanly, a mollycoddle, a sissy, even a pansy. Whereas manhood could be achieved, it could also be lost; it was not simply a quality that resulted naturally and inevitably from one's sex. The calculated character of the everyday rituals of male sociability, solidarity, and competition by which men enacted their manliness and demonstrated their relative virility suggests the remarkable degree to which they regarded their manliness as a kind of ongoing performance, to use Erving Goffman and Judith Butler's term. It also reveals the degree to which relations in this all-male environment were gendered.[33] It was both this self-consciousness about the performativity of gender and the gendering of relations among men that allowed some males to turn themselves into "she-men," so long as they did not question other men's status as men, and allowed other males to confirm their own "he-manliness" by subordinating them. The very theatricality of the fairies' style not only emphasized the performative character of gender but evoked an aura of liminality reminiscent of carnivals at which the normal constraints on men's behavior were suspended, making it easier for men to interact with them without considering it consequential.[34]

One of the reasons fairies were tolerated by tough working-class men and often had remarkably easygoing relations with them was the care they took to confirm rather than question the latter's manliness. Fairies related to men as if they themselves were women—though often the "tough" women who dared venture into the social spaces dominated by tough men—and they did so in a manner that confirmed the complex social conventions of gender deference, inequality, and power characteristic of gender relations in that culture. But some gangs of men regarded fairies, like women, as fair game for sexual exploitation. Sexually using a fairy not only could be construed and legitimized as a "normal" sexual act but could actually provide some of the same enhancement of social status that mastering a woman did.

That this dynamic sometimes influenced the meaning ascribed to homosexual encounters is suggested by the experience of one Italian youth around 1920. He was sexually active with other men (almost always, he said, "act[ing] as a woman"), but he tried to protect his reputation by developing a conventionally masculine style in the other spheres of his life. He did not carry himself as a fairy and sought to establish his masculinity with the other youths he met at a neighborhood gymnasium by deliberately "talk[ing] about women" with them. Participating in the collective sexualization and objectification of women was one of the rituals by which he established himself as a man. At the gym he met a twenty-five-year-old boxer to whom he was attracted, and he eventually agreed to let the boxer, who had sensed his interest, anally penetrate him. To the boy's horror, the boxer promptly went to the gym and told everyone what he had done; the boy, humiliated, concluded he could never go there again.[35] A man who allowed himself to be used sexually as a woman, then, risked forfeiting his masculine status, even if he were otherwise conventionally masculine; in this case, the boy's shame clearly derived from his perception that he had been made a fairy in the eyes of his comrades. The story also illustrates the belief among men in this world that so long as they played the "man's" role, they remained men. The most striking aspect of the story is the confidence the boxer felt that reporting the encounter would not endanger his status among his friends, that, indeed, having sexually subordinated the boy would enhance it. If a man risked forfeiting his masculine status by being sexually passive, he could also establish it by playing the dominant role in an encounter with another man. Sexual penetration symbolized one man's power over another.

Men's sexual relations with fairies were also fundamentally influenced by the character of their sexual relations with women, particularly the prostitutes and other "tough girls" who were the only women with whom many men in the bachelor subculture interacted. The very social organization and meaning of their sexual relations with women made it relatively unobjectionable for them to substitute fairies when such women could not be found. Numerous reports by undercover agents investigating female prostitution in the early decades of the century make it clear that in those social milieus dominated by young, single laborers and seamen, it was understood that men in search of women sexual partners might be willing to make just that substitution. It was not thought that all men *would*, but it was not considered remarkable when any man *did*.

One evening in the fall of 1927 two agents in search of female prostitutes were taken by a sailor to an Italian restaurant on West Seventeenth Street, where sailors and "hardened neighborhood girls" congregated. After failing to lure any of the women away from the sailors (but, presumably, having succeeded in demonstrating their sexual interest in women), they asked their waitress if she knew where they could find a "sporting girl." The woman said she did not, but immediately added that "there is a fairy [who] comes in here," and called him over. One might expect that the fairy was pimping for female prostitutes, but the agents' response indicates they believed they were being offered the fairy in place of a prostitute. Quickly taking advantage of the unexpected opportunity, they "tried to make an appointment with [him] . . . and [made] an effort to learn where he resided or took his trade." The fairy begged off, citing a previous appointment.[36] The fairy's disinclination to cooperate meant that the agents—

and we—learned nothing more of his life, but the fact that the waitress referred the agents to him in the first place tells us much about the understanding of male sexuality she had developed while working in a milieu dominated by sailors and Italian laborers. It evidently seemed plausible—even likely—to her that a man anxious for sexual satisfaction would accept it from a fairy if a woman were unavailable.

The Italian waitress was not the only one who believed this. The general secretary of the city's major anti-prostitution society warned in 1918 that opponents of his anti-prostitution campaign might use the "apparent increase of male perversion" during World War I as "evidence to sustain their argument that vice driven out of one form will appear in another."[37] His fear that such reasoning would seem plausible was well founded. One of his own investigators had used it to explain the homosexual liaisons he had observed on the streets surrounding the Brooklyn Navy Yard late one summer night in 1917, when no women were to be found:

> The streets and corners were crowded with the sailors all of whom were on a sharp lookout for girls. . . . It seemed to me that the sailors were sex mad. A number of these sailors were with other men walking arm in arm and on one dark street I saw a sailor and a man kissing each other. . . . It looked like an exhibition of mail [sic] perversion showing itself in the absence of girls or the difficulty of finding them. Some of the sailors told me that they might be able to get a girl if they went 'up-town' but it was too far up and they were too drunk to go way up there.[38]

The belief that fairies could be substituted for female prostitutes—and were virtually interchangeable with them—was particularly prevalent among men in the bachelor subculture whose opportunities for meeting "respectable" women were limited by the moral codes, gender segregation, or unbalanced sex ratios of their ethnic cultures. Indeed, many of these men found the sexual services of fairies to be both easier and cheaper to secure than those of women. They could be found around the Navy Yard and along the waterfront, on well-known streets and in many saloons frequented by sailors and workingmen, and even in many subway washrooms, where a man could find quick release on the way home from work merely by presenting himself. A finely calibrated map of the sexual geography of the neighborhood was usually part of men's gender-specific "local knowledge." Many workingmen knew precisely where to go to find fairies with whom, if they chose, they need not exchange a word to make their wishes clear.[39]

Still, the relative accessibility of fairies to men isolated from women hardly explains the latter's willingness to turn to them. After all, thousands of women were working as prostitutes in the city, and workingmen often *did* have recourse to them; the immense number of single men in the city with few other means of meeting women supported the business of prostitution on a scale that would never be repeated after the 1920s.[40] If men had risked being stigmatized as queer on the basis of a single homosexual encounter, most of them would have sought sex exclusively with such women.

But the very character of their sexual relations with prostitutes and other "tough" women made it possible for them to turn to fairies as well. The moral codes governing the sexual practices of many men in the bachelor subculture (as in the larger culture of men) divided the world into "pure women," with whom men did not expect sexual contact until after marriage, and "impure women" or "whores," whom men felt free to pursue aggressively for sexual purposes.[41] In the eyes of such men, the simple willingness of a woman to enter the saloons, pool-rooms, and other social spaces they dominated was a sign that she was a prostitute. In a culture in which men regarded themselves as highly lustful creatures whose health would be impaired if their explosive sexual needs did not find release (or, as they usually termed it, "relief" or "satisfaction"),[42] a phallocentric economy of sexual pleasure governed relations with such women. Sex was something a man did *to* them, not *with* them: a man's phallic dominance and "satisfaction" were his paramount concern. A man might have a close romantic relationship with one woman, whom he hoped to marry and treated with affection and respect, but still feel free to use a prostitute to satisfy his immediate sexual needs. Few men would ever even imagine substituting a fairy for their beloved (although they might develop feelings of affection for some fairies, just as they did for some prostitutes, and might even find it easier to relate to fairies than to prostitutes because they found it easier to relate to men than to women).[43] But many men did find it relatively easy to substitute a fairy for a prostitute, since both offered immediate sexual satisfaction, as well as the pleasures and amusements of bawdy "female" companionship. In a world in which "every woman is just another place to enter," as one Italian teenager described the attitude of men at his neighborhood pool hall in 1930, the body to enter did not necessarily have to be a woman's.[44]

Gang rapes and other phallocentric sexual practices highlighted the cultural logic that allowed men to substitute fairies for women as objects of sexual penetration. Loop-the-loop, the fairy prostitute mentioned previously, reported to a doctor in 1906 that on a single day he had had sex with "no fewer than twenty-three men . . . one immediately after the other . . . in a room in Brooklyn."[45] His boast is more plausible than it may at first seem, for he would have engaged in a well-established practice when he had sex with a line of men, even if he exaggerated the number. "Line-ups," in which men ("anywhere from three to seventeen," by one account from an Italian neighborhood in the late 1920s) formed a queue to have intercourse, one after another, with a single woman, were not uncommon. Some line-ups constituted nothing less than gang rapes (in which the women "were the victims of a planned scheme on the part of the men," according to the same account). In a smaller number of cases, the women had enough control of the situation to stop it when they chose and to charge the men for the encounter. Every line-up allowed men to find sexual satisfaction and to enact their solidarity with other men by establishing their collective difference from and dominance of the woman they used. In a similar manner groups of young men and boys sometimes forced younger boys to provide them with sexual "relief," either by submitting to anal penetration, or, when the number of boys was too large, by masturbating the older boys, one after another.[46] The very structure of such encounters and the interchangeability of fairies, women, and boys in them highlights the degree to which men were simply using the body of the fairy and sometimes the body of a boy, just as they might use the body of a woman, as a vehicle for phallic satisfaction and manly solidarity.

The phallocentric presumption that a man's sexual satisfaction was more significant than the gender or character of the person who provided that satisfaction allowed gay men to make certain arguments in their approach to "normal" men that would seem utterly incredible in the absence of that presumption. Most commonly, gay men simply offered to perform certain sexual acts, especially fellation, which many straight men enjoyed but many women (even many prostitutes) were loath to perform. In such cases it was the particular phallocentric pleasure, rather than the gender of the person providing the pleasure, that men found appealing, although fairies, who were commonly called "cocksuckers," were especially known for this service, in part because so many women refused to provide it. As one gay man observed of the Irish and Italian young men from South Brooklyn with whom he associated in the 1940s and 1950s, they "do not (necessarily) despise fellators—including these 'nice' Brooklyn boys. Or especially they. They find the fellator desirable. . . . The same with sailors."[47] But even though men found the queer man's services desirable, they also believed that a man lost status if he fellated another man. This was not simply a matter of his losing gender status, however, for women also lost status by performing fellation, which is one reason so many women refused to do it. The act itself— a nonreproductive sexual act whether performed by man or woman and thus "unnatural" by the tenets of a reproductively oriented sexual ideology—was considered perverted for men and women alike to do. Its transgressive character was, indeed, part of its appeal, whether performed by men or women.

Some gay men interested in sex with "straight" men also portrayed themselves as less dangerous than women by arguing that there was no chance they would infect the men with the venereal diseases women were thought to carry. Their success with this remarkable line becomes more understandable when one considers the focus of the highly publicized education campaigns launched to curb venereal disease during World War I. The campaigns, controlled by officials concerned with preserving the sexual morality of young men from rural homes as much as with protecting their health, had tried both to heighten men's fear of venereal disease and to use that fear to persuade them to shun contact with prostitutes or the other "loose" women they might encounter in the nation's port cities and training camps. Some educational materials explained that condoms could protect men from venereal disease (and a measure of their success was that condoms came to be called "protectors" in the slang of the 1920s). But most leaflets and posters identified sex with a woman, rather than sex without a condom, as the source of venereal disease.[48] Ironically, one quite unintentional effect of such moralistic campaigns was to reinforce the traditional belief among men that they could catch syphilis or gonorrhea *only* from female prostitutes or other women, whereas sexual contacts with another man were safe—a misconception men interested in seducing other men were quick to seize upon. An investigator posing as a seaman recounted the following conversation with a thirty-year-old Swede employed by the United Fruit Line, in a waterfront cafeteria's washroom in 1931:

> I was about to leave and he said "It smells like a c . . . house. Did you have a woman lately?" I said "No, I am looking for one. Do you know a place?" He said "Wouldn't it be much safer to have it blown?" I said "Do you know a woman who would do that?" He said "Why do you want a woman, they are not safe." I said, "I want only a woman." He then took hold of my arm and said, "Let's get inside. I'll do it for you."[49]

This view was shared by the police as well. A crackdown on homosexual activity after World War I came to an end, in part, because the chief of the vice squad grew concerned that the campaign had diverted too much attention from the squad's efforts against prostitutes, who, he apparently feared, posed a medical, as well as moral, danger to their customers, and through them to their families. Telling his men that "one prostitute was more dangerous than five degenerates," he ordered them to give more attention to the former, a shift in priorities soon reflected in the squad's arrest statistics.[50] Concern about the relative health risk posed by sexual relations with fairies and prostitutes was possible only because it was presupposed that men could substitute fairies for women without undermining their masculine status. Indeed, men's ability to calculate the relative rewards and risks involved in each kind of encounter provides the most powerful evidence possible that the hetero–homosexual axis did not govern their thinking about sexual practices. In the right circumstances, almost any man might choose to experiment with the queer pleasures of sex with a fairy.

HUSBANDS, WOLVES, AND PUNKS

If every workingman was thought to have the capacity to respond to the advances of a fairy, it was nonetheless the case, as gay men themselves realized, that some men were more interested in sexual contacts with fairies and boys than others were. And although some men treated fairies in the same way they treated prostitutes, not every relationship between a man and a fairy was brief, coercive, or loveless, nor did all men orchestrate the relationships in a way that established their distance from the fairies. Some men sought love and even marriage with fairies, and others at least made no bones about their sexual preference for them. Parker Tyler found many of the Italian men who lived in the Village to be responsive to his charms, for instance, but in his 1929 account of his interaction with the cameramen in a Village speakeasy, he regarded the one who seemed the most anxious about the meeting and who made the most earnest entreaties *to him* as a more distinctive character: a "wolf."

Such men, known as "husbands," "wolves," and "jockers" (terms sometimes used interchangeably, sometimes for different groups of men in different social milieus), occupied an ambiguous position in the sexual culture of the early twentieth century. They abided by the conventions of masculinity and yet exhibited a decided preference for male sexual partners. From a late-twentieth-century perspective they might be regarded as homosexuals more easily than the men just described, since they engaged in homosexual activity on a more exclusive basis than most men who were trade. But the fact that neither they nor their peers regarded them as queer, even if they sometimes regarded them as *different* from other "normal" men, highlights the degree to which gender status superseded homosexual interest as the basis of sexual classification in working-class culture.

Some men involved in marriages with fairies were so confident of their status as "normal" men that they readily acknowledged their relationships to others. One such man, a band musician, told a doctor in 1906 that he did not limit himself to brief, anonymous, and infrequent sexual encounters with other men, but considered himself the "husband" of a fairy (the prostitute Loop-the-loop), with whom he was involved in an ongoing relationship. He "apparently [did] not care an iota," Dr. Shufeldt reported, "whether I was aware of his sex relations with [the fairy] or not," an impression strengthened by the man's willingness to confide to the doctor, man to man as it were, that Loop-the-loop was "the most passionate mortal he had ever heard of, and one of the most difficult to satisfy." Given the doctor's middle-class and professional background, his response to the man was ambivalent. By remarking on the man's nonchalance, the doctor implied that he, in contrast to his subject, considered the arrangement noteworthy and somewhat objectionable. He also expressed his "surprise [that] he was an intelligent young man," although his surprise was probably due at least in part to the fact that he would have predicted a less respectable husband for the fairy, whom he considered "very uncouth." But he did not feel compelled to comment directly on the man's sexual character, and clearly did not regard him in the same terms as he regarded the fairy. The relationship reproduced the conventions of a highly role-differentiated marriage between a man and a woman, and the "husband," since he played the conventional masculine role, even though with a wife who was anatomically male, did not seem so "abnormal."[51]

The male partners of men such as the musician were not always fairies, nor were the relationships always so close. Indeed, some sexual relationships were organized on the basis of a power and status hierarchy dictated by age rather than by gender (although that age hierarchy was sometimes thematized as one of gender) and sometimes took on a more coercive edge. Known as "active pederasts" or, most commonly, "wolves," the term Tyler used, such men acknowledged having a particular predilection for playing the "man's role" in sex with fairies and, more typically, youths, the latter usually referred to as "punks." *Punk* generally denoted a physically slighter youth who let himself be used sexually by an older and more powerful man, the wolf, in exchange for money, protection, or other forms of support.

The punk's sexual character was ambiguous: he was often neither homosexually interested nor effeminate himself, but was sometimes equated with women because of his youth and his subordination to the older man. He was regarded by some men as simply a young homosexual, by others as the victim of an aggressive older man, and by still others as someone whose sexual subordination was merely an aspect of his general subordination to a dominant older man.[52] In a west Pennsylvania prison in 1892, for instance, an older prisoner explained the meaning of *punk* to the anarchist Alexander Berkman in the following manner: "Ever read Billy Shakespeare? Know the place, 'He's neither man nor woman; he's punk.' Well, Billy knew. A punk's a boy that'll . . . give himself to a man. . . . It's done in every prison, an' on th' road [by which he meant among hoboes], everywhere." This may have been the original derogatory meaning of *punk,* which only later passed into underworld and then more general slang as an epithetic diminutive without specifically sexual connotations.[53]

The erotic system of wolves and punks was particularly widespread (and tended to take somewhat different form) among three groups of men who were exceptionally disengaged from the family and neighborhood systems that regulated normative sexuality: seamen, prisoners, and the immense number of transient workers (or hoboes) who passed through American cities before the 1920s. That the wolves regarded themselves as something other than queer attests both to the absence of a sharp hetero–homosexual binarism in their culture, which would inevitably have classified them as homosexual, and to the centrality instead of effeminacy to the definition of sexual abnormality among working-men. Their behavior in prison or on shipboard could be dismissed as a product of the situation (the absence of women) rather than of predisposition (a preference for boys or fairies), but such explanations became implausible when the behavior persisted in settings where women were available. Wolves combined homosexual interest with a marked masculinity. None of them behaved effeminately or took feminine nicknames, and few played the "woman's part" in sexual relations—and then only secretly. On the contrary, their very appellation, *wolf,* evoked the image of the predatory man-about-town intent on seducing young women, and their masculine dominance over punks was further emphasized by the fact that the latter were also referred to as *lambs* and *kids.* Wolves generally did not seek sexual encounters with other "men," in which they might have been forced into sexual roles that would have compromised their own masculine identification, but only with punks or fairies, males ascribed lower status because of their youth or effeminacy.[54]

Thus a seaman blithely explained to an undercover agent whom he met on the lower Manhattan waterfront in 1931 that he liked sex with "fairies or c . . . -s . . . . . . ," particularly fifteen- and sixteen-year-old boys he called "punks." "I had one of those punks living with me at the [Seamen's Church] Institute for quite some time," the man bragged. "He was a young kid about 15 years old, [and] pretty." The fact that he found a boy attractive, regularly had sex with him, and supported him financially did not make the older man, in his own mind or in the opinion of the investigator, a fairy or queer. Critical to both was the fact that, in the seaman's version of the relationship, the boy "satisfied me the same as a woman." At the same time, the seaman appears to have believed that some men—possibly including the investigator—were more likely than others to take an interest in punks; he mentioned his relations with the punks only after learning that the investigator had not visited the "sporting houses" (tenement brothels) that he had previously shown him.[55] Indeed, their interaction suggests that having recourse to a punk or fairy did not have the same reputability in this milieu that going to a prostitute did. When the seaman introduced the agent to a punk prostitute, the agent was able to put off meeting with him by indicating he did not want to make an appointment in front of his friend. This concern evidently seemed plausible to the boy, who accepted the excuse but assured the agent that he could find him anytime around the Seamen's Church Institute.[56] Nonetheless, the seaman's willingness to boast about his relationship with a punk to a man he barely knew suggests that he did not expect to lose much, if any, status because of it. If one man might be reticent about admitting such interests (as he might be about any sexual matter), they were acceptable enough that another man could take pride in commenting on them.

The seaman's interest in punks and fairies was not unusual, nor were such interactions kept carefully hidden. The investigator accompanied the man to Battery Park, whose benches were filled with young men waiting to be picked up by sailors. The punk to whom the seaman introduced him, a sixteen-year-old named Julius, assumed he wanted a rendezvous and immediately offered to find a room in a lodging house in Chatham Square. He also offered a straightforward account of his prices: along with the room, which cost a dollar, he charged 50 cents for oral sex and 75 cents for anal sex. The investigator frequently saw punks and fairies talking with seamen at the Institute, in nearby lunchrooms, and in the park; on one occasion a seaman identified fifteen male prostitutes in the park, sitting "on separate benches, always leaving room for a [man] to sit down."[57] Although the openness and even the existence of such men was news to the investigator, it must have been common knowledge among workers and residents of the waterfront.

Long-term relationships or "marriages" between wolves and punks seem to have been even more common among hoboes, although precisely how many hoboes participated in such relationships is, of course, impossible to determine. A study of a hundred "vagrants" in New York City in 1916 identified a quarter of them as "perverts"; studies conducted in other cities produced lower figures, although any such estimates need to be regarded with suspicion.[58] The prevalence of homosexual relations was so "generally assumed to be true among hoboes," wrote the sociologist and former hobo Nels Anderson in a 1931 hobo handbook, "that whenever a man travels around with a lad he is apt to be labeled a 'jocker' or a 'wolf' and the road kid is called his 'punk,' 'preshun,' or 'lamb.' It has become so that it is very difficult for a good hobo to enjoy the services of an apprentice."[59]

As Anderson's comment suggests, partnerships between older and younger men on the road were common, and while they were presumed to have a sexual element, many did not. In both sexual and nonsexual partnerships, the older man usually took responsibility for teaching his apprentice the arts of the road as well as providing for his material needs. The younger man performed a host of services for his mentor, including shaving him, and also contributed to their supply of cash. In many respects their relationship reproduced the sexual roles, division of labor, and conventions of mutual dependence that were characteristic of husbands and wives in the dominant culture. In his classic 1923 sociological study of hoboes, Anderson noted that "it is not uncommon to hear a boy who is seen traveling with an older man spoken of as the 'wife' or 'woman.' "[60] As with heterosexual marriages, the quality of the partnerships varied widely: some were brutal and coercive, others were close and affectionate, and still others simply instrumental.

The character of such relationships needs to be explored more fully by historians, but it seems likely that the widespread existence of hobo partnerships made it easier for men in sexual relationships to fit into the social world that took shape in rural hobo camps and in urban "hobohemias," the districts, such as the Bowery, where many transient workers spent the winter. Some men doubtless entered into such relationships only because of the circumstances in which they found themselves, but other men must have sought out such circumstances precisely because they made it possible for them to engage in homosexual intimacies.[61]

Another locus of relations between wolves and punks, the New York City Jail on Welfare Island, deserves scrutiny because the organization of sexual relations in it illuminates the boundaries drawn between different kinds of men who engaged in homosexual practices. Although the homosexual world that took shape among prisoners was a peculiar one, it was not so exceptional as is often thought. Nor does the culturally blind concept of "situational homosexuality" offer an adequate framework for analyzing that world. In a remarkable study of homosexual relations in an American prison in the 1970s, Wayne S. Wooden and Jay Parker showed that the social organization of such relations varied among Chicanos, African Americans, and Euro-Americans. Men did not react to being deprived of other sexual contacts by engaging in homosexual practices in a spontaneous and unstructured way, but organized those relations in accordance with the sexual norms they brought to the prison from their own cultures.[62] Similarly, the homosexual world that evolved in the New York City Jail in the early twentieth century, rather than being a singular world cut off from wider cultural patterns, was profoundly shaped by those patterns. It drew especially on the patterns of the bachelor subculture, whose members, as the men least socialized into the dominant social order, were disproportionately represented in the jail.

The dominant pre–World War II conceptualizations of homosexuality were inscribed in the spatial organization of prisons and in the everyday interactions of prisoners. The central position of the fairy in the dominant cultural conception of homosexuality was signaled by the decision of prison authorities not only to segregate homosexual prisoners from other men but to classify as "homosexuals" only those men who exhibited the typical markers of effeminacy. It is not clear when this policy was initiated, but it had become a well-established practice by the 1910s. All prisoners who had been convicted of homosexual solicitation or transvestism were incarcerated in this unit, of course, but the majority of inmates identified as "perverts" had been convicted of drug use or other nonsexual offenses; the authorities segregated any man whose dress or mannerisms suggested he might be homosexual. Segregation from the other prisoners was complete. "Fags" were confined to the prison's South Annex, the most isolated and secure section of the prison; they ate separately, saw movies separately, and worked in separate work gangs, which were assigned "women's work" in the prison laundry and in the warden's home. Within the South Annex (which many prisoners called the Fag Annex), men were informally allowed to wear long hair, wigs, makeshift dresses, and homemade rouge and lipstick. Guards and other prisoners alike usually referred to them by their camp names—"Greta Garbo," "Lillian Russell," "Broadway Rose"—and at Christmas the South Annex inmates staged a bawdy show called the "Fag Follies" for a select audience of guards and well-connected prisoners. Normally the only contact between the "fags" and other prisoners came when the former were marched past the latter on their way to the mess hall.[63]

If the basis on which the authorities segregated homosexual prisoners confirms how widely the fairy was regarded as a distinct social type, the reasons they gave for segregating them confirm how widely it was believed that any man might be attracted to a fairy. Most authorities did not think that men isolated from women would randomly engage in homosexual behavior, but they did assume that such men would be susceptible to the fairies. When a new administrator took over the jail in 1934 he announced that he would force the fairies with long hair to get "military hair cuts," in order, he explained to the press in a revealing comment, to "cut down their attractiveness."[64] Although most prison authorities found inmates' having sex with fairies to be reprehensible, they hardly considered it unusual. Indeed, their fear was not just that fairies would induce other men to engage in homosexual practices but that rivalries between men for a fairy's attentions would escalate into violent confrontations. "Perverts, frank and under cover, stimulate tortured men to indulge in perversion, often by direct solicitation," one prison doctor and reform advocate warned in 1934. "The constitutional type, the one the man in the street recognizes under the optimistic title of 'fairy,' should be segregated in colonies, such as now utilized for mental defectives; only in this way can their moral leprosy be prevented from spreading."[65]

Prison officials generally refused to acknowledge the existence of homosexual activity in their prisons, but reformers brought it to the attention of the public in 1934. Shortly after the newly elected mayor, Fiorello La Guardia, appointed his own commissioner of corrections, Austin H. MacCormick, the commissioner conducted a raid of Welfare Island. His purpose was both to seize control of the prison from the crime-boss inmates who exercised effective suzerainty within it—running numbers rackets, selling liquor, and leading as luxurious a life as prison conditions would allow—and to discredit both the old prison administration that had allowed such conditions to develop and the Tammany Hall mayoral administration preceding La Guardia's.[66] The raid produced sensational newspaper stories that destroyed the credibility of the old administration. Some of the most lurid stories concerned the homosexual segregation unit. The new administrators used the "freedoms" granted homosexuals as well as gang lords to attack the old administration; when they invited the press to tour the prison on the day of the raid, they pointed to the spectacle of homosexual depravity to demonstrate the depths to which the prison had sunk.

The *New York Herald Tribune* cooperated fully in the effort. It described the scene witnessed by the crusading commissioner on the day of the raid when the "sex perverts" entered the mess hall: "These men appeared for lunch, some of them heavily rouged, their eye brows painted, their lips red, hair in some instances hanging to the shoulder, and in most cases hips swinging and hands fluttering. . . . Mr. MacCormick [said] he could see no reason 'for permitting them to flaunt themselves in front of the rest of the prisoners in this way,' " and he "intimated" that this was "but a slight example of the liberties this group had previously had in the prison." The *Daily Mirror* offered a fuller account of their "liberties" when it noted they "had been permitted by the prison bosses to roam the Island, visiting various buildings and cell-tiers 'in drag'—or female costume," although even it only hinted at the sordid purpose of their visits. When the raiding party entered the South Annex, the *Herald Tribune* continued, it was "greeted by cries and howls in high falsetto voices. . . . Inside the cells were found every conceivable article of women's wearing apparel. Dozens of compacts, powder puffs, and various types of perfume were found, while silk step-ins, nightgowns and other bits of negligee were strewn about the cells." The paper also described the dramatic scene as "one man . . . clung desperately to a set of false eyelashes, which he did not want disturbed," in an apparent effort to turn the confiscation of the false eyelashes into a symbol of the reformers' struggle to restore order to the New York City Jail.[67] The sensational news articles were soon followed by a flurry of more "authoritative" studies by prison doctors and reformers with titles like *Sex in Prison* and *Revelations of a Prison Doctor*.[68]

The segregation of "fags" hardly put an end to homosexual liaisons in the city jail, though. As numerous reformers and prisoners themselves testified, the jail was the quintessential home of the "wolf" and the "punk," and the treatment accorded the wolf by inmates and prison authorities alike attests to the degree to which he was regarded as a "normal" man. The wolf's behavior led him to lose little status among other prisoners; if anything, he gained stature in many men's eyes because of his ability to coerce or attract a punk. Prison authorities did not try to segregate the highly masculine and aggressive older wolves by confining them in the "degenerate" unit in which they segregated the effeminate fairies, primarily because they did not think it was possible to distinguish wolves from other prisoners.

Whether the wolf could be distinguished from the other inmates was subject to debate. Some prison reformers, such as Thomas Mott Osborne, thought that " 'wolves,' who by nature or practice prefer unnatural to what we may call natural vice," should be distinguished from other homosexually active men "who have no liking for unnatural vice [and] outside of prison would never be guilty of it." Several reformers recommended that wolves be segregated from vulnerable youths.[69] But most prisoners, like the prison authorities, seem to have regarded the wolves as little different from other men; their sexual behavior may have represented a moral failure, but it did not distinguish them from other men as the fairy's gender status did. As one prisoner wrote in 1933, "The 'wolf' (active sodomist), as I have hinted before, is not considered by the average inmate to be 'queer' in the sense that the oral copulist, male or female, is so considered. While his conduct is felt to be in some measure depraved, it is conduct which many a prisoner knows that he himself might resort to under certain special circumstances." The "special circumstances" he envisioned were not so special after all and presumed that any prisoner might be attracted to a youth. "If the prisoner can find a good-looking boy, and the opportunity, and is sufficiently 'hard up' for sexual satisfaction," he explained, "he will not usually disdain to make use of him for purposes of relief."[70] The line between the wolf and the normal man, like that between the culture of the prison and culture of the streets, was a fine one indeed.

The ability of many workingmen to alternate between male and female sexual partners provides powerful evidence that the hetero–homosexual axis—the dichotomy between the "homosexual" and the "heterosexual"—governed neither their thinking about sexuality nor their sexual practices. While fairies, trade, wolves, and punks all engaged in what we would define as homosexual behavior they and the people who observed them were careful to draw distinctions between different modes of such behavior: between "feminine" and "masculine" behavior, between "passive" and "active" roles, between desire for sex with a man and desire for sex. The organization of the relationships between fairies or punks and their husbands, trade, wolves, and customers (sometimes overlapping groupings of men) serves to highlight the cultural presumption that the men in such relationships were defined by their *differences*—manifested in their different sexual roles or their differently gendered modes of self-presentation—rather than by their *similarities*—their shared "homosexuality." Even evidence of persistent and exclusive interest in sexual relations with another man did not necessarily put a man in the same category as his partner. The band musician's marriage to Loop-the-loop did not turn him into a fairy, after all, but into the husband of a fairy. While today we might regard all of them equally as "homosexuals," they recognized no "homosexual" category in which they all could be placed. In the very different sexual culture that predominated at the turn of the century, they understood themselves—and were regarded by others—as fundamentally different kinds of people. To classify their behavior and identities using the simple polarities of "homosexual" and "heterosexual" would be to misunderstand the complexity of their sexual system, the realities of their lived experience.

As this chapter's ethnography of sexual practices and identities demonstrates, men did not just use different categories to think about a sexuality that, despite appearances, was fundamentally the same as that of men today, for those different cultural categories governed and were manifest in men's everyday social practices. Even in the terms of the late-twentieth-century hetero–homosexual axis, in other words, it would be difficult to argue that the "normal" men who had sex with fairies were *really* homosexuals, for that would leave inexplicable their determined pursuit of women sexual partners. But neither could they plausibly be regarded as heterosexuals, for heterosexuals would have been incapable of responding sexually to another male. Nor were they bisexuals, for that would have required them to be attracted to both women as women and men as *men*. They were, rather, men who were attracted to womanlike men or interested in sexual activity defined not by the gender of their partner but by the kind of bodily pleasures that partner could provide.

Not all men in working-class New York had the same degree of interest in sex with a fairy (and many had none at all), just as not all men had the same degree of interest in sex with a dark-skinned woman or a middle-aged woman or a blue-eyed woman. But almost all workingmen—from the liquor authority agents who watched "fags" trying to pick up sailors at the Happy Hour Bar to the newsstand owner who watched sailors trying to pick up fairies at the Times Square Building—considered it unremarkable that a man might go with a fairy and as little revelatory about his sexual identity as his preference for one kind of woman over another. A man's occasional recourse to fairies did not prove he had homosexual desire for another man, as today's hetero–homosexual binarism would insist, but only that he was interested in the forms of phallic pleasure a fairy could provide as well as a female prostitute could. Men's identities and reputations simply did not depend on a sexuality defined by the anatomical sex of their sexual partners. Just as the abnormality of the fairy depended on his violation of gender conventions, rather than his homosexual practices alone, the normality of other men depended on their conformity to those conventions rather than on an eschewal of homosexual practices which those conventions did not require. Heterosexuality had not become a precondition of gender normativity in early-twentieth-century working-class culture. Men had to be many things in order to achieve the status of normal men, but being "heterosexual" was not one of them.

1. Report on Times Square Building by J. K., May 2, 1927, Committee of Fourteen papers, New York Public Library (hereafter COF). "D—" in the original.

2. *Happy Hour Bar & Grill, Inc., v. Bruckman et al.,* 256 A.D. 1074 (2nd Dep't 1939), reports on the Happy Hour Bar & Grill by investigators Tierney and Kirschenbaum, dated October 10 and October 17, 1938.

3. E. S. Shepherd, for example, specifically referred to "fairies" as "the male prostitute of the streets" in "Contribution to the Study of Intermediacy," *American Journal of Urology and Sexology* 14 (1918): 245.

4. Richard Meeker, *Better Angel* (New York, 1933), p. 259; Kennilworth Bruce, *Goldie* (New York, 1933), p. 105.

5. Gershon Legman, "The Language of Homosexuality: An American Glossary," in *Sex Variants,* ed. George W. Henry (New York, 1941), vol. 2, appendix VII, p. 1176, quoting a study of prostitutes' slang; *Report and Proceedings of the [Lexow] Senate Committee appointed to investigate the Police Department of the City of New York* (Albany, 1895), Captain Ryan testimony, p. 5591.

6. Charles W. Gardner, *The Doctor and the Devil; or, the Midnight Adventures of Dr. Parkhurst* (New York, 1894), p. 52.

7. R. W. Shufeldt, "Biography of a Passive Pederast," *American Journal of Urology and Sexology* 13 (1917): 451–60. Although the interview was reported in 1917, it took place in 1906. "Looping the loop" had become a generic slang expression for such amusement park rides in the 1900s; see Jane Addams's reference to "looping the loop" in *The Spirit of Youth and the City Streets* (New York, 1909), p. 69, as quoted in John F. Kasson, *Amusing the Million: Coney Island at the Turn of the Century* (New York, 1978), p. 100, who also discusses the ride on pp. 81–82.

8. Quoted in George Chauncey, "Christian Brotherhood or Sexual Perversion? Homosexual Identities and the Construction of Sexual Boundaries in the World War One Era," *Journal of Social History* 19 (1985): 195. The sailor was questioned at the Newport, Rhode Island, naval training station, but had spent time in New York and was involved in a gay world not far removed from that of the city.

9. Alfred Kinsey, Wardell Pomeroy, and Clyde Martin, *Sexual Behavior in the Human Male* (Philadelphia, 1948), pp. 650–51. Kinsey's statistical methods were subject to criticism almost from the moment of their publication, and this criticism has mounted in recent years in the wake of several new studies that have produced lower estimates of the incidence of homosexual behavior: R. E. Fay, C. F. Turner, A. D. Klassen, and J. H. Gagnon, "Prevalence and Patterns of Same-Gender Sexual Contact among Men," *Science* 243 (1989): 343–48; S. M. Rogers and C. F. Turner, "Male–Male Sexual Contact in the USA: Findings from Five Sample Surveys, 1970–1990," *Journal of Sex Research* 28 (1991): 491–519; J. O. G. Billy, K. Panfer, W. R. Grady, and D. H. Klepinger, "The Sexual Behavior of Men in the United States," *Family Planning Perspectives* 25 (1993): 52–60. It is not necessary to defend Kinsey's sampling methodology or to assert the infallibility of his estimates, however, to object on historical grounds to the effort by recent critics to prove Kinsey was "wrong" by contrasting his figures with the lower figures produced in recent studies. The fact that a certain percentage of the population engaged in homosexual practices in the 1990s does not mean that the same percentage did so fifty years earlier, when Kinsey conducted his study. It is precisely the argument of this book that such practices are culturally organized and subject to change, and that the prewar sexual regime would have made it easier for men to engage in casual homosexual behavior in the 1930s than in the 1980s, when such behavior would ineluctably mark them as homosexual. Kinsey's methodology makes his precise statistical claims unreliable, but the fact that they are higher than those produced by recent studies does not by itself demonstrate they are wrong. Moreover, Kinsey's study had the merit of trying to measure the incidence of homosexual activity rather than presuming that there was a clearly defined population of "homosexuals"

whose size he could measure. Even if Kinsey's study overestimated the incidence of homosexual activity twofold or threefold, his numbers are still astonishingly high.

10. Kinsey, *Sexual Behavior*, pp. 612, 614.

11. Ibid., p. 616.

12. The reputation of Italian men for trade in the gay world was noted by Frank Burton, Bruce Nugent, and Sebastian Risicato in interviews; see also the role of Italian men in Charles Henri Ford and Parker Tyler, *The Young and Evil* (Paris, 1933), which was based on Tyler's experiences in the Village, where he regularly encountered "straight" Italian men interested in sex with men. On Irish men, see the discussion of Charles Tomlinson Griffes and policemen in George Chauncey, *Gay New York: Gender, Urban Culture, and the Making of the Gay Male World, 1890–1940* (New York, 1994), ch. 4. I have been unable to locate sufficient evidence concerning the sexual cultures of other immigrant groups in New York to propose even a tentative analysis of them. New York City's small Chinatown community, for instance, consisted almost entirely of bachelors as a result of restrictive immigration policies. While slender oral history evidence hints at homosexual activity among some of the bachelors, there is not a single gay-related reference (and virtually no reference of any kind) to Chinese men in the records of the Committee of Fourteen and Committee of Fifteen I have examined. The single sodomy case I have found concerns an unmarried twenty-four-year-old Chinese laundryman, who allegedly forced sex on two Jewish boys he enticed into the premises of a laundry on East Broadway one evening in 1898. He was acquitted, and the district attorney case file contains no additional information (*People v. Ong*, Manhattan District Attorney's papers, New York Municipal Archives (hereafter NYMA) 22,086 [Court of General Sessions, New York City, 1898]).

13. Frederick H. Whitin, "Sexual Perversion Cases in New York City Courts, 1916–1921," bulletin 1480, November 12, 1921, Box 88, COF. My review of the backgrounds of the two hundred men arrested by the police (with the assistance of the Society for the Suppression of Vice) for degenerate disorderly conduct in 1920–21 suggests that almost twice as many Italians than Jews were arrested (see the eleven-page list, untitled, in "Homosexuality" folder, Box 63, COF). Religious and national backgrounds for most (but not all) of the men arrested were supplied in the records of the Society itself, volumes 3–5 (Society for the Suppression of Vice Papers, Library of Congress, Washington, D.C.). These figures, of course, may reveal as much about the enforcement priorities of the police as about the actual incidence of homosexual conduct. I include them, however, as one piece of evidence for the pattern of ethnic differences suggested more conclusively by the greater visibility and institutionalization of gay life in the Italian than Jewish Lower East Side.

14. 207 Canal St. report, "Court of Special Sessions [cases]," Box 65, COF. A judge ultimately refused to close the saloon on the basis of "disorderly conversation" alone.

15. Report of J. R., March 22, 1901, Box 7, Committee of Fifteen papers, New York Public Library (hereafter NYPL).

16. Report of H. S. Conklin, March 5, 1901, Box 5; report of Salomon and Robinson, February 1901, Box 7, Committee of Fifteen papers, NYPL. According to the typed transcript of the investigators' notes cited here, the five boys were known as "faniss," by which they may have meant "finocchio," the Italian-American term for fennel, used in the production of licorice, which Italian-Americans used synonymously with the English term cocksucker. (This presumably was the origin of the name of Finocchio's, a famous club in San Francisco featuring a female-impersonation act in the 1940s and 1950s.) Other investigators' reports refer to such men as "fairies," as well as "perverts" and, most commonly, "cock suckers." "Pansy" did not become a common term for gay men until the 1920s.

17. Report of Captain Titus [to the Mayor], December 20, 1900, Box 9, Van Wyck papers, Mayors' Papers, NYMA. The same report notes that the police investigated rumors that 138 Chrystie St. was a disorderly house, but does not indicate what kind of "disorder" was said to occur there. I am indebted to Timothy Gilfoyle for this reference.

18. Unfortunately, no ethnographic studies have been made of the social organization of homosexual relations in southern Italy or the Jewish Pale of Settlement in Russia at the turn

of the century, for example, that might shed light on the behavior of immigrants from those regions. As a result, my comments here must remain highly tentative and can only suggest directions for future research by historians of Europe as well as of American immigrants. Such research would not only help us understand the social organization and cultural meaning of same-sex relations in those cultures, but would also offer a revealing new vantage point for thinking more generally about gender relations in each group.

19. Kinsey, *Sexual Behavior,* p. 483. On Italian immigrants' response to church teachings, see Robert Orsi, *The Madonna of 115th Street: Faith and Community in Italian Harlem, 1880–1950* (New Haven, 1985), pp. xvi–xviii, 219–21; Gary R. Mormino and George E. Pozzetta, *The Immigrant World of Ybor City: Italians and Their Latin Neighbors in Tampa, 1885–1985* (Urbana, 1987), pp. 210–32.

20. Kinsey also noted that many sexologists in Italy itself considered southern Italy "the most homosexual place in the world," although he continued to believe that homosexual behavior was more widespread in several countries in the Middle and Far East. See Wardell Pomeroy, *Dr. Kinsey and the Institute for Sex Research* (New Haven, 1972), pp. 423–27. On the general openness of Italian men to sexual contacts with men, see also the letters from one of Kinsey's informants reprinted in Martin Duberman, *About Time: Exploring the Gay Past* (New York, 1986), pp. 173–77. For one gay veteran's view of homosexual life in Italy, see John Hope Burns's postwar novel *The Gallery* (New York, 1947). On instrumentalist approaches to the body, see Pierre Bourdieu's observations in "Sport and Social Class," *Social Science Information* 17 (1978): 819–40. Bourdieu argues that such attitudes are more characteristic of (French) working-class men than middle-class men, but unfortunately does not historicize that assessment. Although the homosexual culture on the Lower East Side bears a remarkable resemblance in many respects to the limited accounts we have of Mediterranean sexual patterns, the subtle variations in those patterns, both within the Mediterranean basin and between Europe and the United States, need to be studied with care. "Mediterranean" cultures are often represented as more homogeneous in such matters than they actually are. On the dangers of such homogenization, see, for example, Michael Herzfeld, "The Horns of the Mediterraneanist Dilemma," *American Ethnologist* 11 (1984): 439–54. See also John J. Winkler, *Constraints of Desire* (New York, 1990).

21. On the different demographic patterns of Italian and Jewish immigration to New York, see Thomas Kessner, *The Golden Door: Italian and Jewish Immigrant Mobility in New York City* (New York, 1977), pp. 26–32. On the unusually large number of single men who immigrated to the United States from Italy, see also Dino Cinel, *From Italy to San Francisco: The Immigrant Experience* (Stanford, 1982), pp. 162–72. For an analytic overview of the circumstances in Europe and the Americas that resulted in European emigration and of the significance of family networks to migration, see John Bodnar, *The Transplanted: A History of Immigrants in Urban America* (Bloomington, 1985), pp. 1–84. Numerous historians have studied Italian and Jewish immigration to New York. See, for example, Moses Rischin, *The Promised City: New York's Jews, 1870–1914* (Cambridge, Mass., 1962); Irving Howe, *World of Our Fathers* (New York, 1976); Donna R. Gabaccia, *From Sicily to Elizabeth Street: Housing and Social Change among Italian Immigrants* (Albany, 1984); as well as the other studies cited elsewhere in this section.

22. Sophonisba Breckinridge, *New Homes for Old* (New York, 1921), pp. 176–77. See also Susan A. Glenn, *Daughters of the Shtetl: Life and Labor in the Immigrant Generation* (Ithaca, 1990), pp. 81–82, 159–60, 162, 215–16. On the greater degree of social interaction between men and women in Jewish than Italian neighborhoods, see also Kathy Peiss, *Cheap Amusements: Working Women and Leisure in Turn-of-the-Century New York* (Philadelphia, 1986), pp. 30, 68; Elizabeth Ewen, *Immigrant Women in the Land of Dollars: Life and Culture on the Lower East Side, 1890–1925* (New York, 1985), pp. 210–11; Elinor Lerner, "Family Structure, Occupational Patterns, and Support for Women's Suffrage," in *Women in Culture and Politics: A Century of Change,* ed. Judith Friedlander et al. (Bloomington, 1986); and Gabaccia, *From Sicily,* p. 97.

23. Orsi, *Madonna of 115th Street,* pp. 21, 115–17, 135–43. On living arrangements, see Kessner, *Golden Door,* pp. 99–101; and Gabaccia, *From Sicily,* chs. 5–6. On the use of leisure time, see Perry R. Duis, *The Saloon: Public Drinking in Chicago and Boston, 1880–1920* (Urbana, 1983), pp. 146–48, Louise C. Odencrantz, *Italian Women in Industry: A Study of Conditions in New York* (New York, 1977), pp. 203–5, who notes that in such families "the mother had no recreation and [even] the father took his alone" (p. 203), and Gabaccia, *From Sicily,* p. 97.

24. John H. Mariano, *The Second Generation of Italians in New York City* (Boston, 1921), pp. 140–43. For a fine analysis of such social clubs and gangs, see Leonard H. Ellis, "Men Among Men: An Exploration of All-Male Relationships in Victorian America" (Ph.D. diss., Columbia University, 1982), pp. 1–60. Ellis assumes too readily that boys usually left such gangs for poolrooms and saloons once they reached the age of sixteen or eighteen, but he offers a thoughtful analysis of the role of all three such neighborhood-based all-male social groupings and spaces in the everyday lives of late-nineteenth-century men.

25. These men have received remarkably little attention in recent studies of immigration and working-class culture. In response to an older historiographical and sociological tradition that viewed social "disorganization" and instability as the inevitable consequences of immigration, a generation of historians has sought to document the social cohesiveness of the extended kinship systems of immigrants and their central role in organizing migratory networks and settlement patterns. In response to older studies that made universal claims about the process of immigration on the basis of men's experience alone, a generation of historians has offered a finely nuanced analysis of the role of women and families in immigration. These studies have corrected and deepened our understanding of immigration in significant ways, but an inadvertent consequence of their focus has been to ignore the ubiquitous presence of unattached men in immigrant neighborhoods and to limit inquiry into the social worlds they created. Although such men often migrated to the United States to serve the interests of a larger family-oriented and family-determined economic strategy (to raise capital for investment in land in southern Italy, for instance), once in this country many of them moved in an all-male world.

26. For a fascinating analysis of the origins and social organization of the Irish bachelor culture, see Richard Stivers, *A Hair of the Dog: Irish Drinking and American Stereotype* (Philadelphia, 1976). For evidence of the concern the high rates of bachelorhood and spinsterhood provoked among Irish and Catholic leaders, see the articles cited by Stivers: James Walsh, "Catholic Bachelors and Old Maids," *America* (August 12, 1922): 389–90; idem, "The Disappearing Irish in America," *America* (May 1, 1926): 56–57; idem, "Shy Irish Bachelors," *America* (March 29, 1930): 592–93; and M. V. Kelly, "The Suicide of the Irish Race," *America* (November 17 and 24, 1928): 128–29, 155–56.

27. The paintings by Cadmus and Demuth of sailors in homoerotic situations appear in many of the catalogs of their work. See the paintings reproduced in the catalog for the Demuth retrospective at the Whitney Museum of American Art, *Charles Demuth* (New York, 1987). For later pornographers, see almost any issue of *Tomorrow's Man, VIM, Physique Pictorial,* and the other gay-oriented "physique magazines" published in the 1940s–1960s.

28. On the decline of the transient workforce, see Nels Anderson, *Men on the Move* (Chicago, 1940), pp. 2–5, 12.

29. There were also ethnic, occupational, and generational differences among the men in the various male subcultures that collectively constituted the "bachelor subculture," but most of them shared its distinctive characteristics to some degree.

30. Ralph Werther, *Autobiography of an Androgyne* (New York, 1918), pp. 83–84, 88.

31. Report on the Subway Cabaret, Fourteenth St. near Fourth Ave., 10 P.M., January 12, 1917, COF.

32. On the importance of what he calls "masculine conviviality" to such men, the character of the bachelor subculture, and the relationship between the culture of the "rough" work-

ing class and the respectable, see David Montgomery, *The Fall of the House of Labor: The Workplace, the State, and American Labor Activism, 1865–1925* (Cambridge, 1987), pp. 87–92; Roy Rosenzweig, *Eight Hours for What We Will: Workers and Leisure in an Industrial City, 1870–1920* (New York, 1983), pp. 57–64, 74–81; Elliott J. Gorn, *The Manly Art: Bare-Knuckle Prize Fighting in America* (Ithaca, 1986), pp. 129–45, esp. pp. 140–45; Ned Polsky, *Hustlers, Beats, and Others* (Chicago, 1967), pp. 31–37, 90, 105, 109–10; Ellis, "Men among Men," pp. 1–60; and Peter Bailey, "'Will the Real Bill Banks Please Stand Up?' Towards a Role Analysis of Mid-Victorian Working-Class Respectability," in *Expanding the Past: Essays from the Journal of Social History,* ed. Peter N. Stearns (New York, 1988), pp. 73–90.

33. For two distinct perspectives on the performativity of everyday life, see Erving Goffman's classic study, *The Presentation of Self in Everyday Life* (Garden City, N.Y., 1959); and Judith Butler's splendid *Gender Trouble: Feminism and the Subversion of Identity* (New York, 1990).

34. On the carnival, see Peter Stallybrass and Allon White, *The Politics and Poetics of Transgression* (Ithaca, 1986).

35. Antonio L., quoted in Henry, *Sex Variants,* p. 420.

36. Report on Italian Restaurant, 207 W. 17th St., October 6, 1927, Box 36, COF.

37. Frederick H. Whitin to Captain T. N. Pfeiffer, War and Navy Departments Commission, Washington, April 3, 1918, Box 25, COF.

38. J. A. S., Conditions about the Brooklyn Navy Yard, June 6, 1917, Box 25, COF. See also, for example, Harry Benjamin's 1931 article arguing that "the suppression of prostitution [in New York] has probably increased and favored homosexual tendencies and practices" ("For the Sake of Morality," *Medical Journal and Record* 133 [1931]: 380–82).

39. For more on the sexual mapping of the city, see Chauncey, *Gay New York,* ch. 7.

40. On the magnitude of the business of prostitution in nineteenth- and early-twentieth-century New York City, and its decline after the 1910s, see Timothy J. Gilfoyle, *City of Eros: New York City, Prostitution, and the Commercialization of Sex, 1790–1920* (New York, 1992).

41. Kinsey, *Sexual Behavior,* p. 38; William Foote Whyte, "A Slum Sex Code," *American Journal of Sociology* 49 (1943): 24–31.

42. On the belief that men had to have regular orgasms to maintain their health, see Charles Rosenberg, "Sexuality, Class, and Role in Nineteenth-Century America," in *The American Man,* ed. Elizabeth H. Pleck and Joseph H. Pleck (Englewood Cliffs, N.J, 1980), pp. 230–32; and E. Anthony Rotundo, *American Manhood: Transformations in Masculinity from the Revolution to the Modern Era* (New York, 1993), pp. 121–22. Both accounts focus on the nineteenth century, but it is clear that the belief persisted into the twentieth. For examples of the term *satisfaction* used casually to mean orgasm, see, for example, Salvatore N., quoted in Henry, *Sex Variants,* p. 176; and Victor F. Nelson, *Prison Days and Nights* (Boston, 1933), pp. 157–58.

43. Will Finch, a middle-class gay man who had pursued and constantly associated with straight working-class men since the 1930s, believed that the homosocial character of "rough" working-class culture gave gay men an advantage over women in one respect: "*We* can be *buddies* of men, whereas a woman never can." For most of the unmarried working-class men he knew, women were for sex, men for "companionship," a situation, Finch thought, comparable to that in classical Greece. One of his sex partners, whom Finch wryly christened "the voice of the urban proletariat," had commented, typically enough, "that he is not at ease with a girl socially and intellectually and emotionally, but only with other males. But girls are lots of fun to fuck." Finch diary, August 8, 1949, Kinsey Institute for Research in Sex, Gender, and Reproduction Library, Indiana University, Bloomington.

44. "Social Contagion in the Pool-room," pp. 14–15, in Frederic M. Thrasher, "The Use of the Superior Boy in Research," Bureau of Social Hygiene papers, Rockefeller Archives Center, North Tarrytown, N.Y., Box 11, folder 229 ("NYU Boys Club Study, 1930"), microfilm reel 6.

45. Shufeldt, "Biography of a Passive Pederast," p. 457.

46. "Sex Practices and Stimuli," pp. 12–13, in Thrasher.

47. Finch diary, January 3, 1951. Committee of Fourteen investigators regularly reported that even prostitutes were unwilling to engage in oral sex; see, for example, the reports on 269 1/2 W. 22nd St., May 26, 1927; tenement, 756 Eighth Ave., December 4, 1928; tenement, 2544 Eighth Ave., June 21, 1928; Navarre Hotel, Seventh Ave. and 38th St., March 16, 1928, Box 36, COF. Not all women rejected such requests, however; see the reports on tenement, 954 Eighth Ave., September 20, 1927 ("I don't make a practice of it, but if you want it, I'll accommodate you"); tenement, 42 W. 46th St., July 22, 1927; and B&G Sandwich Shop, 140 Fulton St., December 19, 1927 (the woman there said "the only way I do it is the French way," explaining that she did not want to risk pregnancy), all in the same file.

48. Allan M. Brandt, _No Magic Bullet: A Social History of Venereal Disease in the United States Since 1880_ (New York, 1985), chs. 2–3, provides the best account of such campaigns. On men's fear of catching a disease from a prostitute, see, for example, Report on Maxim's, 108 W. 38th St., September 25, 1916, Box 31, COF. In significant respects such campaigns prefigured the AIDS education campaigns of the early 1980s, which often identified sex with a gay man or an IV-drug user, rather than sex without a condom, as the source of AIDS. Such campaigns led many people to fear that the most casual contact with certain categories of people was unsafe, while reassuring them, with deadly inaccuracy, of the safety of the most intimate contact with other categories of people.

49. Report on Hanover Lunch, 2 South St., June 12, 1931, Box 35, COF. Gene Harwood and Frank Burton, in discussing their memories of the 1920s and 1930s in an interview with the author, also pointed to men's fear of getting venereal diseases from women as a reason for their willingness to have sex with gay men. The sociologist Nels Anderson also reported that hoboes argued they were less likely to catch a venereal disease from homosexual than from heterosexual intercourse (_The Hobo: The Sociology of the Homeless Man_ [Chicago, 1923], pp. 134, 147–48), a view shared by the Chicago Vice Commission in its 1911 report, _The Social Evil in Chicago_, pp. 296–97, cited in Anderson, p. 148. See also Samuel Kahn, _Mentality and Homosexuality_ (Boston, 1937), pp. 50–51. For indications that this belief was of long standing, see Randolph Trumbach, "The Birth of the Queen: Sodomy and the Emergence of Gender Equality in Modern Culture, 1660–1750," in _Hidden from History: Reclaiming the Gay and Lesbian Past_, ed. Martin Duberman, Martha Vicinus, and George Chauncey (New York, 1989), pp. 129–40.

50. Bulletin 1504, March 24, 1922, Box 88, COF.

51. Shufeldt, "Biography of a Passive Pederast," pp. 459, 456.

52. Will Finch thought the latter, although he sometimes substituted the older Navy word _pogue_ for the more generally used _punk_. As he commented of one young Norwegian sailor, an older sailor's "boy" who nonetheless ended up in bed with Finch one summer night in 1946 and made it clear he expected Finch to anally penetrate (or "brown") him: "I decided that he was either queer and _liked_ to be browned or the big guy's pogue and _expected_ to be browned" (Finch diary, July 14, 1946). On the widespread use of _pogue_ by sailors in the World War I era to mean a man who desired to be browned, see Chauncey, "Christian Brotherhood or Sexual Perversion?" especially pp. 192, 196. The evidence suggests that the young men to whom the term was applied fell into all three camps.

53. Alexander Berkman, _Prison Memoirs of an Anarchist_ (New York, 1912), pp. 170, 172. Joseph F. Fishman, the first federal Inspector of Prisons and, in the late 1920s, the Deputy Commissioner of the New York City Department of Corrections, used the word _wolf_ for the aggressive party in homosexual encounters in his description of prison homosexuality among non-homosexuals, in _Sex in Prison_ (New York, 1934), p. 152, as did his critic, Louis Berg, _Revelations of a Prison Doctor_ (New York, 1934), pp. 120, 142. For evidence of the use of such terms among hoboes in the 1910s–1930s, see Anderson, _Hobo_, pp. 99, 101, 103, 144–48 (_wolf, jocker, lamb, kid, wife_, and _punk_), and _Broadway Brevities_ (November 9, 1931): 10. In the novel _Goldie_, a sailor approached the protagonist, who was hustling on Times Square, called himself "the slickest wolf in ther navy," and added, in reference to the hustler, "I guess I ought ter

know a regular punk when I sees one" (p. 116). The terms were also used in Los Angeles by the 1920s, according to Aaron J. Rosanoff, "Human Sexuality, Normal and Abnormal, from a Psychiatric Standpoint," *Urologic and Cutaneous Review* (1929): 528. *Punk* was also widely used in the criminal underworld beyond the prison walls, specifically to refer to the underlings in a criminal gang and more generally as an epithet; see, for example, its use in Cornelius Willemse, *Behind the Green Lights* (New York, 1931), pp. 336–37. On the term's diffusion into general slang, see Legman, "The Language of Homosexuality," p. 1174. The terms were still used with similar sexual meanings in prisons in the 1970s; see Wayne S. Wooden and Jay Parker, *Men behind Bars: Sexual Exploitation in Prison* (New York, 1982).

54. The distinction between "wolves" and homosexuals (or "queers") persisted. One hustler picked up in 1949 by a conventionally masculine queer, Will Finch, queried whether he were "just queer or a wolf," adding that there was "no use in 'getting up there and finding out it's no use,'" which Finch took to mean that "he won't be pedicated" (Finch diary, May 20, 1949). The hustler, in other words, insisted on remaining the man in the encounter, which he could do if he were sexually serviced by a queer, and refused to be feminized by being pedicated by a wolf. Finch's response, that he was "not a wolf—unless [the hustler] wants me to be," suggests that, at least by the postwar period, *wolf* described a sexual role as much as a social or characterological "type."

55. Report on the Seamen's Church Institute and vicinity, July 15 and 16, 1931, COF.

56. Reports on the Seamen's Church Institute and vicinity, May 27, June 22, July 2, and July 15 and 16, 1931, COF.

57. Ibid.

58. Frank Charles Laubach, "Why There Are Vagrants: Based upon an Examination of One Hundred Men" (Ph.D. diss., Columbia University, 1916), pp. 13–14, reported that twenty-four of the hundred men were perverts. A 1935 survey of ninety men housed in a Chicago shelter for the homeless noted that "7 percent stated they were engaging in homosexual practices" (Edwin J. Sutherland and Harvey J. Locke, *Twenty Thousand Homeless Men: A Study of Unemployed Men in the Chicago Shelters* [Chicago, 1936], p. 131). The 7 percent figure is almost surely low: not only does it report the number of men who "stated" they were homosexually active, something many such men would doubtless deny to people surveying them in a homeless shelter, but the figure was produced during the Depression, when a more diverse group of men had been made homeless.

59. Dean Stiff [pseudonym of Nels Anderson], *The Milk and Honey Route: A Handbook for Hoboes* (New York, 1931), p. 161.

60. Anderson, *Hobo*, p. 145.

61. Indeed, homosexual relationships appear to have been so widespread among seamen and hoboes that historians need to recognize the desire to live in a social milieu in which such relationships were relatively common and accepted—or to escape the pressure to marry in a more family-oriented milieu—as one of the motives that sent men on the road or to sea. More work needs to be done on the patterns of same-sex relations in all-male work settings where "hoboes" and other transient laborers worked, such as lumber camps, cattle ranges, and many mining camps. Important early efforts to investigate such social worlds from this perspective include Susan Lee Johnson's "'The Gold She Gathered': Difference, Domination, and California's Southern Mines, 1848–1853" (Ph.D. diss., Yale University, 1993); B. R. Burg, *Sodomy and the Pirate Tradition: English Sea Rovers in the Seventeenth-Century Caribbean* (New York, 1984); and Chad Heap, "The Melting Pot of Trampdom," unpublished seminar paper, University of Chicago, 1993.

62. Wooden and Parker, *Men behind Bars.*

63. Berg, *Revelations of a Prison Doctor*, pp. 137, 152–61; Kahn, *Mentality and Homosexuality*, pp. 23–24, 129; see also Perry M. Lichtenstein, "The 'Fairy' and the Lady Lover," *Medical Review of Reviews* 27 (1921): 369–74.

64. *New York Herald Tribune*, January 27, 1934: 2.

65. Berg, *Revelations of a Prison Doctor,* pp. 161–63.

66. The raid has not received much attention from historians, but for La Guardia's appointment of Austin H. MacCormick as Commissioner of Corrections and his insistence that the Tammany influence be driven from the Corrections Department, see Lowell M. Limpus and Burr W. Leyson, *This Man La Guardia* (New York, 1938), pp. 378, 381; and Thomas Kessner, *Fiorello H. La Guardia and the Making of Modern New York* (New York, 1989), ch. 8.

67. "M'Cormick Raids Welfare Island, Smashes Gangster Rule of Prison; Warden Relieved, Deputy Seized: Commissioner Discovers Top Notch Thugs Living at Ease in Hospital . . . Private Section Housing Degenerates Revealed in 'World's Worst' Bastille; Flare-up Feared," *New York Herald Tribune,* January 25, 1934: 1, 9; "McCann Admits 'Convict Rule,' " *Daily Mirror,* January 26, 1934: 10. In yet another article in the same issue, "Welfare Milk Racket Bared," p. 3, the paper asked "why 'Greta Garbo,' alias 'Top and Bottom,' the drug-eaten former U.S. Navy gob, wears his hair to his waist." The *New York Times* also gave the prison raid extensive coverage. Although it paid less attention to the most scandalous elements, even it described the "altogether different line of contraband" found in the homosexual cell block, including "rouge, powder, mascara, perfume, even a woman's wig," and went on to describe how "several of the inmates of this cell block affected long hair. Silk undergarments were found in the cells" ("Welfare Island Raid Bares Gangster Rule over Prison; Weapons, Narcotics Found . . . Vice Carried on Openly," January 25, 1934: 3).

68. In addition to the studies already cited, see Joseph F. Fishman, *Sex in Prison: Revealing Sex Conditions in American Prisons* (New York, 1934). The growth of interest in homosexuality in prisons may account for the publication of Samuel Kahn's study, *Mentality and Homosexuality,* in 1937, even though it had been written more than a decade earlier.

69. Thomas Mott Osborne, *Prisons and Common Sense* (Philadelphia, 1924), pp. 89–90. He also recognized a third category: "the degenerates, whose dual nature [combining male and female elements] has been a problem to the psychologist since the days of ancient Greece."

70. Nelson, *Prison Days and Nights,* pp. 157–58. Note the assumption that male and female fellators were equally anomalous and virtually interchangeable.

TOWARD A "VALUE-FREE" SCIENCE OF SEX

The Kinsey Reports

JANICE M. IRVINE

I hardly ever see him at night any more since he took up sex.

—Clara Kinsey

The development of sexology in the Kinsey era is best understood in light of widespread changes in sexuality and the family early in the century. The social and economic changes that reshaped marital ideology and gender roles in the wake of World War I form the cultural backdrop for the emergence of the scientific study of sex. Increasingly, women were moving into the cities, living on their own, and working in the public sector. Having achieved a sense of independence in college or in jobs, women were less content to settle for the exclusivity of wife/mother roles.[1] Sociosexual mores for women changed rapidly in the 1920s. Smoking in public vied with sexual adventure as the epitome of female licentiousness. An official of the National Reform Bureau noted that smoking "is the beginning of the end" and prophesied, "Virtually all the male vices will be feminine vices, too."[2] Much later, Alfred C. Kinsey would document that public anxiety about loosening sexual morality was based in reality. The generation of women born in the first decade of the twentieth century showed twice the incidence of premarital intercourse of those born earlier. And more of these women were having sex with men other than their intended husbands.

Throughout the 1920s and 1930s, traditional sexual morality was increasingly at variance with people's actual behavior. Discussion of sexual matters was becoming more acceptable, and with the confidence and authority of all popular magazines, *Fortune* proclaimed, "Sex is no longer news."[3] The era moved toward an attitude that Estelle Freedman and John D'Emilio describe as sexual liberalism—an emphasis on erotic pleasure as an integral part of personal and marital satisfaction and a rejection of the belief that sex is inevitably oriented toward reproduction.[4] Heterosexual relations outside marriage became more normative, amid popular cries that the family was in peril and home life was disintegrating.

Yet sexual ideology was merely one arena of the more widespread shift in gender roles. As the Victorian sociosexual boundaries of separate spheres blurred, it was becoming harder to define what it meant to be a man and what it meant to be a woman. A popular poll in the *Ladies Home Journal* in the mid-1930s reflected the ambivalence about men's and women's traditional roles. Of the women polled, 60 percent objected to the word "obey" in the marriage ceremony; 75 percent believed that husbands and wives should make decisions together; and 80 percent believed an unemployed husband should perform household duties. Yet 60 percent of the women added that they would lose respect for their husband if they earned more than he did, and 90 percent stated that a woman should quit her job if her husband demanded it.[5] The tension between traditional demands and the emerging order was palpable.

This flux in gender roles was accelerated by World War II. Women were propelled even more dramatically out of traditional roles by the war mobilization. And, since definitions of appropriate gender roles are inextricably related, historians have noted how the increasing liberation of women precipitated a crisis of masculinity among men.[6] Gender insecurity during the war led to an idealization of images of women and the family that were invoked with a vengeance in the postwar era. Heavy-handed propaganda called for the reinstitution of gender polarities along traditional, conservative lines. The celebration of heterosexuality and marriage led to the baby boom of 1946 to 1964, a cohort of 75 million whose movement from phase to phase of the life cycle has had a profound effect on U.S. culture at each stage.[7] Yet one can discern the signs of intense cultural anxiety about sex, gender, and marriage in this period. The witch-hunts of the early 1950s, directed against communists and homosexuals, spoke to a pervasive fear of Otherness. The crisis of gender was reflected in fears that our men weren't man enough (to protect us from the Red scare) and our women were too strong and overbearing (which would lead to a decline in the moral fabric and subsequent communist takeover). As journalist Michael Bronski has observed, such films as *The Incredible Shrinking Man* and *Attack of the 50-Foot Woman* capture the gender anxiety of the era.[8]

It was in this context that Kinsey published his work. Sex and gender, both socially constructed concepts, were heavily influenced by the changes of the early to mid-twentieth century. Thus, while Kinsey documented and verified the quantitative dimensions of sexual behavior, he also tapped the public's ambivalence about fluctuating sexual mores. For some his work was reassuring and for others outrageous. Yet Kinsey spoke to the cultural confusion about sexuality by offering the hope of scientific solutions to the crisis of gender and heterosexuality.

He presented data that he hoped would help men and women understand each other and thus improve both the marriage contract and the marriage bed. It was a vision in which he deeply believed, and which simultaneously functioned as a strategy to secure acceptance of sex research.

In the 1930s, as issues of birth control, sexuality, and marriage were increasingly dealt with by professionals, as opposed to feminists and sex radicals, the professionalization of sexology appeared logical.[9] Science and medicine had established themselves as the mechanisms for solving social problems, and elite institutions dedicated to preserving the traditional social order, like the Rockefeller Foundation, funneled millions of dollars into hard, scientific research. Until the 1960s, when political movements once again organized around issues of sex and gender, scientific sexology was a major option for individuals who needed information or help with sexual problems.

THE KINSEY ERA

To most people the name Kinsey is evocative of the emergence of scientific sex research in the United States. Alfred C. Kinsey was undeniably a pioneer and indeed a landmark figure in the scientific study of sex. Other scientists in Europe and America had conducted research before Kinsey, and J. M. Exner, Katherine Davis, Clelia Mosher, and Robert Latou Dickinson had in the early 1900s conducted sex surveys in the United States that foreshadowed Kinsey's empirical methodology. Yet none approached the magnitude of the research Kinsey produced.

By Kinsey's time, a number of factors had converged to loosen traditional religious strictures on the secular approach to sexuality in the United States. The work of Sigmund Freud had achieved wide currency in the early decades of the twentieth century, providing new paradigms for understanding the social and emotional significance of sexuality. Other writers such as Havelock Ellis and Theodore van de Velde had produced popular books and marriage manuals, which were available to the general public. Several empirical sex surveys had been published, and "health" issues such as birth control, venereal disease, and abortion provided a forum for discussing sex. Widespread demographic changes triggered public concern about marriage and sexuality. In this context, sexual behavior was being widely discussed by groups as varied as physicians, clergy, eugenicists, feminists, radicals, and social reformers.

By 1910 the Rockefeller Foundation had already committed over $5 million to the study of prostitution and the "white slave" trade, convinced that sexual biology, then a fledgling science, was the means by which social "problems" of sexuality would be solved. Breakthroughs in endocrinology at the turn of the century fueled this belief. Hormones, and their relationship to certain sexual characteristics, had just been discovered, and many physicians were hoping that questions about sexual "problems" such as homosexuality would be answered by research on the sex glands.[10] Chemicals extracted from the ovaries and the testes had been labeled "female" and "male" sex hormones, reflecting the underlying ideological hope that research would explicate the essential differences between the sexes. Although later research revealed the presence of both hormones in both sexes, the labels stuck, and these biological interpretations were directly used by some scientists to imply that gender differences, and by extension women's "inferiority," were inborn.[11]

Two prominent sex endocrinologists persuaded the National Research Council to establish the Committee for Research in Problems of Sex in 1921. The stated intent of the committee's founders was that "by their concerted effort and with the prestige of the National Research Council, they could raise to scientific favor in the United States a subject which up to that time had remained in relative dispute, and that they could stimulate and coordinate research in all the related sciences that bear upon human behavior."[12] The committee was funded by the Rockefeller Foundation and from its inception until the late 1940s was both umbrella and impetus for much of the scientific sex research conducted in the United States. The research that the committee funded reflected the ideological agenda of the officers of the Rockefeller Foundation. Some were opposed to the direct study of sex; others were interested in "backing brains" in order to solve "the social and moral problems of sex behavior in the community"— divorce, illegitimacy, prostitution—all reducible, in the opinion of the Foundation, to some biological or psychological etiology, and thus amenable to "objective" empirical analysis. The research funded consisted of "the kind of morphological, functional studies that appealed to the sexologists for their scientific definition of the socially normal, and to the biologists for their mechanical insight into the animal organism." From 1922 to 1949, the Foundation gave the committee between $60,000 and $75,000 a year, most of which, until 1934, was allocated to hormonal research.[13] At that point, the committee broadened its focus and took the risk of funding what would prove to be the most pivotal sex research of the century.

It was to the Committee for Research in Problems of Sex that Alfred Kinsey, the quintessential scientist, turned for funding in 1941. After a nominal grant the first year, the committee increased its funding to him exponentially over the years, so that by 1947 Kinsey's Institute for Sex Research was receiving half of the committee's entire budget. His rigorously empirical approach to the study of sex mirrored the Foundation's intents. But in 1954, prompted by a congressional investigating committee, the Rockefeller Foundation completely terminated his funding. The Foundation was apparently unwilling to weather the moral and political outrage engendered by Kinsey's research.

Kinsey's research was a logical outcome of his own evolving interests and professional predilections. He was a professor of zoology at Indiana University whose area of expertise was the gall wasp. A taxonomist and collector par excellence, he had amassed over four million wasps during the course of his fieldwork. Kinsey's shift to the study of sexuality can be traced to his involvement with a marriage course instituted at Indiana University in 1938. As coordinator of the course, he was dismayed by the dearth of scientific literature on sex and his consequent inability to answer his students' questions. He was critical of all previous sex research as methodologically unsound or, in contrast to his own penchant for collecting, too narrow in scope. Thus he began compiling his own data, initially by taking the sexual histories of his students.[14]

The cultural idealization of science in American society was Kinsey's inspiration as well as his validation. He was convinced of the relevance and necessity of the application of the scientific method to the study of human sexuality, and he devoted considerable space in his texts to arguments for the viability of sexual science. Any increase in knowledge, he believed, would increase "man's capacity to live happily with himself and with his fellow men."[15] Kinsey squarely faced challenges to the right of scientists to conduct research in the area of human sexuality. Psychology and philosophy, he said, "ignored the material origins of all behavior"; only direct observation could provide reliable information on material phenomena—and for Kinsey, sex was essentially a material phenomenon. A true son of science, Kinsey was committed to the value-free objectivity of his research. In his first volume, *Sexual Behavior in the Human Male* (*SBHM*), he wrote,

> The present study . . . represents an attempt to accumulate an objectively determined body of facts about sex which strictly avoids social or moral interpretations of the fact. Each person who reads this report will want to make interpretations in accordance with his understanding of moral values and social significance; but that is not part of the scientific method, and indeed, scientists have no special capacities for making such evaluations.[16]

From the purview of the 1980s, when science has, at least in some circles, been removed from its pedestal, Kinsey's naiveté is obvious. Radical critiques of science emphasize that, far from being value-free, science embodies a white, middle-class, heterosexual imperative. And, as we shall see, Kinsey's work is grounded in this dominant ideology. Yet, in that particular historical era of sex research, Kinsey's claim to objectivity was, in some respects, quite radical. The scientific study of sex was still suspect in a climate where discussions of sex were typically conducted under the aegis of religion and philosophy. The work of the early sexologists such as Krafft-Ebing and Ellis categorized forms and classes of behavior as "abnormal" and "perverse." When Kinsey proclaimed his "objectivity," he was eschewing both the moralism of religion and the pathologizing tendency of the social sciences. It was essentially, for Kinsey, a claim that he would make no negative judgments, point no fingers, and condemn no behavior.

But though scientists may avoid explicit moral judgments, research is implicitly striated with values and biases. In fact, Kinsey's values permeate his work. Kinsey conveys his belief, cloaked in the rationale that what is "natural" is right, that sex is good and more is better, thus effecting an important ideological shift for sexology. His pro-sex stance inheres in modern sexology and accounts for some of the field's ideological complexity, particularly with respect to female sexuality.

Kinsey's belief in scientific objectivity had another consequence that persists within modern sexology: his refusal to take public stands on political or social issues of the day. Wardell Pomeroy, one of Kinsey's research associates, cites Kinsey's dogged continuance of his research during World War II as if he were untouched by it. "He never joked about politics," Pomeroy says, "no doubt because he was completely apolitical."[17] Neutrality was a logical outcome of Kinsey's belief that scientists were not necessarily equipped to make political evaluations, yet it was also a strategy to maintain his growing social legitimacy. Kinsey's work was controversial enough and could be threatened by partisan stances. In the first pages of *SBHM*, Kinsey describes some of the difficulties he encountered:

> During the first year or two we were repeatedly warned of the dangers involved in the undertaking, and were threatened with specific trouble. There was some organized opposition, chiefly from a particular medical group. There were attempts by the medical association in one city to bring suit on the ground that we were practicing medicine without a license, police interference in two or three cities, investigation by a sheriff in one rural area, and attempts to persuade the University's Administration to stop the study, or to prevent the publication of the results, or to dismiss the senior author from his university connection, or to establish a censorship over all publications emanating from the study. Through all of this, the Administration of Indiana University stoutly defended *our right to do objectively scientific research, and to that defense much of the success of this project is due.* In one city, a school board, whose president was a physician, dismissed a high school teacher because he had cooperated in getting histories outside of the school but in the same city. There were other threats of legal action, threats of political investigation, and threats of censorship, and for some years there was criticism from scientific colleagues. It has been interesting to observe how far the ancient traditions and social custom influence even persons who are trained as scientists. [Emphasis added.][18]

Kinsey's claim to objectivity and neutrality was in many ways a careful presentation of self. For his books make it clear that he had deep convictions regarding social and political mores. He was critical of the church, educational institutions, and homes for being "the chief sources of the sexual inhibitions, the distaste for all aspects of sex, the fears of the physical difficulties that may be involved in a sexual relationship, and the feelings of guilt which many females carry with them into their marriages."[19] And he railed against sex laws in the beginning of *Sexual Behavior in the Human Female* (*SBHF*):

Our present information seems to make it clear that the current sex laws are unenforced and are unenforceable because they are too completely out of accord with the realities of human behavior, and because they attempt too much in the way of social control. Such a high proportion of the females and males in our population is involved in sexual activities which are prohibited by the law of most of the states of the union, that it is inconceivable that the present laws could be administered in any fashion that even remotely approached systematic and complete enforcement. The consequently capricious enforcement which these laws now receive offers an opportunity for maladministration, for police and political graft, and for blackmail which is regularly imposed both by underworld groups and by the police themselves.[20]

Both *SBHM* and *SBHF* contain impassioned critiques of the "sexual psychopath" laws that originated in the 1930s and swept through many states and the District of Columbia. These laws were enacted in the wake of moral panics, often triggered by sexual crimes against children, but doing little, in fact, to protect their intended beneficiaries. Rather, they served to crystallize public sexual discourse around normality and deviance,[21] categories that Kinsey despised. Kinsey attempted to deconstruct the category of "sex offender" by pointing out that most people engaged in sexual behavior that was illegal.[22] To arrest and imprison some of them for relatively common activities was the height of hypocrisy. Kinsey also opposed the sodomy laws that, as a gay male writer noted in the 1950s, rendered "every homosexual in this country . . . a potential felon and traitor."[23] Yet despite the vehemence of his critique, Kinsey simultaneously believed that the only function of the Institute was to present factual data and their significance, not to lobby politically.[24]

This strategy has persisted at the Kinsey Institute for Research in Sex, Gender, and Reproduction, as the Institute is now known. Sex researchers there have refused, for example, to take public stands on pornography.[25] Kinsey's dilemma is inherent in the scientific study of sex. For both political and strategic reasons, many sexologists have attempted, like Kinsey, to ignore sexual politics and attend simply to the "facts." Since sex is so highly politicized in this culture, sexologists are continually sought out by special interest groups, legislators, lobbyists, and social activists who want them to act as advocates and give their expert opinions. The founders of the Sex Information and Education Council of the United States (SIECUS) realized this in 1965 when they were asked to sign a petition in support of Ralph Ginzburg, whose conviction for publishing *Eros* was being reviewed by the Supreme Court. In a letter to founder Mary Calderone, board member Lester Kirkendall wrote, "I think myself that we must take some stand in such matters. We can't deal with sex without getting into controversy."[26] Yet this realization of the inherently political implications of sexuality and sex research has throughout the century collided with many sexologists' aspirations to value-neutrality. Sexology has yet to resolve the tension between sexual politics and sexual science.

Kinsey's commitment to the scientific method is palpable in both *SBHM* and *SBHF.* Both are replete with passages that reflect his passion for, even awe at, the potential of science to expand the boundaries and improve the lot of humankind. One can almost hear him persuading the average reader of the wonders of the emergent sexual science. Yet, subtextually, it is clear that Kinsey felt that the success of his research depended on scientific rigor and, perhaps more important, on his ability to convince the public of the stringency and objectivity of his approach. He went to great lengths at the beginning of *SBHM,* published in 1948, to satisfy would-be critics as to his precision. In painstaking detail he described the research team's objectives and methods. He reviewed the foundations of taxonomy, the nuances of interviewing, statistical analysis, sampling problems, and the validity of the data. (Kinsey acknowledged that his subject called for a different procedural approach from those used in "less intimate and less complex" areas.[27]) He even included a proviso, which has gotten lost over the years as researchers authoritatively quote the Kinsey findings, that the data presented throughout the volume should be recognized as "probably fair approximations, but only approximations of the fact."[28] Nevertheless, Kinsey boasted a proficiency of method and uniformity of data that, he claimed, many would have thought impossible for "as taboo a subject as sex."[29]

The style and content of his research, as well as his fundamental sexual ideology, were both profoundly affected by Kinsey's background in biology and taxonomy. He was a collector of the "natural" and an observer fascinated by the minutiae of variation. In his introduction to *SBHM,* Kinsey lists nineteen taxonomic studies of sexuality that preceded his. Yet the major early figures in the scientific study of sex (e.g., Krafft-Ebing, Ellis, Freud, Davis, and Bloch) had essentially based their work on case studies or small samples. Although Kinsey ostensibly defers to the contribution of these pioneers, one can often detect scorn in his references to their theories or findings. He questioned their methodology, dismissing certain field methods as "barbershop techniques":

> Some persons are appalled at the idea of having to undertake a large-scale coverage of thousands of individual cases before they are allowed to generalize about the whole. Contacts with the statistics of small samples have provided rationalizations for some of this inertia; but no statistical techniques can make a small sample represent any type of individual which was not present in the original body of data.[30]

Whether the subject was the gall wasp or sex, the key to valid research, for Kinsey, was identical: amass a vast sample. In this case, his nonrandom sample consisted of the sex histories of individuals as varied as college students, prisoners, mental patients, white- and blue-collar workers, ministers, and prostitutes. His technique was the interview. The average interview lasted from ninety minutes to two hours, and covered from 350 to 500 items, or more. Kinsey devoted considerable space in *SBHF* to describing this method and defending it against critics who objected that subjects might exaggerate, distort, or simply forget the specific details of their sexual pasts:

> The testing of the reliability and validity of our data is as yet insufficient, and we shall continue to make such tests as the research program allows; but it may be noted that this is the first time that tests of either reliability or validity have been made in any study of human sexual behavior, and that there are few other case history studies of any sort which have made as extensive tests as we have undertaken in the present study.[31]

The interview was one of the most controversial aspects of the Kinsey research; even today curiosity persists about what exactly went on. It is clear that Kinsey's interviewing format was highly idiosyncratic. He admitted that certain techniques worked better for some interviewers than others and that approaches to different informants might vary in language, style, and the definition and construction of questions. He believed that an experienced interviewer (one trained in the Kinsey method) would be alert and responsive to intangibles that called for a modification in technique. In a rare lapse of his usual aspirations to scientific objectivity, he acknowledged that effective interviewing could require empathy from the researcher: "The interviewer who senses what these things can mean, who at least momentarily shares something of the satisfaction, pain, or bewilderment which was the subject's, who shares something of the subject's hope that things will, somehow, work out right, is more effective, though he may not be altogether neutral." He went so far as to describe the interview as "a communion between two deeply human individuals, the subject and the interviewer."[32] This was a striking departure from the traditional stimulus–response approach to the interview.

Given his devotion to rigor and objectivity, however, it is not surprising that Kinsey attempted to standardize his subjective and even idiosyncratic interviewing behaviors. He described such "technical devices in interviewing" as "putting the subject at ease" (by letting him or her smoke; engaging in comfortable chatter, etc.) and "establishing rapport" (treating the subject as a friend, establishing eye contact, since "people understand each other when they look directly at each other"). The goal was to present a more universalized and objective interviewer–respondent interaction that was consistent with a positivist research tradition. Social scientists have traditionally attempted to standardize and neutralize the interview with the hope of reducing bias,[33] yet more than usual was at stake in Kinsey's quest for standard, objective research techniques: the viability of his project and, by extension, sex research as a whole.

Kinsey's studies are a pageant of counting and categorizing. *SBHM* is based on data from the sex histories of 5,300 men. Kinsey divided the population on the basis of twelve demographic factors: sex, race–cultural group, marital status, age, age of the subject at the onset of adolescence, educational level, occupational class of subject, occupational class of subject's parent, rural–urban background, religious group, religious adherence, and geographic origin. Kinsey believed that it was necessary to have at least three hundred cases from a particular subgroup for it to be adequately represented. His ultimate plan was to obtain a hundred thousand sex histories, but he died before achieving that goal.

Although his sample was unprecedented in its diversity, neither *SBHM* nor *SBHF,* published in 1953, includes data from non-whites. *SBHF,* based on 5,940 histories, fails even to mention race in its breakdown of population characteristics. This shortcoming is a result of Kinsey's obsession with numbers; he felt that he had not obtained enough sex histories from Black men and women to permit valid extrapolation. In *SBHM* he wrote: "The story for the Negro male cannot be told now, because the Negro sample, while of some size, is not yet sufficient for making analyses comparable to those made here for the white male."[34] Although Kinsey planned to make revisions when he had more histories from Black people, he never did so, and he thus unwittingly colluded in the racial exclusion so pervasive in sex research. The most comprehensive sex research ever published, which has been used for decades to generalize and form conclusions about people's sexual activity (and has drawn new attention with the advent of the AIDS epidemic), is based exclusively on whites. The invisibility of Black people in sexology as subjects or researchers has undermined our understanding of the sexuality of Black Americans and continues to be a major problem in modern sexology.

Kinsey's approach to hiring staff and interviewers reflected his basic assumptions and values. (It also influenced later research decisions and interpretations of data and was related to the exclusion of Blacks from his reports.) His major criteria for interviewers were as follows:

1. They must be happily married, but able to travel at least half-time. This criterion allowed him to exclude women, since, he explained to a colleague, "it is much more difficult for a woman to stay happily married and travel away from home a good deal."[35]
2. They should have either a medical degree or a doctorate, yet be able to get along with individuals from lower socioeconomic levels.
3. They must have been born and raised in the United States, exposed to American customs and attitudes, yet be able to refrain from evaluating what others did sexually.[36]

In addition, Kinsey would never hire anyone with an odd or an ethnic name, since he thought it might interfere with establishing rapport with subjects. He particularly avoided Jewish names for fear of alienating Protestants.[37] He adamantly insisted that his staff composition did not interfere with research efficacy or interviewing. Although Kinsey confessed that it was "astounding," given the cultural taboo against revealing personal sexual activities, that anyone had agreed to be interviewed, he did not believe the process would be enhanced if subjects were approached by a member of their own community. Against the need for women or Black interviewers he argued that if one had to match interviewer and subject on the basis of sex or race, then one should also do so for other social groups, such as prostitutes—a practice that he considered unworkable. His staff, then, consisted of male, heterosexual, white Anglo-Saxon Protestants, since for Kinsey these characteristics represented the yardstick of normality. WASPs, he believed, would be able to interview anybody.

This decision reveals two related features of Kinsey's worldview: his devotion to the scientific method, and the strength of his covert biases about gender, race, and sexual preference. His ideology was so based in numbers and frequencies that he inevitably viewed the characteristics of any numerical majority as "natural," normative, or good. Since male WASPs represent, if not the statistical, at least the cultural, norm in the United States, Kinsey considered them to be natural researchers. With enough scientific training in the fine points of interviewing, he believed they could be neutral, win the trust of their subjects, and elicit information from anyone. It apparently never occurred to him that there was anything political about representing the dominant social group as the norm and refusing to hire more diverse interviewers.

It is impossible to say whether, and how, a different research team might have influenced the studies. A group of women, homosexuals, Blacks, and prostitutes might perhaps have asked different questions, elicited more accurate information from the interviewees, or even provided new perspectives calling for a reconceptualization of the entire project. And it is important to note that, as with all scientific endeavors, values and biases would inhere in the research whatever the composition of the team. Kinsey's unwillingness to consider the potential impact of his interviewers' profiles, however, reveals his inability to acknowledge research itself as a social intervention.

KINSEY ON THE ORIGINS OF SEXUALITY

The question of sexuality and the origins of sexual behavior was far from esoteric for Kinsey. Rather, the answer was central both to the arguments he would propound and to his efforts to convince the public of the viability of sexual science. Yet his analysis of sexuality is sometimes vague and often contradictory. In contrast to earlier major sexual theorists, notably Freud, for whom sex represented a profoundly mysterious force, Kinsey viewed the sex drive as straightforward. Repeatedly he asserts that human sexual behavior is the outcome of the interplay of biological, psychological, and sociological influences. On the other hand, despite his own scientific background and the penchant of his major funding source for biologically oriented study, Kinsey frequently cites the enormous importance of psychological and social factors in sexual development. Depending on the point he wanted to make, Kinsey identified one of three factors as preeminent in the origin of sexual behavior: "our mammalian ancestry," anatomical and physiological capacity, and social conditioning.

Kinsey's manifest goal was to persuade skeptics that sex was a topic suitable and appropriate for scientific investigation. Thus, in his description of human sexual response, he frequently emphasized physiological processes, with psychological factors treated as mitigating effects: "Erotic arousal is a material phenomenon which involves an extended series of physical, physiologic, and psychologic changes. Many of these could be subjected to precise instrumental measurement if objectivity among scientists and public respect for scientific research allowed such laboratory investigation."[38] Describing sex as a "material phenomenon" meant, for Kinsey, that it had a basis in biology or the physical world. There was nothing magical for Kinsey about sex, and, indeed, he was committed to demystifying the aura of secrecy that surrounded it. By the time *SBHF* was published, he was determinedly addressing his critics:

> With the right of the scientist to investigate most aspects of the material universe, most persons will agree; but there are some who have questioned the applicability of scientific methods to an investigation of human sexual behavior. Some persons, recognizing the importance of the psychologic aspects of that behavior, and the relation of the individual's sexual activity to the social organization as a whole, feel that this is an area which only psychologists or social philosophers should explore. In this insistence they seem to ignore the material origins of all behavior. It is as though the dietician and biochemist were denied the right to analyze foods and the process of nutrition because the cooking and proper serving of food may be rated a fine art, and because the eating of certain foods has been considered a matter for religious regulation.[39]

Moreover, emphasizing the primacy of biological and physiological factors enabled Kinsey to criticize societal proscriptions against behavior that he believed was rooted in nature:

> Whatever the moral interpretation, . . . there is no scientific reason for considering particular types of sexual activity as intrinsically, in their biological origins, normal or abnormal. . . . Present-day legal determinations of sexual acts which are acceptable, or "natural," and those which are "contrary to nature" are not based on data obtained from biologists, nor from nature herself.[40]

Kinsey was an essentialist for whom "natural" equaled good. He defended whatever behavior he saw as originating from biological impulses, distilled from the contaminating effects of psychological or sociological variables. Eschewing the judgments of earlier sex theorists, Freud in particular, based on perceived "normality," he adopted instead a yardstick based on "naturalness": "It is unwarranted to believe that particular types of sexual behavior are always expressions of psychoses or neuroses. In actuality, they are more often expressions of what is biologically basic in mammalian and anthropoid behavior, and of a deliberate disregard for social convention."[41]

An analysis that emphasized biology would render sexuality less amenable to societal restriction, Kinsey noted. In *SBHM* he pointed out that cultures with purely social or religious interpretations of sexuality tend to institute restrictions on behavior, whereas a view of sex as simply biological would afford greater freedom: "A third possible interpretation of sex as a normal biologic function, *acceptable in whatever form it is manifested,* has hardly figured in either general or scientific discussions" (emphasis added).[42]

In *SBHF* he intensified this argument, no doubt in response to criticism of the nature of sex research as well as public outrage at the range of sexual behavior he had documented.

SBHF emphasized his two essentialist themes: the mammalian ancestry of humans and the notion of sexual capacity. At the beginning of every section, Kinsey undertook a review of historical and anthropological data on whatever behavior was under discussion. This was an attempt to contextualize human behavior and, ultimately, to illuminate the repressiveness of Western customs. He painstakingly reported, for example, on the "phylogenetic origins" of petting in cattle, hogs, dogs, rats, ferrets, and other mammals. Similarly, he noted that anthropologists have documented extensive petting in "primitive, pre-literate cultures." Petting, he concluded, is not unique or outrageous: "the independent but parallel development of such similar patterns in these widely scattered races is, again, further evidence of their phylogenetic origins in anatomic and physiologic characteristics which must have been part of the heritage of the ancient ancestors of all mankind."[43]

Kinsey bravely carried these discussions to absurd lengths, as when he observed that distinguishing between premarital and marital activity among animals is problematic, "since there is no institution of marriage among the lower mammals." Yet he quickly recovered and pointed out the implications of this fact. Our fuss about pre- and extramarital affairs is specious because "while human custom and man-made law may make a sharp distinction between coitus which occurs before marriage and the identical physical acts when they occur within a marriage, it is important to realize that physically and physiologically they are one and the same thing in man, just as they are in the lower mammals."[44]

The presentation of information on "our mammalian origins," "infrahuman species," and "primitive human cultures" allowed Kinsey to challenge or support social customs. On the one hand, to shatter the assumed rationality and sanctity of what he considered cultural constraints, he pointed out that avoidance of nudity during coitus was "a perversion of what is, in a biological sense, normal sexuality."[45] On the other hand, he found it just as easy to defend the status quo as an artifact of mammalian history. He frequently justified the double standard as a biological imperative: "The human male's interest in maintaining his property rights in his female mate, his objections to his wife's extra-marital coitus, and her lesser objection to his extra-marital activity, are mammalian heritages."[46]

And he surmised that extramarital affairs sprang from an ancient desire for multiple sex partners that would not be resolved "until man moves more completely away from his mammalian ancestry."[47]

Kinsey's reliance on an essentialist understanding of the sexual patterns of other mammals and "primitive" cultures as the yardstick for natural human behavior was a logical outcome of his empirical methods. The scope of his research was vast and unprecedented, and his use of interviews was intriguing; still, Kinsey was ultimately simply counting the incidence and frequency of orgasms. Focusing his lens on the most quantifiable unit of sexual behavior allowed him to talk about patterns of behavior but never about its significance. Kinsey saw culture simply as an obstacle to the realization of a potential level of sexual activity, rather than as a set of influences that affect and shape the meaning of sexuality. His romantic gaze back to mammalian ancestors reveals a view of sexuality as a seamless, transhistorical force that, but for the impediments of modern social relations, we could extend into the present. In his discussion of homosexuality, for example, he notes that if all persons with any trace of homosexual history were eliminated from the population, there is no reason to think that the incidence of homosexuality in the next generation would be diminished. "The homosexual has been a significant part of human sexual activity ever since the dawn of history, primarily because it is an expression of capacities that are basic in the human animal."[48] From the perspective of outlets and behavior patterns, this is no doubt true. But his unwillingness to consider homosexuality as more than a particular configuration of orgasms kept him from considering that homosexuality, as both an activity and an organizing principle for a community of people, would be constructed very differently at different moments in history. This narrow view of the development and expression of sexuality forecloses a more nuanced analysis of the ways in which sexual behavior and identity evolve and change in their purposes and meanings both for individuals and for a society. This lack of vision is endemic in sex research and modern sexology in general. It was not, as some of his critics have charged, that Kinsey ignored the cultural constructs of sex. However, when he did acknowledge sex laws, social mores, ethnic or religious traditions, or other cultural infusions of meaning, it was to describe them as fetters on what would otherwise be an untroubled, "natural" expression of sexuality. These customs, he notes, "originate neither in accumulated experience nor in scientific examinations of objectively gathered data. The sociologist and anthropologist find the origins of such customs in ignorance and superstition, and in the attempt of each group to set itself apart from its neighbors."[49]

Sexual capacity, the second essentialist theme of *SBHF*, is a fundamental, if inchoate, part of Kinsey's sexual worldview. Without ever operationally defining it, he seems to have used the term in place of "libido" to connote an inner wellspring of sexual energy. The concept makes its strongest appearance in *SBHF*, where it is linked to anatomy and physiology: "We now understand that this capacity to respond depends upon the existence of end organs of touch in the body surfaces, nerves connecting these organs with the spinal cord and brain, nerves which extend from the cord to various muscles in the body, and the autonomic nervous system through which still other parts of the body are brought into action."[50] Functionally the term is related, rather simplistically, to sexual frequency: those with a low sexual capacity had sex less often than those with higher capacities. Kinsey made several uses of the concept. One, as we shall see, was to justify differences in sexual behavior between men and women. Women, he thought, had less sex and fewer sexual variations because of their lower capacity. Second, he used it to criticize Freudian theories of sublimation. Kinsey thought it was a mistake to believe in a fixed amount of sexual energy, some of which can be channeled into "higher" things, "as nervous energy is shunted from one to another portion of a nervous system, or electricity short-circuited into new paths and channels."[51] Although he conceded that health and opportunity for sexual contact might affect sexual functioning, he believed that people typically manifested whatever variable amount of sexual energy they had. "Inactivity is no more sublimation of sex drive than blindness or deafness or other perceptive defects are sublimation of those capacities,"[52] he declared, his analogies making it clear that he considered those with less capacity to be less physically able. Kinsey hated sublimation theory because it resonated with traditional religious proscriptions against sex and implied that there were "higher levels of activity" in which one could engage rather than having sex. Sublimation theory, he believed, was merely moralism codified into scientific doctrine.

Finally, Kinsey wielded the concept of capacity to argue for the validity of every form of sexual expression. Although there might be differences in degree, all humans have the physiological equipment to respond to effective stimulation. He noted, for example, that daily orgasm is within the capacity of the average human male, and if humans were unrestricted by custom or culturally imposed inhibition, the more than daily rates observed in some primates could be matched by man. Similarly, all men and women have the capacity for homosexual behavior. It is simply the vagaries of experience that allow some people to engage in homosexual activities more readily than others. This concept of capacity enabled Kinsey to locate sexuality as a basic, intrinsic human drive and consequently to criticize cultural repression of such fundamental impulses.

A third element in Kinsey's sexual worldview is the centrality of social conditioning. According to his learning-theory model of sexual behavior, humans' fundamental capacity for a wide range of expression is channeled in a particular direction by external influences, among them religion, the educational system, and the family. Sex laws, for Kinsey, were a prime example of custom and a metaphor for the destruction that cultural influences inflicted on sexual expression.

Analysts of Kinsey have alternately accused him of biological reductivism and cultural relativism. While such accusations would appear to be mutually exclusive, in fact both accounts are accurate. Kinsey simultaneously located himself on the far end of both sides of the argument over biological versus social influences on sexuality. He believed that sexual behavior was in some senses "predestined by its morphologic structure, its metabolic capacities, its hormones, and all of the other characters which it has inherited or which have been built into it by the physical environment in which it has developed."[53] And, as noted, he thought of sexual behavior in terms of outlets and orgasms, whose frequency might vary but whose meanings are consistent across history and culture. On the other hand, he professed that sexual conventions are normal only because culture deems them so.

Kinsey's sexual ideology is a complex weave of essentialist strands with social influences. His disdain for culture, which he saw as an inevitably restricting force on an otherwise robust sexual energy, was palpable. It is not surprising that his research aroused such ire, since he overturned traditional sexual morality. Freudian as well as religious tenets focus on the civilizing effects of culture and its ability to tame the potentially wild, uncontrollable libido. Kinsey, on the other hand, was arguing for the inherent health and naturalness of sexuality. His arguments were simplistic in many ways, ignoring, for example, the role of power relations in sociosexual hierarchies. But since he valorized *anything* he believed was rooted in nature, even when it challenged conventional morality, he subverted the traditionally oppressive use of essentialism to support the dominant ideology. In its historical context, Kinsey's essentialist impulse was basically a move to affirm sexual desire and all varieties of sexual expression in a culture where sexual attitudes and norms were intensely repressive.

SEX AND GENDER IN THE KINSEY RESEARCH

Kinsey's emphasis on the primacy of physiological response and his insistence on empiricism led him, as we have seen, to adopt orgasm as an accessible and quantifiable unit of measurement. He defined orgasm operationally, as "the moment of sudden release."[54] This formulation was less viable, however, in his research on women. He briefly mentioned in *SBHF* the difficulty of basing statistical calculations on orgasms, as had been done for the male, since he found that much female sexual activity did not result in orgasm. There is, he concluded, "no better unit for measuring the incidences and frequencies of sexual activity,"[55] but he attempted to supplement his information on women's sexuality by including in *SBHF* more qualitative data, such as diaries, letters, and other anecdotal material.

In the era in which Kinsey was writing, his use of orgasm as a measuring unit for women's sexuality was progressive. Given the aura of shame around female sexuality, and the lack of widespread support for women's pleasure, modifying the basic sexual yardstick for research on women could have underscored the popular impression that women's sexuality was more "diffuse" and orgasm less important for them. By retaining orgasm as the measure for both groups, he conveyed the legitimacy and importance of the female orgasm.

Armed with a unit of measurement, Kinsey turned to collecting data on the types of activities people engaged in and counting the number of times they engaged in them. A major construct of his research was "sexual outlet"—a taxonomy of the six major sources of orgasm (masturbation, nocturnal emissions, heterosexual petting, heterosexual intercourse, homosexual relations, and intercourse with animals). The sum of the orgasms attained from these varied sources was called the individual's total sexual outlet. The most significant ramification of this conceptualization was its elevation of typically marginalized behaviors (bestiality, nocturnal emissions) and stigmatized activities (homosexuality, masturbation) to an equivalent status with heterosexual behavior. Anticipating Masters and Johnson's conclusion that, physiologically, an orgasm is an orgasm is an orgasm, Kinsey accorded all equal dignity.

The sheer magnitude of the statistics Kinsey amassed was startling to many. With extreme care, he documented the minutiae of thousands of people's experiences with premarital sex, petting, intercourse, homosexuality, and sex with animals. Both volumes are thick with statistics that clearly document the gulf between mainstream morality and what people actually did. He noted, for example, that masturbation, common among women, was almost universally engaged in by men. Similarly, extramarital sex was widespread among men, and 26 percent of women had had affairs by the age of forty. Women were increasingly having orgasms during marital coitus. The rate of premarital intercourse among women reached 50 percent, and a large majority claimed to have no regrets. Even among children, sex play was reportedly extensive. With dispassion, Kinsey lifted the veil of privacy covering the scope and variety of white Americans' sexuality. He especially seemed to delight in reporting the ubiquity of culturally taboo sexual behavior. He stated, for example, that at least 37 percent of the male population had some homosexual experience: "more than one male in three of the persons that one may meet as he passes along a city street."[56] Since, for Kinsey, the very existence of a behavior was an indication of its naturalness, he hoped that societal sanctions against certain outlets would be modified if the public understood the frequency with which they occurred.

Another major construct was the homosexual–heterosexual continuum. Believing that sexual behavior was not discretely dichotomous, Kinsey utilized a seven-point scale on which he rated individuals after considering both physical response and psychological experiences:

0. Exclusively heterosexual with no homosexual
1. Predominantly heterosexual, only incidentally homosexual
2. Predominantly heterosexual, but more than incidentally homosexual
3. Equally heterosexual and homosexual
4. Predominantly homosexual, but more than incidentally heterosexual
5. Predominantly homosexual, but incidentally heterosexual
6. Exclusively homosexual

This scale has been criticized as having no advantages over the preexisting classifications of heterosexual–bisexual–homosexual. It was subsequently abandoned by later researchers at the Kinsey Institute because of its lack of empirical usefulness.[57] Yet for all its empirical shortcomings, the scale has been utilized through the 1980s to denote the variability of sexual behavior. In addition, its ideological significance for its own time should not be dismissed. The notion of the range and fluidity of sexual expression as embodied in the homosexual–heterosexual continuum represented a challenge to a more rigid nineteenth-century conceptualization that linked one's identity with a particular sexual behavior. Both Krafft-Ebing and Ellis wrote about homosexuality (or, more precisely, "inversion") as a congenital identity type. In contrast, Kinsey refused to talk about homosexuality as an identity or about homosexual persons. He believed everyone had the "capacity" for homosexuality, and so he spoke only of homosexual patterns of behavior: "There may be considerable fluctuation of patterns from time to time. . . . For instance, there are some who engage in both heterosexual and homosexual activities in the same year, or in the same month or week, or even in the same day. . . . The world is not to be divided into sheep and goats."[58] Again Kinsey was emphasizing that cultural norms are arbitrary, the sexual hierarchy hypocritical. If the scale was not extremely successful as a research tool, therefore, it still had pedagogical usefulness for gay people, who used it to question sexual labeling and assert the fluidity of sexual behavior and the existence of sexual oppression.

Kinsey's research on homosexuality came at the time when an urban gay subculture was forming in the United States. The massive mobilization for the war had entailed the temporary restructuring of family and gender roles, separated men and women with what some feared was "a barrier of indescribable experience," created opportunities for intense same-sex bonding,[59] and made it possible for thousands of men and women to discover their homosexuality and join in communities with others like themselves.[60] Kinsey's data on gay men and lesbians, published after the war, had contradictory effects. On the one hand, his figures reassured gay individuals, provided a statistical basis for the consolidation of the budding gay community, and exploded the myth that homosexuals could be easily identified. One lesbian wrote, "Probably the reams of material written in passionate defense of the homophile have done less to further the cause of tolerance than Kinsey's single, detached statement that 37 per cent of the men and 19 per cent of the women whom he interviewed admitted having had overt homosexual relationships."[61] On the other hand, the same information fueled the cultural panic of the early 1950s and paranoia about "sex perverts." Although Kinsey had hoped that his data would engender tolerance, they were in fact utilized to legitimate the McCarthy witch-hunts against both communists and homosexuals.[62] Sexual perverts were considered by many to be as dangerous as communists, and this conflation of the Red menace and the lavender menace was apparent in the popular culture of the day. Films like *I Was a Communist for the FBI* (1951), *The Red Menace* (1949), and *My Son John* (1952) portrayed communists as effeminate, seemingly invisible infiltrators who undermined family life and "seduce[d] 'impressionable' young men into joining the Party."[63] Paradoxically, Kinsey's work was utilized by vigilantes to fuel the postwar backlash and cited by gay activists, who rightly considered him an ally. The two-edged use of sexological research would become a familiar pattern.

Despite his background as a biologist, Kinsey's work is often considered to be sociological, since one of his major goals was to determine the factors (age, sex, class, etc.) that influenced choice and frequency of sexual outlet. Undoubtedly, his landmark finding was the significance of social class for male sexual behavior. He used three criteria to measure social stratification: educational level, occupational class of the interviewee, and occupational class of the interviewee's parents. Ultimately, however, he found classification by occupation too imprecise, and he came to rely on educational level as the most convenient criterion for statistical use. He rarely used the term "social class," preferring to describe findings for the "upper level" and "lower level." Journalists reporting on his work paid a good deal of attention to class distinctions in sexual behavior, but Kinsey's categories bear more definitional resemblance to the Weberian concept of status group than to a Marxist concept of class.

True to the descriptive nature of his work, Kinsey presented his findings and hinted at some of the social implications, but provided no broader analysis concerning the origins or function of the differences among social levels. "We do not yet understand, to the full, the origins of these diverse sexual philosophies," he concluded; "but it will be possible to record what the thinking of each group is in regard to each type of activity."[64] The data on males showed little variation among classes in frequency of sexual outlet, but major variances occurred in choice of sexual outlet and in sexual technique. Essentially, "upper-level" males masturbated more frequently and engaged in less premarital intercourse, homosexual behavior, or sex with prostitutes, but more petting; they experienced more nocturnal emissions. The "lower-level" males were found to be more genitally oriented and very sexually active, but to have little interest in foreplay or erotic activities other than intercourse.

In addition, a portrait of differing sexual worldviews emerged from Kinsey's descriptions. He noted that upper-level men tended to focus on issues of morality and rationalize their sexual activity according to notions of right and wrong. Lower-level males, by contrast, described their behavior in terms of what they considered to be natural or unnatural. Given Kinsey's own bias toward the "natural," it is not surprising that his sympathies fell squarely with the working class. When he discussed the wider implications of these social differences, he criticized the upper-level professionals—clinicians, lawyers, judges, teachers—who, he felt, judged all behavior by their own philosophy and imposed their sexual norms on the lower level. This practice, of which he gave examples, was anathema to him, given his idealization of nonjudgmental description and his implicit bias toward the working-class worldview. His summary of the sexual conflict went as follows:

> In general, the upper level feels that "lower level morality" lacks the ideals and the righteousness of the upper level philosophy. The lower level, on the other

hand, feels that educated and upper level society has an artificial and insincere pattern of sexual behavior which is all the more obnoxious because the upper level tries to force its patterns upon all other levels. Legends about the immorality of the lower level are matched by legends about the perversions of the upper level.[65]

Kinsey believed, however, in the healing power of scientific data. All polarities, he hoped, whether between social classes or between men and women, could be harmonized once people had the facts that facilitate understanding.

Kinsey's analysis of the role of social level in the sexual behavior of women contrasts sharply with his analysis in *SBHM*. The significance of class (or social level) was virtually dismissed in *SBHF*. Kinsey discounted a woman's occupation as a criterion for determining her social level, since her social status after marriage depended on the occupational class of her husband as well as upon her own social background (i.e., the occupational class of the parental home). His classifications are based on these latter factors. Using this derivative definition of class, Kinsey found that class (and other demographic variables) had little to do with women's sexual behavior. He concluded that males are more conditioned by the social groups in which they live than females are.[66] Since a major focus of *SBHF* is an attempt to delineate gender differences in sexual activity, it is at first surprising that Kinsey could not conceive of the category of "woman" as itself a social group in which women are taught historically and culturally bound expectations of sex and gender-appropriate behavior. Yet the male composition of the research team, the sociopolitical climate of the early 1950s, and Kinsey's own apolitical stance and biologistic emphasis were all more conducive to a generalization that carried psychophysiological implications than to an analysis of conditioning and socialization on the basis of gender.

In examining differences in sexual behavior between men and women, Kinsey focused on psychophysiological variables. Having devoted extensive sections to anatomy and physiology, he concluded that "in spite of the widespread and oft-repeated emphasis on the supposed differences between female and male sexuality, we fail to find any anatomic or physiologic basis for such differences."[67] And this knowledge should contribute to harmony between the sexes, since "males would be better prepared to understand females, and females to understand males, if they realized that they are alike in their basic anatomy and physiology."[68] This was a radical departure from the Victorian gender schema that mythologized and polarized differences between women and men.

Those sex differences that Kinsey found were attributed to the lesser "conditionability" of the female. The evidence came from what he interpreted as women's lower interest in pornography, voyeurism (described by Kinsey as vicarious sharing of sexual activity), writing graffiti in bathrooms, indulging in cross-dressing, and the like. Kinsey's interpretation of these findings was that although females are as capable of responding to tactile stimulation as males, they differ in their capacity to respond to psychological stimulation. Ostensibly this was a psychological difference, yet he struggled to reduce it to a biological one by, again, blurring the distinctions between physiology and psychology:

> Such specious distinctions between form and function have, unfortunately, lent encouragement to the opinion that the psychologic aspects of human sexual behavior are of a different order from, and perhaps more significant than, the anatomy or physiology of sexual response and orgasm. Such thinking easily becomes mystical, and quickly identifies any consideration of anatomic form and physiologic function as a scientific materialism which misses the "basic," the "human," and the "real" problems in behavior. . . . Those aspects of behavior which we identify as psychologic can be nothing but certain aspects of that same basic anatomy and physiology.[69]

Kinsey continually and explicitly rejected a cultural analysis suggesting that women are sexually socialized differently from men. The disinclination of women to indulge in certain behaviors was not due to their adherence to moral or social conventions, he believed, but to their lack of erotic interest in them. And this, Kinsey thought, must depend on some internal mechanism that functions differently in men and women. Thus, he turned to neural and hormonal research in an attempt to explain these differences. After an extensive review of the research, Kinsey could state nothing conclusively, but, like many sexologists more than forty years later, he continued to believe that more research would reveal the origins of gender differences in sexual behavior in the physiological realm.

It was to these hypothesized variations in physiological structure that Kinsey attributed what he referred to as individual differences in sexual capacity. As we have seen, he believed in individual variations in sex drive almost as genetic givens, resembling differences in acuity of sight or hearing. In *SBHM* he referred to "fundamentally apathetic persons" who would go indefinitely without orgasm.[70] Not surprisingly, given that his concept of "capacity" was rooted in frequency of sexual activity, Kinsey believed that males had a greater sexual capacity than females. He stated that 30 percent of women were more or less sexually unresponsive.[71] This, for Kinsey, was merely a physiological fact that should be accepted graciously:

> There is an inclination among psychiatrists to consider all unresponding individuals as inhibited, and there is a certain skepticism in the profession of the existence of people who are basically low in capacity to respond. This amounts to asserting that all people are more or less equal in their sexual endowments, and ignores the existence of individual variation. No one who knows how remarkably different individuals may be in morphology, in physiologic reactions, and in other psychologic capacities, could conceive of erotic capacities (of all things) that were basically uniform throughout a population. Considerable psychiatric therapy can be wasted on persons (especially females) who

are misjudged to be cases of repression when, in actuality, at least *some of them never were equipped to respond erotically.* [Emphasis added.][72]

Unfortunately, this biologically deterministic theory of sexual capacity supported the very stereotypes about female sexual indifference of which Kinsey was so critical. And it could be used to dismiss other reasons, such as power inequities or inadequate lovers, for female sexual dissatisfaction. In addition, Kinsey used it to explain the double standard as inevitable. Women, he noted, had been regulated more than men because their lower sexual capacity, and hence lower level of activity, made them more controllable.

AN IDEOLOGICAL PRECURSOR

Kinsey blazed a trail for the later sex researchers, Masters and Johnson. Secretly (for fear of losing funding), he observed and filmed sexual activity in the laboratory: twenty homosexual couples, ten heterosexual couples, and twenty-five men and women masturbating.[73] (The first step in this direction had been paying prostitutes to allow researchers to measure the length of their clitorises so that Kinsey could document anatomical differences.) Kinsey's associate Wardell Pomeroy notes that this quest for "original data" was a logical outcome for an empirical scientist.[74] Some of the physiological data presented in *SBHF* were derived from this work. In fact, much of the second half of the volume is devoted to the anatomy and physiology of human sexual response. Kinsey charted, in minute detail that foreshadowed the work of Masters and Johnson, changes in pulse, respiration, genital secretions, and body movement during sexual activity.

It was on the basis of this research that he planted a timebomb that would not explode until the work of Masters and Johnson—his challenge to the concept of the vaginal orgasm. He repeated continually that the walls of the vagina are devoid of nerve endings and so, for most women, insensitive.[75] Thus, he claimed that vaginal orgasm was a physiological impossibility and criticized Freud and other theorists for projecting male constructs of sexuality onto women. This led inevitably to questions about whether sexual intercourse could satisfy women sexually—an issue to be raised again by Masters and Johnson. Since Kinsey viewed the clitoris as the main center of sexual response and the vagina as relatively unimportant, he questioned the erotic merits of penetration. He noted that few women inserted fingers or objects into their vaginas when they masturbated and concluded that satisfaction from penile penetration was mainly psychological, or perhaps the result of referred sensation. This deemphasis of intercourse was consistent with Kinsey's schema of six sexual outlets. So although he accorded a certain primacy to intercourse, particularly marital coitus, he clearly challenged its sacredness in the arena of women's sexual pleasure.

Like Masters and Johnson, Kinsey emphasized the significance of masturbation. He found that it was the one sexual activity in which women most often reached orgasm and, like Masters and Johnson, he attributed this in part to effectiveness of technique and in part to the absence of distraction by or accommodation to a partner. Kinsey took exception to Freudian and psychoanalytic interpretations of masturbation as an immature activity, which he believed generated needless worry and conflict for individuals who masturbated. He justified his attempts to destigmatize masturbation by invoking the importance of improving both marriages and women's sociopsychological well-being. No other sexual activity was so worrisome to women, he claimed: "Whatever may affect the efficiency of some millions of individuals may be considered of social concern. Whether masturbation provides a satisfactory source of sexual outlet or becomes a source of psychologic disturbance is, therefore, a question of some social import."[76] In addition, his data showed that women made better sexual adjustments in marriage if they had been regularly attaining orgasm (by any means) before marriage. Masturbation was especially significant in this respect, since it provided women with the quickest and most reliable orgasms.

Kinsey's emphasis on the similarity of the genders, both anatomically and physiologically, also helped lay the groundwork for Masters and Johnson. There is a reason for this emphasis. Kinsey devoted considerable space to discussion of the family and frequently analyzed certain sexual behaviors in terms of their impact on marriage. In his chapter on marital coitus, he noted that it "is socially the most important of all sexual activities, because of its significance in the origin and maintenance of the home."[77] He then provided a brief description of the origin and history of the family, one of the few places in which he offered more than a cursory account of the social context of a sexual behavior.

Whereas Masters and Johnson and later sexologists have shown a romantic investment in marriage, however, Kinsey believed in its functional importance. His functionalism was all the more striking given the post–World War II idealization of home and the nuclear family. While critical of anachronistic customs, Kinsey believed that history had proved the viability of the family as the foundation of the social order. It provided an effective partnership for men and women, produced a stable environment for raising children, and served to control promiscuity by furnishing a regular sexual outlet. In his view no alternative structure with which communal groups or communist countries had experimented provided a satisfactory substitute for marriage.

Kinsey noted the increasing divorce rate with alarm, and he focused on women as a causal factor. Fundamental conceptualizations about marriage were changing because of "the emergence of the female as a significant force in the political, industrial, and intellectual life of our Western culture."[78] He believed marriages were evolving out of male domination into a more equal partnership between men and women. As a scientist, Kinsey believed that the present challenge to home and family life could be approached pragmatically:

There is developing in this country, as well as in some other parts of the world, an increasing interest in understanding some of the factors which contribute to the effectiveness of a home, and an increasing emphasis on training modern youth and adults to be more effective marital partners. It is in these terms that the significance of sex education, of pre-marital sexual outlets, of non-marital sexual activities for adults, and of the techniques and frequencies of marital coitus are being evaluated today.[79]

He viewed his own research as a major contribution in this area, and believed that emphasizing the similarities between men and women would foster understanding, harmony between the sexes, and a conceptualization of marriage as a partnership.

Significantly, like Masters and Johnson, Kinsey focused on the importance of good sex for better marriages. While noting that a good sex life was not the primary variable in maintaining a marriage, he frequently warned that "the female's failure to respond to orgasm in her sexual relationship is, nonetheless, one of the most frequent sources of dissatisfaction in marriage, and it is not infrequently the source of other types of conflict which may lead to a dissolution of a marriage."[80] According to his data, sexual factors accounted for as many as three-quarters of the divorces in his sample. Kinsey believed that science was the answer to this social problem. He thought that freer discussion of sex, prompted by scientific sex research and marriage manuals, had led to the greater frequency of female orgasm during the early decades of the twentieth century. One of his rationales for conducting research was his concern that many marriage manuals of the day were inaccurate and his hope that an increase in scientific data would filter down, via clinicians and new marriage manuals, to improve the sex lives of the general public. He reassured skeptics who worried that sex research might undermine marriage:

> There are some who have feared that a scientific approach to the problems of sex might threaten the existence of the marital institution. There are some who advocate the perpetuation of our ignorance because they fear that science will undermine the mystical concepts that they have substituted for reality. But there appear to be more persons who believe that an extension of our knowledge may contribute to the establishment of better marriages.[81]

Kinsey's pragmatic, functional commitment to marriage was the filter through which he evaluated other sexual behavior. His advocacy of masturbation and premarital sex sprang from data that indicated their role in increased sexual responsiveness in marriage. Similarly, he was tolerant in his approach to extramarital coitus, since he believed that it was based on "our mammalian ancestry" and need not lead inevitably to marital conflict. This focus on solving the crisis of marriage and heterosexuality is not unique to Kinsey; rather, it is thematic in sexology. Yet Kinsey's commitment to marriage was considerably more tepid than that of Masters and Johnson, who began publishing at the height of the "sexual revolution" when, like all institutions, marriage was increasingly challenged.

KINSEY, AMERICAN SOCIETY, AND SEXOLOGY

Kinsey's work is of great importance for many reasons: his role in the development of modern American sexology; the scope of his work; the vast amount of data he accumulated; and his ideology. His research reflects the sociopolitical tenor of the time and helped consolidate sexology's right to intervene in gender relations and the crisis of the family.

The implications of Kinsey's research about women are complex. On the one hand, he channeled some of his findings toward promoting and maintaining conventional heterosexual relations. He consistently ignored the ways in which women as a social group may have been taught to avoid or dislike sex and sought biological explanations for their supposedly lower sexual capacity. However, Kinsey's relentless empiricism and sexual enthusiasm were generalized to his research on women in a fashion that was truly supportive of female sexuality. He was relatively dispassionate about marriage and assumed that equality in marriage was desirable and important. He challenged the primacy of the penis and sexual intercourse as a source of pleasure for women. In many ways he assessed women's sexuality on its own terms, and he afforded it a certain importance and validity through the seriousness with which he studied women's sexual behavior. In a sense his actual interpretations (for example, his emphasis on clitoral as opposed to vaginal orgasms) were less important than his reporting that women engaged in a wide variety of sexual activities with great frequency. Though *SBHF* was published in a repressive time for women, Kinsey discussed their sexual pleasure, separated the concept of sexual pleasure from reproduction, cited the pleasures of masturbation, and regarded women as sexual agents. These were all issues of sexual liberation that feminists would not discuss until well over a decade later.

Such groundbreaking challenges to received ideas about women's sexuality were not welcomed by Kinsey's contemporaries. Several years after the publication of *SBHF,* one journalist noted the lack of substantive response to it, compared with the reception of the volume on men: "My opinion is that the American public, both male and female, was afraid to read the report on female sexuality because it was afraid to confront what it knew it would find there— confirmation of the unsettling idea that in their sexual behavior women are just as good, or bad, as men."[82] This was a radical concept, cloaked in scientific neutrality, in an era that lacked a radical political movement to organize around these issues.

It has been suggested that Kinsey had more interest in male sexuality and so his work had little impact on attitudes toward female sexuality.[83] Yet his data on females were as extensive as his data on males. It seems likely that the lack of public attention to his findings about female sexuality had more to do with sociopolitical variables than with Kinsey's personal research interests. *SBHF* was, after all, published in 1953—the period of the Cold War and McCarthyism. In 1954 a conference of the American Medical Association passed a resolution publicly criticizing Kinsey for contributing to a "wave of sex hysteria,"[84] and he was attacked by many doctors who had concluded that the book's effects were not beneficial.[85] A *Newsweek* article entitled "Sex vs. America" reported the criticisms of Representative Louis Heller of Brooklyn, who had proposed a congressional investigation of Kinsey and asked the Post Office to bar *SBHF* from the mails. Kinsey was, Heller charged, "hurling the insult of the century" at American women and contributing "to the depravity of a whole generation, to the loss of faith in human dignity . . . to the spread of juvenile delinquency, and to the misunderstanding and confusion about sex."[86] Not surprisingly, in this atmosphere of repression and paranoia, many professionals ignored Kinsey's conceptual challenges to their work. And, more important, there was no feminist movement to publicize Kinsey's findings on women. Publishing in the late 1960s in the context of a reemerging women's movement, Masters and Johnson were credited with revolutionizing female sexuality when they presented findings that Kinsey had published over a decade before.

But if Kinsey's specific observations were ignored, his work was not. The predominant response was outrage. Social scientists objected to what they perceived as Kinsey's reductionism. They criticized him for draining sex of its social and emotional meaning and for concentrating on performance to the exclusion of relationships. Psychoanalysts in particular were incensed. In general, Kinsey had either ignored basic psychoanalytic tenets (developmental theories of sexuality) or refuted them (sublimation, vaginal orgasm), and the analysts in turn saw him as naive. Popular critics, such as Lionel Trilling, complained that Kinsey was materialistic and that his work was rife with unsubstantiated assumptions about sex.[87] Ironically, it is quite likely that it was Kinsey's commitment to science, and a particular scientific method, that generated this impassioned and vehement response to his work. Although the transition from reverence for philosophical/theological authority to a scientific, medical approach to knowledge was well under way, Kinsey differed from early sexologists such as Freud and Ellis both stylistically and methodologically. He was blunt, practical, and obsessed with numbers. His empiricism and derision of psychoanalysis left him with an atheoretical approach to sex. This lack of a psychodynamic theory would not be remedied by Masters and Johnson and would eventually, in the 1980s, result in a clinical crisis around disorders of sexual desire.

Whatever conservative politicians and professionals thought, the reading public was enthralled. Working at a time when sexology was focused on establishing itself as a science and was not searching for a clientele, Kinsey demonstrated that there was, in fact, a potential market. His research was popularized and sensationalized, and his books quickly became best sellers. In part, this success was due to the sophistication of the mass media and the growing awareness that sex sells, whether in magazines, movies, or other commodities. Yet beyond the surface clamor, Kinsey had clearly touched a cultural nerve. People had concerns, questions, and problems related to sex and wanted somewhere to turn. Scientific sexology was becoming a place to turn. The Kinsey reports provided people with basic information about sex. Best-selling books about sex throughout the century, from Radclyffe Hall's lesbian novel *The Well of Loneliness* to Masters and Johnson's physiological research, would evoke thousands of letters from readers around the country who wanted advice or information about a troubling sexual issue. The two volumes popularly referred to as the Kinsey reports were no exception. They were the first large-scale empirical studies and so served as standards by which people could evaluate their own sexual behavior. This could reassure, or it could engender anxiety. In later decades the work of sexologists would do both. When Kinsey—the taxonomist and quantifier— transferred his method of studying the gall wasp to the study of human sexuality, he helped open the door to a rapid intensification of sex research. By omitting questions about ethics, emotions, and the social context of sex, Kinsey played a powerful role in reinforcing the transition from religious to scientific hegemony over matters of sex and sexuality. The debates surrounding his research had as much to do with content and method as with the appropriateness and morality of the application of science to a hitherto profoundly personal and emotional arena. Ultimately, the Kinsey research advanced the ongoing shift of the discourse on sexual issues from the private to the public arena.

Though Kinsey had made the scientific study of sex more legitimate, it was still an enterprise profoundly influenced by politics. In 1954 the Rockefeller Foundation, headed by Dean Rusk, began to reconsider its funding commitment to Kinsey after learning that it was under congressional investigation for its support of his Institute. After hearings by the House Committee to Investigate Tax-Exempt Foundations, chaired by ultra-right-wing representative B. Carroll Reece, the Rockefeller Foundation terminated the Kinsey Institute funds. As Wardell Pomeroy, one of the original Kinsey investigators, wrote: "The truth was that the Foundation had simply quit, under pressure and out of fear, in direct contradiction to its frequently reiterated principles. . . . Its staff wanted to continue support but the Foundation could not take the heat."[88] Kinsey died of a heart attack two years later, and the Institute foundered for some time after his death and the termination of funding.

Around this time a young gynecologist in St. Louis named William Masters, who wanted to embark on sex research, was warned by his mentors that such research could ruin his career if he did not establish himself within the medical profession first. Kinsey, as Masters later said, "opened the door."[89]

1. Peter Gabriel Filene, *Him/Her/Self* (New York, 1974), p. 143.

2. Quoted in ibid., p. 149.

3. Quoted in Susan Ware, *Holding Their Own: American Women in the 1930s* (Boston, 1982), p. 62.

4. John D'Emilio and Estelle Freedman, *Intimate Matters: A History of Sexuality in America* (New York, 1988).

5. Filene, *Him/Her/Self,* p. 184.

6. Michelle Perrot, "The New Eve and the Old Adam: Changes in French Women's Condition at the Turn of the Century," in *Behind the Lines: Gender and the Two World Wars,* ed. Margaret Randolph Higonnet et al. (New Haven, 1987), p. 57.

7. See, for example, Michael Delli Carpini, *Stability and Change in American Politics: The Coming of Age of the Generation of the 1960s* (New York, 1986); Paul C. Light, *Baby Boomers* (New York, 1988); Pamela Reynolds, "What Lies Ahead for Baby Boomers," *Boston Globe,* June 15, 1987.

8. Personal conversation, Michael Bronski, June 12, 1987.

9. Linda Gordon, *Woman's Body, Woman's Right: Birth Control in America* (New York, 1974).

10. Diana Long Hall, "Biology, Sex Hormones, and Sexism in the 1920s," in *Women and Philosophy: Toward a Theory of Liberation,* ed. Carol Gould and Marx Wartofsky (New York, 1979), pp. 81–96.

11. Diana Long Hall, "The Social Implications of the Scientific Study of Sex," paper presented at the Barnard Conference, 1976.

12. Quoted in ibid., p. 14.

13. Ibid., pp. 14–16, quotation at p. 14.

14. Sexual consciousness has changed so much that a researcher who attempted this mode of questioning with his female students in the 1990s would likely be vulnerable to accusations of sexual harassment.

15. Alfred C. Kinsey, Wardell B. Pomeroy, Clyde E. Martin, and Paul H. Gebhard, *Sexual Behavior in the Human Female* (New York, 1953), pp. 9, 8; hereafter cited as *SBHF.*

16. Alfred C. Kinsey, Wardell B. Pomeroy, Clyde E. Martin, and Paul H. Gebhard, *Sexual Behavior in the Human Male* (Philadelphia, 1948), p. 5; hereafter cited as *SBHM.*

17. Wardell D. Pomeroy, *Dr. Kinsey and the Institute for Sex Research* (New York, 1972), p. 21.

18. *SBHM,* pp. 11–12.

19. *SBHF,* p. 264.

20. Ibid., p. 20.

21. Edwin Sutherland, "The Diffusion of Sexual Psychopath Laws," *American Journal of Sociology* 56 (1950): 142–48; Estelle Freedman, " 'Uncontrolled Desires': The Response to the Sexual Psychopath, 1920–1960," *Journal of American History* 74 (1987): 83–106.

22. Kinsey's opposition to sex laws seems clearly resonant with his admiration for those with rich and varied sex lives. He saw sex laws as simply another impediment to sexual realization. In this respect, Kinsey frequently pits males against females, males being pursuers of sexual gratification and females reluctant gatekeepers. His texts are peppered with examples of lusty, male adolescents unjustly chastened by rigid female authorities who lack the capacity to empathize with them. He goes even further, in his criticism of sex laws, by asserting that often young girls misunderstand sexual advances made by older men. In *SBHM,* he writes, "Many small girls reflect the public hysteria over the prospects of 'being touched' by a strange person; and many a child, who has no idea at all of the mechanics of intercourse, interprets affection and simple caressing, from anyone except her own parents, as attempts at rape. In consequence, not a few older men serve time in penal institutions for attempting to engage in a sexual act which at their age would not interest most of them, and of which many of them are

undoubtedly incapable" (p. 238). This is one of several instances of his denial of the possible validity of girls' claims of sexual abuse.

23. Peter Jackson, "The Tender Trap," *Mattachine Review*, February 1957, 9.

24. Pomeroy, *Dr. Kinsey*, p. 395.

25. See, for example, Elizabeth Hall, "New Directions for the Kinsey Institute," *Psychology Today*, June 1986, 33–39.

26. Letter, Lester Kirkendall to Mary S. Calderone, January 4, 1965, SIECUS Library, New York.

27. *SBHF*, p. 7.

28. *SBHM*, p. 153.

29. Ibid., p. 147.

30. Ibid., p. 19.

31. *SBHF*, p. 67.

32. *SBHM*, p. 42.

33. Ibid., p. 47. See Elliott G. Mishler, *Research Interviewing: Context and Narrative* (Cambridge, Mass., 1986).

34. *SBHM*, p. 6.

35. Pomeroy, *Dr. Kinsey*, p. 102.

36. Ibid., p. 101.

37. Ibid., p. 103.

38. *SBHM*, p. 157.

39. *SBHF*, p. 8.

40. *SBHM*, p. 202.

41. Ibid., p. 201.

42. Ibid., p. 263.

43. Quotations from *SBHF*, pp. 230–32.

44. Ibid., p. 283.

45. Ibid., p. 365.

46. Ibid., p. 412.

47. Ibid., p. 436.

48. *SBHM*, p. 666.

49. Ibid., p. 203.

50. *SBHF*, p. 102.

51. *SBHM*, p. 207.

52. Ibid., p. 209.

53. Ibid., p. 327.

54. Ibid., p. 158.

55. *SBHF*, p. 46.

56. *SBHM*, p. 650.

57. Alan Bell, Martin Weinburg, and Sue Hammersmith, *Sexual Preference: Its Development in Men and Women* (Bloomington, 1981).

58. *SBHM*, p. 639.

59. Sandra Gilbert, "Soldier's Heart: Literary Men, Literary Women, and the Great War," in *Behind the Lines*, ed. Higonnet et al., p. 201.

60. Allan Berube, "Marching to a Different Drummer: Lesbian and Gay GIs in World War II," in *Powers of Desire: The Politics of Sexuality*, ed. Ann Snitow, Christine Stansell, and Sharon Thompson (New York, 1983), p. 89.

61. Valerie Taylor, "Five Minority Groups in Relation to Contemporary Fiction," *The Ladder* 5/4 (1961): 10.

62. See, for example, Michael Bronski, *Culture Clash: The Making of Gay Sensibility* (Boston, 1984); John D'Emilio, *Sexual Politics, Sexual Communities: The Making of a Homosexual Minority in the United States, 1940–1970* (Chicago, 1983).

63. I am grateful to Michael Bronski for pointing out this connection to me. See Nora Sayre, *Running Time: Films of the Cold War* (New York, 1982), p. 81.

64. *SBHM*, p. 375.

65. Ibid., p. 389.

66. See *SBHF* pp. 685–89, for this discussion of men, women, and social conditioning.

67. Ibid., p. 641.

68. Ibid.

69. Ibid., p. 642.

70. *SBHM*, p. 209.

71. Ibid.

72. Ibid.

73. Ibid., p. 177.

74. Pomeroy, *Dr. Kinsey,* p. 172.

75. This notion was challenged in the early 1980s by sexologists who proclaimed the existence of a highly sensitive area in the vagina, which they named the G-spot after sex researcher Ernst Grafenberg. Grafenberg's research is noted by Kinsey in *SBHF* pp. 576, 580, 587, 635.

76. Ibid., p. 171.

77. Ibid., p. 346.

78. Ibid., p. 347.

79. Ibid.

80. Ibid., p. 358.

81. Ibid., p. 13.

82. *Herald Tribune,* May 16, 1958.

83. Paul Robinson, *The Modernization of Sex*, New York, 1976: p. 116.

84. *Catholic News,* July 10, 1954.

85. *New York Mirror*, August 27, 1953.

86. "Sex vs. America," *Newsweek,* September 7, 1953: 20.

87. Lionel Trilling, "The Kinsey Report," in *The Liberal Imagination* (New York, 1957).

88. Pomeroy, *Dr. Kinsey,* p. 380.

89. Quoted in "Repairing the Conjugal Bed," *Time,* May 25, 1970: 49–52.

PART 6

PUNISHING SEX

NEGOTIATING SEX AND GENDER IN THE ATTORNEY GENERAL'S COMMISSION ON PORNOGRAPHY

CAROLE S. VANCE

Larry Madigan began his testimony in the Miami federal courthouse. Dark-haired, slight, and dressed in his best suit, he fingered his testimony nervously before he was recognized by the chair. The podium and microphone at which he stood were placed at the front of the auditorium, so when the thirty-eighty-year-old looked up from his typed statement, he saw only the members of the Attorney General's Commission on Pornography. They sat on the raised dais, surrounded by staff aides, federal marshals, the court stenographer, and flags of Florida and the United States. Behind him sat the audience, respectfully arrayed on dark and immovable wood benches that matched the wood paneling which enveloped the room.

"At age 12," he began earnestly, "I was a typical, normal, healthy boy and my life was filled with normal activities and hobbies." But "all the trouble began a few months later," when he found a deck of "hard-core" pornographic playing cards, depicting penetration, fellatio, and cunnilingus. "These porno cards highly aroused me and gave me a desire I never had before," he said. Soon after finding these cards, his behavior changed: he began masturbating, attempted to catch glimpses of partially dressed neighbor women, and surreptitiously tried to steal *Playboy* magazines from the local newsstand. His chronicle went on for several minutes.

"By the age of 16, after a steady diet of *Playboy, Penthouse, Scandinavian Children,* perverted paperback books, and sexology magazines, I had to see a doctor for neuralgia of the prostate." His addiction worsened in his twenties, when he began watching pornographic videos. He went on to "promiscuous sex" with "two different women," but eventually found Christ. He concluded,

"I strongly believe that all that has happened to me can be traced back to the finding of those porno cards. If it weren't for my faith in God and the forgiveness in Jesus Christ, I would now possibly be a pervert, an alcoholic, or dead. I am a victim of pornography."[1]

The audience sat in attentive silence. No one laughed. Only a few cynical reporters sitting next to me quietly elbowed each other and rolled their eyes, although their stories in the next day's papers would contain respectful accounts of Mr. Madigan's remarks and those of his therapist, Dr. Simon Miranda, who testified as an expert witness that many of his patients were being treated for mental problems brought on by pornography.

The Attorney General's Commission on Pornography, a federal investigatory commission appointed in May 1985 by then Attorney General Edwin Meese III, orchestrated an imaginative attack on pornography and obscenity. The chief targets of its campaign appeared to be sexually explicit images. These were dangerous, according to the logic of the commission, because they might encourage sexual desires or acts. The commission's public hearings in six U.S. cities during 1985 and 1986, lengthy executive sessions, and an almost two-thousand-page report[2] constitute an extended rumination on pornography and the power of visual imagery. Its ninety-two recommendations for strict legislation and law enforcement, backed by a substantial federal, state, and local apparatus already in place, pose a serious threat to free expression. Read at another level, however, the commission's agenda on pornography stands as a proxy for a more comprehensive program about gender and sexuality, both actively contested domains where diverse constituencies struggle over definitions, law, policy, and cultural meanings.

To enter a Meese Commission hearing was to enter a public theater of sexuality and gender, where cultural symbols—many dating from the late nineteenth century—were manipulated with uncanny intuition: the specter of uncontrolled lust, social disintegration, male desire, and female sexual vulnerability shadowed the hearings. The commission's goal was to implement a traditional conservative agenda on sexually explicit images and texts: vigorous enforcement of existing obscenity laws coupled with the passage of draconian new legislation.[3] To that end, the commission, dominated by a conservative majority, effectively controlled the witness list, evidence, and fact-finding procedures in obvious ways that were widely criticized for their bias.[4] But the true genius of the Meese Commission lay in its ability to appropriate terms and rhetoric, to deploy visual images and create a compelling interpretive frame, and to intensify a climate of sexual shame that made dissent from the commission's viewpoint almost impossible. The power of the commission's symbolic politics is shown by the response of both spectators and journalists to Larry Madigan's testimony, as well as by the inability of dissenting commission witnesses who opposed further restriction to unpack and thus counter the panel's subterranean linguistic and visual ploys.

Convened during Ronald Reagan's second term, the commission paid a political debt to conservatives and fundamentalists who had been clamoring for action on social issues, particularly pornography, throughout his terms of office. Pornographic images were symbols of what moral conservatives wanted to control: sex for pleasure, sex outside the regulated boundaries of marriage and procreation. Sexually explicit images are dangerous, conservatives believe, because they have the power to spark fantasy, incite lust, and provoke action. What more effective way to stop sexual immorality and excess, they reasoned, than to curtail sexual desire and pleasure at its source—in the imagination. However, the widespread liberalization in sexual behavior and attitudes in the last century, coupled with the increased availability of sexually explicit material since the 1970s, made the conservative mission a difficult, though not impossible, task.[5] The commission utilized all available tools, both symbolic and procedural.

PROCEDURES AND BIAS

Appointed to find "new ways to control the problem of pornography," the panel was chaired by Henry Hudson, a vigorous anti-vice prosecutor from Arlington, Virginia, who had been commended by President Reagan for closing down every adult bookstore in his district. Hudson was assisted by his staff of vice cops and attorneys and by executive director Alan Sears, who had a reputation in the U.S. Attorney's Office in Kentucky as a tough opponent of obscenity.[6] Prior to convening, seven of the eleven commissioners had taken public stands opposing pornography and supporting obscenity law as a means to control it. These seven included a fundamentalist broadcaster, several public officials, a priest, and a law professor who had argued that sexually explicit expression was undeserving of First Amendment protection because it was less like speech and more like dildos.[7] The smaller number of moderates sometimes tempered the staff's conservative zeal, but their efforts were modest and not always effective.

The conservative bias continued for fourteen months, throughout the panel's more than three hundred hours of public hearings in six U.S. cities and lengthy executive sessions, which I observed.[8] The list of witnesses was tightly controlled: 77 percent supported greater control, if not elimination, of sexually explicit material. Heavily represented were law-enforcement officers and members of vice squads (68 of 208 witnesses), politicians, and spokespersons for conservative anti-pornography groups like Citizens for Decency through Law and the National Federation for Decency. Great efforts were made to find "victims of pornography" to testify,[9] but those reporting positive experiences were largely absent. Witnesses were treated unevenly, depending on whether the point of view they expressed facilitated the commission's ends. There were several glaring procedural irregularities, including the panel's attempt to withhold drafts and working documents from the public and its effort to name major corporations such as Time, Inc., Southland, CBS, Coca-Cola, and Kmart as "distributors of pornography" in the final report, repeating unsubstantiated allegations made by the Reverend Donald Wildmon, executive director of the

National Federation for Decency. These irregularities led to several lawsuits against the commission.

The barest notions of fair play were routinely ignored in gathering evidence. Any negative statement about pornographic images, no matter how outlandish, was accepted as true. Anecdotal testimony that pornography was responsible for divorce, extramarital sex, child abuse, homosexuality, and excessive masturbation was entered as "evidence" and appears as supporting documentation in the final report's footnotes.

GENDER NEGOTIATIONS

The commission's unswerving support for aggressive obscenity law enforcement bore the indelible stamp of the right-wing constituency that brought the panel into existence. Its influence was also evident in the belief of many commissioners and witnesses that pornography leads to immorality, lust, and sin. But the commission's staff and the Justice Department correctly perceived that an unabashedly conservative position would not be persuasive outside the right wing. For the commission's agenda to succeed, the attack on sexually explicit material had to be modernized by couching it in more contemporary arguments, arguments drawn chiefly from anti-pornography feminism and social science. So the preeminent harm that pornography was said to cause was not sin and immorality, but violence and the degradation of women.

To the extent that the worldviews and underlying ideologies of anti-pornography feminism and social science are deeply different from those of fundamentalism, the commission's experiment at merging or overlaying these discourses was far from simple. In general, the commission fared much better in its attempt to incorporate the language and testimony of anti-pornography feminists than that of social scientists. The cooptation of anti-pornography feminism was both implausible and brilliantly executed.

Implausible, because the panel's chair, Henry Hudson, and its executive director, Alan Sears, along with the other conservative members, were no feminists. Hudson usually addressed the four female commissioners as "ladies." He transmuted the term used by feminist anti-pornography groups, "the degradation of women," into the "degradation of femininity," which conjured up visions of Victorian womanhood dragged from the pedestal into a muddy gutter. Beyond language, conservative panelists consistently opposed proposals that feminists universally support—for sex education or school-based programs to inform children about sexual abuse, for example. Conservative members objected to sex-abuse programs for children, contending that such instruction prompted children to make hysterical and unwarranted accusations against male relatives. In addition, panelists rejected the recommendations of feminist prostitutes' rights groups like COYOTE and the U.S. Prostitutes Collective,[10] preferring increased arrests and punishment of women (though not their male customers) to decriminalization and better regulation of abusive working conditions. More comically, conservative panelists tried to push through a "vibrator bill," a model statute that would ban as obscene "any device designed or marketed as useful primarily for the stimulation of human genital organs." The three moderate female commission members became incredulous and upset when they realized that such a law would ban vibrators.

During the course of the public hearings, conservative and fundamentalist witnesses made clear that they regarded the feminist movement as a major cause of the family breakdown and social disruption which they had observed during the past twenty years. Feminists advocated divorce, abortion, access to birth control, day care, single motherhood, sexual permissiveness, lesbian and gay rights, working mothers—all undesirable developments that diminished the importance of family and marriage. Conservatives and fundamentalists were clear in their allegiance to a traditional moral agenda: sex belonged in marriage and nowhere else. Pornography was damaging because it promoted and advertised lust, sex "with no consequences," and "irresponsible" sex.

Anti-pornography feminists, in their writing and activism dating from approximately 1977, saw the damage of pornography in different terms, though other feminists (and I include myself in this group) objected to their analysis for uncritically incorporating many conservative elements of late-nineteenth-century sexual culture.[11] Nevertheless, the anti-pornography feminist critique made several points that differed sharply from those made by conservatives. It argued that most, if not all, pornography was sexist (rather than immoral). It socialized men to be dominating and women to be victimized. Moreover, pornographic imagery led to actual sexual violence against women, and it constituted a particularly effective form of anti-woman propaganda. At various times, anti-pornography feminists have proposed different remedial strategies ranging from educational programs and consciousness-raising to restriction and censorship of sexually explicit material through so-called civil rights anti-pornography legislation, first drafted in 1983. But a consistent theme throughout anti-pornography feminism, as in most feminism, was intense opposition to and fervent critique of gender inequality, male domination, and patriarchal institutions, including the family, marriage, and heterosexuality.

The conflict between basic premises of conservative and anti-pornography feminist analyses is obvious. Nevertheless, the commission cleverly used anti-pornography feminist terms and concepts as well as witnesses to their own advantage in selective ways, helped not infrequently by anti-pornography leaders and groups themselves. Anti-pornography feminist witnesses eagerly testified before the commission and cast their personal experiences of incest, childhood sexual abuse, rape, and sexual coercion in terms of the "harms" and "degradation" caused by pornography. Anti-pornography feminist witnesses, of course, did not voice complaints about divorce, masturbation, or homosexuality, which ideologically give feminists no cause for protest, but they failed to comment on the great divide that separated their complaints from those of fundamentalists, a divide dwarfed only by the even larger distance between their respective political programs. Indeed, some prominent anti-pornography feminists were willing to understate, and most avoided mentioning, in their testimony their support for those cranky feminist demands so offensive to conservative ears: abortion, birth control, and lesbian and gay rights. Only one feminist anti-pornography group, Feminists Against Pornography from Washington, D.C., refused to tailor its testimony to please conservative members and attacked the Reagan administration for its savage cutbacks on programs and services for women.[12] Their testimony was soon cut off on the grounds of inadequate time, though other anti-pornography groups and spokespersons—including Andrea Dworkin, Catharine MacKinnon, and Women Against Pornography (New York)—would be permitted to testify at great length.

In the context of the hearing, the notion that pornography "degrades" women proved to be a particularly helpful unifying term, floating in and out of fundamentalist as well as anti-pornography feminist testimony. By the second public hearing, "degrading" had become a true crossover term—used by moral majoritarians, vice cops, and aggressive prosecutors, as well as anti-pornography feminists. Speakers didn't notice, or chose not to, that the term "degradation" had very different meanings in each community. For anti-pornography feminists, pornography degrades women when it depicts or glorifies sexist sex: images that put men's pleasure first or suggest that women's lot in life is to serve men. For fundamentalists, "degrading" was freely applied to all images of sexual behavior that might be considered immoral, since in the conservative worldview immorality degrades the individual and society. "Degrading" was freely applied to visual images that portrayed homosexuality, masturbation, and even consensual heterosexual sex. Even images of morally approved marital sexuality were judged "degrading," since public viewing of what should be a private experience degraded the couple and the sanctity of marriage. These terms provided by anti-pornography feminists—"degrading," "violence against women," and "offensive to women" (though conservatives couldn't resist adding the phrase "and children")—were eagerly adopted by the panel and proved particularly useful in giving it and its findings the gloss of modernity and some semblance of concern with human rights.

Although the commission happily assimilated the rhetoric of anti-pornography feminists, it decisively rejected their remedies. Conservative men pronounced the testimony of Andrea Dworkin "eloquent" and "moving" and insisted on including her statement in the final report, special treatment given to no other witness. But anti-pornography feminists had argued against obscenity laws, saying they reflected a moralistic and antisexual tradition that could only harm women. Instead, they favored ordinances, such as those developed for Minneapolis and Indianapolis by Dworkin and MacKinnon,[13] that would outlaw pornography as a violation of women's civil rights. The commission never seriously entertained the idea that obscenity laws should be repealed; given its conservative constituency and agenda, it couldn't have.

The commission's report summarily rejected Minneapolis-style ordinances. These had been "properly held unconstitutional" by a recent Supreme Court decision, the panel agreed, because they infringed on speech protected under the First Amendment. But the panel cleverly, if disingenuously, argued that traditional obscenity law could be used against violent and degrading material in a manner "largely consistent with what this ordinance attempts to do," ignoring anti-pornography feminists' vociferous rejection of obscenity laws. The panel recommended that obscenity laws be further strengthened by adding civil damages to the existing criminal penalties. This constitutes a major defeat for anti-pornography feminists. But unlike social scientists, who protested loudly over the commission's misuse of their testimony, the anti-pornography feminists did not acknowledge the panel's distortion. Instead, they commended the panel for recognizing the harm of pornography and continued to denounce obscenity law,[14] without coming to grips with the panel's commitment to that approach.

Even more startling were MacKinnon's and Dworkin's statements to the press that the commission "has recommended to Congress the civil rights legislation women have sought,"[15] and this comment by Dorchen Leidholdt, founder of Women Against Pornography: "I am not embarrassed at being in agreement with Ed Meese."[16] Over the course of the hearings, it seems that each group strategized how best to use the other. However, the vast power and resources of the federal government, backed by a strong fundamentalist movement, made it almost inevitable that the Meese Commission would benefit far more in this exchange than anti-pornography feminists.

The commission attempted another major appropriation of feminist issues by recasting the problem of violence against women. Since the backlash against feminism began in the mid-1970s, conservative groups most decisively rejected feminist critiques of violence in the family, particularly assertions about the prevalence of marital rape, incest, and child sexual abuse. Such sexual violence was rare, they countered, and exaggerated by feminists only because they were "man-haters" and "lesbians" who wanted to destroy the family. Accordingly, conservatives consistently opposed public funding for social services directed at these problems: rape hotlines, shelters for abused wives, programs to identify and counsel child victims of incest. Such programs would destroy the integrity of the family, particularly the authority of the father, conservatives believed.

The commission hearings document inequality, patriarchy, and women's powerlessness—a startling reversal in the conservative discourse on sexual violence. Conservative witnesses now claimed that there is an epidemic of sexual violence directed at women and children, even in the family. Unlike the feminist analysis, which points to inequality, patriarchy, and women's powerlessness as root causes, the conservative analysis singles out pornography and its attendant sexual liberalization as the responsible agents. Men are, in a sense, victims as well, since once their lust is aroused, they are increasingly unable to refrain from sexual aggression. It is clear that the conservative about-face seeks to respond to a rising tide of concern among even right-wing women about the issues of violence and abuse, while at the same time seeking to contain it by providing an alternative narrative: the appropriate solution lies in controlling pornography, not challenging male domination; pornography victimizes men, not just women. In that regard, it is striking that the victim witnesses provided by anti-pornography feminist groups were all female, whereas those provided by conservatives included many men.

Ironically, the conservative analysis ultimately blames feminism for violence against women. To the extent that feminists supported a more permissive sexual climate, including freer sexual expression, and undermined marriage as the only appropriate place for sex and procreation, they promoted an atmosphere favorable to violence against women. The commission's symbolic and rhetorical transformations were skillful. The panel not only appropriated anti-pornography feminist language to modernize a conservative agenda and make it more palatable to the mainstream public, but it also used issues of male violence successfully raised by feminists to argue that the only reliable protection for women was to be found in returning to the family and patriarchal protection.

THE PLEASURES OF LOOKING

The commission's campaign against sexually explicit images was filled with paradoxes. Professing belief in the most naive and literalist theories of representation, the commissioners nevertheless shrewdly used visual images during the hearings to establish "truth" and manipulate the feelings of the audience. Arguing that pornography had a singular and universal meaning that was evident to any viewer, the commission staff worked hard to exclude any perspective but its own. Insisting that sexually explicit images had great authority, the commissioners framed pornography so that it had more power in the hearing than it could ever have in the real world. Denying that subjectivity and context matter in the interpretation of any image, they created a well-crafted context that denied there was a context.

The foremost goal of the commission was to establish "the truth" about pornography—that is, to characterize and describe the sexually explicit material that was said to be in need of regulation. Pornographic images were shown during all public hearings, as witnesses and staff members alike illustrated their remarks with explicit, fleshy, often full-color images of sex. The reluctance to view this material that one might have anticipated on the part of fundamentalists and conservatives was nowhere to be seen. The commission capitalized on the realistic representational form of still photos and movie and video clips, stating that the purpose of viewing these images was to inform the public and themselves about "what pornography was really like." Viewing was carefully orchestrated, and a great deal of staff time went toward organizing the logistics and technologies of viewing. Far from being a casual or minor enterprise, the selection and showing of sexually explicit images constituted one of the commission's major interventions.

The structure of viewing was an inversion of the typical context for viewing pornography. Normally private, this was public, with slides presented in federal courthouse chambers before hundreds of spectators in the light of day. The viewing of pornography, usually an individualistic and libidinally anarchic practice, was here organized by the state—the Department of Justice, to be exact. The ordinary purpose in viewing, sexual pleasure and masturbation, was ostensibly absent, replaced instead by dutiful scrutiny and the pleasures of condemnation.

These pleasures were intense. The atmosphere throughout the hearings was one of excited repression: witnesses alternated between chronicling the negative effects of pornography and making sensationalized presentations of "it." Taking a lead from feminist anti-pornography groups, everyone had a slide show: the FBI, the U.S. Customs Service, the U.S. Postal Service, and sundry vice squads. At every "lights out," spectators would rush to one side of the room to see the screen, which was angled toward the commissioners. Were the hearing room a ship, we would have capsized many times.

Alan Sears, the executive director, told the commissioners with a grin that he hoped to include some "good stuff" in their final report, and its two volumes and 1,960 pages faithfully reflect the censors' fascination with the thing they love to hate. The report lists in alphabetical order the titles of material found in sixteen adult bookstores in six cities: 2,370 films, 725 books, and 2,325 magazines, beginning with *A Cock between Friends* and ending with *69 Lesbians Munching.* A detailed plot summary is given for the book, *The Tying Up of Rebecca,* along with descriptions of sex aids advertised in the books, their costs, and how to order them.

The commission viewed a disproportionate amount of atypical material, which even moderate commissioners criticized as "extremely violent and degrading."[17] To make themselves sound contemporary and secular, conservatives needed to establish that pornography was violent rather than immoral and, contradicting social science evidence, that this violence was increasing.[18] It was important for the panel to insist that the images presented were "typical" and "average" pornography, but typical pornography—glossy, mainstream porn magazines directed at heterosexual men—does not feature much violence, as the commission's own research (soon quickly suppressed) confirmed.[19] The slide shows, however, did not present many carefully airbrushed photos of perfect females or the largely heterosexual gyrations (typically depicting intercourse and oral sex) found even in the most hard-core adult bookstores. The commission concentrated on atypical material, produced for private use or for small, special-interest segments of the market or confiscated in the course of prosecutions. The slides featured behavior that the staff believed to be especially shocking: homosexuality, excrement, urination, child pornography, bestiality (with over twenty different types of animals, including chickens and elephants), and especially sadomasochism (SM).

The commission relied on the realism of photography to amplify the notion that the body of material shown was accurate and therefore, they implied, representative. The staff also skillfully mixed atypical and marginal material with pictorials from *Playboy* and *Penthouse,* rarely making a distinction between types of publications or types of markets. The desired fiction was that all pornography was the same. Many have commented on the way all photographic images are read as fact or truth, because the images are realistic. This general phenomenon is true for pornographic images as well but it is intensified when the viewer is confronted by images of sexually explicit acts which he or she has little experience viewing (or doing) in real life. Shock, discomfort, fascination, repulsion, and arousal all operate to make the image have an enormous impact and seem undeniably real.

The action depicted was understood as realistic, not fantastic or staged for the purposes of producing an erotic picture. Thus, images that played with themes of surrender or domination were read as actually coerced. A nude woman holding a machine gun was clearly dangerous, a panelist noted, because the gun could go off (an interpretation not, perhaps, inaccurate for the psychoanalytically inclined reader). Images of obviously adult men and women dressed in exaggerated fashions of high-school students were called child pornography.

Sadomasochistic pornography had an especially strategic use in establishing that sexually explicit imagery was "violent." The intervention was effective, since few (even liberal critics) have been willing to examine the construction of SM in the panel's argument. Commissioners saw a great deal of SM pornography and found it deeply upsetting, as did the audience. Photographs included images of women tied up, gagged, or being "disciplined." Viewers were unfamiliar with the conventions of SM sexual behavior and had no access to the codes participants use to read these images. The panel provided the frame: SM was nonconsensual sex that inflicted force and violence on unwilling victims. Virtually any claim could be made against SM pornography and, by extension, SM behavior, which remains a highly stigmatized and relatively invisible sexuality. As was the case with homosexuality until recently, invisibility reinforces stigma, and stigma reinforces invisibility in a circular manner.

The redundant viewing and narration of SM images reinforced several points useful to the commission—pornography depicted violence against women and promoted male domination. An active editorial hand was at work, however, to remove reverse images of female domination and male submission; these images never appeared, though they constitute a significant portion of SM imagery. Amusingly, SM pornography elicited hearty condemnation of "male dominance," the only sphere in which conservative men were moved to critique it throughout the course of the hearing.

The commission called no witnesses to discuss the nature of SM, either professional experts or typical participants.[20] Given the atmosphere, it was not surprising that no one defended it. Indeed, producers of more soft-core pornography joined in the condemnation, perhaps hoping to direct the commission's ire to groups and acts more stigmatized than themselves.[21] The commission ignored a small but increasing body of literature that documents important features of SM sexual behavior, namely consent and safety. Typically, the conventions we use to decipher ordinary images are suspended when it comes to SM images. When we see science fiction movies, for example, we do not leave the theater believing that the special effects were real or that the performers were injured making the films. But the commissioners assumed that images of domination and submission were both real and coerced.

In addition, such literalist interpretations were evident in the repeated assertions that all types of sexual images had a direct effect on behavior. The idea that sexual images could be used and remain on a fantasy level was foreign to the commission, as was the possibility that individuals might use fantasy to engage with dangerous or frightening feelings without wanting to experience them in real life. This lack of recognition is consistent with fundamentalist distrust and puzzlement about the imagination and the symbolic realm, which seem to have no autonomous existence; for fundamentalists, imagination and behavior are closely linked. If good thoughts lead to good behavior, a sure way to eliminate bad behavior is to police bad thoughts.

The voice-over for the visual segments was singular and uniform, which served to obliterate the actual diversity of people's response to pornography. But sexually explicit material is a contested ground precisely *because* subjectivity matters. An image that is erotic to one individual is revolting to a second and ridiculous to a third. The object of contestation *is* meaning. Age, gender, race, class, sexual preference, erotic experience, and personal history all form the grid through which sexual images are received and interpreted. The commission worked hard to eliminate diversity from its hearings and to substitute instead its own authoritative, often uncontested, frequently male, monologue.

It is startling to realize how many of the Meese Commission's techniques were pioneered by anti-pornography feminists between 1977 and 1984. Claiming that pornography was sexist and promoted violence against women, anti-pornography feminists had an authoritative voice-over, too, though for theorists Andrea Dworkin and Catharine MacKinnon and groups like Women Against Pornography, the monologic voice was, of course, female. Although anti-pornography feminists disagreed with fundamentalist moral assumptions and contested rather than approved, male authority, they carved out new territory with slide shows depicting allegedly horrific sexual images, a technique the commission heartily adopted. Anti-pornography feminists relied on victim testimony and preferred anecdotes to data. They, too, shared a literalist interpretive frame and used SM images to prove that pornography was violent.

The Meese Commission was skilled in its ability to use photographic images to establish the so-called truth and to provide an almost invisible interpretive frame that compelled agreement with its agenda. The commission's true gift, however, lay in its ability to create an emotional atmosphere in the hearings that facilitated acceptance of the commission's worldview. Its strategic use of images was a crucial component of this emotional management. Because the power of this emotional climate fades in the published text, it is not obvious to most readers of the commission's report. Yet it was and is a force to be reckoned with, both in the commission and, more broadly, in all public debates about sexuality, especially those that involve the right wing.

RITUALS OF SEXUAL SHAME

An important aspect of the commission's work was the ritual airing and affirmation of sexual shame in a public setting. The panel relentlessly created an atmosphere of unacknowledged sexual arousal and fear. The large amount of pornography shown, ostensibly to educate and repel, was nevertheless arousing. The range and diversity of images provided something for virtually everyone, and the concentration on taboo, kinky, and harder-to-obtain material added to the charge. Part of the audience's discomfort may have come from the unfamiliarity of seeing sexually explicit images in public, not private, settings, and in the company of others not there for the express purpose of sexual arousal. But a larger part must have come from the problem of experiencing sexual arousal in an atmosphere where it is condemned. The commission's lesson was a complex one, but it taught the importance of managing and hiding sexual arousal and pleasure in public, while it reinforced secrecy, hypocrisy, and shame. Unacknowledged sexual feelings, though, did not disappear but developed into a whirlwind of mute, repressed emotion that the Meese Commission channeled toward its own purpose.

Sexual shaming was also embedded in the interrogatory practices of the chair. Witnesses appearing before the commission were treated in a highly uneven manner. Commissioners accepted virtually any claim made by anti-pornography witnesses as true, while those who opposed restriction of sexually explicit speech were often met with rudeness and hostility. The panelists asked social scientist Edward Donnerstein if pornographers had tried to influence his research findings or threatened his life. They asked actress Colleen Dewhurst, testifying for Actor's Equity about the dangers of censorship in the theater, if persons convicted of obscenity belonged to the union, and if the union was influenced by organized crime. They questioned her at length about the group's position on child pornography.

Sexual shame was also ritualized in how witnesses spoke about their personal experiences with images. "Victims of pornography" told in lurid detail of their use of pornography and eventual decline into masturbation, sexual addiction, and incest. Some testified anonymously, shadowy apparitions behind translucent screens. Their first-person accounts, sometimes written by the commission's staff,[22] featured a great elaboration of the sexual damage caused by visual images. To counter these accounts there was nothing but silence: descriptions of visual and sexual pleasure were absent. The commission's chair even noted the lack and was fond of asking journalists if they had ever come across individuals with positive experiences with pornography. The investigatory staff had tried to identify such people to testify, he said, but had been unable to find any. Hudson importuned reporters to please send such individuals his way. A female commissioner helpfully suggested that she knew of acquaintances, "normal married couples living in suburban New Jersey," who occasionally looked at magazines or rented X-rated videos with no apparent ill effects. But she doubted they would be willing to testify about their sexual pleasure in a federal courthouse, with their remarks transcribed by the court stenographer and their photos probably published in the next day's paper as "porn-users."

Though few witnesses chose to expose themselves to the commission's intimidation through visual images, the tactics used are illustrated in the differential treatment of two female witnesses, former *Playboy* Playmate Micki Garcia and former *Penthouse* Pet of the Year Dottie Meyer. Garcia accused Playboy Enterprises and Hugh Hefner of encouraging drug use, murder, and rape (as well as abortion, bisexuality, and cosmetic surgery) in the Playboy mansion. Her life was endangered by her testimony, she claimed. Despite the serious nature of some of these charges and the lack of any supporting evidence, her testimony was received without question.[23] Meyer, on the other hand, testified that her association with *Penthouse* had been professionally and personally beneficial. At the conclusion of her testimony, the lights dramatically dimmed and large blow-ups of several *Penthouse* pictorials were flashed on the screen; with rapid-fire questions the chair demanded that she explain sexual images he found particularly objectionable. Another male commissioner, prepared by the staff with copies of Meyer's nine-year-old centerfold, began to pepper her with hectoring questions about her sexual life: Was it true she was preoccupied with sex? Liked sex in cars and alleyways? Had a collection of vibrators? Liked rough-and-tumble sex?[24] The female commissioners were silent. His sexist cross-examination was reminiscent of that directed at a rape victim, discredited and made vulnerable by any admission or image of her own sexuality. Suddenly, Dottie Meyer was on trial, publicly humiliated because she dared to present herself as unrepentantly sexual, not a victimized woman.

The ferocious attack on Dottie Meyer—and by extension on any displays of women's sexual pleasure in the public sphere—is emblematic of the agenda of conservatives and fundamentalists on women's sexuality. Although they presented their program under the guise of feminist language and concerns, their abiding goal was to reestablish control by restricting women—and their desires—within ever-shrinking boundaries of the private and the domestic. The falsity of the panel's seemingly feminist rhetoric was highlighted by the moment when a lone woman speaking of her own sexual pleasure was seen as a greater threat than all male "victims" of pornography who had assaulted and abused women. The conspicuous absence of any discourse that addressed women's definitions of their own sexual pleasures, that enlarged rather than constricted the domain of their public speech or action, unmasked this agenda. Unmasked, too, was the commission's primary aim: not to increase the safe space for women, but to narrow what can be seen, spoken about, imagined, and—they hope—done.

The invisibility and subordination of female sexual pleasure in the commission's hearings is that which conservatives and fundamentalists would like to extend to the entire culture. Feminist language, disembodied from feminist principles and programs, was used to advance the idea that men, women, and society could be protected only through the suppression of female desire. In the face of false patriarchal protections embedded in shame and silence, feminists need to assert their entitlement to public speech, variety, safety, and bodily and visual pleasures.

NOTES

1. Attorney General's Commission on Pornography, Miami transcript, public hearing, November 21, 1985.

2. Attorney General's Commission on Pornography, *Final Report,* 2 vols. (Washington, D.C., 1986).

3. See *Final Report,* pp. 433–58, for a complete list of the panel's recommendations. These include mandating high fines and long jail sentences for obscenity convictions, appointing a federal task force to coordinate prosecutions nationwide, developing a computer data bank to collect information on individuals suspected of producing pornography, and using punitive RICO legislation (the Racketeer Influenced and Corrupt Organizations Act, originally developed to fight organized crime) to confiscate the personal property of anyone convicted of the "conspiracy" of producing pornography. For sexually explicit material outside the range of legal prosecution, the commission recommended that citizen activist groups target and remove material in their communities which they find "dangerous or offensive or immoral."

4. For a detailed critique of procedural irregularities, see Barry Lynn, *Polluting the Censorship Debate: A Summary and Critique of the Attorney General's Commission on Pornography* (Washington, D.C., 1986).

5. For changes in sexual patterns in the last century, see (for England) Jeffrey Weeks, *Sex, Politics, and Society: The Regulation of Sexuality since 1800* (New York, 1981); and (for America) John D'Emilio and Estelle B. Freedman, *Intimate Matters* (New York, 1988). For a history of pornography, see Walter Kendrick, *The Secret Museum* (New York, 1987).

6. Sears went on to become the executive director of Citizens for Decency through Law, a major conservative anti-pornography group. (The group has since changed its name to the Children's Legal Foundation.)

7. Attorney Frederick Schauer argued that sexually explicit expression that was arousing was less like speech and more like "rubber plastic or leather sex aids." See "Speech and 'Speech'—Obscenity and 'Obscenity': An Exercise in the Interpretation of Constitutional Language," *Georgetown Law Journal* 67 (1979): 899–923, esp. pp. 922–23.

8. My analysis is based on direct observation of the commission's public hearings and executive sessions, supplemented by interviews with participants. All the commission's executive sessions were open to the public, following the provision of sunshine laws governing federal advisory commissions. Commissioners were specifically prohibited from discussing commission business or engaging in any informal deliberations outside of public view.

Public hearings were organized around preselected topics in six cities: Washington, D.C. (general), Chicago (law enforcement), Houston (social science), Los Angeles (production and distribution), Miami (child pornography), and New York (organized crime). Each public hearing typically lasted two full days. Commission executive sessions were held in each city in conjunction with the public hearings, usually for two extra days. Additional work sessions occurred in Washington, D.C., and Scottsdale, Arizona.

9. Victims of pornography, as described in the *Final Report*, included "Sharon, formerly married to a medical professional who is an avid consumer of pornography," "Bill, convicted of the sexual molestation of two adolescent females," "Dan, former Consumer of Pornography [*sic*]," "Evelyn, Mother and homemaker, Wisconsin, formerly married to an avid consumer of pornography," and "Mary Steinman, sexual abuse victim."

10. Los Angeles transcript, public hearing, October 17, 1985.

11. Major works of anti-pornography feminism include Andrea Dworkin, *Pornography: Men Possessing Women* (New York, 1979); Susan Griffin, *Pornography and Silence: Culture's Revenge against Nature* (New York, 1981); Laura Lederer, ed., *Take Back the Night* (New York, 1980); Catharine A. MacKinnon, "Pornography, Civil Rights, and Speech," *Harvard Civil Rights–Civil Liberties Law Review* 20 (1985): 1–70.

Opinion within feminism about pornography was, in fact, quite diverse, and it soon became apparent that the anti-pornography view was not hegemonic. For other views, see Carole S. Vance, ed., *Pleasure and Danger: Exploring Female Sexuality* (New York, 1984); Varda Burstyn, ed., *Women against Censorship* (Vancouver, 1985); and Kate Ellis et al., eds., *Caught Looking: Feminism, Pornography, and Censorship* (New York, 1986).

12. Washington, D.C., transcript, public hearing, June 20, 1985.

13. For the version passed in Indianapolis, see Indianapolis, Ind., code section 16–3 (q) (1984); and Andrea Dworkin, "Against the Male Flood: Censorship, Pornography, and Equality," *Harvard Women's Law Journal* 9 (1985): 1–19. For a critique, see Lisa Duggan, Nan Hunter, and Carole S. Vance, "False Promises: Feminist Antipornography Legislation in the U.S.," in *Women against Censorship*, ed. Burstyn, pp. 130–51.

14. Women Against Pornography press conference, July 9, 1986, New York.

15. Statement of Catharine A. MacKinnon and Andrea Dworkin, July 9, 1986, New York, distributed at a press conference organized by Women Against Pornography following the release of the Meese Commission's *Final Report*.

16. David Firestone, "Battle Joined by Reluctant Allies," *Newsday*, July 10, 1986: 5.

17. Statement of commissioners Judith Becker and Ellen Levine, *Final Report*, p. 199. In addition, they wrote: "We do not even know whether or not what the Commission viewed during the course of the year reflected the nature of most of the pornographic and obscene material in the market; nor do we know if the materials shown us mirror the taste of the majority of consumers of pornography."

18. Recent empirical evidence does not support the often-repeated assertion that violence in pornography is increasing. In their review of the literature, social scientists Edward Donnerstein, Daniel Linz, and Steven Penrod conclude, "At least for now, we cannot legitimately conclude that pornography has become more violent since the time of the 1970 obscenity and pornography commission" (in *The Question of Pornography: Research Findings and Policy Implications* [New York, 1987], p. 91).

19. The only original research conducted by the commission examined images found in the April 1986 issues of best-selling men's magazines (*Cheri, Chic, Club, Gallery, Genesis, High Society, Hustler, Oui, Penthouse, Playboy, Swank*). The study found that "images of force, violence, or weapons" constituted less than 1 percent of all images (0.6 percent), hardly substantiating the commission's claim that violent imagery in pornography was common. Although the results of this study are reported in the draft, they were excised from the final report.

20. For recent works on SM, see Michael A. Rosen, *Sexual Magic: The S/M Photographs* (San Francisco, 1986); Geoff Mains, *Urban Aboriginals* (San Francisco, 1984); Samois, ed., *Coming to Power*, 2nd ed. (Boston, 1982); Gini Graham Scott, *Dominant Women, Submissive Men* (New York, 1983); Thomas Weinberg and G. P. Levi Kamel, *S and M: Studies in Sadomasochism* (Buffalo, 1983); Gerald and Caroline Greene, *S-M: The Last Taboo* (New York, 1974).

21. The proclivity of mildly stigmatized groups to join in the scapegoating of more stigmatized groups is explained by Gayle Rubin in her discussion of sexual hierarchy (Gayle Rubin, "Thinking Sex: Notes for a Radical Theory of the Politics of Sexuality," in *Pleasure and Danger,* ed. Vance, pp. 267–319).

22. Statement of Alan Sears, executive director (Washington, D.C., transcript, June 18, 1985).

23. Los Angeles transcript, public hearing, October 17, 1985.

24. New York transcript, public hearing, January 22, 1986.

AIDS AND THE DISCURSIVE CONSTRUCTION OF HOMOSEXUALITY

STEVEN SEIDMAN

AIDS appeared during a period of significant change in Western sexual conventions. A series of movements in the 1960s and 1970s pointed in the direction of expanded erotic choice and tolerance for diversity. The women's movement struggled for women's erotic autonomy. Feminists demanded that women be able to define and control their own sexuality, and that included choosing a lesbian alternative. Less visible were the struggles by sexually disenfranchised groups like the elderly or the disabled to be accepted as full sexual beings. The counterculture made a more open and expressive eroticism a prominent part of its social rebellion. Furthermore, changes in our sexual norms that reflected long-term trends became evident. For example, the norm that sex is legitimate only as an act of love or a sign of relational fidelity was challenged. Sex discourses and representations (e.g., pornography, sex manuals, and radical sex ideologies) appeared that constructed sex as an autonomous sphere of pleasure and self-expression with its own intrinsic value and justification. A libertarian sex ethic accepted sex for its pleasurable qualities in any context of mutual consent and respect. This has expanded the types of relationships in which sex is permitted. Indeed, the exclusivity of marriage as the proper site for sex has given way to a more flexible convention that tolerates sex in varied relational settings. In short, while it would be misleading to assert that a revolution occurred, there did transpire important changes in our sexual norms and behavior during this period.

Indicative of this more liberal sexual culture was the increased tolerance for homosexuality. By the mid-1970s gay subcultures were visible in virtually every major urban center.[1] These provided gay people with institutional protection, a source of social support, and a mass base for a politics of civil rights reform and gay liberation. Within these gay spaces a cultural apparatus emerged that included gay-oriented publications (books, magazines, and newspapers), theatre groups, movies, and so on. Of particular importance is that this new gay intelligentsia articulated affirmative images of homosexuality. Constructions of "the homosexual" as a morally perverse, deviant, or pathological figure were assailed. Homosexuality was reconceived to refer to a morally neutral need or behavior that is not indicative of a distinctive personality type. New models viewed the homosexual as a person with merely an alternative sexual or affectional preference or as a member of an oppressed minority. In fact, some gays endorsed the notion of homosexuals as different but reconceived this in affirmative ways. Finally, gay people made important gains in political empowerment and social inclusion. For example, by the mid-1970s more than half the states in the United States had repealed their sodomy laws; dozens of cities had passed anti-discrimination ordinances, the civil service commission had eliminated its ban on hiring homosexuals, and so on.

The trend towards sexual liberalization and, in particular, the tolerance of homosexuals, encountered a lot of resistance and hostility. In the late 1970s this tolerance narrowed considerably as anti-gay themes became integral to a revived conservative politics. The explanation for this lies perhaps in social developments that paralleled sexual liberalization. Specifically, the conjunction of a series of events, including an economic recession, political legitimation problems stemming from Watergate, military setbacks in Vietnam and Iran, and social disturbances arising from the various civil rights, protest and liberation movements, produced a pervasive sense of social crisis and decline. Although social and political responses to this situation were varied, it is not coincidental that a series of purity crusades swept across the country.[2] This was one way people responded to feelings of social danger and sought to gain control over social events. Different groups or phenomena, from pornography to pedophiles, were targeted. However, gay people in particular were singled out. This was not entirely fortuitous. The trend towards the acceptance or at least tolerance of homosexuality challenged the exclusive legitimacy of a heterosexual and marital norm. Moreover, the visibility and political assertiveness of homosexuals, coupled to their symbolic association with social dissolution in a context perceived by many Americans as one of family breakdown and national decline, made them easy prey for scapegoating.

The anxiety and hostility many Americans felt towards recent developments were displaced onto homosexuality. Homosexuals were portrayed as a public menace, as a threat to the family, and as imperiling the national security by promoting self-centered, hedonistic, and pacifist values. An anti-gay backlash crystallized that was initially centered around local and state campaigns to repeal gay rights ordinances. Gradually, it expanded to include national legislation, the resurgence of anti-homosexual discourses, and escalating discrimination and violence towards homosexuals.[3] Its aim was to deny legitimacy to homosexuality; to dismantle gay subcultural institutions; to return homosexuals to a condition of invisibility and marginality; and to reassert a discourse of the dangers of homosexuality.

I argue that AIDS has provided a pretext to reinsert homosexuality within a symbolic drama of pollution and purity. Conservatives have used AIDS to rehabilitate the notion of "the homosexual" as a polluted figure. AIDS is read as revealing the essence of a promiscuous homosexual desire and proof of its dangerous and subversive nature. The reverse side of this demonization of homosexuality is the purity of heterosexuality and the valorization of a monogamous, marital sexual ethic. To be sure, the discourse of homosexuality occasioned by AIDS is not uniform. Liberal segments of the heterosexual media have, in the main, repudiated a politics aimed at the repression of homosexuality. Instead, they have enlisted AIDS in their campaign to construct an image of the "respectable homosexual" and to legitimate a sexual ethic of monogamy and romance. Similar themes are conspicuous in the gay media. In fact, many gays have used AIDS to articulate their own redemptive drama. In imagery that oscillates between the apocalyptic and the millennial, AIDS is seen as marking the failure of a way of life; as signaling, like Stonewall, another critical turning point in the coming of age of homosexuals; and, finally, as the beginnings of a new maturity and social responsibility among homosexuals.

AIDS AND HETEROSEXUAL CONSTRUCTIONS
OF HOMOSEXUALITY

In the heterosexual media the identification of AIDS as a gay disease was made early and has proved persistent despite overwhelming evidence to the contrary. Initially, the appearance of Kaposi's sarcoma and other rare cancers among young homosexual men led researchers to designate the term GRID (gay-related immune deficiency) for this new syndrome. Taking their cue from medical researchers, the mass media referred to this disease as the "homosexual cancer," the "gay epidemic." These terms suggest an intrinsic tie between homosexuality and AIDS. The causal link was identified as homosexual behavior.

The two most prominent epidemiological theories directly joined AIDS to homosexual acts. The so-called "overload theory" held that "the gay lifestyle" (the combination of drug use, poor health habits, and a history of sexually transmitted diseases resulting from sexual promiscuity) is responsible for the collapse of the immune system. The currently more accepted theory asserts the existence of a virus which combined with other factors breaks down the body's resistance to disease. The introduction of semen into the body during sex releases the virus into the bloodstream. The typical scenario that is postulated holds that repeated anal intercourse tears the delicate tissue of the anus. This allows the semen and therefore the virus of the infected person to pass into the blood circulation of the unsuspecting other. Both theories underscore the association between sexual behavior and AIDS among homosexuals. They highlight sexual "promiscuity" as the intermediary or connecting link. The overload theory posits a more direct, ironic, and insidious dynamic: the immediate sensual pleasures of "promiscuous" sex set in motion a hidden telos of disease and death. The very act of sexual union—with its cultural resonances of love and the production of life—is turned into an act of death as bodily defenses collapse. Although the viral hypothesis does not view AIDS as the very signature of homosexual behavior, it asserts an indirect tie between promiscuity and AIDS among homosexual men. It is, after all, only under conditions of non-monogamy that sex can threaten viral infection. Both the overload and the viral theory, then, represent medical frameworks that center on the causality between sexual promiscuity, disease, and death.

In the heterosexual media's response to AIDS, promiscuity became the defining property of gay sexuality. Headlines and feature stories in all the major national media dramatized a gay lifestyle, a fast-lane life of indiscriminate casual sex. A piece in the *San Francisco Examiner* found in AIDS confirmation of the conventional wisdom that gays are "a population whose lifestyle is based on a freewheeling approach to sex."[4] John Fuller in *Science Digest* observed that AIDS is simply further evidence of what science has told us about homosexual men: "Sociologists and psychologists had long noted that the constant search for new sexual partners is a persistent pattern among many gay males."[5] Some commentators underlined the paradoxical aspects of homosexuality. "Ironically, the freedom, the promiscuity . . . that many gays declared an integral part of their culture have come to haunt them."[6] I want to here underscore a key point regarding this discourse: the promiscuity of homosexual men is not considered incidental or a historically specific behavioral property of homosexuality. Rather, it is viewed as essential to homosexuality. In other words, this discourse resurrects an older notion of the male homosexual as a type of person with unique physical, emotional, and behavioral traits. His essence is that of a hypersexual human type. Homosexual men sexualize themselves and others; they reduce persons to eroticized bodies; they frame sex as mere physical release or pleasure-seeking. Promiscuity manifests the lustful, amoral nature of the homosexual. Homosexual desire symbolizes pure sexual lust or unrestrained desire subject only to the quantitative limitations of physical exhaustion. It is this compulsive, hyperactive, insatiable desire that compels homosexuals to eroticize the forbidden and to transgress all moral boundaries, rendering themselves dangerous. Homosexuality is constructed as the very antithesis of the heterosexual marital ideal where sex is joined to romance, love, and relational permanence and fidelity.

The AIDS discourse on homosexuality is a moral one. The juxtaposition of homosexuality and heterosexual romantic love carries a moral distinction between the dangers of homosexual promiscuity and the purity of heterosexual love and monogamy. From this vantage point, AIDS reveals not only the truth of homosexuality but is its just punishment. Some commentators have seen in AIDS proof of the unnaturalness or perversity of homosexuality. "The poor homosexuals—they have declared war upon nature, and now nature is exacting an awful retribution," writes President Reagan's former aide Patrick Buchanan.[7]

Reverend Charles Stanley, head of the 14.3 million-member Southern Baptist Convention remarked, "It [homosexuality] is a sinful lifestyle, according to the scripture, and I believe that AIDS is God indicating his displeasure and his attitude towards that form of lifestyle."[8] Finally, arriving at the same moral judgment but framed within a medical-scientific discourse, Dr. James Fletcher writes in the *Southern Medical Journal*, "If we act as empirical scientists can we not see the implications of the data [AIDS and STDs among homosexual men] before us? Might not these 'complications' be 'consequences' [of homosexuality]? Were it so a logical conclusion is that AIDS is a self-inflicted disorder. . . . Indeed from an empirical medical perspective alone current scientific observation seems to require the conclusion that homosexuality is a pathologic condition."[9]

In the above moral rhetorics, AIDS represents a just punishment for homosexuals since they have violated a basic law of God, Nature and Society. There is, however, another more subtle logic of moral judgment presented in the AIDS phenomenon. AIDS is seen as the homosexual's death wish turned upon himself. In modern mythology, homosexuality indicates an unconscious will to subvert and destroy society. Images of subversion surround the homosexual. The ubiquitous association of homosexuals with the corruption of children—the very symbol of purity and social order—is indicative of their link to death. It is, I believe, precisely because in our symbolic universe homosexuality is constructed as a social danger evoking resonances of decline and chaos, that AIDS is seen not only as the truth of homosexuality but as its just punishment. AIDS signals the wish for the annihilation of "the other" being turned inward, back against the homosexual himself. It's because homosexuality symbolizes a threat to life and society that even in the face of the mass suffering and death among homosexuals the public reaction has often been complacent, indifferent, and vengeful. For threatening social existence and "killing the innocent," homosexual men have received their just desert in AIDS. This, at least, appears to be a perhaps unconscious moral sentiment conveyed in the heterosexual response to AIDS.

AIDS has contributed to reviving a notion of the homosexual as a dangerous and polluted figure. Moreover, the revitalization of a discredited image of homosexuality structured the public response to AIDS. As the principal victim of AIDS but also identified as its chief perpetrator, homosexual men were doubly victimized: by the disease and by society's response to it. Blamed for their own affliction, accused of spreading disease and death to innocent people, criticized as a drain upon scarce national resources, homosexual AIDS victims felt socially scorned and shunned.[10] Stories circulated of hospital staff, police, and criminal justice personnel refusing physical contact with AIDS victims, and of AIDS victims left unattended in hospitals, leaving friends and family responsible for their care. Feature stories told of AIDS victims being fired from their jobs, evicted from their homes, ejected from public places. Numerous reports narrate how homosexual AIDS victims had to manage, often alone, a social death in anticipation of their physical one.

AIDS served as an ideal pretext for upgrading the surveillance and oppression of homosexuals. By the end of 1985 demands were being made for stepped-up state regulation of homosexual AIDS cases through administering an "AIDS" test as a condition of employment, military service, health and life insurance, blood donation, and so on. Quarantining AIDS cases was seriously discussed, and in some states statutes were amended to give the government the power to implement a quarantine. Suggestions were heard of empowering the state to rehabilitate sexually promiscuous homosexual men through drugs or confinement. Beyond the repressive measures sought in response to AIDS, backlash forces held that the AIDS crisis rendered homosexuals a public health threat. By claiming that AIDS had produced a national health crisis, backlash forces tried to enlist the state to dismantle gay subcultural institutions. Efforts to close gay bars and baths were part of a broader strategy of withdrawing public tolerance for homosexuals. There were renewed efforts to press for the remedicalization and recriminalization of homosexual behavior. For example the Dallas Doctors Against AIDS issued the following declaration: "Such a sexual public health concern must cause the citizenry of this country to do everything in their power to smash the homosexual movement in this country to make sure these kinds of acts are criminalized."[11] Movements in support of gay rights ordinances were frustrated and efforts to reinstitute or endorse anti-sodomy laws were given a fresh impetus. At a more immediate level, gay men felt the intensification of oppression through an increase of reported acts of discrimination, harassment, and physical assault.[12]

Although the liberal media have sought to avoid the politicizing of AIDS, liberals, no less than conservatives, have seized on AIDS to propagate their own sexual morality. They have used AIDS to reaffirm the morality of monogamy and romantic love. In fact, the liberal media have sought to rehabilitate a pre-gay liberation ideal of the "respectable homosexual": discreet, coupled, monogamous, and cohabiting.

The *New York Times,* for example, has virtually campaigned to create and legitimate this ideal of the respectable homosexual.[13] Its coverage of AIDS has regularly included interviews with prominent figures in the gay community or relevant "experts" who uniformly criticize the immature and irresponsible promiscuous lifestyle accepted in the gay subculture of the 1970s. Articles appeared that reported changes in the behavior of homosexuals. Key indicators of the fast-lane gay lifestyle, e.g., number of sex partners, STDs, and bathhouse attendance were scrutinized to detect indications of a retreat from promiscuity. Reports of a new emphasis upon dating, courting, and nonsexual attendance were given prominence. The *Times* did more than report these developments; it clearly endorsed them. In fact, by virtue of its prestige and its enlisting of experts and community leaders, the *Times* became a major social force in promoting these changes. It ran pieces on homosexual couples who were obviously intended to serve as role models to a crisis-ridden and anomic gay community. One such piece, entitled "Homosexual Couple Finds a Quiet Pride," focuses on two professional men who have lived together for some forty years. They are, in appearance, indistinguishable from conventional heterosexuals. In other words, there is

no trace of a more unconventional gay subcultural style to their self-presentation. There is an implied discreetness to their homosexuality, and their
demeanor exudes an almost exaggerated sense of staid respectability. They are
described as preoccupied with typical heterosexual concerns such as career, family, domestic affairs, hobbies, and anniversaries. The "success" or longevity of
their relationship is summed up by the remark, "You have to work at it." Quite
clearly, the *Times* is offering them, or its construction of them, as a model of
what is an acceptable homosexual style. With moral codes and identity-models in
flux, and with homosexuality itself assailed by backlash forces, this image of a discreet, monogamous, coupled, and conventional homosexual life is endorsed as an
alternative to more unconventional gay socioerotic models. In fact, the principal
thesis of the article is that a "heterosexual model" is now being adopted by homosexuals. "In recent years, some homosexual couples have begun to adopt many of
the traditions of heterosexual marriage. Besides having wedding and anniversary
parties, couples are exchanging vows . . . in religious services known as 'gay
unions.' They are drawing up contracts, wills . . . to provide legal protections for
themselves and their partners. They are adopting children."[14] Setting aside for the
moment the credibility of this argument, the message seems indisputable: AIDS
is a positive catalyst encouraging homosexual men to adopt heterosexual relational patterns. Because of AIDS homosexual men are rediscovering the charm,
civility, security, and safety of romance and monogamy. Liberals, no less than
conservatives, have exploited AIDS for their own moral purposes. Whereas the
latter enlist AIDS as part of their backlash politics, the former use AIDS to relate
a moral tale of the virtues of romantic love and monogamy.

AIDS AND THE CRISIS OF HOMOSEXUALITY
IN THE GAY COMMUNITY

Sexual promiscuity stands at the center of the gay media's response to AIDS. It
is seen as a product of an historically unique gay subculture. It is, moreover, seen
as having a direct causal relation to the current epidemic and to the anti-gay
backlash. For homosexual men with a traditional cultural background, for older
homosexuals who came of age in a milieu emphasizing heterosexual models, for
those men uncomfortable with their sexuality, or for gay liberationists whose
ideals are perceived to have faded behind a wave of self-indulgence, AIDS has
functioned as an appropriate symbol of the failure of current gay life. AIDS provides an ideal opportunity for gays to vocalize their discontents. I am suggesting,
to be perfectly clear, that for heterosexuals and homosexuals, AIDS has served as
a pretext to speak critically about homosexuality and to advocate reforms of the
gay subculture. Perhaps gay men felt that the suffering and intensified oppression they have experienced in the AIDS crises could be somewhat neutralized or
even made self-confirming by reconceiving AIDS as a moral drama. AIDS
comes to signify the beginnings of a great reformation in gay life.

The notion that AIDS has ushered in a time of trial and marks a turning point for gays is neatly captured in the apocalyptic imagery of Larry Kramer's eloquent and moving piece "1112 and Counting." Kramer frames the AIDS phenomenon as a test of collective survival. "Our continued existence as gay men . . . is at stake. . . . In the history of homosexuality we have never been so close to death and extinction before."[15] Survival hinges on a shift from the current hedonistic preoccupations of gay men to a new social consciousness and a responsible erotic ethic. Where Kramer is somewhat pessimistic, other gay men speak in an oddly defiant and upbeat tone of AIDS initiating a new era of maturity and respectability. Toby Marotta observes that "most gays share my view—that [AIDS] is the most profound, maturing incident for the gay community in its history."[16] David Goodstein couples a critical view of pre-AIDS gay life to the prospects for renewal and reform initiated by AIDS. "During the last half of the 1970s, it wasn't chic in gay male circles to place a high value on life-companions or close friendships. Now [i.e., with AIDS] we have another chance for progress: to acknowledge the value of intimate relationships."[17] Stephen Harvey is even more direct in acknowledging the redemptive possibilities of AIDS. "It's a perverse and maybe [!] tragic irony that it took the AIDS outbreak . . . to at last . . . integrate [our] sexual natures with the rest of what [we] are."[18] A central feature of this emerging gay maturity is the appropriation of the behavioral models and rituals of heterosexual interpersonal patterns. Arthur Bell comments: "Indiscriminate sex with phantom partners in backrooms is beginning to diminish. The grudge and filth bars are losing their appeal. Fistfucking is fading. Barbarity is on the way out. Romance [is] . . . on the way in."[19] Stories abound in the gay press of homosexual men rediscovering the quiet joys and healthy lifestyle of romantic love and monogamy. Typically, such narratives set off a pre-AIDS period which is now described as one of immaturity and indulgence. AIDS marks the great turning point where after a protracted period of soul-searching one is reborn: the profligate, self-destructive ways of the past are given up for the new morality of monogamy and romance. Typical is the piece by Arnie Kantrowitz: "Till Death Us Do Part." He begins by recalling the liberating experience of sexual promiscuity. "My experiment in sexual anarchy was a rare delight, a lesson in license, an opportunity to see both flesh and spirit glaringly naked. I will never apologize to anyone for my promiscuity." Yet, that is exactly what he does as he narrates his odyssey of personal growth. From the standpoint of a post-AIDS sexual morality his early sensual delights now appear to him as compulsive and narcissistic. The endless cycle of excitement, release, and exhaustion left him jaded and empty. "I decided to trade self-indulgence for self-respect." Having personally witnessed the guilt-ridden, self-destructive ways of his pre-AIDS days, he "decided to get healthy." Exercise and proper diet replaced drug abuse and sleepless nights. With health and self-respect intact, there could be only one proper dramatic finale. "Finally, I rediscovered the difference between lust and love and began an affair."[20] The transfiguration of AIDS into a moral and mythic drama of reformation and renewal has allowed some gays to be so emotionally distanced from the enormity of suffering it has brought that the current period is defined as one of optimism. One gay writer observes in what is a common motif that "the energy formerly reserved for the sexual hunt [can now be] channeled into the community in other ways [such as] . . . the growth of gay community centers, sports clubs, choruses, and a host of other groups." He concludes by remarking: "all of which I believe makes 1983 a time for optimism and joy."[21]

AIDS AND HOMOSEXUALITY: THE LIMITS OF A DISCOURSE

The public heterosexual and gay responses to AIDS share a common moral theme: the dangers of promiscuity which are asserted to be a defining feature of homosexuality today. The former frequently derives promiscuity from the very essence of homosexual desire. The latter traces promiscuity to the contemporary gay subculture. In both the heterosexual and gay media, promiscuity is taken as the decisive link between homosexual men and AIDS. It is moreover, considered the essence of a universal or more historically specific homosexual desire. Yet, one looks in vain for a definition or a serious analysis of its meaning. Its sense, however, is conveyed by references to having many sex partners. This, however, is misleading. Promiscuity cannot be defined by the sheer number of one's sex partners. For example, a serial monogamous pattern which involves a sequence of changing partners is not promiscuous behavior. Similarly, promiscuity is not synonymous with nonmonogamy. We would not consider, say, an extramarital affair as promiscuous behavior. In general, we must distinguish promiscuity from polygamy or "sexual pluralism." The latter involves multiple sex partners, but there may also be established relationships of intimacy and responsibility with each partner. Promiscuity involves a sexually active person whose sex partners change frequently, and with each there is an absence of personal intimacy and extended responsibilities. Furthermore, the line between serial monogamy, polygamy, and promiscuity cannot always be drawn in a hard and fast way. A serial monogamous pattern involving a sequence of short-lived, emotionally distant relationships has a promiscuous aspect. A polygamous pattern involving one primary long-term relationship and sex with anonymous others suggests a more salient promiscuous element.

At stake is more than a matter of conceptual clarification. The categories used to describe homosexuality carry moral and practical implications. Homosexual behavior cannot be characterized as promiscuous in some generic or essential way. The available studies of current behavior highlight a diversity of homosexual patterns ranging from a monogamous, marital model to promiscuity.[22] Any attempt to frame homosexual desire as some abstract, universal, and homogeneous entity whose essence is promiscuity will not find much empirical support in behavioral research. Researchers agree that a more typical pattern for gay men—at least in the 1970s—has been to combine an ongoing love relationship with secondary affairs centered on sex.[23] The pattern of these secondary involvements ranges from having a few erotically centered relationships involving extended responsibilities to having high numbers of changing, anonymous sex partners. To the extent that the latter is more common then the line between polygamy and promiscuity is blurred. In fact, according to some observers, this more promiscuous style characterized a segment of the urban gay population in the 1970s. Indeed, surveys of sexual behavior show that during this period gay men had, on the average, a much higher number of sex partners—many of whom were anonymous—than heterosexuals and lesbians.[24] It is reasonable to assume some connection between this behavior and AIDS among homosexual men. The error is to assume a generic causal tie between homosexuality, promiscuity, and disease or to take AIDS as evidence of the pathological nature of homosexuality.

There is a series of wrong moves here. Promiscuity is *not* the cause of AIDS but a risk factor. To be even more precise, it is a risk factor *if* one engages in high-risk sex and *if* one does so in circumstances where the HTLV-III virus is widely circulated. Homosexuals do *not* have to be promiscuous or non-monogamous to acquire AIDS. It is *not* legitimate to take AIDS as indicative of a particular type of sexual pattern or lifestyle. Furthermore, given its appearance among heterosexuals, who in some nations are primarily afflicted, it is wrong to interpret AIDS as a homosexual disease. There is no evidence that AIDS is congenital or that it is produced by homosexual behavior or that it favors homosexual men. The only statement that can be endorsed unequivocally is that *specific homosexual acts* are today high-risk. This fact does not, however, require that homosexual men adopt any particular lifestyle or sexual ethic. It mandates only safe-sex practices, but how these are incorporated into a lifestyle or pattern of intimate relationships is open to diverse possibilities.

CONCLUSION

Foucault has shown how the original intent and political purpose of a discourse on sexuality can be reversed. For example, the scientific-medical discourse of "the homosexual" as a perverse or pathological human type promoted new forms of social control. Yet, taking the issue of homosexuality out of a religious context and placing it in a scientific one has allowed an appeal to empirical evidence to challenge stereotypes and, ultimately, to contest the medical model itself. Moreover, this medical discourse contributed to creating a common homosexual consciousness and culture that eventuated in a politic aimed at legitimating homosexuality.

It is, then, possible that AIDS may have a long-term beneficial effect. AIDS requires credible empirical knowledge of homosexuality. This will stimulate and legitimate research on homosexuals, much of which will challenge stereotypes. Finally, this knowledge will be disseminated throughout society and will be taken seriously because of its link to a health crisis. This could provide a favorable setting for legitimating homosexuality and gaining the social inclusion of homosexuals. In the end, this will not result merely from a process of mass enlightenment. Rather, it will require gay people, in particular, to mobilize in order to play a greater role in shaping public discussions. Homosexuals must have a political presence if they expect to shape public policy decisions emerging from the AIDS crisis.

NOTES

1. Dennis Altmann, *The Homosexualization of America* (Boston, 1983); John D'Emilio, *Sexual Politics, Sexual Communities* (Chicago, 1983).

2. Gayle Rubin, "Thinking Sex," in *Pleasure and Danger,* ed. Carole Vance (Boston, 1984).

3. Altmann, *Homosexualization of America.*

4. *San Francisco Examiner,* October 24, 1982: 14.

5. John Fuller, "AIDS: Legacy of the '60s?" *Science Digest,* December 1983.

6. Vincent Cuppola, "The Change in Gay Life Style," *Newsweek,* April 18, 1983.

7. Patrick Buchanan, "AIDS Disease: It's Nature Striking Back," *New York Post,* May 24, 1983.

8. *Times Union,* January 18, 1986.

9. Quoted in James E'Eramo, "The New Medical Journal Homophobia," *New York Native,* May 21, 1984.

10. Mark Starr and David Gonzalez, "The Panic over AIDS," *Newsweek,* May 4, 1983; John Lee, "The Real Epidemic: Fear and Despair," *Time,* July 4, 1983.

11. Quoted in Cindy Patton, *Sex and Germs* (Boston, 1985), pp. 3–4.

12. William Greer, "Violence against Homosexuals Rising," *New York Times,* November 23, 1986.

13. See Richard Lyons, "Homosexuals Find a Need to Reassess," *New York Times,* May 29, 1983; Lyons, "Homosexuals Confronting a Time of Change," *New York Times,* June 16, 1983; Lyons, "Sex in America: Conservative Attitudes Prevail," *New York Times,* October 4, 1983; Lyons, "AIDS Education Takes on Urgency," *New York Times,* September 22, 1985.

14. Georgia Dullea, "Homosexual Couple Finds a Quiet Pride," *New York Times,* December 10, 1984.

15. Larry Kramer, "1112 and Counting," *New York Native,* March 14, 1983.

16 Quoted in Tom Morgenthau, "Gay America in Transition," *Newsweek,* August 8, 1983: 33.

17. David Goodstein, "Editorial," *The Advocate,* August 6, 1985.

18. Stephen Harvey, "Defenseless: Learning to Live with AIDS," *The Village Voice,* December 21, 1982.

19. Arthur Bell, "Where Gays Are Going," *The Village Voice,* June 29, 1982.

20. Arnie Kantrowitz, "Till Death Us Do Part," *The Advocate,* 1983.

21. Steve Martz, "A Quick Look Back and Some Thoughts on the Year Ahead," *Washington Blade,* January 7, 1983.

22. Alan Bell and Martin Weinberg, *Homosexualities* (New York, 1970).

23. Joseph Harry and William Duvall, *The Social Organization of Gay Males* (New York, 1978); Letitia Peplau and Steven Gordon, "The Intimate Relationships of Lesbians and Gay Men," in *Gender Roles and Sexual Behavior,* ed. Elizabeth Allgeier and Naomi McCormick (Palo Alto, 1983); C. A. Tripp, *The Homosexual Matrix* (New York, 1975); Edmund White, *States of Desire* (New York, 1980).

24. Bell and Weinberg, *Homosexualities*; Philip Blumstein and Pepper Schwartz, *American Couples* (New York, 1983).

REGULATED PASSIONS

The Invention of Inhibited Sexual Desire and Sexual Addiction

JANICE M. IRVINE

In recent years, several different headlines bannered the covers of *Cosmopolitan* magazine. In November, 1988, "When You're Not Interested in Sex, He's Not Interested: How to Reawaken Your Desire." In July, 1989, "Girls Who Are Addicted to Sex: Why They Can't Stop." And finally, in November, 1989, the plaintive question, "How Much Sex Is Enough?" The *Cosmo* girl was embroiled in the labyrinthine contemporary debate about sexuality and sexual desire. The latest questions about the nature and limits of desire issue from the invention in the mid-1970s of two distinct diagnostic constructs: inhibited sexual desire (ISD) and sexual addiction. Clearly these are recognizable concerns—that one might have too little desire for sex, or conversely, experience oneself as sexually insatiable. The medicalization of these two conditions, however, with elaborate systems of diagnostic categories and treatment interventions, charts a sexual condition or "sick role"[1] and, in the case of sexual addiction, an entire identity constructed around a specific sexual pattern.

In our culture, disease constructs frequently exceed the bounds of a simple biological entity with clear and objective organic etiology, but rather serve as expanded paradigms imbued with diverse meanings. Diseases are artifacts with social history and social practice. In the area of sexuality, the discursive practices of medicine since the nineteenth century have spawned what Foucault terms a "proliferation of sexualities,"[2] most of which carry the stamp of perversion reborn as disease. Thus, the invention of sexual addiction and inhibited sexual desire can be understood in light of two related historical factors of the late nineteenth century. First, a range of socioeconomic changes prompted a commercialized sexuality in which sex is increasingly privileged as fundamental to individual identity and happiness.[3] Second, the medical profession usurped moral and religious authority in the area of sexuality, generated new and highly visible discourses, and promulgated the diversification of new sexual identities. As Foucault suggests, "Sex was driven out of hiding and forced to lead a discursive existence."[4] Inhibited sexual desire and sexual addiction are two of the most recent medical constructions of sexual disease and disorder.

It would be a mistake, however, to impute sole and uncontested power to the medical profession in the invention of the new disorders. Rather, new diseases emerge within the triangulation of medical imperatives, the demands and experiences of individuals, and cultural traditions and anxieties. This chapter will examine these three axes of influence. First, it will analyze the history of professional intervention in problematic behavior subsequently defined as desire dysfunctions. Second, it will explore the complexities of definition and treatment, and the implications for the afflicted individual. Finally, it emphasizes the ways in which disease reflects the cultural style of a period.[5] It suggests that, in the late twentieth century, these new diseases chart the medically legitimated boundaries of acceptable contemporary sexual experience and serve as signifiers for powerful cultural anxieties about sexuality and desire.

DISEASE NARRATIVES

The construction of disease categories entails a complex set of negotiations among professionals, the general public, and afflicted individuals, which is always mediated by broader cultural ideologies. The particular configuration of very different circumstances for the emergence of ideas about inhibited sexual desire and sexual addiction in the mid-1970s offers clues about their powerful individual and social valence.

Although modern clinicians have anecdotally noted cases of low sexual desire as early as 1972, ISD was first identified in the medical literature in 1977 by two sexologists working independently: Harold Leif and Helen Singer Kaplan.[6] Both are well-known sex therapists who reported the increasing prevalence of complaints about low libido in their clinical practices. This was a noteworthy departure from the presenting problems of most patients during this heyday in sex therapy. With the publication of Masters and Johnson's *Human Sexual Inadequacy* in 1970, sex therapy had grown throughout the decade to become the most visible, lucrative, and widespread enterprise of sexology.[7] On the basis of their research and clinical work, Masters and Johnson had identified several major categories of sexual problems, which were eventually adopted by the third edition of the *Diagnostic and Statistical Manual of Mental Disorders* (DSM-III). For men, the basic sexual dysfunctions included premature ejaculation, primary and secondary impotence, and ejaculatory incompetence (a rare condition in which a man cannot ejaculate intravaginally). Female sexual dysfunctions included dyspareunia (painful intercourse), vaginismus (a tightening of the vaginal muscles that prohibits penile penetration), and several types of orgasmic dysfunctions, broken down into primary or secondary and coital or masturbatory categories.[8] These dysfunctions encompassed the range of technical difficulties to which a couple might be vulnerable, and undeniably, Masters and Johnson's sex therapy program helped scores of people improve their sex lives. Their brief, symptomatic treatment seemed perfect for those with little experience or information about sex.

The mere discovery of the program's existence was enough to instill hope and confidence in some couples. By the late 1970s, sexologists, with their appeal to scientific legitimacy and medical authority, were riding a wave of popularity in a vast market eager for a new approach to sexual problems. Rumors of dramatic, near-miraculous success rates for interventions with sexual problems were so persuasive that clients began reporting cures merely from sitting in the waiting room. By the end of the decade, however, sex therapists voiced a common lament about the disappearance of the "easy cases"—specifically, those problems which were essentially the result of ignorance or misinformation, and which responded well to the simple behavioral methods of Masters and Johnson. The new difficulties were reported in different ways: sexual boredom, low libido, sexual malaise, and even sexual aversion and sexual phobia. Harold Leif recommended that the diagnosis of inhibited sexual desire be applied to those patients who chronically failed to initiate or respond to sexual stimuli. The dysfunction is now routinely referred to as either inhibited sexual desire or hypoactive sexual desire. The American Psychological Association estimates that 20 percent of the population has low or absent sexual desire. Among sex therapists, ISD is now reported as the most common presenting problem, constituting half of all diagnoses, and it is considered to be the most difficult sexual problem to treat.[9] More women than men are diagnosed with inhibited sexual desire, although many therapists report that the rate among males is rising.[10]

The concept of sexual addiction had a quite different beginning, springing to life independently in several cities almost simultaneously. Not surprisingly, the idea of being addicted to sex emerged in the addiction movement among those who were in recovery from substance use. Its first manifestations were in the establishment of 12-Step groups to contain what their members describe as "sexual unmanageability." Sex and Love Addicts Anonymous was the first such group, started by a musician in Boston in 1977.[11] He had been a member of Alcoholics Anonymous for years, had a wife, a mistress, engaged in other sexual affairs, and masturbated several times a day. His perception that his sexuality was out of control led him to find others with a similar problem so that they could "get sober." Initially they met in private homes, but the growth of the group led them to seek public meeting space. A local pastor was sympathetic, but skeptical that his parishioners would support a group of sex addicts, so he suggested a name change. Sex and Love Addicts Anonymous is now also know as the Augustine Fellowship, since one of the members had been reading Augustine's *Confessions,* and claimed, "He's obviously one of us." There are now seven different nationwide fellowships for sex addicts and co-addicts, with such names as Sex Addicts Anonymous, Sexaholics Anonymous, and Sexual Compulsives Anonymous. All were founded under similar circumstances as the Augustine Fellowship.

Every week close to two thousand meetings for sex addicts are held across the country, and the groups are said to be growing at an annual rate of 30 percent.[12] Unlike with ISD, a thriving grassroots movement of individuals who claimed to suffer from the disorder was already in place by the time professionals engaged with the issue. Now, however, experts and clients work in tandem, since sexual addiction has spawned a robust treatment industry. The diagnosis has attracted two types of professionals: the dominant group are "addictionologists" (as they now call themselves), who are joined by a smaller cohort of clinicians who treat sex offenders. Professional awareness of sex addiction was fostered by the "opponent-process" theory of addiction introduced in the early 1970s, which suggested that a substance was no longer requisite for addiction.[13] This proposal that any behavioral excess could lead to dependence fit nicely with the popular and widespread generalization of ideas about addiction represented by such figures as the workaholic, shopaholic, and compulsive gambler. Proponents of the syndrome view sexual addiction within this expanded paradigm of addiction disorders. There are now scores of texts on sex addiction, and treatment programs dot the landscape. The first inpatient program for sexual addicts was begun in 1985 at Golden Valley Health Center's Sexual Dependency Unit in Minneapolis. Addictionologists claim that 6 percent of the population are sex addicts, and approximately 30 percent of these are women. Patrick Carnes, one of the foremost popularizers of the sexual addiction concept, claims that 1 in 12 people in the United States is a sex addict.[14]

THE PROFESSIONAL DIVIDE

The construction of new medical definitions does not simply mirror a perception of illness or problematic conditions. Rather, the discursive elaboration of disease is shaped by myriad and complex factors, including the ideological and economic imperatives of the defining professionals. It is noteworthy that the new diseases of ISD and sexual addiction have each been fashioned by highly different professional cohorts, so that the medical discourses have progressed on parallel and quite distinct trajectories. There has been little connection or communication between addictionologists and sexologists and little overlap in specialization. There has been some veiled hostility between the groups, however, deriving from the clash of underlying ideologies and overt treatment goals. These conflicts highlight the constructed nature of the new diseases and reveal the nature of the loyalties and interests of each profession.

The field of addictionology has been marked by rapid professional expansion, particularly since Solomon's opponent-process theory of addiction provided theoretical legitimacy for the identification of almost anything as an addictive agent. Although the subsequent proliferation of addictions widened the professional domain of addictionologists into new areas, such as gambling and sexuality, their medical gaze remains one of vigilance about excess and admonitions for control and management. This sexual ideology of temperance and abstinence directly opposes the vision of sexual expansion and freedom so implicit in sexology. Addictionologists have criticized many of the sex-enhancing technologies, ideologies and practices that comprise standard sex therapy models. For example, some believe that penile implant surgery, a lucrative procedure that is quite acceptable among sexologists, signifies and reinforces sex addiction.[15] And addiction experts challenge sexologists on their unbridled enthusiasm for the unrestricted use of fantasy and pornography, for their encouragement of masturbation, and for their celebration of virtually any sexual activity between consenting adults. Sex addicts, it is thought, may need to practice celibacy and eliminate fantasy and sexually explicit material "in order to attain and maintain sobriety," and sex therapists may simply re-traumatize them or facilitate a relapse by the espousal of sexual freedom.[16] While addictionologists may accept the dominance of sexologists in many areas of sexuality, they are staking out their turf and becoming more visibly critical of sex therapists for an alleged lack of effectiveness in the treatment of sex addicts.[17]

Sexologists, on the other hand, have struggled for professional legitimacy and a viable commercial market for over a century.[18] They pride themselves on scientific rigor in their work and on fairly unqualified acceptance and support of all sexual expression. The very concept of sexual addiction—that there can be too much sex—threatens the foundations of the profession. Until the early 1990s, sexologists have largely responded to the emerging diagnosis of sexual addiction with sarcasm, disavowal, or attacks on its scientific credibility. In a 1988 anthology on sexual desire disorders, sexologists Sandra Leiblum and Raymond Rosen noted that sexual addiction was beginning to receive considerable attention. They described the affected individuals as "sexual enthusiasts," and noted that they "tend to be admired or envied rather than diagnosed."[19] Helen Singer Kaplan claimed that sexual addiction is exceedingly rare[20] and is "a media term that doesn't have any scientific validity or meaning."[21] Possibly because of his work treating sex offenders with Depo-Provera,[22] noted sexologist John Money was initially a supporter of the new diagnosis, telling the *New York Times* in 1984 that he had seen many patients who were sex addicts. "Their hypersexuality often exceeds normal capacities," he noted.[23] By 1989, however, Money vehemently reversed his position, charging that "the pathologizing of sex by inventing a hitherto unknown disease, sexual addiction," constituted a strategy of "the sexual counterreformation" that has exercised a destructive effect on the advancement of the science of sexology.[24]

Professional antagonisms have slowly begun to dissipate into mutual ambivalence, largely because of the impact of the AIDS epidemic; sexologists, who have been unable to avoid widespread social anxiety about freer sexual mores, have begun fashioning their practices accordingly. Workshops and interventions, such as one entitled "Falling in Love Again," abound for the sexually and relationally bored who are terrorized into monogamy by fear of HIV infection. It is not uncommon for sexologists to chart their professional course through the changing currents of cultural ideologies about sex and gender. Sexology has never presented an uncomplicated vision of sexual liberation. Rather, the field has historically managed the contradictions of a progressive sexual message and the need for conservatism and scientific credibility in order to achieve cultural legitimacy and economic viability. Despite these antinomic imperatives, sexologists generally advance a sexual value system of greater freedom and participation. Yet the cultural sex panic exacerbated by AIDS has foregrounded the addictionologists' message of sexual chaos, as well as the terror of sexual excess. The sexologists' exhortations to sexual pleasure and experimentation look increasingly unwise and unhealthy, and sexologists have begun integrating some of the ideas, if not the wholesale diagnosis, of the sexual addiction field.

The historical narrative, then, of the construction of inhibited sexual desire and sexual addiction reveals a clear bifurcation between two professional cohorts, marked by ideological tensions and distinct border anxiety. As experts laboring at opposite poles of the same continuum of sexual anxiety and control, however, these professionals share a possibly insoluble conundrum: the task of precise clarification and definition of their disease.

DEFINING AND TREATING THE DISORDERS OF DESIRE

The assertion of exact definitional and diagnostic criteria poses an enormous challenge when "disease" is a generalized set of signifiers of cultural chaos and social control. The fabric of overdetermined diseases such as sexual addiction and inhibited sexual desire is woven from the diverse threads of professional expertise and ideologies, cultural beliefs about sex, and the attempts of individuals to make sense out of their own sexual experiences. Nevertheless, the medical legacy of the doctrine of specific etiology[25] has inspired each field to generate myriad hypotheses concerning the individual causes of the disorders. These etiological theories of inhibited sexual desire and sexual addiction are not totalizing discourses but rather an amalgam of diverse and sometimes nebulous perspectives. There is conflict within sexology and addictionology over the origins and nature of their respective disorders, and it would be incorrect to imply a simple unity or consensus. Despite few rigorous research studies, there has been much speculation on the basis of clinical samples and case studies. There are debates over the influences of environment, family, individual personality, and such biological factors as neurochemistry.

Since the nineteenth century, however, professionals have assiduously tracked the etiology of sexual conditions within a biomedical tradition that quantifies desire and locates "this search for the primeval urge in the subject itself."[26] It is this impulse to map desire and its varied disorders in the body itself that represents historical congruence among sexuality professionals and establishes a common theoretical terrain for both inhibited sexual desire and sexual addiction. A pervasive and largely assumed underpinning of both sexual addiction and ISD is the representation of sexual desire as a biological drive or surging energy that is either flooding uncontrollably or woefully diminished. There is the intuitive belief that sex, and specifically sexual desire, resides in the body. This essentialist assumption is not surprising, since it infuses mainstream cultural norms about sexuality with the theoretical foundation of sexual science.[27] As historian Jeffrey Weeks noted about nineteenth-century sexology's search for the origins of sexual behavior, "biology became the privileged road into the mysteries of nature."[28] More than one hundred years later, although few theorists would unequivocally advance a strict biological determinism in the etiology of ISD or sexual addiction, strong essentialist themes resonate throughout the discourses of the desire disorders.

The literature of both professional cohorts reflects a striking emphasis on the brain as the site of sexual desire and the source of its myriad manifestations. Advances in neurochemistry converged with the technological revolution in computers to produce a cyborgian vision of sexuality and desire characterized by images invoked by such phrases as "hardwiring," "circuitry," "programmed into the brain," and "fixed into the system." In this representation, the bedrock of desire and its concomitant sexual possibilities reside within regulatory mechanisms of the brain that are alternately perceived as impervious to change or quite vulnerable to disruption.

The biological basis of sexual desire is most advanced in the work of Helen Singer Kaplan, who pioneered the notion of inhibited sexual desire and who is likely one of the most unreconstructed essentialists within sexology. In her 1979 landmark text on ISD, *Disorders of Sexual Desire*, Kaplan defines sexual desire as an "appetite or drive which is produced by the activation of a specific neural system in the brain."[29] In sociobiological terms, Kaplan describes the importance of sexual desire:

> Sexual desire is a drive that serves the biologic function of species survival. It instills a strong erotic hunger that prods us to engage in species specific behavior that leads to reproduction. It moves us to find a mate, to court, to seduce, to excite, to impregnate, to be impregnated.[30]

For Kaplan, desire is experienced when a specific neural system in the brain is activated, prompting genital sensations and an openness to and interest in sex. When this system is inactive or inhibited, the person "loses his appetite" or "the brain has 'decided' that it is too 'dangerous' to have sex."[31]

Addictionologists tend to discuss sexual desire very little, other than to implicitly regard it as an inherent physiological drive that has spiraled out of control. This discourse harks back to the eighteenth-century perspective described by Weeks that "desire was a dangerous force which pre-existed the individual, wracking his (usually his) feeble body with fantasies and distractions which threatened his individuality and sanity."[32] Significantly, within the sex addiction literature, the moniker "desire" is generally superseded by its moral ancestor, "lust."

Even so, brain-centered sexual theories are even more prolific among addictionologists than sexologists. The most dominant theme proposes that a finite number of polymorphous sexual possibilities are locked into the brain in early childhood, and subsequent behavior is virtually predetermined. The "lovemap" theory of sexologist John Money has been enthusiastically deployed by addictionologists, who find the notion of behavioral options programmed into the brain in childhood a compelling explanatory concept. Money describes the lovemap as "a developmental representation or template, synchronously functional in the mind and the brain, depicting the idealized lover, the idealized love affair, and the idealized program of sexuoerotic activity with that lover, projected in imagery and ideation, or in actual performance."[33] The lovemap allegedly incorporates into the brain a range of social inputs transmitted through sensory mechanisms. In addition, scientific breakthroughs in neurochemistry have informed the development of an essentialist sexual-addiction model, since, as Patrick Carnes notes, "studies generated greater scientific awareness that addiction could exist within the body's own chemistry."[34] Sexual desire and addiction are thus viewed as coterminus physiological events inside the body.

These models enable addictionologists to explain the intransigence of repetitive problematic sexual behavior. It has been encoded into the hardwiring of the brain. It is not uncommon to hear addictionologists suggest, for example, that our brains spontaneously move into preset programs of activities;[35] that the linchpin of codependency is the inability to change behavior because it has been programmed in as a child;[36] or that male and female brains are crucially different, so that the identical early-childhood trauma can affect a female differently than a male.[37] As we will see, these theoretical perspectives on sexual desire disorders are crucial in that they shape treatment strategies.

Although they occupy considerable space, the brain-centered theories of sexuality are not hegemonic. More recently, sexologists have been divided on the centrality of a biologically based model of desire. Many still adhere to a solidly essentialist theory, and scores of studies claim the androgens as the "libido" hormone.[38] Other sexologists have posited multidimensional models that privilege psychological and cognitive factors as shaping desire.[39] The medical literature frequently describes marital difficulties, fear, and anger as underpinnings of inhibited sexual desire. As Helen Singer Kaplan notes about women who experience ISD in the context of ongoing relational discord, "it is not possible for most people to feel sexual desire for 'the enemy.' "[40] And many addictionologists link sexual addiction and codependency to trauma, child sexual abuse, and a breakdown in spirituality.[41] On infrequent occasions, clinicians will point to the role of broader cultural messages that result in complex and often contradictory imperatives about sex.

Even when these professionals invoke more expansive hypotheses to explain the desire disorders, however, they are largely theoretically located in what anthropologist Carole Vance terms the "cultural influence model."[42] In this view, sexuality, although influenced by culture, is thought to encompass universal forms of expression driven by an inner force or impulse. Vance notes, "Although capable of being shaped, the drive is conceived of as powerful, moving toward expression after its awakening in puberty, sometimes exceeding social regulation, and taking a distinctively different form in men and women."[43] While the cultural-influence model as it appears in professional theories of desire disorders is a marked improvement over rigidly essentialist frameworks, it retains determinist assumptions. And, unlike social construction theory, it leaves unexamined the radical mediation of sexuality by history and culture. Only on rare occasions, for example, do sexologists and addictionologists acknowledge the role of societal norms of sex in shaping desire.

Aside from theoretical congruence concerning the nature and origins of desire, however, both professional cohorts face the challenge of precisely elucidating the parameters of their new diseases. The experts constructing sexual addiction and inhibited sexual desire share a common conceptual and practical problem of definition: the decisive question of how much is too much and how little is too little. This indeterminacy is a familiar dilemma in describing sexual disorders. Kinsey was famous for anecdotally defining the promiscuous individual as "someone who's getting more than you are." Similarly, Masters and Johnson struggled for a reasonable definition of premature ejaculation. For example, given the range of partners a man might have, he might be premature with one partner and not with another.

For ISD and sexual addiction, professionals have given diagnostic weight to outside referents. For sex addicts, repeated criminal offenses can serve as a surrogate marker for the subjective experience of being out of control sexually. An angry and dissatisfied partner is often the impetus for someone to seek professional treatment for ISD. Yet again, the fundamental subjectivity is inescapable, and calls to mind the exchange between Woody Allen's and Diane Keaton's characters in *Annie Hall* when their therapists asked how often they had sex. Woody said, "Hardly ever. Maybe three times a week," while Diane replied, "Constantly. I'd say three times a week." Clinicians admit that, especially with ISD, the concept of desire discrepancy is inevitably relational, so that individuals can easily shift diagnoses, depending on their partner. Ultimately, both ISD and sexual addiction rely heavily on self-diagnosis and serve as beacons for the individual who feels a sense of inadequacy or incongruence with cultural or interpersonal sexual norms. Yet despite its inevitably subjective character, professionals have tried to establish quantifiable frames for their diseases.

The nomenclature committee of the American Psychiatric Association recognized inhibited sexual desire as a clinical entity in 1980 and it was included in the *Diagnostic and Statistical Manual of Mental Disorders* (DSM-III), thus making it an official mental illness. The revised third edition (DSM-IIIR) elaborated this classification further by dividing the disease into two categories: Hypoactive Sexual Desire Disorder and Sexual Aversion Disorder.[44] The definition of HSD is vague but implies that the person must be distressed or that there must be an inherent disadvantage to low sexual interest (anger of a spouse, for example). Helen Singer Kaplan describes HSD as either primary—a rare, lifelong history of asexuality—or secondary, in which there is a loss of sex drive after a history of "normal sexual development." Kaplan describes the typically situational HSD woman as the one who:

> feels very erotic during the many years of her precoital experiences. She felt desire and erotic pleasure during "petting," but she loses sexual interest after she has engaged in coitus, or after marriage, or after childbirth, i.e., in situations which on a symbolic and unconscious level represent danger.[45]

The diagnosis of ISD remains controversial among sexologists, with little consensus regarding operational criteria. Some sexologists have even suggested that the disorder is so vague and the diagnostic boundaries so blurred that ISD, as a "catch-all" diagnosis, represents the schizophrenia of sex therapy.[46] Many negotiate these difficulties with the strategy summarized by sex therapists Sandra Leiblum and Ray Rosen as "you know it when you see it."[47]

Proponents of the sexual addiction diagnosis suffer similar definitional quandaries, resulting in a myriad of checklists and screening questionnaires to determine one's vulnerability. Many subscribe to the AA maxim: If you think you've got a problem, you probably do. The Sexual Dependency Unit at Golden Valley defines sexual addiction as "engaging in obsessive/compulsive sexual behavior which causes severe stress to addicted individuals and their families."[48] Sex becomes the organizing principle of the addict's life, for which anything will be sacrificed. In addition, sexual addiction can include the following behaviors when they have "taken control of addicts' lives and become unmanageable: compulsive masturbation, compulsive heterosexual and homosexual relationships, pornography, prostitution, exhibitionism, voyeurism, indecent phone calls, child molesting, incest, rape and violence."[49] Among the several 12-Step groups, definitions of sexual addiction vary, as do the concepts of what constitutes "sobriety." Yet among both professionals and recovering sex addicts, two themes are consistent. First, whatever the behavior, it is practiced compulsively. And second, the common enemy is lust, which is thought to drive the sexual addiction cycle. In a manner reminiscent of the social-purity movements of earlier centuries, lust is thought to lead the victim into uncontrollable and destructive behavior. Lust, therefore, must be eliminated. Sexaholics Anonymous is perhaps the most restrictive in this sense, in that freedom from lust occupies center stage in the definition of sobriety. The literature states:

> Any form of sex with one's self or with partners other than the spouse is progressively addictive and destructive. Thus, for the married sexaholic, sexual

sobriety means having sex only with the spouse, including no form of sex with one's self. For the unmarried . . . freedom from sex of any kind. For all . . . progressive victory over lust.[50]

Again, as with the social-purity movements, addictionologists view sex as simply one of the falling dominoes in a downward-spiraling cycle of destruction that may include, among other elements, gambling, eating disorders, drugs, and alcohol. One professional, for example, described as vulnerable "a particular kind of woman very involved with fantasy who is a compulsive masturbator, compulsive overeater, and reads romance novels."[51] Addictions are described as multiple and often interchangeable. Ann is another case described in the treatment literature.

Ann spent almost every night in cocktail lounges searching for men. After several years of emotionally empty one night stands, she came to the realization that she and the men she seduced were simply using each other sexually. In desperation she swore off the bar scene and joined her friend Judy in small stakes bingo and card games. Within one month, Ann had identified several high stakes poker and bingo games and had become totally absorbed in her new-found gambling compulsion.[52]

To discourage such symptom substitution, professionals are warned that treatment must include all the addictions. Self-help groups thus cast an ever-widening net to include such compulsions as excessive masturbation, gambling, bingo, and romance novels.

In her landmark, bestselling text, *Women, Sex, and Addiction,* Charlotte Kasl expands the system of addiction even further by intertwining sexual codependency with sexual addiction in women. Codependent (or co-addict) was a term originally created to describe the partner of an alcoholic. Kasl has broadened the definition to refer to a "devastating disease" in which a woman has sex when she doesn't want to, in order to maintain a relationship or placate a partner. Codependency, Kasl notes, is "women's basic programming" and is only a slight exaggeration of the culturally prescribed norm for women.[53]

Despite internal disagreement and confusion among sexologists and addictionologists over the etiology, definitions, and operational criteria of their diseases, some consistent treatment strategies have evolved. These are shaped by the biomedical infrastructure central to the construction of the desire disorders; for, regardless of documented social correlatives such as abuse, power differences in heterosexual relationships, or cultural pressures as possible etiological factors, the disease model of sexual desire disorders retains prominence. Sexual addiction is considered dangerous, and by some, such as Anne Schaef, "a progressive, fatal disease."[54] Likewise, sexologists view inhibited sexual desire as a serious and intractable disease. Unlike the other sexual dysfunctions, it has a poor prognosis with available treatment. Treatment strategies for both sexual addiction and inhibited sexual desire remain steadfastly fixed on the individual (or often in the case of ISD, the couple) with the goal of management, adjustment, or regulation of sexual desire and sexual behavior. The most common interventions are individual or couples therapy, sometimes supplemented with pharmaceuticals. For sexual addiction, 12-Step groups are an essential complement to either inpatient or outpatient treatment.

The professional reliance on organic, neurochemical explanations for both ISD and sexual addiction has predictably led to the search for a "magic bullet," as experts in both fields look hopefully and confidently to the future of neurochemistry for unlocking the determinants of their diseases. Meanwhile, drug treatment is used as an adjunct to treatment for both dysfunctions. The antidepressant drug Wellbtruin was once the great treatment hope for ISD, until it was found to trigger seizures. Now, despite a lack of evidence of efficacy, testosterone is being prescribed for low sexual desire in premenopausal women.[55] Prozac is often prescribed for sex addiction, although there is much controversy and suspicion among sex addicts about using a drug to treat an addiction.

MEDICALIZING DESIRE

In our culture, both disease and desire are medical events, individual experiences, and social signifiers. There is no linear relationship between medical ideology and individual behavior. We are not passively shaped by broader medical ideas; yet neither does our medical discourse directly reflect an internal, universal experience of individuals. The content of medical diagnoses is shaped by social, economic, and political factors. And a both specifically medical and broader cultural ideology operates in the construction of individual experiences of sexual desire. Not simply a biological urge, sexual desire is a culturally constructed composite. It is imperative, therefore, to analyze the contemporary medicalization of sexual desire along these three dimensions.

The nineteenth century marked a shift to scientific investigation of sexual matters. Hence, sexuality has represented a site of expansion and control by the medical profession, with its interests in delineating the nature of sexual impulses and constructing new psychological categories of behavior. The themes in ISD and sexual addiction of sexual conflict, chaos, and disorder are familiar legacies from more than a century of a medical gaze on sexual expression. The invert, the sexual psychopath, the hypersexual female, and the onanist are but some of the historically demonized characters who step from the text of a medical discourse of definition and regulation.[56] It is not surprising, then, that professionals in the late twentieth century would conceptualize concerns regarding sexual desire as major medical problems, since physicians have historically played a significant role not only in the management of sexual behavior but in defining the existence, appropriateness, and ideal object of sexual desire or passion.

Broader societal constructs of desire have largely been based not on the felt experiences of individuals, but on ideological beliefs about sexuality and gender.

For example, permission for any individual woman to experience desire, discuss sexuality, initiate a sexual encounter, or present herself as passionate varies historically and culturally. Carl Degler has documented the variability in nineteenth-century medical-advice literature regarding desire in middle-class women. One theme speaks to the strength of women's passion; another articulates the stereotypic Victorian view that women approach sex "with shrinking, or even with horror, rather than with desire."[57] Further, Nancy Cott has related variations in the dominant ideology about women's passion through the eighteenth and nineteenth centuries not to changes in individual and interpersonal sexual experiences, but to cultural shifts in metaphoric systems about the nature of women. Passionlessness, she argues, transformed women's image in the nineteenth century to one of spirituality, away from the eighteenth-century view of women as lustful creatures prone to sexual excess.[58] The most recent medical constructions of desire disorders reinscribe historically familiar themes of morality, regulation, the ambivalence of pleasure, and the ruin of excess and depravity.

The power of medical ideology in the construction of sexual desire derives from its expansion, its authoritative voice. There must be cultural recognition that desire problems are diseases, with a subsequent adoption of the language and concepts of dysfunction. This process is facilitated by popular representation, and by the early 1990s both ISD and sexual addiction had achieved a certain currency within popular culture. For sufferers of low sexual desire, articles abound on DINS (dual-income, no sex), casting ISD as the latest malady for yuppies too tired from an active day on Wall Street to have sex. And at least one popular self-help manual has appeared; in *Not Tonight, Dear,* the author promises that "the mental nature of desire makes it particularly amenable to improvement through reading."[59] Given that our cultural balance consistently tilts away from pleasure and toward prohibition, the idea of sexual addiction has more thoroughly captured the popular imagination. In addition to the thousands of 12-Step groups, there is a National Sexual Addiction Hotline; the *National Enquirer* reported that Rob Lowe had entered a sexual addiction clinic;[60] and Arnie Becker on *L.A. Law* began to describe his sexual exploits as "satyriasis." The shift in the sexual spirit of our times is perhaps best captured by the book by Erica Jong, *Any Woman's Blues,* in which the central female character is a sex addict who joins a 12-Step group by the end.[61] The *New York Times* ad blazoned, "In the seventies, Erica Jong taught women how to fly . . . now she shows them how to land."[62] Through their widespread dissemination of the concepts of inhibited sexual desire and sexual addiction, these popularizations continually reassert and legitimate the idea that cultural ideologies about appropriate sexual expression are valid medical conditions responsive to individual intervention and cure.

The existence of inhibited sexual desire and sexual addiction as medical diagnoses ensures that proposed solutions will be individual and not structural and cultural. In part ideological, this therapeutic trajectory is also driven by a financial motor, and, clearly, economic incentives are central to medical expansion.

Treatment for sexual desire problems is a vast and lucrative commercial venture. The revenues of Sex and Love Addicts Anonymous, for example, soared to over $100,000 after Hazelden took over distribution of their central text in 1988.[63] Golden Valley Health Center employs an international public relations firm to manage the scores of daily calls received from around the world about the Sexual Dependency Unit. And sexologists report that at least half of the clients coming for sex therapy present with claims of low sexual desire.[64] The large numbers of individuals engaged in treatment for desire problems speaks to the widespread acceptance of medical constructs and the availability of professionals who offer medical diagnosis and treatment. But perhaps most importantly, it indicates the pain and confusion experienced by so many people concerning their sexual desire and behavior.

In this respect, then, it is important to evaluate the medicalization of desire by its therapeutic impact—how the medical creation of the sexual desire disorders operates in the lives of individuals. How does the existence of ISD and sexual addiction as disease entities shape individual experiences of sexuality? Has the creation of these diseases either limited or expanded other options for thinking about sexual desire? What does it mean to someone to take on the identity of a sex addict? If one feels little sexual desire, is it helpful to define that absence as a disease? Does it matter that it is clinicians who will offer the range of answers to the *Cosmo* girl who wonders "how much sex is enough"? While there are anecdotal or clinical reports, the desire disorders are too new for the emergence of a nuanced ethnographic and phenomenological literature on the meanings of these diagnoses for men and women. Some speculation about the broader cultural implications and the limits of individual impact is possible, given our knowledge about the nature of medicalization and of the particular theoretical contours of both inhibited sexual desire and sexual addiction.

The imposition of a biomedical paradigm over social events or problems may suggest potential advantages. These include the increased recognition it promotes and the conceptual framework it offers for worried individuals. Further, a medical diagnosis confers legitimacy on a particular set of difficulties. The seemingly neutral and scientific language of disease may offer palpable relief to those who secretly worry that their sexuality is inadequate or out of control. Especially when the definitional options are those of morality or personal failure, a medical diagnosis may sound more dispassionate and, significantly, admits one to a high-tech arena of research and psychotechnology.[65] According to one clinician, "Lack of desire is like a fever. Something is going on."[66] As with contracting the flu, feeling too much or too little desire is nobody's fault. All that remains is the breakthrough treatment discovery.

Ultimately, however, medical diagnosis offers a false neutrality, for, "as illnesses are social judgments, they are negative judgments."[67] Disease designations connote discomfort, deviance, treatment, and cure. Sexologists and addictionologists, for example, have reified the desire disorders into static and simplistic categories. Diagnostic profiles and checklists are purposely vague so as to be inclusive of a wide range of behaviors. One profile for sexually addicted women includes and indicts behavior as diverse as "multiple and serial relationships; affairs; one night stands; cruising bars, health clubs, etc.; personal columns; masturbation; fantasy; preparing and dramatizing; s/m; exposing; dangerous situations; self abuse; suicidal and homicidal; relationships with sexual compulsive men."[68] The ideal model presented for sexually addicted women is a social purity vision of a spiritually based, monogamous sexuality that is always relationally oriented.[69] Any variation from this is pathologized, and within the sexual addiction field, retro-purity terms have reemerged, such as "promiscuity," "nymphomania," and "womanizer." Accepting the disease model of inhibited sexual desire and sexual addiction in exchange for a moral framework proves, then, to be a bad bargain, for the taint of stigma and deviance inheres in the expansive diagnostic categories.

Reliance on individual treatment solutions remains a major shortcoming of the medical model. In the case of ISD and sexual addiction, the obvious limitation is that, in the absence of social and historical insight, the problem is located within the individual chemistry or psyche and is presumed amenable to medical intervention. The inadequacy of a biomedical approach to treatment of the desire disorders is glaring even when one looks at etiology as defined by the professionals themselves. Despite the preoccupation with lovemaps and brain circuitry, professional literature suggests a broader range of social correlatives. ISD is frequently related to fear, anger, and marital problems; some studies suggest that power struggles and lack of respect are major dynamics for ISD in women.[70] Sexual addiction is linked to childhood sexual trauma.[71] Given this data, a sociohistorical approach to treatment would suggest the need for a more encompassing strategy for change. Yet clinicians articulate no social vision to end sexual abuse, challenge the primacy of the nuclear family, end the double standard, improve sex education, or expose destructive and coercive sexual ideologies. Significantly, there are no treatment outcome studies for sexual addiction, and ISD is widely considered the most difficult sexual problem to treat.

Medicalizing desire, then, cannot really be said to eliminate moral stigma or enhance "cure." Other potential effects are difficult to discern clearly. There is some concern that the message from the proliferation of sexual diseases privileges certain styles of sexual expression and marginalizes others. At least one sex therapist has been critical of the broader therapeutic milieu of sex therapy, whose emphasis on sexual enhancement techniques increases the "pressure we all are under to 'always say yes.' "[72] It is widely recognized that the discourse of sickness can readily become coercive, and there is evidence that this is increasingly true for the sexual dysfunctions.[73] One client in therapy for ISD voiced precisely this complaint about her husband's appropriation of the disease frame:

> But he's got this hang-up about my having to have sex the way he does. "Doesn't it feel good to you?" he asks. So, I rub my earlobe and say, "yeah, and this feels good, too, but I never think about rubbing my earlobe and if I do I

don't say, 'Wow, I can't wait to do it again.'" I like Chinese food, but if I had to go a year without any, I wouldn't be miserable. He says I'm inhibited and don't know it and that I need therapy. When he gets angry he calls me an uptight, frigid bitch, and says I'm sick.[74]

Yet individuals internalize disease models in highly variable ways, and it is important to acknowledge that, despite coercive potential, scores of people report relief and validation from the desire diagnoses. Individuals also negotiate these diagnostic systems idiosyncratically. With sexual addiction, for example, there are clearly individuals who instrumentally select from the menu of treatment options, attending recovery groups for the structure, support, and community, but eschewing the adoption of a full-blown identity. Countless others, however, opt for wholesale acceptance of the addiction ideology as an explanatory device for their fears, and they find solace in their "sobriety" from the disease. The AIDS epidemic has been the perfect impetus for many to define as out of control behavior that once would have been perfectly acceptable to them, and in 1986 the national gay newsmagazine, *The Advocate*, reported that thousands of gay men were reporting that they suffered from the disease of sexual addiction.[75] The out-of-control behavior defined by the men themselves ranged from masturbation once or twice a month (by a devout Catholic) to relentless cruising of peep shows. All claimed to experience great relief through their "sexual recovery plans."

This underscores the importance of individual needs and cultural anxieties in the construction of disease categories. Inhibited sexual desire and sexual addiction serve as contemporary disease categories that help people create meaning out of their sexual experiences. The diagnoses offer the hope of achieving "normalcy" to those who experience their sexual desire as either inadequate or out of control. They are bipolar constructs that map the contradictory cultural landscape of the negotiation and management of appropriate sexuality. These disorders emerged in the mid-1970s and flourish during an era of distinct and palpable tensions regarding sexual norms. They are informed by the dichotomous contemporary ideology in which sex is simultaneously heralded as the linchpin of individual fulfillment and denigrated as the source of chaos, exploitation, and death.

Desire, too, is a cultural trope for both pleasurable satisfaction and dangerous, possibly alien, hunger. Historian Joan Jacobs Brumberg and philosopher Susan Bordo speak to this ambivalence and fear in their analyses of anorexia nervosa.[76] Women are terrified and repelled by visions of themselves as voracious, needy, yearning, and hungering without restraint. "Appetite," Brumberg writes, "is an important voice in female identity."[77] Yet appetite, whether for food or for sex, carries with it the hopes of satisfaction and the fears of wanting too much or of needing and not getting. Desire is not neutral. Cultural attitudes toward high levels of sexual desire reflect this pleasure/danger dichotomy.[78] We are assured by experts on ISD that "an increase in sexual desire is invariably beneficial," since high levels of sexual desire inspire people to exercise, watch their weight, dress with flair, groom themselves carefully, and otherwise operate as healthy, attractive individuals.[79] For sex addicts, however, it is "the athlete's foot of the mind. It never goes away. It always is asking to be scratched, promising relief."[80] Desire, then, will either make you a better person or ruin your life.

These bifurcations, so dramatically visible in this era of sexual epidemics such as AIDS, were apparent in the sexual ethos of the 1970s as well. The glut of media information about sex during that time reflected both a growing openness and an increasing sexological expertise. Further, the public challenges of the feminist and lesbian and gay liberation movements to hetero/sexist imperatives created new sexual space. Many women were empowered not merely to avoid exploitive sex, but to seek out fantasy, orgasms, and thrills. Feminist consciousness-raising groups facilitated both a critique of existing sexual relationships and the exploration of new sexual terrain. A study of married couples in the early 1970s revealed greater sexual experimentation among white couples of all classes. Mainstream books such as *The Joy of Sex, The Sensuous Woman,* and *My Secret Garden* spoke to a new sexual spirit. By the late 1970s, women had become increasingly active partners, and couples were enthusiastically proclaiming the importance of sex to a good relationship.[81]

Yet this sexual enthusiasm was striated with oppositional impulses. The persistence of the double standard thwarted many women pursuing sexual freedom. Feminist organizing drew greater public attention to sexual violence as a mechanism for the social control of women. And the plethora of sexual options touted by sexologists and the media were experienced by many merely as increased pressure. The glaring disjuncture between expectations of an easy sexual pleasure and the realities of failed sex helped create a cultural basis for the successful development of clinical programs of sex therapy. The growing New Right launched challenges to sex education, legalized abortion, and gay liberation, reinscribing notions of abstinence, morality, and sexual self-control on the collective psyche. The calls for sexual restraint became, of course, even more widespead and entrenched throughout the 1980s with the emergence of the AIDS epidemic. On parallel tracks, then, inhibited sexual desire and sexual addiction mark these contradictory themes of sexual freedom contrasted with growing sexual fear and prohibition. Together they constitute a set of regulatory discourses and serve as social signifiers that shape individual experience.

However, medical diagnoses function differently for individuals and may operate fluidly and unpredictably in the culture. While constructed diseases like ISD and sexual addiction may play a central role in the creation and reinforcement of the traditional sociosexual order, the diagnoses also contain the seeds of disruption and opposition. The diagnostic binarisms of inhibition and excess easily suggest gendered sexual norms, and, in fact, early on, the demographics revealed more women diagnosed with ISD, while men largely filled the ranks of sex addicts. The disorders therefore reified a normative system of sex/gender relations. For women, ISD was simply a reformulation of historical diagnoses of frigidity. It implied withholding responsiveness. Conversely, the male sex addict merely occupied a position a few degrees further on the continuum of male sexual energy and aggression.

Currently, the more equivalent gender ratios suggest how, in a cultural moment of instability and ambivalence, the diagnoses of ISD and sexual addiction may signify the manner in which sex/gender boundaries are also being eroded. ISD, as it is recently constructed, draws on feminist assertions of the importance of pleasure and desire for women. Despite its many shortcomings, the diagnosis of ISD can serve as a cultural protest by women, a demand for satisfaction in sex and a refusal to settle for less. Similarly, the construct of sexual addiction is sometimes formulated as a complaint against sexual accommodation and exploitation of women. Feminists in the field claim that addiction often represents women's escape from "the powerless feelings of codependency." Codependency is described as a "disease of inequality," in which oppressed people must understand and accommodate those in power.[82] For these women, then, the struggle against sex addiction is a fundamental challenge to restrictive gender roles. Similarly, some men who identify with either ISD or sex addiction have criticized traditional male sexual expectations. It is too soon to tell whether the male who identifies with ISD will simply be silently ridiculed and despised, while the female sex addict will remain an anomaly destined for *Oprah*. But the new diagnoses clearly allow for more than the simple recuperation of normative roles.

These deconstructions simply suggest that, like the nineteenth-century proliferation of sexualities, the invention of contemporary medical categories is not one-dimensional in effect. Discourse, as Foucault notes, produces and reinforces power but also exposes and destabilizes it.[83] The creation of new sexual disorders reinscribes traditional sex/gender relations, while providing a site for resistance. Central to this resistance, however, is a consistent and sharp awareness of how these new diseases, as signifiers of social relations and anxieties, are generally supportive of dominant political interests and social structures. This is especially true in an era when, as medical experts are asserting guidelines about "safer" and hence "appropriate" sex, many individuals feel more vulnerable and therefore susceptible to medical definition, intervention, and control.

Continual challenge of medical definitions is essential, particularly as the new desire disorders become widespread. For despite the potential for some regrounding of sex/gender relations, the tendencies of medicalization are such that ISD and sex addiction can easily become social practices inimical to the goals of feminism and the lesbian/gay movement. We must remember that in the earlier social-purity movements, feminist themes resounded through movements that were otherwise conservative and anti-sex.[84] The social-purity themes of lust, degradation, and loss of control inherent in the sexual addiction construct should give us pause, particularly, for example, as the model is being suggested as salient to the area of sexual abuse and sex offenders.[85] After decades of scholarship suggesting that power inequities and gender oppression underpin most sexual violence, feminists should be wary of models that suggest that rapists and sexual abusers suffer instead from individual dysfunctions. And despite enthusiastic identification by scores of lesbians and gay men, sex addiction has gotten little, and decidedly negative, attention in the gay press. The one major article in *The Advocate,* entitled "Reinventing the Sex Maniac," rightfully worried that sex addiction was simply a new expression of homophobia and self-hatred.[86]

Inhibited sexual desire and sexual addiction are not demon diagnoses; they have offered validation and community to many. But since the biomedical model is a severely limited paradigm for understanding sexuality on either a social or personal level, it is clearly time for an alternative popular and accessible frame for people to understand their experiences or engage in collective discussion and support for sexual concerns. Progressive movements currently articulate a public and oppositional discourse that inserts the elements of history, cultural ideologies, and power relations into any analysis of sexuality. It is the next challenge for them to create the space for individuals to determine how the personal might be political in their sex lives. Otherwise, the new desire disorders stand as uncontested models in which sexual anxieties, discomfort, and problems inhere in the individual body or psyche, rather than in the body politic.

NOTES

1. Talcott Parsons, "The Sick Role and the Role of the Physician Reconsidered," *Health Society* 53 (1975): 257–78.

2. Michel Foucault, *The History of Sexuality. Vol. 1: An Introduction,* trans. Robert Hurley (New York, 1978), p. 48.

3. John D'Emilio and Estelle B. Freedman, *Intimate Matters: A History of Sexuality in America* (New York, 1988).

4. Foucault, *The History of Sexuality,* p. 33.

5. Elizabeth Fee, "Henry E. Sigerist: From the Social Production of Disease to Medical Management and Scientific Socialism," *The Millbank Quarterly* 67, suppl. 1 (1989).

6. See Sandra R. Leiblum and Raymond C. Rosen, eds., *Sexual Desire Disorders* (New York, 1988), p. vii.

7. See Janice M. Irvine, *Disorders of Desire: Sex and Gender in Modern American Sexology* (Philadelphia, 1990), for this discussion of sexology's history.

8. William H. Masters and Virginia E. Johnson, *Human Sexual Inadequacy* (New York, 1980).

9. Leiblum and Rosen, eds., Introduction, in *Sexual Desire Disorders.*

10. Anthony Pietropinto and Jacqueline Simenauer, *Not Tonight, Dear: How to Reawaken Your Sexual Desire* (New York, 1990).

11. This history is from Richard F. Salmon, "A History of the 12-Step Fellowships for Sexual Addicts and Co-Addicts," National Conference on Sexual Compulsivity/Addiction, Minneapolis, Minnesota, May 21, 1990.

12. Ibid.

13. Richard Solomon, "The Opponent-Process Theory of Acquired Motivation," *American Psychologist* 35 (1980): 691–712.

14. Daniel Goleman, "Some Sexual Behavior Viewed as an Addiction," *New York Times,* October 16, 1984.

15. Audience discussion during Carole G. Anderson, "Assessment and Treatment of the Sexual Dependency, Eating Disorders, Sexual Trauma Complex," National Conference on Sexual Compulsivity/Addiction, Minneapolis, May 20, 1990.

16. Ginger Manley, "Sexual Health Recovery in Sex Addiction: Implications for Sex Therapists," *American Journal of Preventive Psychiatry and Neurology* 3 (1991).

17. Mark Schwartz, "Four Paraphilias: Victim to Victimizer Triumph over Tragedy," National Conference on Sexual Compulsivity/Addiction, Minneapolis, May 20, 1991; and Manley, "Sexual Health Recovery."

18. See Irvine, *Disorders of Desire*, for a discussion of sexology's strategies to achieve professional legitimacy.

19. Leiblum and Rosen, eds., Introduction, in *Sexual Desire Disorders*.

20. Goleman, "Some Sexual Behavior."

21. Craig Rowland, "Reinventing the Sex Maniac," *The Advocate*, January 21, 1986, 45.

22. Judy Foreman, "Drugs May Help Sex Offenders," *Boston Globe*, March 5, 1984.

23. Goleman, "Some Sexual Behavior."

24. John Money and Margaret Lamacz, *Vandalized Lovemaps: Paraphilic Outcome of Seven Cases in Pediatric Sexology* (Buffalo, 1989).

25. Rene J. Dubos, *Mirage of Health* (New York, 1959).

26. Jeffrey Weeks, *Against Nature: Essays on History, Sexuality, and Identity* (London, 1991), p. 70.

27. See Jeffrey Weeks, *Sex, Politics, and Society: The Regulation of Sexuality since 1800* (New York, 1981); Weeks, *Against Nature*; and Irvine, *Disorders of Desire*.

28. Weeks, *Against Nature,* p. 70.

29. Helen Singer Kaplan, *Disorders of Sexual Desire and Other New Concepts and Techniques in Sex Therapy* (New York, 1979), p. 9.

30. Ibid., p. 78.

31. Ibid., p. 25.

32. Weeks, *Against Nature,* p. 70.

33. Money and Lamacz, *Vandalized Lovemaps,* p. 43.

34. Patrick J. Carnes, "Sexual Addiction: Progress, Criticism, Challenges," *American Journal of Preventive Psychiatry and Neurology* 2/3 (1990): 1.

35. Ian Forster, "Co-dependency: A New Description and Theory—A Correlation between Co-dependency and the Development of Addictive Disease," National Conference on Sexual Compulsivity/Addiction, Minneapolis, Minnesota, May 21, 1991.

36. Ibid.

37. Schwartz, "Four Paraphilias."

38. Leiblum and Rosen, eds., Introduction, in *Sexual Desire Disorders*.

39. See ibid., for the parameters of this debate.

40. Kaplan, *Disorders of Sexual Desire,* p. 90.

41. See, for example, Patrick Carnes, *Out of the Shadows: Understanding Sexual Addiction* (Minnesota, 1983); and Charlotte Kasl, *Women, Sex, and Addiction: A Search for Love and Power* (New York, 1989).

42. Carole S. Vance, "Anthropology Rediscovers Sexuality: A Theoretical Comment," *Social Science and Medicine* 33 (1991): 875–84.

43. Ibid., p. 878.

44. Leiblum and Rosen, eds., Introduction, in *Sexual Desire Disorders*.

45. Kaplan, *Disorders of Sexual Desire,* pp. 63–64.

46. Cited in *Sexual Desire Disorders,* ed. Leiblum and Rosen, p. 9.

47. Leiblum and Rosen, eds., *Sexual Desire Disorders,* p. 8.

48. "Sexual Addiction," brochure of the Golden Valley Health Center.

49. Ibid.

50. Quoted in Richard Salmon, "Twelve-Step Resources for Sexual Addicts and Co-Addicts," National Association on Sexual Addiction Problems of Colorado, 1989.

51. Keziah Hinchen and Anne McBean, "Sexually Compulsive or Addicted Women," National Conference on Sexual Compulsivity/Addiction, Minneapolis, May 21, 1990.

52. Marvin A. Steinberg, "Sexual Addiction and Compulsive Gambling," *American Journal of Preventive Psychiatry and Neurology* 2/3 (1990): 40.

53. Kasl, *Women, Sex, and Addiction.*

54. Anne Wilson Schaef, *Escape from Intimacy: The Pseudo-Relationship Addictions* (San Francisco, 1989), p. 34.

55. See Irvine, *Disorders of Desire*, for a discussion of ISD and drug treatment.

56. Gayle Rubin, "Thinking Sex: Notes for a Radical Theory of the Politics of Sexuality," in *Pleasure and Danger: Exploring Female Sexuality*, ed. Carole S. Vance (Boston, 1984), pp. 267–318.

57. Carl Degler, "What Ought to Be and What Was: Women's Sexuality in the Nineteenth Century," in *Women and Health in America: Historical Readings*, ed. Judith Walzer Leavitt (Madison, 1984), pp. 40–56.

58. Nancy Cott, "Passionlessness: An Interpretation of Victorian Sexual Ideology, 1790–1850," in *Women and Health in America*, ed. Leavitt, pp. 57–69.

59. Pietropinto and Simenauer, *Not Tonight, Dear*, p. 6.

60. "Rob Lowe in Sex Addiction Clinic," *National Enquirer*, June 5, 1990.

61. Erica Jong, *Any Woman's Blues* (New York, 1990).

62. *New York Times Book Review*, February 4, 1990.

63. Salmon, "A History."

64. See Leiblum and Rosen, eds., *Sexual Desire Disorders*; and Pietropinto and Simenauer, *Not Tonight, Dear.*

65. S. Chorover, "Big Brother and Psychotechnology," *Psychology Today*, October 1973: 43–54.

66. Pietropinto and Simenauer, *Not Tonight, Dear*, p. 4.

67. Peter Conrad and Joseph W. Schneider, *Deviance and Medicalization: From Badness to Sickness* (St. Louis, 1980), p. 31.

68. Handout from Keziah Hinchen and Anne McBean, "Sexually Compulsive or Addicted Women."

69. See Kasl, *Women, Sex, and Addiction.*

70. See Irvine, *Disorders of Desire*, for an expansion of this argument.

71. See Kasl, *Women, Sex, and Addiction,* and press release from Golden Valley Health Center, 1990.

72. Bernard Apfelbaum, "An Ego-Analytic Perspective on Desire Disorders," in *Sexual Desire Disorders*, ed. Leiblum and Rosen, p. 78.

73. See Irvine, *Disorders of Desire*, for a broader examination of these issues.

74. Pietropinto and Simenauer, *Not Tonight, Dear*, p. 20.

75. Rowland, "Reinventing the Sex Maniac."

76. Joan Jacobs Brumberg, *Fasting Girls: The History of Anorexia Nervosa* (New York, 1988); and Susan Bordo, "Anorexia Nervosa: Psychopathology as the Crystallization of Culture," in *Feminism and Foucault: Reflections on Resistance,* ed. Irene Diamond and Lee Quinby (Boston, 1988), pp. 87–118.

77. Brumberg, *Fasting Girls,* p. 265.

78. Vance, ed., *Pleasure and Danger.*

79. Pietropinto and Simenauer, *Not Tonight, Dear*, pp. 15–16.

80. Carnes, *Out of the Shadows,* p. vii.

81. See Irvine, *Disorders of Desire*, for a discussion of these cultural patterns.

82. Kasl, *Women, Sex, and Addiction,* p. 31.

83. Foucault, *The History of Sexuality.*

84. See Ellen Carol DuBois and Linda Gordon, "Seeking Ecstasy on the Battlefield: Danger and Pleasure in Nineteenth-Century Feminist Sexual Thought," in *Pleasure and Danger,* ed. Vance, pp. 31–49; and Margaret Hunt, "The De-Eroticization of Women's Liberation: Social Purity Movements and the Revolutionary Feminism of Sheila Jeffries," *Feminist Review* 34 (1990): 23–46.

85. Judith Lewis Herman, "Considering Sex Offenders: A Model of Addiction," *Signs: Journal of Women in Culture and Society* 13 (1988): 695–724.

86. Rowland, "Reinventing the Sex Maniac."

HOTTENTOT 2000

Jennifer Lopez and Her Butt

MAGDALENA BARRERA

> Jennifer Lopez's big break may have been as a frizzy-haired, brunette fly-girl on *In Living Color*, but take one look at her new sleek, sophisticated look and the difference is black and white.
>
> —*Glamour*

One need not have seen all or even part of the 2000 Grammy Awards show to have heard about Jennifer Lopez and "The Dress." Hot off Donatella Versace's pret-a-porter line, it was a sea-green, see-through chiffon splash of a tropical leaf pattern, of which all $10,000 worth draped gracefully to the floor. It had a daringly low-cut V neck that extended several inches below her navel, where it barely fastened with a sparkly brooch, and then opened out again, exposing all of her legs. Thus, the popular Puerto Rican celebrity announced the first award of the evening, standing nearly naked in what some have called a "glorified bathrobe." Yet even in an industry in which most starlets show off their bodies in random states of undress, Lopez caused a sensation like no other. Indeed, "the Versace dress caused stunned chatter because of what it threatened to reveal: a womanly body of breathtaking proportions."[1]

What is not at all stunning is that so much attention should be focused on Lopez and her body. Since the beginning of her career, journalists have filled magazine and newspaper articles with references to, and puns on, the word "butt." Interestingly enough, what rarely receives mention is her race; when it is noted, it is from a distance, as in "Jennifer Lopez, of Puerto Rican *descent*" or "whose *parents* are from Puerto Rico." No one seems to be able to say, "Jennifer Lopez *is*

Puerto Rican." Instead, what we read is along the lines of "Jennifer Lopez, whose spectacular ass juts out as expressively as her swollen mouth, is terrific."[2]

Such discourse easily inspires comparisons between Lopez and the most famous nineteenth-century butt, that of Saartje Baartman, better known as the "Hottentot Venus." Lopez shares with Baartman the fact that no one needs to mention race, precisely because their butts are shorthand for "otherness." This single body part comes to represent them and, by extension, racialized sexuality. While Lopez has been the subject of much media and even academic attention, few authors have placed her body in historical context and in direct dialogue with discourse regarding Baartman. Indeed, if we take a closer look at how Lopez herself discusses the issues and how she has had a hand in shaping the discourse on her own rear, we can appreciate the general difficulties mainstream culture has in thinking critically about race and sexuality. Lopez occupies a curious place in the U.S. entertainment industry: while she might be imagined as a variety of ethnic "types"—anything from various kinds of Latina to Apache to Italian—that somehow magically transcend certain class markers, she is simultaneously and consistently racialized via her butt.

DOIN' DA BUTT

The first and foremost question to be asked at this point is: Why the butt? Indeed, the body generally has been the subject of fascination and discussion at both popular and academic levels throughout history. For example, in *Discipline and Punish*, Foucault describes in detail the eighteenth-century drive to organize and discipline the body, to make it productive and therefore subjected. "Docile" bodies are those that can be molded to stay in synch with social norms; the bodies that fail to fall in line are the ones that must be punished.[3] Nowadays, one such way of "disciplining" the body includes aesthetic surgery, or attempting to disguise what are thought to be troublesome parts of the body, in part because the "boundaries between the beautiful and the ugly, between the happy and the unhappy, are also those between the erotic and unerotic."[4] People fixate on the body because they equate happiness with sexual attractiveness. Given my focus on Lopez and Hollywood, what I would add here is that not only is the "unerotic" disguised by plastic surgery, but the body is "sculpted" by specialized, highly paid trainers who go by one name—like Radu (Lopez's trainer). The butt is the one body part that everyone focuses on "sculpting," in part because "the buttocks have ever-changing symbolic value. They are associated with the organs of reproduction, with the aperture of excretion, as well as with the mechanism of locomotion through discussions of gait. They never represent themselves. . . . When aesthetic surgery is performed upon the buttocks, it is to enhance their sexual attraction."[5] Should one "fail" to discipline one's body and meet the standards of mainstream beauty, not only does society deal punishment, but one is compelled to take action as well, particularly in Hollywood entertainment circles. For instance, British model/actress Elizabeth Hurley recently has remarked,

"I've always thought Marilyn Monroe looked fabulous, but I'd kill myself if I was that fat."[6]

Psyche and self-esteem are not the only elements that make up the symbolic value of the butt. Laura Kipnis, in "(Male) Desire and (Female) Disgust: Reading *Hustler*," attempts to bring notions of class and social norms to discussions of sexuality (specifically, the porn versus erotica debates of mainstream U.S. feminism). In comparison with magazines such as *Playboy* and *Penthouse*, *Hustler* stands out because the body featured on its pages "is often a gaseous, fluid-emitting, *embarrassing* body, one continually defying the strictures of bourgeois manners and mores and instead governed by its lower intestinal tract—a body threatening to erupt at any moment."[7] While Kipnis certainly does not suggest that the content of *Hustler* in any way represents a progressive political project, she points out that the depiction of unsettling bodies has the important effect of unsettling class. "Given that control over the body has long been associated with the bourgeois political project, . . . *Hustler*'s insistent and repetitious return to the iconography of the body out of control, rampantly transgressing bourgeois norms and sullying bourgeois property and proprieties, raises certain political questions."[8] In other words, the bourgeoisie tries to mirror in the upper and lower halves of their bodies the same distance they would like to have between themselves and the lower, working classes. Thus working-class-affiliated cultural productions like *Hustler* can use butts as a "critique of dominant ideology."[9] In embarrassed laughter, the low succeeds in asserting its authority over the high, and challenging its traditionally inferior position.

Yet the one element that is absent from Kipnis's discussion is race, which would have enlarged the scope of her very useful remarks in intriguing and crucial ways. Specifically, there is a need to relate Latina bodies to her discussion of "an homology between the lower bodily stratum and the lower social classes—the reference to the body being invariably a reference to the social."[10] Many white feminists have ways of universalizing their own notions of what is pleasurable versus what ventures into the realm of pornography or the grotesque, without noting that these preferences are culturally specific. In Latino communities—especially Caribbean ones—butts are "huge," in terms of size and popularity. *Hustler* is not unique in highlighting the "lower bodily stratum" as a sight of contestation—Latinos self-consciously do this on a daily basis.

Fortunately, Puerto Rican movie critic Frances Negrón-Muntaner goes where Kipnis would not dare. In her article with its to-the-point title, "Jennifer's Butt," she explains, "A big culo [butt] does not only upset hegemonic (white) notions of beauty and good taste, it is a sign for the dark, incomprehensible excess of 'Latino' and other African diaspora cultures. . . . A big Latin rear end is an invitation to pleasures construed as illicit by puritan ideologies, heteronormativity, and the medical establishment through the three deadly vectors of miscegenation, sodomy, and a high-fat diet."[11] What is construed as illicit in mainstream white society, then, is not necessarily so in Latino communities in and out of the United States, where *culos* are good, the site of much pleasure, affection, and attention. In Brazil, for example, *Playboy* is filled not with glossy images of soft-focused breasts, but instead with glossy, soft-focused butts. Similarly, many young Latinos joke that that one can predict the quality of a merengue or salsa CD by how much of a woman's butt is featured on the cover (the more, the better). Moreover, most of the popular Latin American dances—merengue, salsa, samba, lambada, cumbia, rumba—prominently feature the exclusive wiggling of the lower strata (hands, shoulders and chests are not as important). Appreciation of the butt in song and dance is common in African-American communities as well. Humorous songs like Sir Mix-A-Lot's "Baby Got Back" and EU's "Doin' da Butt" offer further evidence of this cultural force.

THE HOTTENTOT VENUS

Race adds much to the discussion of what buttocks mean, and how they can act as shorthand for "non-whiteness." No one's buttocks inspired more discussion, analysis, and controversy regarding racial difference than those of Saartje Baartman, the young Khoikhoi woman from southwestern Africa whose body was exhibited throughout Europe in the early 1800s. Fascination with her body ran so deep that after her death, doctors dissected her body and preserved the parts—specifically, her genitals—in order to continue displaying them. Her steatopygia, or protruding buttocks caused by fat deposits, was common among Khoikhoi females, but clearly did not fall into contemporaneous European notions of beauty. In fact, Europeans understood her body as pathology. When they paid to see her "perform"—she was held in a cage and made to dance half-naked in order to receive any food—"some spectators [requested] that a 'real' European woman be present to mediate the encounter with this potentially horrific and monstrous sight."[12] People were so perplexed upon seeing her that they debated whether she was even human.

Despite the horror, or perhaps because of it, Baartman became a collection of sexual parts that stood in for "blackness." The logic of the time determined that not only did black women look different in terms of skin color, but also that their bodies were made differently. Their overdeveloped buttocks "proved" that they were hypersexual. Blackness became a metaphor for "deviant sexuality." For instance, in *Difference and Pathology*, Sander Gilman includes drawings of European prostitutes whose lasciviousness is represented in grossly exaggerated Hottentot-style buttocks. Later, in his history of aesthetic surgery, *Making the Body Beautiful*, Gilman contends, "Beginning with the expansion of European colonial exploration, describing the forms and size of the buttocks became a means of describing and classifying the races. The more prominent, the more primitive. . . . This is a continuation of the cultural presupposition that 'primitive' races have a 'primitive' sexuality, which is represented in their bodies by physical signs of their 'true' nature."[13] This is an excellent example of how we cannot afford to ignore class and race in our understanding of buttocks. Because of her race, Baartman cannot move into the realm of bourgeois sociosexual norms as described by Kipnis. As one scholar explains, "it is both the horror of too much to see, of genital excess, and her Blackness (according to aesthetic and philosophical treatises of the period) that, in tandem, inhibit her movement from 'exhibition' to the space of 'chaste retreat' (which is the space of Whiteness)."[14]

Perhaps the saddest part of Baartman's story is the fact that she had no say in how she was shown; nothing was recorded of her voice. Feminist scholars and artists have attempted to recuperate it. Elizabeth Alexander chooses Baartman as the narrator of one of her poems. In "Venus Hottentot," she writes,

> Since my own genitals are public
> I have made other parts private.
> In my silence I possess
> mouth, larynx, brain, in a single gesture.
> . . . If he were to let me rise up
> from this table, I'd spirit
> his knives and cut out his black heart,
> seal it with science fluid inside
> a bell jar, place it on a low
> shelf in a white man's museum
> so the whole world could see
> it was shrivelled and hard,
> geometric, deformed, unnatural.[15]

Unfortunately, all that remains of Baartman—aside from her body parts still languishing in glass jars—are medical drawings and newspaper cartoons and accounts of her shows. Because these are written and drawn by white men, discourse regarding her focuses only on what were imagined to be her deformities and sexual habits. She died at twenty-five years of age, after being displayed by an animal showman for fifteen months.[16]

I'M EVERY WOMAN

Jennifer Lopez, on the other hand, was only starting to come into her superstardom at the age of twenty-five. Aside from Broadway legend Rita Moreno, through the mid-1990s, few people knew of successful and highly recognizable Puerto Rican female entertainers. While Rosie Perez enjoyed a measure of success on-screen, she seemed to be stuck playing loud and heavily Bronx-accented, money-hungry Latina girlfriends in films like *Do the Right Thing* and *White Men Can't Jump*. Lopez spent the better part of the decade working her way up from dancing professionally (with the Fly Girls on Fox's *In Living Color*) to TV pilots (*South Central* and *Second Chances*), eventually earning small roles in Hollywood movies (*Jack* and *Money Train*). Her big break came in 1997 with the starring role in Gregory Nava's biopic, *Selena*, which established her name in Latino households throughout the United States. But it was her role as FBI agent Karen

Sisco, opposite George Clooney in *Out of Sight*, that made her visible not only to mainstream white audiences, but also as the highest paid Latina actor in history. She banked on this success to take time off from movie-making to record an album. *On the 6* quickly rose on the *Billboard* charts, in part thanks to videos that afford Lopez the opportunity to dance in tight pants, short skirts, and otherwise show off her amazing body.

Though Lopez is becoming ever more a sensation, a June 2000 photo spread in *Vanity Fair* entitled "La Vida Lopez" reveals two very distinct Jennifers. In one photo, Lopez poses aristocratically in Oscar de la Renta haute couture, while two men dressed in eighteenth-century livery serve her a glass of red wine. Then, in the other, she dances in a low-cut, wispy blue dress on a tabletop, and is surrounded by brightly clad, clapping Latino men. As they cheer her on, she joyously lifts her arms in the air, and a breeze blows her dress in just such a way that her butt and hips look huge—beyond sensuously rounded, and venturing into the realm of Hottentot caricature. Our gaze is naturally drawn to her butt by the hands of the man standing behind her; caught in a mid-clap, his hands look as if they are about to squeeze her butt. A caption calmly explains, "Lopez is equally at ease with the socialites who populate the Metropolitan Museum's Costume Institute Benefit and the posses of the hip-hip world."[17] The observation is ironic; perhaps Lopez does manage to feel at ease in both worlds, but are viewers just as comfortable? What does it mean to see the sexualized, dance-salsa-on-the-tabletop Jennifer alongside the high-class, costume-benefit one? Why must the photographer mark her butt so obviously? And why does Lopez allow herself to be photographed in such a way?

As in the case of Baartman, discussion of Lopez's butt is a substitution for race, though mainstream audiences, and even Lopez herself, claim to move beyond it. "It's not a question of, are people ready to see a Latina actress in big movies," explains the director of *Out of Sight*. "The point is, people are ready to see *Jennifer* in high-profile movies."[18] Lopez affirms this line of thinking. "My managers and agents and I realized that I'm not white . . . so I've always wanted to show that I could play any kind of character. Not only a range of emotions, but also race-wise."[19] However, despite her talents to win such non-race-specific roles, her body is an undeniable factor in the roles she does get, and the difficulties she encounters in Hollywood. Lopez observes, "It's not like you can hide [my butt]. But when I get in with the wardrobe designer, they're thinking, 'Let's see, she's looking a little hippy. She's got a big butt, what should we do?' They're always trying to minimize it—put it that way—and it's because we all see these actresses who are so thin and white. . . . Latinas and black women have a certain body type. We're curvy."[20] Because of her backside, outfitters can barely imagine how to dress her for an everywoman role. Her commentary on her body wavers between celebration and exasperation, revealing a tension deeper than that openly discussed in interviews.

Discourse on Lopez's backside rarely is put into historical frame, or in context with the racialized meanings ascribed to it. When one reporter asked her to trace the beginnings of the public's obsession with her butt, she answered, "I think it started with *Selena* and all those tight pants."[21] However, Lopez might have thought about her answer a little more, because even when she was on *In Living Color* during the early 1990s, she already was talking about her rear. An early newspaper feature noted of the young dancer, "Jennifer Lopez loves the designers [the Fly Girls] get to wear. . . . But then there are her . . . hips. 'I'm real funny about what goes on my hips . . . I have a big butt,' she explains."[22] Even before she found wider recognition and success, her efforts to transcend race were hampered by her butt and its long-predetermined cultural codes. The same articles that quote her desire to win roles that call "for a 'woman' with interesting problems and such" identify her primarily as "young, tough, sexy and Latina."[23] Her butt makes such a description redundant.

Lopez often humbly frames discussions of her butt in terms of her own self-esteem: "I love my butt and I was never ashamed of it, and I guess not being ashamed of something like that, which is uncharacteristic, made it become a focal point."[24] Yet according to Negrón-Muntaner, those buttocks come to represent something much larger. She argues that Lopez's success as the highest-paid Latina actress ever represents a three-part victory for the Puerto Rican community as a whole: " 'showing ass' as a sign of identity and pride, 'kiss my ass' as a form of revenge against a hostile cultural gaze, and 'I'm going to kick your ass' vis-à-vis the economic exploitation implicated in racism."[25] While Negrón-Muntaner's comments may be true, there is still the danger that Lopez reifies and reaffirms the stereotype of the spicy, oversexed Latina. When one reporter asked Lopez how she would like people to think of her, she responded, "The 'Butt Girl.' . . . It's all me and men love it."[26] At this point, we must ponder a number of important questions: How do we distinguish celebration/appreciation from a racialized trap? Would a greater awareness of cultural codes on Lopez's part make any difference to what her body comes to represent for Latinas and sexuality generally? As one Los Angeles producer quipped, "One false move, and she's Charo."[27] In other words, she must do some fancy footwork in order to avoid being written off as a ridiculously hypersexual Hollywood sideshow.

Lopez certainly must be aware of her tenuous position as the highest-paid Latina celebrity. While her butt has brought her much attention and success, she cannot let it get out of control—she must continue to discipline it. After her stint as a Fly Girl, she decided to try acting, but her manager suggested that she first lose some weight. "The very next day she had a trainer and was out jogging. She knew she had to or she'd be a fat girl."[28] When she did emerge into the limelight, flurries of newspapers and magazine articles—with titles such as "Plus-Size Posteriors Fashion Forward?"; "Lopez Defines Sensuality without Being Razor Thin"; and "The Curve Is Back"—heralded the end of the waif look. Though some women's magazines featured her alongside full-figured actress Camryn Manheim rather than fellow starlet Cameron Diaz, Lopez claimed not to mind. "I don't take it as an insult, because they're identifying me as a real person."[29] Yet moments later, she shares her typical meals: egg whites in the morning, carbs for lunch, and a salad for dinner. "I think it's so funny that people look at me and say, 'Oh, bigger bodies are okay. I can eat now,' because I watch my diet and exercise an hour and a half every day."[30] The fact that in her latest videos Lopez's butt appears to be shrinking has led some to speculate whether she finally is feeling the pressure of conforming to Hollywood's obsession with thinness. She has begun insisting, "I'm not big, I'm in shape. I don't eat all I want. I work really hard to have my body the way it is."[31] She is fighting not only to keep her butt in line and on the good side of "erotic," but also to influence how people identify her — as another sexy Latina.

BABY GOT BACK

What comes through in more recent interviews is the fact that Lopez may be starting to regret all the emphasis on her butt, as well as the fact that she might not have the love–love relationship with it that she claims. Her tone has changed: "at the mention of it, Lopez groans, 'Enough already.' "[32] As for her status as one of the sexiest stars, with the most-talked-about derriere in America, Lopez sounds a philosophical note: "I understood it because I brought it out at first. I would talk about my butt to interviewers. I guess people picked up on it, and now they concentrate on it. The media is driving it into the ground."[33] It is interesting to note that race never enters either Lopez's or the reporters' vocabulary. "The media" is indeed to blame, insofar as it is a reflection of ideology. And what taking a closer look at ideology would tell us is that the butt continues to be as powerful a cultural symbol as it was in Baartman's day. It functions as shorthand for race exactly it did two hundred years ago.

Apparently only one journalist, Dream Hampton, makes a clear connection between the objectification of Lopez's rear and "white America's gaze on ethnic bodies." In fact, she even relates to Lopez the story of Baartman. The Puerto Rican star "responds appropriately, I guess. 'That's disgusting.' " Hampton continues,

> It's not really [Lopez's] responsibility to contextualize other people's fetishes (or some ancient girl's containment). When a miscellaneous white-boy late-night-talk-show host makes comments bordering on lewd but meant to be complimentary about her ass, why not smile and work it? When she says, kind of finally, 'I glorify in the fact that my mother bore me and I came out with her body,' I'm certainly ready to throw a prideful fist in the air. But there is always reason to be suspicious when objectification gets tangled with celebration and your very cultural body part damn near requires its own publicist. 'I would love to read an article where it's not even mentioned,' she sighs. Sorry.[34]

Hampton's article, "Boomin' System," does an excellent job of coolly taking Lopez to task for not responding more critically to the attention on her ass. The ironic "she responds appropriately, I guess" reveals at least one author's disappointment with her reaction to Hottentot history. Similarly, the curious, distancing aside referring to "some ancient girl's containment" points us toward Lopez's apparent unwillingness to mark the similarities between Baartman and herself. Thus, she very much considers attention given to her ass to be a nuisance to her career, if only because by now all that talk is tiresome and played out. Can't people just get over it?

Just as was the case with Baartman, Lopez has tremendous difficulty moving back into the realm of the chaste (not that it would even be possible for a Latina with a butt like hers to do so). The public remains hungry for and fascinated by her ass. Following her cover feature in one popular men's magazine, the only printed response to the interview complained, "You guys are criminals! How can you feature Jennifer Lopez and not show even a little of her backside?"[35] Apparently, Lopez posing in a wet tube top did not provide enough titillation for some readers. People expect to see her butt, and are surprised when they do not see it. Many were disappointed to note that in her last movie Lopez looked skinnier; journalists scrambled for explanations. Reporter Jeannie Williams wrote, "Jennifer Lopez is known for her generous derriere, and she's proud of it. But in *Out of Sight*, she's nothing but slim. Director Steven Soderbergh said . . . that he didn't go out of his way to slenderize her."[36] Hmm. Where could her butt have gone? "The body she once proudly described in *Movieline* magazine as 'the shape of a guitar' is now as thin as a reed instrument."[37] For some audiences, this may signify that she is somehow less Latina now.

Such discourse leads us to doubt whether Hollywood and the people to whom it caters are aware of Lopez's victories (as outlined by Negrón-Muntaner), or envision themselves as kissing her ass in any way. Even though many magazine editors have hailed her as the "new American face"—a curious phrase in itself—the butts of other stars are never featured so prominently. If anything, they are like Elizabeth Shue and Gretchen Moll on the covers of *Vanity Fair*, smiling coyly, wearing see-through sweaters and gauzy camisoles, hinting at the flesh and nipples underneath. Meanwhile, Jennifer poses inside, foot tapping, and hand on butt.[38]

Race is essential to our understanding of how body parts represent one's sexuality. No one is interested in seeing or talking about the butts of white celebrities. On the other hand, a healthy Puerto Rican butt like Lopez's points to something "different" racially. Even supermodel Cindy Crawford has paused to wonder why she cannot be as brazen as Lopez in showing off her butt: "Is it cultural? I mean, what was it that she was given in confidence that I wasn't?"[39] Indeed, perhaps it was in the food Lopez ate as a little girl, as Sir Mix-A-Lot (humorously and ironically) suggests about big-butt girls: "Red beans and rice didn't miss her—baby got back!" The source of such difference is understood to lie with Lopez: it's something "in her nature," in her biological race, not in an ideology or a notion of race that takes into account its social construction.

Most people will continue to attribute their fascination with her attention-grabbing buttocks to other reasons: "[Lopez] is a visual flash point for our cultural conflict between beauty and sexuality—in short, our modern-day reverse

Puritanism."[40] Whether or not one believes that such "reverse Puritanism" actually exists, beauty and sexuality continue to be defined so that "normal" is synonymous with "white." Throughout her success, Lopez has been well on her way to becoming a fetish—people displace their desires onto her for a variety of historical, economic, and sexual reasons. How wonderful for Jennifer that she is shaking her booty all the way to the bank, but we must wonder how comforting this is for those Latina and black women who are told that they are just plain old "fat." We cannot dismiss the ironic and complex ways that race and gender collude in moments past and present: Baartman lived a life physically contained, making money for someone else; today Lopez pretends to contain her butt and is able to make money for herself. Nevertheless it seems that no one can look away from the body part that is the source of their fame.

NOTES

1. Robin Givhan, "Jennifer Lopez Astonishes Many with Her Fashion Moxie, Fit Body," *The Plain Dealer*, March 2, 2000, F3.

2. Kelvin Tong, "Curvy? Butt It's in the History Books," *The Straits Times*, October 15, 1998, L7, quoting a *Los Angeles Weekly* film reviewer.

3. Michel Foucault, "Docile Bodies," in *The Foucault Reader*, ed. Paul Rabinow (New York, 1984), pp. 180–82.

4. Sander Gilman, "After the Nose," in *Making the Body Beautiful: A Cultural History of Aesthetic Surgery* (Princeton, 1999), p. 206.

5. Ibid., p. 215.

6. Patricia Falvo, "The Hurley Burly," *Allure*, January 2000: 52.

7. Laura Kipnis, "(Male) Desire and (Female) Disgust: Reading *Hustler*," in *Cultural Studies*, ed. Lawrence Grossberg, Cary Nelson, and Paula A. Treichler (New York, 1992), p. 375. Emphasis in original.

8. Ibid., p. 376.

9. Ibid.

10. Ibid.

11. Frances Negrón-Muntaner, "Jennifer's Butt," *Aztlán* 22 (1997): 189.

12. Richard Collin Green, "The (Outer) Limits of Femininity: The 'Hottentot Venus,'" in "Figuring Resistance: Black Bodies, Buttocks and Hottentot Venus" (Ph.D. diss., New York University, 1999), p. 7.

13. Gilman, "After the Nose," p. 212.

14. Green, "The (Outer) Limits of Femininity," p. 11.

15. Elizabeth Alexander, *The Venus Hottentot* (Charlottesville, 1990), pp. 6–7. Quoted in Green, "The (Outer) Limits of Femininity."

16. Green, "The (Outer) Limits of Femininity," p. 2.

17. Evgenia Peretz, "La Vida Lopez," *Vanity Fair*, June 2000: 171.

18. David Handelman, "A Diva Is Born," *Mirabella*, July–August 1998: 84. Emphasis in original.

19. Ibid., p. 82.

20. Christopher Goodwin, "Bum's the Word," *Sunday Times*, September 20, 1998: 1.

21. Brantley Bardin, "Woman of the Year: Jennifer Lopez," *Details*, December 1998: 199.

22. Elizabeth Snead, "For the Fly Girls, Designer Duds Are for Dancing," *USA Today*, May 3, 1993: D6.

23. Robert Dominguez, "Fly Girl Boards 'Money Train,'" *Daily News*, November 17, 1995: 65.

24. Bardin, "Woman of the Year," p. 199.

25. Negrón-Muntaner, "Jennifer's Butt," p. 187.

26. Goodwin, "Bum's the Word," p. 2.

27. Bob Morris, "Could This Be Love?" *Talk*, March 2000: 88.

28. Ibid., p. 89.

29. Elysa Gardner, "She's All That," *InStyle* 6 (June 1999): 281. In order to appreciate the ideal female figures in the entertainment industry, please note that the same issue of *InStyle* magazine that featured Lopez on the cover (June 1999) also ran a photo spread entitled "Asset Management." It gave advice on how to dress various body types, and offered a popular young Hollywood actress as an example of each. Readers learn that Winona Ryder is "petite and curvy," Ashley Judd is "sensuously rounded," and super-thin Gwyneth Paltrow is "small and perfect" (pp. 266–74).

30. "Ooh La Lopez," *Cosmopolitan* 226 (March 1999).

31. Jennifer Tung, "Shaking Her Booty," *New York Post*, February 29, 2000: 2.

32. Gardner, "She's All That," pp. 276–77.

33. Stephen Schaefer, "Lopez Is Steaming up the Charts," *USA Today*, June 15, 1999: D12.

34. Dream Hampton, "Boomin' System," *Vibe*, August 1999: 104.

35. "Letters," *Details*, February 1999: 24.

36. Jeannie Williams, "Jennifer Lopez: She's Proud of Her 'Bottom Line,'" *USA Today*, July 2, 1998: D14.

37. Tung, "Shaking Her Booty," p. 1.

38. Kevin Sessums, "Nimby Girl," *Vanity Fair*, July 1998: 114.

39. "Buzzwords," *Hispanic* (January–February 1999): 12.

40. Barbara Thomas, "Lopez Defines Sensuality without Being Razor-Thin," *Los Angeles Times*, March 3, 2000: E3.

PART 7

UNSETTLING SEX

LEATHERDYKE BOYS AND THEIR DADDIES

How to Have Sex without Women or Men

C. JACOB HALE

> There are times in life when the question of knowing if one can think dif-
> ferently than one thinks, and perceive differently than one sees, is
> absolutely necessary if one is to go on looking and reflecting at all.
> —Michel Foucault, *The Use of Pleasure*

Contemporary queer theory sees gender as a regulatory construct, a site of shifting power relations. Although queer theorists have made many claims about the
power of queerly gendered bodies and performativities to disrupt enforced normative sex/gender systems, theory lags far behind community discourses here.
In sexual-minority communities, such as queer leather communities, there are
rich and subtly nuanced discourses of gendered pleasure, practice, desire, and
subjectivity. These community discourses sometimes reflect rich and subtly
nuanced embodiments of gender that resist and exceed any simple categorization into *female, male, woman, man,* and thus into *homosexual, bisexual,* or *heterosexual.*[1] Further, queer theory has tended to neglect "the implications of an
enforced sex/gender system for people who live outside it," as Ki Namaste has
argued with regard to queer theory's erasure of transgendered subjectivity.[2]
When transgendered subjects participate in minority communities organized
around radical sexual practice, new and theoretically interesting configurations
of sex, gender, and sexuality arise. In this paper, I will theorize the genderings of
U.S. leatherdyke boys and their leatherdyke daddies. I am especially concerned
to explore how leatherdyke genderplay functions as a means for gender interrogation, solidification, resistance, destabilization, and reconfiguration. From this

investigation, I will draw some tentative conclusions about multiple gender statuses already available in the United States.

First, I need to address briefly my qualifications to write on this topic and my subject position in relation to leatherdyke communities and practices. My birth certificate bears witness that when I was born, I was diagnosed "female" and given a heavily gendered feminine name. I was raised girl-to-woman, with a fairly unambiguous female body until I began injections of exogenous testosterone on 19 May 1995. For most of my adult life, I lived as a bisexual woman whose primary sexual relationships were with heterosexual men. In 1991, I "came out" as a lesbian, and two years later I began exploring SM and participating in leatherdyke friendship circles and community structures, primarily in Los Angeles. In 1995, I began transitioning female-to-male (ftm), leatherdyke-to-leatherfag.[3] I retain strong ties with a number of Los Angeles leatherdykes and continue to participate in some leatherdyke community public events, such as serving as a VIP boy for the 1997 Ms. Fallen Angels Contest, although I do not attend women-only play parties even when invited. Since I have not undertaken research even approximating careful ethnography, any generalizations must be tentative. Furthermore, it is crucial to note that not only are uses of leatherdyke genderplay as ftm transitioning technologies different for different ftms, but that many ftms have never participated in leatherdyke or other lesbian practices or communities at all.

From an external-to-leatherdyke-culture point of view, and as a first approximation that I will complicate later, "leatherdyke boys" are adult lesbian (dyke) females who embody a specific range of masculinities intelligible within queer leather (SM) communities; their "daddies" may be butch leatherdykes or, less frequently, gay leathermen. This delineation is, of course, vague insofar as it replicates the haziness of the boundaries between the categories *female, lesbian, dyke, queer, leather,* and *butch.* In this paper, I restrict my focus to leatherdyke boys and their leatherdyke daddies, leaving aside investigations of how gender works in interactions between leatherdyke boys and their gay leathermen daddies.

Leatherdyke boys perform masculinity in a wide range of ways. Playing as a boy does not necessitate age-play; status as a boy may simply indicate a masculine bottom status—submissive or masochistic or both—different from that of a slave. However, in my experience age-play is more common in leatherdyke boy-daddy settings than it is in gay male ones. When boy-daddy age-play occurs, play ages may bear no relation to the legal ages of the players; daddy may be younger than her boy, according to their birth certificates. Leatherdyke boys may have specific play ages, or may locate themselves vaguely as young children or as teenagers; some leatherdyke boys are little boys, some are big boys. Leatherdyke boys may relate to their daddies in loving, respectful, and attentive manners, or they may be bratty, rebellious, withdrawn, or distant. They may signal their status as boys with age- and gender-specific clothing—such as a Boy Scout shirt, schoolboys' short pants, a Catholic schoolboy uniform, school sports uniforms, or youthful hip-hop styles that are at odds with more traditional leather-community styles—or clothing may give no clues as to their status as boys. Cloth-ing is very likely, however, to indicate their statuses as SM bottoms and as butches. Clothing may also vaguely indicate levels of SM experience and, in more precise ways, interest in particular sexual activities. In short, the range of masculinities open for leatherdyke boys' performativities is at least as wide as that open to young males, though it is inflected both through lesbian commu-nity butch styles and through leather-community means of signaling bottom status and interest in specific sexual activities.

Since leatherdyke boys' masculine performativities often occur in contexts separate from interactions with workmates, family (as defined by law), neigh-bors, and other friends and acquaintances outside of SM contexts, they are less bounded by cultural constructions of masculinity, which are inflected by such vectors of power as race, ethnicity, class, sexual orientation, or occupation, than by the performativities of young males. For example, an upper-middle-class pro-fessional woman can become a sixteen-year-old headbanger rockerdude with a change of clothing and attitude.

Gayle Rubin has argued that "there are more ways to be butch" than "there are ways for men to be masculine," since "when women appropriate masculine styles the element of travesty produces new significance and meaning."[4] Rubin's point extends even further when applied to leatherdyke masculinities as enacted in leatherdyke play spaces: when leatherdyke boys' masculine performativities occur in conjunction with fairly unambiguous female embodiments in settings, such as play parties, where heavily gender-coded bodily zones are visible, their performativities are less bounded by cultural regulations of masculinity than young males' are.[5]

This is not to suggest that leatherdyke boys' masculine performativities are unregulated in leatherdyke contexts. Gender performativity, just as any other form of performativity, must occur within social constraints to be intelligible; it must be intelligible if it is to be efficacious; and if it is not efficacious it cannot succeed as performative. Further, wider lesbian community anxieties about mas-culinity, manhood, and maleness circulate throughout leatherdyke communities. These anxieties become especially acute in determining the boundaries of the category *woman* for admittance to women-only sexual spaces, due to a felt need to protect women's sexual safety in sexual spaces. Transsexuals—male-to-female (mtf) and, more recently, female-to-male—have become the major threat to the apparent purity of this boundary. Indeed, other than disputes about whether or not male-to-female transsexuals—with or without surgical alterations of their genitals—may attend the Michigan Womyn's Music Festival, the most anxiety-fraught and vociferous struggles around political boundaries of the category *woman* in lesbian communities have been disputes about how to define *woman* for purposes of admittance to leatherdyke play parties. Although most organiza-tions that host such parties are geographically local, these disputes have been international, because people travel to attend parties out of their geographical regions and because of community discussions in publications such as the now-defunct leatherdyke magazine *Venus Infers* and on-line. Such disputes may reflect different local play-party traditions that shape policy. For example, as the predominantly separatist Seattle leatherdyke community involved in organizing Powersurge attempted to create an event that would draw national attendance and yet enforce their local separatist traditions and policies, they ran into friction with leatherdykes from other regions, such as San Francisco, with deliberately nonseparatist traditions and policies.[6]

In these disputes, anxieties centered around both male embodiment and masculine behaviors. Usually, however, when unclothed embodiment is unambiguously female, a much wider range of masculine behaviors are tolerated than when embodiment is partially male. As Gayle Rubin has observed, "Obnoxious behavior that would be tolerated in a butch will often be considered intolerable in an FTM."[7] While a butch with a fairly unambiguous female body may be called up short for behaving badly, her behavior will not likely be attributed to her sex/gender status, embodiment, self-identifications, or history. In contrast, if an mtf or an ftm engages in the same behaviors, these behaviors are more likely to be labeled "male" and to be attributed to sex/gender history, identification, or embodiment. Further, the person engaging in such behaviors may be banned from attending future play parties and exiled from leatherdyke communities and friendship circles, and causal attributions of objectionable behaviors to sex/gender may be cited as justificatory grounds for changing definitional policies to exclude other mtfs or ftms in the future.

Play party invitations, instruction in SM techniques, inclusion in community organizations and friendship circles, and access to sex/play partners are powerful means for leatherdyke community regulation of leatherdyke conduct, perhaps more so than are their analogs within broader lesbian communities. Despite these regulatory mechanisms, masculine gender performativities, in conjunction with female embodiment, are given a wider range of expression within leatherdyke contexts than in many other lesbian or dyke settings.

Leatherdyke boy-daddy play sometimes functions as a means of gender exploration, solidification, resistance, destabilization, and reconfiguration. This can be illustrated by examining some of the ways in which boy or daddy play within leatherdyke contexts can facilitate female-to-male transitioning paths. In this section, I will rely on my own personal experiences as a leatherdyke boy and the experiences of Spencer Bergstedt as a leatherdyke daddy prior to his transition.

There are at least three ways in which leatherdyke boy or daddy play can function to consolidate a leatherdyke boy's or daddy's self-identification as male or as a man. One, which is not exemplified by either Bergstedt or myself, is through a conception of submission, especially to pain, as the most masculine SM position, especially when the person to whom one submits is also masculine. A second is that which Bergstedt described to me in an interview on 9 August 1995: leatherdyke daddy play enabled him to explore his masculine dominance more thoroughly than he could in other areas of his life. A third is through exploration of masculine boyhoods or periods of adolescence that were missing from our lives as we developed pubescent female bodies—bodies that were supposed to end our lives as tomboys and signal the beginnings of womanhood. I will illustrate this by recounting some of my own personal experiences.

While still identifying as a dyke, Bergstedt served as International Ms. Leather 1994.[8] He currently sits on the executive board of the National Leather Association, holding the same position he did prior to transition. An attorney practicing in Seattle, Bergstedt has served on the boards of numerous other community organizations, including the Seattle City Commission on Lesbians and Gays. Active in transgender community work as well, Bergstedt was the treasurer for the Second Annual FTM Conference of the Americas in Seattle in August 1996 and is family law director of the International Conference on Transgender Law and Employment Project (ICTLEP). A topman who identifies as heterosexual, at the time of our interview Bergstedt had a significant other and was a "daddy with nine leatherkids" with whom he did not play at all. He describes himself as a "Daddy's daddy," someone to whom other daddies, including very experienced gay topmen, turn to for daddying, especially for advice about problems in their lives. Bergstedt characterized his daddying as providing "stable, nurturing male energy."

Bergstedt described SM as "a resource or a means of learning more about myself and growing more spiritually." Later in our interview, "tool" was the word he used. Bergstedt said that SM play has "little to do with sexual pleasure" for him; he is not sexual with most of the people he plays with and views SM play as more of a "spiritual exercise" through which he learns "who I am." Through leatherplay itself, Bergstedt was able to explore his masculinity and his dominance. He is well aware that dominance can be feminine and did not simply equate masculinity with dominance. Instead, he said that SM allowed him to explore "masculine ways of being dominant" to a greater extent than he could in other areas of his life. In SM, he said, "I could really *live* that." He illustrated the contrast with other areas of his life by recounting experiences he had while serving on the Seattle City Commission on Lesbians and Gays during a time when he identified as a dyke: "A number of the women who were on the commission at the time objected to my leadership style as being too male and too dominant and not processing enough, . . . too goal-oriented, whereas the men had very little problem with me at all." When I asked him whether the women on the commission raised similar objections to the leadership styles of the men, he answered, "No, just me." Bergstedt said that the message he was getting in this experience was that "the way that I was expressing my dominance and my personality was inappropriate for the gender role that those people perceived me to be in." In SM play, Bergstedt could "really live" his masculinity through exploring his masculine dominance. This was enabled by the "reinforcement and acceptance" he found for his expressions of masculine dominance in leather community circles, though Bergstedt's leather community participation, both before his transition and now, has been more extensive in pansexual and gay male circles than in leatherdyke ones. He asserts that, "to a person," all of the leatherfolk he knows have been supportive of his transition. Participating in SM has allowed him to form a chosen leather family, a family which is "tolerant of difference and change," thus giving him a safe and supportive environment for self-exploration.

In 1993, I identified as a lesbian and had for two years. For many years, I had not done solosex because the fantasies that came unbidden into my head scared me. I stayed away from reading books about male adolescence because I was frightened and ashamed by the arousal I experienced in response to scenes in which adolescent boys were punished. As I moved further into lesbian communities, my boy-identification strengthened, and I began exploring queer SM community events and literature. Eventually, I started seeing a young post-punk SM dyke whom I met at a Ron Athey performance. Within a few weeks, I started wearing more boyish clothes and jockey shorts, and I gave myself a boy name: first "Alex" and then "Jake." My play age quickly settled in at fourteen years of age. Scenes with this dyke, when she played daddy to my boy, centered on punishments in which invented junior high school locker-room sexual high jinks among boys and basketball played elaborate roles. That is, we engaged in fairly extensive psychological play, sometimes dissolving into giggles when our scripts got stuck. After she and I stopped seeing each other, I ran a personal ad for a dyke daddy in the *Lesbian News,* a free Los Angeles monthly. This time I found someone with many years of leather experience who treated me as "boy" and "son" most of the time we were together. Daddying, for this one, was about love, support, nurturance, and guidance, about helping and teaching, more than it was about punishment. I began to be introduced to other people as "Jake" in settings other than leatherdyke play parties, trying out different styles of masculine self-presentation and behavior, acquiring a leather family, and extending my queer leather community connections and participation. During this time, pronoun usage varied somewhat randomly: either feminine or masculine pronouns were used to refer to Daddy, to Daddy's best butch buddy who became my uncle, and to me.[9] My discomfort with hearing feminine pronouns used to refer to myself solidified here.[10]

Bergstedt's stories and mine are quite different, and we construct our stories quite differently. For him, SM as gender technology allowed him to explore, more fully than he could in other areas of his life, "who I really am," as he put it. For me, SM as gender technology allowed me to experiment with masculinities as part of a process of self-construction in which I became more masculine, in embodiment, in self-presentation, and in identification.[11] In my self-conception, who I "really" am is a matter of social/cultural facts about my categorical locations; there is facticity here, but it is not natural or essential and is continually changing as culturally available categories change and as I change relative to them. Yet there are some common themes to Bergstedt's story and mine: themes of explorations of masculinities, and of the reinforcement and acceptance we found in our leather worlds.

Leatherplay can create, so to speak, a culture of two, composed of those two people who are playing together. When I was a boy with my dyke daddy, in that culture of two I was a boy. I was not an adult woman playing a boy's role or playing a boy, nor was I an adult woman doing boy in some other way. Daddy's participation was necessary for me to be a boy with her. I was a boy with her by engaging in a gender performativity that made sense to both of us as a *boy's* gender performativity. Importing the words Bergstedt chose to speak of himself, Daddy gave me "reinforcement and acceptance" for being a boy. In this culture of two, informed and structured by leatherdyke community gender codes, my communication of a masculine gender identification was legible to someone else, despite my female body. I needed to know that my gender identification could be enacted legibly to at least one other person for it to be convincing enough to me that it could transform from a self-identification fully contained within my fantasy structure to a self-identification with a broader social sphere of enactment. Daddy, of course, could not have read my gender performativity as a boy's gender performativity if there had not been culturally available constructs of *boy* into which she could fit it. For my performativity as boy to be legible to Daddy, I had to cite gender codes she understood as a boy's, though I was not limited to only those boyish codes she had already encountered. Indeed, there were times when I blew it, when what I said or did was way off the boy mark; sometimes these were painful moments, other times they were pleasantly amusing, and some other times they shifted our interaction into one between two adult butches. Los Angeles's leatherdyke community, particularly as it intersected with Los Angeles's gay male leather community and hip-hop youth cultures, provided those cultural constructs of *boy* through which my gender performativity was intelligible as that of a leatherdyke boy at first, then as that of a leatherboy as I moved further into the leathermen's world and as my self-presentation became more masculine. Extending the realm of my gender performativities as boy, or man, beyond situations in which Daddy and I were the only people present opened up new possibilities of gender performativity into which I could fit as a boy or as a man; circumscribed those possible performativities in other ways; and extended the realms in which I could create a masculine self, or masculine selves, in relational gendered communications/communications of gender. Relationality of gender, I think, becomes clear in both Bergstedt's story and mine.

Another aspect of SM as gender technology, which did not come out clearly in my interview with Bergstedt, perhaps because I did not think to ask him about it then, is that leatherdyke genderplay enables a phenomenon sometimes called "retooling" or "recoding" our bodies in trans community discourse. Sexual interactions, along with public restrooms and medical settings, are some of the sites at which dominant cultural connections between genitals and gender are the tightest, so many transpeople must remap the sexualized zones of our bodies if we are to be sexually active. Through leatherdyke SM practice, I was able to disrupt the dominant cultural meanings of my genitals and to reconfigure those meanings. There was already precedence for such deterritorialization and reterritorialization in the leatherdyke communities in which I participated. SM practices that decouple genital sexuality from bodily pleasures provide the backdrop for such phenomena of remapping.[12] One such phenomenon is that inanimate objects—dildoes—sometimes take on some of the phenomenological characteristics of erogenous body parts. So, when Powersurge defined a woman as someone who could slam her dick into a drawer without hurting it, a common response among some butch leatherdykes and some ftms was to say that it sure would hurt if their dicks got slammed into a drawer; a dildo may not be a dick only in the conception, it may be a dick phenomenologically as well. Furthermore, sometimes leatherdykes resignify sexed bodily zones. Among some leatherdyke faggots, an important desideratum is to keep masculinity as seamless as possible during scenes, and gay leathermen's masculinities often provide the paradigms of masculinity here. Thus, if the body part a leatherdyke daddy is fisting is that which a physician would unequivocally deem a "vagina," it may be resignified so that its use for erotic pleasure is consistent with male masculinity. It may become a "hole," "fuckhole," "manhole," "boyhole," "asshole," or "butthole," and a leatherdyke boy pleading, "Please, Daddy, fuck my butt!" may be asking daddy to fuck the same orifice into which a physician would insert a speculum to perform a pap smear. Of course, this resignification may prove painful if this boy's daddy does not understand it. For some ftms who used to be leatherdykes, our abilities to rechart our bodies—I would even say to change our embodiments without changing our bodies, that is, to change the personal and social meanings of our sexualized bodies—began in the queer resignifying practices available to us in leatherdyke cultures. If we invent novel, idiosyncratic reconfigurations, there is an already-given precedence for male reconfigurations of our bodies, which enables our novel reconfigurations to emerge into the realm of efficacious performativity and social production.

Yet some ftms who used to be leatherdykes may have found, as I did, that there were limits to our abilities to reconstitute the sexualized social spaces of our bodies. Some of these limits are constituted personally in that we cannot ourselves reconfigure the social meanings of certain bodily zones, and others may be externally imposed in that we cannot manage to communicate our attempts at idiosyncratic rechartings in ways that others are able and willing to read. Leatherdyke practice may help us discern those aspects of our embodied subjectivities that are susceptible to our own agency, and those parts of our bodies that we must change if we are to live in our own skins.

Is a leatherdyke daddy a woman or a man? Is a leatherdyke boy a woman or a man or a boy? These questions, I think, are badly misguided: they presuppose overly simplistic understandings of how gender categories work, and in so doing they reinscribe the hegemonic stranglehold of the dominant sex/gender/sexuality system. Elsewhere I have argued that the dominant cultural category *woman* in the contemporary United States is not defined in terms of necessary or sufficient conditions, but rather in terms of thirteen criteria, none of which is necessary nor sufficient for membership in that category. The notion that there is one characteristic—usually, though not always, understood as genital—sharply differentiating women from men is part of an oppressive sex/gender/sexuality system which Harold Garfinkel dubbed "the natural attitude toward gender" to indicate its status as a culturally constructed system to which we, as members of this culture, are held morally accountable for upholding and for which we are held morally accountable for upholding as fully natural. Careful analysis of leatherdyke boys' and daddies' performativities in light of both my earlier descriptive reconstruction of the category *woman* and Garfinkel's work on "the natural attitude" would show that, according to the dominant culture's principles, some leatherdyke daddies and boys are women, some are not, and that in many cases there is no fact of the matter. Furthermore, as I shall argue, such a question is culturally imperialistic in ways that foreground interesting contemporary gender formations within the United States.[13]

I take it as fairly noncontroversial that gender is culturally constructed and that leatherdyke communities constitute cultures that, though they are influenced by and may influence the dominant culture, are distinct if not autonomous from the dominant culture insofar as they produce cultural formations and structures different from those found in the dominant culture. Thus, we may legitimately consider "subcultures" as analytically separate from the dominant culture. Given this, we can see that a question that presupposes that a person has a unitary gender status across cultures with varying gender categories is conceptually misguided, even if some of the cultures in question are subcultures. Instead of speaking of a person's gender status, we might do well to speak of a person's gendered status in a given cultural location, at a given time, and for a given purpose.

In a short interlude, I would like to motivate this notion of multiple gendered statuses further by looking at a simpler case, one which does not involve different cultures, but one in which I, again, am my own example. Currently, I do not have a unitary sex/gender status under the law, even under the law in the state in which I was born and reside. My California driver's license bears the sex/gender designation "M," and my California birth certificate bears the sex/gender designation "F." This *apparent* discrepancy is due to the fact that different state laws and regulations govern change of sex/gender designation on these documents; while I have met the legal requirements to change that "F" to "M" on one, I have not met the legal requirements to make that change on the other and, further, have no particular need to change it. Indeed, my earlier use of "the law" was a setup, for there are multiple laws and regulations that define sex/gender status differently. Birth certificates and driver's licenses serve different state purposes. For example, one functions for medical record keeping (among many other purposes) in ways that the other does not. Thus, my sex/gender status is specific to state interests and purposes, and my sex/gender status is different relative to different state interests and purposes. Consequently, unitary sex/gender status is, in part, a juridical construction that falls apart on some transsexed (and intersexed) bodies. Unitariness of sex/gender status is a juridical *fiction* in the strictest of senses; despite appearances to the contrary, there is absolutely no discrepancy between the gender/sex designations on my driver's license and my birth certificate.

In a broader sense, unitary sex/gender status is a culturally constructed fiction produced by the state, by medicine, by psychotherapy, and by other institutions and discursive structures. This construction of sex/gender status as unitary also breaks down on genderplaying leatherqueer bodies situated in "subcultures" with gender orchestrations different from dominant cultural constructs. From medical points of view, most leatherdyke boys and daddies are women; some male-to-female and female-to-male transsexual leatherdyke boys and daddies may count as men; and some leatherdyke boys and daddies may not have a unitary sex/gender status according to law or according to medicine if their sexed characteristics are not unambiguously female or male. This will vary from jurisdiction to jurisdiction, even from law to law within one jurisdiction, from medical specialty to medical specialty, and even from physician to physician within one medical specialty. From a broader cultural point of view, some nontranssexual, nonintersexual leatherdyke boys and daddies may not be easily classifiable if they do not clearly enough satisfy the defining criteria of the categories *woman* and *man*. Relative to leatherdyke cultural spaces, *woman* and *man* may be the most relevant gender categories, and the only two available in addition to neither, for purposes of deciding who gets to participate. These are not, however, the most relevant gender categories for other purposes, such as making sense of another person's behavior, determining how to interact with that person, or organizing sexual desire and sexual practice. For example, when my daddy goes to a women-only play party, probably the first thing she does is pay an admission fee and sign a release form. During this encounter, her operative sex/gender status is *woman,* since she must be a woman (however that is defined by the party organizers) to be admitted. Probably the next thing Daddy does is stow her toybag and hang up her leather jacket if it's a hot night, because Daddy likes to socialize a little and get into a party headspace before playing. During this time, her operative sex/gender status is *leatherdyke daddy,* for this is the category through which her interactions with others are organized, especially but not only those interactions in which eroticism is present. Once Daddy is in a scene with a butch faggot boy, once Daddy's dick has become a sensate dick in Daddy's phenomenological experience of his own embodiment and in Daddy's boy's phenomenological experience of Daddy's embodiment, Daddy may be simply a very butch gay male leather bear-daddy. Or something else entirely, depending on the specific content of the interactions between Daddy, Daddy's boy, and any other participants or observers. Thinking in terms of multiple, context-specific, and purpose-specific gendered statuses allows us to make better sense of this cultural phenomenon than does thinking in terms of (two or more) unitary sex/gender statuses.

The sense of multiple, context-specific, and purpose-specific sex/gender statuses I am urging is not simply one in which sex/gender varies from one cultural/historical location to another, nor even one in which individual persons may change their sex/gender statuses over the course of their lifetimes if they make comparably grand changes in themselves, such as those kinds of changes that transsexuals are expected to make. Nor is this the familiar point that gender identity is constructed in interaction with identities along other vectors of subjectivity and power. A very small amount of time elapses while Daddy walks from the entrance of the play-party to stow her toybag, and she has not left one culture and entered another during that short walk, nor does she alter her body. Rather, the play-party entrance is a spatial and discursive boundary between cultures, a boundary at which dominant cultural sex/gender categories operate for a specific purpose: to protect members of another, though not fully separate, culture from certain types of interference and violence. Once that boundary is passed, dominant cultural sex/gender categories are not entirely suspended, but they are superseded by another, incommensurable set of sex/gender categories. Furthermore, as I sit writing this I lack a unitary sex/gender status under California state law, although my historical and cultural location stays put. The type of multiplicity for which I am arguing is more profusely multiple than that with which we have all become familiar.

One could claim, of course, that Daddy is a woman who is also a leatherdyke daddy, that being a leatherdyke daddy is one way to be a woman. However, this culturally imperialist claim misses the point that to insist that leatherdyke boys and their daddies are women, all the time, in all situations, and for all purposes, is to insist on ignoring the cultural situatedness—or, more accurately, the multiple cultural situatednesses—of leatherdyke gender performativities. Further, it is to insist on ignoring this in favor of upholding a patently oppressive hegemonic sex/gender/sexuality system that imposes the overarching categories *woman* and *man* at the expense of eliding the specificities of how sex/gender works in queer cultural discourses and practices. The decision about which of these views to accept is a *political* decision, a decision about whether or not the dominant culture's sex/gender discourse will be given discursive primacy over leatherdyke sex/gender discourse. One discourse is constituted and enforced by much greater power than the other, yet there is powerful agency in refusing to agree that one is entirely contained within its discursive structures. There is also power in the creative production of new, alternative gender formations.

When we consider the same leatherdyke boy or leatherdyke daddy in different cultural locations, such as competing for a leather title and working as attorney, we will likely be confronted with a fluidity of gender performativity, and perhaps of gender identification as well. Analytically replacing the notion of unitary gender status with that of multiple gendered statuses helps make sense of this sort of gender fluidity. Making this discursive change, however, does absolutely nothing to suggest that gender fluidity is more radical, subversive, transgressive, or disruptive than more stable gender performativities and identifications. Fluidity of gender performativity and identification is clearly not necessary to disrupt unitariness of sex/gender—as is shown by the examples of Daddy walking to stow her toybag and my current situation/s under California state law.

Wild gender multiplicity abounds, and we have some, though not unconstrained, agency within, and along, the soft, permeable edges of the multiple, overlapping boundaries of gender categories and incommensurable gender systems. Our urgent creative political work is not the proliferation of genders, nor are genders countable marks on one line or countable points within a flat, geometric space. Rather, we must familiarize ourselves and others with the multiplicity of genders already available in the curvatures of gendered spaces; we must develop further adept tactics—opened up by the purpose-relativity of gendered statuses—of naming and claiming multiply shifting, resistant sex/gender identifications; and we can use soft, permeable edges as sites for creative production of new, more just genderqueer discursive locations and structures for those of us who are thrust into black holes by location in any of the already given structures of sex/gender/sexuality and who are dislocated from them all.

NOTES

1. Personal ads in sexual-minority community publications sometimes confound readers who do not participate in the communities in which the publications are produced. For an analysis of one personal ad that illustrates my claims, see Jacob Hale, "Are Lesbians Women?" *Hypatia* 11 (1996): 100–1.

2. Ki Namaste, " 'Tragic Misreadings': Queer Theory's Erasure of Transgender Subjectivity," in *Queer Studies: A Lesbian, Gay, Bisexual, and Transgender Anthology,* ed. Brett Beemyn and Mickey Eliason (New York, 1996), pp. 183–206.

3. While this formulation accurately represents a limited slice of my self-identification when I began transition, it obscures the more complex self-identifications I have since formed in resistance to hegemonic constructions of transsexuality and to dominant manhood. For further investigation of the complexities of ftm self-identifications, see C. Jacob Hale, "Tracing a Ghostly Memory in My Throat: Reflections on Ftm Feminist Voice and Agency," in *Men Doing Feminism,* ed. Tom Digby (New York, 1997).

4. Gayle Rubin, "Of Catamites and Kings: Reflections on Butch, Gender, and Boundaries," in *The Persistent Desire: A Femme-Butch Reader,* ed. Joan Nestle (Boston, 1992), p. 469.

5. In addition to using *embodiment* with its more common meanings, I follow Steven G. Smith in thinking of embodiment as a process through which the community stipulates what counts as a male/female body, what life will be like in a male/female body in relation to other bodies, what norms (and latitudes) of character and conduct are associated with these bodies, and who is male and female. See Steven G. Smith, *Gender Thinking* (Philadelphia, 1992), p. 91.

6. Tala Brandeis, "Dyke with a Dick," in *The Second Coming: A Leatherdyke Reader,* ed. Pat Califia and Robin Sweeney (Los Angeles, 1996), pp. 52–62; Pat Califia, "Who Is My Sister? Powersurge and the Limits of Our Community," *Venus Infers* 1/1 (n.d.): 4–7, 34–35; Michael M. Hernandez, "Boundaries: Gender and Transgenderism," in *Second Coming,* ed. Califia and Sweeney, pp. 63–70; Gayle Rubin, "The Outcasts: A Social History," in *Second Coming,* ed. Califia and Sweeney, pp. 339–46.

7. Gayle Rubin, "Catamites," p. 482, n. 29.

8. Anne Williams, "And the Winner Is . . . 1994 International Ms. Leather Is Anne C. S. Bergstedt," *Venus Infers* 2/1 (n.d.): 26–30.

9. My use of feminine pronouns to refer to leatherdyke boys and daddies in this article is an artificial and problematic means of communicating with readers who do not participate and have not participated in leatherdyke community circles.

10. For my former Daddy's perspective on some of these events, see Lee Lambert, "Daddy's Home! Raging Hormones," *Leather Journal* 76 (1995): 29.

11. This should not be misunderstood as invoking a butch-ftm masculinity continuum on which ftms are more masculine than butches. When I say that I became more masculine, I am

describing changes I made during a specific time period and do not mean to suggest that I am more masculine now than I was then, nor that ftms are more masculine than butches. If anything, I am less masculine in some respects now than I was before exogeneous testosterone, and I am certainly less masculine in some respects than a number of my butch friends. See Judith Halberstam, *Female Masculinity* (Durham, 1998); JordyJones, "Another View of F2M," *FTM Newsletter* 29 (1995): 14–15.

12. Bob Gallagher and Alexander Wilson, "Michel Foucault: An Interview: Sex, Power, and the Politics of Identity," *The Advocate* (August 7, 1984): 26–30, 58; David M. Halperin, *Saint Foucault: Towards a Gay Hagiography* (New York, 1995), pp. 85–91.

13. Kate Bornstein, *Gender Outlaw: On Men, Women, and the Rest of Us* (New York, 1994), pp. 46–50; Joseph C. Finney, "Transsexuality and the Laws on Sexual Mores," in *Proceedings of the Second Interdisciplinary Symposium on Gender Dysphoria Syndrome,* ed. Donald R. Laub and Patrick Gandy (Stanford: Division of Reconstructive and Rehabilitation Surgery, Stanford University Medical Center, n.d.), pp. 117–22; Harold Garfinkel, "Passing and the Managed Achievement of Sex Status in an 'Intersexed' Person, Part One," in his *Studies in Ethnomethodology* (Oxford, 1967), pp. 116–85; Hale, "Are Lesbians Women?"; John Heritage, *Garfinkel and Ethnomethodology* (Cambridge, 1984), pp. 179–98; Suzanne J. Kessler, "The Medical Construction of Gender: Case Management of Intersexed Infants," in *Theorizing Feminism: Parallel Trends in the Humanities and the Social Sciences,* ed. Anne C. Herrmann and Abigail J. Stewart (Boulder, 1994), pp. 218–37; Suzanne J. Kessler and Wendy McKenna, *Gender: An Ethnomethodological Approach* (New York, 1978), pp. 112–15.

THE GAME GIRLS OF VNS MATRIX

Challenging Gendered Identities in Cyberspace

KAY SCHAFFER

We are the virus of a new world disorder
Disrupting the symbolic from within.
—VNS Matrix

Early in 1992 VNS Matrix released its "Cyberfeminist Manifesto for the 21st Century" to the world. The venue: Adelaide, South Australia—hardly a prominent city in worldwide, cyberculture terms. The format: a visually and textually arresting 6-by-18-foot billboard on a major, arterial road. The message: "the clitoris is a direct line to the matrix . . . VNS Matrix . . . mercenaries of slime . . . corrupting the symbolic from within . . . we make art with our kunst . . . we are the future" (figure 1). In her book *Zeroes and Ones* Sadie Plant refers to the event as a nodal point for cyberfeminist activity, an extension of Donna Haraway's essay "A Cyborg Manifesto" of the 1980s (the essay, interestingly, also was first published in Adelaide).[1] The manifesto presaged the opening of VNS Matrix computer art installation All New Gen at the Experimental Art Foundation Gallery in Adelaide in 1993. The installation received national interest, critical acclaim, and wildly enthusiastic reviews.[2] Since the time of that modest, low-budget installation augmented versions of All New Gen have traveled around the world. The installation has been displayed at cybernetic art exhibitions, multimedia conferences, and international electronic media art shows, gathering devotees in its wake. Soon the prototype for an All New Gen CD-ROM interactive disc, entitled "Bad

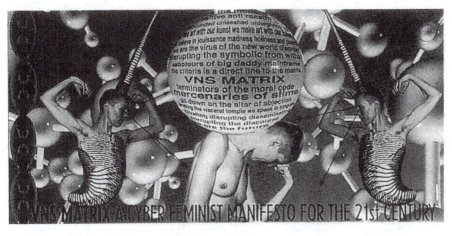

Figure 1   VNS Matrix, "Cyberfeminist Manifesto for the 21st Century." (Courtesy of Julianne Pierce and VNS Matrix.)

Code," will be released, affording new audiences further subversive pleasures, compliments of All New Gen and her emergent matricicial creatrix, in the VNS Matrix team.

This essay examines cyberfeminism's contributions to postmodern understandings of gendered bodies and gendered selves through an investigation of the cyberfeminist artwork of VNS Matrix. The work of VNS Matrix conjoins an oppositional feminist politics with explorations of alternate sexual modalities and postmodern subjectivities. A growing number of postmodern feminist theorists couple these new forms of nongendered (or post-phallic) explorations with radical transformations within the social and cultural order. A number of feminist and queer theory contributors to the anthology *Sexy Bodies: The Strange Carnalities of Feminism,* for example, critically attend to transformations in culture effected through alternative modes of pleasure and desire. These alternate modes depend not on Freudian hierarchical models of sexuality but on feminine collaborative ones; on horizontal rather than vertical zones of desire; on a sexuality that assumes no a priori body. Contributors to *Sexy Bodies* explore the "perverse" undertones of carnality that might lead to new alliances and connections about and between bodies, desires, pleasures, and power.[3] The cyber-art experiments of VNS Matrix are one such example. Are they, and others like them that proliferate in an ever-expanding cyber-community, capable of producing personal, social, and political transformations as these contemporary feminist and queer theorists suggest? What are their subversive elements? Are they capable of dismantling present forms of subjectivity and desire? To what extent might alternative modes of identity, subjectivity, sexuality, and politics offered within the realm of interactive technology lead to a transformation of social and cultural practices?

Welcome to the world of ALL NEW GEN: the radically transgressive, inter-active computer game for non-specific genders.

Thank you for playing.

You are invited to join All New Gen and her DNA Sluts—the super pow-erful Patina de Panties, Dentata, and the Princess of Slime—in their battle against Big Daddy Mainframe and his technobimbo sidekicks—Circuit Boy, Streetfighter and other total dicks—whom you will encounter in the Con-tested Zone. This is a zone where gender is a shuffable six-letter word and power is no longer centered in a specific organization.

Rules of the Game:

All battles take place within the Contested Zone, a terrain of propaganda, subversion, and transgression. Your guides through the Contested Zone are the renegade DNA Sluts, abdicators from the oppressive superhero regime, who have joined All New Gen in her fight for data liberation.

The path of infiltration is treacherous and you will encounter many obsta-cles. The most wicked—Circuit Boy—a dangerous technobimbo, whose direct mindnet to Big Daddy renders him almost invincible.

You may not encounter All New Gen, as she has many disguises. But do not fear; she is always in the matrix, an omnipresent intelligence, anarcho cyber terrorist acting as a virus of the new world disorder.

You will be fuelled by G-slime. Please monitor your levels. Bonding with DNA Sluts will replenish your supplies.

Be prepared to question your biological construction.

There will be opportunities throughout the game for pleasurable distraction.

Be aware that there is no moral code in the Zone.

Enjoy.[4]

Thus begins one's journey into All New Gen, an interactive computer artwork and multimedia installation piece produced by the Sydney-based VNS Matrix collective in 1993. Although the call to arms echoes the pitch of Gameboy com-puter games like Nintendo's popular Donkey Kong and Super Mario Brothers or Sega's Sonic the Hedgehog, this is no game for children. All New Gen mirrors the world of high-tech games but in an ironic and transgressive way. It has been designed for big (bad) girls who understand that the enemies, hazards, and obstacles they face mirror those of the high-tech, top-down world of contempo-rary, masculine technoculture. Players of the game immerse themselves within a politics of resistance to that culture while at the same time exploring new forms of postmodern sexuality and subjectivity.

After logging on to All New Gen, the first question asked of game players is: "What is your gender? Male, Female, Neither." "Neither" is the correct answer, since clicking the Male or Female icon sends players spinning on a loop that takes them out of the game. Having taken up one's nonspecific gendered iden-

Kay Schaffer

tity, players align themselves with ANG (All New Gen) and the DNA Sluts in the Contested Zone. Their aim is to "screw up" Big Daddy Mainframe, would-be Master of the World. ANG's mission, like that of her creatrix, the VNS Matrix collective, is to "hijack the toys from techno-cowboys and remap cyber-culture with a feminist bent."[5] In this their approach is similar to other cyber-feminist projects, such as those of Sadie Plant, Linda Dement, Netchicks, and Geekgirls. But, unlike their techno-abled sisters, these girls blend technological skill with a keen sense of politics and a sophisticated grasp of feminist theory. The combination produces a unique inducement to ludic play that not only extends Donna Haraway's call for new cyber-forms of postmodern subjectivity but also retains her call for an oppositional politics.

In the cyber-art installation, in which the computer plays a central role, play-ers are confronted with a complex interactive environment. The display space of the All New Gen includes light boxes, quick-time animations, wall-sized poster art, rows of telephones with lines connected to the All New Gen characters, and a Bonding Box. The Bonding Box affords players the physical pleasures of com-fortable foam flooring, cushions, a serving tray, and a bottle of ("real" not vir-tual) sake, and computer access to the Matrix, where an erotic video plays, featuring female bonding in nonspecific gendered scenarios.

Players interact with the computer by clicking on icons that introduce them to a number of narratives, characters, settings, and scenarios. They can access multiple All New Gen technoworld narratives, which shift from the tight, hard, clipped feel of a Raymond Chandler thriller (*Beg, Bitch and Snatch were in a dark place, superbonding with some exotic tribal constructs. The feathers were fly-ing*); to identity games infused with techno-babble (*She weeps tears of code. Her thoughts are classified. She has forgotten her password. She is corrupt*); to the femi-nine, erotic, free verse imaginings of Luce Irigaray (*Some Codekids had distrib-uted a message over the Net: You must find your own bliss . . . jouissance is in the cunt of the beholder*).[6] Proceeding into the game, players move between their pos-sible habitation in several environments. These include: the Patriarchal domain of Big Daddy Mainframe; the Contested Zone (where the major action takes place); and the Matrix, home of ANG (the All New Gen, a nonlinear network of possibilities enmeshed in an omnipresent, intelligent mist). With their virtual partners, the DNA Sluts, players can visit the Alpha Bar, where Game Girls seduce the servile waiter-bimbots with promises of nonphallic erogenous plea-sures, or they can replenish their own energy resources with G-slime by bonding with the fantastic DNA Sluts (figure 2).

Stories, scenarios, and settings abound; sidetracks beckon. Players access phone lines where the rhetoric of technoculture meets the erotics of transgres-sive sexuality. Through phone lines to the Matrix, players call down the Oracle Snatch to help them detect and deactivate the drone clones of Circuit Boy; or enter the domain of the abstract, where the abject Mistress of Detestable Plea-sures seduces Circuit Boy; or visit the Perfumed Garden, where "pulse poets beam their Stein lines over the ocean of messages"; or activate Gen's hostile mist

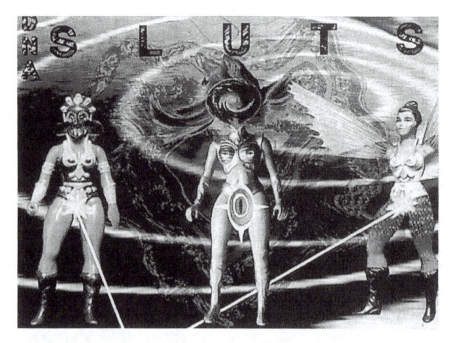

Figure 2   VNS Matrix, "DNA Sluts." (Courtesy of Julianne Pierce and VNS Matrix.)

and intelligent slime to "annihilate the transglobal fathernet of power and ambition" who is Big Daddy Mainframe. "Dirty work. For slimy girls."

> Access:
> The name of the game is infiltration and re-mapping the possible futures outside the (chromo) phallic patriarchal code. . . . Now, with All New Gen in her role as a virus of the new world disorder, this code, like that of DNA, is interfered with and changed so that it just won't reproduce, or alternatively mutates in ways outside the binary oppositions of The Man.

The game engages players in a cheeky game of gender politics in the techno age as they, along with their countercultural cyborg-heroines, confront, with irony and tongue-in-cheek humor, a form of technologically generated, male-controlled, patriarchal politics of the late twentieth century. All New Gen invites players to take up postmodern subjectivities in which mind, body, memory, desire, and experience are combined to make possible new forms of narrative and representation, new intertextual subjectivities.

Since its inception the VNS Matrix team has toured a number of galleries and art spaces in Australia, Europe, the United States, Canada, and Japan with their multimedia installation. In 1994 Gen met with an enthusiastic audience at the International Symposium on Electronic Art in Helsinki, attracting an international cyber-art audience. In the wake of international acclaim VNS Matrix team secured an initial $100,000 grant from the Australian Film Commission to develop a prototype of an All New Gen CD-ROM game for international marketing and distribution. The New CD-ROM prototype, called Bad Code, is based on All New Gen but is enhanced with a number of sophisticated new images, 3D graphic spaces, animations, video sequences, characters, and zones. Beside these projects, members of the VNS Matrix collective operate on a number of sites on the World Wide Web. Their cyber-art experiments offer ever-expanding possibilities for imaginative, transgressive, transgendered, corporeal, libidinal, and intersubjective desires.

BACKGROUND

All New Gen is the invention of VNS Matrix, a Sydney-based art collective whose members describe themselves as "cyberfeminists with attitude." Four Australian artists make up the group: Virginia Barrett, Francesca da Rimini, Julianne Pierce, and Josie Starrs. The two later members began some of their theoretical investigations in Adelaide while enrolled in a postgraduate women's studies course. I taught a subject in the course for which they produced a sophisticated, interactive, participatory assessment project based on readings from Lacanian psychoanalysis and French feminist theories, including Luce Irigaray's and Julia Kristeva's critiques of binary logics, sameness and difference, and investigations of the maternal body, abjection, *jouissance,* and feminine alterity. Their classroom project foreshadowed some of the inventions of the VNS Matrix collective.

The four visual artists formed a collective in 1992, united in their eclectic interests in photography, film, video, music, performance, writing, feminism, and cultural theory. They share an interest in exploring the possibilities for feminist art practice within cyberculture and enticing more girls and women into the world of cybernetics. According to the artists, "the impetus of the group is to investigate and decipher the narratives of domination and control which surround high technological culture, and explore the construction of social space, identity and sexuality in cyberspace."[7]

According to their Artists' Statement,

VNS Matrix are working primarily in the areas of computer-based technologies including graphics, animation, multimedia and, in future, virtual reality systems. Although these advanced systems hold the potential for the creation of entirely new forms of art and communication the cultural products arising from the use of new technologies are often conceptually barren. Form has rapidly become cliched as computer artists have focused on technical challenges rather than structural and conceptual possibilities such as the development of new forms of narrative and representation.

VNS Matrix believe that it is vitally important for new technologies to be used in a critical fashion, and that women have access to the production and consumption of these exciting new tools. VNS Matrix actively engages in the international cross-disciplinary debate surrounding technological development.[8]

The group takes its cues from Donna Haraway's "A Cyborg Manifesto," utilizing computers and optical technologies to critique male-centered theories of the self. Specifically, the collective "reconstruct[s] a socialist-feminist politics . . . through theory and practice addressed to the social relations of science and technology, including crucially the systems of myth and meanings structuring our imaginations."[9] Their project seems to adopt Haraway's criteria, being "oppositional, utopian, and completely without innocence" while remaining "resolutely committed to partiality, irony, intimacy, and perversity."[10] French feminist theories of feminine desire also underlie the Game Girls' narratives, with particular reference to the theories of feminine alterity explored by Luce Irigaray and explorations of the Kristevan abject body as well as the Deleuzian imaginings of the body as desiring machine.

The name, VNS Matrix, carries within its signature elements from the discourses of myth, psychoanalysis, and French-influenced feminist theory, elements that register multiple and contradictory significations (*VNS*, a techno-code word, also pronounced "Venus" = the goddess of love, from the Greek, which also belongs to the word series *to venerate*, in Latin; and *Matrix* = referring to the womb in Latin, or *hystera* in Greek, with its multiple allusions to the maternal and women's bodies in myth, science, and psychoanalysis; the paranoid fantasies of men; and the generative space of feminine). The group's first work, the provocative billboard poster that announced their "cyberfeminist manifesto for the 21st century" (see figure 1), proclaimed that "the clitoris is the direct line to the matrix . . . VNS Matrix." The billboard featured the upper torsos of three female forms, all of which displayed well-muscled arms and cropped hair. Two forms seemed to be mutating from their marinelike fossil base, their arms raised up into pseudo-ironman postures of power, their heads sprouting phallic unicorn horns borne out of popular images from science fiction fantasy. The figures signify both (and neither) masculine and feminine bodies; the products of earth, air, sky, water, and technology; aligned to the past, present, and future. The central figure, posed as an intertextual image that combines Rodin's Thinker with the Greek god Atlas, balances on her shoulders not the heavens but a celestial globe that carries the manifesto: "we are the virus of the new world disorder rupturing the symbolic from within . . . we are the future kunst." (The word *cunt* had to be altered to meet the objections of Adelaide censors.) The figures float in a dreamlike, surreal sea of mutating molecular forms. The left side of the poster features a series of vaginal cells, or cybercunts. The poster announces a new era in cyberfeminist art—one that comments ironically on masculine fantasies of domination from a new postmodern space of feminist revisioning. The poster offers a radical alternative to phallic desire. Here, as Steffensen suggests, "the 'cunt' signified scenarios are not deployed as sites for the production or reproduction of maternity or symbolically inscribed motherhood for women. They are redeployed as a site for the construction of libidinal pleasures: in sex, in horizontal rather than oedipal (vertical) relationships (i.e., collaborations), in technical production, in sexy technology—a feminized and feminist erotics of technocultural production and politics."[11]

The central Thinker/Atlas figure signals the VNS's propensity to mime and parody patriarchal myth. Students of Greek mythology will remember that Atlas was a recalcitrant Titan god who, in retribution for his inhospitality to Perseus, was shown the head of the Gorgon (or, in psychoanalytic terms, the female genitalia), whose gaze turned men into stone. He later took part in an unsuccessful war against Zeus and, as a result, was condemned to hold up the heavens. In the VNS Matrix billboard poster, the mutating feminized bodies register the contradictory elements of the Atlas myth: the god's resistance to and subversion of the patriarchal order and his threatened punishment—the masculine threat of castration. The difference in this emanation of the myth is that the Atlas figure is signified as feminine. The poster can be read from several gendered positions. From a masculine perspective the Atlas figure and its position within the VNS Matrix billboard manifesto invokes the fantasy of the phallic woman, or the monstrous power of the castrating Gorgon/Medusa, about to unleash a new world disorder. But the poster can also be read from a feminine perspective; that is, as a significant mythic revisioning of its Greek origins, one in which the full-breasted Atlas figure upholds the power of female sexuality. It is this power, the power of transgression, seduction, boundary crossing, and viral infiltration, that the All New Gens enact in order to disrupt and corrupt "Big Daddy Mainframe." The signifiers in the poster slide between masculine and feminine codings, registering "Woman" as both a threat to man (the realization of his worst fantasies) and also a conceptual space/Matrix of alterity for women *and men,* beyond phallocentric constructions.

The billboard poster, although situated within a Western Symbolic Order, is at the same time involved in a radical disruption of its sureties. It takes up Donna Haraway's call to exploit feminine otherness in order to transgress the boundaries of self and other within the contested zone of cybernetics. The manifesto announces VNS Matrix as a new voice of bad-girl feminism: "We make art with our cunt." The statement rejects the biological feminine and replaces it with new forms of cultural production. Zoë Sofoulis refers to this element in VNS Matrix as "sublimation"—the creation of a mythic feminine space, a matrix of an "omnipresent intelligence."[12] The space of desire organizes sexuality in a field other than that of the penis/phallus. The cyborg, the "illegitimate offspring of patriarchy," can be imagined as a postmodern mythological figure in a postgendered, postdualistic, and post-oedipal world: the world of the All New Gen.

PLAYING THE GAME

VNS Matrix engages players in a world of hybrid bodies, mutating forms with no fixed gendered identities and no fixed boundaries. In cybertalk these All New

Gens are the illegitimate offspring of techno-man: unreliable and dangerous to Patriarchy. In the All New Gen game and installation the DNA Sluts (or cyber-terrorists) are named, in a playful parody of the fantasy of the phallic woman: Patina de Panties, Dentata, and the Princess of Slime. This trio act as the "mercenaries of slime." They represent, however, not Kristevan bodies of abjection but an Irigarian metaphorics of feminine alterity—a space conjured up by gaps in the narrative, holes in the social fabric. Their bodies call attention to the "slime" of eroticized female genitalia. The forms, rewritten for pleasure, are aestheticized, made abject, and turned into science fiction parodies simultaneously. They thrive on contradiction, assisting the players of the game to infiltrate and remap the future beyond patriarchal codes. The DNA Sluts guide the players through the Contested Zone of a gender politics styled by popular culture. Players refuel with G-slime when they bond with the DNA Sluts, slime that metaphorically lubricates the binary logic system in and beyond the game. Thus, the game reinvents the body, sexuality, and subjectivity beyond modernist visions.

> Instructions:
> Please monitor your levels. Bonding with the DNA Sluts will replenish your supplies. . . . Be prepared to question your gendered biological construction.

Within the Matrix there are no coded binaries of masculine/feminine. The "slime in the matrix" represents a fluid substance between liquid and gas. It slides within a feminine coded cyberspace of fluidity and mutation, an in-between world of new possibilities; a generative space of new feminist imaginings. As Sofoulis comments, "Horrific secret of the masculine sublime, slime can take on quite different connotations in female-centered myths. In proclaiming themselves 'mercenaries of slime,' VNS Matrix call attention to the phenomena of exchange, friction, lubrication, of traffic at the borders of categories, entities, and meaning systems."[13] Further, since "the clitoris is in direct line with the matrix," it appropriates the penis/phallus as a magical signifier of power and agency. The game constructs a feminine mythic space in opposition to that of Big Daddy Mainframe.

> Instructions:
> The path of infiltration is treacherous and you will encounter many obstacles.
> The most wicked is Circuit Boy—a dangerous techno-bimbo.

Circuit Boy is a cyberform with a detachable penis, a feminist parody of the sexy, techno/mechanical, fembot sidekicks of male science fiction fantasy (figure 3). Read "otherwise," the cyborg figure becomes a clever digital enactment of the feminist theoretical question "penis/phallus—same difference?"[14] Or: Can the phallus as signifier ever be detached from the penis as referent? In this game the answer is definitely yes. As a sidekick, he is to Big Daddy Mainframe what AT&T is to IBM and the military-industrial complex. His powers, however, are

Figure 3   VNS Matrix, "Big Daddy Mainframe and Circuit Boy." (Courtesy of Julianne Pierce and VNS Matrix.)

limited. It is the Matrix that is everywhere and everything: an omnipresent mist of intelligence that hovers over, around, and in the environment, threatening to infiltrate Big Daddy's domain with the ultimate virus of a new world disorder. Circuit Boy's penis transforms into a cellular phone that accesses the brain matter of the Matrix, but only indirectly and with the intervention of the Cortex Crones. He must first unscrew the phone / be detached from his penis. He has only indirect and limited access, whereas the DNA Sluts, and players aligned with them, have direct access to the Matrix. In addition, the Sluts are capable of independent action, whereas he must enlist the help of his Masters. Players access the Matrix through phone lines or by bonding with the DNA Sluts. The Matrix signifies a space of feminine alterity, a pre-oedipal, feminine sexual economy articulated beyond the Symbolic Order of language and meaning.

The "click on" instructs players that

All New Gen and the DNA Sluts reveal and generate paths and mappings that not only work in the box, but take you beyond, into the frame, out of the frame, into words, into images, into new connections and allow you to wrap your arms around this new world like radio in a web of the electronic and the erotic, where gender is a shuffable six letter word and power no longer centered in a specific organ-isation.

The game engages players in a perverse alliance between humans, machines, and techno-organisms—into a world in which all become disloyal to (masculine) civilization.

The body here is more than the organic body, more than a textual construction. It becomes a screen onto which cultural fantasies, desires, fears, anxieties, hopes, and utopias are projected. In a parody of cyberpunk and chaos culture players in cyberfeminist space identify with the replicating computer virus that is capable of infiltrating/infecting Big Daddy Mainframe (in opposition to the hacking metaphor of geek boy technological intervention). They manipulate the body; they trade in slime. Participating in fantasies of the fragmented body, they conjure up the blissful, the grotesque, and the uncanny. Steffensen argues that "in VNS the matrix is resignified . . . as a pleasurable site for both the construction and practice of an erotics of a female signified subject, and as a site of epistemological production and pleasure in that knowledge (informatics). . . . Within this 'futures' fantasmatic, the female subject(s) are represented as active agent(s) of their own desires."[15]

Sadie Plant may have had them in mind when she wrote,

Cyberpunk and chaos culture are peppered with wild women and bad girls, transgressions of organisation, the freaks and mutants who find their own languages, the non-members, the nomads, the sex that are not one; leftovers from history; those who have slipped past its filters too soon and accessed the future before its time, hybrid assemblages of what were once called human and machine on the run from their confinement to the world of man and things. Cyborgs are aliens, addicts and trippers who burn past security and through the ice of a culture devoted to spectacle, hacking the screens, and exceeding the familiar. Avatars of the matrix; downloading from cyberspace. They are no longer human. Perhaps they never were.[16]

SUBVERSIVE IMPLICATIONS

Just how politically subversive can a game like All New Gen be? What are the possibilities for and the limits of pleasure and subversion for players in the inter(net)space of technology? Contemporary science fiction is replete with cyborgs—technological organisms that are both *and* neither human and machine. Traditionally the world of technology has been identified as a man's world, one in which he exercises his fantasies of control over cultural (re)production. But the theoretical work, performances, and writings of VNS, like that of Donna Haraway, Sadie Plant, Sandy Stone, Linda Dement, Zoë Sofoulis, and other cyberfeminists, urges new forms of cyberfeminist political engagement on the Net, forms that cyberfeminist artists like VNS Matrix turn into a playful, erotic politics within popular culture.

Linda Dement cogently comments that "the computer is the prized toy of our essentially male culture. To use technologies which are really intended for a clean slick commercial boy's world, to make personal, bodily, feminine work, and to re-inscribe this work into mainstream culture, into art discourse and into society, is a political act."[17] The "politics" to which Dement refers is one played out on the terrain of sameness and difference. Computer technology can engage its audience in this play. Within phallocratic imaginings Woman is the Other of Man. In a history of masculine narratives, women, nature, and technology stand in the place of the other, that which is passive, receptive, and under the control of masculine prerogatives. One thinks of Mary Shelley's *Frankenstein,* an investigation of the critical prototype of masculine desire: the desire to create and control human form through technology, to exert dominance over the biological processes of creation. The dream of Dr. Frankenstein, renamed and analyzed as a paranoid fantasy by Alice Jardine, is to liberate men from real women through reproductive technologies. Jardine suggests that these fantasies represent the last desperate attempt at the stage of nature's final exhaustion to drain the female human body of "the feminine."[18] She writes:

> technology always has been about the maternal body and it does seem to be about some kind of male phantasm, but, more, it perceives that the machine *is* a woman in that phantasm. According to this perception we need to find some access to this phantasm, and it seems that one of the few ways is through two particular kinds of discourses: myth and psychoanalysis.[19]

For her, feminine technoproduction through the reinvention of myth and psychoanalysis allows for a reconstruction of what it means to be female within the Symbolic Order of language.

Donna Haraway also reimagines feminine otherness with reference to technology. For her, technology is not the other of humanity but within technology otherness is brought home to coexist with the human. Technology encourages a denaturalization of the relationship between the body and cultural identity. Women can interact with technology in ways that confound humanist understandings of the unified self. Utilizing Haraway's framework, feminists can not only play a game of subversion with the unified self but also imagine new mythic spaces within which they can generate new myths, arts, and technologies.[20]

In her book *Life on the Screen: Identity in the Age of the Internet* Sherry Turkle describes the Internet as "a significant social laboratory for experimenting with the constructions and reconstructions of self that categorize postmodern life."[21] She aligns cybernetics with elements of postmodern life, including the precedence of surface over depth, of simulation over the real, of play over seriousness. Within technocultures one can image and imagine selves beyond modernist representations in which the Grand Narratives become simulacra, the unified self dissolves into fluidity, Truth gives way to situated knowledges, and multiple identities displace the search for origins.

For all of these writers, as well as their sister-practitioners on the Net, more is at stake here than the staging of new culltural myths. Cultural production is linked to a feminist politics of social and historical change. In 1987 Donna Har-away remarked, in the high feminist rhetoric of the time, that feminists must seize the tools of domination that construct the other and employ them in the service of radical revisionings: "Cyborg writing," she wrote, "is about the power to survive, not on the basis of original innocence, but on the basis of seizing the tools to mark the world that marked them as other."[22] Postmodern feminisms may be less concerned with "seizing the tools of power" than in exercising power in more strategic ways. But they remain committed to exploring reinventions of the body beyond its modernist constraints and to expanding the corporeal and libidinal possibilities of its pluralist forms. VNS Matrix aligns this exploration with a politics that directly confronts the masculine economic power of con-temporary culture (Big Daddy Mainframe). The collective, through their elec-tronic games and art practices, encourage viewers to ask not only who has control of technology (now that the girls have their hands on the tools) but how it is used, who controls it, and to what ends.

As feminists have discovered, cybernetics enables the formation of new sub-jectivities, of hybrid selves beyond the binary dualisms of a phallocratic cul-ture. Within utopian versions/visions of cyberfeminism, of which the VNS Matrix posters, installations, and computer games form a part, the postmod-ern self can be imagined and encountered as plural and fluid. Within this techno-field, gender identifications, oedipal narratives, phallic fictions, the mind/body, nature/culture split, even the boundaries of the body can be trans-gressed.

Computer-generated technology, like that of All New Gen, makes possible the (virtual) realization of what Luce Irigaray calls a feminine alterity. Irigaray rehearses some of the elements of that alterity, elements that can be detected in the cyberfeminist world of the All New Gens. They include:

the construction of a feminine sexual economy, rearticulated through the Imaginary and Symbolic Order, including myths and fantasies within them;

a space of feminist imagining beyond phallocentric constraints;

the end of linear narratives and readings, not only in theory but also in practice through intertextuality (read: hypertextuality);

a multiplicity of possibilities for subjectivity and postphallic formations;

the conceptualization of a maternal genealogy, symbolizing contiguous and non-hierarchical social relationships modeled after the relation-ships between mothers and daughters;

a different sort of social organization based in a non-market economy;

and an alterity in which the feminine is aligned with the Maternal body, with jouissance, plurality, fluidity, and tactility: a boundless body of fluids, a body of prolific orgasmic energies, of orgasmic jouissance.[23]

For postmodern feminists like VNS Matrix, cybernetic worlds imagine Irigaray's alterity, where "woman" is reformulated through narratives and representations within a new Symbolic Order inspired by cyberspace. Utilization of the new technologies enables artists and players to engage in feminine mythic and technologically inspired spaces and struggles. New alignments and engagements follow matricicial patterns of connections where collaborations are encouraged. Cyborg bodies escape the visceral, libidinal investments of phallocratic desire. Cyberspace alters aesthetic sensibilities and offers new pleasures in a world where identities/sexualities are fluid, plural, and playful.

Many feminist theories believe that new forms of narrative and visual creation and new cultural productions of post-oedipal bodies, desires, and erotics have the potential to alter radically sexual and political practices. Catherine Waldby, one of the contributors to *Sexy Bodies,* posits an intimate relationship between fantasy, erotic practice, and the imaginary anatomy of the sexed body that, she argues, can bring about a transformation in cultural practices. She considers sexual fantasies as resources for renegotiating power relationships between men and women, male and female bodies.[24] She begins her article by analyzing how the erotics of heterosexual desire within Western phallocentric economies depend on masculine dominance, ownership of the phallus, bounded impermeable bodies, and violence against women juxtaposed against feminine subordination, lack/castration, permeable and receptive bodies, and receptivity to violence. Given this, she concludes,

> Perhaps feminism needs to develop something like a pornographic imagination in relation to masculine bodies, and bodies in general. By this I mean that it should allow itself to think through and in pleasure, in order to develop ways of fantasizing erotic surfaces and orifices, of relations between organs and parts, that depart from the monotonous imagos described earlier.[25]

Waldby considers a transgressive but familiar pornographic fantasy that defies the dominant heterosexual norm: the fantasy of the receptive heterosexual masculine body, one desirous of a receptive anal eroticism in partnership with a dominant phallic female partner. Waldby posits that such a fantasy imagines the female body imago as one not marked by castration, that is, one that severs the "natural" relation between the penis/phallus, but as one in possession of the phallus. Within the fantasy the phallus is a transferable property.

One of the scenarios in All New Gen offers such a male receptive fantasy. It is enacted in the Alpha Bar, where Dentata begins a seduction with Circuit Boy (figure 4). She sings a Siren Song, teasing him into a seduction that involves a transgression of his bodily boundaries. She proposes a "butt fuck." He is an easy

Figure 4   VNS Matrix, "Dentata's Battle with Circuit Boy." (Courtesy of Julianne Pierce and VNS Matrix.)

seduction. *Their boundaries merged forming new objects. She mapped his changing parameters, calculating the pleasure options. She was object-oriented desire to his subject. It was in this way that Circuit Boy learnt the rewards of willing submission* ("The Triple Temptation of Circuit Boy").[26] This scenario provides an alternative seductive fantasy for heterosexual men and women. It moves normative heterosexual desire beyond the stereotypical images of homosexual deviance. Here the VNS team present the receptive, desiring man and the phallic, sexually active woman to lure both male and female players with the temptations of a "perverse" (but not uncommonly imagined) pleasure. The game is replete with such scenarios. One is reminded of the requirement that all players bond with the DNA Sluts to refuel their G-Slime. This engagement, contrary to Freudian psychoanalytic principles, participates in a refusal to relinquish the pre-oedipal bond with the Mother/Matrix and also to imagine the abject feminine body as a body of pleasure. Similarly, the quite visibly feminine but phallic bodies of the DNA Sluts, Dentata, Patina de Panties, and the Princess of Slime transgress the Freudian boundaries of normative sexuality and the attendant feminine body imago (see figure 2). VNS Matrix challenges all forms of normative sexuality: it brings out the worst fantasies of a conservative, economic rationalist culture—the monstrous feminine of masculine fantasy; the phallic, desiring and desired female; the castratrice; and the receptive, submissive male—and transforms them. Their scenarios provide alternative possibilities for feminine erotic power and pleasure.

A number of VNS narratives and cyber-artworks engage with "the sexual" in ways suggestive of the erotics of Deleuze and Guattari. For example, they experiment with the principle of horizontal proliferation, of bodies as "desiring machines," and "bodies without organs" as opposed to the oedipal dynamics of hierarchical sexual and political relations. The scenarios refuse a theory of desire founded on lack. In the world of All New Gen desire is always positive and in movement. Narratives flow and break off across circuits and surfaces of desire. Neither homosexual nor straight, the scenarios occupy a third space of erotic relations. Sometimes they engage in cheeky confrontations with Freudian theory and its fears of the phallic woman, the abject body, and the like. But at other times, and in other zones of pleasure, narratives enact scenarios of Deleuzian delight. They connect bodies and machines to energies and intensities of feeling without predetermined erotogenic zones. They give rise to new forms of sexual desire.

At the end of the All New Gen installation players encounter the Bonding Booth (complete with cushions and sake), where they can link directly into networks within the Matrix, "a clitorally activated zone." The bonding booth's computer, in addition to providing a nonphallic, ungendered erotic video, enables players to create their own characters, environments, scenarios, and stories. The computer program stores, accumulates, and updates an inventory of the players' contributions, which then travel to new sites with the installation. Four nonspecific gendered, postphallic narratives, prepared by the VNS team, are available to stimulate the user's imagination. VNS rewards players' initiative by offering the possibility of unending, virtual life through the ongoing proliferation of (their) stories. Through these multiple dimensions of the game VNS Matrix articulates alternative forms of desire in the realm of public culture. In this VNS extends the erotic imaginary of theoretical feminism, providing one of Waldby's necessary resources of perversity and fantasy.

All New Gen might be defined as a "postphallic formation" in a number of ways:

it is a collaborative effort in which four women form a creative matrix to bring about new narratives, images, and representations;

those representations disrupt the modernist sureties about masculinity and femininity and the boundaries between them;

they require new linguistic codes—mutations—and new forms of text/body/technology;

they reimage/reimagine the cultural boundaries between the natural, the human, and the technological;

they give rise to new myths and new imaginings for postphallic bodies;

they invent new strategies of subversion;

they invite intersubjective interaction with new technological and intertextual bodies that presage new forms of sexuality, subjectivity, and
desire;

they enable players to partake of "perverse" fantasies beyond the embodied
understandings and bodily unities underwritten by psychoanalysis,
patriarchal ideologies, and representations;

and their subversions take place within the largest possible political realm,
Big Daddy's "transglobal fathernet of power and ambition."

The virtual space of All New Gen proliferates these possibilities endlessly.

Big claims for a computer game. Despite these new directions in theory and
imaginary practice, critics of VNS Matrix question the degree to which the
game is subversive to present power relations. Thom Corcoran differs from the
utopian view, positing that in its plot of the All New Gen against Big Daddy
Mainframe the game mirrors the operation of power and knowledge that cyber-
feminism seeks to dismantle.[27] He argues that the game (at least in its initial formation) does little more than reverse the roles, giving female players access to
masculine positions of power. Similarly, problems arise in the claim that the
game allows players to construct a postmodern subjectivity in the "Contested
Zone" where players are encouraged to question their gendered biological and
cultural constructions. He claims that the game both invents a mythic, intertextual body and presents a number of scenarios that consist of fairly classic sex-role
reversals. And in the final analysis All New Gen *is a game*—an experience to be
encountered in the rarefied space of an experimental art gallery or on a number
of websites. It does not engage the larger body politic. This perspective argues
that the All New Gen project is both complicit with and subversive to present
power relations at the same time.

Julianne Pierce, one of the VNS members, agrees that the prototype developed
for All New Gen in 1993 partially relied on a sex-role reversal strategy. Since that
time the group has become more sophisticated in its thinking about characters,
narratives, desire, and subjectivity. (Many of the references to All New Gen in
this essay are taken from the more recent narratives.) Pierce explains,

It's hard to find narratives that don't fit a genre because we are so influenced
by generic types. Our present challenge is how to represent nonspecific gender. We talk about gender identity and politics, constructions of identity and
subjectivity and we are working on scripting these things both visually and in
the narrative structure.

This is for us the main challenge of cyber-feminism: how you incorporate a
feminist language into technology, how you incorporate the body into tech-

nology, how you incorporate feminist ideology into technology and how you subvert technology for our own means and purposes. This is our prime project.[28]

Perhaps the relevant question is not whether VNS Matrix games and installations succeed in producing a postmodernist subjectivity but how the experimentations locate us in both modernist/patriarchal as well as postmodern/postphallic feminine realms. The game both opens up questions of alternate cultural identities (a form of resistance) and also partially forecloses the questions (a recontainment). The game, as a game, has its limitations. But, more important, as Lykke claims for the Internet in general, VNS Matrix offers women (and men) a site of resistance to hegemonic discourses and the potential for interventions into the practices of sexuality, science, and technology.[29] How it will be received and what its effect will be on actual users is another matter. Its effects may be extended considerably, however, when taken as one of many experimentations that engender new virtual selves within cyberspace.

Sherry Turkle raises similar issues in her conclusion to *Life on the Screen*. She cautions that we cannot simply reject the world of cybernetics or consider the Internet as an alternative life for a minority of users. Her research leads her to concur that the Internet is an arena capable of transforming the personal and political dynamics of contemporary life. Aligning herself with the perspectives of postmodern feminism, she argues that the Net encourages us to think of ourselves and our subjectivities as "fluid, emergent, decentralized, multiplicitous, flexible, and ever in process."[30] Despite the possibilities for recontainment, our associations with the Internet and with projects like those imagined and imaged by VNS Matrix allow for new alliances, new subjectivities, and new possibilities for power relations, for desire, and for "perverse" bodily pleasures.

As Teresa de Lauretis and others have argued, myths and fantasies are not eternal truths but are structured through personal, historical, and cultural processes and practices. As such, they are open to change. When cyberfeminists reinvent the myths and fantasies that underpin masculine preoccupations with technology and technocultural production, they also make possible a revisioning of female subjectivity and feminine cultural production. It would be premature to suggest that cyberfeminist productions like those of VNS Matrix presage a new world order. They don't, at least not yet. But they do allow players to imagine the emergence of a new politics, a new erotics, and a new space for the evolution of postmodern subjectivities. They trouble the techno-terrain.

NOTES

1. Sadie Plant, *Zeroes and Ones: Digital Women and the New Technoculture* (London, 1997), pp. 58–59. Plant cites Donna Haraway, "A Cyborg Manifesto: Science, Technology, and Socialist Feminism in the 1980s," in *Simians, Cyborgs, and Women: The Reinvention of Nature* (London, 1991). This essay first appeared in the Adelaide-based journal *Australian Feminist Studies* 4 (1987): 1–41.

2. I take up some of this analysis in my article "The Contested Zone: Cybernetics, Feminism and Representation," *Journal of Australian Studies* 50–51 (1996): 157–64.

3. Elizabeth Grosz and Elsbeth Probyn, Introduction, in *Sexy Bodies: The Strange Carnalities of Feminism,* ed. Elizabeth Grosz and Elsbeth Probyn (New York, 1994), pp. ix–xv.

4. VNS Matrix, All New Gen. Multimedia installation at the Experimental Art Foundation, Adelaide, South Australia, 1993.

5. "The VNS Matrix," www.next.com.au/spyfood/geekgirl/001stick/vns/vns.html, 1997.

6. Ibid.

7. VNS Matrix, "Artist's Statement," http/www.gold.ac.uk/difference/vns.html, 1995.

8. Ibid.

9. Haraway, "Cyborg Manifesto," p. 163.

10. Ibid, p. 151.

11. Jyanni Steffensen, "Queering Freud: Textual (Re)-constructions of Lesbian Desire and Sexuality" (Ph.D. diss., University of Adelaide, 1996), p. 333.

12. Zoë Sofoulis, "Slime in the Matrix: Post-phallic Formations in Women's Art in New Media," in *Jane Gallop Seminar Papers,* ed. Jill Julius Matthews (Canberra: Australian National University, Humanities Research Centre, 1994), p. 100.

13. Ibid, p. 102.

14. The title of an essay by Jane Gallop.

15. Steffensen, "Queering Freud," pp. 311, 312.

16. Sadie Plant, "Cybernetic Hookers," *ANAT News* (April–May 1994): 2–8.

17. Linda Dement, "Artist's Statement about *Typhoid Mary, Working with New Imaging Technologies*" (Melbourne: National Gallery of Victoria, 1995), p. 30.

18. Alice Jardine, "Of Bodies and Technologies," in *Discussions in Contemporary Culture,* ed. Hal Foster (Seattle, 1987), p. 156.

19. Ibid.

20. Sofoulis, "Slime in the Matrix," p. 105.

21. Sherry Turkle, *Life on the Screen: Identity in the Age of the Internet* (New York, 1995), p. 105.

22. Haraway, "Cyborg Manifesto," p. 30.

23. These positions are taken up and discussed variously in Luce Irigaray, *This Sex Which Is Not One,* trans. Gillian G. Gill (Ithaca, 1985); and Margaret Whitford, *Luce Irigaray: Philosophy in the Feminine* (New York, 1991).

24. Catherine Waldby, "Destruction: Boundary Erotics and Refigurations of the Heterosexual Male Body," in *Sexy Bodies,* ed. Grosz and Probyn, pp. 267–68.

25. Ibid, p. 275.

26. "The VNS Matrix."

27. Thom Corcoran, "'Lost in Cyberspace' or Remaking the Modern" (Honours diss., University of South Australia, 1994), p. 55.

28. Julianne Pierce, interview with author, 1996.

29. Nina Lykke, Introduction, in *Between Monsters, Goddesses, and Cyborgs: Feminist Confrontations with Science, Medicine and Cyberspace,* ed. Nina Lykke and Rosi Braidotti (London, 1996), pp. 5–6.

30. Turkle, *Life on the Screen,* p. 263.

NOTES ON THE CONTRIBUTORS

PETER BAILEY is Professor of History at the University of Manitoba. His most recent book is *Popular Culture and Performance in the Victorian City* (1998).

MAGDALENA BARRERA is a Ph.D. candidate in the Program in Modern Thought and Literature at Stanford University. Her research explores the intersections between cultural production and history of Mexican Americans from the 1920s through the 1940s.

DAVID LORENZO BOYD is Clinic Director of Complementary Medicine, St. Vincent Medical Center, and Academic Dean, Samra University of Oriental Medicine, Los Angeles.

PETER BROWN is Professor of History at Princeton University. His most recent books include *Body and Society* (1988), *Power and Persuasion* (1992), *Authority and the Sacred* (1995), and *The Rise of Western Christendom* (1996). He is currently working on attitudes to wealth and poverty in late antiquity and the early Middle Ages.

GEORGE CHAUNCEY is Professor of History at the University of Chicago and the author of the prize-winning *Gay New York: Gender, Urban Culture, and the Making of the Gay Male World, 1890–1940* (1994). He is the coeditor of *Hidden From History: Reclaiming the Gay and Lesbian Past* (1989), and a special issue of *GLQ, Thinking Sexuality Transnationally* (2000). Professor Chauncey is currently completing *The Strange Career of the Closet: Gay Culture, Consciousness, and Politics from the Second World War to the Gay Liberation Era.*

ANNA CLARK is Associate Professor of History at the University of Minnesota, and the author of *Women's Silence and Men's Violence: Sexual Assault in England, 1770–1845* (1987), and *The Struggle for the Breeches: Gender and the Making of the British Working Class* (1995). She is completing a book on sexual scandals in British politics, 1760–1820.

ROBERT DARNTON is Professor of History at Princeton University. He has published a dozen books on European history, the latest being *The Forbidden Best-Sellers of Prerevolutionary France* (1995), and *The Corpus of Clandestine Literature in France, 1769–1789* (1995). He is currently writing an electronic book on the history of books.

JOHN D'EMILIO is Professor of Gender and Women's Studies and History at the University of Illinois at Chicago. His books include *Making Trouble: Essays on Gay History, Politics, and the University* (1992), *Sexual Politics, Sexual Communities: The Making of a Homosexual Minority in the United States, 1940–1970* (1998), and *Creating Change: Sexuality, Public Policy, and Civil Rights* (2000) (coedited with William Turner and Urvashi Vaid). He is currently working on a biography of Bayard Rustin, an American radical pacifist and civil rights activist.

MARY FISSELL is Associate Professor in the History of Medicine at Johns Hopkins University. She is the author of *Patients, Power and the Poor in Eighteenth-Century Bristol* (1991), and essays on topics ranging from patients' narratives to the history of vermin. She is currently completing a cultural history of women's bodies in English cheap print, 1500–1750.

ESTELLE B. FREEDMAN is Professor of History at Stanford University and the author of *Their Sisters' Keepers: Women's Prison Reform in America, 1830–1930* (1981), and *Maternal Justice: Miriam Van Waters and the Female Reform Tradition* (1996), and coauthor of *Intimate Matters: A History of Sexuality in America* (rev. ed., 1997). She coedited *Victorian Women: A Documentary Account* (1981), and *The Lesbian Issue: Essays from Signs* (1985).

C. JACOB HALE is Associate Professor of Philosophy at California State University, Northridge, and author of several influential articles on issues of sexuality.

DAVID M. HALPERIN is the W. H. Auden Collegiate Professor of English Language and Literature at the University of Michigan, Ann Arbor, and Honorary Visiting Professor in the School of Sociology at the University of New South Wales. He is the author of *One Hundred Years of Homosexuality* (1990), and *Saint Foucault* (1995), and an editor of *The Lesbian and Gay Studies Reader* (1993) and *GLQ*. His most recent contribution to the subject matter of this volume is "How to Do the History of Male Homosexuality," *GLQ* (2000).

TIM HITCHCOCK is Reader in Eighteenth-Century History at the University of Hertfordshire. His books include *English Sexualities, 1700–1800* (1997) and (edited with M. Cohen) *English Masculinities 1660–1800* (1999). He is currently working on a monograph on the experience of poverty in eighteenth-century London.

ALBERT HURTADO holds the Paul H. and Doris Eaton Travis Chair in Modern American History at the University of Oklahoma. His publications include the prize-winning *Indian Survival on the California Frontier* (1988), and *Intimate Frontiers: Sex, Gender, and Culture in Old California* (1999). He is working on a biography of Herbert E. Bolton.

JANICE M. IRVINE is Associate Professor of Sociology at the University of Massachusetts. She is the author of *Disorders of Desire: Sex and Gender in Modern American Sexology* (1990). Her most recent book is *Talk about Sex: The Cultural Politics of Sexuality Education* (2001).

RUTH MAZO KARRAS is Professor of History at the University of Minnesota. She is the author of *Common Women: Prostitution and Sexuality in Medieval England* (1996), and various articles on gender and sexuality in medieval Europe. She is currently at work on a book on masculinity in the fourteenth and fifteenth centuries.

HARRY OOSTERHUIS is Lecturer in History at the University of Maastricht in the Netherlands. He is the author of *Homosexuality and Male Bonding in Pre-Nazi Germany* (1991), *Homoseksualiteit in Katholiek Nederland* (1992), and *Stepchildren of Nature: Krafft-Ebing, Psychiatry, and the Making of Sexual Identity* (2000). He is also coauthor of *Gay Men and the Sexual History of the Political Left* (1995).

KIM M. PHILLIPS (Editor) is Lecturer in History at the University of Auckland. She is coeditor of *Young Medieval Women* (1999) and author of the forthcoming *Medieval Maidens: Young Women and Gender in Late Medieval England*.

BARRY REAY (Editor) is Professor of History at the University of Auckland. His most recent books are *Microhistories: Demography, Society, and Culture in Rural England, 1800–1930* (1996), *Popular Cultures in England, 1550–1750* (1998), and *Watching Hannah: Sexuality, Horror, and Bodily De-Formation in Victorian England* (2002).

KAY SCHAFFER is Associate Professor in the Department of Social Inquiry at Adelaide University. Her books include *Women and the Bush* (1988), *In the Wake of First Contact: The Eliza Fraser Stories* (1995), and the edited anthologies *Indigenous Australian Voices: A Reader* (1988), *Constructions of Colonialism* (1998), and *The Olympics at the Millennium* (2000).

JAMES A. SCHULTZ is Professor of German and Director of the Lesbian, Gay, Bisexual, and Transgender Studies Program at the University of California, Los Angeles. Most recently he has published *The Knowledge of Childhood in the German Middle Ages, 1100–1350* (1995), and *Sovereignty and Salvation in the Vernacular, 1050–1150* (2000). He is also the coeditor of *Constructing Medieval Sexuality* (1997). His next book will study courtly love as a distinctively medieval "sexuality."

STEVEN SEIDMAN is Professor of Sociology at the State University of New York at Albany. His many books include *Embattled Eros: Sexual Politics and Ethics in Contemporary America* (1992), *Difference Troubles: Queering Social Theory and Sexual Politics* (1997), *Queer Theory/Sociology* (1996), and *Contested Knowledge: Social Theory in the Postmodern Era* (1998). He is the editor of the forthcoming *Handbook of Lesbian and Gay Studies*.

CAROLE S. VANCE, an anthropologist, teaches at Columbia University, where she is Director of the Program for the Study of Sexuality, Gender, Health, and Human Rights. She is also a Visiting Professor at the University of Amsterdam, where she is Co-Director of the Summer Institute in Sexuality and Culture. She has written widely on controversies about visual imagery, sexuality and science, and pornography, as well as on gender, sexuality, and health. She is the editor of the influential book *Pleasure and Danger: Exploring Female Sexuality* (1984, 1993).

JEFFREY WEEKS is Professor of Sociology and Dean of Humanities and Social Science at South Bank University, London. He is the author of numerous articles and books on the history and social organization of sexuality. His recent publications include *Invented Moralities: Sexual Values in an Age of Uncertainty* (1995), *Sexual Cultures* (with Janet Holland) (1996), *Making Sexual History* (2000), and *Same Sex Intimacies* (2001).

PERMISSIONS ACKNOWLEDGMENTS

Peter Bailey, "Parasexuality and Glamour: The Victorian Barmaid as Cultural Prototype," *Gender and History* 2 (1990): 148–72. Reprinted by permission of Blackwell Publishers. Illustrations by permission of The British Library. The article has appeared most recently in Bailey's *Popular Culture and Performance in the Victorian City* (Cambridge, 1998), ch. 7.

Magdalena Barrera, "Hottentot 2000: Jennifer Lopez and Her Butt." Printed by permission of Magdalena Barrera.

Peter Brown, "Bodies and Minds: Sexuality and Renunciation in Early Christianity," in *Before Sexuality: The Construction of Erotic Experience in the Ancient Greek World*, ed. David M. Halperin, John J. Winkler, and Froma I. Zeitlin (Princeton, N.J.: Princeton University Press, 1990). Reprinted by permission of Princeton University Press.

George Chauncey, "Trade, Wolves, and the Boundaries of Normal Manhood," in Chauncey, *Gay New York* (New York: Basic Books, 1994). Copyright © 1996 by George Chauncey. Reprinted by permission of Basic Books, a member of Perseus Books, L.L.C.

Anna Clark, "Anne Lister's Construction of Lesbian Identity," *Journal of the History of Sexuality* 7 (1996): 23–50. Copyright © 1996 by University of Texas Press. All rights reserved. Reprinted by permission of University of Texas Press.

John D'Emilio and Estelle B. Freedman, "Family Life and the Regulation of Deviance," in D'Emilio and Freedman, *Intimate Matters: A History of Sexuality in America,* 2nd ed. (Chicago: University of Chicago Press, 1997). Reprinted by permission of The University of Chicago Press.

Robert Darnton, "Sex for Thought," *The New York Review of Books,* December 22, 1994: 65–74. Reprinted by permission of Robert Darnton.

Mary Fissell, "Gender and Generation: Representing Reproduction in Early Modern England," *Gender and History* 7 (1995): 433–56. Reprinted by permission of Blackwell Publishers.

C. Jacob Hale, "Leatherdyke Boys and Their Daddies: How to Have Sex without Women or Men," *Social Text* 52–53 (Fall–Winter 1997): 223–36. Copyright © 1997 by Duke University Press. All rights reserved. Reprinted by permission of Duke University Press.

David M. Halperin, "Forgetting Foucault: Acts, Identities, and the History of Sexuality," *Representations* 63 (Summer 1998): 93–120. Reprinted by permission of The University of Chicago Press. Appearing in David M. Halperin's forthcoming book *Foucault and Gay Cultural Politics: Representations.*

Tim Hitchcock, "Redefining Sex in Eighteenth-Century England," *History Workshop Journal* 41 (1996): 73–90. Reprinted by permission of Oxford University Press.

Albert L. Hurtado, "Sexuality in California's Franciscan Missions: Cultural Perceptions and Historical Realities," in Hurtado, *Intimate Frontiers: Sex, Gender, and Culture in Old California* (Albuquerque, N.M.: University of New Mexico Press, 1999). Reprinted by permission of University of New Mexico Press.

Janice M. Irvine, "Toward a 'Value-Free' Science of Sex: The Kinsey Reports," in Irvine, *Disorders of Desire: Sex and Gender in Modern American Sexology* (Philadelphia: Temple University Press, 1990). Copyright © 1990 by Temple University Press. All rights reserved. Reprinted by permission of Temple University Press.

Janice M. Irvine, "Regulated Passions: The Invention of Inhibited Sexual Desire and Sexual Addiction," in *Deviant Bodies: Critical Perspectives on Difference in Science and Popular Culture,* ed. Jennifer Terry and Jacqueline Urla (Bloomington: Indiana University Press, 1995). Reprinted by permission of Indiana University Press.

Ruth Mazo Karras and David Lorenzo Boyd, "'*Ut cum muliere*': A Male Transvestite Prostitute in Fourteenth-Century London," *GLQ* 1/4 (1995): 459–66.

Harry Oosterhuis, "Richard von Krafft-Ebing's 'Step-Children of Nature': Psychiatry and the Making of Homosexual Identity," in *Science and Homosexualities*, ed. Vernon A. Rosario (London: Routledge, 1997). Reprinted by permission of Routledge.

Kay Schaffer, "The Game Girls of VNS Matrix: Challenging Gendered Identities in Cyberspace," in *Virtual Gender: Fantasies of Subjectivity and Embodiment*, ed. Mary Ann O'Farrell and Lynne Vallone (Ann Arbor: University of Michigan Press, 1999). Reprinted by permission of The University of Michigan Press. Illustrations courtesy of Julianne Pierce and VNS Matrix.

James A. Schultz, "Bodies That Don't Matter: Heterosexuality before Heterosexuality in Gottfried's *Tristan*," in *Constructing Medieval Sexuality*, ed. Karma Lochrie, Peggy McCracken, and James A. Schultz. (Minneapolis: University of Minnesota Press, 1997): 91–110. Reprinted by permission of University of Minnesota Press.

Steven Seidman, "AIDS and the Discursive Construction of Homosexuality," *Social Text* 9 (1988): 187–206. Copyright © 1988 by Duke University Press. All rights reserved. Reprinted by permission of Duke University Press. Published later in *The New American Cultural Sociology*, ed. Philip Smith (Cambridge, 1998).

Carole S. Vance, "Negotiating Sex and Gender in the Attorney General's Commission on Pornography," in *Uncertain Terms: Negotiating Gender in American Culture*, ed. Faye Ginsburg and Anna L. Tsing (Boston: Beacon, 1990). Copyright © 1990 by Carol S. Vance. Reprinted by permission of Carol S. Vance.

Jeffrey Weeks, "Sexuality and History Revisited," in *State, Private Life, and Political Change*, ed. L. Jamieson and H. Corr (London: Macmillan Press, 1990). Reprinted by permission of Macmillan Press.

INDEX

A

Abelove, Henry, 187–89
abortion, 151, 179, 191
Adam and Eve. *See* Fall, the
adultery, 54–56, 76, 91, 114, 129, 133,
    144, 146, 149–50, 152–54, 166–69,
    174–75, 185, 400
AIDS, 16–17, 28, 38, 42, 336, 375–85,
    390–91, 401, 402
anthropology, 4, 7, 19, 30, 32, 35,
    105–6, 168
Apuleius, 54–57
Aquinas, Thomas, 75
Aretino, Pietro, 11, 205, 207–8, 214
Ariès, Philippe, 194
Aristotle, 118
Aristotle's Masterpiece, 145, 192,
    194–95, 258
Armstrong, Nancy, 115
Augustine of Hippo, 137

B

Baartman, Saartje, 17, 407–17
bachelor subculture, 302–310
Bailey, Peter, 12
Bakhtin, Mikhail, 105
barmaids, 12, 222–44
Barrera, Magdalena, 17
Barrett, Virginia, 439
Barthes, Roland, 76, 78
bastardy. *See* illegitimacy
Baudrillard, Jean, 42, 61
Bayle, Pierre, 253
beauty: female, 71–75, 80, 215–16;
    male, 71–75, 79–80, 216
Beerbohm, Max, 239–40
berdache, 155, 169, 171–72
Bergstedt, Spencer, 424–27
bestiality, 76, 143, 154, 169
biblical texts, 108–9, 117, 129–40,
    150

birth control. *See* contraception

bisexuality, 3, 7, 13, 52, 92, 343–44, 421, 422

Boccaccio, Giovanni, 54–57, 208

bodies, 8, 9–11, 17–18, 31, 33, 35, 43; ancient, 51–59; early Christian, 129–40; early modern, 105–126, 186, 189–90, 215–16; medieval, 71–89; postmodern, 434–52; racial, 174, 407–17; transsexual, 421–33

Bordo, Susan, 401

Boswell, James, 251

Boswell, John, 58

Boyd, David Lorenzo, 9

Bray, Alan, 95

Bristow, Joseph, 13

Brooten, Bernadette, 8

Brown, Peter, 10

Bruce, Kennilworth, 295

Brumberg, Joan Jacobs, 401

Brundage, James A., 5

Bullough, Vern L., 5

bundling, 147, 240

Burney, Fanny, 251

Burns, E. Jane, 75

Butler, Judith, 9, 17, 71–77, 79, 98, 249, 261, 262, 305

Bynum, Caroline Walker, 72

Byron, George Gordon, Lord, 252, 256

C

Cadden, Joan, 74

Camille, Michael, 75

Carnes, Patrick, 389, 393

Cassian, John, 137–39

Castle, Terry, 13, 248, 256

Catullus, 11, 252

celibacy, 10, 129–40, 175, 187

chastity: female, 113–14, 133–34, 143, 186; male, 114, 129–40

Chaucer, Geoffrey, 97

Chauncey, George, 14, 248

childbirth, 111, 150–51, 157, 178, 207, 216

Christianity. *See* sex: Christianity

Chrysostom, John, 136–37

cinaedus. See kinaidos

Clark, Alice, 116, 189

Cleanness, 96-97

Cohen, David, 8

conception. *See* reproduction

conduct books, 106, 113–16, 189

constructionist view of sexuality, 4–6, 18–19, 29–32, 39, 45–59, 92

contraception, 28, 145, 151, 157, 178, 191, 193, 207, 209

Corcoran, Thom, 450

Cott, Nancy, 398

courtship, 146–47, 185–86, 191

cross dressing. *See* transvestism

cuckoldry, 143, 154, 168, 210, 218

Culpeper, Nicholas, 107–8, 112, 118

D

D'Emilio, John and Freedman, Estelle B., 11, 328

da Rimini, Francesca, 439

Darnton, Robert, 12, 19

Darwin, Charles, 275

Davidoff, Leonore, and Hall, Catherine, 189

Davidson, Arnold, 4, 76

de Lauretis, Teresa, 251, 256

Degler, Carl, 398

Dekker, Rudolph, and van der Pol, Lotte, 196
Deleuze, Gilles, 449
Dement, Linda, 444–45
Descartes, René, 206, 209
deviance, 13–14, 45–48, 49–57, 141–65, 271–92
dildos, 196, 260
divorce, 150–51, 155, 160, 168–69, 349–50
Donaghue, Emma, 196, 248, 262
Donnerstein, Edward, 370
Donzelot, Jacques, 10
double standard, 144, 152–53
Dworkin, Andrea, 210–11, 364, 365, 369

E

Elias, Norbert, 105
Ellis, Havelock, 329, 331, 344, 352
Encratites, 132–33
Ennodius, 95
essentialist view of sexuality, 6, 12, 19, 31, 45–46, 82, 327–56

F

Fabricant, Carole, 109
fairies, 15, 293–326
Fall, the, 132, 134–35, 137
family, 4, 10–11, 19, 28, 33, 34, 35, 116, 119, 141–65, 167–69, 186–9, 349–51
Fausto-Sterling, Anne, 7
fetishism, 5, 14, 276–77, 278
Fissell, Mary, 10
foreplay. See sex: non-penetrative

fornication, 76, 91, 93, 114, 131, 133, 136, 141, 144, 146–48, 152–53, 159, 168–69, 178, 185–86
Foucault, Michel, 6, 8, 12, 17, 28, 30, 32–33, 35, 42–61, 79, 105, 129, 186, 247–48, 254, 272, 274, 384, 386, 387, 403, 408, 421
Franciscans, 166–82
Freud, Sigmund, 5, 30, 57, 228, 278, 329, 337, 341, 352

G

Galen, 108, 112, 129–31, 133–4, 138–9, 193–4, 209
Gallagher, Catherine, 190
Gallop, Jane, 7
Game Girls, 434–52
Garber, Marjorie, 72
gay sex. See homosexuality: male
Gay, Peter, 28
gender. See sex: and gender
Giddens, Anthony, 3, 288
Gilman, Sander, 17, 410
glamour, 226–31, 238–40
Gleason, Maud, 51–53
Goffman, Erving, 305
Gottfried von Straßburg, 71–89
Goulemot, Jean Marie, 214–15
Gregory of Nyssa, 134–35
Greven, Philip, 144–45
Guattari, Felix, 449

H

Hale, C. Jacob, 18, 421–33
Hall, Radclyffe, 72, 353

Halperin, David, 6, 8

Haraway, Donna, 434, 437, 440, 441, 444, 445, 446

hermaphrodites, 44, 209, 262

heterosexuality, 1–3, 6–7, 9, 12–19, 32, 71–89, 191, 194, 197, 240, 253, 327–56, 378–81, 383–84

Hirschfeld, Magnus, 283

Hitchcock, Tim, 11

Hite, Shere, 2

homosexuality, 3, 6–7, 9, 13–16, 18, 28–29, 31–32, 37, 44, 57–59, 79, 83, 169, 248–49, 252, 329–30, 340, 343–45, 375–85; female. *See* lesbianism; male, 7–8, 11, 14, 16–17, 37–39, 44–59, 75, 90, 94–98, 137, 154–55, 171–72, 195–96, 248–49, 252, 271–92, 293–326, 333, 375–85

Hottentot Venus. *See* Baartman, Saartje

Howe, Irving, 250–51

humors, 4, 190

Hunt, Lynn, 12, 188

Hurtado, Albert, 11

hysteria, 193

I

illegitimacy, 28, 114, 145, 148, 152, 156–58, 175, 179, 186–87, 191

impotence, 149, 150, 195, 208, 216, 387

incest, 114, 144, 150–52, 168–69, 173, 175, 219

infanticide, 152, 157–8, 175, 179

inhibited sexual desire, 386–406

inversion, 99, 271–92

Irigaray, Luce, 439, 440

Irvine, Janice, 16, 18

J

Jamieson, Lynn, 3

JanMohamed, Abdul R., 17

Jardine, Alice, 445

Justin, 129–31, 134

Juvenal, 252, 253, 257

K

Kaplan, Helen Singer, 387, 390, 392, 393, 395

Karras, Ruth Mazo, 9

Katz, Jonathan Ned, 6, 18

Kennard, Jean, 252

kinaidos, 8, 49–57

Kinsey, Alfred, 2, 16, 27, 297–98, 300, 327–56

Kipnis, Laura, 409, 410

Kolodny, Annette, 109

Kosofsky Sedgwick, Eve, 1

Krafft-Ebing, Richard von, 13, 18, 271–92, 331, 344

Kristeva, Julia, 439, 440

L

Laqueur, Thomas, 9, 35, 106, 119, 187–90

Leatherdyke: boys, 421–33; daddies, 421–33

Leif, Harold, 387

lesbianism, 6, 8, 12, 18, 29, 39, 44, 79, 195–97, 210, 247–70, 421–33

Levine, David, 187

Lévi-Strauss, Claude, 203

Lister, Anne, 13, 247–70

Lopez, Jennifer, 17, 407–17

Lubinus, 253

Luhmann, Niklas, 288

M

MacKinnon, Catherine, 210, 214, 364, 365, 369
Malinowski, Bronislaw, 30
Marcus, Steven, 16
marriage, 1–4, 11, 13, 16, 19, 28, 32, 34, 116, 133, 135–36, 167–69, 169–70, 170–72, 188–89, 349–51, 375
Martial, 252, 253–54
Martin, Emily, 106–7
masochism, 4, 13, 271, 276–77, 278
Masters, William and Johnson, Virginia, 2, 28, 343, 348–51, 352, 353, 387, 388, 394
Masters, William, 27–28, 353
masturbation, 12, 76, 141, 144–45, 154, 169, 185, 192–95, 207, 211–13, 219, 274–75, 309, 349, 390, 395, 396, 400
Mather, Cotton, 144, 149, 158
Maubray, John, 107–8, 110
McIntosh, Mary, 31
midwifery, 117–18, 156–57, 189
miscegenenation. See race: sex and
misogyny, 112, 133, 189
mollies, 7, 14, 248
Money, John, 390, 393
Moore, George, 237–39
Morel, Bénédict Auguste, 275
Mort, Frank, 38
Muchembled, Robert, 11
Munby, Arthur, 251
music hall, 238–39

N

Namaste, Ki, 421
nature: acts contrary to, 47–48, 76, 160, 171
nudity, 136, 174
Nussbaum, Felicity, 251

O

Onania, 192–94
Oosterhuis, Harry, 14
orgasm: female, 2, 10, 35, 110, 145, 149, 186, 190, 209–10, 260, 340, 342–43, 348; male, 10, 109–10, 145, 149, 190–92, 208–9, 223, 340, 342–43
Origen, 134, 137
Original Sin. See Fall, the
Ovid, 258–59

P

Padgug, Robert, 6
parasexuality, 12, 222–44
pederasty, 8, 56, 252, 311. See also punks
Penthouse, 359, 368, 371, 409
perversion. See deviance.
Pierce, Julianne, 439, 450–51
Plant, Sadie, 434, 437, 444
plastic sexuality, 3
Plato, 130, 252, 280
Playboy, 359, 368, 371, 409–10
Plummer, Ken, 27, 32
polygamy, 169, 172, 174–75
Pomeroy, Wardell, 332
Poovey, Mary, 2

pornography, 11, 16, 109, 186, 188–89,
    191–92, 194, 203–21, 333, 346,
    359–74, 390, 395
Porter, Roy, 188, 194–95
pregnancy: premarital, 148, 156–58,
    175, 186–87, 191. *See also*
    reproduction
prostitution, 9, 12, 14–15, 28, 35–36,
    38, 91–94, 137, 169, 175, 177, 205,
    207, 211, 217, 220, 293–326
psychiatry, 30, 46–48, 57, 190,
    271–92, 386–406
pubs, 222–40
punks, 311–17
Puritans, 10, 141–46, 148–49,
    161–62, 188

Q

queer theory, 60, 421

R

Rabelais, François, 208
rape, 28, 52, 76, 114, 144, 147, 152,
    155–56, 160–61, 166, 169, 175–77,
    211, 218, 308–9
Rattray Taylor, G., 5
reproduction, 2, 7, 10–11, 19, 28,
    31–32, 34–35, 37, 46, 106–12, 136,
    142–58, 168, 169, 179, 190, 194–95,
    277
Richlin, Amy, 8, 53–54
Roeslin, Eucharius, 111–12, 117
Rogers, Katherine, 116
romantic friendships, 12–13, 79, 196,
    251, 259
Romantic texts, 255–56
Roof, Judith, 254

Rousseau, Jean-Jacques, 255–56
Rubin, Gayle, 32, 423, 424
Rykener, John/Eleanor, 90–104

S

Sade, Marquis de, 188, 205
sadism, 13, 276–77, 278
sado-masochism, 367–68, 424,
    425–28
sapphists, 7, 248, 253–54, 260,
    263–64
Sappho, 248, 253
Schaffer, Kay, 18
Schultz, James A., 9
separate spheres, 186, 189–90, 192
sex: addiction, 17, 386–406; anal, 2,
    49–53, 54, 95, 137, 155, 309,
    293–326; ancient Greek, 7–8, 10,
    31, 33, 49–57, 75, 252–54; ancient
    Roman, 7–8, 10–11, 33, 49–57,
    252–54, 257, 258–59; and children,
    32, 142–46; and Christianity, 4,
    10–12, 15, 27, 32–34, 37–38,
    44–48, 90, 93, 129–40, 141–65,
    166–82, 205–21, 254–55; and class,
    3–4, 8–9, 14–15, 33, 35–36, 74–76,
    83, 145, 156, 160, 196, 209, 234,
    235–36, 239, 293–326, 345–56; and
    clergy, 91, 100–1, 129–40, 206–9,
    211, 219–20; cyber, 17–18, 434–52;
    and death, 10, 129–40, 375–85;
    early Christian, 129–40, 254; early
    modern, 7, 9–11, 28, 45–46, 141–65,
    166–82, 185–202, 203–21; and eco-
    nomics, 31, 33, 46, 142, 150, 156,
    169, 177, 187–88, 222–23, 240;
    eighteenth-century, 7, 9, 11–12, 14,
    35, 47, 105–19, 141–65, 166–82,

185–202, 247–70; and feminism, 5–6, 29, 35, 37, 39, 210–11, 213, 362–66, 369, 372, 402–3, 434–52; and gender, 3–4, 8–10, 12, 14–15, 17–19, 30, 33–35, 46, 49–59, 76–79, 90, 95–99, 110, 119, 137, 170, 195–96, 248, 251, 259–60, 262, 264, 293–326, 327–56, 402–3, 421–33, 434–52; and immigrants, 298–302; and Islam, 32–34; and Judaism, 130–31, 298–301; and Latino communities, 407–17; and law, 9, 28, 44–8, 90–104, 141–65, 275, 282–83, 333, 359–74; liberation, 5, 12, 16, 30, 42, 44, 188; marital, 2–3, 9–11, 14, 19, 76, 93–94, 135–36, 141–65, 169, 187, 190, 195, 218–19; and medicine, 4, 7, 9–15, 17, 27–28, 34, 38, 39, 47–48, 57-59, 74, 106–12, 145, 188, 190, 192–95, 271–92, 386–406; medieval, 5, 7, 9–10, 44–59, 71–89, 90–104; and missionaries, 166–82; nineteenth century, 6–7, 11–13, 16–18, 28, 35, 38, 44–49, 57–59, 204, 222–44, 247–70, 271–92; non-penetrative, 185, 191, 195; oral, 11, 51, 293–326; and politics, 4, 8, 10, 12, 29, 32–37, 48, 114–15, 212–13; postmodern, 17–18, 29, 421–33, 434–52; and prisons, 314–17; and race, 4, 11, 17, 36, 146, 152, 155, 158–61, 166–82, 336–37, 407–17; repression of, 5–6, 12, 16, 30, 141, 188, 359–74, 375–85, 401–4; and science, 7, 9, 13–15, 18, 28, 30, 47–48, 57–59, 74, 194, 271–92, 327–56; and slavery, 159–61; surveys, 1–3, 12, 15–16, 18, 327–56; twentieth century, 13–19,

27–41, 293–326, 327–56, 359–74, 375–85, 386–406, 407–17, 421–33, 434–52; and violence, 28, 37, 113, 176–77, 211

sexology, 5, 7, 12–13, 18, 30, 39, 190, 271–92, 327–56, 386–406

sexual identity, 3, 5–8, 13, 15, 18, 28, 44–59, 62n. 8, 64n. 11, 90, 92, 247–70, 271–92

sexual orientation. *See* sexual identity

sexual scripts, 248

Sharp, Jane, 107–10, 117–19

Shiebinger, Londa, 190

Shorter, Edward, 187, 192, 197

Simpson, Antony, 195

slander, 143–44

slang, 107, 112–13

Smith, Hilda, 116

sociology, 29, 30, 32

sodomy, 44–58, 76, 90–92, 94–98, 144, 152, 154–55, 171, 196, 247–48, 333, 376

Sofoulis, Zoë, 441, 442, 444

Spacks, Patricia Meyer, 251

Starrs, Josie, 439

Steffensen, Jyanni, 440–41, 444

Stein, Edward, 6

Stewart, Susan, 16

Stoler, Ann Laura, 17

Stone, Lawrence, 28, 187–88

Szasz, Thomas, 273

T

Taylor, Charles, 256

Terry, Jennifer, 14, 18

Tertullian, 131–32

Tissot, Samuel, 192–94

trade, 293–326

transgenderism, 18, 169, 421–33
transsexuality, 7, 17–18, 421–33
transvestism, 9, 31, 90–92, 98–104,
    169, 171–72, 196, 261–62
Trumbach, Randolph, 14, 195, 248,
    262
Turkle, Sherry, 445, 451
Tyler, Parker, 310, 311–12

U

Ulrichs, Karl Heinrich, 276
Urnings, 271–92

V

van der Meer, Theo, 248
van de Velde, Theodore, 329
Vance, Carole, 16, 18, 39, 394
venereal disease, 12–13, 31, 35, 38, 150,
    177–78, 208, 218, 220, 239,
    309–10
Venette, Dr Nicholas, 192, 194–95
Vicinus. Martha, 12, 248
Vickery, Amanda, 189

virginity, 2, 10, 108, 129–40, 168, 185,
    211, 218–19
VNS Matrix, 434–52

W

Waldby, Catherine, 447, 449
Walters, Jonathan, 54–55
Weeks, Jeffrey, 4, 6, 7, 16, 249,
    392–93
Weil, Rachel, 114
Weisner-Hanks, Merry, 10
Westphal, Karl, 276
Whitbread, Helena, 249
Williams, Craig, 52–53
Winkler, John J. 49–50, 53
Wolfram von Eschenbach, 73, 74
Wollstonecraft, Mary, 256
wolves, 15, 293–326
Wrigley, E. A., 187

Y

youth, 54–56, 73, 133–35, 142–47,
    195, 252, 309, 310–14